KT-119-512

Business Finance

Applications, Models and Cases

MICHEL SCHLOSSER

 Prentice Hall

FINANCIAL TIMES

An imprint of **Pearson Education**

Harlow, England • London • New York • Boston • San Francisco • Toronto
Sydney • Tokyo • Singapore • Hong Kong • Seoul • Taipei • New Delhi
Cape Town • Madrid • Mexico City • Amsterdam • Munich • Paris • Milan

Pearson Education Limited

Edinburgh Gate
Harlow
Essex CM20 2JE
England

and Associated Companies throughout the world

Visit us on the World Wide Web at
www.pearsoneduc.com

First published 2002

ISBN 0 132 64649 8

British Library Cataloguing-in-Publication Data
A CIP catalogue record for this book can be obtained from the British Library.

Library of Congress Cataloging-in-Publication Data
A catalog record for this book can be obtained from the Library of Congress.

10 9 8 7 6 5 4 3 2 1
06 05 04 03

Typeset in 10/12pt Stone by 35
Printed and bound by Bell & Bain Limited, Glasgow

Business Finance
Applications, Models and Cases

We work with leading authors to develop the
strongest educational materials in business and
finance, bringing cutting-edge thinking and
best learning practice to a global market.

Under a range of well-known imprints, including
Financial Times Prentice Hall, we craft high quality
print and electronic publications which help
readers to understand and apply their content,
whether studying or at work.

To find out more about the complete range of our
publishing please visit us on the World Wide Web at:
www.pearsoneduc.com

Contents

PART *III*

Modelling business processes and simulating their dynamics   105

PART *IV*

Managing the trajectories of commitment
in decline and growth situations

PART *VI*

Deciding to commit to external growth opportunities   395

Introduction

This new text takes a highly-applied and practical approach to the use of finance in creating effective business solutions.

- It integrates theory and cases drawn from real business situations within a spreadsheet-modelling, learning framework and is structured around solving critical business issues.
- It allows readers to conduct their own systematic analysis, to build innovative strategies and action plans, to understand and manage risk and to create more profit, cash and value for their organisation.

For whom is this book written?

I wrote this book with two main audiences in mind:

- students of management attending MBA programmes, as well as advanced undergraduate business or finance courses;
- practising executives who want to use financial tools effectively to solve business problems (as opposed to 'pure financial' problems). This book is designed to be used in executive programmes and also as a self-learning tool.

The approaches and material in this book have been developed and tested in learning and consulting situations with practising executives in America, Asia and Europe.

Website

When working with this book, you can access my website: www.michel-schlosser.com, where you will get a user name and a password. This will give you access to:

- background material and links related to creation of value and other business finance issues;
- additional business cases and models.

A special section of the site is reserved for management educators and consultants.

An *Instructor's Manual* is also available to download from the lecturer's section of the website for the book at http://www.booksites.net/schlosser, or on application to the publishers, free of charge to lecturers adopting the textbook.

What will you learn from working with this book?

This book will enable you to learn how to use finance effectively for understanding and resolving business issues in the age of spreadsheets.

Finance

I strongly disagree with the view that finance is a matter for specialists only. On the contrary, finance is part of the toolkit that any manager can – and probably should – use for understanding and resolving business issues. A knowledge of finance enables managers to understand how they can influence the process of creation of value and the good news is that finance has become much easier to use with the widespread access to personal computers and spreadsheets. This book covers all the topics of finance except those that are only of interest to specialists.

Business issues

The book will give you a chance to learn how to use finance in most of the typical business situations that you encounter as a manager. The unique advantage of the book is its discussion of the use of finance in the rich context of case studies drawn from actual business situations. This will make it much easier to apply what you have learned in your own business context. (See Table 1.)

Spreadsheets

Spreadsheets, like most other powerful technologies, can be used very effectively or very badly, depending on the methodological skills of the user. With this book, you will learn how to use spreadsheets effectively – a new management skill. The book does not assume any prior knowledge of personal computers and spreadsheets.

How will you best learn from this book?

This book consists of text, case studies drawn from real business situations and models. In order to benefit fully, I recommend that you:

● try to solve these cases by yourself – do not look at my solution;
● then compare your solution with mine;
● finally, try to solve these cases again by yourself.

The unique benefits of the modelling approach

The modelling approach has enabled me to use an original structure for the material that will help you develop a progressive, step-by-step understanding of the essentials of finance: cash flow, value, risk, etc.

The models in this book will provide you with many more opportunities to experiment than the material in traditional textbooks. The modelling approach will enable you to

Table 1 • Case studies relevant to typical business situations

Business context	Models within a business case context	More general models
Creating value out of commitment to **growth**	Modelling the impact of growth: *Delta Metal* (p. 177). Redesigning a business to avoid explosive cash requirements: *SW Life* (p. 220). Committing the 'right' resources at the 'right time' in a growing business: *Motion-Control* (p. 246). Investing in the growth of a market while keeping flexibility: *The CLS project* (p. 382). Assessing alternatives for external growth: *I, in the United Kingdom* (p. 415). Understanding an opportunity for co-operation: *I* (p. 432).	Assessing the value of growth (p. 179). Managing the trajectories of commitment for creating value out of growth (p. 271).
Creating value out of commitment to **innovation**	Designing the best strategy for launching a new product: *BA International* (p. 284). Assessing the value of a commitment to an R&D programme: *Eagle* (p. 355).	Modelling the profitability of a new product (p. 279).
Creating value out of commitment to **new business designs and processes**	Redesigning a contract for reducing risk and increasing value: *Gatefield* (p. 100). Sequencing payments as a source of value – going for collect-then-pay business: *Delta Metal* (p. 186). Order-driven businesses: *Relais Electriques* (p. 205). Going for a joint venture rather than for a straight acquisition: *I and F* (p. 415).	Value of an order-driven business (p. 196).
Creating value out of commitments to **turnarounds** and **divestments**	Gradual change vs. aggressive turnaround: *Tyler Welding* (p. 237). Maximising the value of a divestment: *F* (p. 452) and *RFa* (p. 470).	Managing the trajectories of commitment for creating value out of decline (p. 271).
Creating value out of **value pricing**	Value pricing: *Jilin (II)* (p. 45).	Price/volume trade-offs (p. 159) Price vs. volume (p. 161). Impact of changes in product mix (p. 162).

Table 1 ● (*continued*)

Business context	Models within a business case context	More general models
Creating value out of *negotiation*	Effective preparation of a negotiation of a contract: *Jilin* (p. 16). Negotiating a joint venture: *I* (p. 440). Modelling 'the other side': *Jilin (II)* (p. 6) and *F* (p. 452).	
Assessing performance In creating value	Cash vs. profit and the cash-income parity matrix: *Delta Metal* (p. 111). Analysing the trajectories of orders, spending and collection: *Relais Electriques* (p. 211). Assessing performance and risk: *Swedish Timber* (p. 84).	Performance and transfer price (p. 217).
Financial plans and models for creating value	Financial model and plan of a business: *Delta Metal* (p. 106). Financial model and plan in a multi-currency environment: *PT PharMa* (p. 226). Financial model and plan of a project: *Jilin* (p. 60). Financial model and plan of a manufacturing business: *Tyler Welding* (p. 255). Financial plans and models for new products and new product concepts: *BA International* (p. 284) and *Eagle* (p. 355). Financial models and plans of businesses that are going to be acquired or divested: *I, in the United Kingdom* (p. 415) and *RFa* (p. 470). Model and plan of a joint venture (p. 461). Modelling forecasting mistakes: *Delta Metal* (p. 186). Building robust financial plans: *Tyler Welding* and *Motion-Control* (p. 259).	Trajectory models (pp. 151 and 167). Per-cent-of-sales models (p. 126). NPV as the outcome of models (p. 136). Comprehensive income, cash flow and balance sheets model with interest and ratios (p. 141). Price/volume models (p. 152). Order-driven model (p. 213). Model structured by decreasing degree of commitment (p. 265). Global, full life non-discounted model (p. 298). Quarterly model (p. 41). Modelling cost trajectories and experience effects (pp. 315–17). Modelling sales trajectories with the product life cycle concept (p. 316). Inflation and real prices (p. 319). Assessing continuing value (p. 404). Making a model 'easy to use' (p. 334).

Table 1 • (*continued*)

Business context	Models within a business case context	More general models
Portraying and managing **risk and flexibility**	Portraying risk and structuring the sequence of decisions and events with decision diagrams: *Swedish Timber* (pp. 71 and 78), *Dhahran Roads (II)* (p. 96), *BA International* (p. 344) and *I and F* (p. 440). Evaluating alternative value-risk contributions: *Swedish Timber* (p. 74), *BA International* (p. 344) and *Eagle (II)* (p. 373). Risk as a portfolio issue: *Swedish Timber* (p. 69) and *CLS* (p. 384). The value of reacting to adverse events: *Dhahran Roads (III)* (p. 98). Changing the conditions of a business: *Gatefield* (p. 100). Strategic 'what-if': *Tyler Welding and Motion-Control* (p. 259). Comparing two types of capital expenditure: *CLS* (p. 382). The value of a joint venture (p. 463). Flexibility value when launching a new product: *BA International* (p. 349). Flexibility in the decision to commit to a new product concept: *Eagle* (p. 355)	Generating distributions (p. 76). Speed vs. flexibility (p. 375). Value of an order-driven business (p. 196). Managing the trajectories of commitment for creating value out of growth (p. 271). Currency risk. *Swedish Timber* (p.64), *PT PharMa* (p. 233) and *BA International* (p. 342).

acquire a full understanding of finance and to develop the capability to use it. The case studies and their analyses will help you develop skills in:

● specifying problems so that they can be analysed in value creation terms;
● searching for and analysing relevant information;
● selecting adequate financial approaches, and defining relevant variables and relationships;
● building these into effective models, understanding the outcome of these models and testing them against concepts and theories.

The modelling approach will enable you to develop and understand the different topics of finance as a whole. In order to work with it effectively, you need to acquire a global understanding of the discipline. The material presented and analysed in this book will help you to develop that global perspective on finance and financial modelling.

The modelling approach will enable you to develop the skills required to use personal computers and spreadsheets effectively. It will help you to develop the capability of using personal computers and spreadsheets as learning tools.

For users of *Corporate Finance: A model building approach*

This book uses the same learning approach as *Corporate Finance: a model building approach*. However, except for Part VI, all the material is new.

In this book, the users of *Corporate Finance* will find a series of new cases – including new versions of Delta Metal and BA International. They will also find a discussion of new business issues:

- the value and risk of alternative business designs: pay-then-collect vs. collect-then-pay designs;
- flexibility: when to keep and when to exercise options in a variety of business situations – contracts and projects (Gatefield), acquisitions (I/F and RFa), research and development (Eagle), turnarounds (Tyler Welding) and growth (Motion-Control).

They will also find new approaches to building models and, in particular, the new '**trajectory of receipts and payments**' framework.

Finally, they will realise that this book is more focused on value and value creation.

Acknowledgements

When writing a book based on the experience of designing and running learning situations, it is a great pleasure for me to think about all the people I had the chance to work with and to learn from. Among those I would like to pay a special tribute to are all the executives who participated in the courses and programmes on which I taught how to use finance for creating value. I would also like to pay a tribute to the colleagues with whom I enjoyed working and learning about helping others to learn. Among these, two deserve a very special tribute as this book draws on many exciting joint-teaching experiences with them: Sherwood Frey and the late Bernard Dubois.

Also I would like to thank the educational institutions and companies I had the chance to be associated with:

- The Centre HEC-ISA (France) where I started my career as a teacher of management.
- The Harvard Business School, which helped me to understand what is excellence in teaching.
- IFL (Sweden), where I discovered the unique value of executive education as a co-operative venture between industry and academia.
- AGA, which gave me the opportunity to work at creating a 'Corporate University'.
- AGA Linde Healthcare, where I have the chance today, as an executive, to help the organisation and the people who make it develop superior growth and value creation capabilities.

Michel Schlosser
Versailles, July 2002

Publisher's acknowledgements

We are grateful to Sherwood Frey for permission to reproduce the Dhahran Roads and Gatefield Project cases; to the Financial Times Limited for Figure 5.9 Losses on currency dealings embarrass Lufthansa, © *Financial Times*, 24 February 1986; to The Jakarta Post for permission to reproduce Figure L.1 Medicine prices tell a horror story, © *The Jakarta Post*, 15 September 1996. Whilst every effort has been made to trace the owners of copyright material, in a few cases this has proved impossible and we take this opportunity to offer our apologies to any copyright holders whose rights we may have unwittingly infringed.

EVA® is a registered trademark of Stern Stewart and Co. Many of the designations used by manufacturers and sellers to distinguish their products are claimed as trademarks. Pearson Education has made every attempt to supply trademark information about manufacturers and their products mentioned in this book.

PART *I*

Shareholder value

CHAPTER 1

Personal financial spreadsheet models for creating maximum shareholder value

Value is nothing like a new idea and finance textbooks have been advocating for decades that shareholder value should be considered as a central business objective. What is novel is that:

- The concept of shareholder value has spread well outside the community of finance specialists and has become an important issue for many managers. In many companies all over the world, managers are now invited to act every day as 'value managers'.[1]
- Every person in business has access to spreadsheets and related software.

This has created the need for simple and robust tools that can be used to address a wide range of business situations by almost anyone engaged in business. The purpose of this book is to help you develop your personal mastery of using these tools for creating maximum value.

In this first chapter, I should like to single out two of the many reasons that explain why shareholder value has become so popular:

- In recent years a lot has happened on stock markets all over the world. For more than a decade, a significant number of companies showed stellar performance, then the 'bubble' burst and the markets experienced brutal readjustments. This has reminded investors that equities are a risky investment. It has also raised a series of questions: what can investors 'reasonably' expect from investing long term in equities? What standards of value creation does that create for companies? Has the use of new technologies led to new standards for value creation?.

● Maximizing shareholder value is a very good – some people would even say the best – metric for setting targets and measuring performance.

I shall conclude the chapter by explaining what I mean by 'personal' financial models: what is especially valuable in these models? How can these models help you become a more effective 'value manager'?

1.1 Shareholder value: how does the value performance of your company compare with the top global value performers?

The shareholder value of a company is the monetary market value of the interests of its owners. In a company that is listed on the stock market, the shareholder value is very simply calculated as the product of the price of each share by the number of shares outstanding. In a company that is not listed, it is more difficult to find out its market value as one has to estimate the price at which shareholders could sell their holdings. In recent years, it has become common practice to rank companies by the size of their shareholder value rather than by the size of their sales. An example of such rankings is the 'Global 1000' of *Business Week* which lists the 1000 most valuable business firms in the world. The 15 most valuable firms in the world are shown in Table 1.1.[2]

In Table 1.1, focus on the top three companies in 2000: General Electric (GE), Intel and Cisco Systems. Finding GE at the top of the list is no surprise: GE is a very large company ($130 billion sales in 2000) with a very long record of successful performance. The companies coming second and third are a bit more of a surprise: Intel is a much smaller company ($34 billion sales) which was worth $8.9 billion only in 1990. Cisco Systems is an even smaller company ($19 billion sales), which only became public in 1990. For the sake of simplicity, let us ignore the impact of dividends and of possible new equity issues. Table 1.1 shows us that:

● Somebody who might have invested $63 billion in buying all the shares of General Electric in 1990 would have seen the value of that investment multiply by 4.9 in 12 years (1990 to 2002), which corresponds to an annual return of 14%. Note that this investment would be multiplied by 8.3 in 10 years (1990 to 2000) – an annual return of 23%![3]
● Somebody who might have invested $8.9 billion in buying all the shares of Intel in 1990 would have seen this $8.9 billion investment grow to $417 billion in 2000 – or to multiply 46.9 times, which corresponds to an annual return of 47% over 10 years, and then go down to $178 billion in 2002, still an annual return of 28% over 12 years.[4]

Table 1.1, and all the data you may gather on the stock markets,[5] shows that there were really great investment opportunities in the markets in the 1990s.[6]

What will these opportunities be in the future? Nobody knows, but it seems that new benchmarks have been established. This is very good news for all of us as investors. At the same time it is definitely a great challenge for all of us as managers and value creators. **All companies listed on the stock markets compete in one very special arena: they all compete with the top value creation performers for the attention and money of the investors – and of the public.** Within their other competitive arenas, many companies want to be 'number one' or 'number two', or leave. What establishes a company as a top

Table 1.1 ● The 15 most valuable companies in the world (values[8] in $ billion)

1990		1995		2000		2002	
	Value		Value		Value		Value
1 NTT	119	1 NTT	129	1 General Electric	520	General Electric	309
2 IBM	69	2 Shell	108	2 Intel(1)	417	Microsoft	276
3 Industrial Bank		3 General Electric	98	3 Cisco Systems(1)	395	Exxon Mobil	271
of Japan	68	4 Exxon	89	4 Microsoft(2)	323	Wal-Mart Stores	241
4 Shell	67	5 AT&T	80	5 Exxon Mobil	290	Citigroup	223
5 General Electric	63	6 Coca-Cola	79	6 Vodafone			
6 Exxon	60	7 Toyota	72	Airtouch	278		
7 Sumitomo Bank	56	8 Mitsubishi Bank	69	7 Wal-Mart Stores	257		
8 Fuji Bank	53	9 Industrial Bank		8 NTT-Docomo	247		
9 Toyota	50	of Japan	68	9 Nokia	242		
10 Mitsui Tayo		10 Fuji Bank	66	10 Shell	214		
Kobe Bank	50	11 Sumitomo Bank	65	11 Citigroup	210		
11 Dai-IchiKangyo		12 Sanwa Bank	62	12 BP Amoco	208		
Bank	50	13 Philip Morris	62	13 Oracle	204		
12 Mitsubishi Bank	47	14 Roche Holding	61	14 IBM	192		
13 AT&T	47	15 Dai-Ichi		15 NTT	189		
14 Sanwa Bank	46	Kangyo Bank	59				
15 Tokyo Electric							
Power	42						

(1) In May 2002, the value of Intel was $178 billion and the value of Cisco was $96 billion.
(2) In the 1999 ranking, Microsoft was the most valuable company ($407 billion). The value of Microsoft in 1990 was $8.1 billion.
Source: Business Week, The 'Global 1000'[9] for 1990, 1995 and 2000. The author for 2002.

competitor on the stock market? When comparing companies, do investors look at the businesses these companies are in, and limit their expectations of stellar performance to some industries only?[7] Or, rather, do they expect that more or less all great companies in all industries quickly reinvent themselves to join the value creation leaders? What do you personally expect when you put yourself in the position of an investor? Maybe it is time really to look into the value creation process of your own company!

1.2 Shareholder value maximization: a responsibility and a discipline for all managers

A very effective business metric

Among all the metrics for setting targets and measuring performance (sales growth, profit, cash flow, return, etc.), creation of value, and creation of shareholder value in particular, is probably the most meaningful:

● Creation of value is the most comprehensive business metric. Value has the potential to describe the totality of a business activity over its whole economic life. Value is future related. Value takes into account all revenues and costs incurred (including the cost of money). Value has the potential to reflect risk. Value reflects the time effectiveness of a business, and so on. In a corporation with publicly traded shares, any creation of value is immediately and directly reflected into the value of the shares of the company. Value is the only metric that enables managers to test each of their business ideas against an external, 'objective' benchmark.[10] How does *this* idea stand out in front of all other comparable business ideas? How much value do external investors attach to *this* idea?

● Focusing on shareholder value enables broad decentralization. Maximizing shareholder value is a simple rule that is sufficient to guarantee that any manager acts in the best interests of the corporation and of each of the corporation's owners – regardless of differences in their wealth and tastes.

● Creating value is one of the very few business ambitions that has the power to unite all the parties – or 'stakeholders' – involved in a business: employees, customers, suppliers, local and national state authorities, society at large, owners, etc. If it directly benefits its owners, any increase in the value of the shares of a corporation also reflects a much broader success. A corporation is a complex system of contractual relationships that brings a variety of interests into a working equilibrium. The shares of a corporation – a residual claim on its cash flows and assets – can be traded freely and their value reflects the success of the whole contractual system and not only the success of the sole owners. As an investor, would you really be willing to put your money in a company that tries to create value against the interests of its employees, against the interests of its customers, against the interests of society at large? The only effective way for a company to create value in a sustainable manner is to work at continuously satisfying its customers and motivating its employees.

● Focusing on shareholder value is a very effective way of using external pressure to drive continuous change and improvement. It helps companies to monitor the competitiveness of their operations, to really scrutinize all their strategic investments, to demonstrate the value of synergies, to eliminate waste, to identify the areas that should be re-engineered, and so on.

● Finally, creating value corresponds to positive, progressive and motivating behaviours. Creating value is a matter of looking for opportunities, of creating alternatives, of redefining situations, of innovating and so on.

A 'discipline' for all managers

The position expressed in this book is that maximizing shareholder value is not only a management responsibility, it is also a discipline for managers and for all the people working in a business firm. Following Peter Senge, let us define a discipline as 'a body of theory and practice that must be studied and mastered to be put into practice ... To practice a discipline is to be a life long learner. You never arrive; you spend your life mastering disciplines.'[11] The discipline of maximizing shareholder value invites you to put yourself in the position of the owners and continuously to invent better solutions for doing business in ways that maximize shareholder value. The goal of this book is to help you enhance your personal mastery of designing and using those financial models that will enable you to:

● better understand how to measure your own contribution to the continuous process of creating value;

- better understand why some courses of action and changes increase value more than others;
- find better ways to explain to the people you work with how you can all contribute to the process of creating value. It is not sufficient that business leaders be sensitive to shareholder value. Business leaders also have the responsibility to enlist all the people they work with in the discipline of creating shareholder value and to design a learning organization that is always keen to create new ways to maximize shareholder value.

Accounting and finance do not need to be used in a mechanical way[12]

For some people, finance and accounting have the reputation of being a bit mechanical but we should like to show you in this book that this is not necessarily the case. Using an accounting and finance framework does not mean that you have to assume simplistic cause-and-effect relationships. Also, using an accounting and finance framework often offers an opportunity for looking at the whole and for avoiding fragmenting the analysis too much. In this book we are interested in modelling as an activity that helps us understand and influence the processes of creating value. We shall use the framework of accounting and finance to build models that focus on:

- understanding the impact of various changes;
- leveraging those changes;
- exploring the outcomes of different trajectories: different price, volume, costs, etc., as well as different trajectories in commitment;
- controlling the dynamics of growth and recession;
- understanding the risks and the dynamics of different business designs;
- helping to design structures that thrive on conflicting interests, etc.

Maximization is the relevant goal

If most managers would probably agree that enhancing shareholder value is a legitimate goal, it is also fair to say that very few of them would spontaneously accept that, in a competitive world, the relevant objective is to **maximize shareholder value**. Maximization is not an easily accepted idea and is often associated with such negative attitudes as greed and short-term thinking. Without entering an extremely rich and complex – and at times heated – debate, let us just make a few remarks aimed at helping you realize, if needed, that shareholder maximization is nothing like a simplistic, short-term rule:

- Shareholder value should be maximized within a co-operative system: a corporation is a co-operative system in which the various stakeholders have to co-operate to create value. Conflicts may happen at times, especially when it comes to sharing value, but these conflicts should be kept to a minimum for the co-operative system to function effectively,[13] to satisfy the various stakeholders and to provide an effective governance.[14] The game in Appendix I.1 at the end of this chapter illustrates this idea of maximization within a co-operative system.
- The goal is to aim continuously at bringing the shareholder value to a maximum that is sustainable over the long run. This is the same idea as that expressed by Max Weber

about capitalism: 'Unlimited greed for gain is not in the least identical with capitalism, and is still less its spirit. Capitalism may even be identical with the restraint, or at least a rational tempering, of this irrational impulse. But capitalism is identical with the pursuit of profit, and forever renewed profit, by means of continuous, rational, capitalistic enterprise. For it must be so: in a wholly capitalistic order of society, an individual capitalistic enterprise which did not take advantage of its opportunities for profit-making would be doomed to extinction.'[15]

● Finally, maximizing shareholder value is a matter of doing the maximum that anybody could do in the circumstances they are in. It is not trying to reach some kind of theoretical maximum in the absolute.

1.3 Personal models for creating maximum value

Modelling is a very fundamental and common human activity as, if we believe Patrick Rivett: 'The whole history of man, even, in his most non-scientific activities, shows that he is essentially a model-building animal.'[16] This book is very much about what we call **personal modelling**. By personal, we mean an activity which can be undertaken by any manager for his or her own benefit. This activity is not necessarily individual as it may equally involve a manager or a team of managers, but it is private to those members and often unique to that group.

● In many instances, personal modelling simply helps a manager or a group of managers to understand and master a unique situation. In these cases the model is often scrapped as soon as the situation is mastered; learning and experience accumulate but learning aids lose their value as soon as they have served their purpose. The discipline of creating value is a complex activity that can be greatly helped by personal models and this is an experience that we would like to share throughout this book.

● In some instances, personal modelling also helps managers to develop models which will become of standard use (corporate planning models, budgetary models, etc.). This generality of use will require a complete change in the nature of the original model which will have to lose its personal character and become a heavy-duty operational tool to be used by a wide range of people in the organization. This transformation will generally be done by specialists in charge of corporate modelling and procedures. We do not deal with heavy-duty models in this book.

This book is based on the assumption that you will build the various models by yourselves.

● The learning you can achieve from models is not limited to the analysis of their results. In general you learn most from your models while you are building them. With computers you can easily build models and really 'learn by doing'. As expressed by Nicholas Negroponte, 'do not dissect frogs, build them!'[17]

● Building models is usually much more fun than using them. As Russell Ackoff has said: 'One can enjoy a game played by others, but one can only have fun by playing it oneself.'[18]

The consequence is that models should be kept reasonably simple. In this book, we only consider models that any generalist can build by him or herself.

Building the models by yourself does not mean that you should work with this book alone: rather, join with your colleagues and use the book as a way to engage them in a conversation focused on the many methods of creating value in business.

Thriving in the spreadsheet culture

Spreadsheets are everywhere. As expressed by Michael Schrage: 'Within a decade, North America's financial culture has become a spreadsheet culture. Spreadsheets became the medium, the method, the tool and the language of all serious financial analysis.'[19] This book will help you develop your mastery of spreadsheet modelling.

Notes

1. A. Rappaport (1986), *Creating Shareholder Value*, The Free Press. G. Bennett Stewart III (1991), *The Quest for Value, The EVA™ Management Guide*, HarperBusiness. T. Copeland, T. Koller and J. Murrin (1996), *Valuation, Measuring and Managing the Value of Companies*, John Wiley. J.A. Knight (1997), *Value Based Management*, McGraw-Hill. A.L. Ehrbarr (1998), *Stern Stewart's EVA, The Real Key to Creating Wealth*, John Wiley.
2. In 2002, *Fortune* was also publishing its 'Global 500' (http://www.fortune.com). The three companies with the largest sales were: (1) Exxon Mobil ($210 billion), (2) Wal-Mart ($193 billion), and (3) General Motors ($185 billion). General Motors' value was $37 billion only.
3. As shown in Chapter 2, the formula for calculating the annual return is:

    $4.9^{1/12} - 1 = 0.14$ (where 12 is the number of years in the period). $8.3^{1/10} - 1 = 0.23$

4. $46.9^{1/10} - 1 = 0.47$; $20^{1/12} - 1 = 0.28$
5. On MSN's website (http://www.msn.com) you can get simulations that will tell you how much you would have today if you had invested $10 000 in any one of all the listed US companies over periods up to 10 years. This is a much more reliable calculation than our estimate above.

    - $10 000 invested in GE in early May 1990 would have grown to $115 767 in May 2000 (a 28% annual return) and to $70 397 in May 2002 (an 18% annual return).
    - The same $10 000 invested in Intel would have grown to $416 625 in May 2000 (a 45% annual return), and to $195 850 in May 2002 (a 28% annual return).
    - The same $10 000 invested in Cisco would have grown to $6 281 636 in May 2000 (a 90% annual return) and to $1 812 638 in May 2002 (a 54% annual return).

6. This is confirmed by Jeremy Siegel in *Stocks for the Long Run* (1998), McGraw-Hill. Siegel shows that in the USA, over the period 1802–1997, stocks have produced an **average real – above inflation – annual return of 7%**, bonds 3% and gold 0%.

    In the USA, over the same period, the real return on stocks has been fairly stable at around 7% with two exceptional periods: a period of very low returns (1966–81) and a period of higher returns (13%) most recently (1982–97).

    Other countries show fairly similar data: the long-term return on stocks in the period 1926–97 has been 7.2% in the USA, 6.6% in Germany, 6.2% in the UK but only 3.4% in Japan.

    A site for long-term investment data is Globalfindata (http://www.globalfindata.com).
7. The 25 February 2002 'shareholder scoreboard' available on the web edition of the *Wall Street Journal* (http://www.wsj.com), reported wide variations in the return provided by different industries to their shareholders. Over the period 1996–2001 (USA only): *Top returns*: Internet services 66% a year; biotechnology: 30%; advanced medical devices: 25%, security brokers: 24%; home construction: 23%. *Bottom returns*: mining and metals: –1%; consumer services: –3%; recreational products and services: –3%; lodging: –6%; office equipment: –10%.
8. The shareholder values in Table 1.1 show what each company was worth at the end of May 1990, May 1995 and May 2000 but not really the amount of value that has been created by these

companies. In order to know this, one would have to deduct from these values the amounts that have been invested by the shareholders in the process of creating this value. The net shareholder value created – or market value added (MVA) – is calculated by several consulting companies and in particular by Stern Stewart & Co. (http://www.sternstewart.com).

9. Published each year by *Business Week* – in its first July issue. *Business Week* also publishes the value of companies listed on emerging markets. The 'Top 200 Emerging-market Companies' showed that the most valuable emerging-market company, China Mobile (Hong Kong), was worth $90 billion in 2001. This was a little higher in value than Deutsche Telekom, ranking 37 in the 'Global 1000' list. *Business Week* is at http://www.businessweek.com

10. Many senior executives seem to have difficulties when it comes to accepting the control exerted by stock markets which – contrary to customers – are rarely seen as being 'right'. Stock markets are typically, 'greedy', 'short-term oriented', 'excessively impatient', etc. We suggest that you invest time in reading one of the many books that espouse the point of view of shareholders, for example: G.P. Schwartz (1995), *Shareholder Rebellion*, Irwin.

11. From P. Senge (1990), *The Fifth Discipline*, Century Business, p. 10.

12. How good are you – or any of us – at thinking in a non-mechanistic way? How can we improve the quality of our thinking? These important issues which have been around for a long time in other disciplines are quickly gaining popularity in the field of management. The main issue is how to adopt a more complex, more systemic, more dynamic view of the world. Among a very long list of references: G. Simmel (1908), *Conflict and the Web of Group Affiliations*, The Free Press (1955). G. Nicolis and I. Prigogine (1989), *Exploring Complexity An Introduction*, W.H. Freeman. I. Prigogine and I. Stengers (1990), *Order Out of Chaos*, Flamingo. D. Bohm (1992), *Thought as a System*, Routledge. J.H. Holland (1995), *Hidden Order*, Addison-Wesley. T.I. Sanders (1998), *Strategic Thinking and the New Science*, The Free Press. R. Axelrod and M.D. Cohen (1999), *Harnessing Complexity*, The Free Press. For corporate governance, refer to X. Vives (2000), *Corporate Governance*, Cambridge University Press; refer also to the websites of the major investing institutions where they describe their corporate governance philosophy: Calpers – The California Public Employees Retirement System: www.calpers.org; TIAA-CREF (Teachers Insurance and Annuity Association – College Retirement Equities Fund): www.tiaa-cref.org.

13. R. Axelrod (1984), *The Evolution of Co-operation*, Penguin.

14. For the 'stakeholder theory', refer to R.E. Freeman (1984), *Strategic Management: a Stakeholder Approach*, Pitman Publishing. A discussion of value maximization and of its effectiveness as an economic rule is in M.C. Jensen, (2000), *Value Maximization and the Corporate Objective Function*, Harvard Business School Working Papers 00–058.

15. Max Weber (1905), *The Protestant Ethic and The Spirit of Capitalism*, Charles Scribner, New York (1958–76).

16. P. Rivett (1980), *Model Building for Decision Analysis*, John Wiley.

17. N. Negroponte (1995), *Being Digital*, Alfred A. Knopf.

18. R. Ackoff (1978), *The Art of Problem Solving – Accompanied by Ackoff's Fables*, John Wiley.

19. M. Schrage (2000), *Serious Play – How the World's Best Companies Simulate to Innovate*, Harvard Business School Press.

Appendix to Part I
Maximizing value in a co-operative system

This game is one of the many versions of the famous 'prisoners' dilemma'. The game is to be played by two people who role-play two division managers of the same corporation. Each player has to make the decision to behave either:

- according to the strict and immediate interest of their division ('my division first'); or
- according to the broader interests of the company as a whole ('company first').

Each player has a mission: to maximize his or her own interests or more precisely the interests of his or her own division.

The brief for each player

1. You have just been appointed local division manager of Maxima – a global company with two very strong divisions. The president of your own division is very clear: *'You should maximize the value of our business! Do not spend any time talking to the guy who is running the other division in your country! Just mind our own division!'*
2. In each of the next nine quarters you are going to make nine successive business decisions (one in each quarter).[1] Each of these decisions will result in more or less value depending on how you behave and also how the local manager of the other business behaves.

	The other manager behaves 'company first'	The other manager behaves 'my division first'
You behave 'company first'	**Value created: +3** (other player +3)	**Value created: –6** (other player +6)
You behave 'my division first'	**Value created: +6** (other player –6)	**Value created: –3** (other player –3)

3. You have to make your decision without knowing what the other player will decide – and the other player also has to decide without knowing your choice. Obviously, you may decide to behave differently in each of the nine decisions.

4. Each player receives two cards, marked respectively 'my division first' and 'company first'. For each decision, the players make their choice and disclose simultaneously the card that corresponds to their decision.

5. **Making decisions one to three**. The players are not allowed to talk to each other. They just make the three decisions and record their scores (see the score table below).

6. **Making decisions four to six**. In between decisions three and four the players have the option to talk to each other. If they decide to talk, they are allowed to discuss their strategies and to agree on how they will behave in the future. There is no obligation to make such an agreement and, if an agreement is made, each player may decide to breach it. Decisions four to six have to be actually played – especially if an agreement has been made! The players are not allowed to talk again before they have played decision six.

7. **Making decisions seven to nine**. In between decisions six and seven the players have a second option to talk. If they decide to talk, they are again allowed to make an agreement – that they will again be free to respect or to breach.

   An important feature of the last three decisions is that they result in double scores. When both players adopt the same behaviour, they each score +6 if they both behave 'company first' and –6 if they both behave 'my division first'. When the two players make different decisions, the one who behaves 'my division first' scores +12 and the one who scores 'company first' scores –12.

   Decisions seven to nine have to be actually played – especially if an agreement has been made. The players are not allowed to talk again.

8. There is one individual winner: the player with the highest total score.

The game is even more interesting when it is played simultaneously by several pairs of players: where this is the case there is also one single individual winner in the whole group.

The score table

Value score	Value score	Value score
Quarter 1	Quarter 4	Quarter 7
Quarter 2	Quarter 5	Quarter 8
Quarter 3	Quarter 6	Quarter 9
Subtotal:	Subtotal:	**Total:**

The winning behaviour: 'maximization in a co-operative system'

There is a very easy way to win. You always play 'company first' and you score 36! This obviously assumes that the other player will also play 'company first', but what would motivate him or her to play differently, since always playing 'company first' enables the other player to get the very high score of 36?

   These very simple behaviours correspond to what we call 'maximization in a co-operative system':

- You start with adopting a simple, positive, non-aggressive behaviour – even if you are not sure that the other party will be equally positive.
- You continue behaving in the same non-aggressive way, always keeping a long-term point of view. The long-term thinking is essential to help you take care not to destabilize the game by pursuing immediate gains. Achieving immediate ('short-term') gains may cause retaliation and counter-retaliation and completely destabilizes the process.
- You focus on your own gains and progress. Looking enviously at the gains and progress of the other player is no good.
- You do not make explicit agreements. Agreements are not really needed and they actually create the opportunity for cheating.

Life is not that simple, however, and you have to think about what you should do in the case of the other party being aggressive. You should be prepared to retaliate and the recommendation is retaliate fast and forgive fast!

Experience of running this game shows that some players do follow the simple rules described above and score 36 each without any formal agreements, but this is not very common. Many players often decide to adopt 'smarter' strategies and experience shows the following:

- **Most 'smart' strategies result in low** (lower than 36) **or very low** (negative) **scores** for both players. It is actually very easy for two players to destabilize the game and when this happens there is no agreement that typically helps – quite the contrary!
- Some 'smart' strategies result in high – higher than 36 – scores for one of the players. This is typically due to the fact that one player has managed to be aggressive at some stage without causing retaliation. It is always interesting to ask the two players who have reached such a result to play nine new decisions – especially when the 'victory' has been achieved by a 'my division first' in round nine.
- Some 'smart' strategies also result in average scores – around 18. This typically happens when people following aggressive strategies very quickly switch to co-operative approaches.

Note

1. Imagine that you and the other player are running the two divisions of Maxima in a foreign country. You are the two most senior managers and there is no local country president. The activities of the two divisions are very independent. However, since the two divisions are part of the same company there are situations (sharing of information, sharing of resources, etc.) where it pays to take the overall perspective of the company. Even though it might look easier and more 'profitable' for you to focus on the sole interest of your division it is probably more effective to think overall company first.

APPENDIX

PART *II*

Value and risk

Part II introduces modelling tools for understanding how the changes and the decisions that you can make today will improve the future of your business.

Chapters 2, 3 and 4 discuss how to estimate the value created by such changes and decisions.

Chapter 5 proposes a first set of tools that acknowledge that it is impossible to predict the future. Typically we cannot foresee what the value created by a decision will be. However, we can generally estimate all the possible values that may result from this action and decide based on the distribution of these possible values.

***Value** is discussed from the practical example of a negotiation in the telecommunications industry. How can we design a model that will help prepare for the final negotiation of the Jilin project? A very important idea in this book is that models are especially useful for creating new business solutions – not so much for performing post-mortem analysis. A key table here is Table 2.6 which summarizes **what net present values (NPVs) really mean**.*

***Risk** is discussed from another business case, Swedish Timber. Swedish Timber is exposed to substantial currency risk in its business of trading wood in Egypt. Would currency hedging be an effective solution?*

*A key tool introduced in Chapter 5 is the **decision diagram**. See Figures 5.1 and 5.5.*

*In Chapter 4, we also discuss how to measure the progress made in the process of creating value. We discuss the difference between value and **income**. We open the discussion about matching and other related accounting principles: are they more related to the old 'economy of things' than to the 'economy of information'? A key part of Chapter 4 is Section 4.4 which compares **cash** and income: which of the two gives the best picture of the annual outcome of your operations?*

In the Appendix to Part II you will find additional compounding and discounting tools, as well as two case studies. Dhahran Roads is about how to assess the value and risk of a project. In Dhahran Roads, the company has an option to react: we will deal with options later in the book. Gatefield is about how to deliver a better service at a lower price while achieving the same profit and incurring less risk!

The Jilin project

On 15 October 2001, Marcel Dubois, Senior Network Area Manager at French Telecom (FT), was busy reviewing his files on the Jilin project. He was due to leave for China that evening and he wanted to make sure that he had all the elements needed for the final negotiations that he was going to lead with the Chinese authorities.

Negotiations with the Chinese authorities about the Jilin project had been going on since early 2000 and after lengthy discussions about the technical specifications of the project several international telecommunication companies were invited to submit bids by 15 September 2001. Finally, FT was awarded the project and was invited to China for the contract's signing. Marcel Dubois was delighted to have succeeded in winning the project but he was very well aware that the Chinese authorities would most likely come up with last minute requirements. Once again, he would probably have to use all his negotiating ability to protect and hopefully improve the value of the project. He was not actually expecting to get a final signature before a few weeks of discussions had taken place.

Experience of similar negotiations had taught Marcel Dubois that many events could occur in this final round of negotiations: requests for an outright discount, requests for changes in the timing of the implementation of the project, requests for changes in payment conditions and even requests for financing . . . as well as the discovery by FT of some unexpected operational problems leading to higher costs. Finally, he was very well aware that some 'surprises' could also happen after the contract had been signed.

The project, as defined in the bid submitted by FT, is described in Figure A.1. FT's policy was to engage only on those projects that created shareholder value. Minimum return requirements had been defined: for such projects return should be higher than 15% a year (or 3.6% a quarter).

Project description

Long-distance optical-fibre line communication system for the Jilin oil field. Total contract value: €34 million plus €2 million maintenance contract. Duration: two-year execution (2002 and 2003); two-year guarantee (2004 and 2005).

Billings and costs

	2002	2003	2004	2005	Total
Billings					
Main contract	20.4	13.6	–	–	**34.0**
Maintenance	–	–	1.0	1.0	**2.0**
Costs, labour and material	7.2	4.8	0.9	0.9	**13.8**

In addition to labour and material costs, FT would also have to face equipment costs amounting to a total of €18.6 million:

- *Cables*: €5.8 million, bought from FT's cable division. As they were needed on site early in order to get the civil work started, cables would be bought as soon as the contract was signed and paid for in December 2001 or January 2002.
- *Electronic equipment*: €12.0 million. This equipment would be bought from FT's information systems division: 9.0 million bought and paid for in December 2001 or January 2002, and 3.0 million bought and paid for in the first quarter of 2002.
- *Testing equipment*: €0.8 million. To be acquired and paid in the second quarter of 2002.

Some people had argued that it could be simpler to buy all the equipment as soon as the contract was signed and ship all of it at once on the same boat.

As the project was expected to benefit from a tax exemption, no allowance for tax had been made.

Payment conditions

Main contract
A 15% advance on the €34 million.
A 5% retention to be repaid in two equal amounts in the fourth quarter of 2004 and the fourth quarter of 2005. Customer's payments were to occur in the same quarter as the quarter of invoicing. However, experience of recent projects had shown that payment delays were not unusual with this type of customer.

Maintenance
€0.25 million paid in each quarter of 2004 and 2005.

Costs
All material and labour costs were to be paid in the quarter in which they occurred.

Figure A.1 The Jilin contract

CASE

Quarterly breakdown of billings and costs incurred (€ million)

	2002				2003			
	1	2	3	4	1	2	3	4
Main contract	0	3.80	8.20	8.40	5.40	3.20	3.20	1.80
Maintenance	–	–	–	–	–	–	–	–
Equipment	14.8[a] 3.00	0.80	–	–	–	–	–	–
Other costs	1.60	1.80	1.80	2.00	2.00	1.20	0.80	0.80

	2004				2005			
	1	2	3	4	1	2	3	4
Main contract	–	–	–	–	–	–	–	–
Maintenance	0.25	0.25	0.25	0.25	0.25	0.25	0.25	0.25
Equipment	–	–	–	–	–	–	–	–
Other costs	0.24	0.22	0.22	0.22	0.22	0.22	0.22	0.24

[a] *Or in the last quarter of 2001.*

Figure A.1 continued

CHAPTER 2

Is it worth doing this business?

Before meeting the customer for the 'final' negotiation of the Jilin project, let us answer three questions:

- If signed as it is and executed exactly as planned, how much value will this project create?
- What may happen during the final negotiation – and after the contract is signed?
- How can we make the best of the final negotiation and maximize the value of the project?

Let us start with the first question. Assuming that it is signed exactly as it is now and executed exactly as planned, how much value will the Jilin project create?

2.1 Two initial questions

Assessing the value created by a project is a simple matter of comparing:

- all that you are going to get from it (all cash receipts or revenues[1]) over the whole duration of its execution

with,

- all that you are going to have to pay for it (all cash disbursements or costs[2]) including possible financing costs.

As estimating financing costs often requires lengthy calculations the best way is to proceed in two steps.

**Step 1: Ignoring financing costs, how much additional cash or income[3]
will this business generate in the end?**
Data in the case suggest that if the contract is signed as it is and if execution goes as planned, then completing the project will enable the company to create a cash surplus – or profit – of €3.6 million (*see* Table 2.1). This surplus, which ignores financing costs, is generally called the **'operating cash surplus'** or **'operating income or profit'**.[4]

Table 2.1 ● Value created by the Jilin project (in million euros, over the period 2001–04) ignoring financing costs

Total cash receipts from the customer	36.00
Total payments to the suppliers of equipment	18.60
Other payments for labour, material, travel, etc.	13.80
Operating cash surplus/income generated by the project	**3.60**

If the completion of the Jilin project were to take place instantaneously when the contract is signed, then we could simply say that the project will increase the shareholder value by €3.6 million. Unfortunately, things will not happen instantaneously as the company will need four years to complete the project. As soon as the completion of an activity requires time, then suddenly everything becomes more complicated:

● The outcome – the value created – becomes uncertain. Receipts and disbursements become future events that may well differ from expectations. Assessing shareholder value suddenly becomes a matter of estimating an uncertain quantity. A distribution of possible values has to be estimated. Let us ignore this dimension of the problem for the time being.[5]

● There is a need to take into account the impact of financing. The completion of a project over time typically involves temporary cash deficits and excesses which results in financing costs and gains.

● Finally, when it takes a long time to complete a project, you will probably want to design intermediate measurements that will enable you to assess the progress made over the process of creating value.

Step 2: Once the financing costs are taken into account, how much value will be created by this business?

Even though they will exceed cash outflows in the end, cash inflows will probably not be higher than cash outflows at any moment in time. As is typically the case with projects, receipts and disbursements will not be fully synchronized and temporary cash deficits and excesses will occur. At the beginning of the project spending will go fast and will create a temporary cash deficit. This overspending or 'investment' will cause financing costs that will destroy part of the value created by the project. Later on, receipts will exceed disbursements and the investment of the temporary cash excesses will create additional value. The value created by the project will be equal to: what is left of the operating cash surplus (€3.6 million) once the value destroyed by the temporary deficits and the value created by the temporary excesses have been taken into account.

Money does not come for free. If the execution of a project requires money, then you have to take into account the cost of that money, just as you take into account the cost of any other resource. Let us now have a look at the cash generation process of the project.

2.2 Selecting an adequate period for modelling the cash generation process

How much simplification should you introduce into your models? . . . a few initial considerations

The Jilin case provides us with quarterly data. Should we use these data and model the cash generation process on a quarterly basis, or should we adopt a 'helicopter' view and build an annual model instead? This is a decision that you often face when building models: how much should you simplify reality?

● What are the trade-offs? An annual model is easier to build and use. It may enable us quickly to be in the position to test a large number of scenarios. On the other hand, a quarterly model describes the cash generation process much more accurately. The cash generation process is often a continuous process and bank accounts are calculated and balanced every day.

● What is the goal? We are going to meet the customer very soon for the 'final' negotiation of the contract. We need a model to simulate the impact of possible last minute change requests coming from the customer – and from us. Why not quickly build an annual model and spend as much time as possible using the model and trying to anticipate what may happen when we meet the customer?

● How to get started? If you cannot make up your mind and you realize that in the end you will probably have to build both a quarterly and an annual model, the issue becomes: which model do you start with? Do you start with the quarterly or the annual model; with the 'ground' view or the 'helicopter' view? My recommendation is that you start with the helicopter view. Starting from the helicopter view enables you quickly to have a model that you can play with. It also allows you to develop further your understanding of the situation. This often leads you to improve, modify or even completely redesign your model. Going through this process puts you in a much better position for developing a detailed model – if you feel that it is still needed.

2.3 Building an initial paper-and-pencil model of the annual cash flows of the project

Spreadsheets are very flexible tools and many people would never use anything other than a spreadsheet when they build models. However, I would like to recommend that you consider not rushing to your spreadsheet. Why not start with an old fashioned 'paper-and-pencil' model? This is often a very good way to reflect on the design of your models and to think about the following.

● The **outcome variable(s)**. What do you want to achieve with this project? Here, as in most financial models, the outcome variable is the shareholder value created by the project.

● The **variables** that will enable you to generate the outcome variable. These variables generally belong to different categories:
  – **parameters or drivers**. These are all the variables that you want to be able to play with in order to see how they would increase or decrease the shareholder value. Selecting drivers that really matter is always an important step in the design of a model. A discussion of the drivers of the Jilin model is in Chapter 3 (Section 3.1);

Table 2.2 ● Annual cash flows of the Jilin project

	2001	2002	2003	2004	2005	Cumulated
Initial advance	5.10	–	–	–	–	5.10
Billings	–	20.40	13.60	1.00	1.00	36.00
Recovery of initial advance	–	3.06	2.04	–	–	5.10
Retention for guarantee	–	1.02	0.68	–	–	1.70
Release of retention	–	–	–	0.85	0.85	1.70
Cash receipts	**5.10**	**16.32**	**10.88**	**1.85**	**1.85**	**36.00**
Payments for equipment	14.80	3.80	–	–	–	18.60
Payments for other costs	–	7.20	4.80	0.90	0.90	13.80
Cash disbursements	**14.80**	**11.00**	**4.80**	**0.90**	**0.90**	**32.40**
Net cash	**–9.70**	**5.32**	**6.08**	**0.95**	**0.95**	**3.60**

- **data**, or all the variables that have a value that cannot be changed – or that you choose not to change;
- **intermediate variables**. These are all the variables that enable you to relate the parameters and the data with the outcome variables. In Table 2.2 cash receipts, cash disbursements and net cash are intermediate variables;
- the **relationships** that link all the variables.
● The **general architecture/design** of the model. Since spreadsheets do not impose any special architecture on your models, you are free to chose – and therefore you need to decide – the design that really fits your analysis.

An initial paper-and-pencil model of the cash generation profile of the Jilin project is shown in Table 2.2. (*Note*: I am going to delay the building of the spreadsheet model until Chapter 3. If you want to build the model now, please go to Table 3.2.)

Table 2.2 requires a little explanation. First, when you build an annual model, you aggregate all the receipts and disbursements that occur during the entire year. As a result the net cash that you get for each year is the net cash generated during the whole year as it will show on the bank account on the last day of the year. In the Jilin project, we know that a few cash flows will occur at the beginning of 2002 – or even as early as at the end of 2001. Consequently, it is probably a good idea to describe the early phases of the cash generation profile of the project with two cash flows: 'end 2001' and 'end 2002'.[6] In Table 2.2 the annual modelling of the cash flows project summarizes the entire continuous cash generation process with five – and five only – cash flows:

● On 31 Dec. 2001, the company has to find €9.70 million to start the project as a result of its intention to spend €9.70 million more than it receives at the very beginning of the project.
● On 31 Dec. 2002, the company gets €5.32 million from the project – receipts exceed payments by €5.32 million.
● On 31 Dec. 2003, the company gets €6.08 million more.
● On 31 Dec. 2004, the company gets €0.95 million more.
● On 31 Dec. 2005, the company gets a last payment of €0.95 million.

With this annual modelling, all the cash deficits and excesses that may happen during each year are ignored . . . this is the weakness of the helicopter view.

The second point to consider is that the first receipt that the company will get is the initial advance (15% of €34 million). Then cash inflows will result from the work progressively delivered and invoiced to the customer. In 2002, the company delivers and invoices for an amount of €20.4 million. However, since they have already paid 15% of the value of the whole project through the initial advance, the customer will not have to pay the full €20.4 million but 85% of this amount only. Actually, the customer will further deduct 5% of the invoice in order to build a fund for guarantee that they will release in 2004 and 2005.

2.4 Measuring the shareholder value created: a first algorithm for assessing the net future value (NFV) or market value added (MVA)[7]

Measuring the shareholder value is just a matter of adjusting the €3.6 million with the costs and gains caused by the cash deficits and excesses. Financing costs and gains can be estimated from Table 2.2:

- At the end of 2001 there is a need to find €9.70 million. No one can spend more than they receive! These €9.70 million may come from any source external to the project but they have to come or the project manager will have to slow down the spending. In the case we are told that the company wants to get a return higher than 15%: let us assume that it is because money costs 15% a year.[8] In order not to pay more interest charges than necessary, let us borrow for one year only: if €9.70 million are borrowed on 31 December 2001, then €11.16 million have to be repaid on 31 December 2002 (9.70 plus 1.46 interest).
- On 31 December 2002, the project generates €5.32 million. This is not sufficient to repay the €11.16 million and as a result the company will have to borrow €5.84 million and repay €6.71 million one year later, and so on.

If you continue this process until the end of 2005, you realize, as shown in Table 2.3, that once you have introduced the cost of financing, the project generates an amount of €1.21 million at the end of 2005. **This is the value created by the project as of the end of 2005.**[9]

The €1.21 million shown in Table 2.3 corresponds to:

- the difference between the cash received and paid for the project once it has been adjusted for the costs and the gains caused by the cash generation profile of the project: 3.60 million minus a net interest cost of 2.39 million;[10]
- the value created after financing costs – and gains – have been taken care of. If all the receipts and payments of the project go to the same bank account that charges 15% a year on any cash deficit and pays 15% on any cash excess, then, when the project is fully completed on 31 December 2005, **the final balance of the bank account will be equal to 1.21 million.**

These €1.21 million are what is left after customers, employees, suppliers, etc. have got their fair share. These 1.21 million correspond to the creation of an additional value that technically belongs to the owners. It is **shareholder value** and, as shown above, it is the

---

Table 2.3 ● A first algorithm for calculating shareholder value

	2001	2002	2003	2004	2005
Net cash[a]	−9.70	5.32	6.08	0.95	0.95
interest rate	0.15	–	–	–	–
interest paid/received	–	1.46	0.88	0.09	−0.03
Net cash before financing	−9.70	−5.84	−0.63	0.23	1.21
Borrowing/investment	9.70	5.84	0.63	−0.23	–
Net cash after financing[b]	0.00	0.00	0.00	0.00	–

Formulas

In Table 3.2 (p.36), net cash is in row 24. In A25: Interest rate; in A26: Interest paid/received; in A27: Net cash before financing; in A28: Borrowing/Investment; in A29: Net cash after financing. In B25: 0.15; in B27: +B24; in B28: −B27; copy into C27.E27; B29: in B29: + B27+B28; copy into C29.F29; in C26: +B28*$B$25; copy into D26.F26; in C27: +B29 + C24 − C26 − B28; copy into D27.F27.

---

[a] From Table 2.2.
[b] When financing has been arranged cash is typically equal to zero. Any deficit has been financed and any excess has been invested in order not to keep any idle cash.

Table 2.4 ● Value created by the Jilin project (in € million, over the period 2002–05)

Total cash receipts from the customer	36.00
Total payments to the suppliers of equipment	18.60
Other payments for labour and material	13.80
Net operating cash surplus	**3.60**
Net financing costs	2.39
Value created by the project (2005 value)	**1.21**

money that is left in the bank account of the project at the end of its life and that can be taken out. Shareholder value is a very practical measurement.

We can now come back to Table 2.1, amend it and show the value created by the Jilin project. This is done in Table 2.4. The figure of 1.21 million shown in Table 2.4 is called its net future value (NFV) or 'market value added' (MVA).

The problem though with these 1.21 millions is that they express the shareholder value created as of 31 December 2005, a date that is fairly distant in the future. Business people tend to be impatient. Most of them are eager to know what these 1.21 millions mean in today's terms. How much can they take out today, rather than in four years' time?

2.5 Estimating net present values as sums of present values

In Table 2.3, the calculation of loan repayments and the calculations of the proceeds of investments illustrate what is called the **time value of money**. In a 15% interest rate environment:

- borrowing 9.70 million at the end of 2001 means that you will have to repay 11.76 (9.70 × 1.15) million at the end of 2002;
- investing 0.23 million at the end of 2004 means that you will get 0.26 (0.23 × 1.15) million at the end of 2005.

In other words, in a 15% interest rate environment:

- 9.70 million at the end of 2001 is equivalent to 11.76 million at the end of 2002;
- 0.23 million at the end of 2004 is equivalent to 0.26 million at the end of 2005.

These equivalence relationships have wide implications:

- As soon as you can invest money, which is the normal situation, a cash flow is defined by its **amount** and its **date**. When you have the opportunity to invest money, knowing the amount of a cash flow is not sufficient to define this cash flow. You also need to know the date of this cash flow.
- You cannot directly compare two cash flows that occur at different dates. In order to be able to compare cash flows, to add them up, etc., you need first to put these cash flows on the same date, e.g. you have to calculate their equivalent value at that date. In *A Random Walk Down Wall Street*, Burton Malkiel writes: 'It is often said that the Indian who sold Manhattan Island in 1626 for $24 was rooked by the white man. In fact, he may have been an extremely sharp salesman. Had he put his $24 away at a 6% percent interest compounded semi-annually, it would now be worth over $50 billion!'[11]
- There are two ways to adjust a cash flow for time. Calculating the equivalent value of a cash flow at a future date is a matter of **compounding** this cash flow, or of multiplying this cash flow by a factor equal to (1 + interest rate) as many times as needed. Calculating the equivalent value of a cash flow at a earlier date is a matter of **discounting** this cash flow, or of dividing this cash flow by a factor equal to (1 + interest rate) or of multiplying this cash flow by a factor equal to 1/(1 + interest rate) as many times as needed.[12]

We can use the time value of money concept to express the €1.21 million generated as of 31 December 2005 into their equivalent value today (31 December 2001). This is done in Table 2.5.

If 31 December 2001 is the present, then 0.69 million is the estimate of the shareholder value that the Jilin project is going to create expressed as of today. This value is called the **net present value (NPV)** of the project. This 0.69 million has exactly the same meaning as the 1.21 million. It corresponds to:

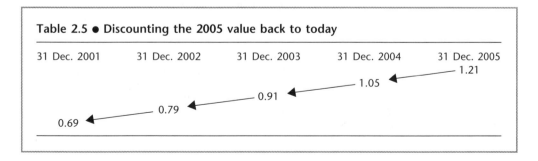

Table 2.5 ● Discounting the 2005 value back to today

31 Dec. 2001	31 Dec. 2002	31 Dec. 2003	31 Dec. 2004	31 Dec. 2005
				1.21
			1.05	
		0.91		
	0.79			
0.69				

- the difference between the cash received and paid for the project including what is paid and or received as a result of the temporary cash balances that will materialize over the life of the project;
- the value created after financing costs and gains have been taken care of. The 0.69 million represents what is left after financing has been accounted for expressed as of today.

2.6 What do NPVs really mean?

Net present values are more than a simple calculation. Experience of teaching finance shows, however, that it is not easy to feel what this number really means. Please use Table 2.6 to check your 'feeling' of what NPV really means.

Table 2.6 ● The meaning of the net present value

Question	Answer
Imagine that French Telecom (FT) announces that it has signed the project. *What impact do you expect this* project, *announcement to have on the value of the whole company?*	**The value of the whole company should increase by the amount of the NPV!** Managers have a direct impact on the value of the company they work with. They increase the value of their company each time they engage in projects that have a positive net present value and execute them according to plans! The net present value is a powerful variable that links operating and strategic business decisions to shareholder value.
FT succeeds in signing the contract but suddenly finds itself unable to execute work in China. FT gets an offer from a contractor that is eager to develop its business in China. *At what price should FT sell the project to that company?*	**At a price equal to the NPV: €0.69 million!**[13] Net present values are used for pricing businesses and companies for acquisition and divestment purposes. In such situations net present values mean real money.
The contract is signed and the shareholders want to take out all the value created as soon as 31 December 2000. *What is the maximum amount that they can they take?*	**They can take as much as the NPV: 0.69 million.** You can use the model to check that if this is done, the annual cash flows become −10.39, 5.32, 6.08, 0.95 and 0.95. The net cash flow decreases to 2.91 (3.60 − 0.69) and interest grows to the same 2.91 and the new NPV is zero. This obviously assumes that the execution of the project will go exactly according to plan!
How much money should you have on 31 Dec. 2001, in order to be able to pay the same amounts as the project: 5.32 on 31 Dec. 2002, 6.08 on 31 Dec. 2003 and 0.95 on 31 Dec. 2004 and 2005? You can invest money at 15%.	**You need €10.39 million (the initial investment of 9.70 million plus the NPV).** You invest 10.39 million for a year, pay 5.32 and reinvest 6.63 for a year. On 31 Dec. 2003 you pay 6.08 and reinvest 1.54. On 31 Dec. 2004 you pay 0.95 and reinvest 0.83. In a year this grows to 0.95!

2.7 How to estimate NPVs in practice: the additive property of value

The net present value can be quickly calculated as the sum of the cash flows, once these have been adjusted for time – or 'discounted'. The net present value can be estimated either:

● as the sum of the discounted net cash flows. This is the usual approach for calculating NPVs;

or

● as the net sum of the present values (PVs) of all the different cash receipts and disbursements. This is an alternative approach that is often very powerful for understanding the process of value creation.

Estimating NPVs from the net cash flows

The usual approach for calculating the NPV of a series of cash flows is shown in Table 2.7. (*Note*: the formulas for building a spreadsheet model are shown in Table 3.2.) It corresponds to a two-step process:

● first, you discount each cash flow and make it equal to its equivalent value today,
● then, you calculate the sum of the discounted cash flows. This is the NPV.

This is a much more powerful algorithm than the one used in Tables 2.3 and 2.5 and it is the one that you should always use when estimating net present values. The first algorithm has one advantage only: for many people, it shows more clearly the meaning of the net present value.

Table 2.7 ● Estimating the NPV from the net cash flows

	2001	2002	2003	2004	2005	Cumulated
Net cash (from Table 2.2)	−9.70	5.32	6.08	0.95	0.95	3.6
Rate	0.15					
Discount factor	1.00	0.87	0.76	0.66	0.57	–
Discounted net cash	−9.70	4.63	4.60	0.62	0.54	–
NPV	0.69					

Notes:
The discount factors are used for adjusting each cash flow and making it equal to its equivalent value as of 31 December 2001 (today). The cash flow received at the end of 2001 does not need to be adjusted, consequently a factor of 1 is applied to this cash flow. The cash flow received in 2002 is worth less than it looks: its face value has to be divided by 1.15 or multiplied by a factor of 1/1.15 which is also equal to 0.87. A cash flow received one year from now is worth only 87% of its face value in a 15% interest rate environment. Each discounted net cash flow is equal to the corresponding net cash flow multiplied by the discount factor that reflects its date of occurrence.
The NPV is the sum of the discounted net cash flows.

Estimating NPVs as the net sum of the present values of all the different receipts and payments

Another way of estimating the NPV is to estimate the present value of each receipt and each disbursement. As shown in Tables 2.8 and 2.9, **the net sum of the present values of all the receipts and disbursements is the NPV of the project**. With this approach you do not need to estimate the net cash flows and the interest cost. Expressing NPV as the difference between the PVs of the cash receipts and disbursements often helps focus on the key factors of the value creation process.

First, as shown in Table 2.9 the value created by the Jilin project (0.69) is a small residual number in comparison to the different cash inflows and outflows of the project. The value created is no larger than 2.3% of the value of the receipts, 3.8% of the value of the equipment and 6.3% of the other costs. This means that a small variation of any of these cash flows must have a very large impact on the value created. In particular, it only takes a very small variation in the value of the receipts from the customer to change significantly the value created by the project. Depending on its direction, a 2% change in the value of these receipts can either double or destroy the whole value of the project!

Tables 2.8 and 2.9 also show that the impact of each cash inflow and outflow is the result of two factors: its amount and its timing. We have just realized that the whole value of the Jilin project would be destroyed by a 2% decrease in the value of the receipts. This 2% decrease may actually have two causes: a discount given in the final negotiation or a delay of payment. Within a 15% interest rate environment, the value of a cash flow decreases very quickly with time: a one-year delay – or a one-year 'collection period' – means 15% less value; a six-month collection period about 7.5% less value; a one-quarter collection period about 3% less value, etc. Without any further calculation we realize that a one-quarter delay is probably enough to destroy the whole value of the project. The high

---

Table 2.8 ● Estimating the NPV from the PVs of all the cash receipts and disbursements

	2001	2002	2003	2004	2005	Cumulated
Rate	0.15					
Discount factor	1.00	0.87	0.76	0.66	0.57	–
Receipts from customer	5.10	16.32	10.88	1.85	1.85	36.00
Discounted values	5.10	14.19	8.23	1.22	1.06	–
Present value (a)	**29.79**					
Payments for equipment	14.80	3.80	–	–	–	18.60
Discounted values	14.80	3.30	–	–	–	–
Present value (b)	**18.10**					
Payments for other costs	–	7.20	4.80	0.90	0.90	13.80
Discounted value	–	6.26	3.63	0.59	0.51	–
Present value (c)	**11.00**					
NPV (a – b – c)	**0.69**					

Table 2.9 ● Expressing NPV as the difference between the present values of all receipts and disbursements vs. expressing NPV as a function of operating surplus

NPV as the difference between the present values (PVs) of all the cash receipts and disbursements[a]		NPV as the result of adjusting the operating surplus for financing costs and gains	
PV of receipts from customers	29.79	Operating surplus	3.60
PV of payments of equipment	18.10	Interest	2.91
PV of other payments	11.00	**Value**	**0.69**
Value	**0.69**		

[a] One can use the same presentation with future values and express the net future value as the difference between the future values of all the cash receipts and disbursements.[14]

sensitivity of the value to the collection period is not as easy to quantify when you estimate the NPV from the net cash flows.

Finally, net cash is a very interesting and important variable but it is often even more interesting to look at its drivers: the various receipts and payments. This enables you to understand what causes interest costs and gains.

The additive property of the NPV is of great help in building financial models. When estimating an NPV you can always break your problem into its components and then add back their individual values.

2.8 Using return to check that the project creates value

The best way to estimate the value created by any new business decision is first to estimate the additional receipts and disbursements that it will cause and then estimate their NPV: this tells you how much value the decision will create. However, there is another way. This consists of:

● looking at the net cash flows resulting from the receipts and disbursements caused by the decision;
● focusing on the investment that exists at the beginning of the project – if there is one – and estimating its return;
● comparing this return with the cost of financing. If the return is higher than the cost of financing then you can conclude that the decision creates value!

Return: a tool for comparing financial investments

Return is used for comparing opportunities for investing money. Let us consider the three opportunities described in Table 2.10.

Investment A is a one-year investment (one anniversary of the investment only); investments B and C are three-year investments (three anniversaries). Estimating return is a matter of answering four successive questions:

Table 2.10 ● Three investment opportunities

	Opportunity A	Opportunity B	Opportunity C
31 December 2001	−1000	−1000	−1000
31 December 2002	1200	200	600
31 December 2003	–	200	600
31 December 2004	–	1200	400

---

1. What is the *amount invested*? This is the same for A, B and C: 1000.
2. What is the *surplus generated* over the life of the investment? This is 200 for A and 600 for B and C.
3. How *long* is the investment? A lasts for one year, B and C last three years. On an annual basis,[15] the surplus represents 20% of the initial investment for A, B and C. For B and C it is (600/1000)/3.
4. How *fast* is the surplus generated? Anybody who has the possibility to invest their money prefers to get the money faster rather than slower in order to put it back to work as soon as possible. Even though both B and C look like having a 20% return, C sounds better than B. Since B has a 20% return – B is actually a typical 20% return investment – then we can say that C should have a return higher than 20%.

Applying the return approach to Jilin: a 'rough cut' estimate of return

The issue is to know whether the return on the project is higher than 15%. The cash flows are as follows:

	2001	2002	2003	2004	2005	Cumulated
Net cash	−9.70	5.32	6.08	0.95	0.95	3.6

When you ask the four questions above, you realize that: the investment is 9.70; the surplus generated is 3.60; and the project lasts four years. These three first answers seem to imply that return is less than 15%: (3.6/9.7)/4 = 9.3%.

Then comes the fourth question: how fast is the cash generation? Jilin's cash generation is very fast – it takes less than two years to recover the money invested! The time needed to recover the investment is called **payback**.[16] The return on the Jilin project should therefore be higher than the 9.3% estimated above. The problem, though, is that the rough-cut approach cannot tell us how much higher it is.

Applying the return approach to Jilin: estimating the internal rate of return or yield to maturity

The way to estimate the rate of return on a project – its 'internal rate of return' (IRR) or yield to maturity[17] – is to proceed by trial and error, progressively applying higher and higher financing costs to the project and observing what happens to the value.

Table 2.11 ● Value as a function of financing costs

Financing cost	Net present value	Net future value
0%	3.60	3.60
15%	0.69	1.21
20%	−0.04	−0.08
19%	0.10	0.20
19.8%	−0.01	−0.02
19.7%	0.00	0.01

- If one applies a 0% financing cost to the Jilin project, then the value (future and present is 3.60).
- If one applies a 15% financing cost to the Jilin project, then the value decreases and becomes 0.69 (present) or 1.21 (future).
- If one continues to apply higher and higher financing costs, then the value will continuously decrease and eventually become negative.

One can find out the financing cost that is needed to make the value equal to zero. Table 2.11 shows that it takes a financing slightly more costly than 19.7% to completely wipe out the value of the Jilin project. If the project almost breaks even with a 19.7% financing cost, this means that its return (IRR) is slightly more than 19.7%.[18] This trial and error process for calculating IRR may seem cumbersome, but unfortunately there is no other way to do it!

Comparing the value and the return approaches

The value and the return approaches both aim at screening among projects based on the value creation criteria. In order only to keep projects that create value you have to keep those projects that satisfy one of the two following criteria:

$$\text{Net present value}_{@ \text{ financing cost}} > 0 \qquad \text{(value approach)}$$
$$\text{Return on the project} > \text{Cost of financing} \qquad \text{(return approach)}$$

In accounting and finance, people tend to use these two approaches almost equally. One may even say that before the recent popularity of shareholder value, the return approach was probably the more popular. These two approaches are very close to each other and you will probably want to use them both, choosing the one more suited to each specific situation. My recommendation, however, is to prefer the value approach. Among the reasons for my preference are the following:

- The return approach tells you that the decision is creating value, but it does not tell you how much.[19] Knowing the absolute amount is very useful when you want to maximize value!
- The return approach focuses too much on the idea of investment and implicitly assumes that you need to invest in order to create value. This is not true and there are many great value-creating ideas that do not involve any over-spending or investment at the early stages.

● Finally, the return approach has some 'technical' drawbacks: returns are not additive,[20] the calculation of return assumes that the intermediate cash flows are reinvested at the internal rate of return,[21] and so on.

Notes

1. The difference between cash receipts and revenues – or sales – is due to time only. Over the whole life of a project cash receipts and revenues – or sales – necessarily have the same cumulative value. Please refer to Chapter 4 (Section 4.2) and Chapter 6 (Section 6.3).
2. The difference between cash disbursements and costs and expenses is only due to time. Over the whole life of a project, payments to the suppliers of equipment, payments for labour, material, travel, etc. and costs of equipment, labour, material, travel, etc. necessarily have the same cumulative value. Please refer to Chapter 4 (Section 4.2) and to Chapter 6 (Sections 6.4 and 6.5).
3. Income and cash are necessarily the same in the end – *see* Chapter 4 (Section 4.4).
4. Typically, when used to describe income or cash, 'operating' means the result ignoring interest income and expenses as well as all other elements which do not correspond to normal operations (and in particular all the exceptional, non-recurring elements).
5. Risk is dealt with in Chapter 5.
6. An alternative is to describe the start of the project with one cash flow only (end 2002). If you do so, then the project is described by four cash flows only: −4.38 at the end of 2002 (−4.38 is equal to −9.70 + 5.32); 6.08 at the end of 2003; 0.95 at the end of 2004 and 2005. This leads to an estimate of 1.64 m for the interest costs (vs. 2.91 m when you use the five cash flows description).
7. MVA® and EVA® are terms used and copyrighted by Stern Stewart & Co. (http://www.sternstewart.com) For more about EVA®, *see* Chapter 4 (Section 4.6).
8. The cost of capital issue is dealt with in the General Appendix at the end of this book.
9. This amount is also called the 'net future (2005) value of the project'.
10. The net cost of interest looks very large. You should however remember that we have waited until the end for taking interest into account. If you compare interest with the other costs, then the picture is different: while 2.39 are paid for interest, 13.80 are paid for labour and supplies and 18.60 for equipment. Interest payments only represent some 7% of the total outflows.
11. Page 88 of the 1990 edition. This was the 1990 value of the $24 received in 1626. The 2001 value of this same $24 still compounded semi-annually at 6% is $96 billion. This is the result of $24 \times (1 + 0.06/2)^\wedge (374 \times 2)$. 374 is the number of years (2001 − 1626).
12. This is when you discount annually. You can also discount for shorter periods. *See* Appendix II.1 for the impact of discounting over shorter periods.
13. If the deal is made at the NPV, then FT will gain as much as doing the project by itself but what about the buyer? How will they create value? Another very interesting issue is how and when the amount will be paid. We will explore these issues later.
14. This would look like this:

Receipts from customers (end 2005 value)	52.11
Payments of equipment (end 2005 value)	31.66
Payment of others (end 2005 value)	19.23
Value (end 2005)	1.71

15. Except in high inflation countries, interest rates are always expressed in annual terms: when people talk about a 3% interest rate, this means 3% a year.
16. The payback of Jilin is less than 2 years: the investment needed is 9.70 million and the project has already generated a cumulated amount of 11.40 (5.32 + 6.08) within 2 years.
17. The term 'yield to maturity' is often used for financial instruments instead of 'internal rate of return'.
18. 19.733% if you like decimals!
19. Which would you prefer: the proceeds of a 100% return on $100, or the proceeds of a 10% return on $100 000?

20. When somebody tells you that you have 10 projects, nine with a great return and just one with a lousy return, you never know what the total outcome may look like!

21. Jilin has a 19.733% return. Does that mean that we can finance Jilin with any loan costing 19.733% and break even? You can check that this is not the case by comparing Jilin with a 19.733% loan that is repaid in full at the end:

	2001	2002	2003	2004	2005	Cumulated
Jilin	−9.70	5.32	6.08	0.95	0.95	3.60
Loan	9.70	−1.91	−1.91	−1.91	−11.61	−7.66
Net	0.00	3.41	4.17	−0.96	−10.66	−4.06

Jilin does not break even with any loan at the IRR rate! The project breaks even with a loan that has the same cash flows or with any loan at the IRR rate provided that any cash excess/deficit is reinvested/financed at the IRR rate. Here, if the 3.41, the 4.17, etc. are reinvested at 19.733%, then you have just enough money to repay the 10.66 in 2005.

CHAPTER 3

Preparing for the negotiation

How to create the maximum value out of a business opportunity

Let us go back to the Jilin contract. The analysis so far has shown that this project has the potential to create value. It has also shown that this value is relatively small[1] and apparently very sensitive to small variations in the amount and timing of receipts (Section 2.7). It is now time to:

- simulate what could happen during the negotiation – and also after the contract is signed;
- find out how we can make the best of the final negotiation;
- set objectives for the increase in value that we want to achieve in the final negotiation.

The first thing to do is to build a spreadsheet model of the project. An additional task will be to check that the results are not biased by the fact that we have adopted an annual – and not a quarterly – framework.

3.1 Building a spreadsheet model of the Jilin project

Defining the drivers that really matter for us in this specific situation

Building a spreadsheet model of the Jilin project is more than simply transferring Tables 2.2 and 2.7 onto a spreadsheet. We need to remember that we are building a model for preparing ourselves for a negotiation:

- What requests might we expect the customer to come up with? Among these possible requests, which are the ones that would hurt the value of the contract most?
- If we have a chance to request a modification to the contract what should we ask for? What are the modifications that could increase the value of the contract most? What are the modifications that could decrease the risk of the contract most?

Table 3.1 ● Defining the drivers that matter most

Possible change requests/proposals	Driver required
Outright discount/Price increase[a]	Contract amount and % change in price
Free maintenance[b]	Maintenance
More/less initial advance	% advance
More/less retention	% retention
Faster/slower delivery and invoices	% delivered/invoiced in 2002
Slower payments[c]	Collection period
Modified equipment specifications/performance	% change equipment costs
More/fewer tasks to be performed/cost overruns[d]	% change other costs
Additional final receipts[e]	Additional final receipts
Additional initial costs[f]	Additional initial costs

[a] An outright price increase may be very difficult to get, but there might be services which are provided for free ('FOC' or free of charges) in the bid. How to try to invoice these?
[b] As they are allowed to retain money until 2005, the customer may consider that the supplier will be motivated to help even if not paid for providing maintenance.
[c] Delayed payments are always a risk. The supplier can also discover in the final negotiation that some procedures – such as the need to have an agent of the customer sign memos specifying the degree of completion before invoices are issued – could slow down the collection of money.
[d] Cost overruns are always a risk. Higher costs may also come from changes in order during the final negotiation and also during the execution of the project.
[e] The testing equipment will still be of value at the end of the contract: why not try to sell it to the customer?
[f] In the final negotiation, the customer may request additional services like technical training. Some custom duties may suddenly be due, etc.

Answering these questions will enable us to define the drivers of the model. Table 3.1 shows a possible set of drivers.

Building a model

Two possible spreadsheet models are shown: the model in Table 3.2 estimates the NPV from the annual net cash flows, while that in Table 3.3 estimates the NPV directly from the PVs of the various receipts and disbursements.

3.2 Using the NPV and IRR built-in formulas of your spreadsheet (and checking that a built-in formula does what you want it to do!)

As with other spreadsheets, Excel has built-in formulas for estimating NPVs and IRRs. The NPV built-in formula is used in Table 3.3. If you meet this built-in formula for the first time, it is a good idea to test it against the formula that is used in Table 3.2. In the model of Table 3.2, enter in B29:[2]

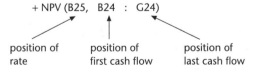

and Excel is going to return 0.60 and not 0.69!

Table 3.2 ● A spreadsheet model of the Jilin project: estimating NPV from the net cash flows

	A	B	C	D	E	F	G	H
1	Main contract	34.00						
2	Maintenance	2.00						
3	Advance rate	0.15						
4	Retention rate	0.05						
5	% of executed in 2001	0.60						
6	Additional final payment	0						
7	Collection period (in quarters)[a]	0						
8	Additional initial cost	0						
9	Change in equipment	0.00						
10	Change in other costs	000						
11	*Year*	*2001*	*2002*	*2003*	*2004*	*2005*	*2006*	*Cum.*
12	Initial advance	5.10						
13	Billings		20.40	13.60	1.00	1.00		36.00
14	Recovery advance		3.06	2.04				5.10
15	Retention		1.02	0.68				1.70
16	Recovery retention				0.85	0.85		1.70
17	Additional final payment							
18	Receivables end year		0.00	0.00	0.00	0.00		
19	**Cash in**	**5.10**	**16.32**	**10.88**	**1.85**	**1.85**	**0.00**	**36.00**
20	Additional initial cost	0						
21	Equipment	14.80	3.80					
22	Labour & other		7.20	4.80	0.90	0.90		
23	**Cash out**	**14.80**	**11.00**	**4.80**	**0.90**	**0.90**		**32.40**
24	**Net cash**	**−9.70**	**5.32**	**6.08**	**0.95**	**0.95**	**0.00**	**3.60**
25	Discount rate	0.15						
26	Discount factor	1.00	0.87	0.76	0.66	0.57	0.50	
27	Discounted net cash	−9.70	4.63	4.60	0.62	0.54	0.00	
28	**Net present value (NPV)**	**0.69**						

[a] Collection period should not be more than 4 quarters.

Background
B1 to B10, B20, B25, B26: inputs
B12: +B1*B3
B19: +B12
B20: +B8
B21: +14.8*(1+B9)
B23: +B20+B21+B22; copy to C23.F23
B24: +B19−B23; copy to C24.G24
B27: +B24*B26; copy to C27.G27
B28: +SUM(B27.G27)
C13: +B1*B5
C14: +C13*$B$3; copy to D14
C15: +C13*$B$4; copy to D15
C18: +(C13−C14−C15+C16+C17)/4*$B$7; copy to D18.F18
C19: +C13−C14−C15+C16+C17−C18+B18; copy to D19.G19

C21: +3.8*(1+B9)
C22: +12*B5*(1+B10)
C26: +B26/(1+$B$25); copy to D26.G26
D13: +B1−C13
D22: +12*(1+B10)−C22
E13: +B2/2
E16: +B1*B4/2
E22: +0.9*(1+B10)
F13: +B2−E13
F16: +E16
H12: =SUM(B12.G12). Copy to H13.H17 and to H19.H24.
F17: +E6
F22: +E22

Table 3.3 ● A spreadsheet model of the Jilin project: estimating NPV from the PVs of all the individual cash receipts and disbursements

	A	B	C	D	E	F	G	H
1	Main contract	34.00						
2	Maintenance	2.00						
3	Advance rate	0.15						
4	Retention rate	0.05						
5	% of executed in 2001	0.60						
6	Additional final payment	0						
7	Collection period (in quarters)	0						
8	Additional initial cost	0						
9	Change in equipment	0.00						
10	Change in other costs	0						
11	Discount rate	0.15						
12	*Year*	*2001*	*2002*	*2003*	*2004*	*2005*	*2006*	*Cum.*
13	Initial advance	5.10						
14	Billings		20.40	13.60	1.00	1.00		36.00
15	Recovery advance		3.06	2.04				5.10
16	Retention		1.02	0.68				1.70
17	Recovery retention				0.85	0.85		1.70
18	Additional final payment							
19	Receivables end year		0.00	0.00	0.00	0.00		
20	Cash receipts	5.10	16.32	10.88	1.85	1.85	0.00	36.00
21	**PV cash receipts**	**29.79**						
22	**PV additional initial costs**	**0.0**						0.00
23	Equipment	14.80	3.80					18.60
24	**PV equipment**	**18.10**						
25	Labour & other		7.20	4.80	0.90	0.90		13.80
26	**PV labour and others**	**11.00**						
27	**NPV**	**0.69**						3.60

Background

B1 to B11: inputs
B13: +B1*B3
B20: +B13
B21: +B20+NPV(B11, C20.G20)
B22: +B8
B23: +14.8*(1+B9)
B24: +B23+C23/(1+B11)
B26: +B25+NPV(B11, C25.F25)
B27: +B21−B22−B24−B26
C14: +B1*B5
C15: +C14*$B$3; copy to D15
C16: +C14*$B$4; copy to D16
C19: +(C14−C15−C16+C17+C18)/4*$B$7; copy to D19.F19
C20: +C14−C15−C16+C17+C18−C19+B19; copy to D20.G20

C23: +3.8*(1+B9)
C25: +12*B5*(1+B10)
D14: +B1−C14
D25: +12*(1+B10)−C25
E14: +B2/2
E17: +B1*B4/2
E25: +0.9*(1+$B$10). Copy to F25
F14: +B2−E14
F17: +E17; F18: B6
H14: =SUM(B14.G14). Copy to H15.H17
    and to H20, H22, H23 and H25
H27: +H20−H22−H23 −H25

If you divide 0.69 by 0.60 – with a formula (= B28/B29) in the spreadsheet – you will get 1.15, which means that the built-in formula of Excel and of most other spreadsheets discounts the initial cash flow. In other words Excel multiplies the first cash flow by 0.87 and not by 1 as we have done. Excel calculates the NPV as of 1 January 2001. There are two ways to make the built in-formula estimate the NPV as of 31 December 2001:

+ NPV(B25, B24 : G24) × (1 + B25)   or   + B24 + NPV(B25, C24 : G24)

Please check that you now get 0.69 and remember to verify that built-in formulas really do what you want them to do before using them! Please also remember to **specify the precise date of your NPVs**. Stating that you have estimated the NPV of Jilin in the year 2001 is not precise enough as there is a 15% difference between the NPV at the beginning of 2001 and the NPV at the end of 2001!

The IRR built-in formula

You can also enter the built-in IRR formula in the model of Table 3.2. In B29:[3]

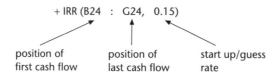

Spreadsheets ask you for a 'start up' or 'guess' rate because their authors want them to return a result quickly even for simulations such as the estimation of an IRR that can be lengthy. Experience will show you that your guess rate does not have to be very close to the actual rate. It will also show that in some cases your guess rate will not be good enough: you will then get an error/'VALUE' message. When this happens, change your guess rate and Excel will manage!

You should check that the result you get with the IRR built-in formula is 0.19733, the same as we got in Table 2.11. Contrary to NPVs, IRRs are not dependent on the date at which they are estimated.

3.3 Checking the model

Spreadsheets are very user friendly. This is great, but it also results in many spreadsheet models being wrong! According to my own experience, about one-third of all spreadsheet models have some kind of flaw that may result in a problem at some time. I therefore urge you always to check your models before you start using them. There are various ways of doing so:

● If you have started with a paper-and-pencil model, check that your spreadsheet agrees with it.
● If you have not built a pencil-and-paper model, try to calculate the outcome variable in more than one way and make sure that all these different ways lead to the same result. For example, calculate the NPV first from the net cash flows and then from the present values of the individual receipts and disbursements.

● Most importantly, verify that your model produces the results that it should generate. Before you start playing with a model, think about some simple 'what ifs' and about the results that they should produce. Then check that your model is able to generate these results. For example, in the case of the Jilin project, it is obvious that the operating surplus (3.6 million) should remain the same whatever the advance rate is, whatever the retention rate is, whatever the percentage executed in 2001 is, whatever the collection period is, and so on. A good idea is to change these drivers and check that the model still generates 3.6. This dynamic verification of models is very powerful and it is a good idea to go through it systematically before starting to use your models.

3.4 Trying to identify those changes that lever value most

Which changes matter most? Are there 'small' contract modifications that we might propose that would increase value in a big way? Are there 'small' change requests that the customer might come up with that could destroy a lot of value? We are now in a position to perform a systematic 'what-if' analysis that can help us answer these questions. Table 3.4 shows the results of a 'one-change-at-a-time' what-if analysis.

A few comments on the results of Table 3.4:

● Timing is very important: a case in point is the relative impacts of an 'additional final payment' and of an 'additional initial cost' of the same nominal value.
● Selling price, collection period and execution timing (realizing that execution can probably be significantly accelerated) have a very large impact on the value created. Executing

Table 3.4 ● Understanding the sensitivity of value

Driver	% change	New NPV	% change in NPV as compared to the base (0.69)
Change in price	+1%	0.98	41.3
	−1%	0.41	−41.3
Maintenance	+1%	0.70	1.8
	−1%	0.68	−1.8
Advance rate	0.16	0.75	8.6
	0.14	0.63	−8.6
Retention rate	0.04	0.76	10.3
	0.06	0.62	−10.3
% executed and invoiced in 2002	0.61	0.71	2.5
	0.59	0.67	−2.5
Collection period	0.5	0.29	−58.2
	1	−0.11	−116.5
Additional final payment	0.5	0.98	41.4
Additional initial cost	0.5	0.19	−72.3
Equipment cost	−1%	0.87	26.2
	+1%	0.51	−26.2
Other costs	−1%	0.80	15.9
	+1%	0.58	−15.9

70% of the contract in 2002 would increase the value of the contract by 25%; executing 80% of it would increase the value by 50%! The potential impact of a payment delay suggests that not only should you ask the customer to commit to a very short collection period but you should also try to find ways to protect yourself against unexpected payment delay. A clause specifying that the customer should pay an interest charge on any overdue payments may prove very valuable.

● However interesting they are, these results have a major limitation as they only show the situation as seen by the supplier. They do not show what the factors are that may increase the value of the project for the customer. In order to understand what is really important for the customer we should also build a model describing the customer's value-creating process.

3.5 'What-if' analyses

What-if analyses are not easy to perform. They require a systematic approach. In Table 3.4 we considered all the drivers, we envisaged similar changes for each of these drivers and looked at the resulting NPVs. This is the one-change-at-a-time type of analysis. This is a good starting point but, as a second step, you will probably also need to analyze the impact of several drivers at a time.

Another problem with sensitivity analyses is deciding the range for changing the drivers. In Table 3.4 most drivers are changed within a ±1% range. This looks fair enough for testing the relative sensitivity of the value to the different parameters. The problem, though, is that for a parameter like 'Change in price', 1% is probably a big change, while for a parameter like 'percentage executed and invoiced in year 2002', 1% is probably a very small change.

When performing one-change-at-a-time analyses, it is a good idea to take advantage of the Save/Open facility of your spreadsheet and to open the base model anew for any new change in a driver. This is a much safer procedure than trying to initialize your model in between two successive changes.

In order quickly to compare the results of a new scenario with the base, it might be a good idea to introduce an additional feature in your model. Based on the model in Table 3.2:

● Copy the value of B28 in C28 (Copy – Paste Special – Value).
● Enter: = B28/C28–1 in D18.

As we shall see in Chapter 5, what-if analyses are not risk analyses: the latter require you to think about the possible favourable and adverse scenarios and the respective chances of their occurring. Of course, the best of the best or the worst of the worst may always happen, but if this is very unlikely, one should perhaps not attach too much importance to such extreme situations.

What-if analyses as a creative process

A basic characteristic of creative solutions is to appear to be new and unfamiliar. Creative solutions cannot, however, be totally new or totally disconnected from previous experience and knowledge, or at least, not from the previous experience and knowledge of their creators. Innovations are the product of human minds and need to be understood by other human minds in order to be accepted. Investigations in the creative process in fields as diverse as art and science show, as Rothenberg has said, that creative people 'dip into the unknown with firm footing in the known'.[4] Fundamental to this process is the concept of **opposition**. Creative people are those who are able to consider simultaneously a solution and its opposite and to achieve new understanding through the resolution of their opposition.

What-if analysis very much pertains to the general process of using opposition for creating new solutions. You start analyzing a situation with the construction of an initial model that corresponds both to your initial understanding of the situation and to the solution which appears to you to be the most adequate, given your previous experience of comparable situations. If you are driven by the need to innovate, you then try to perform what-if analysis, to formulate alternatives, to assess their outcomes, to gain a new understanding from their differences, to formulate new alternatives, to gain further understanding, until you have created a new solution (or recognize that the initial solution was really great). Reconciling opposites, orchestrating tension, designing '**and/also rather than either/or solutions**' is an essential ingredient of organizational change and renewal.[5]

When using what-if analysis as a help in the creative process, you should probably force yourself to explore extreme cases. It is also often effective to use what-if analysis for exploring the consequences of totally opposite strategies. If you are working at simulating the impact of a conservative pricing strategy, invest some time in exploring what if you were to adopt a very aggressive pricing strategy instead. Then, if some ideas emerge from the process, try what if you were to segment your market and simultaneously adopt a conservative and an aggressive pricing strategy. Although it is often a highly productive process, formulating opposites is not easy in practice, as opposites should at the same time be similar in some particular aspects and opposed or specifically resistant to each other in some other respect.

In an organization, creativity is also a social process and what-if analyses are a great tool to create serious conversations about difficult choices. As expressed by Michael Schrage: 'There is an ecological relationship between interaction and iteration: new interactions lead to iterations, and new iterations lead in turn to new interactions: models turn out to be more about mediating interactions between people than mediating interaction between information'.[6]

3.6 Checking that a quarterly model would give similar results

One thing that we should also do before the negotiation is to check that a quarterly model would generate similar results. A quarterly model is shown in Tables 3.5 (foreground) and 3.6 (background).

There tables show us that:

● A quarterly model gives similar results. The NPV estimates of the two models differ by less than 10%.[7] Most importantly, sensitivity analyses performed on the annual and quarterly models lead to similar conclusions. For Jilin the annual model underestimates the NPV. This is due to the fact that the annual model does not capture the fact that positive cash flows start occurring from the second quarter of 2002 onwards.

● The quarterly model is more complicated than the annual model – probably more than four times more complicated! It is also probably less easy to use for simulating the

Table 3.5 ● Quarterly model (foreground)

		1	2	3	4	5	6	7	8	9	10	11	12	13	14	15	16	
1 Main contract	34																	
2 Change price	0%																	
3 Maintenance	2																	
4 Advance rate	15%																	
5 Retention rate	5%																	
6 Collect. period	0																	
7 Final payment	0																	
8 Init. cost	0																	
9 Change equip. costs	0%																	
10 Change other costs	0%																	
11 Discount rate	15%																	
12 *Quarter*	*0*	*1*	*2*	*3*	*4*	*5*	*6*	*7*	*8*	*9*	*10*	*11*	*12*	*13*	*14*	*15*	*16*	
13 Initial advance	5.10																	
14 Billings		0.00	3.80	8.20	8.40	5.40	3.20	3.20	1.8	0.25	0.25	0.25	0.25	0.25	0.25	0.25	0.25	36.0
15 Recov. advance		0.00	0.57	1.23	1.26	0.81	0.48	0.48	0.27									5.10
16 Retention		0.00	0.19	0.41	0.42	0.27	0.16	0.16	0.09									1.70
17 Release ret.													0.85				0.85	1.70
18 Final payment																	0	0.00
19 Due[a]	5.10	0.00	3.04	6.56	6.72	4.32	2.56	2.56	1.44	0.25	0.25	0.25	1.10	0.25	0.25	0.25	1.10	36.0
20 Cash in	5.10	0.00	3.04	6.56	6.72	4.32	2.56	2.56	1.44	0.25	0.25	0.25	1.10	0.25	0.25	0.25	1.10	36.0
21 Initial cost	0.00																	
22 Equipment	14.8	3.00	0.80															
23 Other costs	0.00	1.60	1.80	1.80	2.00	2.00	1.20	0.8	0.8	0.24	0.22	0.22	0.22	0.22	0.22	0.22	0.24	13.8
24 Cash out	14.8	4.60	2.60	1.80	2.00	2.00	1.20	0.80	0.80	0.24	0.22	0.22	0.22	0.22	0.22	0.22	0.24	32.4
25 Net cash	-9.70	-4.60	0.44	4.76	4.72	2.32	1.36	1.76	0.64	0.01	0.03	0.03	0.88	0.03	0.03	0.03	0.86	3.60
26 Quarterly rate	0.04																	
27 NPV	0.75																	

[a] This is the amount due by the customer at the end of a given period (quarter). This intermediate variable is useful to simulate a delay. You can model the delay automatically like here or do it manually using the 'Copy/Paste special/Value' feature of the spreadsheet.

Table 3.6 ● Quarterly model (background)

	A	B	C	D	E	F	G
1	Main contract	34					
2	Change price main co.	0					
3	Maintenance	2					
4	Advance rate	0.15					
5	Retention rate	0.05					
6	Collection period	0					
7	Final payment	0					
8	Initial cost	0					
9	Change in equipment	0					
10	Change in other costs	0					
11	Discount rate	0.15					
12	Quarter	0	+B12.1	#	#	#	#
13	Initial advance	=B1*(1+B2)*B4					
14	Billings	0	#	=3.8*(1+B2)	=8.2*(1+B2)	=8.4*(1+B2)	=5,4*(1+B2)
15	Recovery advance		=C14*$B$4	#	#	#	#
16	Retention		=C14*$B$5	#	#	#	#
17	Release retention						
18	Final payment						
19	Due	=B13+B14−B15−B16+B17+B18	#	#	#	#	#
20	Cash in	=B19	=IF($B$6=0,C19,0)	=IF($B$6=0,D19,IF($B$6=1,C19,0))	b	#	#
21	Initial cost	=B8					
22	Equipment	=14.8*(1+B9)	=3*(1+B9)	=0.8*(1+B9)			
23	Other costs	0	=1.6*(1+B10)	=1.8*(1+B10)	=1.8*(1+B10)	=2*(1+B10)	=2*(1+B10)
24	Cash out	=B21+B22+B23	#	#	#	#	#
25	Net cash	=B20−B24	#	#	#	#	#
26	Quarterly rate	=(1+B11)^0.25−1					
27	NPV	a					

a B27: =IF(B6<2, B25+NPV(B26,C25:T25), FALSE)

b E20: =IF($B$6=0,E19,IF($B$6=1,D19,IF($B$6=2,C19,FALSE)))

	H	I	J	K	L	M	N	O	P	Q	R	S	T	U
12	#	#	#	#	#	#	#	#	#	#	#	#	#	#
13														
14	=3.2*(1+B2)	=3.2*(1+B2)	=1.8*(1+B2)	=B3/8	=K14	=L14	=M14	=N14	=O14	=P14	=Q14	#	#	=SUM(C14:T14) c
15	#	#	#	#	#	#	#	#	#	#	#	#	#	
16	#	#	#	#	#	#	#	#	#	#	#	#	#	
17							=B1*(1+B2)*B5/2				=N17			
18											=B7			
19	#	#	#	#	#	#	#	#	#	#	#	#	#	
20	#	#	#	#	#	#	#	#	#	#	#	#	#	
21														
22														
23	=1.2*(1+B10)	=0.8*(1+B10)	=0.8*(1+B10)	=0.24*(1+B10)	=0.22*(1+B10)	=0.22*(1+B10)	=0.22*(1+B10)	=0.22*(1+B10)	=0.22*(1+B10)	=0.22*(1+B10)	=0.24*(1+B10)			
24	#	#	#	#	#	#	#	#	#	#	#	#	#	
25	#	#	#	#	#	#	#	#	#	#	#	#	#	

c U14: =SUM(C14:T14)

impact of changes in some drivers. In particular, it is less easy to simulate the impact of a different collection period or of a faster or slower possible execution of the contract.[8] The model in Table 3.5 enables us to test the impact of a one or two-quarter collection period only and does not enable us directly to test the impact of a different speed of execution.

In Tables 3.5 and 3.6 the NPV is calculated from the net cash flows. It could as easily be calculated as the net sum of the present values of all the different cash receipts and disbursements.

3.7 Setting ambitious targets for the negotiation

Now that we have worked on the model and have understood the sensitivity of the value to possible modifications of the contract – and to possible implementation problems – it is now time to think about the negotiation and to set our objectives: what would you, yourself, aim at in the final negotiation? To maintain the value at its current level? To increase the value? If so, up to what level? Obviously, it might well be that the customer just has the intention of signing, but what if there were some opportunities to improve the value of the project? *Keeping in mind that the goal is to maximize value, what value target would you set for the team that is going to fly to China and sign the Jilin contract if you were the executive to whom this team is reporting?*[9]

Notes

1. As we said in Chapter 1, the goal is to maximize value, i.e. to create the largest value that can be created in the situation you are in. With this project, is French Telecom really doing the best that it could do?
2. *Warning*: Entering an NPV formula for the first time may be frustrating as (1) the punctuation in the formula depends on your Windows settings, (2) the function wizard is not very friendly.

   ● Windows settings: the punctuation that is given in the text works when your numbers look like this: 100.00 (with decimal point). If, instead, your numbers look like this 100,00 (decimal comma) then try the following punctuation: + NPV (B25 ; B24 . G24).
   ● Function wizard: you do not need to specify each cash flow in the range. Stating where the first and the last cash flows are is enough.

   Another interesting complication is that if you work in a language other than English, you have to find out how your spreadsheet has translated NPV!
3. *Warning*: This is the same warning as note 2. If you are using commas for decimals, try the following punctuation: + IRR (B24 . G24 ; ,15). Finding out how your spreadsheet has translated 'IRR' might also take you some time!
4. A. Rothenberg (1979), *The Emerging Goddess: The creative process in art, science and other fields*, The University of Chicago Press. Refer in particular to Chapter 8, pp. 207–51.
5. Refer to R.T. Pascale (1990), *Managing on the Edge: How the smartest companies use conflict to stay ahead*, Prentice Hall; and R. Moss Kanter (1989), *When Giants Learn to Dance*, Simon and Schuster.
6. M. Schrage (2000), *Serious Play*, Harvard Business School Press.
7. You should keep in mind that estimating the NPV of a project is an attempt at summarizing a whole project with one single number. Estimation errors of 5 to 10% are common with NPVs.
8. One should, however, recognize that this difficulty is linked more to the limitations of spreadsheets which are not exceptionally good at helping you model delays.
9. How should your performance be assessed when you come back from the negotiation? Please refer to Chapter 5 (Section 5.7).

The Jilin project (II)

The customer's position

While preparing for the discussions with French Telecom, the head of the Chinese negotiating party reviewed their position:

- The main objective of the final negotiation with FT was to have FT agree to speeding up the project's execution. The telecommunications infrastructure was needed to exploit the Jilin oilfield. Substantial revenues were expected from this oilfield and there was a lot of pressure from the provincial government to start the exploitation one year earlier. If FT was able to demonstrate that speeding up the project would cause additional costs to them, the negotiators were authorized to agree to compensate FT for such additional costs up to a maximum of €3 million.
- The price quoted by FT was very good: FT had been the lowest bidder. It had been decided not to request any discount on the contract. Obviously, the negotiators had been invited to 'let the supplier talk' and to accept any additional 'offer' from them (e.g. a discount and/or free maintenance).
- Foreign exchange was not a problem: money had been made available by the Central Bank of China. The real issue now was to spend this foreign exchange as fast as possible. Negotiating an increase in the advance rate could be a solution for avoiding being exposed to the Central Bank changing its mind and allocating the money to another project. If the advance rate was going to be increased, the customer would at the same time request an increase in the retention rate with a view to reduce the risk of unsatisfactory execution.

Comments on Jilin (II)
Experiences of negotiation: the challenge of maximizing value

I have used the Jilin case in several executive programmes and have often ended the session by organizing a role-play of the final negotiation with the customer. For this exercise, half of the participants play the role of the customer as described in the case study above and half play the role of French Telecom. Typically, I break the customer and the supplier groups into pairs: this allows for running several negotiations in parallel.

My experience of these negotiations is, first, that the executives involved are very good at recognizing the win-win dynamics of the situation. Two actions at least (faster execution and higher initial advance) create value for both the customer and the supplier. Almost all negotiations end up with the contract to be completed in 2002 and with advance rates higher than 15%.

Second, the participants find it very difficult to extract a price increase from the customer. In spite of the fact that the customer is allowed to pay up to €3 million for getting a faster delivery, most suppliers are not able to get any price increase – some actually end up giving a 'small' discount! This shows how challenging the goal of maximizing value is. Recognizing that there is a win-win situation is not sufficient as you also have to design and implement an effective strategy for sharing the value created.

'Floor' vs. 'ceiling' prices

The modelling that we have done with Jilin has been from the point of view of the supplier and has aimed at making sure that the contract will create value above all the costs involved in implementing the project – including the financing costs. This is something that you should do before any negotiation with a customer, as you cannot create any value if you are not asking your customer for more than your costs.[1] This is not sufficient, however. Focusing on your costs will never make you estimate anything other than your 'floor price', i.e. the price below which you should not agree on any deal. In order to have a chance to create the maximum value for your company, you have to do something more: you also have to estimate the 'ceiling price'. The ceiling price has nothing to do with your costs and cannot be estimated using internal data. The ceiling price is the maximum price that the customer can agree to pay: it can only be estimated through an investigation of the value-creating process of the customer. How much value does the customer create using your products and services? What is the maximum amount of that value that you can capture?

Pricing on value is what you should do and we will explore models that can help you do this in Part V. A few comments at this stage:

● Even though it is essential to think value created and to invest time in trying to find out what the ceiling price is, it is always a good idea to keep assessing your floor price. This floor price should remain your absolute limit. My experience shows that life is full of surprises: in spite of a lot of talk about value, it happens that the ceiling price remains stubbornly below the floor price!
● 'Value pricing' sounds – and is – nice. At the same time, assessing the value created by the customer is a very challenging exercise and capturing this value is an even more difficult exercise. Both require a lot modelling and negotiating capabilities.

Note

1. Knowing your floor price is very much the same idea as knowing your 'best alternative to no agreement' (BATNA) in a negotiation process. See Chapter 23.

CHAPTER 4

Measuring the progress made in the process of creating value

Operating income, 'calculated profit' and EVA®; income statements and balance sheets; income vs. cash flow

Let us assume that there was no bargaining on 17 October 2001 for the Jilin project. When they met in Beijing, the customer and the supplier simply signed the contract described in Figure A.1 and started discussing the next steps in their relationship.

By signing the Jilin contract the supplier has created a value of €0.69 million. The issue now is to execute the contract and to make sure that the execution goes according to plan and results in the creation of the expected value. As it will take four years to execute the project there is a need to put in place measurements that will enable the company to control the value creation process. As in any business, the creation of value will be a complex process involving many different factors and activities: effective organization of the project, building the right project team, procuring the relevant equipment and supplies, successful on-site installation, effective leadership of the project, scrupulous respect of the specifications, on-time delivery, etc.

One way to control the value creation is the key performance indicators or 'balanced scorecard'[1] approach. Starting from the model that describes how the project creates value (Tables 3.2 or 3.3), you identify the key value drivers and you then put in place a system for monitoring that these drivers behave as they should. In order to build an effective measurement system, you probably need to:

- go beyond the very aggregate financial drivers shown in Table 3.3 and define more detailed performance indicators that correspond to things that the people who execute the project can observe and act upon;

● organize these performance indicators into a system – or balanced scorecard – that will help the project team navigate and deliver the expected value.

Another way is to use the accounting approach.[2] Accounting typically claims that value is created progressively and that the progress in value creation over a given period in time can be measured by the **income earned** during that period. In this case cumulative income earned is equal to the value that we estimated earlier.[3] Once you have decided how frequently you want to assess the progress of the project – yearly, quarterly, monthly, etc. – accounting enables you to estimate:

● the specific operating incomes earned in each period. The sum of all the periodic operating incomes will equal the value before financing costs and gains (€3.6 million in Jilin);
● the operating incomes after interest costs or gains earned in each period. The sum of all these incomes – also called 'calculated incomes' or EVA®s – will equal the value itself.

4.1 What 'causes' the progressive[4] creation of value?

The idea that value is created progressively, that one can identify the cause of that creation, and that it is possible to measure the progressive creation of value is a very attractive idea.[5] The problem, though, is that, in a project like Jilin, all the factors that contribute to the creation of value interact in a complex fashion and create **together and in the end** a total value or operating income of 3.6 million. Saying that value is created progressively, and that there is a factor that causes it, is somewhat of an attempt at making reality work in a more mechanistic and linear way than it does. Therefore, you should not be surprised that accountants have not found it easy to agree on what the specific factor is that causes the progressive creation of value. Let us review a few opinions about what this factor could be:

● **Final delivery and acceptance**. To start with, there are accountants who flatly reject the idea of a progressive recognition of value. For these people, value and income can only be recognized when the project is complete or substantially complete (delivered and accepted by the customer). This approach is sometimes used for recognizing the income of projects. It is called the **completed-contract** method. All methods that aim at a progressive recognition of income are labelled **percentage-of-completion** methods.
● **Progressive commitment of resources or progressive implementation of the efforts necessary to complete the project**. One can measure the efforts made or the resources committed by the importance of the amounts progressively spent. It is then possible to say that, in the Jilin project, 46% of the total efforts are made in 2001 when the company spends 14.8 million on the equipment (14.8/32.4 = 0.46); 34% in 2002; 15% in 2003; 3% in 2004 and 3% again in 2005. The progressive creation of total operating income can be recognized accordingly: 46% of 3.60 or 1.64 million in 2002; 34% of 3.60 in 2003; etc. You may, however, realize that not all efforts are of the same nature. As it supports the whole main contract, equipment may be considered as a special effort and be 'allocated' to the other efforts made in 2002 and 2003. If you allocate 60% and 40% of the equipment costs to the operating costs of 2002 and 2003, then you generate a new cost profile over the four years: 57% of the total costs are now allocated to 2002; 38% to 2003; 3% in 2004; and 3% in 2005. This leads to a new assessment of the annual

Table 4.1 • Different causes of the progressive creation of value lead to different annual incomes

Possible 'cause' of the progressive creation of value	Implied annual and cumulated incomes					
	2001	2002	2003	2004	2005	Cumulated
Final delivery					3.60	3.60
Efforts made[a]	1.64	1.22	0.53	0.10	0.10	3.60
Efforts made[b]		2.04	1.36	0.10	0.10	3.60
Deliveries		2.04	1.36	0.10	0.10	3.60
Time elapsed[c]		1.70	1.70	0.10	0.10	3.60
Time elapsed[d]		0.90	0.90	0.90	0.90	3.60

[a] Amount spent with no adjustments.
[b] Amounts spent once the equipment costs have been spread over the life of the main contract.
[c] Time elapsed. Jilin is analyzed as a main contract followed by a maintenance contract.
[d] Time elapsed. Jilin is analyzed as one single contract of €36 million.

operating incomes. **This approach is actually the most commonly used for recognizing the income of projects: it corresponds to the so-called 'cost-to-cost' and 'efforts-expended' methods.** When a project is characterized by large start-up costs – like the equipment costs of the Jilin project – then it is common practice to single out these start-up costs and to spread them over the life of the contract.

- **Progressive fulfilment of the obligations with the customer.** One can also use the deliveries of products and services – or invoices – to measure the degree of fulfilment of the contractual obligations with the customer. With Jilin, the company fulfils 60% (20.4/34) of the total contractual obligations of the main contract in 2002 and as a consequence 60% of the total operating income (2.04) should be recognized in 2002. And so on. **This approach is commonly used for recognizing the income of most business activities.** It is also used for recognizing the income of projects: these are the so-called **units-of-delivery** or **units-of-work-performed** methods.

- **Time elapsed.** If the project is broken into a main contract and a maintenance contract, the income is €1.7 million in 2002[6] and 2003 and €0.1 million in 2004 and 2005. Alternatively, if the project is considered as one single project, then operating income is the same each year: €0.9 million. This very simple approach is used for allocating specific costs (depreciation is an example) but typically not for recognizing income.

Table 4.1 shows the annual and cumulative operating incomes that result from the choice of the 'cause' of value creation. Please check that if the different approaches result in different periodic incomes, they all result in the same cumulative operating income.

How do we want to recognize the annual incomes of Jilin?

Let us decide to use the percentage-of-completion method based on the progressive fulfilment of the obligations with the customer. This method is standard for recognizing the revenues of most business activities and is also used in project activities. It is also worth noting that in the Jilin case this method gives the same results as recognition of income in relation to cost incurred, the most commonly used method in project activities.

4.2 Three key accounting principles: revenues and expenses recognition and matching

Accounting typically considers that the progressive fulfilment of the obligations towards the customer 'causes' the progressive creation of value – or is the event to be used for recognizing income earned.[7] The progressive fulfilment of obligations is done through the delivery of goods and/or services specified in the contract or order. Assessing the operating income earned in any given period is a matter of:

1. Recognizing the revenues or sales.
2. Recognizing the expenses.
3. Estimating the income as the difference between sales and those expenses that 'match' the sales.

Recognizing sales

Accounting principles state that two conditions should be met for a revenue – or a sale – to be recognized. The revenue should be:

● **earned**. This happens as soon as products or services are delivered to the customer; and
● **realized**. This happens as soon as the company has sent an invoice to the customer and can safely consider that it has a promise to pay from the customer.

In the Jilin project, in 2002 sales are equal to €20.4 million. It is worth noting that sales differ from cash received: 20.4 vs. 16.32 million. The difference is due to a series of factors:

● While a total of €20.4 million are delivered and invoiced, only 16.32 million are paid by the customer who is entitled to recover part of the initial advance and to build a fund for guarantee that will be released in 2004 and 2005.
● The €5.1 million received as advance payment at the date of signature should not be considered as sales. The advance does not correspond to the fulfilment of any obligation towards the customer. Quite the opposite, the advance confirms the creation of a series of obligations.

Time is the only factor that makes sales and cash receipts differ from each other. At the end of the project, the cumulative values of sales and cash received are necessarily the same. This value is also equal to the value of the order given by the customer when signing the contract.

Recognizing expenses

Recognizing expenses is similar to recognizing sales. What counts are the goods and services that have been received from the suppliers, not what has been paid to them. In the Jilin project all expenses are paid for in cash. As a result expenses are always the same as cash outflows.

Table 4.2 ● Applying the matching principle to recognize the income of a car dealer

The business issue

A car dealer has sold (and has been paid for) 400 cars in 2001 at an average price of $10 000 each. In the same year this car dealer has purchased (and has paid for) 600 cars at an average price of $8000 each. This car dealer started operating in 2001 and now wants to assess the outcome of his first year of operations. How much cash? How much income?

Cash in $ million	Volume	Unit price	Value	Income in $ million	Volume	Unit price	Value
Cash in	400	0.10	4.0	Sales	400	0.10	4.0
Cash out	600	0.08	4.8	CGS	400	0.08	3.2
Net cash			−0.8	Gross income			0.6

Cost of goods sold (CGS) aims at reflecting the cost of the 400 units that have been sold. Sales and cost of goods sold correspond to the same goods (the volume of sales and of cost of goods sold is the same). **In a physical goods business, the only difference between sales and cost of goods sold is price:**

- at the level of sales the goods are valued at their selling price,
- at the level of cost of goods sold, these same goods are valued at their purchasing price (trading) or at their production price (manufacturing).

The consequence of the matching principle is that the costs that do not match the sales of the period are stored in an **inventory** where they will wait until they are 'recovered' and come to match future sales. Storing costs in an inventory is not necessarily a bad thing, but always involves some risk!

The matching principle

Assessing which expenses should be charged to sales is a matter of applying what accountants call the **matching principle**. According to this principle there is a need to associate the expenses and revenues that are related or to associate 'cause and effect': consequently all expenses incurred in the generation of a revenue should be recognized in the same accounting period as this revenue is recognized. The use of the matching principle is illustrated in Table 4.2.

Back to Jilin

Assuming that the deliveries made in each year all require the same quantity of efforts, then we have to make sure that the expenses in 2002 will be in the same proportion to the total expenses as the revenues in 2002 are to the total cumulative sales. In 2002, sales are 60% of the total sales of the main contract. Expenses in 2002 should also equal 60% of total expenses (30.6 million) i.e. €18.36 million. The problem, though, is that, in 2002, the company incurs more costs than it can charge as expenses (25.80 million vs. 18.36 million). According to generally accepted accounting principles, all costs that cannot be charged to the revenues of the period have to be stored in an asset account of the balance sheet. The difference between 25.80 and 18.36 million (7.44 million) will be stored in an inventory (work-in-progress) account. This inventory account will signal that the company has spent faster than needed for making the sales of the year! Please note that 'inventory' does not necessarily mean easily identifiable physical goods: in a project like Jilin inventory may just be costs that the company has not been able to recover yet. Once costs are estimated, you can then calculate operating income as the difference between sales (20.40) and costs (18.36): 2.04 million. The annual income statements of the project are in Table 4.3. The bottom line of these annual income statements is 'net income' which is defined as the income obtained after having deducted all costs (including financing costs, exceptional costs, tax, etc.). In Jilin there are no taxes and we still ignore financing costs. As a result net income is equal to operating income.

Annual income as a signal of the final outcome of the project

When they report to the external world, companies typically disclose:

● fairly detailed past-related financial statements: income statement, cash flows and balance sheets for the period that has just elapsed (typically a year or quarter);
● very limited future-related data.

When signing the Jilin contract, French Telecom will probably state the total sales involved (this is sometimes and improperly called the 'value' of the contract) but will not disclose how much shareholder value it expects to create with this contract. It is only in 2002 when reporting the first sales and income of the contract that FT will signal to the external world that it believes that this contract will generate a 10% operating income margin. This will be signalled by the fact that the 2002 operating profit is 10% of the 2002 sales.

Table 4.3 ● Annual incomes of the Jilin project (percentage-of-completion)

	2001	2002	2003	2004	Cumulated
Sales	20.40	13.60	1.00	1.00	36.00
Costs	18.36	12.24	0.90	0.90	32.40
Operating income	2.04	1.36	0.10	0.10	3.60
Net income	2.04	1.36	0.10	0.10	3.60
Breakdown of costs					
Costs, equipment	11.16	7.44			18.60
Costs, other	7.20	4.80	0.90	0.90	13.80

Formulas
The full model of Jilin is in Tables 4.8 and 4.9. The following formulas are based on the model built in Table 3.3. Put sales in row 35 in order to keep some space for completing the cash flow statements – *see* Tables 4.8 and 4.9.
In C35: +C14; copy to D14.E14; in D35: +F35+F18
In C36: +(B23+C23+C25+D25+B32)*B5; in D36: +(B23+C23+C25+D25+B32)*(1–B5);
        in E36: +E25; copy to F36.
In C37: +C35–C36; in C38: +C37; Copy C37.C38 into D37.F37

4.3 Value vs. annual income matching: a concept well adapted to the old 'economy of things'

Companies should maximize value, not annual incomes

When it comes to analyzing a business, what counts is the value that it creates or – which is about the same thing[8] – the cumulative income that it generates over its whole life, not so much its periodic incomes. Individual periodic incomes are intermediate assessments and their estimate cannot be considered as totally reliable. We have seen above that allocating the total value of a project over different periods of its life is more a matter of opinion than of facts. When it comes to setting goals and assessing performance, it is the same, what counts is value not individual annual incomes:

● Maximizing value is the relevant objective.
● Maximizing annual income does not mean much. An intermediate, 'short-term' variable such as annual income is not an effective output variable and there are numerous cases where maximizing annual income actually destroys value.[9]

The idea that companies should maximize value and not annual incomes is an idea that is more and more accepted today. This idea is consistent with the finances of some very innovative and aggressive companies of the information economy: very high annual losses and stellar stock market performance. It is also fair to say that the idea of giving priority to value is still facing resistance.

● There is a long tradition in business of focusing on the income statement and its 'bottom line'. Setting and controlling income goals still sounds much more natural to many business people than setting and controlling value goals.
● Many people also like the fact that income earned is something that has been achieved and that is therefore certain[10] – people often tend to forget the allocation problems linked to the estimate of profit. On the contrary, value is a complex concept, it relates to several time periods, it is risky and can be influenced by many factors, and so on.
● Finally, for some people, income earned has the unique advantage of recognizing that a step has been achieved in the process of creating value.

What if matching were to be more adapted to the old economy of things than to the new economy of information?

The matching principle – and the notions of 'cost of goods sold' and 'margin' – are very well adapted to businesses like the car dealer's in Table 4.2. When working with physical products – or with 'atoms' – it is relatively easy to match costs and revenues. It is also very meaningful to do so because, in such businesses, the difference between production cost and selling price is often small and has to be aggressively managed. But in businesses with a high information content – pharmaceuticals have traditionally been a good example – then the margin over the physical or manufacturing cost is not that meaningful. In such businesses manufacturing cost is typically very small when compared with information costs like R&D or marketing. The problem with costs like R&D and marketing is that it is very difficult to match them with sales.[11]

Production cost is typically almost irrelevant to all those companies that trade bits instead of atoms.[12] Cost of goods sold and margin of products or services are not such useful notions for such companies, which often focus much more on customers than on products anyway. As today's economy is made up of a variety of companies ranging from those that deal mostly with bits to those that deal mostly with atoms, matching still has a future but clearly more so with some companies than with others.

A word of caution about the 'relationship' between sales and costs

In order to recognize income, accounting establishes a relationship between sales and costs. In Table 4.2, cost of goods sold is estimated based on sales and as a result looks as though it was driven by sales or, as some people say, 'caused by sales'. This idea is implicit in many financial models which start with an estimate of sales and which calculate almost all the other items as a percentage of sales – the so-called **percentage-of-sales** forecasting method. When analyzing and forecasting income statements you should be very careful, though, and remember that the relationship between sales and cost of goods sold is a relationship that exists more in the minds of accountants than in reality. We shall discuss this issue further in Chapter 9.

4.4 What gives the best picture of the annual outcome of operations: cash or income?

Periodic income and cash assessments often give a very different picture of the outcome of operations. This is the case with the Jilin project. As shown in Table 4.4,

● while income is always positive – and equal to 10% of sales,
● cash starts with showing a very negative figure and then becomes very positive. This is the typical 'investing-harvesting' cycle.

Cash and income give even more conflicting signals for the car dealer of Table 4.2:

● According to the 'cash picture' the operations of the car dealer have been very poor and have resulted in a need to find $0.8 million to support the activity!
● According to the 'income picture' the operations of the car dealer have generated a positive gross income of $0.6 million (20% of sales) which is very satisfactory!

When they give conflicting signals, which of the income and of the cash pictures is right? **Both!** Which of these two pictures best reflects the outcome of the operations? **Neither!** Income and cash reflect two different critical dimensions of the running of a business.

Table 4.4 ● Annual operating incomes and cash flows of the Jilin project

	2001	2002	2003	2004	2005	Cumulated
Operating income	0.00	2.04	1.36	0.10	0.10	3.60
Free cash flow	−9.70	5.32	6.08	0.95	0.95	3.60
Difference (income − cash)	9.70	−3.28	−4.72	−0.85	−0.85	0.00

Income tries to signal how much value the business is expected to create in the end. Income is calculated as if the business was fully synchronized – this is the purpose of matching and all the other allocations.[13] This allows you to check in any given time period that your level of invoicing is high enough for the business to create value. **In a business of atoms, income basically tells you how successful the business is at managing pricing**. The positive income of the dealer in Table 4.2 states that this dealer sells at $10 000, a price significantly higher[14] than the price at which the products are bought ($8000). In an information business, the concept of synchronization is more difficult to apply and as a result the meaning of income is not as clear.[15] One can, however, try to extrapolate the concept and say that income also shows what the business should earn when it is in sync.[16]

Cash tells you how successful the business is at synchronizing its different activities. Cash makes it clear that the car dealer has not been able to synchronize his purchases and sales[17] in 2000. Cash shows synchronization for both the businesses of atoms and the businesses of bits!

Both pricing and synchronization are critical to the process of creating value and both should be continuously monitored. Synchronization of receipts and payments is especially interesting to look at. It is very easy for a company to let its payments and receipts go out of sync.[18] And this is made even easier by the fact that overspending is ambiguous: why would it not be a valuable investment for the future? As a result, it is always worth investigating why receipts and payments may get out of sync:

● *Is it the result of a deliberate strategy or a specific business model?* If the answer is positive (and if you believe that the strategy is valid), then there is generally no need to worry: the 2001 cash deficit at Jilin is just the necessary first step in the process of value creation.
● *Is it the consequence of some unfortunate past decision?* This might well be the cause of the cash deficit experienced by the car dealer of Table 4.2. In this situation there is a need to worry as the poor synchronization might be an early warning signal of future pricing problems. Many dealers tend to get nervous when they find themselves in the situation of Table 4.2. Some actually get so impatient to get rid of their inventory that they consider giving substantial price discounts!

While income and cash provide different and complementary pictures, balance sheets help you understand what drives the possible mismatches between these two pictures.

4.5 Balance sheets: describing what drives the business out of sync

The balance sheet – or **statement of financial position** – aims at reflecting the financial status of a firm in conformity with generally accepted accounting principles. The balance sheet is composed of three elements: assets, liabilities and equity.

Assets

The assets of the project at the end of 2001, 2002, 2003, 2004 and 2005 are shown in Table 4.5. Assets correspond to all the future monetary benefits that are expected to result from past transactions or events. These future monetary benefits are shown at their **historical cost**, i.e. at the cost that was incurred when the transaction was made in the past.[19] In the Jilin project, the assets at the end of 2001 correspond to the equipment costs incurred

Table 4.5 ● Annual cash flows, income statements and balance sheets for the Jilin project

	2001	2002	2003	2004	2005	Cumulated
Free cash flow	−9.70	5.32	6.08	0.95	0.95	3.60
Initial equity	9.70					
Dividend	0.00	0.00	0.00	0.00	0.00	0.00
Change in cash balance	0.00	5.32	6.08	0.95	0.95	13.30
	End 01	**End 02**	**End 03**	**End 04**	**End 05**	
Cash	0.00	5.32	11.40	12.35	13.30	
Retention	0.00	1.02	1.70	0.85	0.00	
Receivables	0.00	0.00	0.00	0.00	0.00	
Inventory	14.80	7.44	0.00	0.00	0.00	
Total	14.80	13.78	13.10	13.20	13.30	
Initial advance	5.10	2.04	0.00	0.00	0.00	
Shareholders' equity	9.70	11.74	13.10	13.20	13.30	
Total	14.80	13.78	13.10	13.20	13.30	

Note:
A necessary step before building the balance sheet is to finalize the cash flow statements. So far we have left the cash flow statement with a cash deficit of 9.70 million without specifying how this cash deficit will be covered. Let us assume that the cash deficit at the end of 2001 is totally covered by equity brought in by the owners. We also have to introduce dividends: dividends correspond to cash paid to shareholders.

The value of cumulated net cash at the end (13.30) is interesting to analyze: it is equal to the cash surplus (3.60) plus the amount invested by the shareholders (9.70)

Formulas
The full model of Jilin is in Tables 4.8 and 4.9.
Cash flows statement
Free cash flow is in row 29: in B29: +B20–B22–B23–B25. Copy to C29.G29
In B30: –B29; in C31.F31: inputs. In B32: +B29+B30–B31. Copy to C32.G32
Balance sheets
Cash is in row 40: In B40: +B32; in C40: +B40+C32; copy to D40.G40
In B41: 0; in C41: +B41+C16–C17; copy to D41.G41
In B42: +B19; copy to C42.G42; in B43: +B22+B23; in C43: +B43+C23+C25–C36
In D43.G43: 0; in B44: +B40+B41+B42+B43; copy to C44.G44
In B46: +B13; in C46: +B46–C15; in D46.G46: 0;
In B47: +B30; in C47: +B47+C38–C31; copy to D47.G47
In B48: +B46+B47; copy to C48.G48

in 2000 and that have not yet been charged to the customer. This is the 14.80 million inventory. It corresponds to a past event (money spent in 2001) and to a future benefit (the equipment is going to be charged to future sales). At the end of 2002, the assets consist of:

● the money retained by the customer in conformity with the 5% retention clause. Money has been retained in 2002 (past event) and will be released in 2004 and 2005 (future benefit);

● the part of the equipment and other costs incurred in 2001 and 2002 that have not been charged to sales – or not expended – yet.

It is interesting to analyze the evolution of the different assets over time together with the progressive completion of the project.

● The retention account continuously grows until the money is released in two successive steps.
● The inventory (equipment costs) account exists at the end of 2001 and 2002 only.

At the beginning of the project – end of 2001 and 2002 – several assets exist. At the end of the project, all assets have disappeared except for one: cash. Assets actually portray all the actions that have been undertaken for a future benefit but which have not yet been completed.

● At the beginning of the project there are a lot of assets because a lot of transactions have been started up but none has yet been completed.
● At the end of the project there are no longer any assets since all the transactions needed for the project have been completed.

From the beginning to the end of the project's life assets show how fast the company is able to transform the project into cash.

How good is it for a company to have assets on its balance sheet? As assets reflect transactions that have not yet been completed, it seems difficult to claim that having assets on the balance sheet is necessarily of great value. Spending money on good projects is very valuable but this spending should be passed to customers as quickly as possible (and paid by them as quickly as possible) rather than being kept on the balance sheet. Assets are typically not popular with some companies that claim that high quality operations should tend towards being **asset free**. Quality is very much about systematically completing actions. Since they correspond to incomplete transactions, it is quite obvious that assets become a target for improvement. Why not adjust production to sales and squeeze inventories? Why not delight the customers and get them to pay faster?

Liabilities

Liabilities correspond to all the future monetary sacrifices that are expected to arise from the present obligations of the company to transfer assets or provide services to other entities in the future as a result of past transactions or events. In the Jilin project, liabilities at the end of 2001 correspond to the outstanding amount of the initial customer's advance: €5.1 million. Over the life of the project this liability continuously decreases with the progressive recovery of the advance by the customer (this is the 'future monetary sacrifice').

Equity

Equity corresponds to the residual interest in the assets that remains after deducting the liabilities. In a business enterprise, the equity is the ownership interest. At the end of 2000, the equity of the project is equal to €13.30 million. This is the amount initially invested (9.70) plus the value created – when the cost of financing is ignored (3.60).

Successive balance sheets show what drives the business out of sync

Table 4.4 shows the differences between the annual income and cash flow figures. Table 4.6 shows how these differences are explained by the changes in the balance sheet accounts:

inventory, retention and initial customer's advance. At the very beginning of the project (2001) cash is very negative due to the very rapid inventory build-up that is fortunately attenuated by the receipt of the initial advance. As early as 2002, cash becomes very positive due to the inventory decrease, but would have been even more positive without the retention build-up and the decrease in the customer's advance account, and so on.

The relationship between income, cash generation and changes in balance sheet accounts is further discussed in Chapter 6.

Table 4.6 ● Explaining the differences between annual operating incomes and cash flows of the Jilin project

	2001	2002	2003	2004	2005	Cumulated
Operating income	0.00	2.04	1.36	0.10	0.10	3.60
– increase in inventory	−14.80	+7.36	+7.44	0.00	0.00	0.00
– increase in retention		−1.02	−0.68	+0.85	+0.85	0.00
+ increase in advance	+5.10	−3.06	−2.04	0.00	0.00	0.00
						3.60
Free cash flow	−9.70	5.32	6.08	0.95	0.95	–

The purpose of balance sheets is not to show the value of a company[20]

Some people find it difficult to use historical cost for valuing assets in a balance sheet. They would intuitively prefer to use a quantity closer to the current value of the assets. The problem, though, is that the purpose of building balance sheets is not to assess the value of a company. Balance sheets are actually not at all a tool designed for assessing value. Value (as measured by NPV) is a future related concept, while balance sheets are basically concerned with what the company has done up to now (the date at which the balance sheet is established). The purpose of balance sheets is to record all that the company has spent and where it has spent it (on which assets) with a view to ensuring that all this spending is going to create value.[21] Using historical cost fits this purpose very well.

The relationship between book equity and shareholder value (market-to-book ratio)

Both book equity (equity as shown in the balance sheet) and shareholder value reflect the monetary interests of the shareholders.

● Book equity reflects what the shareholders have invested up to the date of the balance sheet.
● Shareholder value (as reflected by the stock market) reflects what this investment is worth.

Consequently shareholder value should be higher than book equity and the ratio between shareholder value and book equity (market-to-book ratio) should be higher than 1.[22]

Table 4.7 • Annual incomes of the Jilin project

	2002	2003	2004	2005	Cumulated
Calculated income/EVA®					
Sales	20.40	13.60	1.00	1.00	36.00
Costs	18.36	12.24	0.90	0.90	32.40
Operating income	2.04	1.36	0.10	0.10	3.60
Notional interest	−1.46	−0.88	−0.09	0.03	1.39
Calculated income/EVA®	**0.59**	**0.48**	**0.01**	**0.13**	**1.21**
Accounting income					
Sales	20.40	13.60	1.00	1.00	36.00
Costs	18.36	12.24	0.90	0.90	32.40
Operating income	2.04	1.36	0.10	0.10	3.60
Interest	0.00	0.00	0.00	0.00	0.00
Net Income	**2.04**	**1.36**	**0.10**	**0.10**	**3.60**

The estimate of calculated income/EVA® and the formulas are also in Table 4.8.

4.6 Financing and interest

There are very different ways of taking interest into account. First, when calculating value, we have considered that interest has to be paid on any cash deficit. We have not asked ourselves how this cash deficit is going to be financed, we just charged a notional interest rate (15%). Following the same approach, we can now adjust the annual operating incomes with an interest charge equal to 15% of the cash balance. This is done in Table 4.7 and it corresponds to what some European companies call 'calculated income'[23] and what Stern Stewart & Co call 'EVA®'. Please note that when cumulated, annual calculated incomes/annual EVA®s equal value expressed in end of 2005 terms (€1.21 million).

Secondly, in accounting – and according to the principles that are most commonly accepted today[24] – interest has to be taken into account only when an interest is actually paid (which implies the existence of a loan). This rule is apparently reasonable but when a project is totally financed by its owners, then no interest is to be taken into account and the net income – the bottom line of the income statement – is the same, when there are no taxes, as the operating income! This is also shown in Table 4.7. The fact that equity financing apparently comes for free is even more difficult to accept when you realize that equity necessarily costs more than debt![25]

A business which generates a positive net income does not necessarily create value

Net income takes into account all costs including the costs of loans but ignores the efforts made by the shareholders. The calculation of net income assumes that the money invested by shareholders has been brought in for free! As a consequence, stating that the net income of a business is positive is not sufficient to prove that this business creates value. You also have to establish that this income is sufficiently large in relation to the equity that the shareholders have invested in the business. In order to do so, you have to compare this net income with the amount of equity invested in the business, calculate the 'return on equity' that has been achieved, and compare this return on equity with what this return should be. Then, and only then, will you be able to know about the success of the business.

● If the return on equity is equal to or higher than what it should be (15% in the Jilin project), then you know that the business is successful at creating value.
● If the return on equity is lower than this hurdle, then you have to conclude that the business does not create value – in spite of generating a positive income.[26]

4.7 A comprehensive model for Jilin

A comprehensive model for Jilin is shown in Table 4.8 (foreground) and Table 4.9 (background).

Table 4.8 ● A comprehensive model of the Jilin project (foreground)

A	B	C	D	E	F	G	H
1 Main contract	34						
2 Maintenance	2						
3 Advance rate	15%						
4 Retention rate	5%						
5 % executed in 2000	60%						
6 Collection period	0						
7 Additional final payment	0						
8 Additional initial cost	0						
9 Change in equipment	0%						
10 Change in other costs	0%						
11 Discount rate	15%						
12 *Year*	*2000*	*2001*	*2002*	*2003*	*2004*	*2005*	*Cum.*
13 Initial advance	5.10						5.10
14 Billings		20.40	13.60	1.00	1.00		36.00
15 Recovery advance		3.06	2.04				5.10
16 Retention		1.02	0.68				1.70
17 Release retention				0.85	0.85		1.70
18 Additional final payment					0.00		0.00
19 Receivables end year		0.00	0.00	0.00	0.00		0.00
20 **Cash receipts**	5.10	16.32	10.88	1.85	1.85		36.00
21 **PV cash receipts**	29.79						
22 **PV initial cost**	0.00						
23 Equipment	14.80	3.80					18.60
24 PV equipment cost	18.10						
25 Labour & other		7.20	4.80	0.90	0.90		13.80
26 **PV labour & other**	11.00						
27 **Value**	0.69	0.79	0.91	1.05	1.21		
28							
29 Free cash flow	−9.70	5.32	6.08	0.95	0.95	0.00	3.60
30 Initial equity	9.70						
31 Dividend		0.00	0.00	0.00	0.00		
32 Change in cash balance	0.00	5.32	6.08	0.95	0.95	0.00	13.30
33							

Table 4.8 continued

	A	B	C	D	E	F	G	H
34		2001	2002	2003	2004	2005		
35	Sales		20.40	13.60	1.00	1.00		36.00
36	CGS		18.36	12.24	0.90	0.90		32.40
37	Operating income		2.04	1.36	0.10	0.10		3.60
38	Net income		2.04	1.36	0.10	0.10		3.60
39								
40	Cash	0.00	5.32	11.40	12.35	13.30	13.30	
41	Retention	0.00	1.02	1.70	0.85	0.00	0.00	
42	Receivables	0.00	0.00	0.00	0.00	0.00	0.00	
43	Inventory	14.80	7.44	0.00	0.00	0.00	0.00	
44	Total assets	14.80	13.78	13.10	13.20	13.30	13.30	
45								
46	Advance	5.10	2.04	0.00	0.00	0.00	0.00	
47	Equity	9.70	11.74	13.10	13.20	13.30	13.30	
48	Total liabilities and equity	14.80	13.78	13.10	13.20	13.30	13.30	
49								
50	Net cash	−9.70	−5.84	−0.63	0.23	1.21		
51	Interest for calculating value		1.46	0.88	0.09	−0.03		
52								
53		2000	2001	2002	2003	2004		Cum.
54	Sales		20.40	13.60	1.00	1.00		36.00
55	CGS		18.36	12.24	0.90	0.90		32.40
56	Operating income		2.04	1.36	0.10	0.10		3.60
57	Interest for calculating value		1.46	0.88	0.09	−0.03		
58	**Calculated income/EVA**		**0.58**	**0.48**	**0.01**	**0.13**		**1.21**

Notes

1. Robert S. Kaplan and David P. Norton (1996), *The Balanced Score Card*, Harvard Business School Press.
2. For accounting texts, refer to: Charles T. Horngren, Gary L. Sundem and John A. Elliott (1999), *Introduction to Financial Accounting*, Prentice Hall; and to Barry Elliott and Jamie Elliott (2000), *Financial Accounting and Reporting*, Prentice Hall. For the 'generally accepted accounting principles': US GAAP, refer to: Jan R. Williams (2002), *2002 Miller Gaap Guide*, Harcourt Professional Publishing or Patrick Delaney (2002) *Wiley GAAP 2002* and *Wiley GAAP 2002 for Windows*, Wiley. For International Accounting Standards (IAS), refer to: Barry J. Epstein and Abas Ali Mirza (2002), *Wiley IAS 2002*, John Wiley. You may also consult the following websites: Financial Accounting Standards Board, www.fasb.org; Security and Exchange Commission, www.sec.gov; and International Federation of Accountants, www.ifa.org.
3. We shall see later that when income earned is calculated after interest on both debt and equity, cumulative income earned – also called MVA – equals net future value.
4. Why should the creation of value be a progressive or linear process? Perhaps value is like organizational change, it is not created progressively, it just happens suddenly!
5. Some people would actually not find this idea attractive. In *Relevance Lost* (1987), T. Johnson and R. Kaplan imagine the objectives of the Venetian merchants when accounting was created five hundred years ago: 'To compute overall profitability of the venture and to distribute the net proceeds (the retained earnings) among the initial investors was a worthwhile role for accounting. One has to wonder, however, whether the investors or the Venetian version of the Securities and

---

Table 4.9 ● A comprehensive model of the Jilin project (background)

Rows 1 to 27

B1 to B11 and B26: inputs

B13: +B1*B3

B20: +B13

B21: +B20+NPV(B11, C20.G20)

B22: +B8

B23: +14.8*(1+B9)

B24: +B23+C23/(1+B11)

B26: +B25+NPV(B11, C25.F25)

B27: +B21–B22–B24–B26

C14: +B1*B5

C15: +C14*$B$3; copy to D15

C16: +C14*$B$4; copy to D16

C19: +(C14–C15–C16+C17+C18)/4*$B$7; copy to D19.F19

C20: +C14–C15–C16+C17+C18–C19+B19; copy to D20.G20

C23: +3.8*(1+B9)

C25: +12*B5*(1+B10)

C27: =B27*(1+$B$11); copy

D14: +B1–C14

D25: +12*(1+B10)–C25

E14: +B2/2

E17: +B1*B4/2

E25: +.9*(1+B10)

F14: B2–E14

F17: +E17

H13: =SUM(B13.G13). Copy to H13.H18 and to H20, H22, H23 and H25

H27: +H20–H22–H23–H25

Rows 29 to 48

B29: +B20–B22–B23–B25; copy to C29.G29

B30: –B29; C31.F31: inputs

B32: +B29+B30–B31; copy to C32.G32

H29: +SUM(B29.G29). Copy to H32, to H35.H38 and to H54.H58

B40: +B32; C40: +B40+C32; copy D40.G40

B41: 0; C41: +B41+C16–C17; copy D41.G41

B42: +B19; copy to C42.G42

B43: +B22+B23;

C43: +B43+C23+C25–C36; D43.G43: 0

C35: +C14; copy to D14.E14; D35: +F35+F18

C36: +(B23+C23+C25+D25+B22)*B5

D36: +(B23+C23+C25+D25+B22)*(1–B5)

E36: +E25; copy to F36

C37: +C35–C36; C38: +C37; copy C37.C38 to D37.F37

B44: +B40+B41+B42+B43; copy C44.G44

B46: +B13; C46: +B46–C15

D46.G46: 0; B47: +B30

C47: +B47+C38–C31; copy to D47.G47

B48: +B46+B47. Copy to C48.G48

Rows 50 to 58

B50: +B29; C50: +B50+C29–C51; copy to D50.F50

C51: +B50*–$B$11; copy to D51.F51

C54: +C35; C55: +C36; C56: +C37;

C57: +C51; Copy C54.C57 to D54.F54

C58: +C56–C57; Copy to D58.F58

Exchange Commission or Financial Accountings Standards Board, also asked the accountants to compute the expedition's profit during the third quarter of 1487 when the caravan was traversing the Persian desert *en route* to India.'

6. Let us assume that the contract is signed at the end of 2001 and that it does not make sense to consider 2001 when allocating the total operating income over time.

7. This is what is called the 'transaction approach' to the recognition of income (as opposed to the 'capital maintenance approach'). For a discussion of the different income concepts, please refer to Chapter 3 of R. Schroeder and M. Clark (1997), *Accounting Theory*, John Wiley.

8. It is basically the same if interest is charged on both debt and equity (*see* Table 4.7).

9. Two interesting little books about value destructive income manipulation are Terry Smith (1992), *Accounting for Growth: Stripping the camouflage from company accounts*, Century Business and Charles Mulford and Eugene Comiskey (2002) *The Financial Numbers Game: Detecting creative accounting practices*, Wiley.

10. The new practice of real-time reporting (see 'Making Decisions in Real Time' by Thomas A. Stewart in *Fortune*, 26 June 2000), makes it possible today for a company to know at every minute the income that has been earned so far by a project. This is a very powerful feedback even if it is not exactly the 'right' feedback.

11. The problem with matching is that you should have a good idea of both your costs and your future revenues. In pharmaceuticals R&D expenses are typically related to future sales that are both very distant in time and very uncertain.

12. For an analysis of the 'new economy of information' as opposed to the 'old economy of things', please refer to Philip Evans and Thomas S. Wurster (2000), *Blown to Bits*, Harvard Business School Press.

13. Like depreciation for example.

14. It is the same when you consider a full income statement that reflects all the costs. When this income shows a positive income this means that the price at which the company sells to its customers is sufficiently high to cover its costs and create value.

15. This is one of the reasons why income and value may give such widely different signals for some companies of the e-economy. The stock market value of some of these companies is very high: this means that the market is very confident in their future. At the same time their cash is very negative: this is due to the fact that these companies are in an investing phase. But income is very negative – often close to free cash flow: this is more surprising since a concept like matching should enable these companies to allocate a large part of their current investments to future sales. The problem is that future sales are much too uncertain to allow for the use of an idea like matching.

16. Which means that start-ups that make losses signal with those losses that they have not yet been able to find out the level of pricing/invoicing that they need to have.

17. It is more exact to say that income reflects the quality of pricing only (the process used for recognizing income aims at eliminating the impact of synchronization issues) while cash reflects both synchronization *and* pricing issues.

18. This is made even easier by the fact that in some functional organizations there are entire departments – like purchasing departments – which have the mission to spend.

19. See below: the purpose of balance sheets is not to show the value of a company.

20. This would not be the case if all the items on the balance sheet were to be shown at their net present value. Preparing balance sheets in which assets and liabilities are shown at present value would also require that assets no longer be reported according to categories such as fixed assets, inventories, receivables, etc. but according to projects or markets. One can assess the value of Jilin *as a whole* but not really the value of its retention, inventory, advance, etc.

21. Assets show how much money has been used and where it has been used. Liabilities and equity describe how these uses of money have been financed: through other people's money (liabilities) or by the owners (equity).

22. One of the problems with the market-to-book ratio is that it compares quantities which are not time-homogeneous. As the market value is expressed as of today, it would be useful to restate all the assets and liabilities as of the date of the balance sheet and estimate an 'adjusted book equity' as the difference between adjusted assets and adjusted liabilities. A ratio similar to the market-to-book value is **Tobin's q ratio** which is equal to the market value of the assets over their estimated replacement cost. The numerator q includes all the firm's debt and equity securities, not just the common stock, and the denominator includes all assets, not just the firm's net worth.

23. Calculated income has been used internally for decades by several companies in continental Europe.

24. For an argument in favour of recognizing interest on equity as a cost, refer to R. Anthony, 'Equity interest – its time has come', *Journal of Accountancy*, Dec. 1982.

25. See the General Appendix at the end of the book.

26. The difference between the calculated income/EVA® approach and the return on equity approach is very much the same as the difference between the value and the return approach discussed in Section 2.8.

Swedish Timber[1]

On 27 February 1992, Lars Johansson, the President of Swedish Timber, was preparing the presentation of the hedging policy that he was going to make at the next meeting of the board.

Swedish Timber

Swedish Timber was created on 1 January 1991 by the five largest Swedish forestry companies to sell sawn timber in Egypt and in other countries of the Middle East. Swedish Timber was a trading company acting as a principal, i.e. buying timber from forestry companies – and from its five owners in particular – and selling this timber to wholesalers and construction companies in Egypt and in the Middle East.

Egypt was an important market for Swedish exporters as it was typically buying some 10% of the Swedish production of sawn timber. Egypt was also one of the few markets that were importing growing quantities: 1 000 000 m^3 in 1990. On the other hand, Egypt was a very competitive market with low and volatile prices. Swedish imports were generally the largest in Egypt (200 000 to 500 000 m^3) followed by Finnish and Russian imports. In spite of its importance as a world supplier of wood, Canada exported very little to Egypt as it did not offer the dry qualities required by the local climatic conditions.

In its first year of existence Swedish Timber faced unusual challenges. The overall world market was so depressed that traders used to compare 1991 to 1962, the worst year ever experienced. In 1991 there had also been a lot of currency volatility: surge of the dollar after the Russian coup, devaluation of the Finnish markka (FIM).

In spite of all these challenges, Swedish Timber managed to generate a gross margin of Swedish kronor (SEK) 8 million and sales of 380 million. This was below budget but not that much. Sales corresponded to 126 deals and to a total volume of 410 000 m^3 of timber. The deals were made with Egyptian (90%), Saudi and Syrian customers.

Trading in Egypt

When selling to Egyptian customers Swedish Timber had to quote in dollars (USD).[2] Typically, Swedish Timber would quote a price in dollars based on the wood price in SEK and on the SEK/USD exchange rate. Most often, the cost of freight was included in the price quoted by Swedish Timber. Customers who accepted the offer were asked to confirm their acceptance immediately by fax. They were then allowed time to arrange for a letter of credit with a bank in Egypt. As the Egyptian pound (EGP) was not convertible, it was not always easy for Egyptian importers to get dollars and it was typical for Swedish Timber – and for the other competitors also – to give the Egyptian importers up to two months for arranging the letter of credit. In spite of this long delay, it sometimes happened that the Egyptian importer would come back to Swedish Timber saying that they had not been able to secure the letter of credit. When this happened the deal had to be cancelled.[3] There was no officially published price for wood in Egypt, and the only prices that were tracked by Swedish Timber were the prices of the deals known to the company. On the same day, prices of different deals could differ by as much as 10% depending on the parties involved, the composition of the shipment and the freight cost that differed depending on the harbours. On the Egyptian market, Swedish Timber was competing against other Swedish and Finnish companies.[4]

Contrary to Europe where deals were made to cover the needs of a buyer for a half-year period, deals with Egyptian customers were smaller deals aimed at covering shorter needs (2–3 months maximum).

Exhibit ● Dealing in foreign currencies

Spot, forwards and futures[5]

On foreign currency markets, currencies are traded either for immediate delivery (spot transactions) or for delivery in the future (forward transactions). A **forward** exchange contract is a particularly simple derivative security.[6] It is an agreement between two parties – one typically being a bank – to exchange one currency for another at some future date. The rate at which the exchange is to be made, the delivery date and the amounts involved are all fixed at the time of agreement. A **future** foreign exchange contract is a special type of forward contract that is traded on a regulated exchange.

Fixing future exchange rates as a win-win proposition

It may look like a paradox that on the one hand most people say that it is impossible to predict exchange rates while on the other hand those same people engage in forward transactions and commit themselves to specific exchange rates far ahead into the future. The example in Figure C.1 shows that when you cannot predict what the future market exchange rate will be, the best thing to do may be to create your own future exchange rate and this is just what a forward exchange transaction allows you to do.

Each of the two companies in Figure C.1 is confronted with an unattractive business opportunity. Each business opportunity has a low margin and is risky. In each case, sales are invoiced in a foreign currency and their proceeds are totally dependent on the future exchange rate. When considering the historical currency fluctuations both business opportunities should probably be rejected.

There is, however, a simple solution for making these two business opportunities much more attractive. It just requires that the two companies meet – directly or through an intermediary – and agree to exchange, or swap, the proceeds of their sales at the forward rate mentioned in the figure. If they so agree, then, in 2004:

> On 27 June 2001, the spot GBP/USD rate is 1.49 (1.49 dollars for 1 pound).
> A three-year forward contact has recently been made at a rate of 1.50.
> In the past, the GBP/USD rate has varied by more than 30% in a single year.

A British manufacturer of aero-engines is pricing the sales of three engines to an American airline (price to be made in dollars). The engines will be delivered, invoiced and paid in 2004. The US airline is willing to accept a price of $7.2 million per engine (total: **$21.6 million**). The costs of manufacturing the three engines will all be incurred in pounds and are estimated at **£13.5 million**.	An American contractor is considering signing a contract with a local British authority for an amount of **£14.4 million**. The proceeds of this contract will all be paid in 2004. The costs for executing this contract will all be incurred in dollars and are expected to amount to **$20 million**.

Figure C.1 An opportunity for currency hedging

- the British aero-engine manufacturer will transfer the $7.2 million received from their customer to the American contractor, and
- the American contractor will transfer the £14.4 million received from their customer to the British aero-engine manufacturer.

Through such a transaction, each company now has its sales in the same currency as its costs and all foreign exchange exposure has been dissolved! It is important to realize that when concluding such a transaction, the two companies do not need to forecast the future exchange rate. They should just decide that since it enables each of them to make a reasonable profit, a 1.5 rate is acceptable to both of them. Through this forward transaction, the two companies decide to get the foreign currency issue out of their business world and to make themselves immune to exchange rate fluctuations.[7]

Spot, forward and interest. Covered interest rate parity
Forward rates can be expressed in two ways. They can be quoted at their actual price – outright rate – or as a discount from, or as a premium on the spot rate. A foreign currency is at a forward premium when the outright forward rate is above the spot rate. It is at a forward discount when the forward rate is below the spot. This forward differential is known as the swap rate. Traders establish the forward exchange rate between two currencies in the following way:

- They start from the spot exchange rate between the two currencies.
- They adjust the spot rate in order to offset any interest rate differential between the two currencies.

This is shown in Figure C.2. Forward exchange rates make it possible for different currencies to have different interest rates on the international money market. Whichever currency you invest in, you get – without currency risk – the same interest rate:

- When you invest in a high interest rate currency and sell it forward in order to avoid risk, then the forward rate differential wipes out all the benefit of the high interest.

On 15 August 2000, the spot exchange rate of the Japanese yen is 109.510 (you need 109 yen to buy \$1). On the international money market, the 3-month investment rate for the dollar is $5^{31}/_{32}$ and the 3-month interest rate for the yen is $^1/_{32}$. How much is the 3-month forward rate of the yen?

$$\text{Forward rate} = \text{Spot rate} \times \frac{(1 + \text{interest rate in yen})}{(1 + \text{interest rate in dollar})}$$

$$= 109.510 \times \frac{(1 + 0.003125 / 4)}{(1 + 0.0596875 / 4)} = 107.908$$

If you have dollars, and change them into yen and invest in yen, you will get a very low return for the next 3 months. However, the favourable forward exchange rate will make the amount of dollars that you have at the end of the 3 months exactly the same as if you had invested in dollars at a $5^{31}/_{32}$ rate. As you can fix today all the interest and exchange rates – spot and forward – investing in dollars or changing the dollars, investing in yen and changing back to dollars do not carry any risk.

Figure C.2 Spot rate, interest differential and forward rate

- When you invest in a low interest rate currency and sell it forward in order to avoid any risk, then the forward rate differential compensates for the low interest.

This parity relationship is called 'covered interest rate parity'.

Hedging policy

When dealing in Egypt, sales were invoiced in dollars while purchases were made in kronor. This created a currency risk that had always been perceived as a big issue by the board of Swedish Timber. Since the creation of the company, it had been decided 'to suppress all the currency risk through a strict hedging policy'. As soon as it received the fax confirming an order Swedish Timber was systematically selling forward the dollar amount corresponding to that order. The rationale for this hedging policy was that in a very low margin and very risky business, one should try to eliminate as many risks as possible. A forward sale of the dollars was guaranteeing the rate at which these dollars were going to be changed to kronor.[8]

Even though he was well aware of the need to reduce risk Lars Johansson had been getting more and more unsatisfied with this hedging policy. For him, the central issue was not to suppress the currency risk or any other particular risk, but to reduce the total risk of Swedish Timber, or more precisely to reduce the range of fluctuation of the total gross margin of the company. Johannson was more and more convinced that selling dollars forward was not having any positive impact on the volatility of Swedish Timber's gross margin.

A typical deal

In order to assess the impact of the company's hedging policy Johansson decided to prepare a spreadsheet model. He wanted this model to help him simulate all the possible gross margins that could be generated by a typical deal when this deal was hedged or, on the contrary, not hedged. A typical deal looked as follows:

Price quoted: USD 500 000
  (3 000 000 SEK divided by 6, the 2–month forward USD/SEK rate)
Cost price: SEK 2 880 000

In Lars Johansson's mind, hedging was not the only way of managing risk. Recently, when a number of contracts had been cancelled[9] after the outbreak of the Gulf War, several among the management of Swedish Timber had argued for a reduction of the time allowed to the Egyptian importers to arrange the letter of credit. *'One month or even three weeks should be sufficient for the Egyptian importer and for Swedish Timber to complete the transaction!'*[10]

Notes

1. This case is an abridged version of the case study 'Swedish Timber AB' developed by Michel Schlosser and Anna Jarkestig.
2. In 1991, international trade in wood was conducted in several currencies with the Swedish krona playing a central role. When exporting to Europe, Swedish, Finnish and Russian companies were stating their prices in the local currencies (francs, pounds, etc.) but most contracts had a clause calling for a renegotiation of the price in the case of a change in the SEK rate.
3. When the deal with the customer was cancelled, Swedish Timber could generally also cancel its own deal with the supplier.
4. The Finnish markka was usually moving together with the Swedish krona – except when it devalued sharply in 1991.
5. For a full description of the currency markets, please refer to Cornelius Luca (2000), *Trading in the Global Currency Markets*, Prentice Hall or to Julian Walmsley (2000), *The Foreign Exchange and Money Markets Guide*, John Wiley. Also refer to 'All about the foreign exchange market in the United States', an online report of the Federal Reserve Bank of New York. On their site: http://www.ny.frb.org/pihome/addpub/.
6. A derivative security, also called a contingent claim, is a security the value of which depends on the value of one or several other more basic securities. Forwards, futures, options and swaps are examples of simple derivative securities. For a text on derivatives, please refer to John Hull (2000), *Options, Futures, and Other Derivative Securities*, Prentice Hall International.
7. Are the two companies totally immune to exchange rate risk? They are indeed provided that they actually receive the expected proceeds of their sales (expected amount at the expected date). However, if the business that has motivated the forward transaction does not behave as expected, the two companies should still deliver the currency amount specified in the forward exchange contract. We discuss this issue in Chapter 5.
8. The management of Swedish Timber was well aware that it would have been better to use options rather than forward contracts. They had realized that, unfortunately, the option premium would have totally wiped out their very low margin.
9. In some cases, the customer just 'disappeared'.
10. Statistical studies made on 1991 data had shown to Lars Johansson that both the price of wood and the SEK/USD exchange rate could vary significantly during two months or even one month:

	Within a two-month period	Within a one-month period
Maximum variations of the price of wood in SEK	+15%, −15%	+11%, −11%
Maximum variations between the spot SEK/USD and the forward SEK/USD rate quoted respectively two or one month earlier	+12%, −12%	+8%, −8%

CHAPTER 5

The need to acknowledge risk

Thinking 'ranges and distributions' rather 'one single estimate'[1]

As expressed by Peter Drucker: 'Planning does not deal with future decisions. It deals with the futurity of present decisions'.[2] The main focus of Chapter 5 is the discussion of tools for developing an understanding of the uncertain 'futurity' of business decisions.

We start with the decision diagram, a powerful mapping tool. Clarifying the nature and the sequence of the decisions and of the risks involved is an essential step in developing an effective understanding of the uncertainty of a business situation. Experience shows that it is often very valuable to invest time in structuring the various alternatives and their consequences with the help of one – or a series of – decision diagram(s).

We then introduce the tools that can be used for making a decision once the situation is clearly mapped: how do we generate the possible outcomes of a decision? How do we use simulation tools like @RISK?[3] How do we analyze and compare different distributions of possible outcomes? And finally, how do we make the decision?

At Swedish Timber, the issue is to reduce risk. Let us see how currency hedging can – or cannot – reduce the dispersion of the possible outcomes of trading wood in the Egyptian market.

5.1 The need to approach risk from a total portfolio perspective

Many of the tools for managing risk – or for 'hedging' – are very focused tools. They are each designed to remove a specific form of risk: forward contracts, foreign exchange futures, interest futures, liability insurance, property insurance, etc. However, when using these tools you should never forget that risk can only be approached from a total portfolio perspective:

● Fortunately, all the many different risks of a business are not additive.[4] A company may run a series of individual projects each of which is very risky but which have a relatively low combined risk. This is the virtue of effective diversification, making the total risk less than the sum of the individual risks.[5]

● When analyzing any source of risk – and foreign exchange is no exception – one has to refrain from analyzing this risk in isolation and focus instead on understanding, measuring and managing how this source of risk changes the overall risk and value of the business.[6]

In order to assess whether they should hedge their currency positions, the management of Swedish Timber should try to understand:

● how currency risk impacts the fluctuation of their total margin;
● how hedging may change the fluctuation of this total margin.

When they conclude a deal with an Egyptian customer, Swedish Timber sets the various parameters of the deal in order to earn a 4% margin (SEK120 000 on the typical deal). The problem, though, is that the actual margin will rarely be equal to the target:

● When they conclude a deal, Swedish Timber sets the selling price in USD. This creates a currency risk for the two months that it takes for the customer to arrange for the letter of credit.[7] For as long as the letter of credit is not arranged, Swedish Timber does not know how many SEK it will get from the transaction. This amount is totally dependent on the exchange rate. For the typical deal, a 12% variation in the exchange rate represents an amount of SEK360 000. This can make the margin fluctuate between –SEK240 000 and +SEK480 000.
● In the end, the customer may not be able to arrange for the letter of credit and then the deal is cancelled. Since it has negotiated very good conditions with its suppliers, Swedish Timber also cancels its own deal and as a result cancellation means nothing worse than a zero margin.

Other uncertainties (freight cost, for example) can also affect the margin, but since their impact is much smaller, let us limit ourselves to the risk of cancellation and the currency risk.

As currency risk is the largest individual risk factor, hedging is a tempting solution. If you limit yourself to the currency risk dimension, selling the dollars guarantees that the margin on the typical deal will be SEK120 000 in two months' time! Without hedging, the margin may fluctuate between –SEK240 000 and +SEK480 000. This is the advantage of currency hedging: hedging enables companies to fix the exchange rate today and then to ignore what may happen on the currency markets.

The problem, though, is that currency is not the only source of risk: as we have seen, another important source of risk is cancellation. When the customer cancels its contract, Swedish Timber may also cancel the contract it has with its suppliers but cannot cancel the forward currency sale. When the commercial deal is cancelled, Swedish Timber still has to comply with the forward contact. This means that Swedish Timber has to buy dollars at the market rate in order to sell them at the rate of the forward contract. This is a risky business that may result in a significant profit or loss. If the typical contract is hedged at a rate of 6, Swedish Timber may have to buy the USD at a rate ranging from 5.28 to 6.72 (±12%). When Swedish Timber hedges, any cancelled deal may result in a margin ranging from –SEK360 000 to +SEK360 000!

As indicated in the case, currency options would be a much better tool for Swedish Timber. The big advantage of options is that they would give the company the right and not the obligation to sell the foreign currency. This would solve the problem of contract cancellations. Unfortunately, this solution would totally wipe out Swedish Timber's margin. Options are dealt with in the General Appendix at the end of the book.

When you look – as you should – at the overall business picture, hedging no longer has the power to remove risk:

- Without hedging, the actual margin may easily differ from the target.
- With hedging, the margin may still fairly easily differ from the target but in a different way though: hedging modifies rather than removes risk.

We now need to analyze in a more systematic fashion the impact of hedging: how does it modify the risk profile of a typical transaction?

5.2 Building a decision diagram: structuring the alternatives and their consequences

Decision diagrams are maps of the sequence of decisions and risk factors or events presented in the order in which the decision maker:

- makes a decision,
- learns about the events or risk factors,
- makes new decisions as a result of this learning,
- learns about new events or risk factors,
- and so on.

With Swedish Timber we are going to look at a very simple sequence of decisions and events (Decision–Event). Later on in the book we shall deal with more complex sequences (Decision–Event–Decision–Event– etc.) and discuss the option features attached to such sequences.[8]

Drawing the diagram

Figure 5.1 shows a decision diagram that structures the possible outcomes of either not hedging or hedging. Decision diagrams typically start – on the left-hand side – with a decision node pictured by a square. In the figure, the decision diagram starts from the decision to hedge. From this node two branches emanate, each corresponding to one of the two possible courses of action. Then the diagram pictures what comes next in the sequence. After having decided to hedge or not, Swedish Timber learns that the contract is confirmed or cancelled, then it learns what the exchange rate is when the letter of credit is finally arranged – or not. This rate can be the same as it was at the time of the deal, or more or less.

One important feature of decision diagrams is that the branches emanating from any node should be **collectively exhaustive** and **mutually exclusive**. The term 'collectively exhaustive' means that all the possibilities should be considered, while 'mutually exclusive' means that the branches should not overlap.[9] When looking at Figure 5.1, the description

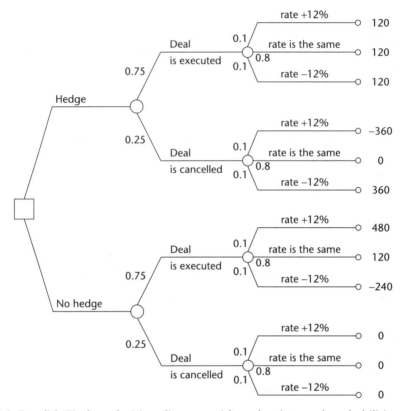

Figure 5.1 Swedish Timber: decision diagram with end points and probabilities

of the possible exchange rate changes is not really satisfactory: the exchange rate can actually take any value in the 5.28 to 6.72 range. We will relax this assumption later and introduce a full distribution (*see* Section 5.4).

Evaluating the end points

Once the decision diagram is drawn, the next step is to evaluate all its end points. Table 5.1 displays the background and the foreground of a model of the typical transaction that can help you generate the different end points.

Weighting the possible end points: probability assessment

The different end points shown in Figure 5.1 confirm that the margin of a typical deal can be significantly more or less than the SEK120 000 target. If Swedish Timber decides to hedge, the margin can be 120 000 but also −360 000, 0 or +360 000. All these end points are not equally likely:

● The 120 000 end point is obtained each time a deal is confirmed and whatever the exchange rate is. This should happen quite often!

Table 5.1 • A model for estimating the outcomes of a typical transaction

	A	B	C
1	Price of wood (SEK)	3000	
2	Margin	0.04	
3	Purchase price (SEK)	2880	
4	SEK/USD rate	6	
5	Price quoted in USD	500	
6			
7	Cancellation, No=1, Yes=0	1	
8	Change in SEK/USD rate	0	
9		No Hedge	Hedge
10	Receipts in USD	500	500
11	Receipts in SEK	3000	3000
12	Cost in SEK	2880	2880
13	**Margin in SEK for Swedish Timber**	**120**	**120**

Background

B3: =B1*(1–B2)
B5: =B/B4
B10: =B5*B7
B11: =B10*B4*(1+B8)
B12: =B3*B7

B13: =B11–B12; copy to C13
C10: =B10
C11: =IF(B7=1,C10*B4,–B5*B4*B8)
C12: =B12

● The –360 000 and the +360 000 end points only occur when the deal is cancelled and when there is an extreme variation in the exchange rate. This may also happen, but not that often!

When describing the chances that one event will materialize, you can do it with words but the problem is that the words describing uncertainty generally have a rather ambiguous meaning.[10] It is therefore more useful to use a quantitative approach and a scale for describing uncertainty. In practice, there are two main approaches: probabilities and odds.[11] With probabilities, the scale goes from zero (absolute impossibility) to one (absolute certainty). By definition, the sum of the probabilities of each of the different possible events is equal to 1. In a decision diagram, you can attach a probability to each of the branches that emanates from an event node. This is done in Figure 5.1. Please check that the sum of the probabilities:

● attached to the branches that emanate from a seam event node are equal to 1;
● attached to each of the different end points (on the extreme right-hand side) are also equal to 1.

The assessment of probabilities is difficult in practice as it is the complex result of using various techniques and procedures based on past data, assumptions and results taken from models, expert advice, and subjective judgement. When used in business situations probabilities often refer to **intensity or degree of belief** (in all situations that occur once, probability can actually only be interpreted as an intensity of belief). The intensity of belief is sometimes based on the experience of comparable situations which allow for estimating

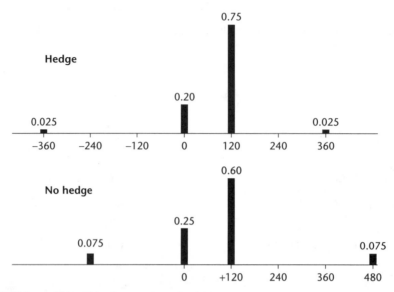

Figure 5.2 Risk profiles of hedge and no hedge

probabilities in terms of **relative frequency**. As they concluded more than a hundred deals in 1991, Swedish Timber is probably in a position to start thinking in terms of relative frequencies: what was the proportion of deals that were cancelled last year?

5.3 Analyzing the possible future outcomes of a decision

Assessing its unique 'expected value–risk' contribution[12]

The decision tree helps us describe the future impact of the decision to hedge on the distribution of possible outcomes. The distributions of the possible margins with hedge and no hedge are portrayed in Figure 5.2.

Distributions or **risk profile diagrams** show both the possible outcomes and their probabilities. Risk is higher when:

● the range of possible outcomes becomes wider;
● the probabilities of non-central outcomes increase.

Figure 5.2 helps us to understand the impact of hedging.

● The good news with hedging is that it allows you to trade the whole distribution of outcomes (–SEK240 000, +120 000 and 480 000) for a unique outcome: 120 000. Hedging is very good at making the margin of all confirmed deals equal to 120 000.
● The bad news is that with hedging you also have to trade the 0 margin of all cancelled deals for a fairly ugly distribution: –360 000, 0, +360 000. The range of this distribution is exactly the same as the range of no-hedge distribution of the confirmed deals that you have just got rid of. The problem, though, is that this distribution is now centred on 0 instead of +120 000. As a result the worst case has moved down from –240 000 to –360 000!

● When considering probabilities, it does not look too bad: on the one hand the worst outcome has a 9% probability, but on the other hand hedging increases the likelihood of the central outcome.

Estimating the 'expected value–risk' contribution of the decision

It is common practice to describe the future impact of decisions with a summary of the distribution of their possible outcomes. These summaries typically describe the impact of a decision with two characteristics of their distributions only:

● centre: expected value, or mean, is the most commonly used summary of the centre of the distribution;
● dispersion, or risk.

Mean or expected value

Mean or expected value (EV) is the average of the different outcomes weighted by their probabilities:

(in SEK 000)

Hedge:

$$EV = 0.75 \times 120 + 0.25 \times (0.10 \times -360$$
$$+ 0.80 \times 0 + 0.10 \times 360)$$

or

$$= 0.75 \times 120 + 0.025 \times -360$$
$$+ 0.20 \times 0 + 0.025 \times 360$$
$$= 90$$

No hedge:

$$EV = 0.75 \times (0.10 \times 480 + 0.80 \times 120$$
$$+ 0.10 \times -240) + 0.25 \times 0$$

or

$$= 0.075 \times 480 + 0.60 \times 120$$
$$+ 0.075 \times -240 + 0.25 \times 0$$
$$= 90$$

The two courses of action generate the same expected value. Hedging does not create any 'cost' or 'gain'. With or without hedging, Swedish Timber generates the same margin on average:[13] 90 000 or 3% of sales.[14] The only impact of hedging is to change the dispersion or the risk of the margin, i.e. the possible values of the margin and their distribution.

Expected value is not the only possible summary measure of the centre of a distribution.[15] Another measure is the **mode**. The mode corresponds to the most likely outcome in the distribution. The mode of the distribution of the margin with hedge is 120 000.

Risk

Dispersion is much more difficult to summarize and – as is the case here – many summaries often fail to capture the complexity of some distributions. One often-used measure of dispersion is the **range** of the distribution or the difference between the largest and the smallest outcome. As indicated above, hedge and no hedge have the same range. The problem with range is that it does not capture the position of this range – here the range of hedge has a less favourable position – and also ignores the probability of the different outcomes. Finally, the range does not apply to distributions with no clearly defined smallest or largest outcomes.[16]

The measure of dispersion that is most frequently used in finance is probably the **variance** and its square root – the **standard deviation**.[17] The variance – or 'second moment' of the distribution – is calculated as the average of the square of the deviations of the different outcomes from the mean weighted by their probabilities:

(in SEK 000)

Hedge:

$$\text{VAR} = (120 - 90)^2 \times 0.75 + (-360 - 90)^2$$
$$\times 0.025 + (0 - 90)^2 \times 0.20 +$$
$$(360 - 90)^2 \times 0.025$$
$$= 9180$$

Standard deviation $= \text{VAR}^{1/2} = 96$

No hedge:

$$\text{VAR} = (480 - 90)^2 \times 0.075 + (120 - 90)^2 \times 0.60$$
$$+ (-240 - 90)^2 \times 0.075 + (0 - 90)^2 \times 0.25$$
$$= 22\ 140$$

Standard deviation $= \text{VAR}^{1/2} = 149$

The variance tells us that hedge has reduced the dispersion of the margin: this is true in the sense that it is, on the whole, more centred, but it is not true in the sense that the worse outcome is more unfavourable: –360 vs. –240. Summarizing dispersion is not easy and my advice is, whenever possible, not to rush and use measures like the variance or standard deviation. Keeping the distributions as they are is often a very effective way to think about risk.

As it seems difficult to make a decision at this stage, let us go back to our description of the business situation and check that we have not missed something important that could help us decide.

5.4 Generating and analyzing distributions with @RISK

The problem with our analysis so far is that we envisage very few – and arbitrary – values for the exchange rate: 5.28, 6 and 6.72. In order better to describe the impact of possible changes in the foreign exchange rate, we can use a piece of software like @RISK and introduce a distribution to describe all the possible values that the exchange rate can take between 5.28 and 6.72. @RISK is an add-in system to Excel that provides you with powerful tools for risk analysis while allowing you to continue working in your Excel environment. The process for using @RISK is as follows:

● Build your model in Excel.
● Get @RISK and open your model in the Excel environment of @RISK.
● Replace your drivers with their distributions.
● Set the parameters for running a simulation.
● Analyze the results of the simulation – a sophisticated risk profile.

Replacing the drivers with their distributions

The exchange rate may take any value between 5.28 and 6.76. Among all the distributions proposed by @RISK, let us select the simple 'Triangular' distribution. Using the model in Table 5.1, you need to enter in B8: = RiskTriang (–.12,0,.12).

When it comes to the cancellation index, we want it to take the value of 0 (cancellation) or 1. We further want non-cancellation to have a probability of 0.75. This can be achieved using the 'Discrete' distribution of @RISK. Still using the model of Table 5.1, you now need to enter =RiskDiscrete({0,1},{1,3}) in B8. Figure 5.3 shows the distributions of the two drivers that will be used by @RISK in the simulations.

Setting the parameters of the simulation

This is a matter of clicking on the 'Sim Sett' icon – on the @RISK toolbar and of, first, defining the numbers of iterations that you want to have. Do not hesitate to go for a fairly

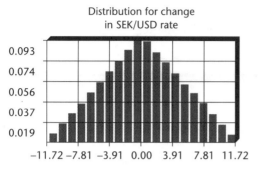

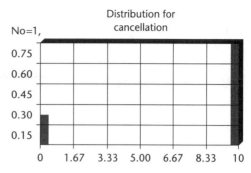

Figure 5.3 Distributions of the input variables

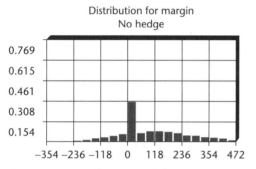

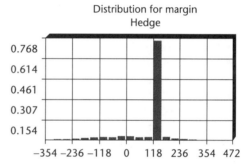

Figure 5.4 Distributions of the margin with hedge and no hedge

large number, such as 1000. Next, you define the sampling method that you want to be used: go for Latin Hypercube.[18] You then say if you want @RISK to continuously update the display of your model during the simulation: go for it.

The next task is to define your output cells: these are B13 and C13. In order to define B13 as an ouput cell, highlight it. Then click on the '+Output' icon.

Running the simulation and analyzing the results

When you have entered the distributions of the drivers, determined the simulation settings and defined the output variables, running a simulation is a matter of clicking on the 'Simulate' icon. Results are presented in several ways with graphs and statistics. Figure 5.4 shows the distribution of the margin when you hedge and when you do not hedge. Table 5.2 shows the statistics of these two distributions provided by @RISK.

These results confirm:

● The good news about hedging: in 75% of cases you get a margin of 120 000. The new information brought by the distributions is the heavy weight of this fixed margin.
● The bad news about hedging: hedging creates the possibility of some unlikely but very bad incomes.

Table 5.2 ● Statistical results of the distributions of the margin with hedge and no hedge

	No hedge	Hedge
Mean	88	88
Mode	0	120
Minimum	−227	−321
Maximum	472	330
Standard deviation	140	88
Skewness	0.51	−2.2
Kurtosis	2.7	8.0

Notes on the statistical results

The statistics confirm that the **mode** of the margin is 120 000 with hedge. They also tell us that the mode of the same margin with no hedge is 0 – all the cancellations cases. In Figure 5.2 the mode with no hedge is 120 000 but this is an illusion because this particular case – no change at all in the exchange rate nor in the price of wood – has a very low likelihood.

When comparing with the results in Figure 5.2, you realize that @RISK has not generated the extreme positive and negative values (−240 000 and 480 000 with no hedge and −360 000 and +360 000 with hedge). This is probably fair since these extreme values are very unlikely.

The **variance** and the **standard deviation** are lower with hedge. The difference is actually more in favour of hedge than we found earlier. Hedging makes the margin equal to 120 000 in about 75% of cases. This results in a lower standard deviation for the margin with hedge.

Skewness and **kurtosis** are measures of the shape of the distribution. The skewness – or 'third moment' of the distribution – is calculated as the weighted average of the deviations of the different outcomes from the mean elevated at the power three. It measures the tilt of the distribution to one side or the other, or indicates the asymmetry of extreme values relative to the mean: skews in financial asset distributions are often temporary phenomena (prolonged bear or bull markets typically create skewness). The kurtosis – or fourth moment of the distribution – is calculated as the weighted average of the deviations from the mean elevated at the power four. The kurtosis measures the thickness – or 'fatness' – of the tails and the peakedness of the centre.

5.5 Revisiting the issue: why do customers cancel their deals?

The commonly accepted view is that customers are 'not always able to arrange for a letter of credit' and as a result may have to cancel the deal. An alternative view is that customers cancel the deal for completely different reasons. Within a period of two months a lot of things may happen and opportunities for better deals may surface. When confronted with the opportunity of a better deal, customers decide to cancel claiming that they have not been able to arrange for a letter of credit. Case C suggests that several factors may create the opportunity of a better deal:

- As soon as the value of the dollar increases, Egyptian importers get an opportunity to buy wood at a lower dollar price. Swedish Timber might really be hurt by such an exchange rate driven cancellation. If they have hedged, they have to buy expensive dollars and sell them at the cheap rate of the forward contract!
- A decrease in the price (in SEK) of wood also creates a new opportunity for the customer. This cause of cancellation is less worrying for Swedish Timber – the company may actually make a foreign exchange gain in this situation!
- A devaluation of the Finnish markka could also have an impact. Provided that the Finnish exporters do not increase their prices, a devaluation of the Finnish currency makes their business more attractive in dollar terms. This has actually happened recently. However, since this is perceived as 'exceptional', let us ignore this potential source of risk.

Our new understanding of the situation leads to a new analysis. Please have a look at the new risk diagram in Figure 5.5, at the new spreadsheet in Table 5.3 and at the new @RISK results. Figure 5.6 shows the distribution of cancellation (now an output). Table 5.4 shows the statistics of the two distributions. Figure 5.7 shows their graphs and Figure 5.8 the graph of their cumulative distributions.

5.6 What should Swedish Timber do? Managing risk vs. redesigning the business

The new analysis confirms the difficulty of making a decision about hedging. When one considers foreign exchange risk only, then the decision looks simple. As hedging removes currency risk, Swedish Timber should go for it! The problem, though, is that risk should be analyzed from a total portfolio point of view. When you do so, you realize that hedging only modifies the distribution of Swedish Timber's total margin.

With the new model you actually realize that hedging does not change this distribution very much. The mean is not changed and the standard deviation hardly at all.

- The positive impact of hedging is to create a most frequent outcome of 120 000.
- The negative impact of hedging is to create the possibility of some extremely negative outcomes and to suppress the possibility of some very favourable outcomes. The negative outcomes are not likely but they may happen and they are worse than anything that the company could experience without hedging. We may wonder if hedging actually reduces risk!

Figure 5.8 displays the cumulative distributions of the margin with no hedge and with hedge.[19] These cumulative distributions intersect twice: this confirms that with hedging you have more chances to get negative numbers and that you have fewer chances to get very large numbers. However, in most cases (73%) you get 120 000.

How can we balance the positive and the negative impacts of hedging? What would you do yourself in this situation?

- If you hedge, you will get 120 000 on each transaction. In the conditions of the second simulation (Table 5.4), you will lose about one-third of your potential margin due to cancellations and you are exposed to very unlikely and very big losses in case of cancellation.

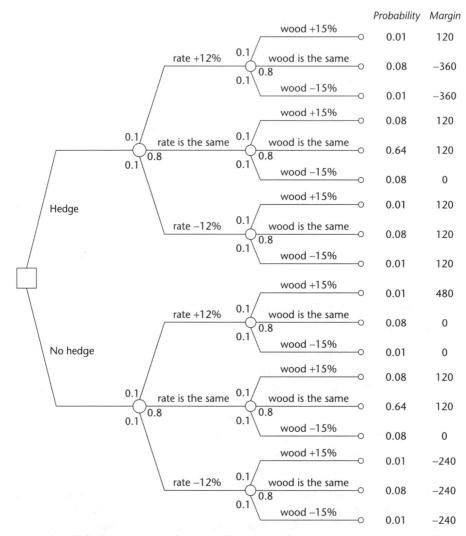

	Probability	Margin
wood +15%	0.01	120
wood is the same	0.08	−360
wood −15%	0.01	−360
wood +15%	0.08	120
wood is the same	0.64	120
wood −15%	0.08	0
wood +15%	0.01	120
wood is the same	0.08	120
wood −15%	0.01	120
wood +15%	0.01	480
wood is the same	0.08	0
wood −15%	0.01	0
wood +15%	0.08	120
wood is the same	0.64	120
wood −15%	0.08	0
wood +15%	0.01	−240
wood is the same	0.08	−240
wood −15%	0.01	−240

Figure 5.5 Swedish Timber: new decision diagram with end points and probabilities

● If you do not hedge, you will get a very uncertain amount on each transaction, but on average this should result in the same 57 000. Cancellations will not impact your margin.[20]

Redesigning the business vs. managing risk

There are always two ways to approach risk.[21] Once you have understood the risk you are exposed to, either you accept this risk and try to hedge it. This is not very promising here! Or you do not accept this risk and you try to redesign your business in order to get rid of it. Personally I have found that this second approach is often very effective and that the new economy of information creates new opportunities for 'destroying risk'.

Table 5.3 ● A new model for estimating the outcomes of a typical transaction

A	B	C
1 Price of wood	3000	
2 Margin	0.04	
3 Price purchase	2880	
4 SEK/USD rate	6	
5 Price quoted in USD	500	
6		
7 Change in price of wood	0	
8 Change in SEK/USD rate	0	
9 Competitive price in USD	500	
10 Acceptable premium (%)	0.05	
11 Cancellation, No=1, Yes=0	1	
12		
13	**No Hedge**	**Hedge**
14 Receipts in USD	500	500
15 Receipt in SEK	3000	3000
16 Cost in SEK	2880	2880
17 **Margin in SEK for Swedish Timber**	**120**	**120**

Background

B3: =B1*(1–B2)
B5: =B1/B4
B7: =RiskTriang (–.15, 0, .15)
B8: =RiskTriang (–.12, 0, .12)
B9: =(B1*(1+B7))/(B4*(1+B8))
B11: =IF(B9<=B5*(1–B10),0,1)
B14: =B5*B11

B15: =B14*B4*(1+B8)
B16: =B3*B11
B17: =B15–B16; copy in C15
C14: =B14
C15: =IF(B11=1,C14*B4,–B5*B4*B8)
C16: =B16

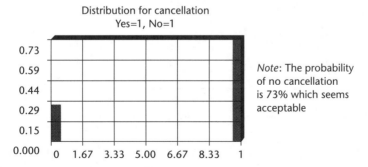

Distribution for cancellation
Yes=1, No=1

Note: The probability of no cancellation is 73% which seems acceptable

Figure 5.6 Distribution of the new output variable: cancellation

Table 5.4 ● Statistical results of the new distributions of the margin with hedge and no hedge

	No hedge	Hedge
Mean	57	57
Mode	0	120
Minimum	−235	−346
Maximum	453	188
Standard deviation	119	121
Skewness	0.53	−1.7
Kurtosis	3.1	4.4

Note:
The results are obviously never exactly the same from one simulation to another.

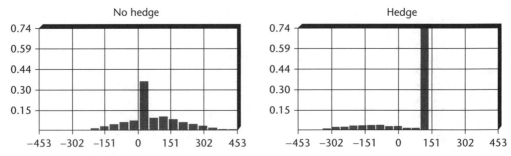

Figure 5.7 New distributions of the margin with hedge and no hedge

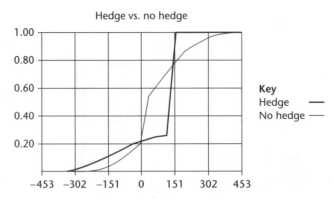

Figure 5.8 Cumulative distribution of the margin with hedge and no hedge

How can Swedish Timber try to redesign its business? Its current business design does not look very effective: is it really necessary for Swedish Timber to give to its customers an option to renegotiate the price with a competitor?

- Even though this does not change the basic design of the business, Swedish Timber could try to limit the size of each individual deal. This may help bring the margin towards the mean.
- In order to start improving its business, Swedish Timber could do as suggested in the case and try to reduce the time allowed for the customer to 'arrange for the letter of credit'. Reducing this time to one month would reduce the range of variation of the price of wood and of the exchange rate.[22]
- Swedish Timber could also try to establish stronger relations with its customers and to reinforce their commitment to the deals. It could try to provide them with various incentives for sticking to the deal: opportunity to renegotiate the price, advance deposit, etc.
- Swedish Timber could also review its strategy for doing business in Egypt. At the moment the company sells to traders who are typically people who always look for a better deal. Would it be feasible to deal with final customers instead? When concluding risky deals why not get into such deals only if the margin is sufficient to allow for buying a currency option?

It is only after the company has explored all these opportunities and discovered ways to change the design of its business that Swedish Timber will be in a position to look again at the opportunity to use hedging tools.

5.7 Analyzing and managing risky situations: the three steps[23]

It is normal to have to analyze and manage risky situations in business. The central activity in this process is to get an effective understanding of the alternatives and of their consequences. When considering a risky – i.e. a typical – business situation, making the final choice is important, but the phase during which you structure this choice is even more important. The decision diagram is valuable in helping you organize the structuring phase. As stated by P.L. Keeney and H. Raiffa, 'the spirit of decision diagrams is one of *Socratic discovery*, of unfolding what you really believe, of convincing yourself, and of deciding'.[24] Decision diagrams help you structure scenarios and strategies for the future. They enable you to identify the decisions which are to be made today, assess the risks involved, identify the choices that you can defer (future options), and think about how these future choices can be helped by additional information and experimentation. The basic condition for using decision diagrams successfully is to find the right balance between trying to look at all the possibilities (what some call the 'British Museum approach') and pruning promising solutions too quickly. Decision diagrams invite you to adopt a holistic perspective and to defer your decision until you have visualized all the consequences. They prevent you from falling into the trap of comparing and selecting alternatives on a one-to-one basis, and of comparing and eliminating alternatives on the basis of one feature at a time.[25]

Once you have really understood the situation, then comes the second step which is a matter of taking a proactive attitude and of trying to modify the situation in your favour by gaining information, time and control. In a number of cases, this second step will lead you to redesign your business itself. As a part of this second step, or as a third step of its own, will then come the time for deciding to use tools for managing the residual risk.

5.8 The challenge of assessing performance

In our uncertain world, assessing performance is not easy and the economic press is rich in stories about dramatic foreign exchange 'losses'[26] and companies which have made 'wrong' hedging decisions. What do you think of the story reproduced in Figure 5.9? Can one really say that the company has paid DM200 million more than it needed to? This is what is often referred to as the cost of hedging. Was it 'reckless speculation' on the part of the company?

This business story reflects the difficulty a number of people have with performance assessment in a risky – typical – business environment:

● What we observe at a later date – the reality – is typically one of the possible events, not the mean or expected value, nor the distribution of all the possible events. This is the problem with uncertainty: a bad manager may be lucky and get a great outcome and conversely a good manager may be unlucky and get a poor outcome.

● When you decide to go for a lower risk route, you explicitly decide that you may pass up great bargains. This is what you have to accept in order also to pass up major losses. We may imagine that when deciding to hedge, the management of Lufthansa decided to go for an acceptable price in DM for its planes rather than a price in DM that could be very low or very high due to the position of the exchange rate. Is it fair, once you know the event, to come back and lecture people about how they should have managed risk? The DM200 million cannot be considered as a 'cost' of hedging. They are only 'regrets'. As expressed by Bell, 'Regret is a psychological reaction to making a wrong decision, where wrong is determined on the basis of actual outcomes rather than on the information available at the time of the decision'.[27]

Losses on currency dealings embarrass Lufthansa

Losses on currency dealings which could total over DM200 m (£59.8 m) are causing embarrassment at Lufthansa, the West German state airline and are fuelling ill-disguised political sniping against its chairman, Mr Heinz Runhau. Mr Runhau was summoned last week to meet Mr Werner Dollinger, the Transport Minister, to explain the losses. Unconfirmed reports were circulating this weekend that a decision by the airline's supervisory board on whether to extend his term of office when it expires in 1987 would be postponed until at least June. The currency problems stem from dollars purchased in 1985 to cover roughly half the purchase price of more than $500 m (£357 m) which Lufthansa is paying for Jumbo jets and 10 Boeing 737s due to be delivered this year. The dollars, it is understood, were bought at the price of DM3.20 in the fear that the dollar might rise even further against other currencies. In the event it has fallen steeply to around DM2.30, meaning that the airline has paid over DM200 m more than it needed . . . Last week . . . a partner in the present centre-right coalition demanded that Mr Runhau 'be dismissed for reckless speculation'.

Figure 5.9 Hedging vs. reckless speculation
Source: Rupert Cornwell, *Financial Times*, 1986. Reprinted with permission.

Risk and risk management are an essential part of business. At the same time risk is still a difficult idea to live with in business.

Notes

1. A recommended book is S.E. Bodily, R.L. Carraway and S.C. Frey (1997), *Quantitative Business Analysis: Text and Cases*, Irwin.
2. In 'Long Range Planning', *Management Science* (April 1959), p. 239.
3. @RISK is a product of the Palisade Corporation, Newfield, NY: www.palisade.com. A similar software program is Crystal Ball, a product of Decisioneering Inc, Denver, Colorado: www.decisioneering.com.
4. This is one major difference between value and risk analyses. When assessing value, you can break the whole into parts and use the fact that the value of the total is equal to the sum of the values of the parts. When assessing risk, you have to keep working at the level of the whole.
5. The concept of diversification within a portfolio is one of the basic building blocks of the whole insurance industry. It is also a building block of modern portfolio theory in finance.
6. With the rapid growth of derivative instruments and the development of financial engineering, corporate risk management has become a major part of the finance function. Please refer to: Neil A. Doherty (2000), *Integrated Risk Management, Techniques and Strategies for Managing Corporate Risk*, McGraw-Hill and to C. Culp (2001) *The Risk Management Process*, John Wiley.
7. Global companies often make a distinction between the future cash flows in foreign currencies that appear in their business plans:

   ● The future cash flows that correspond to a price in a foreign currency that cannot be changed. This is the case for the payments of accounts receivable and payable, the payments of loans and the receipts from financial investments, but also for the orders and the firm quotes. As soon as the price is fixed in a foreign currency, the amount that the company will receive or pay in its own currency is totally dependent on what will happen to the exchange rates. These cash flows are obviously fully exposed to currency risk.

   ● All the other future cash flows that correspond to transactions that have not yet been finalized and for which a price in the foreign currency has not yet been established. One can often see that, if the exchange rate were to change, the company would also have a chance to adjust its price. As a result, it is common to consider that these cash flows are not exposed to currency risk.

8. A first example of such a sequence is the Dhahran Roads (III) case on p. 98. A more elaborate example is the Eagle case on p. 355.
9. Mutually exclusive also means that outcomes should be defined in such a way that only one at a time can occur. Collectively exhaustive means that outcomes should be defined in such a way that one or another of them must occur.
10. See P.G. Moore, 'The Manager Struggles with Uncertainty', *Journal of the Royal Statistics Society*, Series A (General), (1977) **140**: 129–48.
11. Odds are expressed in the form of '2 to 1', '10 to 1', etc. Even though both methods are equivalent, we will mostly use probabilities in this book.
12. As an example, the mean-variance rule has been extensively used in finance for making decisions related to investments in risky assets. Other approaches are also used to analyze and decide in risky situations:

    ● expected utility: refer to P.H.J. Shoemaker (1982) 'The expected utility model: its variants, purposes, evidence and limitations', *Journal of Economic Literature*, XX, June; R. Schlaifer (1969) *Analysis of Decisions under Uncertainty*, McGraw-Hall; H. Raiffa (1970), *Decision Analysis: Introductory lectures on choices under uncertainty*, Addison-Wesley; P.L. Keeney and H. Raiffa (1976) *Decisions with Multiple Objectives: preferences and tradeoffs*, John Wiley; and D. Bell, H. Raiffa and A. Tversky (eds) (1988) *Decision Making: Descriptive, normative and prescriptive interactions*, Cambridge University Press.

    ● Stochastic dominance: refer to H. Levy and M. Robinson (1998) *Stochastic Dominance: Investment decision making under uncertainty*, Kluwer Academic Press.

13. Here we may underestimate the value created by hedging when it transforms the distribution of the non-hedged margins (confirmed deals) into one single margin number. This reduction of risk probably creates value that should come and increase the mean. In *Integrated Risk Management* (McGraw-Hill, 2000), Doherty shows (Chapter 7, pp. 193–233) that decreasing risk also decreases the transaction costs faced by a firm in doing business. Reducing risk decreases the average tax bill (tax convexity), reduces the average cost of debt, facilitates the financing of investments after loss, and helps use incentive compensation for managers. The problem, though, is that hedging also creates additional risk. Let us assume that these two effects offset each other.

14. Which is more than the actual margin: $8/380 = 2\%$ indicated in the case.

15. The median is a third summary measure of centrality. Loosely speaking, the median is that outcome which divides the range of possible outcomes in half, 'probabilistically'.

16. This is the case of the normal and of the exponential distributions, for example. For such distributions one can quote the range between the 0.10 and the 0.90 fractile. The k fractile is the outcome for which the probability of being below that value is k. The median is the 0.50 fractile.

17. When the distribution is the bell-shaped normal distribution, then you can interpret the standard deviation in terms of the chances that the outcome will be within one or two standard deviations of the mean.

18. Latin Hypercube is a relatively new sampling technique used in simulation modelling. Its advantage is to recreate accurately the distribution functions in fewer iterations than other techniques.

19. The statistics of @RISK also provide you with the fractiles of the distributions:

	5%	10%	15%	20%	25%	30%	35%	40%	45%	50%
No hedge	−126	−79	−41	−9	0	0	0	0	0	10
Hedge	−231	−158	−102	−34	68	120	120	120	120	120

	55%	60%	65%	70%	75%	80%	85%	90%	95%
No hedge	36	64	88	111	134	159	190	232	286
Hedge	120	120	120	120	120	120	120	120	120

If you do not hedge . . .
You have a 5% chance of having   −126   or   less
You have a 10% chance of having   −79   or   less
You have a 15% chance of having   −41   or   less
You have a 20% chance of having   −9   or   less

You have a 75% chance of having   0   or   more

You have a 25% chance of having   134   or   more
You have a 5% chance of having   286   or   more

If you hedge . . .
You have a 5% chance of having   −231   or   less
You have a 10% chance of having   −158   or   less
You have a 15% chance of having   −102   or   less
You have a 20% chance of having   −34   or   less

You have a 70% chance of having   120   or   more

20. The lack of attractiveness of currency hedging for Swedish Timber is consistent with the results of several studies that show that currency hedging typically is not a very effective tool. See for example: 'Why Derivatives Don't reduce FX Risk', by T.E. Copeland and Y. Joshi, *The McKinsey Quarterly Journal* (1996), **1** pp. 66–79.

21. This is what some authors call the 'duality' of managing risk.
22. If you run the simulation model with a –0.11, +0.11 range for the price of wood and a –0.08, +0.08 range for the exchange rate, you get results like the following:

	No hedge	Hedge
Mean	85	85
Minimum	–116	–232
Maximum	346	154
Standard deviation	96	80
Skewness	0.48	–2.2
Kurtosis	2.4	6.3

23. For how to approach risky decisions, refer to K.R. MacCrimmon and D.A. Wehrung, *Taking Risks: The Management of Uncertainty* (1988), The Free Press.
24. *Decisions with Multiple Objectives: Preferences and Value Tradeoffs* (1976), John Wiley.
25. For more about this process of choice, refer to A. Tversky: 'Elimination by Aspect: a theory of choice', *Psychological Review* (1972), **79**: 281–99.
26. Foreign exchange losses are often used as excuses for bad results, but foreign exchange gains are not used so often to explain good results.
27. Bell (1985), 'Disappointment in Decision Making Under Uncertainty' in D. Bell, H. Raiffa and A. Tversky (1988), *Decision Making: Descriptive, normative and prescriptive interactions*, Cambridge University Press.

Appendices to Part II

Appendix II.1
Compounding and discounting: some additional tools

Cumulative values of discounting and compounding factors

Present value of annuities

It happens that the future cash flows in a savings plan are the same each year. Such a level stream of cash flows is called an **annuity**. If the cash flows start immediately, it is called an **immediate annuity**. If the cash flows start at the end of the current period rather than immediately, then it is called an **ordinary annuity**. How do you calculate the present value of an ordinary annuity of 1000 to be received in the next four years?

$$PV = 1000 \times 1/(1+r) + 1000 \times 1/(1+r)^2 + 1000 \times 1/(1+r)^3 + 1000 \times 1/(1+r)^4$$
$$PV = 1000 \times (1 + 1/(1+r) + 1/(1+r)^2 + 1/(1+r)^3 + 1/(1+r)^4)$$

Rather than estimate each discount factor and then calculate their cumulative value, you can use the following relationship:

$$\sum_{n=1}^{k} 1/(1+r)^n = (1 - (1+r)^{-k})/r$$

where,

    r = discount rate, and
    k = number of years (or more generally of periods)

When the cash flow of the annuity grows at a constant rate g, starting from an initial amount in period 1, then the cumulative discount factor, or multiplier, to be applied is:

$$(1 - ((1+g)/(1+r))^k)/(r-g)$$

where,

    g = growth rate
    r = discount rate, and
    k = number of years (or of periods).

Earning multiples

Annuities with a stream of cash flows that continues for ever are called **perpetuities**. The formula for calculating the NPV of a perpetuity is:

$\text{NPV} = 1000 \times 1/r$
when the 1000 remains the same
for ever r is the discount rate

$\text{NPV} = 1000 \times 1/(r-g)$
when the 1000 continuously grows at a
rate of $g\%$ r is the discount rate

This is the paradox with perpetuities: you cannot estimate the total nominal amount that you will receive from them (it is infinite), but you can calculate their value (NPV). The perpetuity formula is often used when valuing streams of earnings: the factor $1/r$ or $1/(r-g)$ is called 'earnings multiple'.

Cumulative value of compounding factors

A problem: *The sales of a company are growing 20% a year. Sales in 2002 were 12 000. Assuming that there is no seasonality and that monthly sales are growing at a constant rate, what was the value of the sales in January 2002? What was the value of the sales in the last quarter of 2002?*

The formula for calculating the cumulative value of the compounding factors over several periods is:

$$\sum_{n=0}^{k} (1+r)^n = ((1+r)^{k+1} - 1)/r$$

The monthly growth rate g that corresponds to a 20% annual growth is: $g = (1.2)^{1/12} - 1 = 0.015$.

Estimation of the sales in January:

If s = sales in January and S = sales for the year, then
$s \times (1 + (1+g)^2 + (1+g)^3 + \ldots + (1+g)^{11}) = S$
$s \times ((1+g)^{12} - 1)/g = S$
$s = S \times g/((1+g)^{12} - 1) = 918.57$

Estimation of the sales in the last quarter of 2002:

$\text{Sales}_{10}^{12} = \text{Sales}_{1}^{12} - \text{Sales}_{1}^{9}$ $\text{Sales}_{10}^{12} = 12\,000 - s \times ((1+g)^9 - 1)/g = 3208$

where:

Sales_{10}^{12} = last quarter sales; Sales_{1}^{12} = annual sales; Sales_{1}^{9} = sales in the first three quarters.

Compounding with periods shorter than one year

In high inflation countries, banks compound interest on a monthly basis, 8% per month for example. If you invest 1000 for one year at an 8% a month compounded rate, you will have at the end of the year: $1000 \times (1.08)^{12} = 1000 \times 2.518 = 2518$.

This is the same as if you had invested your money at an annual rate r (annually compounded) of 152%:

$$2518/1000 = 2.518 = 1 + r$$

Hence $r = 1.52$.

When interest is compounded on a monthly basis, the annual equivalent/annually compounded rate is more than twelve times the stated monthly rate: 152% vs. 96%. The annual equivalent rate (152%) is called the **effective rate** and the monthly rate multiplied by twelve (96%), the **stated rate**.

The relationship between the stated and the effective rates is as follows:

$$(1 + \text{stated rate}/m)^m - 1 = \text{effective rate}$$

where m = number of compounded periods in a year

Continuous compounding

We can rewrite the relationship between the stated and the effective rate denoting m/stated rate as x:

$$(1 + 1/x)^{x \times \text{stated rate}} - 1 = \text{effective rate}$$

When the compounded period is shortened and the number of periods increase to infinity, the value of $(1 + 1/x)^{xk}$ approaches e^k, where e is a mathematical constant whose value is approximately 2.72 and the value of $(1 + 1/x)^{x \times \text{stated rate}}$ approaches $e^{\text{stated rate}}$. The relationship between stated and effective rate becomes:

$$e^{\text{stated rate}} - 1 = \text{effective rate}$$

In Excel, the formula is: =EXP(stated rate) – 1 = effective rate.
Another useful formula is:

$$\log(1 + \text{effective rate}) = \text{continuous return}$$

Discounting continuously generated cash flows

Even though cash flows are usually generated continuously, it is common practice to simplify NPV calculations and to assume that cash flows are generated once a year at year end. What kind of bias does this simplification introduce in NPV calculations?

Let us assume that in 2002, a project generates a 1200 cash flow and that this cash flow is generated in equal amounts each month. The annual discount rate is 20%. The monthly rate is $(1.2)^{1/12} - 1 = 0.015$.

From the annual cash flow:
NPV = 1200/1.2
= 1000

From the monthly cash flows:
$$NPV = 100/1.2^{1/12} + 100/(1.2^{1/12})^2 + \ldots + 100/(1.2^{1/12})^{12}$$
= 1089

If you repeat this calculation with different discount rates, you get the following results:

Annual discount rate	NPV calculated from monthly cash flows	NPV calculated from annual cash flow	Difference
0.08	1151	1111	−3%
0.10	1140	1091	−4%
0.12	1129	1071	−5%
0.15	1113	1043	−6%
0.20	1089	1000	−8%
0.30	1044	923	−12%

When cash flows are generated continuously – evenly each month – and when you ignore this reality and use one single end of year cash flow only, you tend to underestimate the NPV and this bias increases with the discount rate. How to remove this bias? You can use shorter periods than the year for your models, but your models may quickly become unmanageable. You can also adjust the discount rate.[1]

In the example above, you need to discount the annual cash flow at a rate of:

$$1200/1089 - 1 = 0.102$$

This rate can be estimated with the formula for the present value of an ordinary annuity:

$$0.102 = \sum_{n=1}^{k} 1/(1 + r)^n = (1 - (1 + r)^{-k})/r$$

where $r = 1.2^{1/12}$

What would you do in practice? The first thing to remember is that NPVs are estimates. A 5–10% estimation error is very common with NPVs. Estimating cash flows at year end and discounting them on an annual basis is generally acceptable. However, it is a good idea to check that this simplification is valid. In order to do so, you must think about the distribution of cash flows within each year and work out the pattern of the quarterly or monthly cash flows. You can then calculate the NPV based on these cash flows and compare it with the NPV calculated from the year end cash flows. If the difference is small keep your annual model. If the difference is large either go for shorter periods or adjust the rate.

Present value of a continuously generated cash flow discounted continuously

$$PV = C \ (1 - e^{-n \ (k-p)})/(k - p)$$

where

C = annual cash flow
n = number of years
k = equivalent continuous discount rate. With r the annual rate: $k = \ln(1 + r)$
p = equivalent continuous growth rate. With g the annual rate: $p = \ln (1 + g)$

Note

1. You should be aware that in a multi-annual model, you have to use a different discount rate for each year end cash flow. For example, the adjusted rate for the second year is: $((1 + \text{adjusted rate year 1}) \times (1 + \text{unadjusted rate}))^2 - 1$.

Appendix II.2
Two additional cases focusing on value and risk

The Dhahran Roads series describes a project situation. It enables you to address questions such as: what is the value created? What are the major risks? How to portray these risks? How to manage them? Dhahran Roads (III) enables you to model a richer sequence of decisions and events than Swedish Timber. When you have an option to react risk becomes different. The only risk which has a negative impact is the risk that corresponds to events from which you have no future flexibility to escape. The Dhahran Roads series was developed by the author and Sherwood Frey, Professor of Business Administration at the Colgate Darden Graduate School of Business (USA).

Gatefield is a case that focuses on the substantial value that can be created through redesigning the way we do business. What does it take to create a new business situation in which:

● the customer gets a better service at a lower price, *and*
● the supplier achieves the same profit while incurring less risk?

This is an abridged version of the Gatefield case study developed by Sherwood Frey. The business situation from which the case is derived is also described in 'ABB and Ford: Creating Value though Cooperation' (1993), Sherwood Frey and Michel Schlosser, *Sloan Management Review*, Fall 1993, pp. 65–72.

APPENDIX

Dhahran Roads

On 15 January 2002, Mr Malik, the financial manager of SADE, a Bahraini civil engineering company, was reviewing the contract which the company had just been awarded by the municipality of Dhahran in Saudi Arabia for the construction of a new road network linking the airport complex and the city. The characteristics of the contract awarded to SADE are described in the exhibit. Mr Malik was planning to estimate the value of the contract and to check that it was yielding more than the 25% return requested by SADE on projects in Saudi Arabia.

Exhibit ● The contract awarded to SADE

Total project amount: 168 million Saudi rials (SR).

Advance made by the client: 15% of the total project amount.

Schedule of costs and billings (in million SR):

	Cost incurred	Billings
2002	7	11
2003	28	43
2004	31	48
2005	25	39
2006	17	27

In addition to these costs, SADE will have to buy equipment for an amount of SR 38 million (to be paid in 2002). The equipment will be depreciated over five years and SADE does not expect to be able to use it again for other projects. It is also reasonable to assume that SADE will not be able to resell this equipment.

All costs will be paid in the year they occur.

Amounts billed to the customer should be paid in the same year. The customer is expected, however, to pay only 80% of each invoice. The 20% deduction corresponds to:

- the recovery by the customer of the initial advance (15%);
- a 5% retention for guarantee. Half of this retention is to be reimbursed upon completion (in 2006) and the remaining half in 2007. The release of the retention funds is, however, subject to the completed construction being approved by the customer.

Project organization

The contract is to be executed by a Saudi company created specifically for the purpose. SADE will own 100% of the capital of this company. SADE wishes to invest a minimum and to be able to draw dividends as quickly as possible.

Risks

During the past several months, the SADE engineering department has inspected the site, confirmed the surveying and reviewed the drawings that have been provided by the municipality of Dhahran. In the opinion of the head of the engineering department, the project presents no unusual problems. It is very similar to several SADE projects in other countries and these have progressed without any serious difficulties.

The project is to be managed by one of SADE's most experienced project managers, Mr H.K. Jones. Mr Jones has just completed a major waterworks project in Africa and is noted for strong engineering skills and tight cost control.

As the Bahraini dinar is pegged to the Saudi rial, the risk of currency variations is very small.

Taxes

There are no corporate taxes to be paid in Saudi Arabia and no corporate taxes will have to be paid in Bahrain on the profit of this project.

CASE

CASE *E*

Dhahran Roads (II)

While Mr Malik was delighted that the Dhahran Roads contract would generate a substantial value to SADE, he recognized that a favourable result such as this depended on everything proceeding smoothly. Unfortunately, it seemed to him that it would be pure luck if the necessary combinations of events were all to occur in his favour. Even though it was unpleasant, his thoughts began to turn to those aspects of the project that could go wrong.

He first wondered which of the various inputs to his evaluation were particularly critical. He decided to make changes to one assumption at a time so that he could see which assumptions had the largest impact on the value of the Dhahran Roads contract.

As he continued to think about the risk inherent in the project, it seemed that there were two key areas in which former projects had run into trouble: delayed payments and cost overruns.

Delayed payments by the client

There had been occasions when SADE had experienced problems in making the contracting agency pay in accordance with the agreed schedule. SADE was not the only contractor facing these problems. In fact, there had been several informal discussions among contractors in which they had shared their experiences in this area. During these conversations, a pattern of behaviour seemed to emerge. If there were going to be problems in keeping to the billing schedule, the delay seemed to appear in the third year of the longer-term contracts and, recently, one-year postponements of that payment and of all subsequent payments had been experienced. It was felt by many of the contractors that the delay occurred at a point in time when the project had gone so far that they could not abandon it, but at a point where delayed payments represented an effective cost reduction to the client. The delays seemed to have occurred recently in about a quarter of the projects and were often justified by the client on the basis of the slightest of deviations from the performance terms of the contract.

Cost overruns

Even though SADE prided itself on its ability to control costs, it occasionally experienced overruns, sometimes rather substantial ones. After reviewing the files of 10 completed projects, it seemed that projects could be grouped into four categories:

96

1. Those projects for which actual costs were very close to the original estimate.
2. Those projects that experienced mild cost overruns in the range of 5% to 10%.
3. Those projects that got into substantial difficulties and had overruns in the vicinity of 15% to 20%.
4. Those projects for which actual costs were lower than expected, in the range of 3% to 5%.

Unfortunately, there had been only one project of this latter variety, while there had been one with serious overruns and two with mild overruns. A close examination of the files showed that, when cost overruns did occur, they spread fairly equally over the whole life of the contract.

CASE F

Dhahran Roads (III)

Mr Malik was very pleased to have succeeded in building a diagram describing the combined impact of possible cost overruns and payment delays. But he was still not fully convinced that SADE should go ahead with the contract. Certainly the decision to go ahead corresponded to a positive NPV, but the dispersion of the possible outcomes was wide and some very unfavourable outcomes could occur, especially if SADE were unfortunate enough to experience both payment delays and cost overruns.

When analyzing the problem further, Mr Malik realized that the contract could look much more attractive if SADE had the ability to react against those adverse events that might materialize.

He decided to review previous contracts in which SADE had experienced delayed payments. When such problems occurred, SADE always tried to exert some pressure on the customer and in one case, it even decided to stop the execution of the contract. This firm reaction impressed the customer a great deal and, as a result, he changed his attitude completely. The contract was then restarted and no more payment delays occurred.

Mr Malik thought that such a strategy could be adopted if delays in payments occurred in the Dhahran Roads contract. From the discussions he had with commercial and technical managers, he tried to estimate what the billings and costs could be in such a case.

Impact of a strong reaction to payment delays

If payment delays occurred in the third year, SADE would try to convince the customer that such delays were a breach of the original contract and it therefore should be brought to a halt. If this approach failed, SADE could well decide to stop the execution of the contract. It was likely that such an action would:

● causes losses for SADE as it was impossible to stop all the expenses;
● impress the customer sufficiently to enable the contract to be restarted and completed with no further payment delays.

The schedule of costs and billings corresponding to such a situation had been estimated as follows:

	2002	2003	2004	2005	2006
Billings	11	43	0[1]	60	54
Costs	7	28	5[2]	39	34

1 No receipt at all in 2004. All remaining billings are paid in 2005 and 2006.
2 Costs incurred in 2004 in case the execution is interrupted.

Mr Malik estimated the probability of success of a strong reaction strategy to be at least 80%. He had also estimated the schedule of costs and billings in case this strategy failed:

	2002	2003	2004	2005	2006	2007
Billings	11	43	0	15	45	54
Costs	7	28	5	39	34	

In this latter case it was reasonable to assume that recoveries of the retentions would occur in 2006 and 2007.

CASE

The Gatefield project

An 'incredible' month

The events of the past months have been extraordinary. On December 23, 2000, just hours before our office holiday party, I was notified by KHW that their $150 million North Carolina paint finishing project had been canceled. The announcement was a complete surprise. Both KHW and us had invested heavily in the planning and engineering of the plant and the cooperative spirit enkindled by the new 'collaborative engineering' concept recently adopted by KHW had made work on the project very satisfying. On the day after New Year, apparently in response to my inquiries regarding other project opportunities, I received an invitation from KHW, to present our capabilities to undertake the construction of Gatefield, a facility twice the size of North Carolina. The presentation we made on January 5, 2000 went well and KHW asked for a formal proposal within a week. Although the deadline was incredibly short, we completed the bid proposal on January 12 and quoted a price of $300 million. KHW's response echoes in my ears: 'You must be joking!'

Henry Jones, President and CEO of ABC

The Gatefield project

The Gatefield project was a full service contract for the design and construction of one of the largest automotive paint finishing plants in the world: a 730 000 square foot, 75-car-per-hour, $300 million facility attached to KHW's Gatefield, Canada, assembly plant. KHW had decided to use leading-edge paint finishing technology at Gatefield. This was a very large project that would require ABC, the main contractor, to involve subcontractors satisfying something like 200 bid packages. At its peak Gatefield would have more than 1000 people employed on the site. In addition to its size, Gatefield also presented some unusual complications. Canada had a short 36-hour working week, overtime pay was very costly, weather conditions could be tough and cause delays, there was some exchange risk, and so on. In spite of all these complexities, the management of KHW had committed to ambitious targets:

- A 30% cost reduction. The target was to complete Gatefield at a cost of $210 million instead of the $300 million typical for such a project.
- A two-year time period from bid invitation to the turnover of an operational facility. This was a substantial reduction from anything in KHW's prior experience.

At the end of 2000, KHW had prepared the detailed specifications for the project and had sent them to ABC on 2 January. These specifications envisaged a fairly traditional facility with a very large building and a well-established process.

Paint finishing

The combined pressures of the market, the technology and the environment had created considerable technical challenges for paint finishing and called for state-of-the-art responses.

The quality of an automobile finish (visual appearance as well as durability) had become increasingly important in a customer's purchase decision. In the manufacturing of an automobile, paint finishing was a sensitive process comprising many steps, each of which compounded the chances of defect and the risk of increasing the manufacturing through-put times. Paint finishing also had significant potential emission problems that demanded sophisticated environmental controls. In addition to these challenges, the construction of a paint finishing facility was a complex undertaking, with complicated designs and intricate interfaces with the manufacturing process.

Experimenting with new relations with suppliers

The management of KHW had been concerned with the fact that the very competitive relations that the automotive industry was having with its suppliers could present barriers to innovation and cost reduction.

American car companies had been very surprised to realize that their Japanese competitors could build new manufacturing facilities in the USA at something like 70% of the typical cost of the same plant built by an American company. Japanese companies were using the same suppliers but they were working differently with them:

● American manufacturers were used to fixing all the detailed specifications before inviting the suppliers to bid. Japanese manufacturers used to work a lot with their suppliers at developing the final project design.
● Japanese manufacturers often used a turnkey approach in which a single full-service supplier assumed the management responsibility of the whole project. A company like KHW would rather assign the responsibility of each discipline involved (building, structural work, electrical services, conveyor systems, ovens, booths and spraying processes) to specific internal teams. Each small team would then work with a specific supplier to perform its portion of the job. This approach was rendered even more complex by the constant involvement of central engineering and central purchasing, two departments which often had 'problems talking to each other'.

In the late 1990s, KHW decided to:

● set a 30% cost reduction target for all its new plants;
● start experimenting with new relations with its suppliers.

KHW had decided to use the North Carolina plant project – the one that had just been cancelled – as its first 'collaborative engineering' project. This enabled KHW and ABC to experiment with a new approach. Rather than designing the building first and ending up with having a 'big and expensive barn', the two companies decided to start with the design of the industrial process. 'We will then design the best building to host this process.' ABC had put together a 20-person team on the project but unfortunately KHW decided to cancel.

ABC

ABC was the paint finishing global business of a large international group that was one of the world leaders in industrial equipment engineering and supply. In the 1990s and in the face of the difficulties met in the paint finishing business ABC reaffirmed its commitment to this business provided that more effective relations could be developed with the auto-mobile manufacturers. With some manufacturers relations could actually be described as 'adversarial' with the customer typically trying to exploit its strength to a maximum: extremely detailed specifications, very low prices, systematic competitive bidding, last minute cancellations, and so on.[1] ABC had been close to believing that the North Carolina project would be a major step in the establishment of new relations with KHW. Unfortunately the project was cancelled and now the debilitating discussion about price was restarting!

Executive summary prepared by Henry Jones on 13 January 2001

When considering the numbers, it is very difficult to see how one could quote a price anywhere close to the $210 million that KHW seems to be expecting.

Base case

The $300 million is made up of four main components:

- engineering and management (ABC at cost): $12 million,
- building (subcontracted): $78 million,
- process (ABC at cost): $64 million; sub-contractors: $110 million.

This leads to a total of $264 million, to which we have added the usual 2.5% contingency and a 10% profit margin: this makes $300.7 million.

As there are risks involved in all the items, it is difficult to reduce the contingency. Obviously, the subcontracted costs also include some contingency and some profit. The building subcontractor has included his own contingency and profit and the process con-tractors will do the same.

Risks

We are very confident of our cost estimates. We should, however, accept the fact that the actual costs may end up within range of the estimate above. This is based on the experience of previous projects and taking into account the very limited time that we had to prepare this estimate:

- Engineering and management may range between $11m (−5%) and $12.6m (+5%).
- Building may range between $74 million (−5%) and $85.8 million (+10%).

- Internal process costs may range between $61 million (–5%) and $67.2 million (+5%); external process costs between $105 million (–5%) and $121 million (+10%).

One cannot also ignore the 'worst' case scenario. The building is not completed in time and then the end of the project is delayed by one quarter year. In this case costs are incurred as planned (except for the costs of the building which are delayed by one quarter). The payments to the customer are delayed by one quarter and a 5% penalty has to be paid to the customer. With the traditional design, this worst case scenario is extremely unlikely.

Schedules and payments

The schedule of costs and payments is in Figure G.1. KHW will pay with a delay of one quarter. A retention of 10% is made on all invoices. This retention is released one year after the reception of the facility. Internal costs are paid in the quarter they occur. External costs are paid with a delay of one quarter.

The new design

The only possibility to reduce the cost to KHW would be to adopt a completely different design of the facility: more efficient building with two levels and a smaller footprint, lighter building structure, more efficient process flows and more effective automation. The implementation of this new design would result in a better and cheaper facility. However, this is a more risky undertaking for ABC. The high risk related to the implementation of the new ABC design is primarily due to our current lack of knowledge of the details of the final solutions that will be implemented. The North Carolina project was cancelled too soon! The pessimistic cost estimates typically reflect the following scenario. 'We fix the specifications today; we then realize that there are mistakes; we have to correct those mistakes through change in orders!'[2]

Costs and risks of the new design

- Engineering and management: $20 million (with –15%, +10% range)
- Building (subcontracted): $66 million (with –25%, +25% range)
- Process: ABC $64 million (with –20%, +10% range); sub-contractors: $82 million (with a –25%, +20% range)

The 'best guess' estimate was amounting to a total cost of $232 million. With this cost level, a price of $265 million allowed ABC to create the same value as with the traditional design.

Once again, one cannot ignore the 'worst' case scenario: the building is not completed in time and then the end of the project is delayed by one quarter. In this case, costs are incurred as planned (except for the costs of the building which are delayed by one quarter). The payment of customers is delayed by one quarter and a 5% penalty has to be paid to the customer.

Schedules and payments

The schedule of costs and payments is in Figure G.1. KHW will pay with a delay of one quarter. A retention of 10% is made on all invoices. This retention is released one year after the reception of the facility. Internal costs are paid in the quarter they occur. External costs are paid with a one quarter delay.

Discount rate

We have been using the usual 12% rate (annual).

Figure G.1 ● Schedule of costs and invoices

Traditional design (base)

Quarter		1	2	3	4	5	6	7	8
Engineering & management	12	10%	30%	30%	10%	5%	5%	5%	5%
Building	78	0%	10%	20%	30%	30%	10%		
Process	174	0%	0%	0%	15%	25%	25%	25%	10%
Invoices	300	0%	5%	5%	10%	20%	20%	20%	20%

New design

Quarter		1	2	3	4	5	6	7	8
Engineering & management	20	10%	30%	30%	10%	10%	5%	5%	
Building	66	0%	30%	30%	30%	10%			
Process	146	0%	0%	15%	15%	25%	25%	20%	
Invoices	265	0%	5%	15%	20%	20%	20%	20%	

Notes

1. This adversarial climate was, however, not always turning in favour of the customer. Contractors could also make a lot of money with changing orders. This could happen each time the customer made a mistake in the specifications.
2. A solution would be to start today and put together a team of 25 people that would start working with KHW on defining the detailed specifications of the new ABC design. If our hopes regarding this design come true, which is very likely, then in 3 to 4 months time, we will have the detailed specifications for a plant that could really be built at a cost very close to the optimistic scenario (with a +/–5% range: large projects always have some uncertainty).

Modelling business processes and simulating their dynamics

In Part III we discuss how we can effectively model:

● *the **value creation dynamics** of business processes and of whole companies. A key model here is the recommended **trajectories-of-payments-and-receipts** model in Table 10.5 (p. 174). This is a superior alternative to the traditional 'per-cent-of-sales' approach.*

● *how **price shocks** affect the value creation process. This is discussed in Chapter 9. In the appendices, the case study on PT PharMa illustrates this issue again in a turbulent price and currency environment.*

● *the impact of **growth** on the 'pay-then-collect' business designs: this is discussed in Chapter 11. In the appendices, the case study on SW Life shows the extent to which growth, here of a pure information business, can very much destabilize the cash trajectory.*

● *the **dynamics of alternative business designs**. Chapter 12 discusses the value of '**collect-then-pay**' or '**sense-and-respond**' business designs. Even though they are not new, these more customer-centric than product-centric business designs have become popular with the new economy. We discuss why these business designs are much less risky and often create more value than the traditional '**pay-then-collect**' or '**make-and-sell**' approaches. In the appendices, the case study on Relais Electriques explores how alternative organizational designs ('**process orientated**' vs. '**functional**') impact the dynamics of cash flows.*

*Following the introduction of our case study on Delta Metal, we start Part III with an analysis of all the time factors that may make income and cash deviate in the short run. A central idea here is the **cash–income parity** relation and its visualization in the **cash–income matrix**. We also pursue the discussion of accounting principles and argue that depreciation – like cost of goods sold – is a concept more adapted to the economy of things than to the economy of information.*

   *In Table 8.3, we introduce a **comprehensive model for generating the financial statements of a business** (income statement, balance sheets and cash flows).*

Delta Metal[1]

In November 2001, Mr Lauru, the President of Delta Metal SA, was preparing the company's financial plan for 2002. Mr Lauru expected that this planning exercise would help him find answers to a number of questions related to the future of the company. Among these questions, two were very important for him:

- Should Delta Metal introduce the plan proposed by the Finance Manager which was aimed at reducing the accounts receivable?
- How would the new market regulations which the EU planned to introduce in 2002 affect the operations of Delta Metal?

When trying to answer these questions, Mr Lauru wanted to focus on how Delta Metal's cash generation could change. The company's cash generation had been generally poor in the past and Mr Lauru wanted to improve it.

Delta Metal

Delta Metal was the French subsidiary of the Delta Metal group, one of the few large independent traders in special steel in Europe. Delta Metal, like other subsidiaries of the group in Europe, was in competition with trading companies belonging to the large steel manufacturers as well as with a large number of small independent distributors. Over the past 10 years, the market for special steels in Europe had been growing in volume but, due to the harsh competition prevailing in the sector, margins had been gradually eroded at the same time. Despite being of a different nature, 2000 and 2001 had both been very difficult years for Delta Metal:

- In 2000, sales had developed well, but the company had faced a severe cash shortage and had difficulties in securing new loans with its banks.
- In 2001, the market had been sluggish and, in order to remove excess inventory, Delta Metal had decided to conclude several contracts at what could be considered 'sacrificial prices'. This had resulted in a loss; the company was able, however, to decrease its borrowings as requested by its bankers.

Tables H.1, H.2, H.3 and H.4 show Delta Metal's financial statements.

Table H.1 ● Delta Metal: cash flow statements 'direct' presentation

(in €000)	2000	2001[a]
Receipts from customers	107 715	120 124
– Payments to suppliers	105 636	78 942
– Payments to employees	16 760	16 090
– Payments to tax authorities	0	0
– Payments to suppliers of capital expenditures	380	2 001
= Free cash flow	–15 061	23 093

[a] Estimates.

Table H.2 ● Delta Metal: cash flow statements 'indirect' presentation

(in €000)	2000	2001[a]
Sales	129 386	114 934
Cost of goods sold (CGS)	103 515	95 625
Operating expenses	16 760	16 090
Depreciation	300	340
Operating income before tax	8 811	2 880
Corporation tax	0	0
Operating income after tax	**8 811**	**2 880**
Depreciation (+)	300	340
Receivables open (+)	41 944	63 615
Receivables end (–)	63 615	58 425
Inventory open (+)	20 255	26 993
Inventory end (–)	26 993	17 367
Payables open (–)	28 459	33 076
Payables end (+)	33 076	40 132
Cash from operating activities	–14 681	25 093
Capital expenditures (–)	380	2 001
Free cash flow	**–15 061**	**23 093**
Interest after tax[b]	6 048	6 234
Long-term debt repayment	11	3 076
New short-term debt	13 283	–12 865
New long-term debt	5 000	0
Dividends	0	0
Change in cash	–2 836	918

[a] Estimates.
[b] As no corporation tax was paid in 2000 and 2001 (carry forward of losses), interest after tax is equal to the actual amount of interest paid.

Table H.3 ● Delta Metal: income statements

(in €000)	1999	2000	2001[a]
Sales	**96 794**	**129 386**	**114 934**
Cost of goods sold	75 493	103 515	95 625
Operating expenses	14 084	16 760	16 090
Depreciation	203	300	340
Operating income	7 013	8 811	2 880
Interest	3 048	6 048	6 234
Income before tax	3 965	2 764	−3 354
Corporation tax[b]	0	0	0
Income after tax	**3 965**	**2 764**	**−3 354**
Growth rate of sales	*5%*	*34%*	*−11%*
Cost of goods sold/sales	*78%*	*80%*	*83%*
Operating expenses/sales	*15%*	*13%*	*14%*
Operating income/sales	*7%*	*7%*	*3%*
Profit after tax/sales	*4%*	*2%*	*−3%*

[a] Estimates.
[b] Corporate tax rate is 33%. A total amount of 4588 can be carried forward against future profits.

Table H.4 ● Delta Metal: balance sheets

(in €000)	End 1999	2000	2001
Cash	3195	359	1 277
Accounts receivable	41 944	63 615	58 425
Inventory	20 255	26 993	17 367
Net fixed assets	2 464	2 544	4 204
Total	67 858	93 511	81 272
Bank short term	23 560	36 933	24 068
Accounts payable	28 459	33 076	40 132
Long-term debt current[a]	11	3 076	2 534
Long-term debt	5 000	6 924	4 390
Net worth	10 738	13 502	10 148
Total	67 858	93 511	81 274
Collection period (months)	*5.20*	*5.90*	*6.10*
Inventory turnover	*3.73*	*3.83*	*5.51*
Payment period (months)	*4.40*	*3.60*	*5.60*
Debt/equity	*2.67*	*3.48*	*3.05*

[a] The 'current portion' is the part of long-term debt that is due within a year. The balance sheet at the end of 2001 shows that an amount of 2534 will have to be repaid in 2002.

Prospects for 2002

Mr Lauru expected the market to remain extremely competitive in 2002. He was convinced that margins would stay low, but not as low as in 2001 when Delta Metal had decided to remove its excess inventory. A cost of goods sold equal to 80% of sales was to be expected in 2002. The other assumptions which Mr Lauru considered reasonable for 2002 were:

- operating expenses: 14% of sales;
- inventory turnover: four times a year;
- collection period: six months;
- payment period: four months.

The sharp reduction in the payment period envisaged for 2002 was motivated by the urgent need to improve relationships with the suppliers. In 2001, Delta Metal had delayed its payments a great deal and this could not be continued indefinitely.

The new credit plan

During its history, Delta Metal had often experienced cash shortages caused by excessive volumes of inventories and accounts receivable. The success of the actions taken in 2001 for reducing the inventory reinforced Mr Ladouce's position as Finance Manager; he had for many years been arguing in favour of shortening the collection period. Mr Ladouce recommended that Delta Metal would use discounts to motivate its customers to pay faster. According to Mr Ladouce, it was possible to reduce the average collection period to four months, losing only 4% of the sales price on average.

The new EU regulations

The EU was trying to introduce new regulations aimed at promoting healthier competition in the steel industry. For Delta Metal, these new regulations (which were not yet fully defined) were likely to mean:

- an increase in the gross margins: cost of goods sold could well fall to 74% of sales (instead of 80%) due to subsidised prices;
- a need to increase the level of inventories. Mr Lauru believed that the inventory turnover could fall to three (instead of four as expected in the absence of the new regulations).

Market volume in 2002

Mr Lauru was not very optimistic for 2002. He expected the market to remain sluggish. There would be a small increase in sales (4%) for Delta Metal, however, due to better selling prices. Mr Lauru did not completely disregard the hypothesis of a volume increase (5% to 10%).[2] The steel market should grow in the long run but nobody could tell when growth would start again. Data on the industry are given in Figure H.1.

Throughout western Europe the demand for special steels had been growing in the 1990s (with the modernization of numerous production facilities) and more growth was expected in the future. In spite of this basic growth trend, the market was very cyclical.

Production of special steel was concentrated in a very small number of manufacturers (four major ones in Europe) and distribution was ensured by the trading companies of these manufacturers, hundreds of small brokers and a few large stockists, among which was Delta Metal. In the late 1990s price competition had been severe on this market and some manufacturers had not hesitated to cut their prices when the market was low.

Buyers of special steel had the choice either to purchase direct from the manufacturers or to go to the independent traders:

● In the first case, the price was lower but a long lead time was to be expected (manufacturers were normally producing to order and lead times were typically in the range of six months).
● In the second case, delivery was almost immediate but the price was higher.

In the late 1990s, more and more customers seemed to prefer buying from the factory, even for small volumes, but some experts believed that the new EU regulations could reverse this trend. In the segment in which Delta Metal operated, the customers were relatively few (about a hundred in France). Very often these customers had special technical requirements which obliged their engineering departments and those of the manufacturers to co-operate. Due to the diversity of the problems raised by the customers and the variety of the possible technical solutions, even large traders like Delta Metal could not afford to have their own engineering departments. In the late 1990s, the manufacturers' trading companies had become more aggressive on the market and there was no sign that this aggressiveness would decrease.

Market conditions were different in each country but the trend described above existed everywhere in Europe. In some countries, the situation for stockists like Delta Metal was made even more difficult by the existence of long collection periods: this was the case in Italy, France and Spain, for example.

Figure H.1 Delta Metal: evolution of the industry

Notes

1. This material was developed by Michel Schlosser from an actual business situation that has been modified in order to serve as a basis for learning and class discussion.
2. This would lead to a total sales growth of 9.2 to 14.4%:

   ● If volume grows by 5% and prices by 4%, then sales will be multiplied by a factor equal to 1.05×1.04 and the sales growth rate will be $1.05 \times 1.04 - 1 = 0.092$.
   ● If volume grows by 10% and prices by 4%, then sales will be multiplied by a factor equal to 1.10×1.04 and the sales growth rate will be $1.10 \times 1.04 - 1 = 0.0144$.

CHAPTER 6

Cash–income parity

Analyzing deviations from parity

6.1 Cash and income trajectories: cash–income matrix

Cash and profit are equivalent. We should always keep in mind the cash–income parity relation when we observe that cash and profit differ in a given time period. As they are equivalent, the **cash and income of a successful company should 'naturally' move together** up the diagonal shown in Figure 6.1. However, this is not always the case and income and cash may follow different trajectories and bring any business into each one of the four cells of the matrix of Figure 6.1:

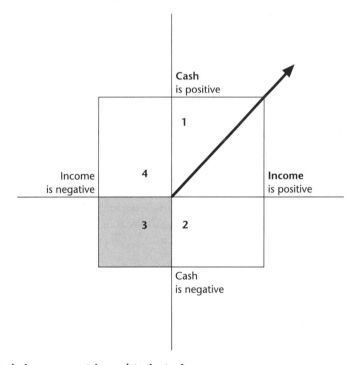

Figure 6.1 Cash–income matrix and trajectories

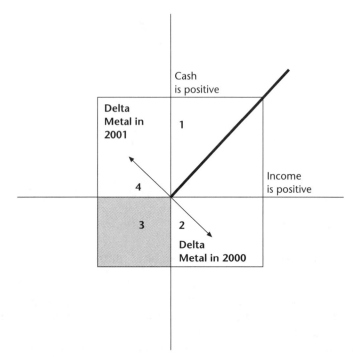

Figure 6.2 Delta Metal in 2000 and 2001: from cell 2 to cell 4

- Cell 1: Income and cash are positive; this is the normal situation.
- Cell 2: Income is positive and cash is negative. Pricing is fine, at least for the time being. But receipts and disbursements are out of sync and this is not sustainable. The issue is to assess if the overspending is a value-creating investment.
- Cell 3: Income and cash are negative. This is consistent but often means death.[1]
- Cell 4: Cash is positive and income is negative. Receipts and disbursements are out of sync. Pricing is wrong – income is negative – but 'over-receiving'[2] hides the problem at the level of cash.

At Delta Metal (*see* Case H) cash and income have not moved up together in 2000 and 2001. As shown in Figure 6.2, they have followed divergent trajectories and have brought the company from cell 2 to cell 4. What has made Delta Metal – and what makes other companies – end up in each of the two non-sustainable situations 2 and 4? Are there specific problems associated to these out-of-balance situations? Why has Delta Metal gone from situation 2 to situation 4, and not from situation 2 to situation 1 as Jilin did after 2002? How is it possible for a company continuously to experience situation 1 and never go into situations 2 and/or 4?

6.2 Free cash flow and income

Free cash flow is a measure of performance that has gained a lot of acceptance since the expression started being used in the late 1980s.[3] The free cash flow generated by a company over a period is equal to the amount of money that is left after the company has

Table 6.1 • Free cash flows and operating incomes at Delta Metal in 2000 and 2001

	2000	2001		2000	2001
Sales	129 386	114 934	Receipts from customers	107 715	120 124
CGS	103 515	95 625	Payments to suppliers	105 636	78 942
Operating expenses	16 760	16 090	Payments to employees	16 760	16 090
Depreciation	300	340	Payments to tax		
Taxes	0	0	authorities	0	0
			Payment of capital		
Operating income			expenditures	380	2 001
after tax	8 811	2 880	Free cash flow	−15 061	23 093

cashed all its receipts and paid for all its disbursements, ignoring the receipts and payments which are of a financial nature. Financial receipts and payments are those that relate to:

● shareholders (money received as initial equity or as the proceeds of new equity issues and money paid as dividends);
● banks and various financial firms (proceeds of loans and various financing schemes, interest and various payments related to financing contracts, cash paid for repaying loans, etc.).

The free cash flow generated by a company over a given period is equal to the difference between:

● all the money received by the company from its customers

and

● all the money paid by the company to all its various suppliers, its employees and to the tax authorities.

When stating that free cash flow equals income after tax (or 'net income'), you have to deal with the potential complication introduced by interest on loans. Interest on loans is a financial item that impacts corporate taxes. There are several ways to deal with this difficulty:

● You compare income and cash on a before-tax basis. This is what you do when there are no corporate taxes. This was the case at Jilin.[4] This is the case again at Delta Metal: due to previous losses no corporate taxes have been paid in the recent past. In these situations cumulated operating income equals cumulated free cash flow.
● You work on an after-tax basis and you adjust net income. You remove interest paid on loans and recalculate corporate taxes.[5] Then cumulated adjusted net income[6] equals cumulated free cash flow.
● Another solution – which is not the best but which is commonly used – is to keep working on an after-tax basis and to 'adjust' the definition of free cash flow and consider it 'after interest on loans'. Then, once again, over the long run free cash flow equals net income.[7]

Table 6.1 compares Delta Metal's operating incomes and free cash flows in 2000 and 2001. Let us spend some time reviewing the relationship between the respective drivers of free cash flow and of operating income.

6.3 Sales, receivables and cash receipts

Sales and cash receipts

Completing transactions with a customer is typically a three-step process:

1. An order is received, or a contract is signed with the customer.
2. Goods and or services are delivered.
3. Goods and or services are fully paid for (cash receipt).

As discussed in Chapter 4, sales or revenues are recognized at step 2 when the revenue is earned (products or services have been delivered) and realized (an invoice has been sent). While they are necessarily the same in the end, sales and cash received from customers often have a different timing:

● Cash receipts may lead on sales. This happens each time a customer pays when placing an order. This is what customers who buy on the web typically do. This is also what happens when customers make an advance payment, like in Jilin.

● Cash receipts may come at the same time as sales. This happens when customers pay cash on delivery.

● Cash receipts may lag behind sales. This is the traditional ('old') way to do business. When credit is granted to customers, cash receipts lag behind sales by a time period equal to the duration of the credit granted, called the 'collection period'. Those sales that are not yet paid are recorded in a 'receivable' or 'debtors' account.

Which is the more meaningful description of a transaction with a customer: sales or cash receipts?

● When the environment is very volatile, when inflation is high, when transactions are made in foreign currencies, etc., cash receipts often tell more than sales![8]

● Cash receipts may also be the most effective yardstick to motivate 'sales' people. It has been something of a tradition to think functionally and to consider that sales people should focus on sales and that accountants should focus on collection. It is, however, often a much better idea to give a broader responsibility to sales people, to involve them in the collection of cash and to motivate them to contribute to bringing the transactions with customers to their full completion.[9]

Sales, accounts receivable and cash receipts at Delta Metal

In order to estimate the amount of cash received by Delta Metal in 2000 and 2001, you have to adjust the amount of sales by the change in accounts receivable. This is shown in Table 6.2.

What drives the difference between sales and cash receipts?

In 2000 cash came slower than sales. In 2001 cash came faster than sales. When sales are made on credit, the difference between sales and cash is driven by the changes in two factors:

● **Changes in collection period.** When the collection period increases, then cash generation is slowed down and cash looks small when compared with the sales of the current period. When the collection period decreases then cash generation is accelerated.

Table 6.2 ● Sales and cash receipts at Delta Metal in 2000 and 2001

	2000	2001
Sales (goods delivered and invoiced during the year)	129 386	114 934
+ **Accounts receivable end** (goods delivered and invoiced during the year but not yet paid by the end of the year)	(63 615)	(58 425)
− **Accounts receivable open** (goods paid for during the year but delivered and invoiced during the preceding year)	41 944	63 615
= **Cash receipts** (cash received in relation to goods delivered during the current and the preceding year)	107 715	120 124

or:

	2000	2001
Sales	129 386	114 934
− **Increase or + decrease in accounts receivable** from the beginning to the end of the year	−21 671	+5 190
= **Cash receipts**	107 715	120 124

Table 6.3 ● Analyzing the difference between sales and cash receipts at Delta Metal

	2000	2001
Collection period	*Increases* Cash receipts are slowed down	*Increases* Cash receipts are slowed down
Level of activity	*Increases* Cash receipts look small	*Decreases* Cash receipts look large
Net impact	Current cash receipts are less than current sales	Current cash receipts are more than current sales

● **Change in level of sales.** With growth, the sales in a given period are larger than the sales in any earlier period. When customers pay with a delay the cash that you get relates to earlier sales and is necessarily smaller than current sales. When a recession occurs, the opposite phenomenon materializes. Cash looks large when compared with current sales.

Table 6.3 shows how these two factors have impacted the cash generation of Delta Metal in 2000 and 2001.

6.4 Cost of goods sold, inventories and purchases

Matching and cost recovery principles: product and period costs

The income statement shows the margin earned on goods or services sold. As discussed in Chapter 4, this is done through charging to sales the costs that 'match' these sales. However, the matching principle does not apply to all the costs incurred in a business firm:

Table 6.4 ● Two applications of the matching principle

Matching (usual CGS approach)		Matching (traditional continental European)	
Sales	114 934	Sales	114 934
− CGS	95 625	+ Inventory end	17 367
= Gross income	19 309	− Inventory open	26 993
		− Purchases	85 999
− Operating expenses[a]	16 430	− Personnel costs	16 090
		− Depreciation	340
− Interest	6 737	− Interest	6 737
= Income before tax	−3 857	= Income before tax	−3 857
= Income after tax	−3 857	= Income after tax	−3 857

[a] Or 'selling and administrative' expenses.

● Some costs – expenses is a word that is also used – are called **product costs**. These are the costs that are considered to be 'directly related to sales'. They are charged to sales according to the matching principle. When a company incurs product costs faster than it sells, then all the product costs that exceed sales are stored in an inventory. When a company sells faster than it incurs product costs, then the costs stored in the inventory are **recovered**. In the extreme case where no sales are made, then the cost of goods sold in this period should be zero and all the product costs should be stored in an inventory.

● All the other costs are called **period costs**. These correspond to items the benefit of which is consumed by the passage of time rather than by the level of sales. These costs are charged to the period in which they occur whether or not sales are made and they are never stored in an inventory. General, administrative and selling expenses are typical examples of period costs.

The distinction between product and other costs allows for assessing the margin made on the products sold by a company. This is an interesting idea but you should be aware that it is an idea which is more useful in the economy of things than in the economy of information. Also, it is not an idea that is easy to put into practice. Even in the economy of things, the distinction between product and period costs is often a matter a judgement and depends very much on the cost system that is used.[10] As a result, you should always be careful when you try to compare your gross margins with those of your competitors – and especially when your competitors operate in another country!

Two different ways to apply the matching principle

The format of the income statements of Delta Metal (Table H.3) is the most commonlyused. There is an alternative format that has been traditionally used in continental Europe. Rather than showing cost of goods sold, this presentation shows purchases – or manufacturing cost, inventories open and inventories end (opening and closing stock). The two presentations are compared in Table 6.4.

Table 6.5 ● CGS and purchases at Delta Metal in 2000 and 2001

	2000	2001
CGS (goods sold during the year at cost price)	103 515	95 752
− **Inventory open** (goods sold during the year and purchased in the preceding year)	(20 255)	(26 993)
+ **Inventory end** (goods purchased during the year and that are going to be sold in the subsequent year)	26 993	16 367
= **Purchases** (goods received during the year)	110 254	85 999

or:

	2000	2001
CGS	103 515	95 752
+ **Increase in inventory or − decrease in inventory** from the beginning to the end of the year.	6 739	(9 754)
= **Purchases**	110 254	85 998

Both presentations apply the same matching principle and obviously lead to the same income. The difference between the two approaches comes from the way in which they aggregate costs:

● The 'product cost approach' aggregates the costs into two categories: product and period costs or CGS and operating expenses. This allows for the calculation of **gross margin** (or gross result). Depreciation is included in CGS and/or operating expenses. Product costs and other costs are typically given without any breakdown describing their nature (personnel, purchases, etc.)
● The 'traditional continental European' approach **typically aggregates costs according to their nature**: personnel, purchases, depreciation but does not state whether these costs should be considered as product costs or as selling or administrative costs. As a result, they do not allow for a calculation of gross margin.

Cost of goods sold, inventory and purchases at Delta Metal

In order to estimate what Delta Metal paid to its suppliers, we should first estimate what the company purchased. Estimating purchases is a matter of adjusting the cost of goods sold with the change in inventory. This is shown in Table 6.5.

6.5 Purchases, payables and payments to suppliers

It is a generally accepted principle of accounting to recognize purchases and expenditures when the goods and services are received and not when these goods and services are paid for. This is symmetric to the revenues recognition principle.

Table 6.6 shows what Delta Metal paid to its suppliers in 2000 and 2001.

Table 6.6 ● Purchases and payments to suppliers at Delta Metal in 2000 and 2001

	2000	2001
Purchases (goods received during the year)	110 254	85 998
− **Accounts payable end** (goods received during the year and not yet paid at the end of the year)	(33 076)	(40 132)
+ **Accounts payable open** (goods received during the preceding year, not paid during the preceding year, paid during the current year)	28 459	33 076
= **Payments to suppliers** (payment of goods purchased during the year and during the preceding year)	105 636	78 942

or:

	2000	2001
Purchases	110 254	85 998
− **Increase or + decrease in accounts** payable from the beginning to the end of the year end	(4 618)	(7 056)
= **Payments to suppliers** (payment of goods purchased during the year and during the preceding year)	105 636	78 942

6.6 Depreciation and capital expenditure

The money spent on physical resources (property, plant and equipment) is called 'capital expenditure'. In all those companies involved in the economy of things, investing in capital expenditures is a major strategic issue[12] that is described differently by the cash and the income approaches:

● From the cash point of view capital expenditure are taken into account when they are paid for.
● From the income point of view, it is common practice to distribute the cost of tangible assets, less salvage value if any, over the estimated useful life of the asset. Tangible assets are recorded as fixed assets in the balance sheet. At a given moment in time, the amount of net fixed assets in the balance sheet shows how much is still to be allocated to future sales.

Table 6.7 shows how a specific capital expenditure is dealt with from the cash and income points of view.

The depreciation process calls for a few comments: the only difference between depreciation and capital expenditure is time. Cumulated allowances for depreciation necessarily equal capital expenditure (provided that historical cost is used for valuing assets and allowance for depreciation).[13]

Just like the cost of goods sold, depreciation is more related to the economy of things – it applies to tangible assets – than to the economy of information. In the economy of information:

● Companies tend to invest more in intangible (research and development, business development, brand building, etc.) than in tangible assets.[14]

Table 6.7 ● Capital expenditure and allowance for depreciation

ISSUE. *In 2002, the Taylor company buys a piece of equipment at a cost of $3 million. This equipment is to be used equally in 2002, 2003 and 2004.*

Cash

A disbursement of $3 million, called capital expenditure, occurs in 2002. If the supplier of the equipment grants a credit, the disbursement will be delayed and any amount still to be paid will be recorded as accounts payable in the balance sheet.

Income

Income statements

	2002	2003	2004
Allowance for depreciation	1	1	1

Balance sheets

	1 Jan. 2002	31 Dec. 2002	31 Dec. 2003	31 Dec. 2004
Gross fixed assets	3	3	3	3
Cumulated depreciation	0	1	2	3
Net fixed assets	3	2	1	0

What happens if:
- *The company decides to keep the equipment running in 2005?* No depreciation allowance is charged, gross fixed assets remain equal to 3 and net fixed assets to zero for as long as the equipment is kept.
- *The company stops using the equipment at the end of 2004 and, very unexpectedly, is able to sell it at $1 million?* This means that too much allowance for depreciation has been charged in 2002, 2003 and 2004. Since the current practice does not allow you to modify past records, you will recognize an 'exceptional gain' of 1 when the asset is disposed of.

- The concept of distributing the cost of an asset over its life requires that this asset has a well-defined use. This is often the case with physical resources but not with information resources which typically have unlimited uses.
- Investments in information resources are not made like investments in physical resources. Investments in physical resources often correspond to one big irreversible investment made for a long period of time. Investments in information resources typically correspond to a much more complex and much more flexible process. Investment can be staged, some decisions can be deferred, there are many options to abandon and to expand, there are many options to switch, etc. This process is much too complex for using a concept like depreciation.

Depreciation has an impact on corporate taxes. The quicker you depreciate, the slower you pay taxes. This is why, in most countries, tax authorities define very precise guidelines for

Table 6.8 ● Allowance for depreciation, income tax and deferred tax

ISSUE. *Early in 2002, the Luleo company purchases a SEK 300 000 physical asset which is expected to have a three-year economic life. The company is entitled to claim a 100% capital allowance in 2002. It expects its income before depreciation and tax to be 600 000 in 2002, 700 000 in 2003 and 900 000 in 2004. How can the company estimate its profit after tax?*

Alternative 1: 'tax income'

	2002	2003	2004	Cumulated
Income before depreciation and tax	60	70	80	210
Depreciation (capital allowance)	30			30
Income before tax	30	70	80	180
Tax at 40%	12	28	32	72
Income after tax	18	42	48	108

Alternative 2: 'fair income'

	2002	2003	2004	Cumulated
Income before depreciation and tax	60	70	80	210
Depreciation ('fair' depreciation)	10	10	10	30
Income before tax	50	60	70	180
Tax at 40%	20	24	28	72
Income after tax	30	36	42	108

The two alternatives lead to the same cumulative tax. The advantage of alternative 1 is a timing effect only. The problem with this alternative is that it underestimates income in 2002 and overestimates it afterwards (provided that the allowance for depreciation is really fair). The solution is to introduce the deferred tax concept:

	2002	2003	2004	Cumulated
Income before depreciation and tax	60	70	80	210
Depreciation ('fair' depreciation)	10	10	10	30
Income before tax	50	60	70	180
Tax paid (from alternative 1)	12	28	32	72
Provision for tax (deferred tax)	8	−4	−4	0
Income after tax	20	24	28	108

Each year, the provision for tax is equal to the difference between actual tax paid (from alternative 1) and 'fair' tax. Provisions for tax are accumulated in a balance sheet account called deferred tax. This account cancels itself out automatically at the end of the life of the asset.

computing the allowance for depreciation, sometimes called the capital allowance. In some countries, tax authorities may grant very generous capital allowances which enable investing firms to defer their income tax to a very significant extent. However, the existence of generous capital allowances creates a problem for the reporting of income. Table 6.8 shows the nature of the problem and how it can be solved by the use of **deferred tax**. The thing to note is that the concept of deferred tax is not universally accepted. Although it is common practice in the UK, the USA and countries with similar accounting philosophies it is not used in most continental European countries. In these countries, profit should be reported as it is calculated for tax purposes, as in alternative 1 in Table 6.8. The consequence of this is that when capital allowances are generous, annual reported incomes are not generally 'fair'. This creates difficulties when you want to compare the profitability of companies across countries.

6.7 Direct and indirect assessments of free cash flow

There are two main approaches for estimating free cash flow:

● The 'direct method' estimates free cash flow as the difference between receipts from customers, and payments to all suppliers, employees and tax authorities. This was illustrated in Case H, Table H.1.
● The 'indirect method' estimates free cash flow starting from net income. This method, illustrated in Table H.2, is definitely much more difficult to understand than the direct method. However, it has the great advantage of showing both income and cash in the same statement. This is probably why it is more widely used than the direct approach.

Let us go through the process of estimating the free cash flow of Delta Metal in 2001 with the indirect method. The starting point is the income statement in Table 6.9. Then the challenge is to estimate free cash flow starting from income! This is a matter of making four successive adjustments.

Table 6.9 ● Starting with the income statement

	2001
Sales	114 934
Cost of goods sold	(95 625)
Operating expenses	(16 090)
Depreciation	(340)
Corporation tax	0
Operating income after tax	2 880

Step one: Voiding depreciation and introducing capital expenditure
In the income statement, depreciation is deducted from sales. From a cash point of view we want to consider capital expenditure and not depreciation. In Table 6.10:

● Depreciation is added back to profit; the easiest way to void something that has been subtracted it is to add it back!
● Then actual capital expenditure is deducted.

Table 6.10 • Adjusting for depreciation and capital expenditure

	2001	
Sales	114 934	
− Cost of goods sold	(95 625)	
− Operating expenses	(16 090)	
− Depreciation	(340)	
− Corporation tax	0	
= Operating income after tax	2 880	
+ **Depreciation**	**340**	340 − 340 = 0, depreciation is voided
− **Capital expenditure**	**(2 001)**	
= Temporary estimate	1 220	

Table 6.11 • Adjusting for changes in accounts receivable

	2001	
Sales	114 934	
− Cost of goods sold	(95 625)	
− Operating expenses	(16 090)	
− Depreciation	(340)	
− Corporation tax	0	
= Operating income after tax	2 880	
+ Depreciation	340	
− Capital expenditure	(2 001)	
+ **Receivables open**	**63 615**	114 934 + 63 615 − 58 425 = 120 124
− **Receivables end**	**(58 425)**	(cash receipts from customers)
= New temporary estimate	6 410	

Step two: **Adjusting sales and getting cash receipts**

This is a matter of adding back the accounts receivable open and of deducting the accounts receivable end. This is done in Table 6.11.

Steps three and four: **Adjusting expenses in order to get payments to suppliers**

In order to replace CGS with payments to suppliers, we need to make the two further adjustments shown in Table 6.12:

- We first replace cost of goods sold by purchases. Inventories open are added and inventories end are deducted. Inventories open are goods that have been bought in 2000 and that are going to be sold in 2001. From an income viewpoint the cost of these goods is recovered against sales. From a cash viewpoint, these goods are available and we do not need to purchase them any longer – provided that what we have in stock is exactly what we need!

- Then, we replace purchases with payments to suppliers. Accounts payable open are added and accounts payable end are deducted.

Table 6.12 • Adjusting for changes in inventories and accounts payable

	2001
Sales	114 934
– Cost of goods sold	(95 625)
– Operating expenses	(16 090)
– Depreciation	(340)
– Corporation tax	0
= Operating income after tax	2 880
+ Depreciation	340
– Capital expenditure	(2 001)
+ Receivables open	63 615
– Receivables end	(58 425)
+ Inventory open	26 993
– Inventory end	(17 367)
– payables open	(33 076)
+ payables end	40 132
= Free cash flow	23 093

$-95\,625 + 26\,993 - 17\,367 = -85\,998$
Purchases
$-85\,998 - 33\,076 + 40\,132 = -78\,942$
Payments to suppliers

6.8 Free cash flow, income and changes in working capital needs

Table 6.13 portrays an alternative presentation of the relationship between income and free cash flow. It shows once more that the only difference between income and free cash flow is time:

● Depreciation and capital expenditure are necessarily the same in the end (i.e. on a cumulated basis).
● **Changes in working capital needs** – defined as the net sum of the changes in receivables, inventories and payables – also correspond to time effects. In the end, cash receipts necessarily equal sales, CGS necessarily equals purchases[15] and purchases necessarily equal payments to suppliers.

Table 6.13 • Income, changes in working capital needs and free cash flow

	2000	2001
Income after tax	8 811	2 880
+ Depreciation	+300	+340
– Increase or + decrease in working capital needs[a]		
= Cash from operating activities	–14 681	25 093
– Cash used for investing activities	–380	–2 000
= **Free cash flow**	–15 061	23 093

[a] Defined as the net sum of changes in receivables, inventories and payables.

6.9 What happened at Delta Metal in 2000 and 2001?

Deviations from cash–income parity

In 2000, Delta Metal generated a positive income and a very negative free cash flow, a situation that cannot be sustained. In 2001, the company made a loss and generated a very positive free cash flow, a situation that cannot be sustained either. The 2000 and 2001 deviations from the income–cash parity are of a very different nature.

In 2000, the sales of Delta Metal grow fast – faster than income – but due to the long collection period growth does not result in much cash generation. At the same time, the company decides to accelerate its purchases in order to be well prepared for even higher growth in 2001. This results in heavy payments to suppliers – even if part of the payments are delayed.

The situation in 2001 is very much the opposite. The expected growth does not materialize – betting on growth was the wrong move. This results in two pieces of good news and two of bad news. The first good news is that the high sales of 2000 are cashed: their amount looks big compared with the sales of 2001! The second piece of good news is that the lower growth enables the company to slow down its purchases. This reduces the payments to suppliers, especially since the company takes the risk of delaying its payments to suppliers. The first bad news is that there is still too much inventory. This creates a need to sell at sacrificial prices, something that may have a long-term effect on the price level of the company. The second piece of bad news is that capital expenditure (a new warehouse) was ordered in 2000 when the company was betting on growth. In 2001, when Delta Metal realized that the market had slowed down, it was too late for cancelling the capital expenditure.

Notes

1. This is also the situation of many start-up companies and of e-economy start-ups in particular. A case in point was Amazon.com in the late 1990s:

(in $ million)	1995	1996	1997	1998	1999
Sales	0.5	16	148	610	1640
Income/loss	−0.3	−6	−31	−125	−718
Free cash flow	−0.3	−3	−125	−231	−1013
				May 1999	*May 2000*
Value ($ billion)				14	17

2. Divestment and downsizing often lead companies into cell 4. Divesting typically creates large exceptional receipts and exceptional one-time costs that hurt profit. When downsizing, companies incur severance costs. At the same time decrease in activity generates cash.
3. Free cash flow is a term coined by M. Jensen in 'Agency Costs of Free Cash Flow, Corporate Finance and Take-overs', *American Economic Review*, May 1986, pp. 323–9. Jensen defines the free cash flow of a firm as the 'cash flow in excess of that required to fund all projects which have a positive NPV when discounted at the relevant cost of capital'. The free cash flow of a firm is the surplus or profit it generates after it has exhausted all valuable investment opportunities. Consequently this free cash flow should be distributed to shareholders. See M. Jensen, 'The Eclipse of the Public Corporation', *Harvard Business Review*, Sept.–Oct. 1989, pp. 61–74.

4. In all the models of the Jilin project you can replace 'operating cash surplus' with 'free cash flow'.

5. As interest charges are tax deductible, you need to remove loans as well as their impact on corporate tax.

6. This adjusted income is basically operating income after tax (also called 'NOPAT' – net operating income after tax – by some authors and consultants. You assume that you are going to pay the taxes that would have to be paid if no interest charges on loans could be deducted. It is precisely operating income after tax when there are no financial incomes, or exceptional items.

7. However, you cannot really use this adjusted free cash flow for estimating NPVs. Doing so would make you double-count interest costs.

8. Please refer to the case Relais Electriques in the appendices to Part III.

9. Some people even argue that motivating sales people on the basis of cash received is an excellent way to reveal all the quality problems that may result in payment delays, and to motivate the whole organization to solve them.

10. With activity based costing (ABC) many companies have realized that one cannot really assess the profitability of a product or of a service without analyzing all the costs related to that product or service and not simply its production costs (CGS). Please refer to R.S. Kaplan and R. Cooper (1999), *Cost and Effect*, Harvard Business School Press.

11. You can use two levels of analysis. The first level is product and period costs. The second level corresponds to the breaking down of the product and period costs into material and external services, personnel, depreciation, etc.

12. When formal, this process is called 'capital budgeting' or 'resource allocation'. As it relates to physical assets, this process is very much linked to the economy of things.

13. For internal purposes, some companies sometimes recalculate depreciation in relation to the current value of their assets.

14. The absence of a mechanism like depreciation for capitalizing and spreading the costs related to the future makes the early losses even bigger. The only good news is that taxes are probably slowed down.

15. This is true in a trading company. In a manufacturing company, cumulated CGS equals cumulated production costs (purchases, personnel, depreciation, etc.).

CHAPTER 7

Building and using a per-cent-of-sales, vertical income, free cash flow and value model

In order to try to bring the company back into cell 1 (positive income and positive cash) (Figure 6.1) the management of Delta Metal is considering:

- the decision to adopt a new credit plan;
- the possibility that the market starts growing again and that European authorities decide to implement new market regulations.

Let us build an income and cash flow model and use it to test the impact of these scenarios. In order to get started, we shall build a model that describes the simplest scenario:

> In 2002, things will be almost as they were in 2001: growth will be 4%, there will be no new EU regulations and the company will not implement the new credit plan.

The data for this scenario are given in the case (p. 109).

7.1 An initial per-cent-of-sales model

The advent of spreadsheets has reinforced the popularity of the per-cent-of-sales approach for building income and cash flow models. You start with estimating the sales of the period – typically in relation to the previous period's sales. Then you estimate everything as a percentage or a 'ratio' of these sales: the simplest approach is to assume that most of the items on the income statement and balance sheet will maintain the same ratio to sales as in the previous year.

The popularity of the per-cent-of-sales is probably linked to its closeness to accounting data:

- Most managers feel comfortable with the accounting format. When using the accounting structure, there is no need to establish the credibility of this format for simulating the future.

126

Table 7.1 • A per-cent-of-sales, vertical income, free cash flow model

A		B	Background
1	*Growth*	*.04*	= .04
2	Sales	119.53	= 114.934*(1+B1)
3	*CGS/sales*	*.80*	= .8
4	CGS	95.63	= B2*B3
5	*Operating expenses/sales*	*.14*	= .14
6	Operating expenses	16.73	= B2*B5
7	*Depreciation*	*.60*	= .6
8	Operating income before tax	6.57	= B2–B4–B6–B7
9	Operating income after tax	6.57	= B8
10	Depreciation	.60	= B7
11	Accounts receivable open	58.43	= 58.425
12	*Collection period*	*6*	= 6
13	Accounts receivable end	59.77	= B2/12*B12
14	Inventory open	17.37	= 17.367
15	*Inventory turnover*	*4*	= 4
16	Inventory end	23.91	= B4/B15
17	Accounts payable open	40.13	= 40.132
18	*Payment period*	*4*	= 4
19	Accounts payable end	34.05	= (B4+B16–B14)/12*B18
20	Cash from operating activities	–6.79	= B9+B10+B11–B13+B14–B16–B17+B19
21	*Capital expenditure*	*0.5*	= .5
22	Free cash flow	–7.29	= B20–B21

- Past and present accounting data are easily accessible, accounting data are neatly organized, financial statements – and the income statement in particular – often show some stable patterns.[1]

The problem with extrapolating accounting data patterns[2] is that some of these patterns may result more from the accounting principles themselves (matching and depreciation) than from reality! Table H.2 (page 107) shows the typical architecture of a per-cent-of-sales income and cash flow model. Table 7.1 shows how you can build a spreadsheet model using this same architecture. One of the unique features of this architecture is that the relationships[3] between variables do not typically go across periods but are all within the same current period. All variables are simply related to current sales. Let us call such relationships **vertical** and those relationships that go across periods we shall call **horizontal**.

The typical drivers of per-cent-of-sales, vertical models

Table 7.1 shows the drivers typically used in these models:

- **Growth in sales.**
- Margins: **cost of goods sold/sales** reflects the competitive strength of the products and services of the company. **Operating expenses/sales** is an indicator of its administrative and selling effectiveness.

● Working capital parameters: **collection period, inventory turnover** and **payment period** measure the time effectiveness. The use of these drivers is actually a departure from a strict per-cent-of-sales method that would typically estimate accounts receivable, inventories, etc. as a simple percentage of sales.
● **Capital expenditure** and the related variable, depreciation. As it corresponds to the recovery of capital expenditure, depreciation is not an autonomous variable.

In Table 7.1 the drivers are exactly the same as the measures typically used to monitor the performance of a company and this is the problem with such drivers: except for capital expenditures, they are more output variables than drivers related to actual business decisions. For the Jilin project, we started from the business decisions that we were contemplating and then we selected the most adequate drivers (Table 3.1 on p. 35). Delta Metal is contemplating giving a discount. Why not have 'discount' or 'change in selling price' as drivers? Why not have 'change in purchasing price as a driver? etc.

Estimating depreciation and working capital items

In Table 7.1 depreciation is assumed to be higher than in 2001. As the company has made large capital expenditures in 2001, these expenditures should now be charged to sales (cost recovery). The ending (closing) balances of accounts receivable, inventories and accounts payable are estimated as follows:

● Accounts receivable end equal six months of average sales. This calculation implies that sales are equally spread over the year which is not necessarily true as December is often a very active month. Everybody wants to 'meet the budget'!
● Inventories end are equal to three months of cost of goods sold. It is worth noting that since cost of goods sold and sales are equivalent volume-wise, the quantity of goods stored in the ending inventory corresponds to the quantity needed for selling over three months. The problem, though, is that the goods in inventory end will be sold in the subsequent year (2003) only. Consequently, it would be better to estimate inventory end as a function of next year's sales/cost of goods sold. One major difference among the main components of working capital needs is that **accounts receivable and payable are past-related, and inventory is future-related.**
● Accounts payable end equal three months of average purchases. The use of average purchases implicitly assumes that the company is going to rebuild its inventory progressively over the year.

7.2 Checking the initial results and designing a game plan to use the model effectively

Net income is higher than in 2001: this is consistent with the assumption made for the margin (20% vs. 17% in 2001). Free cash flow is negative. This is not due to the impact of accounts receivable which do not change very much (similar level of activity and similar collection period). It is due to the large increase in inventories (Delta Metal has decided to rebuild its inventory) and to the large decrease in accounts payable (Delta Metal needs to bring its payment period to a more realistic level). Rebuilding stocks and paying suppliers faster are largely the consequence of what was done in 2001. In 2001, Delta Metal has

Table 7.2 • Preparing a game plan

Decision variable	Environment variables		Outcomes variables	
Delta Metal implements the new credit plan	and the EU implements the new regulations	and the market grows by	Income	Cash
1. NO	NO	0%	6.57	−7.29
2. NO	NO	10%	?	?
3. NO	YES	0%	?	?
4. NO	YES	10%	?	?
5. YES	NO	0%	?	?
6. YES	NO	10%	?	?
7. YES	YES	0%	?	?
8. YES	NO	10%	?	?

managed to pull a lot of cash from both the past and the future! The current scenario describes the situation in which: (1) Delta Metal decides not to go for the new credit plan, (2) the market remains sluggish and (3) the EU authorities do not implement any new regulations. This is obviously just one among the many possible scenarios suggested by the case study and which are described in Table 7.2.

7.3 Estimating the drivers: the challenge of modelling the impact of price changes

Table 7.2 shows all the parameters that you need to estimate: it is the game plan of the simulation. Table 7.3 shows the value of all the parameters. Several of these scenarios involve price changes: the new credit plan involves a reduction in the selling price and the new EU regulations involve a reduction in the purchasing price. The problem with, per-cent-of-sales, vertical models is that since none of their drivers explicitly relates to price changes, modelling a change in selling prices obliges you to modify several drivers and, as we are going to see, these modifications are not always easy to make which means that it is very easy to make mistakes. This is one of the reasons why we recommend you not to use the per-cent-of-sales vertical approach in spite of its popularity.

Modelling the impact of selling price changes

Table 7.4 shows the striking feature of changes in selling prices. **They impact two items only in the income statement: sales and income.** The price discount envisaged by Delta Metal results in 4.8 million less sales and in exactly the same 4.8 million less income! Changes in selling prices have a tremendous impact on income. They make income change by an absolute amount that equals the discount itself. At Delta Metal, a 4% decrease in price makes the operating income decrease by 73%! Another interesting characteristic of changes in selling prices is that they impact a whole series of ratios:

Table 7.3 ● Estimating the value of the parameters in 2002

(A)	(B)	(C)	Change in sales 2002 vs. 2001	GCS/sales	Operating expenses/ sales	Collection period	Inventory turnover	Payment period
NO	NO	0.00	0.04	0.80	0.14	6	4	4
NO	NO	0.10	1.04*1.1−1	0.80	0.14	6	4	4
NO	YES	0.00	0.04	a	0.14	6	e	4
NO	YES	0.10	1.04*1.1−1	b	0.14	6	f	4
YES	NO	0.00	1.04*0.96−1	0.80/0.96	0.14/0.96	4	4	4
YES	NO	0.10	1.04*1.1*0.96−1	0.80/0.96	0.14/0.96	4	4	4
YES	YES	0.00	1.04*0.96−1	c	0.14/0.96	4	e	4
YES	YES	0.10	1.04*1.1*0.96−1	d	0.14/0.96	4	f	4

(A) Delta Metal implements the new credit plan (yes or no)
(B) The EU implements the new regulations (yes or no)
(C) The market grows by 0 or 10% – volume growth
[a] $0.74 + 0.06 \times 17.37 / 95.63$
[b] $0.74 + 0.06 \times 17.37 / 105.19$
[c] $(0.74 + 0.06 \times 17.37 / 95.63) / 0.96$
[d] $(0.74 + 0.06 \times 17.37 / 105.19) / 0.96$
[e] $3 \times (0.74 + 0.06 \times 17.37 / 95.63) / 0.74$
[f] $3 \times (0.74 + 0.06 \times 17.37 / 105.19) / 0.74$
Note:
When the inventory is assessed on the future rather than on the current CGS, as in Table 7.8, then there is no need to adjust the inventory turnover.

Table 7.4 ● Impact of the 4% discount at Delta Metal

	Before discount	After discount	Difference
Sales	119.53	114.75	−4.78
CGS	95.63	95.63	0
Operating expenses	16.73	16.73	0
Depreciation	0.60	0.60	0
Operating income	6.57	1.79	−4.78

It is assumed that the discount is offered starting 1 January and that the volume sold does not change.

● the growth in sales is changed;
● all the ratios that were expressed as a percentage of sales are also changed.

Growth in sales will result from two factors: the 4% growth in volume and the 4% price reduction. The relation – a multiplicative relation – between the 2001 and the 2002 sales is:

$$2002 \text{ sales} = 2001 \text{ sales} \times (1 + 0.04) \times (1 - 0.04)$$

which means that sales will grow by $(1 + 0.04) \times (1 - 0.04) - 1 = 0$.

The ratios or percentages expressing CGS, operating expenses, etc. in relation to sales will all be modified. When price decreases, sales change but CGS, operating expenses, etc. remain the same and as a result increase as a proportion of sales. As a result of the 4% discount, the various ratios become:

CGS/sales = 95.63/114.75 = 0.80/0.96 = 0.83

Operating expenses/sales = 16.73/114.75 = 0.14/0.96 = 0.15

Modelling the impact of purchase prices changes and recognizing the delaying effect of inventory

The subsidies attached to the new EU regulations would bring the price of steel from 80% to 74% of the selling price which means that the price of steel would decrease by 7.5%. In order to assess the impact of this price reduction on CGS, you need to take the opening inventory into account. The opening inventory is made up of goods purchased in 2001 before the occurrence of the subsidies. As the cost of these goods will have to be recovered in 2002, CGS/sales will be a bit higher than 74% in 2002. One way to calculate the CGS/sales ratio in 2002 is to adjust the base scenario:

Base scenario
CGS: 95.63 (80% of sales)
Inventory open: 17.37 (we assume that goods are valued at 80% of sales)
CGS is made up of 17.37 (inventory open) and of 78.26 (purchases of the year)

New regulations
With the new purchasing price, CGS becomes:
17.37 (no change) + 78.26 × 0.74/0.80 (new purchasing price) = 17.37 + 72.39 = 89.76
and the CGS/sales ratio becomes:
0.8 × (17.37/95.63) + 0.74 × (72.39/95.63) = 0.750614
or as indicated in Table 7.3 0.74 + (0.80 − 0.74) × 17.37/95.63 = 0.74 + 0.01614

The adjustment for opening inventory has to be made in 2002 only. Once the cost of the goods bought at the old price has been recovered, CGS is equal to purchasing price (provided that prices remain stable). A further adjustment has to be made in the model in 2002. It is reasonable to assume that that the goods in the inventory at the end of 2002 should be valued at the new purchasing price: 0.74. The problem, though, is that the model estimates inventory end in relation to CGS in 2002, that is 0.75 of sales: this results in an overestimation of the closing inventory. In order to remove this bias, you can correct the inventory turnover and make it equal to 3 × (0.74/0.75). This adjustment is to be done in 2002 only (provided again that prices remain stable). As indicated in Table 7.3, you do not need to make this adjustment when you estimate inventory in relation to future sales and cost of goods sold.

7.4 Analyzing the results

The outcomes of the scenarios are in Tables 7.5 and 7.6.

Table 7.5 ● Key results of the initial one-year model

Decision variable	Environment variables		Outcomes variables	
Delta Metal implements the new credit plan	and the EU implements the new regulations	and the market grows by	Income	Cash
1. NO	NO	0%	6.57	−7.29
2. NO	NO	10%	7.29	−10.95
3. NO	YES	0%	12.44	−7.09
4. NO	YES	10%	13.88	−10.65
5. YES	NO	0%	1.79	9.45
6. YES	NO	10%	2.03	7.46
7. YES	YES	0%	7.66	9.64
8. YES	NO	10%	8.62	7.76

Table 7.6 ● Detailed results of the initial one-year model

	Scenario							
	1	2	3	4	5	6	7	8
Growth	4%	14%	4%	14%	0%	10%	0%	10%
Sales	119.53	131.48	119.53	131.48	114.75	126.23	114.75	126.23
CGS/sales	80.0%	80.0%	75.1%	75.0%	83.3%	83.3%	78.2%	78.1%
CGS	95.63	105.19	89.76	98.60	95.63	105.19	89.76	98.60
Operating expenses/sales	14.0%	14.0%	14.0%	14.0%	14.6%	14.6%	14.6%	14.6%
Operating expenses	16.73	18.41	16.73	18.41	16.73	18.41	16.73	18.41
Depreciation	0.60	0.60	0.60	0.60	0.60	0.60	0.60	0.60
Operating income	6.57	7.29	12.44	13.88	1.79	2.03	7.66	8.62
Operating profit/sales	5.5%	5.5%	10.4%	10.6%	1.6%	1.6%	6.7%	6.8%
Corporation tax	0.00	0.00	0.00	0.00	0.00	0.00	0.00	0.00
Operating income after tax	**6.57**	**7.29**	**12.44**	**13.88**	**1.79**	**2.03**	**7.66**	**8.62**
Receivables open	58.43	58.43	58.43	58.43	58.43	58.43	58.43	58.43
Collection period	6.00	6.00	6.00	6.00	4.00	4.00	4.00	4.00
Receivables end	59.77	65.74	59.77	65.74	38.25	42.08	38.25	42.08
Inventory open	17.37	17.37	17.37	17.37	17.37	17.37	17.37	17.37
Inventory turnover	4.00	4.00	3.04	3.04	4.00	4.00	3.04	3.04
Inventory end	23.91	26.30	29.48	32.43	23.91	26.30	29.48	32.43
Payables open	40.13	40.13	40.13	40.13	40.13	40.13	40.13	40.13
Payment period	4.00	4.00	4.00	4.00	4.00	4.00	4.00	4.00
Payables end	34.05	38.04	33.96	37.89	34.05	38.04	33.96	37.89
Cash from operations	−6.79	−10.45	−6.59	−10.15	9.95	7.96	10.14	8.26
Capital expenditure	0.50	0.50	0.50	0.50	0.50	0.50	0.50	0.50
Free cash flow	**−7.29**	**−10.95**	**−7.09**	**−10.65**	**9.45**	**7.46**	**9.64**	**7.76**

Should Delta Metal implement the new credit plan?

The results in Tables 7.5 and 7.6 show that the credit plan would very significantly improve the free cash flow situation: the cash flows of scenarios 4–8 are 17 to 18 million higher than the cash flows of scenarios 1–4! When seeing these results, participants of executive programmes generally split into two groups:

- Some people strongly argue that since 'cash is king' the new credit plan should be implemented right away!
- Other people argue even more strongly that the results shown in Tables 7.5 and 7.6 are an illusion. How could a price reduction generate more cash? The evidence is that a price cut can only result in less cash.

I fully agree with the second opinion. The new credit plan obviously results in less cash and what we observe in Tables 7.5 and 7.6 is nothing like 'more' cash but rather something like 'less and earlier' cash. Table 7.7 and Figure 7.1 show what really happens with the new credit plan. They show that the new credit plan reduces the cash received and at the same time turns 2002 into a 14-month year. Do not expect that to be sustainable!

There are other ways to think about the new credit plan and to reject it:

- You can think in terms of the income–cash parity matrix (Figure 6.1). The new credit plan moves Delta Metal into cell 4, a fundamentally unstable situation. The increase in free cash flow comes from the one-off reduction of the working capital needs. Working capital needs decrease by some 20 million once in 2002 (two months of sales) at the price of a discount of a bit more than 4 million that is going to be given each year

Table 7.7 • Understanding the impact of the new credit plan

	No new credit plan		New credit plan	
	Receipts from opening receivables	Receipts from current sales	Receipts from opening receivables	Receipts from current sales
January	10		10	
February	10		10	
March	10		10	
April	10		10	
May	10		10	9.6
June	10		10	9.6
July		10		9.6
August		10		9.6
September		10		9.6
October		10		9.6
November		10		9.6
December		10		9.6

In 2002, sales are about 10 million per month. Sales made in January 2002 will be paid in July without the plan and in May with the plan (in the plan 9.6 only will be paid). Whatever is done with the new credit plan, accounts receivable will generate cash receipts in the first six months of 2002. These receipts are approximated here as 10 million per month.

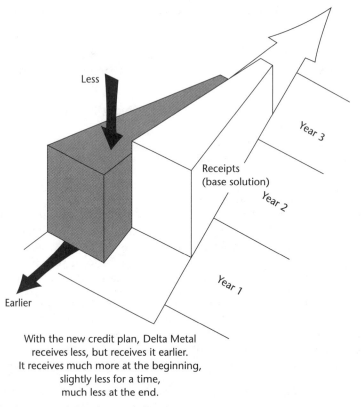

Less

Receipts
(base solution)

Year 3

Year 2

Year 1

Earlier

With the new credit plan, Delta Metal
receives less, but receives it earlier.
It receives much more at the beginning,
slightly less for a time,
much less at the end.

Figure 7.1 The impact of the new credit plan

starting in 2002. In 2002, the net impact is positive (16 million); then it is negative (–4 million) in each of the subsequent years.

● The impact of the new credit plan is only to accelerate the cash receipts. And this acceleration is very expensive: a 4% discount for two months corresponds to 2% per month and more than 24% per year (if you compound the effect).

In spite of all these arguments, it happens in some executive programmes that a few participants are still not totally convinced by the arguments above. The solution is to invite these participants to extend the model along two dimensions:

● Adding a few more years helps demonstrate that if it looks good in the short run, the new credit plan is really bad in the long run. You can also introduce an NPV calculation and show that the credit plan destroys value.

● Adding balance sheets and introducing an interest calculation can help reinforce the idea that the new credit plan is a very costly business proposition.

7.5 Extending the model to a few more years

Extending a model to a few more years involves a bit more than just using the Copy command of your spreadsheet. In most models all the years do not look exactly the same and typically the first and the last years are a bit different from all the other years. For example, in the Delta Metal model, receivable open, inventory open and payables open are fixed quantities in 2002. After 2002 they should be made equal to the value of the corresponding ending accounts in the preceding year.

When extending a model, you have to make a choice as you can:

● Start with copying the whole first year at once and then go through the different rows and correct what needs to be corrected. This is not recommended!
● Copy row by row. This enables you to think and to sort out what can be copied as it is and what should be modified first.
● **Build the second year, check it works and then reward yourself with copying this second year into as many years as you need.** This is my preferred way! Table 7.8 shows the background of column C for Delta Metal. This can be copied into as many years as you need.

The model is shown in Tables 7.8 and 7.9. As you will realize,

● The calculation of the ending inventory has been modified. It is a function of future sales.[4]
● A corporate tax calculation that takes the losses carried forward into account has been introduced.
● All the parameters are now anchored on their value in 2002. This will enable us to test the impact of simple changes in each parameter (more growth for ever, better cost structure for ever, etc.). Starting with simple changes is a very effective way to attack what-if analyses.

7.6 Finalizing the model with an estimate of the shareholder value created

When building financial models we should never forget that their main purpose is to help us create maximum shareholder value. It is now time to introduce an NPV calculation into the model. As with the Jilin project, the relevant variable for estimating the impact of our decisions on shareholder value is the net cash flow which we now call free cash flow.[5]

Checking the cash–income parity relation and adjusting free cash flow

Let us assume that we construct a five-year model.[6] Before estimating the NPV we need to make sure that the cash–income parity relationship is respected. If you cumulate net operating income and free cash flows in column H, then you realize that they are not equal! This is due to three problems:

● A problem at the beginning of the period. Part of the cash flow in 2002 does not correspond to the activity in the 2002–06 period. Receivables, inventories and payables open correspond to activities that took place earlier. They should be deducted from the 2002 cash flow.
● A problem at the end of the period. At the end of 2006, you have not yet recovered the receivables as of the end of 2006 and not yet paid the payables as of the end of 2006. Receivables and payables correspond to money delayed, not to money lost! A solution is

Table 7.8 • Extending the model to a few more years

	A	B	C
1	Year	2002	= B1+1
2	Growth	= 0.04	= B2
3	Sales	= 114.934*(1+B2)	= B3*(1+C2)
4	CGS/sales	= 0.8	= B4
5	CGS	= B3*B4	
6	Operating expenses/sales	= 0.14	= B6
7	Operating expenses	= B3*B6	•
8	Depreciation	= 0.6	= B8
9	Operating income before tax	= B3–B5–B7–B8	•
10	Taxable income	= B9–4.588	a
11	Income after tax	b	•
12	Depreciation	= B8	•
13	Receivables open	= 58.424	= B15
14	Collection period	= 6	= B14
15	Receivables end	= B3/12*B13	•
16	Inventory open	= 17.367	= B18
17	Inventory turnover	= 4	= B17
18	Inventory end	= C5/B16	•
19	Payables open	= 40.132	= B21
20	Payment period	= 4	= B20
21	Payables end	= (B5+B17–B15)/12*B19	•
22	Cash from operations	= B10+B11+B12–B14+B15–B17+B18+B20	•
23	Capital expenditure	= 0.5	= B23
24	Free cash flow	= B21–B22	•

a = C9+IF(B10<0,B10,0); copy.
b = IF(B9<0,B9,IF(B10<B9,IF(B10>0,B9–B10*0.33,B9),B9*0.67)); copy.
• = copy the formula.
Note:
When you estimate the inventory as a function of future sales, then you make a decision regarding the value you want to have for inventory at the end of the last year of your model:

- If you do nothing, the model will automatically set the value of this inventory to zero and a very large cash flow will be released. Some people like this approach which helps them visualize how much money is frozen in inventories.
- If you want to have a more 'normal' level of inventory in the last year, then you have to calculate sales and cost of goods sold for one additional year.

to introduce an additional cash flow in 2007 that is equal to the difference between the ending (closing) receivables and payables.
- More depreciation than capital expenditure. The additional cash flow in 2007 (column G) has been adjusted in order to remove the impact of that imbalance.

Introducing the NPV calculation

Once the cash–income parity relation is respected you can introduce the NPV calculation shown in Table 7.10. As discussed in the General Appendix, we should use a rate that reflects the risk of the business and that is necessarily higher than the cost of a loan. Let us

Table 7.9 ● Foreground of the extended model

1		2002	2003	2004	2005	2006
2	*Growth*	*4%*	*0%*	*0%*	*0%*	*0%*
3	Sales	119.53	119.53	119.53	119.53	119.53
4	*CGS/sales*	*80.0%*	*80.0%*	*80.0%*	*80.0%*	*80.0%*
5	CGS	95.63	95.63	95.63	95.63	95.63
6	*Operating expenses/sales*	*14.0%*	*14.0%*	*14.0%*	*14.0%*	*14.0%*
7	Operating expenses	16.73	16.73	16.73	16.73	16.73
8	Depreciation	0.60	0.60	0.60	0.60	0.60
9	Operating income	6.57	6.57	6.57	6.57	6.57
10	Taxable income	1.98	6.57	6.57	6.57	6.57
11	**Operating income after tax**	**5.92**	**4.40**	**4.40**	**4.40**	**4.40**
12	Depreciation	0.60	0.60	0.60	0.60	0.60
13	*A/R open*	58.42	59.77	59.77	59.77	59.77
14	*Collection period*	*6.00*	*6.00*	*6.00*	*6.00*	*6.00*
15	A/R end	59.77	59.77	59.77	59.77	59.77
16	Inventory open	17.37	23.91	23.91	23.91	23.91
17	*Inventory turnover*	*4.00*	*4.00*	*4.00*	*4.00*	*4.00*
18	Inventory end	23.91	23.91	23.91	23.91	0.00
19	*A/P open*	40.13	34.05	31.88	31.88	31.88
20	*Payment period*	*4.00*	*4.00*	*4.00*	*4.00*	*4.00*
21	A/P end	34.05	31.88	31.88	31.88	23.91
22	Cash from operations	−7.44	2.82	5.00	5.00	20.94
23	*Capital expenditure*	*0.50*	*0.50*	*0.50*	*0.50*	*0.50*
24	**Free cash flow**	**−7.94**	**2.32**	**4.50**	**4.50**	**20.44**

Note:
Except for sales growth, it is assumed that all drivers remain the same over the planning period. This is a reasonable way to start and understand where the current conditions may lead the company to in the long run. As the 4% sales growth corresponds to an exceptional price recovery, it is assumed to happen once only. From 2003 onwards growth is assumed to be zero (no volume growth).

assume that the rate to be used is 14% for after-tax cash flows and 21% for before-tax cash flows.

Working capital needs – a time bomb!

In Table 7.10 the adjusted cash flows – or '2002–06 cash flows' – show a very large cash deficit in the first year, low cash flows during the whole period and very big cash excesses at the end. The very big negative and positive cash flows at the two ends of the period are visible only because we have artificially isolated the 2002–06 period. In normal life operations work as a continuous process and these large negative and positive cash flows continuously offset each other and are never visible. **In a low margin, relatively stable business with high working capital needs the continuity of the operations completely hides the working capital needs problem.** However, the potential impact of these needs is very large. It is a sort of time bomb that is going to destabilize the trajectory of the cash flows as soon as the level of activity starts to fluctuate.

Table 7.10 ● Introducing an NPV calculation

A		B 2002	C 2003	D 2004	E 2005	F 2006	G 2007	H Cum.
8	Depreciation							a
11	Operating income after tax							b
23	Capital expenditure							c
24	Free cash flow							
25	Free cash flow 2002–06	d	=C24	●	●	●	e	f
26	Discount rate	0.14						
27	NPV	g						
	Outcomes (base case):							
	Free cash flow 2002–06	*−43.60*	*2.32*	*4.50*	*4.50*	*20.44*	*35.36*	*23.53*
	NPV	*−4.03*						

[a] =SUM(B8.F8)
[b] =SUM(B11.F11). The result is 23.53
[c] =SUM(B23.F23)
[d] =B24−B13−B16+B19
[e] =F15−F21−H8+H23
[f] =SUM(B25.G25)
[g] =NPV(B26, B25.G25)

Table 7.11 ● Estimating the value of the drivers from 2003 onwards

(A)	(B)	(C)	Change in sales	CGS/sales	Operating expenses/sale	Collection period	Inventory turnover	Payment period
NO	NO	0.00	0.00	0.80	0.14	6	4	4
NO	NO	0.10	0.10	0.80	0.14	6	4	4
NO	YES	0.00	0.00	0.74	0.14	6	3	4
NO	YES	0.10	0.10	0.74	0.14	6	3	4
YES	NO	0.00	0.00[a]	0.80/0.96[a]	0.14/0.96[a]	4	4	4
YES	NO	0.10	0.10	0.80/0.96	0.14/0.96	4	4	4
YES	YES	0.00	0.00	0.74/0.96	0.14/0.96	4	3	4
YES	YES	0.10	0.10	0.74/0.96	0.14/0.96	4	3	4

(A) Delta Metal implements the new credit plan (yes or no)
(B) The EU implements the new regulations (yes or no)
(C) The market grows by 0 or 10% – volume growth
[a] The decrease in price destroys the margin for ever (for as long as the price stays at the new level) but the impact of the price decrease on sales growth is a one-off effect only. Once the price has been decreased, sales continue to grow with volume!

Estimating the value of the drivers from 2003 onwards

From 2003 onwards, the value of the drivers is the same in each year. The value of the drivers for the different scenarios is shown in Table 7.11. Once again, the difficulty is to model the impact of the change in selling price caused by the new credit plan. Chapter 10

Table 7.12 ● Operating income, free cash flows and NPVs for the eight scenarios

	2002	2003	2004	2005	2006	2007	Cum.
1. Base, no new credit plan, 0% growth, no new EU regulations							
Operating income after tax	5.92	4.40	4.40	4.40	4.40		23.53
Free cash flow	−7.94	2.32	4.50	4.50	20.44		
2002–06 Free cash flow	−43.60	2.32	4.50	4.50	20.44	35.36	23.53
NPV$_{end\ 2001\ @\ 14\%}$	**−4.03**						
2. No new credit plan, 10% growth, no new EU regulations							
Operating income after tax	6.40	5.41	5.99	6.63	7.34		31.77
Free cash flow	−13.60	−3.34	−0.37	−0.37	27.85		
2002–06 Free cash flow	−49.26	−3.34	−0.37	−0.37	27.85	57.25	31.77
NPV$_{end\ 2001\ @\ 14\%}$	**−5.69**						
3. No new credit plan, 0% growth, new EU regulations							
Operating income after tax	9.85	9.21	9.21	9.21	9.21		46.68
Free cash flow	−9.68	4.83	9.31	9.31	28.96		
2002–06 Free cash flow	−45.34	4.83	9.31	9.31	28.96	39.61	46.68
NPV$_{end\ 2001\ @\ 14\%}$	**8.83**						
4. No new credit plan, 10% growth, new EU regulations							
Operating income after tax	10.81	11.23	12.39	13.67	15.08		63.17
Free cash flow	−15.88	−0.92	5.02	5.55	40.96		
2002–06 Free cash flow	−51.54	−0.92	5.02	5.55	40.96	64.10	63.17
NPV$_{end\ 2001\ @\ 14\%}$	**11.23**						
5. New credit plan, 0% growth, no new EU regulations							
Operating income after tax	1.79	1.79	1.52	1.16	1.16		7.43
Free cash flow	9.45	−0.29	1.62	1.26	17.20		
2002–06 Free cash flow	−26.21	−0.29	1.62	1.26	17.20	13.84	7.43
NPV$_{end\ 2001\ @\ 14\%}$	**−6.13**						
6. New credit plan, 10% growth, no new EU regulations							
Operating income after tax	2.03	2.29	1.82	1.94	2.18		10.26
Free cash flow	5.70	−4.09	−1.94	−2.20	25.85		
2002–06 Free cash flow	−29.96	−4.09	−1.94	−2.20	25.85	22.60	10.26
NPV$_{end\ 2001\ @\ 14\%}$	**−8.32**						
7. New credit plan, 0% growth, new EU regulations							
Operating income after tax	6.65	6.00	6.00	6.00	6.00		30.67
Free cash flow	8.63	1.63	6.10	6.10	25.76		
2002–06 Free cash flow	−27.03	1.63	6.10	6.10	25.76	18.09	30.67
NPV$_{end\ 2001\ @\ 14\%}$	**6.90**						
8. New credit plan, 10% growth, new EU regulations							
Operating income after tax	7.29	7.35	8.13	8.98	9.92		41.66
Free cash flow	4.26	−2.43	3.36	3.73	38.95		
2002–06 Free cash flow	−31.39	−2.43	3.36	3.73	38.95	29.45	
NPV$_{end\ 2001\ @\ 14\%}$	**8.71**						41.66

Note:
The values of the drivers are in Tables 7.3 and 7.11. For scenarios 3, 4, 7 and 8, please remember that inventory end is estimated from future sales: you do not have to adjust inventory turnover in 2002.

describes a better way to model the income statement that makes it much easier to test the impact of changes in selling prices.

7.7 Reviewing the results

The results of the new model are given in Table 7.12. They confirm that the new credit plan destroys shareholder value and should be rejected.

Notes

1. The problem is that, in business, accounting data are often the few data that we have and that look good for serving as a basis for forecasting. As indicated in N. Resher (1999), *Predicting the Future – An Introduction to the Theory of Forecasting*, State University of New York Press, any sort of rational prediction is based on some kind of pattern fitting, and any forecasting activity requires that:

   ● we can obtain relevant information about the past and present in an adequately timely, accurate and reliable way;
   ● this body of data exhibits discernible patterns;
   ● the patterns so exhibited are stable, so that this structural feature manifests a consistency that also continues into the future.

   Accounting data typically look like satisfying these three conditions!
2. The per-cent-of-sales approach was being used long before PCs and spreadsheets were available. One actually hardly needs a spreadsheet to use the per-cent-of-sales approach!
3. With the exception of sales which are linked to previous year's sales through a horizontal relation that goes across two time periods.
4. With this change the model is no longer strictly vertical and fully driven by current sales.
5. With the indirect presentation of the cash flows you have to estimate the NPV as the NPV of the net cash flows (free cash flows). In order to estimate the NPV as the net sum of the present values of the different receipts and payments, you need to use the direct presentation of the cash flows.
6. The period of study should be the same as the life span of the decision that we are analyzing. How long will the impact of the new credit plan be? The discount given by Delta Metal may depress the level of its selling price for ever! If this is true, a calculation over a period of five years would probably underestimate the impact on shareholder value.

CHAPTER *8*

Building and using a comprehensive income, cash flow and balance sheets model

8.1 A comprehensive financial model: capital employed, calculated income, OVA/EVA® and ROCE

The second extension of the Delta Metal model is the building of a comprehensive income, cash flow and balance sheets model. This will enable us to estimate the accounting return of the various scenarios and to check once more that the new credit plan destroys value. Let us say, however, that in many situations you will not need to build comprehensive models ending with balance sheets. The model in Tables 7.9 and 7.10 with the NPV of the free cash flows as the outcome variable is the typical model you need for selecting among business alternatives. This means that in most cases your modelling work can and should stop at that stage!

The background and foreground of the comprehensive model are shown in Tables 8.1 and 8.2.

From the free cash flow to the construction of the balance sheets

Even though free cash flow is probably the most important variable of the cash flow statement,[1] it is generally not a good idea to leave the cash flow statement before answering two questions:

- What dividends are we going to pay to our shareholders?
- How are we going to invest the cash excesses or finance the cash deficits in order to make 'change in cash' equal to zero? 'Change in cash', the bottom line of the cash flow

141

Table 8.1 ● A comprehensive income, cash flow and balance sheets model (foreground)

Year	2002	2003	2004	2005	2006
Growth	*4%*	*0%*	*0%*	*0%*	*0%*
Sales	119.53	119.53	119.53	119.53	119.53
CGS/sales	*80.0%*	*80.0%*	*80.0%*	*80.0%*	*80.0%*
CGS	95.63	95.63	95.63	95.63	95.63
Operating expenses/sales	*14.0%*	*14.0%*	*14.0%*	*14.0%*	*14.0%*
Operating expenses	16.73	16.73	16.73	16.73	16.73
Depreciation	0.60	0.60	0.60	0.60	0.60
Operating income	6.57	6.57	6.57	6.57	6.57
Taxable income	1.98	6.57	6.57	6.57	6.57
Income after tax	**5.92**	**4.40**	**4.40**	**4.40**	**4.40**
Depreciation	0.60	0.60	0.60	0.60	0.60
Receivables open	58.43	59.77	59.77	59.77	59.77
Collection period	*6.00*	*6.00*	*6.00*	*6.00*	*6.00*
Receivables end	59.77	59.77	59.77	59.77	59.77
Inventory open	17.37	23.91	23.91	23.91	23.91
Inventory turnover	*4.00*	*4.00*	*4.00*	*4.00*	*4.00*
Inventory end	23.91	23.91	23.91	23.91	0.00
Payables open	40.13	34.05	31.88	31.88	31.88
Payment period	*4.00*	*4.00*	*4.00*	*4.00*	*4.00*
Payables end	34.05	31.88	31.88	31.88	23.91
Cash from operations	−7.44	2.82	5.00	5.00	20.94
Capital expenditure	*0.50*	*0.50*	*0.50*	*0.50*	*0.50*
Free cash flow	**−7.94**	**2.32**	**4.50**	**4.50**	**20.44**
Repayment of long-term loans	2.53	2.53	1.86	0.00	0.00
Dividend	0	0	0	0	0
New equity	0	0	0	0	0
New short-term loans	10.47	0.21	−2.64	−4.50	−20.44
Change in cash	0	0	0	0	0
Cash	1.28	1.28	1.28	1.28	1.28
Receivables	59.77	59.77	59.77	59.77	59.77
Inventory	23.91	23.91	23.91	23.91	0.00
Net fixed assets	4.10	4.00	3.90	3.80	3.70
Total assets	89.05	88.95	88.85	88.75	64.75
Short-term loans	34.54	34.75	32.11	27.61	7.17
Payables	34.05	31.88	31.88	31.88	23.91
Long-term loans	4.39	1.86	0.00	0.00	0.00
Shareholders' equity	16.07	20.47	24.87	29.27	33.68
Total liabilities and equities	89.05	88.95	88.85	88.75	64.75
Capital employed at year end	55.00	57.08	56.98	56.88	40.84
Capital employed average	48.07	56.04	57.03	56.93	48.86
Calculated income/OVA/EVA®	**−3.52**	**−5.20**	**−5.40**	**−5.38**	**−3.69**
ROS	5.5%	5.5%	5.5%	5.5%	5.5%
Capital turnover	2.49	2.13	2.10	2.10	2.45
ROCE	**13.7%**	**11.7%**	**11.5%**	**11.5%**	**13.5%**

Table 8.2 ● A comprehensive income, cash flow and balance sheets model (background)

A	B	C
24 Free cash flow	= B22–B23	●
25 Repayment long-term loans	= 2.534	= B25
26 Dividend	= 0	= 0
27 New equity	= 0	= 0
28 New short-term loans	= –B24+B25+B26–B27+B29	
29 Change in cash	= 0	= B29
30		
31 Cash	= 1.277+B29	= B31+C29
32 Receivables	= B15	●
33 Inventory	= B18	●
34 Net fixed assets	= 4.204+B23–B8	= B34+C23–C8
35 Total assets	= SUM(B31:B34)	●
36		
37 Short-term loans	= 24.068+B28	= B37+C28
38 Payables	= B21	●
39 Long-term loans	= 4.39+2.534–B25	= B39–C25
40 Shareholders' equity	= 10.148+B11–B26	= B40+C11–C26
41 Total liabilities and equities	= SUM(B37:B40)	●
42		
43 Capital employed at year end	= B35–B38	●
44 Capital employed, average	= (B35–B38+81.27–40.13)/2	= (B43+C43)/2
45 Calculated income/OVA/EVA®	= B9–0.21*B44	●
46 ROS	= B9/B3	●
47 Capital turnover	= B3/B44	●
48 ROCE	= B46*B47	●

Note:
Free cash flow is estimated in Table 7.9.
The balance sheet is presented as in the case study (Table H.4). In order to simplify the calculation of long-term loans, we have aggregated long-term loans and long-term loans current.
Copying a repayment of loans of 2.534 quickly makes the long-term loan balance become negative (see Table 8.1). You need to correct repayments of loans and make them equal to 1.86 in 2004 and 0 afterwards.

statement is a balancing item only. This change in cash relates to change in the idle cash balance which should always be zero whatever the free cash flow and the dividends are.

Change in cash in row 29 is a target: zero.[2] As a result new short-term loans are used to offset any imbalance between this target and the actual cash generation. When the cash generation – after dividends and repayment of long-term loans – is negative then the model automatically raises new short-term loans, When it is positive, then the model automatically repays the short-term loans. When borrowing more the model does not check that this is possible. You have to do it yourself.

The 'interest problem'

We have already met this problem in Chapter 4 (Section 4.6):

● Accounting considers interest only when it corresponds to interest paid on loans. For accounting, equity financing, the most expensive source of financing,[3] comes for free!
● As a result, one can never be sure that a company that generates a positive income after interest really makes a 'profit'. In order for a company to make a profit it should generate a positive income after the costs of all the sources of financing (debt *and* equity) have been taken into account.

Alternative solutions to this problem are:

● to estimate a variable like calculated income or OVA or EVA®;
● to estimate return on capital employed (ROCE) and to compare it to a target return.

Both solutions require that you estimate capital employed which corresponds to the money needed for running the business.

Capital employed

The equality of total assets and total liabilities and equities provides you with two ways for estimating capital employed:

● either as the difference between total assets[4] and accounts payable – and all other operational or 'non-interest-bearing liabilities'. The money invested by a business into its operations is reported in the assets accounts. However, when you consider the credits to customers as an asset, you also have to consider that at the same time you get credit from the suppliers. This is the rationale for deducting the payables and all other operational liabilities that originate from the operations rather than from a financial institution.[5]
● or as the sum of the equity and of all the loans and other interest-bearing liabilities.

The first equation (assets – non-interest-bearing liabilities) reflects the money that is needed to run the business; the second equation (loan plus equity) reflects how the money is provided (shareholders vs. loans).

Alternative expressions for the term 'capital employed' are **net assets** and **operating capital**.

Return on capital employed (ROCE)

ROCE is a metrics that has been popularized by some European-based multinationals. The formula for calculating it is:

ROCE = operating income/capital employed.[6]

ROCE is calculated in Tables 8.1 and 8.2. ROCE does not mean much before it is compared with a return target. Even though a 12% ROCE may look acceptable, this is not sufficient when it is compared with the required return (21%). ROCE is even lower than the cost of short-term loans (16%). Since Delta Metal uses a lot of loans, it is likely that the net income itself will turn negative as soon as we finalize the model and introduce a calculation of the interest on loans.

Rather than the expression ROCE, some companies use expressions like **RONA** (return on net assets) or **ROC** (return on capital), etc. All these expressions basically correspond to the same metrics. Return on assets (**ROA**) or return on investment (**ROI**) are somewhat different metrics that compare operating income and total assets – non-interest liabilities are not deducted.[7]

Calculated income/OVA/EVA®

Calculated income/OVA/EVA® are estimated as the result of the difference between operating income and a 'calculated interest'. Calculated interest is estimated as the product of capital employed times a notional interest rate – or required return – that reflects the cost of all sources of financing (debt and equity) and not only the cost of loans. As shown in the General Appendix, the notional interest rate typically depends on the risk of the business and is always higher than the cost of a loan. Calculated income/OVA/EVA® is in Tables 8.1 and 8.2. It gives the same signal as ROCE and confirms that the performance of Delta Metal is not satisfactory:

- calculated income is negative (once a 21% cost is charged on capital);
- ROCE is 12% only which is less than the cost of capital (21%).

Return on sales (ROS), capital turnover and ROCE

Tables 8.1 and 8.2 also show a useful way to break ROCE down into two components. return on sales and capital turnover.

$$\text{ROCE} = \frac{\text{Operating income}}{\text{Capital employed}} = \frac{\text{Operating income}}{\text{Sales}} \times \frac{\text{Sales}}{\text{Capital employed}}$$

$$= \text{Return on sales} \times \text{Capital turnover}$$

This analysis of ROCE shows once more that there are two complementary approaches for increasing return and value: you can increase the margins and/or improve the timing of the operations.[8] If you look at the data for the years 2004–05, you can say that the 12% ROCE of Delta Metal results from a 6% ROS and a capital turnover equal to 2. The fact that capital turnover is equal to 2 is interesting: since accounts receivable also have a turnover equal to 2, we can say that accounts payable offset all the other assets, or that the only assets that count are accounts receivable. This gives us a new opportunity to understand what happens with the new credit plan:

- ROS decreases from 6% to 2% – this is a 'rough cut' estimate;
- capital turnover increases from 2 to 3 (collection period decreases to four months);

which results in a ROCE of 6% – we have to check that with the model – which is further away from the target of 21%.

Using this approach you can immediately realize that a credit plan that would involve no discount would bring the ROS to 18% which is much closer to 21% but still not sufficient.

Starting from the model in Table 8.1, insert two blank rows above row 10. Use:

- new row 10 for introducing interest. In B10: = 0.16*(B39+B41); copy.
- new row 11 for income before tax. In B11: = B9–B10; copy.
- correct taxable income in row 12. B12: –4.588+B11, C12: +C11+IF(B12<0,B12,0); copy.
- correct income after tax. In B13: = IF(B11<0,B11,IF(B12<B11,IF(B12>0,B11–B12*0.33,B11), B11*0.67)); copy.

As you have introduced a circular feature, you need to change the default calculation of your spreadsheet. In Excel, this is done through the Tools/Options/Calculation menu. In the calculation sheet, click on the iteration box and select 5 for the number of iterations.

Warning: If you make a mistake and get an error statement ('VALUE', 'NAME', etc.) correcting your mistake will not be sufficient to get the model working again. You will actually have to (1) suppress the formula that creates the circular reference – net income here, (2) correct your mistake, and then (3) reinstall the formula that creates the circular reference.

You should also be careful each time you open a circular model. As the default settings of your spreadsheet most probably do not accept circular references, you have to change these default settings (Tools/Options/Calculation, etc.) before you can use your model.

Figure 8.1 Introducing interest on loans

8.2 Introducing an interest calculation in the model (interest on loans)

The last step in the construction of the model is to introduce a calculation of the interest paid on loans. Contrary to the notional interest introduced above, interest on loans is actually paid. Introducing an interest on loans will therefore change cash, change loans and also change interest. Introducing interest on loans is actually going to introduce a circular feature in the model. Circular features are of two kinds: some converge and some diverge! Diverging features are not nice as they make models explode. Fortunately, interest converges[9] and you can safely force Excel into accepting the circular feature. The process for introducing the interest calculation is described in Figure 8.1. The outcome of the model with interest on loans is shown in Table 8.3.

8.3 Generating a new set of results

The new results in Table 8.3 confirm that the new credit plan is definitely not a good idea. It brings ROCE further away from the 21% target and makes calculated income/OVA/EVA® even more negative. It is interesting to compare the results of the different scenarios in Table 8.4:

- Scenarios 1, 2 and 4 portray value destruction situations: calculated income is always negative, net income is always negative, equity declines continuously and loans increase continuously. All these scenarios are in cell 3 of the cash–income matrix (Figure 6.1) and scenario 2 shows that it does not help to grow a business that destroys value.
- Scenario 3 portrays a value creation situation: calculated income is positive, net income is positive, equity increases continuously and loans decrease continuously. Within this scenario, Delta Metal is finally in cell 1 of the cash–income matrix!

Table 8.3 ● Comprehensive vertical model with interest (base situation)

Year	2002	2003	2004	2005	2006
Growth	*4%*	*0%*	*0%*	*0%*	*0%*
Sales	119.53	119.53	119.53	119.53	119.53
CGS/sales	*80.0%*	*80.0%*	*80.0%*	*80.0%*	*80.0%*
CGS	95.63	95.63	95.63	95.63	95.63
Operating expenses/sales	*14.0%*	*14.0%*	*14.0%*	*14.0%*	*14.0%*
Operating expenses	16.73	16.73	16.73	16.73	16.73
Depreciation	0.60	0.60	0.60	0.60	0.60
Operating income	6.57	6.57	6.57	6.57	6.57
Interest	7.29	7.82	8.04	8.30	5.58
Income before tax	−0.72	−1.25	−1.47	−1.73	0.99
Taxable income	−5.31	−6.56	−8.03	−9.76	−8.77
Income after tax	**−0.72**	**−1.25**	**−1.47**	**−1.73**	**0.99**
Depreciation	0.60	0.60	0.60	0.60	0.60
Receivables open	58.43	59.77	59.77	59.77	59.77
Collection period	*6.00*	*6.00*	*6.00*	*6.00*	*6.00*
Receivables end	59.77	59.77	59.77	59.77	59.77
Inventory open	17.37	23.91	23.91	23.91	23.91
Inventory turnover	*4.00*	*4.00*	*4.00*	*4.00*	*4.00*
Inventory end	23.91	23.91	23.91	23.91	0.00
Payables open	40.13	34.05	31.88	31.88	31.88
Payment period	*4.00*	*4.00*	*4.00*	*4.00*	*4.00*
Payables end	34.05	31.88	31.88	31.88	23.91
Cash from operations	−14.08	−2.83	−0.87	−1.13	17.53
Capital expenditure	*0.50*	*0.50*	*0.50*	*0.50*	*0.50*
Free cash flow	**−14.58**	**−3.33**	**−1.37**	**−1.63**	**17.03**
Repayment of long-term loans	2.53	2.53	1.86	0.00	0.00
Dividend	0	0	0	0	0
New equity	0	0	0	0	0
New short-term loans	17.11	5.87	3.23	1.63	−17.03
Change in cash	0	0	0	0	0
Cash	1.28	1.28	1.28	1.28	1.28
Receivables	59.77	59.77	59.77	59.77	59.77
Inventory	23.91	23.91	23.91	23.91	0.00
Net fixed assets	4.10	4.00	3.90	3.80	3.70
Total assets	89.05	88.95	88.85	88.75	64.75
Short-term loans	41.18	47.04	50.28	51.91	34.88
Payables	34.05	31.88	31.88	31.88	23.91
Long-term loans	4.39	1.86	0.00	0.00	0.00
Shareholders' equity	9.43	8.18	6.71	4.97	5.96
Total liabilities and equities	89.05	88.95	88.85	88.75	64.75
Capital employed at year end	55.00	57.08	56.98	56.88	40.84
Capital employed average	48.07	56.04	57.03	56.93	48.86
Calculated income/OVA/EVA®	**−3.52**	**−5.20**	**−5.40**	**−5.38**	**−3.69**
ROS	5.5%	5.5%	5.5%	5.5%	5.5%
Capital turnover	2.49	2.13	2.10	2.10	2.45
ROCE	**13.7%**	**11.7%**	**11.5%**	**11.5%**	**13.5%**

Table 8.4 ● Results of the new model

Base (scenario 1)

Net income	−0.72	−1.25	−1.47	−1.73	0.99
Free cash flow	−14.58	−3.33	−1.37	−1.63	17.03
Loans (short- and long-term)	45.57	48.90	50.27	51.90	34.88
Shareholders' equity	9.43	8.18	6.71	4.97	5.96
ROCE	14%	12%	12%	12%	13%
Calculated income/OVA/EVA®	−3.52	−5.20	−5.40	−5.38	−3.69

No new credit plan, 10% growth, no new EU regulations (scenario 2)

Net income	−1.03	−1.96	−2.51	−3.19	1.37
Free cash flow	−21.03	−10.71	−8.87	−10.19	21.88
Loans (short- and long-term)	52.02	62.73	71.60	81.79	59.91
Shareholders' equity	9.11	7.16	4.65	1.46	2.83
ROCE	14%	12%	12%	12%	15%
Calculated income/OVA/EVA®	−3.45	−5.68	−6.40	−6.85	−4.38

New credit plan, 0% growth, no new EU regulations (scenario 4)

Net income	−2.31	−3.15	−3.73	−4.42	−2.21
Free cash flow	5.35	−5.23	−3.63	−4.32	13.83
Loans (short- and long-term)	25.65	30.88	34.51	38.83	25.00
Shareholders' equity	7.84	4.69	0.96	−3.47	−5.68
ROCE	5%	5%	5%	5%	7%
Calculated income/OVA/EVA®	−6.04	−5.46	−5.67	−5.65	−3.95

No new credit plan, 0% growth, new EU regulations (scenario 3)

Net income	4.97	4.32	4.85	5.44	8.47
Free cash flow	−14.57	−0.05	4.95	5.54	28.23
Loans (short- and long-term)	45.56	45.61	40.66	35.12	6.90
Shareholders' equity	15.11	19.43	24.28	29.72	38.19
Roce	24%	22%	21%	21%	25%
OVA	1.75	0.54	0.09	0.12	2.20

How can a business go so easily from deadly cell 3 to cell 1? The main difference between scenarios 1, 2 and 4 and scenario 3 is ROCE. In scenario 3 ROCE is higher than both financing cost hurdles. It is higher than the cost of loans (which makes income become positive) and higher than the cost of capital (which makes the business create value as is shown by the positive calculated income/OVA/EVA®).

A basic rule in business is that **ROCE should be higher than financing costs**. If it is not, business just goes down the drain! So when thinking about Delta Metal again, it should be clear that the first and only thing that management has to do is to bring ROCE above 21%. It is also interesting to look at the impact of growth: when the business grows, ROCE remains the same but value as shown by OVA/EVA® decreases. More about this in Chapter 12.

Notes

1. Except for NPV.
2. As of the end of 2001, Delta Metal has a large idle cash balance. Let us assume that a dealer like Delta Metal needs idle cash in order to be able to take advantage of the many unexpected opportunities that materialize on the steel market. If you find this cash balance excessive, then adjust the target for 'change in cash' in 2002. Setting it at −1.277 brings cash to zero.
3. See General Appendix at the end of the book.
4. One issue is how to deal with cash and short-term financial investments and to make sure that the definitions of income and of capital employed are consistent.

   ● When income includes interest gains on cash and short-term financial investments, then capital employed should also include cash and short-term financial investments. This is the approach typically used when estimating capital employed and ROCE at the level of a company as a whole.
   ● When income does not include interest gains on cash and short-term financial investments, then capital employed should not include these items either. In this case capital employed can be estimated as total assets minus cash minus accounts payable, or as equity plus net loans (net loans are equal to loans minus cash). This approach is typically used when estimating the capital employed and the ROCE of a division or of any internal unit.

5. Capital employed is sometimes also defined as the sum of net fixed assets and working capital needs. Working capital needs are equal to the net sum of cash – see note 3 – accounts receivable, inventories, accounts payable and other non-interest-bearing liabilities.
6. One issue is: which is the capital employed to be used: the working capital at the beginning of the year or the working capital at the end of the year? If you consider the way in which return is defined (*see* Chapter 2, Section 2.8), then capital employed open is probably best. The common practice, however, is to use average capital employed.
7. Deducting accounts payable and all other non-interest-bearing liabilities provides you with a better estimate of the operational cash needs. This is a strong argument for using ROCE, RONA and ROC rather than ROA and ROI.
8. Real success is achieved only when you manage to do both: when you manage to grow income *and* to turn it faster into cash.
9. Provided that the interest rate is lower than 100%.

CHAPTER 9

Price, product mix and volume changes

Financial planning as modelling and managing change trajectories

Models are for helping us leverage change. Change is the striking feature of contemporary business. The many change processes that take place today are constantly creating new opportunities – and threats also[1] – and success depends on our ability to:

- recognize these opportunities and threats and to act in a timely way on them;
- manage change trajectories. When both costs and revenues change quickly, success is a matter of keeping their trajectories sufficiently apart. When there is explosive growth the challenge is to keep cash and costs away from erratic trajectories and to maintain some sort of alignment,[2] etc.

In the three coming chapters, we are going to discuss:

- How to build and use models that help leverage such change processes as the explosive growth of a new market, a continuous decrease in selling prices, a progressive shift in demand and product mix, dramatic changes in productivity, etc.
- How to build models that can help us keep the trajectories of the different costs and revenues evolving into value-creating rather than value-destroying dynamics.

Table 9.1 contrasts the 'change-focused' models that we are now going to build with the more traditional per-cent-of-sales models. Before going back to Delta Metal in Chapter 10, let us invest some time in discussing the impact of two critical changes: changes in prices and changes in volume.

- What is the relative impact of changes in prices and in volume?
- What are the most effective levels of aggregation of price and volume variables?

9.1 'Growth' is a very ambiguous driver: stating that sales will grow by 10% does not tell us what will happen to profit and cash!

Growth is often associated with growth in volume – or quantities: selling more products and services, serving more customers, delivering to more markets, etc. The problem, though,

Table 9.1 • Trajectories-of-payments-and-receipts vs. per-cent-of-sales models

	Trajectories-of-payments-and-receipts models	Per-cent-of-sales models
Goal	Assessing the value-creating opportunities/value-destruction threats that result from the convergence and/or the divergence of the trajectories of key business factors.	Producing pro-forma financial statements
Outcome variable	Value (NPV)	Financial statements[a]
Approach	• Investigation of the underlying change processes in the business and in its environment • Research of discontinuities, of breakpoints • Simulation of new business designs and structures	• Replication of past structures of financial statements • Research of stable patterns and ratios in the past and replication of these
Aggregation of variables/relations in between variables	• Depends on the issue at stake • Typically price and volume factors are separated • Simulation of different relations – not necessarily linear – for linking variables	• Same variable as accounting • Most variables are in a linear relation with current sales
Time frame	Typically based on the whole life cycle of the decision	Typically short (3 to 5 years)

[a] Traditional per-cent-of-sales models often do not have a specific output variable. They often only aim at checking that the financial statements do not develop major imbalances (such as an excessive debt-to-equity ratio for example).

is that reporting higher sales does not necessarily mean that growth – i.e. volume growth – has materialized. Sales are driven by volume and price and as a result the same change in sales may result from many different combinations of volume and price changes and, consequently, may result in very different incomes. Table 9.2 shows that the same 10% growth in sales may result in income falling by 108% or in income growing by 106%! Changes in price and changes in volume should be treated as two distinct drivers and growth in sales should be used as an output variable only.

Economy of things vs. economy of information

Table 9.2 makes it clear that the widely different impacts of price and volume are caused by the fact that it costs more to produce more physical goods and services. For pure information businesses, the logic is different: information can be replicated at almost no cost without limits. **For pure information businesses, changes in volume and price have basically the same effect: they both directly and almost equally impact the bottom line.**

Table 9.2 ● How the same growth in sales can lead to very different incomes

A	B	C	D	E	F
Scenario		1	2	3	4
1					
2 Growth in price (input)		10%	0%	−20%	20%
3 Growth in volume (input)		0%	10%	38%	−8%
4 Resulting growth in sales (output)		10%	10%	10%	10%
5					
6	2001	2002	2002	2002	2002
7 Sales	10 000	11 000	11 000	11 000	11 000
8 CGS	7 000	7 000	7 700	9 625	6 417
9 Selling and administration	1 000	1 000	1 000	1 000	1 000
10 Depreciation	500	500	500	500	500
11 Income	1 500	2 500	1 800	−125	3 083
12 Change in income (2002 vs. 2001)		67%	20%	−108%	106%

Background

In B7, B8, B9 and B10: data. In B11: =B7−B8−B9−B10; copy.
In C2: driver. In C3: =(1+C4)/(1+C2)−1. In C4: .10
In C7: =$B$7*(1+C2)*(1+C3); copy.
In C8: =$B$8*(1+C3); copy.
In C9: =B9. In C10: =B10; copy C9 and C10. In C12: =C11/$B$11−1; copy.

9.2 Changes in volumes, prices, product mix and productivity

There are different ways to define the drivers of 'change in sales' and 'change in costs'. Figure 9.1 shows three possible levels of aggregation of these drivers. Going from level 1 to level 3 is a matter of progressively introducing more details into the analysis:

● Level 1 models rely on only two extremely aggregated drivers: change in sales and change in costs.
● Level 2 models rely on more detailed drivers: change in volume and change in prices of sales and costs. Alternatively, level 2 models can also use drivers such as changes in productivity.
● Level 3 models use even more detailed drivers and change in prices are further broken down into change in prices of individual products and change in prices caused by changes in product mix.

Going from level 3 to level 1 is a matter of progressively ignoring phenomena which are taking place anyway. In most businesses the product mix changes and this has an impact on the average selling price, the average unit cost and the income. When you build a level 2 model you think 'change in average price' without explicitly recognizing how the change in mix may influence this change in average price. The risk is that you focus only on the changes in prices of the individual products and miss the influence of the change in mix.[3] Recognizing more of the phenomena that are present in a business often looks very attract-

Level 1	Level 2	Level 3
Change in sales	Change in average selling price	Change in price of each individual product
		Change in product mix (some products grow faster)
	Change in overall volume sold	

Change in costs	Change in overall volume sold	
	Change in average unit cost	Change in product mix (some products grow faster)
		Change in productivity
		Change in price of each individual input

Figure 9.1 Three levels of aggregation of the drivers of change in sales and change in costs

ive, but one should be careful as more detailed/less aggregated models are more difficult to manipulate and require inputs which are not always easy to get. **Additional details should be introduced, on a case by case basis, only when they make a positive difference!**

Level 1 models	Change in sales
	Change in costs

Level 1 models have the major disadvantage of using two drivers only. The value of each of these drivers is the result of many factors interacting in a complex way. As a result, changes in the value of these drivers are often ambiguous. Level 1 models have the great advantage of overall simplicity and they can be used effectively in all those situations where prices do not change much or where changes in price do not really differ from changes in volume: **this is the case for all the information businesses.**

Level 2 models	(1 + change in selling price) × (1 + change in volume sold) − 1
	(1 + change in unit cost price) × (1 + change in volume sold) − 1

Level 2 models allow for an explicit modelling of the relative impacts of changes in price and changes in volume. They analyze the business as if it was a single product business. The existence of different products with different price and margin levels is ignored and changes in selling price correspond to changes in 'average selling price'. The causes of changes in average selling price (changes in individual products' prices vs. changes in product mix) are not made explicit.

There are many different ways to build level 2 models:

● Costs may be all aggregated together or may be broken down into several different categories:
 – purchases, labour, depreciation, etc. or
 – cost of goods sold, administration and selling, R&D, etc.
● Change in volume may be defined in two different ways:
 – One may use different volume metrics for sales and costs. A further option is to use one single metric for all the costs or one specific metric for each cost or resource. Using different volume metrics for sales and costs creates the opportunity for portraying **changes in productivity**. When the volume of outputs (sales) grows faster than the volume of inputs (costs or resources), then productivity increases. When the volume of outputs grows slower, then productivity decreases. Changes in productivity can be identified at the aggregate level of all costs or, better, at the level of each of the different categories of costs or resources.
 – One may also use quantities sold as the one single volume metric for all sales and all costs items. When you do so, then 'change in unit cost' aggregates a series of different changes: changes in the prices of individual cost items, changes in productivity and changes in product mix. You should also be aware that 'change in quantities sold' corresponds to change in overall or net volume sold. In a multi-products business different products typically grow at different rates and some products may even decline.

Level 3 models	(1 + change in individual selling prices) × (1 + change in mix) × (1 + change in volume sold) − 1
	(1 + change in individual cost prices) × (1 + change in mix) × (1 + change in productivity) − 1

Level 3 models allow you to break down the change in average prices (sales and costs) and to make explicit what is due to:

● changes in prices of the individual products,
● changes in the product mix.

This is very useful when a business operates product lines that have very different characteristics (very different price levels and margins) and that grow at very different paces. In such situations, level 3 models help you understand, for example, the dramatic consequences of the rapid growth of a low price-low margin product that experiences a sharp price decline. Table 9.6 displays a level 3 model. The problem with level 3 models is that they have the potential to become excessively big as one may be tempted to break sales down into the sales of a very large number of different products.

9.3 Three models for assessing the relative impacts of price and volume changes (level 2 models)

The first model (Table 9.3) helps us to understand the relative impacts of price and volume changes. The second one (Table 9.4) helps us make decisions that involve price/volume trade-offs: how much additional volume is needed to compensate for a small price concession? How much volume loss is acceptable when price is increased, etc.? The third model (Table 9.5) explores the impact of continuous price decreases over time and shows that very few business structures are sufficiently robust to resist very adverse price trajectories. Adverse price trajectories can only be combated with business reinvention.

A model portraying the impact of price and volume changes on margins

When they both change, price and volume have a multiplicative impact:

Sales = Previous sales × (1 + price growth) × (1 + volume growth)
    = Previous sales
        + previous sales × price growth   *price impact*
        + previous sales × volume growth   *volume impact*
        + previous sales × volume growth × price growth   *combined volume and price impact*

The multiplicative impact of price and volume requires that:

1. One clearly specifies what is measured: is the impact of a price change measured before or after volume has changed? Is the impact of a volume change measured before or after price has changed?
2. One keeps consistency. In order to explain the total impact of a volume and a price change, one has to consider:
   - price change after volume has changed *and* volume change before price has changed, or
   - price change before volume has changed *and* volume change after price has changed, or
   - price change before volume has changed *and* volume change before price has changed *and* combined impact of the price and volume change.

Table 9.3 shows the relative impacts of price and volume changes.

Changes in price vs. changes in volume
Changes in prices – in selling and cost prices – impact income more than changes in volume. Changes in prices impact income both in absolute and in percentage of sales

Table 9.3 ● A model for understanding the impact of changes in prices and volume

	A	B Open/before	C Change	D End/after
1				
2	Number of units	100	0%	100
3	Unit selling price	500	–10%	450
4	Sales	50 000		45 000
5	Change in sales			–10%
6	Unit cost	400	0%	400
7	CGS	40 000		40 000
8	**Margin**	**10 000**	**–5 000**	**5 000**
9	Change in margin			–50%
10	Margin/sales	20%		11%
11				
12		**Sales**	**CGS**	**margin**
13	Impact of change in price at open volume/before volume change	–5 000	0	–5 000
14	Impact of change in volume at end price/after price change	0	0	0
15	**End (post changes) figures . . .**	**45 000**	**40 000**	**5 000**
16				
17	Impact of change in price at end volume/after volume change	–5 000	0	–5 000
18	impact of change in volume at open price/before price change	0	0	0
19	**End (post change) figures . . .**	**45 000**	**40 000**	**5 000**
20				
21	Impact of price at open volume/before volume change	–5 000	0	–5 000
22	Impact of volume at open price/before price change	0	0	0
23	Combined price/volume impact	0	0	0
24	**End (post change) figures . . .**	**45 000**	**40 000**	**5 000**

Background

B2, B3, B10, C2, C3, C6: inputs
B4:+B22*B3; copy to C4
B6:+B3*(1–B10)
B7:+B6*B2; Copy to C7
B8:+B4–B7; Copy to C8
B13: +(D3–B3)*D2
B14: +(D2–B2)*D3
B15: +B4+B13+B14
B17: +(D3–B3)*D2
B18: +(D2–B2)*B3
B19: +B4+B17+B18
B21: +(D3–B3)*B2
B22: +(D2–B2)*B3
B23: +B4*C2*C3
B24: +B4+B21+B22+B23
C8:+D8–B8
C13: +(D6–B6)*B2

C14: +(D2–B2)*D6
C15: +B7+C13+C14
C17: +(D6–B6)*D2
C18: +(D2–B2)*B6
C19: +B7+C17+C18
C21: +(D6–B6)*B2
C22: +(D2–B2)*B6
C23: +B7*C6*C2
C24: +B7+C21+C22+C23
D2:+B2*(1+C2); Copy to D3 and D6
D5:+D4/B4–1; Copy to D9
D10: +D8/D4
D13: +B13–C13; Copy to D14, D17.D18, D21.D23
D15: +B8+D13+D14
D19: +B8+D17+D18
D24: +B8+D21+D22+D23

Table 9.4 ● Changes in price vs. changes in volume

		10% increase in selling price	10% decrease in unit cost	10% increase in volume sold
20% initial margin	Impact (amount)	5000	4000	1000
	Impact (% increase)	50%	40%	10%
12% initial margin	Impact (amount)	5000	4400	600
	Impact (% increase)	83%	73%	10%

Table 9.5 ● Combined changes in selling prices and in cost prices

		Initial margin	After a 10% decrease in price	% decrease in unit cost needed to keep the margin
20% margin	Income (amount)	10 000	5 000	−12.5%
	in % of sales	20%	11%	10%[a]
80% margin	Income (amount)	40 000	35 000	−50%
	in % of sales	80%	78%	10%[a]

[a] Percentage decrease in unit cost needed to keep the margin at the same % of sales.

---

terms. Changes in volume impact income in absolute terms only. In low margin businesses, changes in prices make income change by a large percentage. In low margin businesses, changes in volume make income change by a small percentage. This is shown in Table 9.4.

Combined changes in selling prices and in cost prices
When selling prices and unit costs change by the same percentage, then income increases by the same percentage – and the income to sales ratio is unchanged. In order to maintain the same absolute amount of income, unit cost should decrease more than selling price. In high margin businesses, unit cost should decrease a lot to keep income at the same absolute level. In low margin businesses, a small change in unit cost is sufficient (or, in other words, low margin businesses are very sensitive to changes in unit cost). This is shown in Table 9.5.

Combined changes in selling price and in volume
When the unit cost is assumed to remain the same, changes in selling prices are only offset by a bigger change in volume sold. In a low margin business, only very large increases in volume can enable a business to maintain its absolute amount of income when selling prices decline. When the income reaches zero, then no volume increase, however big it is, can help restore the income. Finally, volume increases can help maintain the absolute level of income but have no impact on the income to sales ratio (which is only a matter of price differentials). This is shown in Table 9.6.

Table 9.6 ● Combined changes in selling price and in volume

		Initial margin	After a 10% decrease in price	% increase in volume needed to keep the income
20% margin	Income (amount)	10 000	5000	100%
	in % of sales	20%	11%	a
15% margin	Income (amount)	7 500	2500	200%
	in % of sales	15%	6%	a

a No increase in volume can bring the income back to 20% or 15% of sales; whatever the volume increase is, income remains equal to 11% and 6% of sales, respectively.

The model in Table 9.3 helps us realize why volume increases are ineffective for restoring margins after these have been destroyed by price decreases. The 10% price decrease has cut income by an amount of 5000 and has brought the margin down to 11% of sales. In order to compensate for the 5000 decrease in income with volume you have to do it with a business that now has a low 11% margin (see rows 13 and 14 of the model). This means that in order to generate an income of 5000 we need an amount of sales equal to 5000/ 0.1111 = 45 000 which corresponds to 100 additional units (at the new price of 450). Doubling the volume sold is what it takes to restore the income! Rows 21, 22 and 23 also show us that, in the conditions at origin – when margin is still 20%:

● change in price increases income by 5000;
● change in volume increases income by 10 000 but the combined price and volume effect (impact of a 10% price decrease on the additional 50 000 business created by growth) finally decreases income by 5000.

Combined impact of changes in selling price, in volume and in unit cost

Even though this does not always happen automatically, it is generally assumed that volume growth should result in some reduction in unit cost. This volume-driven unit cost reduction is typically used as the argument in favour of volume growth. When comparing the relative impacts of changes in prices and in volume, one should compare changes in prices with changes in volumes *and* the implied reduction in unit cost. The model in Table 9.3 and the results in Table 9.7 show that it is possible to completely offset a decrease in selling price with a increase in volume provided that the increase in volume generates a decrease in unit costs that is:

● of the same magnitude as the increase in volume (+10% in volume and –10% in unit cost). This allows for maintaining income in the same percentage of sales;
● a bit larger than the increase in volume (+10% in volume and –10.2% in unit cost). This allows for maintaining the absolute amount of income.

As such decreases in costs are difficult to achieve in the economy of things, changes in prices generally have a larger impact than changes in volume even when unit cost reductions are taken into account.

Table 9.7 • What it takes to offset a price decrease by an increase in volume

		Initial margin	After a 10% decrease in price and a 10% increase in volume	% decrease in unit cost needed to keep the margin
20% margin	Absolute margin	10 000	5 500	−10.24%[a]
	in % of sales	20%	11%	−10%[a]
15% margin	Absolute margin	7 500	2 750	−10.17%
	in % of sales	15%	6%	−10%
80% margin	Absolute margin	40 000	38 500	−13.64%
	in % of sales	80%	78%	−10%

[a] Unit cost needs to be reduced by 10.24% in order to keep the income at the initial absolute level (10 000) and by 10% – the same as the decrease in price – in order to keep income equal to 20% of sales as it was at the origin.

A model for testing the value of volume/price trade-offs

Sales people often attempt to increase income by trying out small marginal price and/or volume changes. They want to implement a small price increase hoping that this will not make them lose too much volume, they consider making a small price concession in order to gain a significant additional volume, etc. The model in Table 9.8 helps in making such decisions. It shows:

● The maximum volume decrease allowed. A small price increase could push the income up, but what if this hurts volume? The model estimates the maximum decrease in volume allowed in order to maintain the original income.

● The minimum volume increase required. A small price concession would hurt the income unless it also increases volume. What is the minimum increase in volume needed to maintain the original income?

● The maximum price decrease allowed. You are eager to increase volume and you believe that this requires a small price sacrifice. What is the maximum decrease in price allowed in order to maintain the original income? (This is the same problem as the previous one but expressed in a different way.)

The model in Table 9.8 assumes that unit cost price does not change, which is realistic when it comes to small price and volume adjustments 'at the margin'. One interesting output of the model is the volume change/price change ratio. This ratio depends on the initial margin of the business:

● In a very high margin business (income is 80% of sales) you need a volume change 1.3 times larger than the price change to compensate for a 5% price decrease. You need a 1.4 times larger volume change when price decreases by 10% and a 1.7 times larger volume change when price decreases by 20%.

● In a high margin business (income is 50% of sales), then the volume/price ratio becomes 2.2 with a 5% price decrease, 2.5 with a 10% price decrease and 3.3 with a 20% price decrease.

Table 9.8 ● A model to test the value of pricing decisions

	A	B	C	D	E	F
1	Gross margin	20%	Gross margin	20%	Gross margin	20%
2	Price increase	10%	Price decrease	10%	Volume increase	10%
3	Volume decrease allowed	33%	Volume increase required	100%	Price decrease allowed	2%
4	Volume/price ratio	3.3	Volume/price ratio	10.0	Volume/price ratio	5.5
5	*Initial situation*		*Initial situation*		*Initial situation*	
6	Sales	1000	Sales	1000	Sales	1000
7	Costs	800	Costs	800	Costs	800
8	Income (absolute)	200	Margin (absolute)	200	Margin (absolute)	200
9						
10	*After the price change*		*After the price change*		*After the volume change*	
11	Sales	1100	Sales	900	Sales	1100
12	Costs	800	Costs	800	Costs	880
13	Margin (absolute)	300	Margin (absolute)	100	Margin (absolute)	220
14						
15	*After the second change*		*After the second change*		*After the second change*	
16	Sales	733	Sales	1800	Sales	1080
17	Costs	533	Costs	1600	Costs	880
18	Margin (absolute)	200	Margin (absolute)	200	Margin (absolute)	200
19		0		0		0

Background

In B6: 1000. In B7: =B6–B8. In B8: =B6*B1; copy in D6:D8 and F6:F8
In B11: =B6*(1+B2). In B12: =B7. In B13: =B11–B12. In B16: =B11*(1–B3). In B17: =B7*(1–B3).
In B18: =B16–B17. In B19: =B18–B8.
In D11: =D6*(1–D2). In D12: =D7. In D13: =D11–D12. In D16: =D11*(1+D3). In D17: =D7*(1+D3).
In D18: =D16–D17. In D19: =D18–D8
In F11: =F6*(1+F2). In F12: =F7*(1+F2). In F13: =F11–F12. In F16: =F11*(1–F3). In F17: =F12.
In F18: =F16–F17. In F19: =F18–F8
In B4: =B3/2; copy to D4 and F4.

To use the model
There are actually three models (in columns A and B, in columns C and D and in columns E and F)
You can use these three models independently. For using any of the three models, you need to:

1. Set the initial margin rate (in B1, D1, or F1)
2. Set the price increase – or the volume increase (in B2, D2 or F2)
3. Use the Goal Seek function of Excel to estimate the value of B3, D3 or H3: For the model in A and B: Tools/Goal Seek. Set cell B9 to value 0 by changing cell B3.

- In a lower margin business (25% gross profit), then the volume/price ratios are large: 5 with a 5% price decrease, 6.7 with a 10% decrease and 20 with a 20% decrease.
- In a zero margin business, there is no way to restore the initial margin through any volume increase.[4] This is obvious but some aggressive sales-minded people may tend to forget it!

When using price/volume trade-off models, different companies typically use different levels of income. While some companies assess the impact of price and volume changes on gross margin (sales – CGS), other companies assess this impact on operating income (sales – all relevant costs). The choice of the level of income is not neutral: the change in volume/change in price ratio is lower – and somewhat underestimated – when assessed at the level of gross margin.

A model for portraying the relative impacts of price and volume trajectories

There are industries in which companies have to cope with a continuous decline in the selling prices of their products. A case in point is the microelectronics industry in which selling prices decline by 20%, or more, a year. The model in Table 9.9 helps to explain what the impact of such price trajectories is and how a business can thrive when its selling prices decline continuously.

As indicated in Table 9.9, ZBZ has to adjust to an unexpected declining trend in price. Initially it plans to counteract this trend by downsizing its workforce, but this proves to be

---

Table 9.9 ● Assessing the impact of adverse price trajectories

A challenging business situation

In 2002, ZBZ finds itself confronted with a new challenging industry-wide environment. ZBZ specializes in producing and selling air gases (oxygen, nitrogen, etc.), a very capital intensive industry. In the late 1990s, the company had invested heavily in order to prepare for growth. In 2002, ZBZ realizes that while volume develops quickly (+16% a year trajectory, much more than the expected 5%), selling prices start declining sharply (–12% a year trajectory instead of the –2% expected). The company realizes that that these trends may well continue for a few years and that it will be very difficult to reach the operating income target: 15% of sales in 2003. The company is also aware that it is probably over-staffed and the question becomes: by how much should we reduce the workforce in order to cope with the adverse price trend?

The spreadsheet

	A	B	C	D	E	F	G	H	I
1		2000	2001	2002	2003	2004	2005	2006	2007
2				Base	1	2	3	4	5
3	Depreciation	1 371	1 644	1 822	2 004	2 004	2 004	2 004	2 004
4	Other costs	6 790	7 535	8 208	8 865	9 574	10 340	11 167	12 060
5	**Change in personnel** expenses				0%	0%	0%	0%	0%
6	Personnel expenses	3 134	3 497	3 300	3 300	3 300	3 300	3 300	3 300
7									
8	**Volume change**				16%	16%	16%	16%	16%
9	**Price change**				–12%	–12%	–12%	–12%	–12%
10	Sales growth				2%	2%	2%	2%	2%
11	SALES	12 860	14 408	15 088	15 402	15 722	16 049	16 383	16 724
12	Operating income	1 565	1 732	1 758	1 233	844	405	–88	–641
13	Operating income/sales	12.2%	12.0%	11.7%	8.0%	5.4%	2.5%	–0.5%	–3.8%

Depreciation is driven by the investments made in the late 1990s. Other costs are costs of external purchases (energy and other supplies and services).

Table 9.9 continued

Background

E3=D3*1.1, F3=E3; copy

E4: +D4*(1+0.5*E8)

E6: +D6*(1+E5)

E10: +(1+E8)*(1+E9)−1

E11: +D11*(1+E10); copy

E12: +E11−E3−E4−E6

E13: +E12/E11

Copy E4: E13 into F4:I4

Using the model

You can use the model to simulate the results expected by ZBZ: set volume change to 0.05 and change in price to −0.02. Operating income/sales becomes: 11.6% in 2003, 12.8% in 2004, 14.0% in 2005, 15.1% in 2006 and 16.2% in 2007. Now using the Goal Seek function of Excel, you can find out the annual change in personnel expenses needed to make operating income (1) remain equal to 12% during the period 2003–07, (2) reach the 15% target in 2006:

	2003	2004	2005	2006	2007
Operating income/sales	0.12	0.12	0.12	0.12	0.12
Decrease in personnel costs required	−0.19	−0.16	−0.21	−0.22	−0.48
Operating income/sales	0.12	0.13	0.14	0.15	0.15
Decrease in personnel costs required	−0.19	−0.22	−0.31	−0.48	−0.80

totally unrealistic: it is possible to reach the 15% income to sales target with downsizing provided that all the workforce is progressively laid off! One interesting result of this model is that the impact of the price trajectory is cumulative and requires bigger and bigger cost reductions to be offset – bigger and bigger in absolute number and obviously even bigger and bigger in percentage. This example may look a bit extreme but it illustrates the issues associated with quickly declining prices:

- Only innovation can drive rapidly declining prices: new product and service designs, new ways to manufacture, new ways to distribute, etc.
- When having to cope with adverse price trajectories a company can only survive through a continuous reinvention of the ways in which it operates. Downsizing is generally not sufficient in such a situation.

9.4 Introducing the impact of product mix changes

Table 9.10 shows the relative impacts of changes in individual product prices, in product mix and in volume. Changes in mix can be assimilated to a change in price. What is unique with them is that they affect both the selling and the cost prices.

Introducing the impact of product mix changes is not always useful but there are cases when making this driver explicit helps explain the evolution of prices and margins. Table 9.11 shows such a situation. ZBZ, the industrial gas company that we met in Table 9.9 is very concerned about the evolution of its selling prices: its fastest growing product is also experiencing an 8% price decline a year. This fastest growth product has a much lower price than the traditional products that still represent 75% of the total sales. Introducing change in product mix as a driver shows that ZBZ is rightly concerned: the rapid growth of this low price, declining price, and low margin product results in:

● a 12% decline in the average selling price. This is much more than the price decline of any product!
● a 5% increase in the unit cost price – another impact of the change in mix!

The consequence of these price trajectories are shown in Table 9.11.

Table 9.10 ● Comparing the impacts of changes in individual product prices, changes in mix and changes in volume

Change in \ Impact on	Sales	CGS	Margin
Selling price	Full impact: sales grow by the increase in selling price	No impact: CGS is unchanged	Very high impact due to the fact that CGS remains constant while sales increase
Product mix (some products grow faster than others)	Full impact: sales grow by the increase in average selling price due to the change in mix	Contingent impact: CGS grows or decreases in relation to the change in average unit cost due to the change in mix	Contingent impact: all depends on the relative growth of sales and CGS. If high margin products replace low margin product, then margin increases
Volume	Full impact: sales grow by the increase in volume	Full impact: CGS grows by the same amount as sales (provided that unit cost does not change)	Full impact: margin grows by the same amount as volume growth (provided that unit cost does not change)

Table 9.11 ● A price, volume mix model applied to a three products business

The issue
An industrial gas company operates three businesses with very different characteristics:

● a high price (600 per unit), high margin (180 per unit) industrial cylinder gas (IG) business that unfortunately experiences a decline in volume (–5% a year). Unit selling prices are stable.
● a high price (750 per unit), high margin (262.5 per unit) pharmaceutical gas (PG) business that is growing 15% a year with stable unit selling prices.
● a low price (50 per unit), low margin (0.25 per unit) commodity liquid gas (LG) business that is growing at a high rate (20% a year) through the implementation of aggressive price cutting tactics (–8% a year).

At the end of 2000, these three businesses are of different sizes: industrial cylinder is 60% of total sales, pharmaceutical cylinder is 15% and liquid is 25%.

Table 9.11 continued

The model

	A	B	C	D	E	F	G	H	I
				Year 1				Year 2	
1									
2		IG	LG	PG	Total	IG	LG	PG	Total
3	Change in price					0%	−8%	0%	
4	Unit price	600	50	750	161	600	46	750	142
5	Change in average price								−12.1%
6	Change in volume					−5%	20%	15%	15.8%
7	Number of units	10	50	2	62	10	60	2	72
8	Sales	6 000	2 500	1 500	10 000	5 700	2 760	1 725	10 185
9	Change in sales					−5.0%	10.4%	15.0%	1.9%
10	Proportion of sales	60%	25%	15%		56%	27%	17%	
11	Change in CGS					0%	0%	0%	5.4%
12	Unit cost	420	48	488	122	420	48	488	111
13	CGS	4 200	2 375	975	7 550	3 990	2 850	1 121	7 961
14	Margin	1 800	125	525	2 450	1 710	−90	604	2 224
15	Margin/sales	0.30	0.05	0.35	25%	30%	−3%	35%	22%
16	Change in margin								−9.2%
17									
18	**Impact of:**						Sales	CGS	Margin
19	**Changes in prices at opening volumes/before volume changes**						−2.0%	0.0%	−8.2%
20	**Changes in overall volume at opening prices/before price changes**						15.8%	15.8%	15.8%
21	**Changes in mix at opening prices/before change in prices**						−10.3%	−8.9%	−14.3%
22	**Combination of changes in price, volume and mix**								0.4%
23	**Total change**						1.9%	5.4%	−9.2%

Formulas

Inputs in ranges B4.D4, B7.D7, B15.D15 – these are the base conditions – and in ranges F3.H3, F6.H6 and F11.H11.

B8: +B4*B7; copy to C8.I8

B10: +B8/$E$8; copy to C10.D10 and F10.H10

B12: +B4*(1−B15); copy to C12.D12

B13: +B12*B7; copy to C13.I13

B14: +B8−B13; copy to C14.I14

E4: +B4*B7/E7+C4*C7/E7+D4*D7/E7

E7: +SUM(B7:D7); copy to I7

E12: +B12*B7/E7+C12*C7/E7+D12*D7/E7

E15: +E14/E8; copy to F15.I15

F4: +B4*(1+F3); copy into G4.H4

F7: +B7*(1+F6); copy into G7.H7

F12: +B12*(1+F11); copy into G12.H12

I4: +F4*F7/I7+G4*G7/I7+H4*H7/I7

I5: +I4/E4−1; I6: +I7/E7−1

I9: +I8/E8−1; I11: +I13/E13−1

I12: +F12*F7/I7+G12*G7/I7+H12*H7/I7

I16: +I14/E14−1

G19: +F3*B10+G3*C10+H3*D10

H19: +F11*B13/E13+G11*C13/E13+H11*D13/E13

I19: +(G19*$E$8−H19*$E$13)/$E$14

Copy content of I19 into I20.I21

G20: +I6; H20: +I6

G21: +(I4/E4)/(1+G19)−1

H21: +(I12/E12)/(1+H19)−1

I22: +(1+I23)/((1+I19)*(1+I20)*(1+I21))−1

G23: +(1+G19)*(1+G20)*(1+G21)−1; copy to H23

I23: +I16

9.5 The issue of 'increasing selling prices'

Changes in price impact income more than changes in volume. This is nothing new for people with business experience. This means that:

- It is a good idea to spend a lot of time understanding how you create value for your customers, how your customers agree to share this value with you, how your customers compare your products and services with those of your competitors, with other alternatives, etc. Please remember from the analysis of the Jilin project in Chapter 4 how difficult it is to extract a price increase – even when it is a win-win situation. Extracting a price increase is often better done in oblique ways.
- Getting a better price is not only a matter of increasing prices. It is also a matter of managing your product and service portfolio as well as your customer portfolio. Focusing on your stronger products and services, and eliminating the weaker ones, focusing on your most profitable customers and eliminating the non-profitable ones are often powerful ways to increase your average selling prices.[5] Adding and invoicing pure information services also works as well as increasing prices.
- Finally, getting better prices is a matter of mobilizing the whole organization on the issue and of getting everybody used to tools for segmenting the market, understanding the customers, adding pure information services, etc.[6]

You should also be fully aware that high prices can hide almost any kind of problem.[7] This is one of the traps into which companies with very strong market positions – monopolies – often fall. Continuous price increases help such companies thrive in spite of very poor business models until a much more effective competitor comes in and kills them.

Notes

1. There is today a very rich literature calling for new approaches to strategy in a rapidly changing world. See for example: S.L. Brown and K.M. Eishenhardt (1998), *Competing on The Edge*, Harvard Business School Press; L. Downes and C. Mui (1998), *Unleashing the Killer App*, Harvard Business School Press.
2. G. Labovitz and V. Rosansky (1997), *The Power of Alignment*, John Wiley.
3. Which, however, is a problem only when the mix has a significant impact.
4. Still assuming that the unit cost does not change.
5. Refer to R.S. Kaplan and R. Cooper (1998), *Cost and Effect*, Harvard Business School Press, Chapter 9, p. 160.
6. For a systematic analysis of how to design effective pricing strategies and tactics, refer to: T.T. Nagle and R.K. Holden (1995), *The Strategy and Tactics of Pricing*, Prentice Hall and to R.J. Dolan and H. Simon (1996), *Power Pricing – How Managing Price Transforms the Bottom Line*, The Free Press.
7. Refer to the Relais Electriques case in the appendices to Part III.

Delta Metal (II)

Additional information on the situation in 2000 and 2001

Mr Lauru had gathered the volume and price information shown in Table I.1. These data helped him understand better what had happened in the company in the past two years:

- In 2000, the company experienced a shock when its purchasing prices increased by 14%. Delta Metal did not manage to pass on this price increase to its customers (selling prices increased by 8% only). This was, however, partly masked by the existence of a large inventory at the beginning of 2000. This delayed the impact of the shock that only produced its full effect in 2001. In 2000 the market was buoyant and quantities sold increased by 24%.
- In 2001, the company was under market pressure and volumes decreased. In this difficult market, the company was not able to increase its selling prices and to catch up with the high purchasing prices. On the contrary, the company had to decrease its selling prices slightly.

In 2002 Delta Metal expects finally to be in a position to recover the higher purchasing costs. This is the rationale for the expected 4% selling price.

Table I.1 ● **Delta Metal: past volume and price data**

	1999	2000	2001	2002(F)
Increase in volume sold		*24%*	*−10%*	*0%*
Volume sold (tons)	18 614.21	23 081.62	20 773.46	20 773.46
Increase in selling price		*7.8%*	*−1.3%*	
Selling price (000)	5.20	5.61	5.53	
Inventory open volume	4 896.33	4 994.21	5 864.05	3 772.75
Unit cost	4.06	4.06	4.60	4.60
Increase in volume purchased		*28%*	*−22%*	
Volume purchased	18 712.09	23 951.47	18 682.15	
Increase in purchase price		*13.5%*	*0%*	
Unit purchase price	4.06	4.60	4.60	

CHAPTER 10

Building and using trajectories-of-payments-and-receipts models

10.1 Trajectories-of-payments-and-receipts models

The need for trajectories-of-payments-and-receipts models was introduced in Chapter 9. When preparing business plans it is not very effective to use the traditional per-cent-of-sales models that are basically made for extrapolating the past.[1] We need models that are really designed for helping us:

- simulate the possible trajectories, including disruptive trajectories, of the different payments and receipts over time;
- understand what the forces are that can make these payments and receipts trajectories keep parallel, or rather start diverging or converging;
- identify all the new opportunities for creating value that may result from the co-evolution of these trajectories. And identify the new threats that may also emerge.

Table 10.1 contrasts the design of the trajectories-of-payments-and-receipts models with that of the traditional models. It complements Table 9.1 which analyzes the goals and approaches of the trajectory models. In this chapter we are going to discuss two different trajectory models:

- The first is an explicit volume–price model that can be built based on the data of Delta Metal and Delta Metal (II).
- The second is a more trajectory-oriented model, and is the one I recommend that you use.

10.2 A first trajectories-of-payments-and-receipts model: explicit volume–price model

The model in Tables 10.2 and 10.3 is an explicit volume–price model in the sense that each of the variables that helps estimate cost of goods sold is decomposed into a volume and a price component. Please note the three sets of relationships in the model:

● The first set of relations is the usual accounting relations: cost of goods sold = inventory open + purchases – inventory end (the same as inventory open for the next coming year). Operating profit = sales – cost of goods sold – operating expenses – depreciation.
● The second set of equations relates all the quantities: volume purchased = volume sold + volume inventory end – volume inventory open. In the model, volume sold and

Table 10.1 ● Trajectories-of-payments-and-receipts vs. per-cent-of-sales models

	Trajectories-of-payments-and-receipts models	Per-cent-of-sales models
Drivers	● Change in selling price ● Change in volume sold ● Change in purchase price ● Change in operating expenses ● Collection period ● Inventory turnover ● Payment period ● Capital expenditure and depreciation	● Growth in sales ● CGS/sales ● Operating expenses/sales ● Collection period ● Inventory turnover ● Payment period ● Capital expenditure and depreciation
Design	● A number of relations between variables are horizontal and go across periods.[b] Key variables are estimated from the value that they had in the previous period and a change factor ● Price and volume changes are made explicit ● There are also vertical relations in the models for calculating income, cash, etc. There are also vertical relations that recognize the co-variation of some variables like volume[c] ● The model does not necessarily mimic the accounting format[d]	● Most of the variables are estimated as a ratio of the current sales. Most relations between variables are vertical in the sense that they exist only between variables belonging to the same period[a] ● Price and volume changes are not explicit ● There are also a few horizontal relations. In particular, sales are estimated in relation to the sales of the previous period ● The model mimics the accounting format

[a] Most per-cent-of-sales models are vertical – all relations are within the same time period – and do not have the relation linking inventory end of the period to sales in the following period. Most of these models link the ending inventory to the sales of the current year.
[b] It is important that the relations across periods are not necessarily limited to relations between consecutive periods:

● For changes in price, the relation is typically between the current price and the price of the previous period; for inventory, the relation is between the inventory at the end of the current period and the sales expected in the following period.
● For changes in the level of manufacturing resources, selling resources, R&D resources, etc. then the relation is between the current period – when you decide the increase – and several periods away in the future.

As soon as a change is made today in relation to the value of one or more variables in the future (sales volume, sales prices, etc.), then an additional problem emerges: what if we make the wrong forecast? This is an issue that we discuss in Chapter 12.
[c] Differences in co-variation of the different volume indicators are interesting to focus on as they reflect improvements of productivity (see in Chapter 9).
[d] This is not the case of the model in Tables 8.2 and 8.3, but it is the case of the model in Table 14.11.

Table 10.2 • Explicit volume–price model (foreground)

	2001	2002	2003	2004	2005	2006
Increase in volume sold		*0%*	*0%*	*0%*	*0%*	*0%*
Volume sold	20 773	20 773	20 773	20 773	20 773	20 773
Increase in selling price		*4.0%*	*0%*	*0%*	*0%*	*0%*
Unit selling price	5.53	5.75	5.75	5.75	5.75	5.75
Sales	114.93	119.53	119.53	119.53	119.53	119.53
Inventory turnover		*4.00*	*4.00*	*4.00*	*4.00*	*4.0*
Inventory open volume	5864	3773	5193	5193	5193	5193
Unit cost price	4.60	4.60	4.60	4.60	4.60	4.60
Inventory open	26.99	17.37	23.91	23.91	23.91	23.91
Increase volume purchases		19%	−6%	0%	0%	−25%
Volume purchases	18 682	22 194	20 773	20 773	20 773	15 580
Increase in price of purchases	*0%*	*0.0%*	*0%*	*0%*	*0%*	*0%*
Unit purchase price	4.60	4.60	4.60	4.60	4.60	4.60
Purchases	86.00	102.16	95.62	95.62	95.62	71.72
CGS	95.62	95.62	95.62	95.62	95.62	95.62
Increase in operating expenses		*4%*	*0%*	*0%*	*0%*	*0%*
Operating expenses	16.09	16.73	16.73	16.73	16.73	16.73
Depreciation	0.34	*0.60*	*0.60*	*0.60*	*0.60*	*0.60*
Operating income	2.88	6.57	6.57	6.57	6.57	6.57
Taxable income		1.98	6.57	6.57	6.57	6.57
Operating income after tax	**2.88**	**5.92**	**4.40**	**4.40**	**4.40**	**4.40**
Receivables open	63.62	58.42	59.77	59.77	59.77	59.77
Collection period	6.10	*6.0*	*6.0*	*6.0*	*6.0*	*6.0*
Receivables end	58.42	59.77	59.77	59.77	59.77	59.77
Payables open	33.08	40.13	34.05	31.87	31.87	31.87
Payment period	5.60	*4.0*	*4.0*	*4.0*	*4.0*	*4.0*
Payables end	40.13	34.05	31.87	31.87	31.87	23.91
Cash from operations	25.09	−7.44	2.82	5.00	5.00	20.94
Capital expenditure	2.00	*0.50*	*0.50*	*0.50*	*0.50*	*0.50*
Free cash flow	**23.09**	**−7.94**	**2.32**	**4.50**	**4.50**	**20.44**
Growth in sales		*4.0%*	*0.0%*	*0.0%*	*0.0%*	*0.0%*
CGS/sales	*83.2%*	*80.00%*	*80.0%*	*80.0%*	*80.0%*	*80.0%*
Operating expenses/sales	*14.0%*	*14.0%*	*14.0%*	*14.0%*	*14.0%*	*14.0%*
Operating income/sales	*2.5%*	*5.5%*	*5.5%*	*5.5%*	*5.5%*	*5.5%*

volume inventory end (through the inventory turnover driver) are drivers. Volume inventory open is a given and volume purchased is calculated by the model.

• The third set of equations deals with prices and makes the price of inventory end equal to the price of purchases made during the year according to the 'first-in-first-out concept'.[2]

In the model, the volume of inventory end is estimated as a function of the volume of sales expected in the next period. As no sales are currently envisaged for 2007, inventory end 2006 is automatically made equal to zero. The calculation of corporate taxes is the same as in Table 7.9.

Table 10.3 ● Explicit volume–price model (background)

	A	B	C
1		2001	=B1+1
2	*Increase in volume sold*		*0*
3	Volume sold	20 773.46	=B3*(1+C2)
4	*Increase in selling price*		*0.04*
5	Unit selling price	5.5327	=B5*(1+C4)
6	Sales	=B3*B5/1000	●
7	*Inventory turnover*		*4*
8	Inventory open volume	5864.06	=B8+B12–B3ᵃ
9	Unit cost price	4.603	=B14
10	Inventory open	=B8*B9/1000	●
11	Increase volume purchases		=C12/B12–1
12	Volume purchases	18 682.15	=C3+D8–C8
13	*Increase in price of purchases*		*0*
14	Unit purchase price	4.603	=B14*(1+C13)
15	Purchases	=B14*B12/1000	●
16	CGS	=B15+B10–C10	●
17	*Increase in operating expenses*		*=1.04–1*
18	Operating expenses	16.09	=B18*(1+C17)
19	Depreciation	0.34	*0.6*
20	Operating income	=B6–B16–B18–B19	●
21	Taxable income		=C20–4.588ᵇ
22	Operating income after tax	=B20	ᶜ
23	Receivables open	63.615	=B25
24	*Collection period*	6.1	*6*
25	Receivables end	=B6/12*B24	●
26	Payables open	33.076	=B28
27	*Payment period*	5.6	*4*
28	Payables end	=(B16+C10–B10)/12*B27	●
29	Cash from operations	=B22+B19+B23–B25 +B10–C10+B28–B26	●
30	*Capital expenditure*	2	*0.5*
31	Free cash flow	=B29–B30	●
32			
33	*Growth in sales*		*=C6/B6–1*
34	*CGS/sales*	*=B16/B6*	●
35	*Operating expenses/sales*	*=B18/B6*	●
36	*Operating income/sales*	*=B20/B6*	●

ᵃ In D8: =D3/C7; copy
ᵇ In D21: +D20+IF(C21<0,C21,0); copy
ᶜ In C22: =IF(C20<0,C20,IF(C21<C20,IF(C21>0,C20–C21*0.33,C20),C20*0.67)); copy

The explicit modelling of volumes and prices has advantages and disadvantages. Among the advantages of volume–price models are the following:

● They help you understand how inventories delay the impact of price changes. Explicit price–volume models are good for understanding the impact of different rules for valuing inventories (see Tyler Welding in Chapter 14), etc.

● They are very useful for analyzing manufacturing situations where there are several types of inventories and different types of costs behaving in different ways. We will actually use a similar model for modelling a manufacturing situation in Part IV (Case M – Tyler Welding).

Among the disadvantages of volume–price models are:

● They tend to be heavy: for variables like purchases and inventory you now have three rows instead of one!
● The data that you need are not all readily available. You have to do some research to get the volume and price data and you may have to use modelling techniques to recalculate some inventory data.
● These models tend to be very personal. When you build an explicit volume–price model by yourself, you quickly realize that the 'volumes' and 'prices' of such a model are not really actual volumes and actual prices of actual products. Rather, they correspond to a volume index and to a series of price indexes. You could actually build a model for Delta Metal with completely different unit prices and volumes that would give exactly the same results! The problem is that many managers feel uncomfortable with using abstract volume and price indexes that they cannot directly relate to actual products. Some people would like to have models that show all the actual products with their actual volumes and prices. These would turn out to be very big models! This is a difficulty that you will not meet when building your own models but you may encounter it when trying to use your models with other people. My advice is to limit your use of explicit volume–price models and keep them mainly for your own use and learning. Trajectories-of-cost-and-revenues models are a bit more difficult to build, but they are much more effective when it comes to communicating with other people.

10.3 Checking that the new model gives the same results

With the new model, it is much easier to test the different scenarios for Delta Metal. The value of the drivers are given in Table 10.4. You can check that they produce the same results as the drivers in Table 7.11. The results of the model in Table 7.11 are given in Table 7.12.

10.4 The recommended trajectory-of-payments-and-receipts model

The model that I would like to recommend to you is the one in Tables 10.5 and 10.6. The only difficulty in building this model comes from the existence of an inventory that complicates the estimation of cost of goods sold, and of the inventory itself.

Cost of goods sold

The estimation of CGS is a three-step process:

Step 1: Estimating CGS as if there was no inventory
If there was no inventory, then cost of goods sold in – let us say 2002 – would be simply estimated as follows:

Table 10.4 ● Estimating the value of the drivers in 2002 and beyond

(A)	(B)	(C)	Change in selling price	Change in purchasing price	Change in volume	Change in expenses	Col. per.	Inv. turn.	Pay. per.
NO	NO	0.00	0.04 in 2002 then 0	0	0	0.04 in 2002 then 0	6	4	4
NO	NO	0.10	0.04 in 2002 then 0	0	0.10	$1.4 \times 1.1 - 1$ in 2002 then 0.1	6	4	4
NO	YES	0.00	0.04 in 2002 then 0	−0.075 in 2002 then 0	0	0.04 in 2002 then 0	6	4	4
NO	YES	0.10	0.04 in 2002 then 0	−0.075 in 2002 then 0	0.10	$1.4 \times 1.1 - 1$ in 2002 then 0.1	6	4	4
YES	NO	0.00	$1.04 \times 0.96 - 1$ in 2002, then 0	0	0	0.04 in 2002 then 0	4	4	4
YES	NO	0.10	$1.04 \times 0.96 - 1$ in 2002, then 0	0	0.10	$1.4 \times 1.1 - 1$ in 2002 then 0.1	4	4	4
YES	YES	0.00	$1.04 \times 0.96 - 1$ in 2002, then 0	−0.075 in 2002 then 0	0	0.04 in 2002 then 0	4	4	4
YES	YES	0.10	$1.04 \times 0.96 - 1$ in 2002, then 0	−0.075 in 2002 then 0	0.10	$1.4 \times 1.1 - 1$ in 2002 then 0.1	4	4	4

(A) Delta Metal implements the new credit plan (yes or no)
(B) The EU implements the new regulations (yes or no)
(C) The market grows by 0 or 10% – volume growth

Note:
Please compare these drivers with those of the per-cent-of-sales model in Tables 7.4 and 6.13. If you want to make your life easier, you can put a formula that estimates selling expenses according to the behaviour we suppose them to have in our simulations: in 2002: $(1.04) \times (1 + \text{sales volume growth}) - 1$; then sales volume growth.

$$CGS_{2002} = CGS_{2001} \times (1 + Vc_{2002/2001}) \times (1 + PPc_{2002/2001})$$

with

$Vc_{2002/2001}$ = change in sales volume from 2001 to 2002

$PPc_{2002/2001}$ = change in purchasing price from 2001 to 2002

Step 2: Readjusting the base CGS for the 'catch-up' effect

There was an inventory of goods at the beginning of 2001. If purchasing prices have increased in 2001 this inventory of goods which was bought at a lower price in 2000 has enabled Delta Metal to see its CGS grow less than it should have done in 2001 (this is the 'price delaying effect' of inventory). This beneficial impact will not happen again in 2002. A catch-up effect will take place in 2002 whatever new price changes may occur in that year. We now have to come back to the CGS calculation formula and make the base CGS equal to what CGS_{2001} should have been without the impact of the inventory that existed at the beginning of 2001.

Without the effect of inventory, CGS_{2001} should have been:

CGS_{2001} + Open inventory$_{2001} \times PPc_{2001/2000}$

with

$PPc_{2002/2001}$ = change in purchasing price from 2000 to 2001

OI_{2001} = inventory at the beginning of 2001

and the formula for CGS becomes:

$$CGS_{2002} = (CGS_{2001} + OI_{2001} \times PPc_{2001/2000}) \times (1 + Vc_{2002/2001}) \times (1 + PPc_{2002/2001})$$

Step 3: Adjusting the new CGS for the 'delaying effect'

The last step is to introduce the delaying effect due to the inventory existing at the end of 2001/beginning of 2002. The formula for calculating CGS finally is:

$$CGS_{2002} = (CGS_{2001} + OI_{2001} \times PPc_{2001/2000}) \times (1 + Vc_{2002/2001}) \times (1 + PPc_{2002/2001})$$
$$- OI_{2002} \times PPc_{2002/2001}$$

with

OI_{2002} = inventory at the beginning of 2002

To summarize, CGS in 2002 depends not only on: what CGS was in 2001 and how the volume of sales and the unit cost price are expected to change, but also – and this is due to inventory – the inventory at the beginning of 2002, *the inventory at the beginning of 2001* and the *change in unit cost price in 2001*.

It is definitely very easy to miss such effects with a per-cent-of-sales model!

Inventory

The model estimates the inventory open as a function of the volume of sales expected to be made during the year. Let us go through the estimation of inventory at the beginning of 2003 (OI_{2003}). In 2003 sales are expected to grow at a rate of $Vc_{2003/2002}$. If it wants the volume of its inventory to be equal to three months of expected sales, then Delta Metal has

Table 10.5 ● The recommended trajectories-of-payments-and-receipts model (foreground)

Year	2001	2002	2003	2004	2005	2006		Cum.
Drivers								
Change in sales price		4%	0%	0%	0%	0%		
Change in volume		0%	0%	0%	0%	0%		
Change in price of purchases		0.000	0.00	0.00	0.00	0.00		
Inventory turnover		4.00	4.00	4.00	4.00	4.00		
Change in operating expenses		4.0%	0.0%	0.0%	0.0%	0.0%		
Depreciation		0.60	0.60	0.60	0.60	0.60		
Collection period		6.00	6.00	6.00	6.00	6.00		
Payment period		4.00	4.00	4.00	4.00	4.00		
Capital expenditure		0.50	0.50	0.50	0.50	0.50		
Outputs								
Sales	114.93	119.53	119.53	119.53	119.53	119.53		
Inventory open	26.99	17.37	23.91	23.91	23.91	23.91		
CGS	95.63	95.63	95.63	95.63	95.63	95.63		
Operating expenses	16.09	16.73	16.73	16.73	16.73	16.73		
Depreciation	0.34	0.60	0.60	0.60	0.60	0.60		
Operating income	2.88	6.57	6.57	6.57	6.57	6.57		
Taxable income		1.98	6.57	6.57	6.57	6.57		
Operating income after tax	**2.88**	**5.92**	**4.40**	**4.40**	**4.40**	**4.40**		23.53
Depreciation	0.34	0.60	0.60	0.60	0.60	0.60		
Receivables end	58.43	59.77	59.77	59.77	59.77	59.77		
Payables end	40.13	34.05	31.88	31.88	31.88	23.91		
Cash from operations	25.09	−7.44	2.82	5.00	5.00	20.94		
Capital expenditure	2.00	0.50	0.50	0.50	0.50	0.50		
Free cash flow	**23.09**	**−7.94**	**2.32**	**4.50**	**4.50**	**20.44**		
Free cash flow 2002–06		−43.60	2.32	4.50	4.50	20.44	35.36	23.53
NPV (end 2001 at 14%)		**−4.02**						
Other output variables								
Sales growth		4.0%	0.0%	0.0%	0.0%	0.0%		
CGS/sales	83.2%	80.0%	80.0%	80.0%	80.0%	80.0%		
Operating expenses/sales	14.0%	14.0%	14.0%	14.0%	14.0%	14.0%		
Operating income/sales	2.5%	5.5%	5.5%	5.5%	5.5%	5.5%		
Apparent inventory turnover	3.54	5.51	4.00	4.00	4.00	4.00		

to build an inventory equal to three months of the CGS of 2002 once this CGS has been increased at the same rate as the 2003 sales. But then there is the problem with the price-delaying effect caused by the inventory at the beginning of 2002. Before you adjust CGS 2002 for growth, you have to make it equal to what it would have been without the impact of the price-delaying effect. When you have done this CGS 2002 is at the same price as inventory open:

$$OI_{2003} = (CGS_{2002} + PPc_{2002/2001} \times OI_{2002}) \times (1 + Vc_{2003/2002}) / IT$$

with:

Table 10.6 • The recommended trajectories-of-payments-and-receipts model (background)

1	*Year*	*2001*	*=B1+1*	•
2	**Drivers**			
3	*Change in sales price*		*0.04*	*0*
4	*Change in volume sold*		*0*	*=C4*
5	*Change in price of purchases*		*0*	*=C5*
6	*Inventory turnover*		*4*	*=C6*
7	*Change in operating expenses*		*0.04*	*0*
8	*Depreciation*		*0.6*	*=C8*
9	*Collection period*		*6*	*=C9*
10	*Payment period*		*4*	*=C10*
11	*Capital expenditure*		*0.5*	*=C11*
12	**Outputs**			
13	Sales	114.934	=B13*(1+C3)*(1+C4)	•
14	Inventory open	26.993	17.367	=(C15–C14+C14 *(1+C5))*(1+D4)/C6
15	CGS	95.625	=((B15–B14+B14 *(1+B5))*(1+C4) *(1+C5))–C14*C5	•
16	Operating expenses	16.09	=B16*(1+C7)	•
17	Depreciation	0.34	=C8	•
18	Operating income	=B13–B15–B16–B17	=C13–C15–C16–C17	•
19	Taxable income		=C18–4.588	=D18+IF(C19<0,C19,0)
20	**Income after tax**	=B18	a	•
21	Depreciation	=B17	=C8	•
22	Receivables end	58.425	=C13/12*C9	•
23	Payables end	40.132	=(C15+D14–C14)/ 12*C10	•
24	Cash from operations	25.093	=C20+C21+B22–C22 +C14–D14–B23+C23	•
25	Capital expenditure	2	=C11	•
26	**Free cash flow**	=B24–B25	•	•
26	Free cash flow 2002–06		=C26–B22–C14+B23	=D26
27	**NPV (end 2001, at 14%)**	=NPV(0.14,C26:H26)		
28	**Other output variables**			
29	*Sales growth*		*=C13/B13–1*	•
30	*CGS/sales*	*=B15/B13*	•	•
31	*Operating expenses/sales*	*=B16/B13*	•	•
32	*Operating income/sales*	*=B18/B13*	•	•
33	*Apparent inventory turnover*	*=B15/B14*	•	•

a C20: = IF(C18<0,C18,IF(C19<C18,IF(C19>0,C18–C19*0.33,C18),C18*0.67))
H27: =G22–G23–SUM(C8.G8)+SUM(C11.G11)

OI_{2003} = inventory at the beginning of 2003; OI_{2002} = inventory at the beginning of 2002
CGS_{2002} = cost of goods sold in 2002; $PPc_{2002/2001}$ = change in purchasing price in 2002
$Vc_{2003/2002}$ = change in volume sold from 2002 to 2003; IT = inventory turnover

The model is organized in such a way that drivers, calculations and output variables are separated. Working capital needs accounts have been made more compact (using the fact that ending and opening accounts are the same). The 'bottom line' of the model is the NPV of the free cash flows. This the model that I recommend you to use when modelling pure trading activities. A similar type of model adapted to more complex business activities is in Part IV (Case N – Motion-Control).

You can check that this model gives the same results as the vertical model (see Table 7.12) and as the explicit volume–price model (Tables 10.2 and 10.3).

Notes

1. Which is a problem when this past has been smoothed by accounting principles.
2. For alternative methods for evaluating inventories, please refer to C. Horngren, G. Sundem and J. Elliott (1999) *Introduction to Financial Accounting*, Prentice Hall.

CHAPTER 11

Growth, cash and value

The need for continuous improvement

Financial planning is a matter of managing the trajectories of all the costs, payments, revenues and receipts. In order to create value you should manage these trajectories in such a way that income and cash are positive in the long run, or on a cumulative basis.[1]

The safe way to make sure that cash and income are positive in the long run is to keep them continuously positive – i.e. always to keep your business in cell 1 of the parity matrix. However, this is not always possible as:

- launching new products, developing new businesses, creating totally new industries, etc. often brings companies into cell 4 – or even cell 3. We discuss this issue in Part V;
- many business processes have a 'make-and-sell', or 'buy-and-sell', or 'push', or '**pay-then-collect**'[2] design that makes it difficult to control the trajectories of costs, disbursements, revenues and receipts.

Chapter 11 starts with modelling the impact of growth at Delta Metal. Growth is a major issue for any business.[3] How can a company that operates according to a 'make-and-sell' design keep its cash and profit positive when there is growth? The dynamics of the make-and-sell business designs are further discussed in Chapter 12 where we also discuss the dynamics of the 'sense-and-respond' or 'pull' or '**collect-then-pay**' approaches. Pay-then-collect and collect-then-pay are business designs that exist in both the economy of things and in the economy of information: you do not need to operate in the economy of atoms to see growth destabilize your cash flows!

For many businesses (all those which operate according to the pay-then-collect design), growth is a process that makes the trajectories of income and cash diverge for a period of time (*see* Figure 11.1). Some businesses accept it and call it 'investing in growth'. Others refuse to believe that cash ever becomes negative. They put improvements in place, keep cash afloat and create even more value, or they just decide to reinvent their business design and go for a collect-then-pay model.

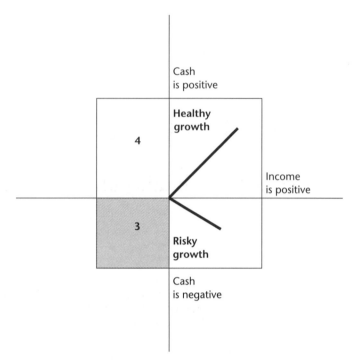

Figure 11.1 Two cash and income trajectories that may result from growth

11.1 The impact of growth at Delta Metal: growth without improvement, value and cash

Four of the eight scenarios of Delta Metal envisage a higher growth – more quantities sold: instead of being flat, the market may start growing and the company may experience a 5 to 10% volume increase. We have already generated the outcomes of the 10% growth scenarios (10% more volume each year). Let us use the horizontal model (Tables 10.5 and 10.6), first to check the results that we already have (Tables 7.11 and 7.12), and then to generate new results with a clearly higher growth: 30%. Let us not forget that in 2000 Delta Metal has grown by 24%.

Table 11.1 shows the impact of what we can call 'growth without improvement'. The different scenarios are grouped within three categories: 'base' (no new credit plan and no new regulations), 'new regulations' (and no new credit plan), and 'new credit plan' (and no new regulations). Within each of these categories, the only difference between the different scenarios is the difference in volume growth. Except for growth, all the other drivers are the same: margins remain the same, operating expenses grow with volume (and as a result remain the same as a percentage of sales), collection period, inventory turnover and payment period remain the same. The results show the three consequences of growth without improvement:

1. It increases both income and cash in the long run.
2. It changes the trajectories of cash payments and receipts and creates cash deficits and excesses.
3. It just leverages the value created.

Table 11.1 ● Analyzing the impact of growth

	2002	2003	2004	2005	2006		Cum.
Base (no new credit plan, no new regulations)							
No volume growth							
Income after tax	5.92	4.40	4.40	4.40	4.40		23.53
Free cash flow	−7.94	2.32	4.50	4.50	20.44		
Free cash flow 2002–06	−43.60	2.32	4.50	4.50	20.44	35.36	23.53
NPV (end 2001 @ 14%)	**−4.02**						
10% growth							
Income after tax	6.40	5.41	5.99	6.63	7.34		31.78
Free cash flow	−13.59	−3.34	−0.37	−0.37	27.86		
Free cash flow 2002–06	−49.25	−3.34	−0.37	−0.37	27.86	57.25	31.78
NPV (end 2001 @ 14%)	**−5.69**						
30% growth							
Income after tax	7.36	7.72	10.16	13.32	17.44		56.00
Free cash flow	−25.86	−18.82	−18.43	−23.87	45.99		
Free cash flow 2002–06	**−61.52**	−18.82	−18.43	−23.87	45.99	132.64	56.00
NPV (end 2001 @ 14%)	**−10.70**						
New regulations, no new credit plan							
No volume growth							
Income after tax	9.85	9.21	9.21	9.21	9.21		46.69
Free cash flow	−9.68	4.84	9.31	9.31	28.97		
Free cash flow 2002–06	−45.34	4.84	9.31	9.31	28.97	39.61	46.69
NPV (end 2001 @ 14%)	**8.83**						
10% growth							
Income after tax	10.81	11.23	12.39	13.67	15.08		63.17
Free cash flow	−15.88	−0.92	5.02	5.55	40.96		
Free cash flow 2002–06	−51.54	−0.92	5.02	5.55	40.96	64.10	63.17
NPV (end 2001 @ 14%)	**11.24**						
30% growth							
Income after tax	12.73	15.84	20.71	27.05	35.28		111.62
Free cash flow	−29.45	−17.09	−12.48	−16.13	74.00		
Free cash flow 2002–06	−65.11	−17.09	−12.48	−16.13	74.00	148.42	111.62
PV (end 2001 @ 14%)	**17.82**						
New credit plan, no new regulations							
No volume growth							
Income after tax	1.79	1.79	1.53	1.20	1.20		7.52
Free cash flow	9.45	−0.29	1.63	1.30	17.24		
Free cash flow 2002–06	−26.21	−0.29	1.63	1.30	17.24	13.84	7.52
NPV (end 2001 @ 14%)	**−6.08**						
10% growth							
Income after tax	2.03	2.29	1.82	1.94	2.18		10.26
Free cash flow	5.70	−4.09	−1.94	−2.20	25.85		
Free cash flow 2002–06	−29.96	−4.09	−1.94	−2.20	25.85	22.60	10.26
NPV (end 2001 @ 14%)	**−8.31**						
30% growth							
Income after tax	2.51	2.99	3.12	4.17	5.55		18.34
Free cash flow	−2.74	−15.15	−14.56	−18.84	52.53		
Free cash flow 2002–06	−38.40	−15.15	−14.56	−18.84	52.53	52.76	18.34
NPV (end 2001 @ 14%)	**−15.01**						

Growth increases both cash and income

In Table 11.1, the cumulative calculations of income and cash enable you to check the positive impact of growth on both income and cash in all the scenarios: growth without improvement always means more profit and cash in the end. You can check in each of the three categories of scenarios that:

● when annual volume growth goes from 0 to 10% cumulated cash and income are multiplied by 1.4;
● when growth goes from 0 to 30% cumulated cash and income are multiplied by 2.4!

When they think about growth, people immediately see the positive effect growth has on income and cash. The effect is true indeed but it does not necessarily mean that growth has a positive effect on value.

Growth disturbs the trajectories of cash payments and receipts

Figure 11.2 shows the impact of growth and working capital needs on the cash generation profile of a business. If there were no working capital needs, then:

● cash receipts would come at the same time as sales;
● cash payments would come at the same time as costs;
● net cash would come at the same time as profit and would increase with growth – just as profit does!

But as shown in Figure 11.2, working capital needs:

● delay receipts. Delta Metal has to wait six months before it collects its sales.
● accelerate disbursements. As a stockist, Delta Metal buys three months in advance of sales in order to have an inventory. Fortunately Delta Metal is able to delay the payment of these purchases!

Working capital needs create cash deficits at the early stages of growth. If the business creates value, net cash is necessarily positive in the end and the early cash deficits will be more than compensated for by cash excesses later. The cash profile created by growth makes it easy to repay a loan raised for financing growth. This is why most banks have tradition-ally been very positive when asked to finance growth, the driver of 'self-liquidating loans'.

Companies that carry accounts receivable and inventories that amount to a larger total than accounts payable are said to experience **positive working capital needs** which also means that such companies pay for their various costs earlier than they get paid for by their customers. This is what we called above the **pay-then-collect**, or 'buy-and-sell' or 'push' business design. For all the companies that operate according to this design, growth means short-term problems and more growth means less cash. Growth tends to push such companies into cell 4 of the cash–income parity matrix. With growth, the operating cash flow of such companies is automatically driven down. If growth also requires large capital expenditure, then their free cash flow may easily turn very negative. This is what some people call 'investing in growth'. Depending on the characteristics of the operations and of the rate of growth, this investment in growth may be extremely spectacular (see Case K – SW Life).

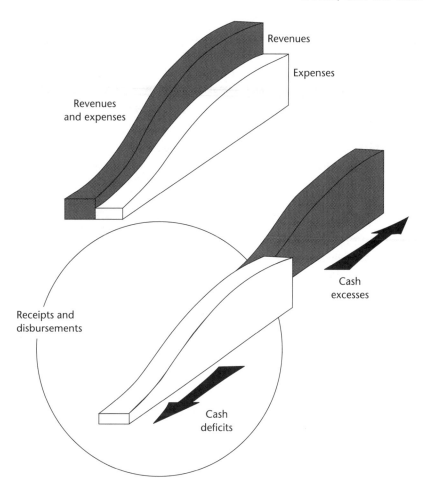

Figure 11.2 Impact of growth on the cash generation profile

At the other end of the spectrum, companies that carry less accounts receivable and inventories than accounts payable are said to experience **negative working capital needs**. Such companies are paid by their customers before they have to pay their suppliers and their other costs. This is what we called above **collect-then-pay** or 'sense-and-respond' or 'pull' business designs. Food supermarkets and contractors who receive large advance payments are examples of companies that enjoy negative working capital needs. When there is growth such companies do not experience any short-term cash problems: for such companies growth means more cash in the short term.

Growth leverages value

Rather than say that growth creates value it is more exact to say that growth just magnifies the value-creating process:

- When a business creates value, then the impact of growth is positive. In the scenarios corresponding to the new regulations, Delta Metal creates value and growth multiplies the value created: 30% growth means 2 times more value than 0% growth!
- When a business destroys value, then the impact of growth is negative. Growth enables such a business to multiply the destruction of value by a factor: when it goes from 0% to 30%, growth makes the negative value of the base scenario 2.7 times larger and the negative value of the new credit plan 2.5 times larger.

Grow good businesses but do not grow bad ones! Make sure that a business creates value before you try to grow it! Do not believe that you can easily 'outgrow your problems'. When you have a difficult business, the top priority is probably to turn it back to a value creation status. Once the business creates value again, then you can start thinking about growing it. It is important to realize that:

- Doing more business necessarily scales up all the features of the business, including the positive and the negative ones. If there are cash deficits at the beginning, these are multiplied by growth. You can check in Figure 11.1 that the cash deficit created by the new regulations in 2001 increases with growth. This is, however, a pure scaling effect. As you do more business, you experience a bigger cash deficit at the beginning, as well as bigger cash excesses later and a greater value.
- The only criterion that matters is value. Businesses that create value have the potential to amplify their success and to displace less successful businesses. Doing more of such businesses necessarily creates more value.

11.2 'Healthy', 'continuously cash-generating' growth: the need for continuous improvements

When you realize that they correspond to a pure timing issue, you may consider that the temporary cash deficits caused by growth are nothing to worry about. The problem, though, is that growth often takes place over a fairly long period of time. Cash deficits come now and cash excesses will come a few years later and since the world is not predictable, these cash excesses may come a bit earlier or later than expected. They may also be bigger or smaller than expected. Companies pursuing aggressive growth strategies heavily financed by loans have often discovered the hazards of growth. The entry of a competitor, unexpected operational problems, etc. can easily delay the harvesting period and banks who believed they had arranged a self-liquidating loan may start getting more and more nervous. In some case the delays and the nervousness of the banks and of the company may even end up in a fatal crisis.

In order to avoid the risks attached to any investment in growth many companies now demand a special type of growth. In spite of the fact that they operate according to the pay-then-collect model[4] these companies want to experience a growth that means:

- more sales and,
- more profit and,
- **more cash now.**

This is what is called 'healthy' growth or 'continuously cash-generating' growth, or 'cell 1' growth. Growing and generating more cash now is not just a matter of increasing volume. It is a matter of increasing volume **and** at the same time of improving the operations. Areas for improvement are:

- Improvements in working capital parameters: reduction of the collection period, increase in the inventory turnover and also increase in the payment period. One should realize, however, that if they work from the point of view of arithmetic, increases in payment period do not necessarily work from a business point of view, especially when you claim that your suppliers are your partners.
- Improvements in prices and productivity: increase in selling prices, reduction in purchasing prices, decrease in selling and administrative expenses.

One question is often asked when discussing the concept of healthy growth in executive programmes: is it realistic to believe that a business could grow and increase its prices at the same time? The answer comes in two parts:

- Yes, some companies manage to increase prices when they grow and this is pure logic. Growth means that there are customers who enjoy creating value with your products and services. Isn't that the best opportunity you have to share the value with them – another way to describe price increases? Do you really believe that it is a good idea to wait and risk finding yourself trying to get a price increase when your products are no longer at the top of your customers' preferences or when there is a recession?
- The concept of 'buying market share', i.e. of aggressively gaining volume through a lot of market investments including aggressive pricing, is very risky and should be undertaken only when one is extremely confident that the strategy will succeed.[5]

The model in Table 11.2 can help you estimate the minimum improvements that are needed at Delta Metal in order that a 10% growth does not result in less at any moment in time. Within the base scenario, this means that the annual cash should be at least:

	Year				
	2002	**2003**	**2004**	**2005**	**2006**
Net cash	−7.94	2.32	4.50	4.50	20.44

Table 11.2 shows what it takes for each driver (acting in isolation) to maintain cash at the level it has without growth. The model actually aims at keeping the cumulative value of cash in 2002 and 2003[6] (−7.94 + 2.32) unchanged. The table also suggests a process for generating these results.

The results also show that value is greatly increased by a very tight control of the trajectories of disbursements and receipts.[7]

Table 11.2 ● How to avoid cash decreasing when there is growth

Process for generating the results
Starting from the model in Table 10.5:

1. Set the drivers for the base solution and insert two blank rows above row 29.
2. Copy the values of the free cash flows (C26:G26) into, for example, C29:G29 (Copy/Paste Special/Values).
3. Estimate the difference between the cash flows of a new scenario and the cash flow of the base in 2002 and 2003: in D30: +C26+D26–C29–D29.
4. Check that operating expenses are driven by volume growth and adjust their formula in order to easily change their level in 2002: in C7: =1.04×(1+C4)*(1+C2)–1. You can now enter in C2 a driver to adjust the level of operating expenses, in D7: +D4; copy.
5. Set the parameters of the model for the solution 10% growth, no new credit plan, no new EU regulations. You should get a value of –13.60 in C26 and of –11.34 in D30.
6. Use the Goal Seek function to estimate the value of the driver that would bring the cash in 2002 back to –7.94, or the value of C29 to zero. To do so, and starting with change in the level of operating expenses, position the cursor on D30, click on Tools, Goal Seek. Excel suggests setting the value of D30. State that you want that cell set to zero by changing cell C2.
7. When Excel has set cell D30 to zero, click on OK and observe the results: how do the free cash flows look in the other years? What is the NPV now? Then reset the cell that has been changed by Excel (again set C2 to zero) and go to the next driver.

Results

Driver	Driver value needed for that driver alone to restore the 2002 and 2003 cash flows to their original cumulated value	Resulting NPV
Change in operating expenses	–44%	16.34
Change in selling price	+14%	27.20
Change in purchase price	–9%	18.26
Inventory turnover	6.3	–1.53
Collection period	5	–0.52
Payment period	5	–0.69

Notes

1. Including financing costs.
2. Unfortunately, there is no commonly accepted pair of expressions for describing the two extreme designs for a business.

   ● In trading activities we use 'stockists' as opposed to 'brokers' (see Chapter 12).
   ● In manufacturing, we use 'forecast-driven' or 'push' manufacturing as opposed to 'order-driven' or 'pull' or 'just in time' manufacturing. Among the many references, you may refer to R. Harmon and L. Peterson (1990), *Reinventing the Factory*, The Free Press; R. Hayes, S. Wheelwright and K. Clark (1988), *Dynamic Manufacturing*, The Free Press; R. Lubben (1988), *Just-in-time Manufacturing*, McGraw-Hill; S. Shingo (1988), *Non Stock Production: the Shingo system for continuous improvement*, Productivity Press; K. Suzaki (1987), *The New Manufacturing Challenge*, The Free Press; R. Hall (1987), *Attaining Manufacturing Excellence*, Dow Jones-Irwin.

- More recently, in strategy and organization, we use the 'make and sell' as opposed to the 'sense and respond' model. Please refer to S.H. Haeckel (1999), *Adaptive Enterprise: Creating and Leading Sense-and-Respond Organizations*, Harvard Business School Press; and E. Goldratt and J. Cox (1989), *The Goal*, Gower.
- And in finance, what counts is the sequence of payments: pay-then-collect vs. collect-then pay.

3. There are many reasons why businesses should grow. The world economy is growing, new technologies and markets are continuously emerging. Most importantly, in an evolutionary perspective, growth is the symptom of success: the success of a new product, of a new business model leads to its diffusion and to the progressive destruction of less successful solutions. Any business that does not grow runs the risk of extinction. In a competitive environment all competitors continuously improve their productivity. Increasing productivity without growth means continuously decreasing resources and personnel in particular.

4. The alternative is obviously to change the business design and to go for a collect-then-pay design. This is what Delta Metal could try to do and become a broker instead of being a stockist. This is discussed in Chapter 12.

5. And that it will be possible to increase prices!

6. You could also do it with 2002 only but cash is such a sensitive variable that it is better to consider a two-year period.

7. The relatively small contribution of the working capital parameters to value may surprise you. The reason for that is that we aim to restore cash over a short period of time. The most effective drivers for restoring cash quickly are the working capital parameters (collection period, inventory turn, etc.). A small change in any of these parameters has an immediate and major impact on cash. To achieve the goal of restoring cash in 2002 and 2003, you need small changes of these drivers only. These small changes obviously cause relatively small value improvements.

CHAPTER 12

Sequencing payments as a source of value

Forecast-driven, pay-then-collect vs. order-driven, collect-then-pay operations

Creating value, although a very simple matter of receiving more than spending, is made difficult by the fact that spending typically comes first. In Chapter 11, we discussed an initial challenge of the pay-then-collect business designs: they make it difficult to manage the trajectory of cash when the business grows. In this chapter, we discuss a second and probably even more difficult challenge of these designs: risk. When it comes first, spending cannot be driven by the actual receipts but only by a forecast of these receipts. Aggressively committing to spending is risky and may result in a large destruction of value. The typical process that leads pay-then-collect companies to destroy value is:

- committing to an aggressive spending trajectory that brings them into cell 2;
- then, after a while, suddenly realizing that the aggressive spending trajectory was not adequate. The next step is to decide, often under pressure, to implement a series of drastic actions aimed at restoring cash. Typically, this brings the company not into cell 2 but rather into cell 4 or even 3.

This is what happened at Delta Metal in 2000 and 2001 (*see* Figure 12.1).

12.1 Forecasting mistakes and their very expensive remedies: the true cost of inventory

Mistakes are of very different kinds. At one extreme there are all the mistakes that can be recognized and corrected fast.[1] Such mistakes do not really matter. At the other extreme there are mistakes which are not easily recognized – or which take a long time to be recognized – and which are finally corrected at a very high cost. The mistakes that we are going to discuss belong to the latter category and we are going to try to simulate the mistake itself as well as the corrective action. Finally, we will try to estimate the cost of

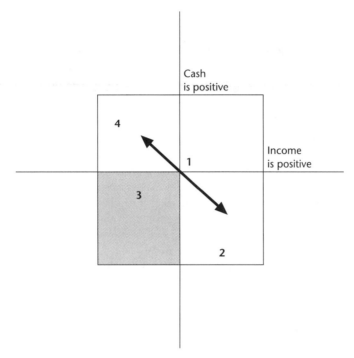

Figure 12.1 Value destruction trajectories

both the mistake and the remedy. When doing such a simulation with a spreadsheet, it is a good idea to start with the study of one mistake only. For Delta Metal, let us simulate the impact of a forecasting error made towards the end of 2001 – in the budget – and not corrected until very late in 2002.

The 'forecasting mistake-and-remedial action' scenario at Delta Metal

The company commits[2] to a spending trajectory

Towards the end of 2001, Delta Metal strongly believes that the market will consolidate in 2002. As result of this strong belief, the company makes a series of commitments:

● Sales are budgeted at Ffr119.53 million.
● The company decides to keep its resources at their current level. Delta Metal decides not to downsize its warehousing facilities. Part of the investment made in 2000 and 2001 could have been reversed. Delta Metal also decides to increase its selling and administrative resources by 4%.
● Finally, the company realizes that the inventory should be rebuilt and more steel is ordered.

All these decisions put the company on a spending trajectory that is going to last for a period of time. Even if new decisions are made it will take time to alter this trajectory.

Then 2002 progressively unfolds

During the first part of the year the market is flat. This does not affect the confidence of the management of Delta Metal in their budget. Just before the summer, the market collapses. Delta Metal sees these difficulties as temporary and believes that the market will recover after the summer. In order not to miss any sales, the company continues to order and to purchase according to budget. However, towards the end of the year the management of Delta Metal has to accept the evidence:

● Sales for the whole year will be 10% less than budget in volume if nothing is done.
● Administrative and selling costs are excessive in relation to these sales. However, it is too late for having a significant impact on these costs by the end of the year.
● Purchases have not been slowed down. This makes inventories surge. This has no impact on the margins so far (matching principle) but creates a cash problem. Short-term borrowing increases. This increases interest costs and makes the banks very nervous.

Finally, the company takes an expensive remedy

As is typically done in similar circumstances, the company starts exploring the possibility of selling part of its inventory at a sacrificial price in order to alleviate the pressure on cash. With a price concession that would result in reducing the overall price increase over the whole year to 2% – instead of 4% in the budget – Delta Metal expects to limit the decrease in volume sold to 4% only in 2002.

The model in Table 10.5 can be used as a base for simulating the 'full impact' of a forecasting mistake: impact of the error itself and impact of a typical remedy. There is a need, however, to make some changes to the model:

● introduction of the balance sheet as of the end in 2002 and of an interest calculation;
● introduction of both the budget and the actual figures.

Table 12.1 shows the foreground of the new model and Table 12.2 its background. With this model we can assess the impact of the forecasting error and of the remedy. Table 12.3 shows the results after the mistake as well as the results after the mistake and the remedy – or the full results of the forecasting mistake.

The forecasting mistake results in a sharp decrease in income and in cash. Delta Metal is really rushing into cell 3! The drop in operating income is due to the high selling and administrative expenses. They were decided in relation to a sales forecast that has proven to be too optimistic. The drop in cash is also due to the increase in inventory. Even though the cash balance is very negative it is important to keep in mind that the inventory might be sold fairly quickly – even though it is 50% more than what is needed for the sales expected in 2003.[3]

The numbers after the reaction look attractive. The loss has been reduced by 1.3 million and cash is even better than in the base solution. Delta Metal is still in cell 3 but on its way to cell 4. The problem, though, is that you cannot really stop analyzing the impact of the forecasting mistake and of the reaction at this stage. You have to think about the possible longer-term side-effects of the medicine that has been administered:

● *What will happen to Delta Metal's selling prices in 2003 and beyond?* If the company is able to return quickly to its previous price level, then the impact on value will be minimal. But if the price cut results in a durable erosion in prices, or if even worse, the price level

Table 12.1 ● Budget vs. actual model

Year	Budget[a]			Actual[b]	
	2001	2002	2003	2002	2003
Drivers					
Change in sales price		4%		4%	
Change in volume sold		0%	0%	−10%	
Change in price of purchases		0.00		0.00	
Inventory turnover		4.00		4.00	
Change in operating expenses		4%		4%	
Depreciation		0.60		0.60	
Collection period		6.00		6.00	
Payment period		4.00		4.00	
Capital expenditure		0.50		0.50	
Outputs					
Sales	114.93	119.53		107.58	
Inventory open	26.99	17.37	23.91	17.37	33.47
Purchases	86.00	102.16		102.16	
CGS	95.63	95.63		86.06	
Operating expenses	16.09	16.73		16.73	
Depreciation	0.34	0.60		0.60	
Operating income	2.88	6.57		4.18	
Interest	6.23	7.29		8.43	
Income before tax	−3.35	−0.72		−4.25	
Taxable income		−5.31		−8.84	
Income after tax	**−3.35**	**−0.72**		**−4.25**	
Depreciation	0.34	0.60		0.60	
Receivables end	58.43	59.77		53.79	
Payables end	40.13	34.05		34.05	
Cash from operations	18.86	−14.08		−21.19	
Capital expenditure	2.00	0.50		0.50	
Free cash flow	**16.86**	**−14.58**		**−21.69**	
Repayment of long-term loans	3.08	2.53		2.53	
Dividends	0.00	0.00		0.00	
New equity	0.00	0.00		0.00	
New short-term loans	−12.86	17.11		24.22	
Change in cash	0.92	0.00		0.00	
Cash	1.28	1.28		1.28	
Receivables	58.43	59.77		53.79	
Inventory	17.37	23.91		33.47	
Net fixed assets	4.20	4.10		4.10	
Total assets	81.27	89.05		92.64	
Short-term loans	24.07	41.18		48.29	
Payables	40.13	34.05		34.05	
Long-term loans	6.92	4.39		4.39	
Shareholders' equity	10.15	9.43		5.90	
Total liabilities and equities	81.27	89.05		92.64	
Output variables					
Sales growth	−11.2%	4.0%		−6.4%	
CGS/sales	83.2%	80.0%		80.0%	
Operating expenses/sales	14.0%	14.0%		15.6%	
Operating income/sales	2.5%	5.5%		3.9%	

[a] The results are the same as in Table 7.4.
[b] Actual is a combination of actual – or rather estimated – data (2003) and of a new forecast (2004).

Table 12.2 ● Background of the budget vs. actual model

A	C	E
	Budget	Actual
Year	2002	2002
1		
2		
3 **Drivers**		
4 *Change in sales price*	0.04	=C4
5 *Change in volume*	0	−0.1
6 *Change in price of purchases*	0	0
7 *Inventory turnover*	4	=C7
8 *Change in operating expenses*	0.04	=C8
9 *Depreciation*	0.6	=C9
10 *Collection period*	6	=C10
11 *Payment period*	4	=C11
12 *Capital expenditure*	0.5	=C12
13 **Outputs**		
14 Sales	=B14*(1+C4)*(1+C5)	=B14*(1+E4)*(1+E5)
15 Inventory open	17.367	=C15
16 Purchases	=C17+D15−C15	=C16*(1+E6)/(1+C6)
17 CGS	=((B17−B15+B15*(1+B6))*(1+C5)*(1+C6))−C15*C6	=(E14*(1.04/(1+E4))*C17/C14)*(1+E6)−C15*E6
18 Operating expenses	=B18*(1+C8)	=B18*(1+E8)
19 Depreciation	=C9	=C19
20 Operating income	=C14−C17−C18−C19	●
21 Interest	=0.16*(C42+C44)	●
22 Income before tax	=C20−C21	●
23 Taxable income	=−4.588+C22	●
24 Income after tax	ª	●
25 Depreciation	=C19	=C25
26 Receivables end	=C14/12*C10	●
27 Payables end	=(C17+D15−C15)/12*C11	●
28 Cash from operations	=C24+C25+B26−C26+C15−D15−B27+C27	=E24+E25+B26−E26+E15−F15−B27+E27
29 Capital expenditure	0.5	=C29
30 Free cash flow	=C28−C29	●
31 Repayment of long-term loans	2.534	=C31
32 Dividends	0	=C32
33 New equity	0	=C33
34 New short-term loans	−C30+C31+C32−C33+C35	●
35 Change in cash	0	=C35
36		
37 Cash	=B37+C36	=B37+E35
38 Receivables	=C26	●
39 Inventory	=D15	●
40 Net fixed assets	=B40+C29−C19	=B40+E29−E19
41 Total assets	=SUM(C37:C40)	●
42 Short-term loans	=B42+C34	=B42+E34
43 Payables	=C27	●
44 Long-term loans	=B44−C31	=B44−E31
45 Shareholders' equity	=B45+C24−C32	=B45+E24−E32
46 Total liabilities and equities	=SUM(C42:C45)	●

Note:
In column B: data from the case.
ª In C24: =IF(C22<0,C22,IF(C23<C22,IF(C22>0,C22−C23*0.33,C22),C22*0.67))
In D15: =(C17−C15+C15*(1+C6))*(1+D5)/C7. In F15: +E15+E16−E17*(1+E6)

Table 12.3 ● Results of the forecasting mistake

	Base scenario	Outcome of the mistake	
		Before reaction	After reaction
Net income	−0.72	−4.25	−2.93
Free cash flow	−14.58	−21.69	−8.61

The remedy

- price concession to maintain volume: prices increase by 2% in 2002 (vs. 4%) and volume decreases 4% (instead of 10%);
- delaying of the payments to suppliers: Delta Metal repeats what was done in 2001 and the payment period becomes 5 months.

---

never returns to its original level, then the loss of value will be large. You can use the model in Table 10.5 to estimate the NPV when you set the price increase in 2002 to 3% instead of the 4% originally planned. NPV falls from −4.02 to −6.43. A one-per-cent-point loss in selling price costs 2.4 million over five years.

- *Who will buy the steel sold at sacrificial prices?* If they do not need steel, customers will not be interested in buying even if the price is attractive. The most likely buyers of cheap steel are other stockists who feel they can take a position at a good price. Steel moving from stockist to stockist may increase the volatility of the market. This may render forecasts even more difficult and increase the chance of making more mistakes in the future.
- *What will happen to Delta Metal's purchasing prices?* The company has delayed its payments again and suppliers may react with a price increase. What if they were to increase their prices by 1% in order to compensate for the delay? The model in Table 10.5 shows that a 1% increase in purchasing price in 2002 and maintained over five years brings the NPV down from 4.02 to 6.08, a 2 million loss in value!

In the end it is not clear that the 'typical' reaction envisaged above is a good move. When you realize that you have made a forecasting mistake, you have to be careful to avoid reacting in a way that will make the situation even worse.[4]

The true cost of inventory

The cost of inventory is often defined as an interest cost. Like receivables and payables, the other main working capital items, inventory corresponds to a delay. However as already mentioned, inventory is of a different nature from receivables and payables: inventory is 'speculative'. Inventory is based on a forecast and one cannot assess its value by considering the outcome of holding inventory in one case only: the forecast was correct. One also has to consider all the cases when the forecast proves to be wrong! The discussion above shows that inventory may prove very expensive. The problem, though, is that inventory is nothing more than one of the consequences of adopting a specific design of operations: the pay-then-collect, forecast-driven model. Talking about the cost of inventory does not actually mean very much and a better approach is to compare different ways to design operations and sequencing payments and assess their respective value and risks. This is done below in Section 12.5.

12.2 The challenge of keeping payments/costs and revenues/receipts trajectories aligned

When looking at the accounts of a business we realize that sales are the top line of the income statement. This should not make us believe that sales drive all the other items: costs, income, cash, etc. The feeling that sales drive everything may also come from the use of the matching principle and from the construction of per-cent-of-sales models. But this is a totally wrong impression. **Sales do not come first! What comes first are costs, and some costs come much earlier than others – and consequently much earlier than sales.**

Spending/costs are engaged first

Spending ahead of sales occurs each time that a company decides that it is worth doing so (or 'investing'). Spending ahead of sales is a decision that is based on an opinion on the near or longer-term future:

● When Delta Metal decides to build a new warehouse, the decision is made and implemented based on what the company thinks that sales will be in the three to five years – or more – to come.
● Building up a sales force, developing administrative systems, etc. are actions that take time to implement and that cannot easily be reversed. Such decisions are typically made within a business plan that goes largely beyond the current year. Once the business plan is accepted, then spending starts, it takes place over a period of time, and then benefits start materializing.
● Delta Metal purchases steel based on a forecast of the sales in the next coming months. Orders are placed with suppliers, steel is received and paid for before a customer places the expected order – e.g. before a customer orders exactly the grade that has been ordered.

All these forecasts imply both volume and price assumptions and we know that price and volume have different impacts. A forecast that guesses volume right but completely misses price is not so effective!

Then, at a later date, orders come and – almost all of them – result in sales

The problem with orders is that they need to correspond to the steel that Delta Metal has in its inventory. If not they cannot be satisfied. When orders that can be satisfied come, then sales immediately occur or more typically some additional costs are committed for fulfilling the order, and then sales occur. Then accounting recognizes intermediate income: revenues are recognized and part of the costs that have been kept in the inventory are recovered. This means that the sales and the costs that are reported by accounting reflect the net result of a complex process:

1. Costs incurred as a result of a commitment made in relation to expected sales.
2. Occurrence of orders.
3. In some cases, recognition of forecasting mistakes and the impact of these mistakes, and of the reactions to these mistakes.[5]

The challenge of aligning cost and revenues trajectories

In business, costs and revenues are not as neatly aligned as they appear to be in an income statement. The fact that spending comes first has two series of consequences: it creates cash deficits and risk.

12.3 Brokers vs. stockists: two business designs leading to very different financial outcomes

Operating as a broker

Delta Metal operates as a stockist but most of its competitors have decided to operate as brokers. Stockists and brokers are at the two extremes of a continuum of solutions for designing and running trading operations. How do the brokers who compete with Delta Metal run their operations? Suppose that you work in the trading company of one of the large steel manufacturers portrayed in the case study. For the past 10 years, you have managed the relations with 20 large customers. Now, you decide that it is time for you to create your own brokerage firm. The great thing about creating a brokerage firm is that it does not really require money. The only thing you need is a good knowledge of the market. With your 10 years of experience you have developed an intimate knowledge of this small market. You know the purchasing managers of most of the customers and you also know how they behave. Some purchasers are able to forecast their needs months in advance. They have no difficulties with the long lead times of the manufacturers and buy from them direct in order to capture a good engineering service and a low price. Other purchasers are often facing unexpected needs and go to the stockists and brokers in order to try to fulfil their needs. You have decided to focus and help these latter purchasers.

A very effective sequence of actions to start your new business is the following:

1. Call potential purchasers until you identify one who is willing to let you help them meet their unexpected needs. Promise this customer your help! A unique feature of brokerage operations is that they start from the actual need of an actual potential customer and not from a forecast of demand.
2. Call everybody who might have the steel needed by your potential customer. Successful brokers are people who find steel in places where nobody else would think of looking. Successful brokers identify the workshop that has produced steel in excess, or the customer who has ordered too much, or the customer who needs to delay a planned purchase, etc.
3. Call your customer back and bring either the good news (you have found the steel!) or the bad news (in spite of all your efforts, you have failed to find the steel). If you have found the steel and are not willing to get involved in any logistics and administration, a very effective solution is to request that your customer transfers the agreed commission to your bank account. Upon receipt of this commission, you will tell him where the steel is. The disadvantage of this approach is obviously letting your customer know where the steel is. However, this is not a problem if there is little chance that the same steel will be in the same place in the future.

From a financial standpoint, the above sequence of actions is remarkable. This way of designing and running operations:

- does not require much investment. Very little spending in advance of receipts is required at any of the three steps described above;
- does not involve much risk. When you are successful, you generate money at step 3 above. When you are not successful, you do not generate any positive result, but you do not lose much either. However, please keep in mind that repeated failures may jeopardize your future as a broker!
- requires very little forecasting. Brokers spend their time at sensing the market and at responding to it, not at making forecasts;
- is very customer orientated. Brokers always start from the actual needs of an actual customer.

Operating as a stockist

The sequence of the operations needed to start and run a stockist business like the one of Delta Metal is very different:

1. Approach a manufacturer, order steel and pay for it. You need to have money to invest to create a new stockist firm! The need for money might actually not be limited to paying suppliers as you may also need it to secure an access to warehouse, transport and office facilities. In addition to raising money, you also need to make forecasts in order to decide what you are going to purchase. Forecasts are probably the very first step in the operations of a stockist.
2. **Wait for a customer to come!** The word 'wait' may sound strange as it does not reflect at all the intensity of the selling activity that a stockist will undoubtedly deploy at this stage, and the further spending of money ahead of sales that it will cause. 'Wait' is, however, an adequate word as it expresses very well the fact that the stockist will get or not get an order depending on a decision made by an external customer. A customer coming with the 'right' request at the 'right' time is the real test of the quality of the forecast.
3. Execute the order – or sell – and wait for the payment: typically Delta Metal has to wait for six months before a sale is paid. And this is the best case as it may also happen that Delta Metal does not have the steel needed.

The sequencing of the payments of Delta Metal creates a lot of challenges:

- A lot of money has to be spent ahead of getting an actual order from an actual customer. Table H.3 shows that, in 2001, Delta Metal's operations generated an income equal to 6% of the sales. This means that Delta Metal has to 'invest' 94 (80 for the purchase of steel and 14 for all the other preparatory and 'waiting' activities) in order to be ready to sell 100.
- Money spent ahead of getting an actual order creates a significant risk due to the relative outcomes of successful and of unsuccessful forecasts. Based on a sale of 100, a successful forecast creates a gain of 6 while an unsuccessful forecast creates a potential loss of 94, i.e. more than 15 times the gain achieved with a successful forecast!
- Forecasting becomes a key factor of success. While brokers hardly do any forecasting, stockists submit their survival to their ability to guess the future.
- This business model is as much concerned with the product as with the customers. The contact with the product comes very early in the process but the contact with the actual customers only comes at the end.

Is it a good strategy for Delta Metal to operate as a stockist? In a cyclical market forecasting is generally not easy. And for Delta Metal the difficulty is compounded by the fact that the company tries to forecast what the customers are not able to forecast themselves. When able to forecast, customers most probably order direct from the manufacturers. Doing so enables them to benefit from low prices and tailor-made products. It is only when they are unable to forecast that customers turn to stockists or brokers in the hope that they have anticipated their unexpected needs (stockists) or that they will be able to find a solution anyway (brokers).

What are the possibilities for Delta Metal to operate in such a way that the benefit derived from successful forecasts largely surpasses the cost of unsuccessful forecasts?

12.4 Forecast-driven, pay-then-collect vs. order-driven, collect-then-pay business designs

The difference between the operations of Delta Metal and those of a broker is basically the same as the difference that exists in manufacturing between forecast-driven or pushed and order-driven or pulled or just-in-time operations. Forecast-driven operations start with a forecast of the future demand. The forecast enables the company to purchase and manufacture in advance of getting the actual customer orders. The theory is that producing ahead of demand brings valuable advantages both to the manufacturing and the selling functions:

● When producing ahead of demand you decouple manufacturing from demand which enables you to organize production according to the optimal manufacturing logic and to benefit from the advantages of scale and stability.
● Goods produced ahead of demand also allows for instantaneous delivery to customers.

There are problems, however, with these forecast-driven, pay-then-collect business designs:

● The sequencing of payments is such that you continuously need to spend money ahead of receiving money (i.e. you need continuously to 'invest' in such operations).
● You need continuously to make good forecasts in order to capture the advantages described by the theory! Forecasting errors can be very detrimental and may even completely destabilize the smooth process that is aimed at with any forecast-driven operations. Following a forecasting error, it is easy to over-react when trying to adjust the level of production, and a succession of forecasting and correction errors can completely destabilize the whole system. With forecast-driven operations, it is not uncommon to end up with a level of manufacturing that is more volatile that the level of customer ordering.[6] The effects of a very volatile manufacturing level can be very damaging. Not only are effects of stability and scale lost but also organizational conflicts tend to surface. Confronted with continued adjustment problems, manufacturing people tend to resent the inability that sales people have to come up with good forecasts: 'Sales people do not sufficiently care about forecasting!' And sales people tend to resent the pressure put by manufacturing people on forecasts as well as their inability to have the right products in stock!
● You end up focusing more on your products than on your customers. With this business design the whole organization tends to focus on its own products and operations and

may be tempted to view marketing and communication tools as a way of trying to impose its product and operational choices on to its customers.[7]

At the other extreme of the many possible ways to design and run operations, **order-driven, collect-then-pay operations** have a much better dynamics. Fully order-driven manufacturing operations would look exactly like the operations of a broker. Everything would start with the receipt of an actual order from an actual customer. Even though it is difficult to imagine operations in which all the spending would be deferred until the reception of actual orders, recent manufacturing experience shows that there is often a lot of room for deferring spending and for designing and running operations that tend towards a fully order-driven approach.

Order-driven operations have many valuable advantages:

● Since you do everything based on real customer orders, you never have to adjust your operations to deal with unexpected orders and you never have to try to find an alternative use for goods that you have produced and that found no customers.
● The sequencing of payments is much more effective. You tend to spend later and closer to the moment when your customers pay you. When you manage to get your customers to confirm their orders with an advance payment, order-driven operations may actually create a sequence of payments in which you always receive money earlier than you pay money for executing your customer orders.
● Finally, deferring all your actions until the order from the customer enables you to sense the needs of your customers – rather than trying to impose your own solutions – to try to really respond to those needs and to offer tailor-made solutions . . . and maybe to increase your selling prices!

Order-driven operations also have their disadvantages:

● Manufacturing is totally coupled to sales and cannot be organized according to its own logic. Manufacturing has to become very flexible and scale effects become more difficult to capture.
● It becomes very difficult to envisage delivering instantaneously when the customer places an order.[8]

12.5 Assessing the value created by redesigning the sequencing of operations

Figure 12.2 describes the operations of a company that is contemplating the redesign of its forecast-driven operations into more order-driven operations:

● With forecast-driven operations the sequencing of payments is such that all disbursements are made before the company knows anything about actual orders. All disbursements are made before knowing if they are worth being made. With this sequencing of payments the company exposes itself to a very large loss each time the expected order does not materialize. Even with the possibility of reusing some of the components a loss of 60 is made for each individual forecasting error. This is four times what is earned on each successful forecast.
● With the current quality of forecasts (one wrong forecast out of 10 on average), half of the operating income is destroyed!

EE is an electric panel builder. Its operations consist in assembling different electric components into panels. At present, the operations are fully forecast driven and this results in the following sequence of cash flows (everything expressed in proportion of a typical sale of 100):

1 Spending on general resources   −15
2 Spending on material, labour and components   −70
3 Sales/cash receipts   +100

When panels find customers, then the income is 15! But recently EE has been suffering from more and more costly forecasting mistakes. When no order comes for a panel that has already been built, only the most expensive components can be reused. The cost of taking out these components and of scrapping a panel are estimated at 45. As the value of the components is 70, this leaves a net value of 25 for any panel that does not find a customer. As 85 have been spent already, any panel that does not find a customer generates a loss of 60. In the past forecasting mistakes were not that common, but recently one could estimate that about 1 in 10 panels built has not found a customer. This has led to a very dramatic drop in income that is now 7.5 on average ($15 \times 0.9 + -60 \times 0.1 = 7.5$).

A redesign of the operations could make them more order driven: EE would wait until getting an order before ordering the components and doing the final assembly work. This would not change the level of spending on general resources. Neither would it change the level of operating expenses but it would change their timing. Now only 28% of these expenses (or 20) would be committed before an order is received. This would also allow for getting an advance payment from the customer when the order is confirmed. The new operational design would have both an advantage and a disadvantage for the customer: the customer will now get customized products but will have to wait a couple of weeks before getting them. EE estimated that the advantage and the disadvantage were going to offset each other. As a consequence selling prices could probably not be increased.

Figure 12.2 The opportunity to make operations more order driven

Two types of solution are possible for improving operating income. You can either improve the quality of forecasts or change the sequencing of spending. Improving the quality of forecasts is the typical solution for all those people who strongly believe in forecast-driven operations. The other solution is to recognize that forecasting will always involve errors and to organize operations in a way that forecasting mistakes do not matter – or matter less. The way to do it is to sequence payments in such a way that as little as possible is spent until one knows for sure that this spending is worth being made.[9] This is the beauty of order-driven or pull operations.

The model in Table 12.4 enables us to compare the relative robustness to uncertainty of:

● purely forecast-driven operations;
● more or less order-driven operations.

When doing this comparison, you can also test what happens when the two types of operation correspond to different levels of costs and selling prices.

How re-sequencing creates value

When payments are re-sequenced and operations made more order driven, value is created from three sources at least:

Table 12.4 ● A model for assessing the value of more order-driven operations

	A	B	C	D	E
1	*Probability that customer does not come*		0.1		
2		Order	Does		
3		comes	not		
4	**Forecast-driven operations**				
5	Payments for general resources	−15	−15		
6	Payments for operating resources	−70	−70		
7	Sales/receipts or disposal value	100	25		
8	**Income/cash in the end**	15	−60	on average:	7.5
9					
10	**Order-driven operations**				
11	*Change in general resources*	0			
12	*Change in operating resources*	0			
13	*Proportion committed before receiving the order*	0.28			
14	*Change in sales price*				
15	*Percentage of advance at order*	0.2			
16	Payments for general resources	−15	−15		
17	Payments for operating resources before order	−20	−20		
18	Advance received at order	20			
19	Payments for operating resources after order	−50			
20	Sales/receipts	80			
21	**Income/cash at end**	15	−35	on average:	10.0

Formulas

In C1, B5, B6, B7, C7, B11, B12, B13, B14, B15 data

In C5: +B5; copy to C6

In B8: +B5+B6+B7; copy to C8

In B16: +B5*(1+B11); in C16: +B16

In B17: +B6*(1+B12)*B13; in C17: +B17

In B18: +B7*(1+B14)*B15

In B19: +B6*(1+B12)*(1−B13)

In B20: +B7*(1+B14)*(1−B15)

In B21: +B16+B17+B18+B19+B20; copy to C21

In E8: +B8*(1−$C$1)+C8*$C$1. Copy to E21

● Operations become more robust to uncertainty. In Table 12.4 the order-driven opera-tions – which are still partly forecast driven – are less impacted by uncertainty. As a result their operating income is better on average (10% of sales instead of 7.5%) and is also more stable. With forecast-driven operations forecasting mistakes do not occur in a regular fashion. It might well happen that EE is very lucky for a whole quarter: no one single mistake and the operating income surges to 15% of sales. Then in the following quarter EE suddenly becomes unlucky and makes several mistakes and a loss surfaces! Order-driven operations are much less volatile.

● Opportunities for product and service customization are created. Order-driven opera-tions create customer value and customers may find customization more valuable than immediate delivery. If this is the case, changing the business design may allow for a price increase.

● Growth becomes easier. Re-sequencing payments reduces working capital needs and the trajectory of cash better resists the impact of growth. This is especially the case when an advance payment is requested at the time of the order.

Notes

1. P. Barnevik, the founder and first CEO of ABB was famous for his action orientation: 'Every ABB manager should be a driving force for change and development. Taking action and doing the right thing is obviously best. Taking action, doing the wrong thing and quickly correcting it is second best. Creating delays or losing opportunities is the worst course of action.' (From ABB's corporate values.)

2. One of the key characteristics of budgets, plans and strategies is to create organizational commitment. Commitment is a two-edged sword. On the one hand it helps companies create performance difference, on the other hand it makes it costly to change one's mind. For a discussion of strategy as a process of managing commitment, refer to: P. Ghemawat (1991), *Commitment. The Dynamic of Strategy*, The Free Press.

3. It may be that Delta Metal's forecast was not totally wrong, perhaps the market decrease in 2002 is only due to the delaying of some big projects. If this is true, then the market in 2003 will be better than expected and the inventory will sell quickly.

4. See J.W. Forrester (1961), *Industrial Dynamics*, Productivity Press.

5. This is the problem with per-cent-of-sales models: they assume wrongly that sales drive costs and then replicate a relation between sales and costs that is the outcome of the complex process described above. If it is safe to assume that the complex costs-orders-sales process is going to repeat itself, it is dangerous to assume that it will probably lead to the same outcome – at least, the mistakes will probably not be the same.

6. See Forrester (note 4) and G. Stalk and T. Hout (1990), *Competing against Time*, The Free Press.

7. According to J.R. Beniger (1986), *The Control Revolution*, Harvard Business School Press, advertising and other communication tools were invented in the late 1800s by companies which needed to control demand following the development of their huge production capabilities.

8. But it often seems possible to organize operations in such a way that customers do not wait for very long. In 1999, Toyota was claiming that it needed only five days to build and a deliver a car made to order. See *Wall Street Journal*, 6 August 1999, p. A4.

9. In decision trees' language (see Chapter 5) this is called 'pulling circles ahead of squares'.

CHAPTER 13

What should Delta Metal do?

Financial numbers as a symptom of operational excellence and strategic fit

Delta Metal has no choice. There is a need for radical change! Even without considering the impact of forecasting risk, the base scenario destroys value (see the model in Table 10.5). Why is this so? Financial numbers do not have any independent existence of their own. They are only the symptom of the quality of the strategy and of the operations.

13.1 Quality of strategy and operations

A low-quality strategy

In order to analyze the quality of Delta Metal's strategy,[1] let us ask ourselves two questions:

- How strong is the competitive position of the company?[2]
- How does the business model fit the transformations that are taking place in its business environment?[3]

The **competitive position** of a company, and of Delta Metal in particular, is very dependent on the forces which prevail in the environment in which the firm operates:

1. **Bargaining power of the customers**. Delta Metal's customers have several alternatives available. When able to forecast, they can choose between the offers of four different manufacturers, a few stockists and hundreds of brokers. When confronted with an unexpected need, they can still choose between numerous stockists and brokers. One may expect the financial statements of Delta Metal to reflect the bargaining power of its customers: low selling prices as well as long delays of payments.
2. **Bargaining power of the suppliers**. Delta Metal is in the difficult position of having to get its supply from its competitors. One may expect the financial statements of the

company to show high purchasing prices as well as short delays of payments. When considering the power of both its customers and its suppliers Delta Metal seems to be squeezed and one should expect both low margins and a difficult cash position.

3. **Rivalry among competitors**. Delta Metal has to compete with other stockists, its own suppliers and also with brokers. Manufacturers are in a strong position and Delta Metal should be worried about their distribution strategy and their apparent intention to further develop direct distribution. Brokers may also represent a difficult challenge for Delta Metal. The design of their operations makes them very flexible and not exposed to forecasting risk. The existence of brokers may result in more downward pressure on prices: one more piece of bad news for Delta Metal.

4. **Threat of new entrants and of substitute products**. The case study does not suggest that the market is sufficiently attractive to appeal to new competitors: this is the first good news for Delta Metal. It does not suggest any threat of substitute products either. However, steel does not appear as a winner in the competition among materials.

5. **Specific characteristics of the local business environment**. When doing business globally, you always have to be ready to recognize the influence of specific local business conditions as these can have a significant financial impact (unstable economy, high inflation, etc.). Here the long payment conditions that seem to be typical in France reinforce the cash difficulties.

A complementary way of analyzing the quality of a company's strategy is to look at the **transformations taking place in its business environment** and to analyze how the **business model** of the company is able to leverage these changes. As is the case in many business environments several transformations are going on concurrently. Adopting the framework of Slywotzky and Morrison in *Profit Patterns*,[4] we can say that:

1. Delta Metal seems to have run out of any strategic idea that would bring it back on the path of creating value. The company seems to be waiting for something external to come and help (market growth, new regulations, etc.). The only 'idea' – the new credit plan – gives away more value than it creates.

2. There is a convergence between the manufacturers and the stockists. The manufacturers seem to have changed their view about the value chain and seem to be willing to integrate distribution.

3. There is a change in technology that allows and will allow for more and more effective – probably faster – order-driven approaches.

4. There might also be a change in the product and information offers: on the one hand there are the solutions offered by the manufacturers (tailor-made and low price) and on the other hand there is the emergency service offered by the brokers and the stockists (which probably has the potential to be a high price service).

Who are Delta Metal's real competitors? Delta Metal does not seem to be able to rival the manufacturers. If Delta Metal is competing with the brokers, then is the company's business model really adapted to an environment where forecasting is difficult and will probably become more and more difficult? Maybe, the best solution for Delta Metal is to become a broker!

An analysis of the customers has shown that it is always the same customers who pay late and who ask for rebates. Without these 'marginal customers', the collection period would probably be less than 4 months (between 3 and 4 months) and selling prices would probably be 2 to 4% higher. The problem, though, is that these marginal customers have come to represent some 30 to 40% of the total sales and cannot really be replaced by 'better' customers.

Figure 13.1 Delta Metal (III)

Low-quality operations

Assessing the quality of operations is a matter of asking ourselves how good the company is at implementing its business model. How good are the systems and procedures, and most importantly, how do the capabilities fit the business model? The case does not provide any information on these issues but we might have our doubts. Companies which tend to give in to their customers (low prices, long collection period, etc.) are typically companies which have systems and capability deficiencies.[5] Even though this would probably not solve its major strategic problems, it might well be that better systems and stronger capabilities could help Delta Metal extend the life of its business model for a few more years.

A more focused strategy?

Figure 13.1 provides additional information on the company. The approach described in the figure corresponds to what is called a focused strategy. If you run the model in Table 10.5 with the numbers of Figure 13.1 you realize that Delta Metal is back on a value creation trajectory – in spite of the loss in sales![6] It is not clear, however, that this would suffice to counteract the profound transformations taking place in the business environment.

Notes

1. For an analysis of the different strategic schools of thought, please refer to H. Mintzberg, B. Ahlstrand and J. Lampel (1998), *Strategy Safari: A guided tour through the wilds of strategic management*, The Free Press. Other recommended books on strategy are: D.J. Collis and C.A. Montgomery (1998), *Corporate Strategy*, Irwin/McGraw-Hill and P. Ghemawat (2001) *Strategy and Business Landscape*, Prentice-Hall; G. Hamel (2000) *Leading the Revolution*, Harvard Business School Press and to *Mastering Strategy* (2000) FT Prentice Hall.
2. This is the traditional and very effective approach developed by Porter. See M.E. Porter (1980), *Competitive Strategy*, The Free Press.
3. This is a more dynamic/change-focused approach that started emerging in the late 1990s. See among other sources: K. Eisenhardt and D. Sull (2001) Strategy as Simple Rules, *Harvard Business Review*, January, p. 107–116; S. Brown and K. Eisenhardt (1998) *Competing on the Edge*, Harvard Business School Press; P. Evans and T. Wurster (2000) *Blown to Bits*, Harvard Business School Press and J. Collins (2001) *Good to Great*, Harper Business.
4. A.J. Slywostzky and D.J. Morrison (1999), *Profit Patterns*, Times Business, Random House.
5. The percentage of operating expenses to sales seems very high for a stockist: this is an area that it would be good to investigate.
6. Assuming obviously that operating expenses are reduced substantially. If operating expenses are reduced in proportion, then the business becomes profitable and profitability – and not size – is the goal.

Appendices to Part III
Mastering the trajectories
of payments and receipts

The material in these appendices is about alignment and derailment of the trajectories of payments and receipts.

The Relais Electriques case study and Appendix III.1 show the value of aligning all the payments and receipts on the trajectory of orders received. As shown in Chapter 12, setting all the cash flows on the same trajectory as orders received is a powerful tool for reducing risk and creating value. Appendix III.1 shows how to build a **model in which orders received – rather than sales – are used as the input variable** (see Table III.1.1 on p. 215).

Figure III.1.2 (p. 214) also shows how to model the impact of **advance payments**, a very powerful source of value creation. Finally, Appendix III.1 shows how powerful it is in analyzing the **past performance** of a business to diagnose the alignment of the trajectories of its various receipts and payments.

Organization and internal conflicts are a very common and often misunderstood source of derailments of cash flows. Relais Electriques and Appendix III.2 help to explain how **functional, non-process orientated organizations** have the potential to put any business – including the ones with a 'collect-then-pay' design – on to erratic cash flow trajectories. This material also shows how the breaking down of the supply process into a **chain of profit centres** may result in conflicts that, unexpectedly, tend to be fuelled by **accounting measurements**: see Table III.2.1 on p. 217.

Case K, SW Life, describes a pure information business that is about to launch a new financial product. The management is convinced that this new product has a very large market and will enjoy an **explosive growth** (with annual growth rates ranging between 50% and 100%). In Appendix III.2, you will find a model that helps explain how explosive growth can completely derail the overall cash flows of a value-creating business. You will also see that a different business design with a more favourable timing of the payments could easily bring cash back under control – whatever the growth might be!

Finally, the PT PharMa case and Appendix III.3 introduce a model for simulating an international business which is exposed to substantial currency risk. The PT PharMa model aims at simulating the simultaneous impact of **prices and currency changes**. The

PT PharMa case takes place in Indonesia at the end of 1996. At that time the company is very concerned with a major local pricing risk: prices of drugs have grown high in Indonesia and there is strong pressure to bring them down. At that time the company – like many international companies operating in Asia at that time – is not preoccupied at all with currency risk.

Relais Electriques[1]

In February 2001, Jean-Luc Pernod was sitting in his office reviewing the 2002 budget of Relais Electriques SA (Relais Electriques). Jean-Luc Pernod had just joined the CFE group[2] where he had been appointed president of the global Relays[3] business area[4] and president of the largest manufacturing and selling unit of this business area: Relais Electriques. Before turning his attention to the future, Jean-Luc Pernod decided to spend time reviewing the performance of the company and finding satisfactory answers to a few questions that had been puzzling him since he joined the company as its president one week earlier:

- How was Relais really performing? On the one hand, the return on investment had been satisfactory for many years, but on the other hand, many customers were complaining about delays. Delays had been a problem since the early 1990s – and, apparently, had been a problem in the late 1970s also.
- Was it really true that the company did better in 1997–9 than in 2000–1?
- Could one really trust the performance measurements of the profit centres? How effective was the profit centre system implemented in 1996? While some managers were very positive, others were very critical and had actually started reorganizing their departments according to a different workflow.

The company

Based in Lyon, Relais Electriques was selling to the French market and to the other CFE companies all over the world. Relais was selling more than 20 000 relays per year (one-third of which were especially made to customer specifications) to more than 5000 customers in the world: power plants, electrical distribution companies, process industries such as paper mills, and so on. The 5000 products offered by Relais had the reputation of being reliable and of high quality. Relays generally made up a minor component of the customers' facilities, but their failure could result in considerable losses. For a power plant, losing a day of operations could result in a million dollar loss. Relais' financial statements are shown in Table J.1.

Reorganizing the business into 'a chain of customers'

Relais' organization is shown in Figure J.1. In 1996 the company was reorganized into seven profit centres: five manufacturing workshops, sales and R&D. This new organization was aimed at increasing the quality, the speed, the implementation and the follow-up of

Table J.1 ● Relais' financial data

	1995	1996	1997	1998	1999	2000	2001
Income and cash							
Order intake	311	357	430	533	500	445	467
Growth		15%	20%	24%	−6%	−11%	5%
Sales	**309**	**320**	**360**	**430**	**579**	**467**	**448**
Growth		4%	12%	20%	34%	−19%	−4%
CGS	206	214	247	299	395	318	312
Selling, administration and development	37	43	49	63	71	85	74
Growth		16%	14%	29%	12%	20%	−13%
Operating income[a]	**66**	**63**	**63**	**69**	**113**	**64**	**62**
Capital employed	196	222	252	299	318	365	330
Return on investment	**34%**	**28%**	**26%**	**24%**	**35%**	**18%**	**19%**
Sales	309	320	360	430	579	467	448
Receivables end	57	70	78	138	147	119	110
Collection period (months)	2.2	2.6	2.6	3.9	3.1	2.9	2.8
Receipts	**299**	**307**	**352**	**370**	**570**	**502**	**457**
Cost of sales	206	214	247	294	397	337	325
Inventory end	70	71	124	175	191	157	157
Production	207	215	300	350	411	284	312
Growth		4%	40%	17%	18%	−31%	10%
Payments	**244**	**258**	**349**	**413**	**482**	**369**	**386**
Cash generated	**55**	**49**	**3**	**−43**	**88**	**134**	**71**
Number of people employed							
Employees	291	307	321	361	378	357	340
Workers	501	484	544	600	699	602	550
Total	792	791	865	961	1077	959	890
Prices and cost increases							
Increase in selling prices			6.5%	5.0%	8.0%	6.3%	6.5%
Inflation rate	9.3%	8.2%	5.7%	3.3%	5.2%	6.3%	6.7%
Increase in salaries (employees)		10.8%	6.8%	7.1%	6.0%	6.9%	9.8%
Increase in salaries (workers)		11.0%	8.1%	7.1%	6.7%	7.4%	9.9%
Exceptional production costs							
Overtime		3	3	4	5	4	3
Other exceptional expenses				2	2	2	
Subcontracted work			10	30	30	8	

[a] Excluding financing costs.

decisions. It was also aimed at increasing the involvement of people as well as their cost awareness. When the company was reorganized, it was stressed that:

● Relais Electriques is one single company serving the needs of its customers as a whole entity.[5]
● The various departments of Relais Electriques are a 'chain of customers'. Each department should consider the previous one in the chain as its supplier and the next one in the chain as its customer.

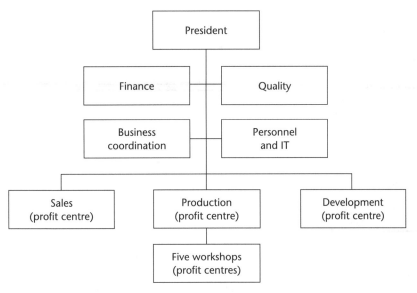

Figure J.1 Relais's organization chart. The four staff functions employed 120 people and the five workshops 770 people

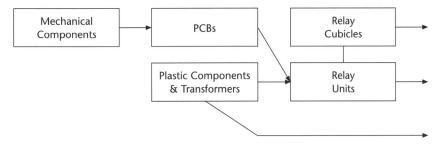

Figure J.2 Organization of the profit centres in production

Manufacturing was especially impacted by the new organization (see Figure J.2).

- Manufacturing was redesigned into a supplier–customer chain of five workshops. Each workshop had between 10 and 20 white-collar workers and between 50 and 200 blue-collar workers. The production manager position was kept and five new workshop managers were appointed.
- All the tasks that had previously been performed centrally (delivery order request, external purchasing, production planning, production preparation, etc.) were put under the responsibility of each of the five workshops.
- A new information system was implemented. This system had the capability of breaking down all the customer orders into component orders for the different workshops.
- It was decided to assess the performance of the workshops based on their profit and capital employed. (See Table J.2.)

Table J.2 ● Evolution of the results of the five workshops

Workshop results	1997	1998	1999	2000	2001
Growth in sales		28%	29%	−26%	−15%
Mechanical components		17%	7%	−18%	17%
Plastic components and transformers		24%	29%	−30%	4%
Printed circuit boards		13%	13%	−37%	−8%
Relay units		33%	19%	−27%	−18%
Relay cubicles		22%	36%	−31%	−23%
Growth in production		30%	13%	−31%	−18%
Mechanical components		12%	−10%	−16%	17%
Plastic components and transformers		23%	21%	−28%	5%
Printed circuit boards		−2%	−4%	−32%	−33%
Relay units		34%	16%	−25%	−24%
Relay cubicles		27%	30%	−41%	−17%
Cost of goods sold/sales	88%	87%	82%	90%	87%
Mechanical components	85%	81%	75%	79%	78%
Plastic components and transformers	81%	76%	74%	83%	83%
Printed circuit boards	94%	88%	82%	88%	81%
Relay units	97%	94%	94%	102%	99%
Relay cubicles	97%	97%	96%	99%	97%
Return on investment	20%	22%	37%	17%	25%
Mechanical components	20%	27%	37%	26%	33%
Plastic components and transformers	38%	49%	55%	24%	28%
Printed circuit boards	12%	22%	41%	17%	32%
Relay units	14%	31%	31%	−6%	5%
Relay cubicles	23%	12%	21%	6%	30%

Order and forecast driven operations

Manufacturing of relays was labour intensive[6] and did not require much capital. The two workshops delivering to external customers (Relay Units[7] and Relay Cubicles) were order driven and did not start production until they had received a firm customer order.

The production of printed circuits boards (PCBs) was done according to forecasts of the future needs of Relay Units and Relay Cubicles. Also, when large orders were received, the planners of the PCB workshop were making assumptions regarding which PCBs were going to be needed and they started manufacturing accordingly. PCBs were often produced in larger series than were actually required. This was mainly due to:

● The difficulty of preparing accurate forecasts. For most products, the 'future need' was automatically estimated as equal to 30% of the actual need of the preceding month plus 70% of the estimated need of that same month.

- Incorrect assumptions regarding the type of PCB needed. Relay cubicles, for example, were often custom designed, and it was not easy for the workshop planner to know which PCBs would be required by engineering when the order was going to be executed.
- The unreliability of the information system. According to one manager: 'Running the business with our system feels like flying a jumbo without a control panel'. One problem was the so-called 'preliminary orders'. Such orders were entered as soon as one believed that the customer would order, so that components, transformers and PCBs would be ready in time. The problem was that the actual order did not always match the preliminary order, which resulted in excesses of certain articles and shortages of others.

Other reasons for manufacturing PCBs in large batches were: long set-up times, low yield (many PCBs did not pass the burn-in test[8]), and long and/or irregular suppliers' lead times. Finally, it was often possible to buy large quantities of some electronic components at very good prices. When large quantities of PCBs were bought, production often decided to start working on them in order to have them ready for use.

In the Plastic Components and Transformers workshop, some components (transformer coils and some plastic mouldings) were produced based on yearly forecasts. Half of the workshop's production was sold to other relay producers and the rest to the Relay Units workshop. The Mechanical Components workshop was located 300 km away from the main Relais Electriques production unit to which it was shipping components.

Since the production of all final products was order driven, finished goods inventory amounted to only 2% of the turnover. Lead times from customer orders to deliveries ranged between three to eight months, depending on the complexity of the product. Delivery reliability, measured as the proportion of orders delivered complete at the delivery date originally offered, had improved from a low 50% in 1998 to 80% in 2001. Jean-Luc Pernod considered this was not satisfactory. Sales and distribution to the final customers were carried out by CFE's national subsidiaries. Most of these subsidiaries were directly connected to Relais' computer system. However, the system did not yet allow for a satisfactory processing of the orders of all non-standard products.

Impact of the 1996 reorganization and further changes

The new organization helped all levels of management to achieve a tighter control of costs. Also, it made people in the workshops focus on profitability even though they did not always fully understand how the income and the capital of their units was calculated. Some workshop managers actually developed the feeling that they only had a limited impact on their return on investment. Profit depended a lot on the transfer prices decided by central management and the high levels of stock were often the result of orders cancelled by the next workshop in the chain.

Another positive impact of the reorganization was the decrease in the throughput times and the reduction of the batch sizes in production. In several workshops, people discovered that set-up times could be reduced, especially when the administrative procedures were simplified. However, workshops started operating with smaller batches for a limited number of components only (components that were relatively easy to forecast as well as components produced with recent and reliable machines).

Delays

Delays became a major problem in the period 1997–9 and gradually customers started to lose patience. The order backlog increased considerably and inventory increased even faster. In 1999, as many as 15% of the production orders were classified as 'top priority orders', following requests from the sales department. The national subsidiaries because increasingly frustrated with the delays of Relais Electriques, which became known as '*Delays*'. One of the frustrated subsidiaries was CFE India. CFE India started assembling relays in 1994. Initially, they imported most components from Relais, but they rapidly increased their own value added. The components bought by CFE were ordered in matching kits to fit the production schedule, carefully co-ordinated by an advanced computer system. The problem was that Relais Electriques's deliveries were late and incomplete! It was common for Relais to ship 85–90% of the components ordered (with the promise to send the rest in a back order three months later). As it did not make much sense for the company to start producing until all components needed were available, CFE India was typically spending the first nine months of each year collecting the components for its orders. Then in the remaining three months CFE India would produce and deliver! In 1998, CFE India decided to send their production manager, C.K. Chugani, to France with the mission to convince Relais Electriques of the importance of following the delivery schedule. Mr Chugani soon realized that the current capacity of the company could only accommodate half of the order backlog and that most other subsidiaries were having the same difficulties as CFE India. Relais Electriques explained that they had plans for expanding capacity by 25% but not earlier than 2000. As a result CFE India decided to post two of its engineers in France for controlling the production of their orders.

Delays were partly caused by planning and scheduling problems. The information system was a standard package for manufacturing control. This system automatically generated production orders for the components of the different workshops, but in the beginning, the system did not work well. Bugs in the system overstated the needs for some components and these were then produced in excess. It also happened that the system failed to initiate the purchase orders needed for the final product. One of the consequences of these planning and scheduling problems was the build-up of stocks. When in doubt people tended to protect themselves by producing more.

In 1999 and 2000, Relais Electriques used a lot of overtime (this represented additional costs of Fr 13 million in 1998, 1999 and 2000), and subcontracted some production to suppliers and other companies in the group. Finally, Relais Electriques used interim personnel and had to rent suitable premises to accommodate people and materials. In 1999, Relais Electriques had plans to increase capacity but these were cancelled at the last minute when management saw orders drop after the summer vacation.

Spontaneous reorganization

After many experiences of delays and of volatile production demand, where it could be panic one week and less work the next, the workshop managers met to discuss the situation. Several of them were convinced that some kind of process or flow organization would be preferable, but others were reluctant to recommend the break-up of the profit centre structure. The practical result of these meetings was the integration of the PCB and the

Relay Units workshops. The wall between the two workshops was torn down and one manager was appointed to head both. In 2000, the Relay Units workshop manager began reorganizing his workshop according to flow groups. Until then, the workshop had been organized around five specialized production jobs. It was now reorganized into three parallel groups of 20 people who could handle the five different production jobs. Two small groups (2–3 people) serving the three parallel groups were organized around the automatic assembly and soldering machines. This reorganization did not cause significant capital expenditure but required a lot of training: in 2000, 15% of the working time was spent learning others' jobs. The throughput time fell from 23 to 10 days.

Notes

1. This case is the abridged version of the Relais Electriques case study developed by Michel Schlosser and Niklas Myhr from a real business situation.
2. A $30 billion sales international group specializing in electrical products and services.
3. Relays within a power system are a bit like brakes in a car. When a dangerous situation arises, it must be possible to stop the car. Similarly in a power system, electric current must be stopped in case of danger. The primary function of a relay is to initiate the isolation of any defective segment in the power network, reliably and quickly.
4. Since 1997 CFE had grown by acquisition and its relays business had become a dominant world leader with a 40% global market share – twice as large as the second largest competitor. In 2001, the whole business area employed 2800 people for a turnover of 1640 million francs. For the years to come, Jean-Luc Pernod expected the sales of the business area to grow about 22% a year (4% due to market increases, 5% to market share gains, 4% to general price increases, and 9% to increases in price related to system offerings).
5. The idea of organizing the company into units specializing in different product groups had been discarded in order to keep economies of scale and customer synergies (large customers used to order several types of products).
6. Labour costs represented 60% of the total manufacturing costs for the traditional products and 40% for the more recent ones.
7. Half of the production of Relay Units was sold externally and half was sold to Relay Cubicles which assembled customer-specific combinations of various relay units.
8. In the burn-in test PCBs were activated for 72 hours. During that time, inferior quality cards malfunctioned and could be sorted out. For some products, the burn-in test of the cards was carried out only after the relay unit had been assembled.

Appendix III.1
Aligning all the cash flows on the trajectory of orders received

Diagnosing the alignment of the trajectories of receipts and payments is a powerful tool for understanding the performance of a business. The Relais Electriques case shows the potential danger of drawing conclusions from the sole analysis of profit and return on investment. How is it possible that a company with such poor operations generates returns on investment ranging between 24 and 35% in the 1995–9 period and between 15 and 19% in 2000–1? How is it possible that several indicators (growth, income, return on investment) point towards:

- continuous success in the period 1995–9, with a peak in 1999, when the operations are clearly not running satisfactorily?

● difficulties in the period 2000–1 when the operations seem to be about to be put back in order?

These paradoxes stem from the calculation of profit that is based on the assumption that the operations of the business are perfectly synchronized – see Chapter 3. As a result, when assessing performance, you cannot look at profit only and you should always ask yourself the question: are the operations of the business perfectly synchronized? If so, then you can trust the profit figures. They tell the 'whole truth'. But when the operations are not in sync, then you should ask yourself a second series of questions: could the misalignment of receipts and payments result in a major destruction of value? If so, then the profit figures only tell – an often small – part of the truth.

A very effective way to understand the nature and the potential consequences of misalignments is to contrast three series of trajectories:

1. Orders received
2. Payments
3. Receipts (with distinguishing volume and price trajectories).

The profit and return performance of Relais Electriques is due to the favourable trajectory of the selling prices. Table J.1 shows that Relais Electriques has been able to increase its selling prices almost as fast as salaries during the period. When you realize that the price of materials (and of electronic components in particular) has probably been decreasing continuously, then it is clear that the inefficiency of the operations of Relais Electriques has been easily hidden by the favourable selling prices trajectory. Selling price trajectories typically set the scene. Rapidly declining prices call for radical – and continuously so – innovation. Continuously increasing prices create a large room from manoeuvre that can be used for delivering superior value or for wasting resources.

An analysis of the trajectories of orders received, payments and receipts helps explain what has happened at Relais Electriques. As shown in Figure III.1.1:

● The trajectories of the different payments have been following the trajectory of orders received. After an initial lag, production spending has very quickly caught up with orders. Unfortunately production spending has not slowed down as fast as orders. This was probably due to two major factors. First, production spending, which was lagging behind orders received had to catch up. Secondly, production is not fully driven by orders. When production is driven by forecasts, it is very typical that production spending slightly misses the 'turning points'. The trajectory of selling, administrative and development spending very much follows the progression of orders but does not slow down until 2001. It is typical that this type of spending is driven by a long-term vision and does not spontaneously respond to short-term changes in activity. Companies often need centrally imposed cost cutting programmes for slowing down this type of spending.
● The trajectory of receipts is very much lagging behind orders. This is due to a series of factors. First, sales (deliveries and invoices) lag behind production. Relais Electriques is not able to make complete deliveries and cannot invoice as fast as needed. Sales grow considerably in 1999, but this is just the necessary catch-up effect, and is followed by a collapse in 2000. The misalignment of the production and sales trajectories results in the build-up of an inventory. Then, as often happens in such a situation, incomplete deliveries and other quality problems cause customers to be dissatisfied and payment delays tend to surface.

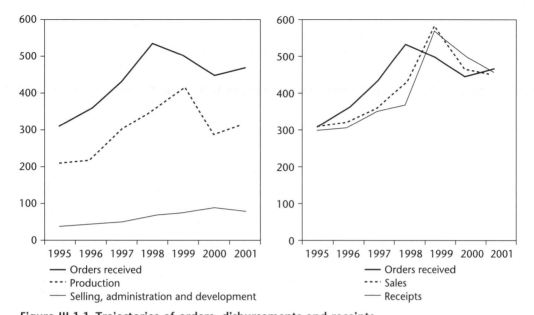

Figure III.1.1 Trajectories of orders, disbursements and receipts

Note: These charts show the trajectories of the different variables based on their values shown in Table J.1. The problem with using past data is that production, sales and receipts in 1995 – the first year of analysis – do not strictly correspond to the orders received in 1995. The model in Table III.1.1 solves this problem by adjusting the first year – and creating an additional year at the end. Such a model is a better basis for drawing charts.

The mismatch of the trajectories of payments and receipts results in cash continuously deteriorating during the 1995–8 period. Cash then improves but falls again in 2001. Let us hope that this does not mean that the company enters a new cycle of problems!

Analyzing 'horizontal' trajectories is often more powerful than the traditional 'vertical' analysis of annual financial statements. In the case of Relais Electriques, analyzing trajectories helps us understand that:

- The rapidly improving performance in 1998–9 is caused by the slow initial reaction to a very strong growth in orders that should have produced much better results in 1996 and 1997.
- The very good results of 1999 are definitely not sustainable. They largely correspond to a catch-up effect and since orders received have started to decrease, sales will also decrease once the artificially created peak is passed. One of the dangerous effects of such a catch-up is that it may make the company focus on growth when the trend in orders calls for adjusting capacity down. One could say that Relais was lucky to face a dramatic drop in orders after the summer vacation. It made them wake up and realize that it was foolish to extrapolate the trend of 1999 and to invest in additional capacity.

An orders received driven model

Table III.1.1 shows a model that can be used to simulate the value destroyed by Relais during the period. Contrary to many financial models, this model is not driven by sales

---

Modelling customer advances

Over the past decade(s) many companies all over the world have exerted considerable pressure for reducing one of the critical components of working capital needs: accounts receivable. In a way accounts receivable and credit granted to customers is very much part of the paper-based 'old economy'. If you have been shopping on the web, you will have realized that the 'new economy' is based on payment with order (or 'advance payments'). Advance payments have two positive impacts on the working capital need:

● *They reduce accounts receivable.* With an advance payment, the formula for calculating accounts receivables is:

Sales × (1 – Advance payment rate) / 12 × Collection period in months

with a 100% advance payment, accounts receivable are always equal to zero!

● *They generate a source of financing or liability that further helps reduce the working capital needs.* Advance payment in the balance sheet is calculated as follows:

Order received × (Advance rate) / 12 × Time between order received and delivery (in months)

Impact of customer advances at Relais

When you set the customer advance rate to 20% (in B16), then the value in B28 becomes 182, a 21% increase. You can check with the model that one of the advantages of advances is to reduce accounts receivable.

Figure III.1.2 Modelling the impact of advance payments

but by orders received. As explained in Chapter 12, orders received is often a much better input variable than sales. Note that the model is structured to mimic the sequence of the operations:

1. It all starts from the trajectory of orders.
2. The trajectory of orders is used to drive spending – or at least part of it.
3. Then deliveries drive sales and receipts. Note the new identity: cumulated orders received equal sales.

The model also features customer advances the impact of which is described in Figure III.1.2.

The data in Table III.1.1 show what actually happened at Relais. You can use the model and simulate an alternative in which:

● orders would have had the same trajectory, but
● payments and receipts would have been aligned with orders, and
● no costs caused by delays and their resolution would have surfaced.

The drivers for such a simulation and its results are given in Table III.1.2. With a better alignment of the trajectories of its payments and receipts Relais Electiques could have generated a value (beginning 2002 value) of FFr 1148 million instead of the value of 347 that it has generated (see Table III.1.1). **Misalignment has dissipated two-thirds of the potential value!**

Table III.1.1 ● Order-driven model

A	B	C	D	E	F	G	H	I
1	1996	1997	1998	1999	2000	2001	2002	Cum
2 *Change in volume ordered*		13.0%	18.1%	−13.1%	−16.3%	−1.4%		
3 *Change in price*		6.5%	5.0%	8.0%	6.3%	6.5%		
4 Volume ordered	100	113	133	116	97	96		
5 Cumulated volume ordered	100	213	346	462	559	655		655
6 **Orders received**	357	430	533	500	445	467		2731
7								
8 *Growth in expenses*		14.0%	29.0%	12.0%	20.0%	−13.0%		
9 **Selling, Operating & Develop.**	43	49	63	71	85	74		385
10 *Change in volume produced*		27.0%	11.0%	13.0%	−40.0%	10.0%		
11 *Change in production cost*		11.0%	5.0%	4.0%	15.0%	0.0%		
12 Volume produced	90	114	127	143	86	95		
13 Cumulated volume produced	90	204	331	475	561	655		
14 **Production cost**	213	300	350	411	284	312		1870
15 **Payments**	256	349	413	482	369	386		2255
16 *Advance rate*	0							
17 Advance account	0	0	0	0	0	0		
18 *Change in volume sold*			14.1%	26.6%	−25.0%	−10.0%		
19 Volume sold	60	97	111	140	105	95	48	655
20 Cumulated volume sold	60	157	268	408	513	607	655	
21 Order backlog end (volume)	40	56	79	55	47	48	0	
22 **Sales**	214	360	431	579	467	448	233	2731
23 *Collection period*	3.9	2.6	3.9	3.1	2.9	2.8		
24 A/R end	70	78	138	147	112	103	0	
25 **Receipts**	144	352	370	570	502	457	336	2731
26 **Cash flow**	−112	3	−43	88	134	71	336	476
27 Discount rate	0.15							
28 **Value**	150						347	
29 Volume inventory end	30	47	63	67	48	48	0	
30 Inventory end	71	124	175	191	157	157	0	
31 CGS	142	247	299	395	318	312	157	
32 **Income**	29	63	69	113	64	62	76	476

Additional data

Price and volume data have been added to the data of Table J.1. Cumulated volume data allow us to check the cumulative volume of orders. Production and sales is equal.

'First and last year adjustments'

The model aims at assessing the value created by the processing of the orders received in the period 1996–2000: as a result, one must:

● take away from the 1996 figures everything that is due to orders received prior to 1996;
● extend the model to 2001 when the final part of the orders received in 2000 is invoiced and cashed.

Input for customers advances

Finally, the model introduces a feature for testing the impact of advances from the customer (rows 16 and 17).

Rows 1, 2, 3, 8, 10, 11, 18, 23: data
B4, B6, B9, B12, B14, B19, B23, B27: data

C4: +B4*(1+C2); Copy
B5: +B4; C5: +B5+C4; Copy
C6: +B6*(1+C2)*(1+C3); Copy
C9: +B8*(1+C8); Copy
C12: +B12*(1+C10); Copy
B13: +B12; C13: +B13+C12; Copy
C14: +B14*(1+C10)*(1+C11); Copy
B15: +B9+B14; Copy
B17: =(B6−B22)*$B$16. In C17: =B7+(C6−C22)*$B$16. Copy to D17.H17
C19: 97[a]
D19: +C19*(1+D18); Copy
H19: +I4−SUM (B19:G19)

B20: +B19; C20: +B20+C19; Copy
B21: +B5−B20; C21: +B21+C4−C19; Copy
B22: +B6−B21*B6/B4; C21: =SUM($B$6:C6)−SUM($B$22:B22)−C21*C6/C4; Copy
B24: +(B22*(1−$B$16))/12*B23; Copy
B25: =B22−B24+B17; C25: =C22+B24−B17+C17; Copy
B26: −B15+B25; Copy
B28: +NPV(B27,B26:H26); H28: +B28*(1+B27)^6
B29: +B12−B19; C29: +B29+C12−C19; Copy
B30: +B29*(B14/B12)
B31: +B14−B30; C31: +C14+B30−C30; Copy
B32: +B22−B31−B9; Copy

In column I please put formulas for checking that cumulative cash equals cumulative income!

[a] The trajectory of sales over the whole period is very sensitive to the values of the sales in the early years. As 1997 is very much higher than 1996 (+62%), a small difference in this high growth rate can create a significant variation in the whole trajectory of sales. As a result it is safer not to use a growth rate and to enter data in C19. This problem is often encountered when simulating the sales of a new product. A solution is to model the cumulative rather than the annual sales – see the case of BA International (II).

Table III.1.2 ● Value gained through an effective alignment of cash flow

1	1996	1997	1998	1999	2000	2001	2002	Cum.
2 *Change in volume*		13%	18%	−13%	−16%	−1%		
3 *Change in price*		7%	5%	8%	6%	7%		
4 Volume	100	113	133	116	97	96		655
5 Cumulated volume	100	213	346	462	559	655		
6 **Orders received**	**357**	**430**	**533**	**500**	**445**	**467**		2731
7								
8 *Growth in expenses*		16%	22%	−10%	−14%	2%		
9 **Selling, operating & devt**	**43**	**50**	**61**	**54**	**47**	**48**		303
10 *Change in volume*		13%	18%	−13%	−16%	−1%		
11 *Change in production cost*		3%	3%	3%	3%	3%		
12 Volume produced	100	113	133	116	97	96		
13 Cumulated volume	100	213	346	462	559	655		
14 **Production cost**	**213**	**248**	**302**	**270**	**233**	**236**		1501
15 **Payments**	**256**	**298**	**362**	**324**	**280**	**284**		
16 *Advance rate*	0							
17 Advance account	0	0	0	0	0	0	0	
18 *Growth sales volume*		22%	17%	−11%	−15%	−4%		
19 Volume sold	92	112	131	117	99	95	8	655
20 Cumulated volume sold	92	204	336	452	552	647	655	
21 Order backlog end (volume)	8	9	11	10	8	8	0	
22 **Sales**	**328**	**425**	**523**	**500**	**453**	**463**	**39**	2731
23 *Collection period*	2.6	2.6	2.6	2.6	2.6	2.6		
24 A/R end	71	92	113	108	98	100	0	
25 **Receipts**	**257**	**404**	**501**	**505**	**463**	**461**	**140**	2674
26 **Cash flow**	**1**	**106**	**139**	**181**	**183**	**177**	**140**	927
27 Discount rate	0.15							
28 **Value**	**496**						**1148**	
29 Volume inventory end	8	9	11	10	8	8	0	
30 Inventory end	17	19	25	23	18	20	0	
31 CGS	196	246	296	271	237	235	20	1501
32 **Income**	**89**	**129**	**166**	**175**	**168**	**181**	**19**	927
33 Target inventory	8	9	11	10	8	8	0	

Notes

- Selling, Operating and Development expenses are assumed to evolve as orders when it comes to volume and to grow 3% per year in price. In C8: =(1+C2)*1.03−1
- Production volume is aligned on orders: in B12: +B4; Copy. Growth in volume produced is corrected in C10: +C12/B12−1; Copy. Change in cost of production is assumed to be 3% per year.
- All the production except for 1 month is delivered in the same year. Target inventory in row 33 estimates the value of 1 month production: in B33: +B12/12; Copy. This target inventory helps you tune annual sales through the selection of an appropriate annual growth rate in row 18 (by trial and error).
- Collection period is assumed to be always equal to 2.6 months.

Appendix III.2
The 'chain of profit centres': a dangerous concept!

Creating a chain of internal customers may look like an attractive idea, but when everybody in the chain tries to maximize their own profits, then the perspective of the whole supply process may easily be lost. Table III.2.1 shows a model that you can use in order to better understand the danger of splitting the overall profit between the components of the chain. This model features a very short chain with two components only: 'production' and 'sales'.

To use the model, it is best to start with estimating the transfer price that should be used in order that each profit centres – 'production' and 'sales' – starts with a similar 29% target return. In order to do so, you can enter a transfer price in B2 and proceed by trial and error.

Table III.2.1 ● A model showing some 'value destruction' tactics

A	B	C	D
1	Production	Sales	Consolidated
2 Sales unit price	0	5	
3 Sales volume	1000	1000	
4 **Sales**	0	5000	5000
5 Production volume	1000		
6 Labour cost	1500		
7 Material unit price	1.5	0	
8 Material volume	1000	1000	
9 Material cost	1500	0	
10 Inventory open unit cost	3	3.75	
11 Inventory open volume	200	200	
12 Inventory open	600	750	
13 Inventory end unit cost	3	0	
14 Inventory end volume	200	200	
15 Inventory end	600	0	
16 Other costs	500	800	
17 Profit	−3500	3450	700
18 Net fixed assets, receivables, etc.	1000	200	1200
19 Average inventory	600	375	1200
20 Capital employed	1600	575	2400
21 **Return on capital employed**	−219%	600%	29%

Background
B2,B3,B5,B6,B7,B10,B11,B16,B18,C2,C3,C10,C11,C16,C18: inputs
B4: =B2*B3. Copy to C4. D4: =C4
C7: =B2
B8: =B5; C8: =B3
B9: =B7*B8. Copy to C9
B12: =B10*B11. Copy to C12
B13: =(B6+B9)/B5. C13: =C7
B14: =B11+B5−B3. C14: =C8+C11−C3
B15: =B13*B14. Copy to C15
B17: =B4−B6−B9−B12+B15−B16. Copy to C17
D17: =D4−C16−B16−B6−B9−B12−
  C11*B10+B15+C14*B13
D18: =B18+C18
B19: =(B12+B15)/2. Copy to C19
D19: =(B12+C11*B10+B15+C14*B13)/2
B20: B18+B19. Copy to C20.D20
B21: =B17/B20. Copy to C21.D21

This will make you realize that the returns of the profit centres are very sensitive to the transfer price which means that the whole system may be easily destabilized. You can then simulate what would happen if:

● *'Production' overshoots its target and produces a bit too much.* In order to simulate the impact of overproduction you can enter numbers higher than 1000 in B5. By doing so, you simulate what happens when nothing changes except for this 'slight' overproduction that is going to be put into inventory.
● *'Production' produces a bit too much and then manages to pass this excess production to 'sales'.* To do this simulation set B5 at 1600 and assess the impact of numbers higher than 1000 in B3. With these numbers in B3, you share the excess inventory between 'production' and sales . . . See what happens when all the excess production is passed to 'sales'.

Table III.2.2 shows the outcomes of these simulations. They reveal that:

● When 'production' increases its activity beyond what is needed, then its return on investment increases. The return on investment of 'sales' does not change and the

---

Table III.2.2 ● Outcomes of the model
(a) Impact of different production levels (transfer price in B2: 3.96)

Production level	Return/production	Return sales	Consolidated
1000	29%	29%	29%
1100	33%	29%	31%
1200	36%	29%	32%
1300	38%	29%	33%
1400	39%	29%	34%
1500	40%	29%	34%
1600	40%	29%	34%
1700	40%	29%	34%
1800	40%	29%	34%
2500	38%	29%	33%
3000	36%	29%	31%
5000	28%	29%	25%

(b) Impact of 'passing the problem to whoever is next in the chain'

Production level	Sales to production	Return/production	Return sales	Consolidated
1600	1000	40%	29%	34%
	1100	49%	24%	34%
	1200	60%	21%	34%
	1300	72%	18%	34%
	1400	85%	16%	34%
	1500	101%	14%	34%
	1600	118%	13%	34%
	1700	139%	12%	34%

consolidated return also improves. This is due to the fact that income increases faster than capital employed for as long as the excess production is not too large. *The incentives are not right: small excess productions are actually rewarded by the system.* It is only when the excess production becomes very big that there is a punishment.

● When 'production' produces in excess of what is needed and manages to pass this excess to the next unit in the chain (here 'sales'), then 'production' really generates great results. This tactic for increasing results is obviously reserved to those units that are far from the real external customers. This is actually consistent with the results at Relais Electriques: in Table J.2, the units that are further away from the customers seem to have better results!

Relais Electriques shows one of the main challenges involved in mastering the payments and receipts trajectories in an organization:

● Any organization needs to be split into different units. When specific units become responsible for a part of the cash flow only, then the alignment of overall payments and receipts is at risk. Think about those organizations in which the purchasing department proudly defines itself as the 'biggest spender of the company!'

● This risk of misalignment varies considerably with the way in which the organization is split. In those organizations that have a strong functional orientation, the perspective of the final external customer may easily be lost and the risk of misalignment is probably maximum. In those organizations which are made up of a series of external customer-related businesses then the risk of misalignment is probably much less. When your own department receives orders from external customers, then it becomes much more practical to align all the cash flows of the department onto the trajectory of orders received. This is one of the reasons behind the efforts made in the 1990s by so many companies to become more 'process orientated' and to get organized around small self-contained (external customers directly related) businesses.

Relais Electriques also shows that when it comes to analyzing the profitability and the value creation of a business, it is essential to break the business down into units of activities that are related to external customers and that encompass all the cash flows caused by the business with these customers.[1]

Note

1. The process of creating value requires that a series of functions (development, marketing, sales, procurement, etc.) co-operate together for delivering a product or a service to a customer. As the value is created by these functions **working as a whole**, one should focus the analysis of value at the level of the whole.

CASE *K*

SW Life[1]

In the spring of 1989, the management of SW Life decided to launch their new 'Variable Deferred Annuities' on the US market. They were convinced that this product was going to enjoy a very positive response. The goal for SW Life was to distribute some $2 billion of annuities per year in 2000. In the short term, the company aimed at reaching 10 million in 1989 and 50 in 1990.

On 5 April 1989 while preparing for his next visit to the USA, Peter Landert, the president of SW Life, wanted to determine the magnitude of the cash that SW Life would have to invest in order to grow the portfolio of these new products. He decided to organize his analysis in two steps.

1. He wanted first to model a 'typical contract': $50 000 invested for 15 years.
2. He then wanted to simulate the cash flow of a growing portfolio of such contracts.

The product as seen by customers

The variable deferred annuity of SW Life was a very efficient long-term investment plan. Efficiency was achieved by a unique combination of asset selection, tax control and administration. Customers had the possibility of investing in the same types of mutual funds as they would have had access to otherwise: 'aggressive growth stocks', 'growth and income stocks', 'small companies', 'global', etc. During the life of the investment plan, customers also had the possibility of adjusting their portfolio. Transfers between mutual funds were tax-free and also free of charge, up to a specified number.[2] The variable annuity contract enabled customers to grow money on a tax deferred basis (tax was due at the maturity of the investment only). When entering a variable annuity contract, customers had to decide:

- for how long they wanted to invest (with a minimum duration of seven years); and
- how they wanted to collect the money at the end of the plan: payment of a lump sum or payment of an annuity; for a determined period of time; for life, and so on.

During the contract, customers also had the possibility of getting out of the plan at a cost.

- If the proceeds were collected before the owner was $59\frac{1}{2}$ years old, a 10% tax penalty had to be paid.
- Cancellation charges, called 'surrender charges', had to be paid to SW Life. Surrender charges were typically a function of the time elapsed between the start of the plan and its cancellation.[3]

In case of death, it was typical for annuities to guarantee a minimum compounded annual growth of the capital invested: at least 5% per annum (up to a maximum of 200% of the capital invested).

Customers were also charged an annual fee typically equal to 1.4%[4] of the value of the money invested.

The product as seen by SW Life

SW Life had designed the product in the following way. They would collect the money from the customer, immediately invest this money in mutual funds, pay the proceeds of the investments to the customers and administer the whole process.

SW Life was going to charge an annual fee equal to 1.4% of the value of the capital invested. This fee, the only revenue, would enable SW Life to cover all its distribution and operating costs and to provide its shareholders with the return they required (15% a year).

SW Life was planning to reach the final customers through brokers and wholesalers.[5] Brokers would charge SW Life a fee equal to 5% of the capital collected. This fee would be charged once, when the money was collected from the customer. Wholesalers would charge a 1% fee (also paid once, when the money was collected).

As far as investments were concerned, SW Life was totally transparent. The company immediately invested all the money collected in the mutual funds selected by the customers[6] and immediately paid the totality of the proceeds received from these funds (investment gains net of the expenses charged by the funds) to the customers.[7]

Being prepared to meet the challenges of explosive growth

Peter Landert was well aware that such growth was going to create very large cash needs. While he knew that the impact of growth was a timing impact only, he was also aware that it was never easy to manage a company that was generating very large negative cash flows.

Notes

1. This case is the abridged version of the SW Life America case study developed by Michel Schlosser and Niklas Mhyr from a real business situation.
2. As with typical mutual funds, customers had to pay for the investment services: typically, an annual fee equal to 1% of the value of the capital invested.
3.

Years elapsed before the cancellation of the contract	1	2	3	4	5	6	7
Surrender charge as a % of the value of the capital	7.5	7.0	6.0	5.0	4.0	3.0	2.0

4. The maximum fee allowed by the regulatory authorities was 1.4% per year. Most companies were charging the maximum fee.
5. While it would be difficult for SW Life to go for 'direct distribution' down to the end customers, it would probably be possible for them to recruit their own wholesalers. It would also be possible to try to design a different agreement with the brokers and wholesalers.
6. These mutual funds were specially created for variable annuities investment and were mimicking the typical funds available on the market. From a customer standpoint, they were very similar to the typical mutual funds available on the market.
7. SW Life could also try to find a way to organize their own funds and to run them at a cost lower than the 1% typically charged.

CASE

Appendix III.3
Modelling the impact of growth on the trajectory of cash

Table III.3.1 shows a model that describes a typical SW Life contract (rows 1 to 12) and the progressive development of the business over time (rows 13–26). In year 1, SW Life sells some contracts, one contract in the model. Then in the following year SW Life sells new contracts: either the same number as in year 1 or more if the selling activity grows. And so on.

The drivers in B3 and B7 enable you to check the quality of the new SW Life product. The individual contracts have been constructed in such a way that they generally create value for SW Life. In order to maximize value, SW Life should sell as many contracts as it can and should definitely welcome the expected 'explosive growth'. The only problem with that is that each individual contract has a very clear 'pay-then-collect' profile with a large negative initial cash flow. The contract shown in Table III.3.1 has the following cash flow profile: –$3000 in year 1, $700 in year 2, $786 in year 3, $882 in year 4, $990 in year 5, etc. With such a cash profile, you cannot easily finance the sales of new contracts with the proceeds of old contracts! As shown in Table III.3.2:

- Selling the same number of contracts each year (B13=0) creates an overall cash profile that needs seven years to break even (cumulative cash). The individual contract needs five years to break even.
- Selling a growing number of contracts each year may lead to very challenging cash profiles. With growth rates higher than 30%, the annual cash in row 25 becomes more negative each year until it suddenly turns to positive.

The charts of the model in Figure III.3.1 can help you visualize the impact of explosive growth:

- With a 50% rate of growth (in B13), then cash, as shown in the right-hand side graph looks fine. However, cumulative cash is negative for 11 years and as displayed in the central graph declines each year in the first 10 years! Put yourself in the position of the shareholders who, for 10 years will see, each year, sales of new contracts increase *and* cumulated cash continuously decrease.
- With 100% and higher growth rates, then the cash profile is really dramatic.

Making the business immune to explosive growth

You can, then, check that the erratic cash profile is only due to the 'pay-then-collect' cash profile of each individual contract. What about changing the timing of the distribution fee? What about passing the same value to the distribution partners but with a different timing? With the present agreement SW Life pays 6% of each contract in year 0 ($3000 for a typical $50 000 contract). If SW Life were to spread the payment of the distribution fee over 15 years, starting in year 1, then an annual payment of $513 would have the same value as the payment of $3000 in year 0.[1] If you set B4 to 0 and C4 to 0.513, then you can check that the value of the typical contract is not changed. What is changed, though, is

Table III.3.1 ● Modelling explosive growth (foreground)

	B	1	2	3	4	5	6	7	8	9	10	11	12	13	14	15
Capital	50	56	63	71	79	89	100	112	126	141	159	178	200	224	252	283
Return on investment	0.15															
Distribution fee	6	0.0	0.0	0.0	0.0	0.0	0.0	0.0	0.0	0.0	0.0	0.0	0.0	0.0	0.0	0.0
Fee SW Life	1.4%	0.7	0.8	0.9	1.0	1.1	1.2	1.4	1.6	1.8	2.0	2.2	2.5	2.8	3.1	3.5
Asset Mgt fee	1.0%	0.5	0.6	0.6	0.7	0.8	0.9	1.0	1.1	1.3	1.4	1.6	1.8	2.0	2.2	2.5
Actual duration	15															
Surrender conditions		7.5%	7.0%	6.0%	5.0%	4.0%	3.0%	2.0%								
Surrender fees		0.0	0.0	0.0	0.0	0.0	0.0	0.0	0.0	0.0	0.0	0.0	0.0	0.0	0.0	0.0
CASH FLOW	**-3**	**0.7**	**0.8**	**0.9**	**1.0**	**1.1**	**1.2**	**1.4**	**1.6**	**1.8**	**2.0**	**2.2**	**2.5**	**2.8**	**3.1**	**3.5**
Rate	0.15															
NPV	4.7															
Growth	0.5															
Number years <0	11															
Yr 1	-3.0	0.7	0.8	0.9	1.0	1.1	1.2	1.4	1.6	1.8	2.0	2.2	2.5	2.8	3.1	3.5
Yr 2		-4.5	1.1	1.2	1.3	1.5	1.7	1.9	2.1	2.4	2.6	3.0	3.3	3.7	4	
Yr 3			-6.8	1.6	1.8	2.0	2.2	2.5	2.8	3.1	3.5	4.0	4.5	5.0	5	
Yr 4				-10.1	2.4	2.7	3.0	3.3	3.7	4.2	4.7	5.3	6.0	6.7	7	
Yr 5					-15.2	3.5	4.0	4.5	5.0	5.6	6.3	7.1	8.0	8.9	10	
Yr 6						-22.8	5.3	6.0	6.7	7.5	8.4	9.5	10.6	11.9	13	
Yr 7							-34.2	8.0	8.9	10.0	11.3	12.7	14.2	15.9	17	
Yr 8								-51.3	12.0	13.4	15.1	16.9	19.0	21.3	23	
Yr 9									-76.9	17.9	20.1	22.6	25.4	28.5	32	
Yr 10										-115.3	26.9	30.2	33.9	38.1	42	
Cash	-3	-4	-5	-6	-9	-12	-17	-24	-34	-49	101	113	127	143	16	
Cum cash	-3	-7	-12	-18	-27	-39	-56	-79	-114	-163	-62	52	179	322	4	

Legends: - - - Cash — Cum cash

Table III.3.1 continued ● Modelling explosive growth (formulas)

Inputs and formulas
B2, B3, B4, B5, B6, C8, D8, E8, F8, G8, H8, I8, B7 and B13: data

C2: =(1+$B$3)*(B2–C5–C6); Copy
C4: =0; D4: =C4; Copy
C5: =IF(C1<=$B$7, $B$5*B2,0); Copy
C6: =IF(C1<=b7, B2*$B$6,0); Copy
C9: =IF(C1=$B$7, C8*$B$2,0); Copy
B10: –B4*B2/100
C10: =C5+C9–C4
B11: =B3
B12: =NPV(B11,C10:Q10)+B10
B14: =SUM (B27:Q27)
B15: =B10; Copy
C16: =B10*(1+$B$13); Copy

D17: =B10*(1+$B$13)^2; Copy
E18: =B10*(1+$B$13)^3; Copy
F19: =B10*(1+$B$13)^4; Copy
G20: =B10*(1+$B$13)^5; Copy
H21: =B10*(1+$B$13)^6; Copy
I22: =B10*(1+$B$13)^7; Copy
J23: =B10*(1+$B$13)^8; Copy
K24: =B10*(1+$B$13)^9; Copy
B25: =SUM(B15:B24); Copy
B26: =B25
C26: =B26+C25
B27: =IF(B26>0, 0, 1); Copy

Graphs
The three graphs show the same two variables: annual and cumulative cash flows (rows 25 and 26). The only difference is scale. The scales of the vertical axes of the three graphs are as follows:

	Left	Centre	Right
Maximum	2.5	25	2500
Minimum	–5	–20	–900

Table III.3.2 ● Overall cash profile with different growth rates

Case 1: each year SW Life sells the same number of new contracts

1 contract sold in year 1	–3.00	0.70	0.79	0.88	0.99
1 contract sold in year 2		–3.00	0.70	0.79	0.88
1 contract sold in year 3			–3.00	0.70	0.79
1 contract sold in year 4				–3.00	0.70
1 contract sold in year 5					–3.00
Total annual cash flows	–3.00	–2.30	–1.51	–0.63	0.36
Total cumulated cash flows	–3.00	–5.30	–6.81	–7.45	–7.09

Case 2: each year SW Life sells 30% more

1 contract sold in year 1	–3.00	0.70	0.79	0.88	0.99
1.3 contracts sold in year 2		–3.90	0.91	1.02	1.15
1.7 contracts sold in year 3			–5.07	1.18	1.33
2.2 contracts sold in year 4				–6.59	1.54
2.9 contracts sold in year 5					–8.57
Total annual cash flows	–3.00	–3.20	–3.37	–3.50	–3.57
Total cumulated cash flows	–3.00	–6.20	–9.57	–13.08	–16.65

Case 3: each year SW Life sells 50% more

1 contract sold in year 1	–3.00	0.70	0.79	0.88	0.99
1.5 contracts sold in year 2		–4.50	1.05	1.18	1.32
2.3 contracts sold in year 3			–6.75	1.58	1.77
3.4 contracts sold in year 4				–10.13	2.36
5.1 contracts sold in year 5					–15.19
Total annual cash flows	–3.00	–3.80	–4.91	–6.49	–8.74
Total cumulated cash flows	–3.00	–6.80	–11.71	–18.20	–26.95

the cash flow profile: the individual contract always shows a positive cash flow (it has become a 'collect-then-pay' business) and the overall cash flow is on a continuously growing trajectory whatever growth is experienced.

Note

1. The sum of $1 + 1/1.15 + 1/1.15^2 +$ etc . . . over 15 years is equal to 5.8474. And $3/5.8474 = 0.5131$.

PT PharMa[1]

On 15 November 1996, Prapti Sukarman, the head of planning, was preparing a model for simulating the possible financial outcomes of PT PharMa. PT PharMa was the Indonesian daughter company of the PM group, one of the world leaders of the pharmaceutical and chemical industries. In 1994, a new group president had taken charge and had stated that the group's target was to achieve a 15% return on equity averaged over an economic cycle. 'This will increase the value of the company and enhance shareholder value over the long term. At the same time, we will safeguard jobs and create new ones by growing successfully.'

The company

With a 3.5% share of the market, PT PharMa was the largest foreign joint venture in Indonesia. The financial statements of the company are shown in Table L.1. In 1996, PT PharMa employed 450 people and was both producing locally (70% of the sales) and importing. PT PharMa had a local partner who was responsible for distribution. The Indonesian pharmaceutical industry was fragmented. There were some 280 companies with the largest company controlling 10% of the market and the 20 largest accounting for 50% of the market. Among the 280 companies, 4 were state owned and 41 were foreign joint ventures. Traditionally, the Indonesian government had controlled the pharmaceutical industry and had limited imports to a strict minimum. However, in 1993, a first major deregulation package was introduced. Patent protection had been traditionally weak and parallel imports were always a threat.

Healthcare in Indonesia

In 1996 Indonesia had a population of 196 million people spread over a vast archipelago of 1.9 million km^2. Urbanization was growing but was lower than in China, Malaysia or the Philippines: Indonesia's urban population was estimated to be less than 7 million. In the 1990s the population had been growing at an annual rate of 1.8% and 75% of the people were younger than 40. Indonesia's economy had achieved impressive success during the first economic 25-year plan (1969–94) and more growth was expected to take place during the second 25-year plan started in 1994. One of the results of the economic growth had been the significant improvement in living standards: people defined as poor by the World Bank decreased from 42.5% of the total population in 1976 to 15.5% in 1990. In 1992 Indonesia's per capita income was US $670 with a wide diversity. Indonesian consumers

Table L.1 ● Past financial statements of PT PharMa (in million rupiahs)

Cash flows	1994	1995	1996
Sales	**41 656**	**54 381**	**63 001**
Income before interest and tax	9 498	12 420	14 690
Interest expenses	85	2 287	1 732
Income before tax	9 413	10 133	12 958
Tax	3 433	3 357	4 000
Income after tax	**5 980**	**6 776**	**8 958**
Depreciation	1 523	2 092	2 092
Receivables – close	8 161	12 804	13 226
Inventory – close	6 767	9 424	9 563
Payables – close	5 232	7 487	5 212
Net capital expenditure	2 915	7 413	7 813
Free cash flow	**3 790**	**–3 590**	**401**
Dividend	2 310	4 710	7 100
New borrowings	–1 480	8 300	6 699
Change in cash	0	0	0
Sales growth	*25%*	*31%*	*16%*
Income after tax/sales	*14%*	*12%*	*14%*
Free cash flow/sales	*9%*	*–7%*	*1%*

Income statements	1994	1995	1996
Sales	**41 656**	**54 381**	**63 001**
Cost of goods sold	17 404	22 812	26 450
Gross margin	24 252	31 569	36 551
Operating expenses	14 754	19 149	21 861
Notional interest	2 547	4 102	5 385
Earnings from operations (EFO)	**6 952**	**8 318**	**9 305**
Reversal of notional interest	2 547	4 102	5 385
Income before interest and tax	9 498	12 420	14 690
Interest expenses	85	2 287	1 732
Income before tax	9 413	10 133	12 958
Income after tax	**5 980**	**6 776**	**8 958**
Cost of goods sold/sales	*42%*	*42%*	*42%*
Operating expenses/sales	*35%*	*35%*	*35%*
EFO/sales	*17%*	*15%*	*15%*

Balance sheets	1994	1995	1996
Cash	2	2	2
Receivables	8 161	12 804	13 226
Inventory	6 767	9 424	9 563
Net fixed assets	7 281	12 602	18 323
Total assets	22 211	34 832	41 114
Payables	5 232	7 487	5 212
Bank borrowings	5 738	14 038	20 737
Equity	11 241	13 307	15 165
Total liabilities and equity	22 211	34 832	41 114
Collection period (months)	*2.35*	*2.83*	*2.52*
Inventory turnover	*2.57*	*2.42*	*2.77*
Payment period (months)	*3.43*	*3.53*	*2.35*
Return on capital employed	*56%*	*45%*	*41%*

were classified into five revenue groups and PT PharMa's market was limited to the top three groups (31 million people).

In spite of the great improvements that had taken place in the late 1980s and early 1990s, the health sector was still facing difficult problems. 'The health care system had not been one of the top beneficiaries of Indonesia's private sector driven economic growth.'[2] World Bank figures for 1990 showed that Indonesia spent 2% of GNP on healthcare as compared to 8% spent by Australia, 6.5% by Japan, 6% by India and 5% by Thailand.

The three growth scenarios

PT PharMa had been very successful in the past but was still short of the financial goal recently set by the group's regional management: earnings from operations (EFO) were now expected to be equal to 18% of sales. The decrease in EFO experienced in 1995 and 1996 was mainly due to an investment of 12 billion rupiahs (6 billion spent in 1995 and 1996). *'The previous management team was not exposed to the same pressure for financial results; today we would probably hesitate investing in such a nice building. Also with the new business area organization, we would now decide by ourselves instead of having to accept the decision of a country manager!'* Another challenge for PT PharMa was to grow its business: in recent years the company had been able to increase its prices freely (from 7 to 10% each year) and had benefited from the natural growth of the market. In the recent past, the company had not been particularly strong at introducing new activities and products. Now the market was changing and the company was very busy preparing for the launch of three new products and for the start of a new logistics project. The management team of PT PharMa had prepared three scenarios (see the detailed assumptions in Table L.2):

Table L.2 ● Inputs for the three scenarios

	'Base' %	'Higher growth' %	'Lower growth' %
Change in volume sold	6.0	6.0	7.0
Inflation	6	6	6
Change in selling price	7	10	3
Price increase above inflation	1	4	−3
Change in sales (rupiah)[a]	13	17	10
Change in sales ($)[b]	7	10	4
Change in price imported products[c]	6	6	6
Change in price local inputs	8	8	8
Change in productivity	2	2	3
Change in price local products[d]	5.9	5.9	4.9
Change in price operating expenses inputs	8	8	8
Change in productivity	2	2	3
Change in operating expenses[e]	12.2	12.2	12.2

Notes
[a] (1 + change in selling price) × (1 + change in volume) − 1
[b] (1 + price increase above inflation) × (1 + change in volume) − 1. It is assumed that prices do not change in the USA and that the change in the rupiah/$ exchange rate offsets the inflation in Indonesia.
[c] Due to change in exchange rate.
[d] (1 + change in price local inputs) × (1 − change in productivity)
[e] (1 + change in price operating expenses) × (1 − change in productivity)

● 'Base scenario'. The central assumption of this scenario was that annual growth would average 13% in rupiah (7% in price and 6% in volume) and 7% in US dollars. This scenario assumed a whole series of productivity gains that were necessary to compensate for the fact that salaries were increasing faster than inflation. The financial outcomes of this scenario are shown in Table L.3.

Table L.3 ● Model of an international business and base scenario

A	B	C	D	E	F	G
1	1996	1997	1998	1999	2000	2001
2 Change in selling price		7%	7%	7%	7%	7%
3 Change in volume sold		6%	6%	6%	6%	6%
4 **Sales**	63 001	71 456	81 045	91 921	104 257	118 249
5 % Imports		30%	30%	30%	30%	30%
6 Change in cost price imports		6%	6%	6%	6%	6%
7 Change in cost price local		5.9%	5.9%	5.9%	5.9%	5.9%
8 CGS	26 450	29 700	33 348	37 446	42 046	47 212
9 Change in operating expenses		12.2%	12.2%	12.2%	12.2%	12.2%
10 Operating expenses	21 861	24 528	27 520	30 878	34 645	38 872
11 Notional interest	5 385	5 724	6 143	6 626	7 180	7 816
12 **EFO**	9 305	11 504	14 033	16 972	20 386	24 349
13 Reversal notional interest	5 385	5 724	6 143	6 626	7 180	7 816
14 Income before interest and tax	14 690	17 228	20 176	23 598	27 566	32 165
15 Interest	1 732	2 725	2 772	2 812	2 842	2 860
16 Profit before tax	12 958	14 503	17 404	20 786	24 724	29 305
17 **Income after tax**	8 958	10 152	12 183	14 550	17 307	20 514
18 Depreciation	2 092	2 301	2 531	2 784	3 063	3 369
19 Collection period	2.52	2.52	2.52	2.52	2.52	2.52
20 Receivables end	13 226	15 006	17 019	19 303	21 894	24 832
21 Inventory turn	2.77	2.77	2.77	2.77	2.77	2.77
22 Inventory end	9 563	10 722	12 039	13 518	15 179	17 044
23 Payment period	2.35	2.35	2.35	2.35	2.35	2.35
24 Payables end	5 212	6 043	6 789	7 623	8 559	9 611
25 Capital expenditure	7 813	2 450	2 744	3 073	3 442	3 855
26 **Free cash flow**	401	7 896	9 385	11 332	13 613	16 276
27 Dividend	7 100	8 122	9 746	11 640	13 845	16 411
28 New loans	6 699	226	362	308	233	135
29 Change in cash	0	0	0	0	0	0
30						
31 Cash	2	2	2	2	2	2
32 Receivables	13 226	15 006	17 019	19 303	21 894	24 832
33 Inventory	9 563	10 722	12 039	13 518	15 179	17 044
34 Net fixed assets	18 323	18 472	18 684	18 973	19 352	19 838
35 Total assets	41 114	44 201	47 745	51 797	56 428	61 717
36 Loans	20 737	20 963	21 324	21 632	21 865	22 000
37 Payables	5 212	6 043	6 789	7 623	8 559	9 611
38 Equity	15 165	17 195	19 632	22 542	26 003	30 106
39 Total liabilities and equity	41 114	44 201	47 745	51 797	56 428	61 717

Medicine prices tell a horror story

Jakarta (JP): Your health is your treasure, a proverb says. Sure it is. The problem is health is too often a luxury that only a lucky few can afford to 'buy' . . . Despite the fact that there are now around 250 medicine factories, 1300 distributors, about 4000 pharmacies and hundreds of thousands of drugs stores, the prices of the estimated 20 000 types of medicines on the market, most of which are made locally, remain high. For many years, the health service, including the pharmaceutical industry, has become a profitable business for government employees, pharmacy owners and medical practitioners.

Collusion involving these three parties is strongly believed to have caused the continuous increase in medicines prices. 'They are criminals', said Prof. Iwan Darmansyah from the School of Medicine at the University of Indonesia. Medicines sold at pharmacies can be over three times higher than those offered by PT Askes, the only health insurance firm assigned by the government to provide low-cost medicines and medical treatment to state employees.

Compared to some other countries, some prices may look only slightly higher or even lower. 'But don't forget that our per capita income is much lower than many other countries' said Iwan.

Some medicines at pharmacies in neighbouring Australia, for instance are still much cheaper than here, even though Australia's Gross National Product per capita is US $19 100, or 20 times higher than Indonesia's $940.

There are many factors behind the high prices of medicines here, including that many government officers routinely ask for money from businessmen involved with medicines. 'I know of high-ranking officials in the Ministry of Health who often ask for money from certain pharmaceutical companies for their official trips overseas', said a source who requested anonymity.

Another factor is attributed to the fact that producers need extra funds to bribe doctors to help sell their medicines.

Another factor is passive consumers who never complain. As a result, only a few out of Indonesia's population of 195 million are able to purchase proper medicines.

Figure L.1 Risk of a price freeze
Source: Copyright *The Jakarta Post*, 15 September 1996.

- **'Higher growth' scenario**. In this scenario, annual growth was assumed to average 17% (10% in price and 6% in volume) and 10% in US dollars. This scenario was extrapolating the situation that had recently prevailed in Indonesia for PT PharMa and the other pharmaceutical companies.
- **'Lower growth' scenario**. In this scenario, average annual growth was 10% only, and 4% in US dollars. In Indonesia, prices of medicines seemed to become an issue (see in Figure L.1 an extract of an article published in *The Jakarta Post* of 15 September 1996). One could not rule out the possibility of a price freeze.

Additional price and currency data are given in Table L.4.

Notes

1. This case was prepared by Michel Schlosser from a real business situation.
2. From *Health Care in Indonesia*, G.P. Farmasi, 1994.

Table L.4 ● Price and currency data

	1987	1988	1989	1990	1991	1992	1993	1994	1995	1996
Price index Indonesia	100	109	116	127	139	145	160	174	189	202
Price index USA	100	104	109	114	119	122	126	129	133	137
Rupiah devaluation rate (actual)	100	105	109	115	121	125	128	133	139	143
Rupiah devaluation rate (PPP)[a]	100	105	106	111	116	119	127	135	143	148
Inflation (annual %)	8	9	6	9.5	9.5	4.9	9.8	9.2	8.6	6.7
Price increase of drugs	10	7	7	9	10	5	10	10	7.5	8

Note
[a] This shows what the devaluation of the rupiah should have been in order to exactly offset the inflation differential:

In 1987, 105 is calculated as $100 \times 109/104$
In 1986, 106 is calculated as $100 \times 116/109$

A comparison with the actual devaluation rate shows that the change in exchange rate has very much offset the inflation differential.

Appendix III.4
Building a model for an international business

The PT PharMa case is an opportunity to build a price–volume model in an international context. The evolution of the margin of a company that imports is a function of two series of changes:

● *Change in local selling prices.* Local selling prices change under the pressure of local inflation and of the specific competitive situation of the company. So far PT PharMa has always been able to increase its price faster than inflation. However, this may not continue and the article in the *Jakarta Post* suggests that one tests a more pessimistic scenario than the 'low growth' one.

● *Change in import prices.* Import prices change under the pressure of inflation in the exporting country, of the change in exchange rate, and of the specific competitive situation of the exporting company.

One thing to keep in mind is that three of these changes tend to offset each other. Purchasing power parity (see Chapters 5 and 19) states that changes in exchange rates and relative changes in inflation tend to offset each other. Purchasing power parity suggests that we:

● Look simultaneously at change in currency and relative changes in inflation. Here since we assume that inflation in the USA is nil, the only inflation that counts is the local inflation in Indonesia.

● Envisage the impact of possible deviations from purchasing power parity. This is important for both for diagnosis and for simulation purposes. When assessing the performance of a business, it is important to have a good understanding of the environment created

---

Table III.4.1 ● Model of an international business (formulas)

Rows 2, 3, 5, 6, 7, 9, 19, 21, 23 and 29: data

B4, B8, B10, B11, B14, B15, B16, B17, B18, B20, B22, B24, B25, C25, B26, B27, C27, B28, B31, B34, B36 and B38: data

C4: +B4*(1+C2)*(1+C3); Copy

C8: +B8*(1+C3)*(C5*(1+C6)+(1–C5)*(1+C7)); Copy

C10: +B10*(1+C9); Copy

C11: +.15*(C35–C37); Copy

B12: +B4–B8–B10–B11; Copy

B13: +B11; Copy

C14: +C12+13; Copy

C15: +.13*C36. Copy. This feature introduces a circular reference. You have to modify Excel's Recalculation option, see page 146.

C16: +C14–C15; Copy

C17: +.70*C16; Copy

C18: +B18*1.1; Copy

C20: +C4/12*C19; Copy

C22: +C8/C21. Copy. This is not a very satisfactory formula. See page 128.

C24: +(C8+C22–B22)/12*C23; Copy

D25: C25*1.12; Copy

C26: +C17+C18–C20+B20–C22+B22+C24–B24–C25

D27: +.8*D17

C28: –C26+C27+C29

C31: +B31+C29

B32: +B20; Copy.

B33: +B22; Copy

C34: +B34+C25–C18; Copy

B35: +SUM(B31.B34); Copy

C36: +B36+C28; Copy

B37: +B24; Copy

C38: +B38+C17–C27; Copy

B39: +SUM(B36.B38); Copy

---

by the situation of the currency. Some foreign subsidiaries may operate in countries with an 'overvalued' currency, e.g. a currency that has lost little value in spite of high local inflation. When a foreign subsidiary operates as an importer in such an environment, then its financial results are naturally biased upwards and one should expect to see very good results![1] At the opposite extreme, a foreign subsidiary that operates as an importer in a country with an undervalued currency has its results naturally biased downwards and one should not necessarily equal these results with poor management. When it comes to simulation, it is important to keep in mind that substantial deviations from purchasing power parity may surface. Even though past data (see Table L.1) show that local inflation and currency changes have been offsetting each other nothing guarantees that this will continue in the future.

A model for PT PharMa is given in Table L.3. The formulas for building this model are in Table III.4.1. This model features the concept of notional or calculated interest, the European ancestor to the MVA and EVA® (see Chapter 3).

Testing the impact of a price freeze

You can use the model to test the impact of a price freeze: it is a matter of setting the change in selling price (row 2) to 0. In 1996, operating earnings before notional interest is equal to 23% of sales, and return of capital employed is 41%. A one-year price freeze (in 1997) brings these two returns down to 19% and 34% respectively. A two-year price freeze (in 1997 and 1998) brings them down to 14% and 26%.

Looking at PT PharMa with hindsight

At the end of 1996, PT PharMa – like many international companies operating in Asia – was not concerned with the risk that the Indonesian currency would dramatically lose a lot of value. The model could have helped test the impact of a change in currency value and could have helped assess by how much local prices should have been increased, provided that a price freeze was not imposed by the government.

In 1997, the Indonesian currency collapsed but PT PharMa managed to survive through a succession of actions:

- less reliance on imports;
- productivity gains;
- currency hedging. Buying currency forward gave PT PharMa two advantages. Hedging enabled the company to fix its purchasing price at a level that was very unfavourable but had the advantage of being known in advance: PT PharMa could then act in order to try to operate at that price. The second advantage only appeared progressively. Forward rates proved to be systematically better than actual rates;
- price increases. Due to the collapse of the currency, prices had to, and did, increase.

Note

1. Foreign subsidiaries that generate poor results in such environments are often excessively aggressive on price.

CASE

Managing the trajectories of commitment in decline and growth situations

·

*Part IV is organized around two business cases that focus on the challenges associated with the two major dynamics of business: **decline** and **growth**.*

- *Tyler Welding (Case M) is a declining business that operates in a declining industry.*
- *Motion-Control (Case N) is a new business in an emerging industry.*

*Part III – and especially Chapter 12 and the appendices – has shown the advantages of 'collect-then-pay' business designs. Unfortunately it is generally not possible for a business to avoid committing to any spending in advance of its receipts. As a result almost all businesses are confronted with one of the most challenging issues of managing through decline and growth: the **selection of trajectories of commitment under uncertainty**.*

  Tyler Welding and Motion-Control operate according to a clear pay-then-collect business design and both companies have to select effective commitment trajectories:

- *Tyler Welding needs to decide how fast and how deep the company should commit to downsizing. On the one hand, the market is declining, but on the other hand some recent actions seem to prove that this market decline might be reversed. In the last two years the company has refocused on its traditional gas welding activity and this refocus has resulted in a significant growth.*
- *Motion-Control needs to decide how fast the company should commit resources to growth. For several years Motion-Control has been working at creating a new industry but the business has been very slow to come. Now there are strong signals that growth might be about to come. The problem though is that committing too many resources too fast may destroy all the potential value of this emerging growth.*

Chapter 14 provides tools and frameworks that will help you set value-creating trajectories of commitment:

- ***Strategic what-if analysis:*** *a tool for designing robust business plans, e.g. business plans that embody strategies of commitment that can cope with the 'surprises' of growth and decline.*
- ***Real options thinking:*** *a powerful framework for helping you decide when you should commit in order to create the maximum value.*

You will also find in Chapter 14 two new models. The model for simulating the operations of Tyler Welding (Table 14.2) is a generic model for simulating manufacturing operations. The model for simulating the business of Motion-Control (Table 14.11) is organized to reflect the actual sequence of business decisions – according to their degree of commitment – rather than the traditional accounting format.

Tyler Welding

On 25 November 1999, Henrik Billgren, the president of Tyler Welding, was not feeling fully at ease. He had just been reviewing the estimate for 1999 that was showing a loss of Swedish kronor (SEK) 9.5 million (see Tables M.1 and M.2). In spite of all the changes implemented since 1993, Tyler Welding had been making losses for five years in a row (see Tables M.3 and M.4) and Henrik Billgren was really wondering about what he should do now.

- Should he persist and continue implementing the gradual change strategy that he had adopted since joining the company in 1997? The growth recently achieved by the company seemed to demonstrate that it was possible to succeed in this challenging industry and Henrik Billgren wanted now to focus his attention to marketing and sales. Another promising opportunity was the possibility of finding a way to stop the war with the most aggressive competitor: Osvald.
- Or should he rather completely stop thinking in terms of gradual change and initiate a radical turnaround process? Henrik Billgren was well aware of the persistent weaknesses of Tyler Welding and of the need for the company to completely re-engineer itself. He was also fully aware that this turnaround would probably be a very time-consuming and very painful internal process.

The company

Tyler Welding was one of the four largest manufacturers of equipment for gas welding and gas cutting in Europe. Their products were regulators, hoses and torches with welding and cutting attachments, and consumable such as nozzles and welding rods. Tyler Welding was a daughter company of Tyler, one of the world leaders in the industrial and medical gases industry.[1]

Tyler Welding's headquarters were situated on the site of the former airport of Malmö in the south of Sweden where the company employed 155 people. Production was located in Malmö and in Oslo, Norway (20 people). Selling was done through Tyler's local gas companies throughout the world except for the UK and Germany where Tyler Welding had its own selling companies and salesforces (5 people in the UK and 2 people in Germany). At its peak, the UK sales company had employed 50 people.

Table M.1 • Financial data for 1999 (estimate)

Income and cash flows (million SEK)

Sales[a]	137.8
Cost of goods sold[b]	103.6
Administrative, selling & development[c]	33.5
Operating income	**0.7**
Interest[d]	10.2
Income before tax	**−9.5**
Depreciation	4.6
Receivables open[e]	22.0
Receivables end	24.1
Inventory open[e]	55.6
Inventory end	68.0
Payables open[e]	20.0
Payables end	21.8
Capital expenditures	7.0
Free cash flow	**−24.7**
New loans	23.7
Change in cash	−1.0

Balance sheet, as at 31 December 1999 (million SEK)

Cash	1.5		
Accounts receivable	24.1	Accounts payable	21.8
Inventory	68.0	Loans[f]	93.0
Net fixed assets	34.4	Net worth	13.2
Total assets	128.0	Total liabilities and equities	128.0

Notes
[a] 344 500 units at an average price of SEK 400 each.
[b] See manufacturing account in Table M.2.
[c] Of which: personnel costs: SEK 20.5 million (46 persons); other costs: SEK 13.0 million.
[d] Interest rate 8%.
[e] Accounts related to the sole gas welding activity.
[f] Part of the loans were inter-company loans.

Relationships within the group

Being part of a large group obviously brought a series of advantages and disadvantages. On the one hand, Tyler Welding had access to more resources than its smaller competitors and could often invest when they were unable to. The company also benefited from the support of a strong network of sales companies all over the world. On the other hand, Tyler Welding could not really have its own independent strategy:

- The Tyler gas companies relied on direct sales only. Tyler Welding would have liked to rely on direct and indirect sales through distributors.
- In 1999 Tyler acquired a Norwegian gas company. As a result, Tyler Welding had to acquire Nova, the gas welding equipment unit of that company. Nova had a plant in Oslo which produced the same range of products as Malmö. If he had been given the choice, it was not clear that Henrik Billgren would have decided to acquire this business!

Table M.2 ● Production account

	Volume (000 units)	Unit price (SEK)	Value (million SEK)
Volume produced	375		
Inventory material open	30	143	4.3
Inventory material end	20	142	2.8
Purchase of material	365	142	51.8
Consumption of material		142	53.3
Other variable costs		21	8.0
Direct and indirect labour cost[a]			44.9
Other fixed costs			7.0
Depreciation			4.6
Manufacturing cost	375	314	117.8
Inventory open finished goods and work in progress	177	290	51.3
Inventory end finished goods and work in progress	208	314	65.2
Cost of goods sold	345		103.6

[a] 136 people.

Table M.3 ● Financial data for the period 1994–98

Income statements (million SEK)

	1994	1995	1996	1997	1998
Sales	136.8	167.0	157.0	157.8	134.1
Cost of production	96.0	106.2	104.5	110.7	98.4
Gross result	40.8	60.8	52.5	47.1	35.6
Operating income	−14.9	−1.9	−11.3	0.6	1.9
Interest	2.3	3.8	5.7	7.7	7.7
Income before tax	−17.1	−5.7	−17.0	−7.1	−5.8
Income after tax	−17.1	−5.7	−17.0	−7.1	−5.8

Balance sheets (million SEK)

	1994	1995	1996	1997	1998
Cash	2.8	5.8	5.1	2.7	2.5
Accounts receivable	36.0	31.7	29.1	26.7	27.5
Inventory	70.6	86.0	75.3	81.8	56.1
Net fixed assets	13.2	14.1	21.2	23.2	32.4
Total assets	122.6	137.6	130.7	134.4	118.5
Accounts payable	25.7	26.0	23.9	24.4	27.1
Loans	50.6	70.4	84.5	85.1	75.3
Net worth	46.3	41.2	22.3	24.9	16.1
Total liabilities and equities	122.6	137.6	130.7	134.4	118.5

Selected ratios

	1994	1995	1996	1997	1998
Growth in sales	21%	22%	−6%	0%	−15%
Cost of production/sales	70%	64%	67%	70%	73%
Operating income/sales	−11%	−1%	−7%	0%	1%
Inventory (months)	8.8	9.7	8.6	8.9	6.8
Collection period (months)	3.2	2.3	2.2	2.0	2.5
Number of personnel	390	378	326	241	164

Table M.4 ● Actual vs. budget and electric welding vs. gas welding

Actual vs. budget (million SEK)

	1993	1994	1995	1996	1997	1998	1999
Sales							
Budget	92.1	131.2	159.4	194.8	189.3	155.8	122.8
Actual	74.0	136.8	167.0	157.0	157.8	134.1	137.8
Operating income							
Budget	4.2	−9.2	0.4	4.8	8.6	7.8	9.9
Actual	−3.1	−14.8	−1.8	−11.3	0.8	1.9	0.5

Electric welding vs. gas welding

	1997	1998	1999
Electric welding			
Sales	75.0	15.6	0.0
Material consumed	27.3	5.8	0.0
Direct labour	7.8	1.7	0.0
Indirect labour	11.6	2.0	0.0
Inventory end	23.2	22.3	0.0
Gas welding			
Sales	82.8	118.5	137.8
Material	25.5	41.0	51.8
Direct labour	8.0	12.9	16.8
Indirect labour	8.8	14.4	18.5
Inventory end	58.6	33.8	67.8

● Finally, the managing directors of the local Tyler gas companies were authorized to select any supplier of gas welding and cutting equipment – as well as any supplier of regulators for other applications.

The refocus on gas welding and the restart of growth

Tyler Welding had been producing gas welding equipment since acetylene cutting and welding was introduced in the 1920s. In the early 1980s, Tyler recognized that offering electric welding equipment would help sell more gas. The company started to produce and sell equipment for the electric welding business but they failed to build a significant position on this market and decided to exit electric welding in 1997. Henrik Billgren was appointed managing director of Tyler Welding to finalize the divestment of electric welding and to organize the refocus on gas welding.

With the refocus on gas welding, sales started to grow again: from 83 million in 1997 to 138 million in 1999.[2] For Henrik Billgren, this demonstrated that a large part of Tyler Welding's problems were self-inflicted: 'With selling electric welding, the company has neglected its core business. Salesmen always prefer to deal with the "exciting" electric welding equipment! Now that electric welding is no longer an issue, Tyler Welding can start rebuilding itself as a profitable business.' Henrik Billgren did not believe, however, that the growth experienced in 1998–9 could be sustained.

A challenging industry

In 1999 the total European market for gas welding equipment amounted to some SEK 1.4 billion. This was 22% of the total world market.[3] The five largest European markets were Germany (420 million), the UK (210 million), France (190 million), Italy (160 million) and the Nordic countries (148 million). Even though it differed from market to market, the overall trend in Europe had been very challenging in the recent past. Recently, volume had decreased by 3–5% a year.

- Most customers belonged to declining industries: the shipbuilding industry, heavy construction and agriculture, heating, ventilation and plumbing, and to light industry, hobby welding and cutting.
- The consumption of steel was still decreasing in Europe. Gas welding, as well as the entire welding business, was heavily dependent on steel consumption.
- Lighter and more resistant metals requiring less cutting and welding were being used more and more. The increased diffusion of materials such as plastics that are glued rather than welded was not helping either.
- Finally, gas welding was suffering from the introduction of new welding and cutting methods – plasma cutting and welding – as well as from the continued but slow substitution to electric welding.

Nobody really knew what the future had in store for the European welding industry. Some experts were convinced that since the traditional customers were about to complete their restructuring, the gas welding market would stabilize. Other experts were convinced that the decline would continue.

Competition

In Europe there were four large competitors, a couple of medium ones and many small ones. The four large competitors were all of a similar size and three of them were part of an industrial gas group:

- Tyler Welding in Sweden, owned by Tyler;
- SAF in France, owned by Air Liquide, the largest gas company in the world;
- Messer Griesheim in Germany (the largest German gas company).

The fourth largest competitor was Osvald in the UK, the former daughter company of BOC, a large international gas company that was now part of the largest electric welding group in the world. Each of the top four gas welding manufacturers controlled 8–10% of the total European market and had a strong position in its home market where it typically competed with a number of small local firms, but not so much with large foreign competitors. With almost 30% of its sales outside the Nordic countries, Tyler Welding was one of the most international companies in the industry.

The two medium sized competitors were Gloor, a Swiss company with limited international activities (SEK 50 million sales in 1998) and Kayser, a German company (SEK 45 million sales).

There were also a large number of small manufacturers. Their presence could be explained by a series of factors:

- Low cost of entry into the industry. Gas welding and cutting equipment used an old, fairly stable and fairly unsophisticated technology.
- Local character of the business with strong national features. *'Professional welders like to work with the same equipment as the one they had learned to use at school!'* In terms of applications and performance all products were similar, but each country had its own preferred design: as an example, the position of the knob that controlled the regulator pointed forward in the UK and downward in Germany. So far, no manufacturer had yet adopted a production process which allowed for meeting all these different national requirements from the same basic design.

Gas welding and cutting equipment was not a very profitable business. Many companies were operating below capacity. Prices were also a matter of concern.[4] In many markets, prices had been continuously declining and typical comments made by sales people were as follows: *'Elga[5] calls our distributors and offers copies at a 45% lower price.'* 'Today a regulator is sold at a price 30% cheaper than in 1980.' 'Osvald has just increased their prices by 5%. They had had a price freeze for more than one and a half years!'

Tyler Welding in the Nordic market

Although Tyler Welding was one of the most international companies in the industry, the Nordic market represented 70% of its total sales, and 88% of its gross profit. In the Nordic market, Tyler Welding had a strong name and a dominant market share (65% of the Nordic market – 65% in Sweden, 76% in Finland, 74% in Norway and 41% in Denmark). *'Nordic customers do not simply purchase a regulator, they purchase a "Tyler"'*. Tyler Welding had always directed its efforts towards improving its products and developing new ones and had earned a reputation as a technological innovator: in the mid 1990s they had introduced a new nozzle which offered a substantial increase in productivity. However, as shown in Table M.5, Tyler had lost ground in some of its key markets and in Sweden in particular. A series of factors had contributed to this decline:

- The company had been slow at detecting the gradual shift from direct sales to indirect sales through distributors. In 1999 Tyler was still making 65% of its sales direct – actually through the Swedish Tyler gas company. Indirect sales were made through a

Table M.5 ● Market share in Sweden

	1989	1996	1999
Tyler	80%	63%	65%
Elga	10%	16%	16%
Osvald	0.3%	8%	8%
Vahli		5%	5%
Others	0.7%	8%	6%

national hardware retail chain and a variety of other channels: welding houses, various specialized shops, farmers' shops, and so on. The Swedish Tyler gas company had 20 salespeople who had started taking care of both the direct and indirect sales of Tyler Welding.

● Tyler had to compete with Elga and Vahli, two small, family-owned businesses. Elga's competitive advantage was its high flexibility and good service to customers. Elga marketed itself as the alternative to the 'big and dominant' Tyler.

● Finally, Tyler Welding had suffered from the entry of Osvald onto the market. In 1991 Osvald acquired a small German company with a product line adapted to the Nordic market. Since then the company had been selling gas welding products as a complement to its electric welding product range. In order to build market share, Osvald attacked the Swedish market with prices 15% below those of Tyler and quickly gained ground until Tyler aligned its prices down and started to retaliate in the UK, Osvald's home market.

Tyler Welding in other markets

Tyler Welding was exporting to a dozen markets, mostly in Europe but also in the USA, in South America and in the Middle East. In 1999, 30% of the sales (41 million) and 12% of the gross margin (4 million) had been generated from export activities. When selling and administrative costs were taken into account, export activities were just breaking even and a consultant had been asked to recommend how to improve the situation. The consultant's analysis confirmed that the company was not very professional on the export market. The export organization was weak: lack of attention to detail, lack of responsiveness and flexibility, lack of an overall sense of direction. The consultant also confirmed that Tyler Welding had a moderate to poor competitive position in most markets. The consultant finally concluded that the attractiveness (size, growth, price level, competition) of most markets was on the low side.

One of the growth prospects for Tyler Welding was the possible restructuring of the European industry. In the long run, the European industry was bound to go through some kind of restructuring and Tyler Welding was one of the few companies which had the potential and resources needed to implement an active strategy of acquisitions and alliances.

Opportunities to cut costs

Henrik Billgren still remembered the first impression he had when he joined the company in 1997: 'How is it possible to have so many people in marketing...and in most of the other departments?'

In Malmö, the plant was organized according to the various production processes: turning, drilling, and so on. Components and finished products were always manufactured in large batches. As an example, regulators were manufactured to cover six months of sales, which represented some 15 000 units! Lead times varied but could reach six months. Set-up times were four hours on average. Flexibility was a difficult issue since production included a great number of components: the product range for the Scandinavian market included 8000 items, and 20 000 part numbers. Roughly 60% of the components were manufactured in-house.

Tyler Welding produced for stock, based on forecasts prepared by the salespeople in the Tyler gas companies. Recently, Tyler Welding had experienced a number of unfortunate incidents in distant export markets. In Algeria, a salesman had booked a SEK 2 million order to be delivered at very short notice. Production was switched over and started working for this order. In the meantime, however, the Algerian customer found another supplier with a price 25% lower and cancelled the order. Since they were specific to the Algerian market, the products had to be kept in stock. Henrik Billgren was also feeling an urgent need to improve the delivery reliability, which did not exceed 50%. On a few occasions he had visited some retailers 'incognito' and had asked: *'Who do you consider to be the least reliable supplier in the industry?'* The name Tyler Welding came up several times as the answer.

Henrik Billgren wanted to reorganize manufacturing into flow groups and to shift the responsibility of the stock from marketing to production. He was also convinced that it was urgent to start focusing on the total manufacturing cost rather than on the unit manufacturing cost. Instead of large batches, the company should go for small series. Such a reorganization would entail an initial investment of SEK 5 million in new machinery with shorter set-up times (one hour instead of four) and changes in the design of the factory floor. Training of the personnel would require an investment of SEK 2–3 million spread out over two years. Henrik Billgren was convinced that this reorganization would generate a lot of benefits. It would help reduce the inventory to 15% of sales, and some 40 people working in production and production-related activities (production planning, co-ordinators, supervisors, shipment, etc.) would become superfluous.[6] He was also well aware that such a reorganization would probably meet heavy resistance from employees as well as trade unions. The recent divestment of electric welding had resulted in a tense atmosphere on the factory floor. Tyler Welding was also considering closing the Oslo plant and integrating its production into the Malmö factory. This would allow for a further reduction in personnel (20 people) but would cause closing costs equal to SEK 2 million.

The reorganization of production would have two other positive impacts: it would enable Tyler Welding to reduce its material costs by 10% and also to start selling regulators for applications requiring higher quality.[7]

Henrik Billgren also believed that the whole organization was still the one that was built in the 1985–90 expansion era (electric welding strategy and international development). He believed that the marketing department could be reduced by as many as 10 people[8] (fewer public relations people and fewer travelling salespeople). The R&D department could probably be reduced by three people at least: this department was running many interesting projects, but very few of them were bringing valuable results. Through an investment of 3–5 million in new computer systems, administration could be reduced by three people.

New competitive developments

Among Tyler's competitors, Osvald had a unique position and represented a special challenge. When it became a gas welding company, Osvald inherited a leading position in the UK and an underdog position in the Nordic markets. This was a position exactly symmetric to that of Tyler Welding: a leader in Nordic countries and an underdog in the UK. When Osvald tested the market and attacked Tyler's market share in the Nordic countries, Tyler retaliated in the UK and both companies stopped attacking each other. Tyler's management was well aware that the welding businesses of Tyler and Osvald were very complementary. One company was strong in electric welding while the other was strong in gas welding. One company was strong in gas welding in the UK while the other was strong in gas welding in the Nordic market, and so on. One of Tyler's senior vice-presidents actually took the initiative and suggested the idea of a strategic alliance to Osvald's president, who showed nothing more than a polite interest. However, when at the end of 1999 Henrik Billgren presented his budget, several senior managers of the group suggested that *'it might be the right time to give a second chance to a possible co-operation with Osvald'*. Henrik Billgren was very much in favour of a strategic alliance. For him it would mean that Osvald would stop putting pressure on prices – which could make selling prices increase by something like 10–14%. This could also mean a bit more volume for both companies (more gas welding business for Tyler and more electric welding business for Osvald).

Notes

1. Tyler Welding did not sell regulators for certain special uses like healthcare. Although these 'special' regulators were basically the same as those for 'basic' use, the Tyler gas companies did not consider Tyler Welding to be a sufficiently reliable supplier.
2. Including the acquisition of the Norwegian company that represented a 30 million increase in turnover.
3. North America 30%, USSR and eastern Europe 20%, Asia Pacific 20%, Africa 3%, South America 3%, Oceania 2%.
4. For the coming years, one could envisage a 2% annual price decline . . . while material costs were not expected to decline by more than 1% a year.
5. A small Swedish producer.
6. It is reasonable to consider that any reduction in personnel has no impact on personnel costs in the year in which the action is taken.
7. These applications often enjoyed better growth and better prices.
8. Henrik Billgren was also considering the possibility of keeping these people and making them work in a better way. He did not believe, however, that this alone could create much growth.

CASE *N*

Motion-Control

We are entering an incredible new era of manufacturing, where a mix of mass customization, mass production and craft manufacturing systems co-exist to bring us a wider variety of products and services than before. Advances in technology are giving us an incredible array of choices for controlling automation in this new era.

Extract from the website of a supplier of control systems

In November 2001, Maurice Dulac, the president of Motion-Control[1] was busy preparing plans for growth and in particular plans for growth in 2002.

The motion control business

Electric motors had become key components in many industrial applications and new control systems for electric motors based on microprocessors and power electronics had developed in the 1990s. These control systems were giving designers new possibilities of developing easily adjustable, more accurate and faster production machines. The market for new control systems – motion controllers and servo drives – had a rapid growth, 5–15% a year.

This growth was, at the same time, fuelled by the trend towards increased automation and the shift from mechanical control to electronic control – half of the machines were still mechanically controlled; and limited by the conservatism of some machine builders and the higher investment cost. New electronic machines were 10–15% more expensive, and this additional investment had a three to four year payback.[1]

Motion-Control

Motion-Control specialized in motion products for advanced multi-axis machines. The latest technology was implemented both in hardware and software. The company planned to release a second generation of products in 2003, while most competitors had only recently launched their first generation. The company had succeeded in getting the business of a few reputed machine builders in the fields of packaging, wiring, printing and textile printing. Motion-Control was a Swiss company located close to Zurich. In 2001 the company employed 67 people and had budgeted sales of SFr 13.5 million. It had sales companies in Germany and the UK and sales offices in Italy and France. The company was family owned until its ownership changed in 2001.

The development of Motion-Control

Motion-Control was founded in 1976 to develop motion control and management products. The company started by developing control systems for NC machines produced by one of the leading Swiss machine builders. Activity progressively shifted towards special machines, and the execution

---

Figure N.1 The development of Motion-Control

CASE

of a contract for a textile printing machine builder enabled the company to develop strong competencies in dealing with complex motion problems involving a lot of axes. In 1997 the company became involved with packaging machines when it won a bid organized by a reputed international company. Since 1992 the company had developed a unique system for the control of a large number of axes – more than 4. This system was based on the use of a separate control module that simplified the functional interconnections between the axis drives[2] both from a hardware and programming point of view. One of the unique features of the system was the use of fibre optics for connecting the separate control module and the axis drives: this had considerably increased the reliability of the system. Since 1998, the company had been working at developing a new generation of axis controllers and separate control modules: these new products, initially expected to be released in 2002, were now planned for introduction late in 2003. This new generation of product would correspond to a change in production: the new products required the use of a new technology that was making it impossible to subcontract part of manufacturing as the company was currently doing. Motion-Control had almost made its choice: rather than totally subcontracting, the company was in favour of investing[3] and manufacturing the new products.

One of the characteristics of the company had been its reliance on a relatively small number of customers[4]: this resulted in advantages and disadvantages. For a number of years – 1978 to 1997 – it enabled the company to grow at a steady pace.[5] In 1997 the company employed 80 people and sales amounted to SFr 14 million. But on two occasions this had resulted in very serious shocks:

● In 1997, the Swiss NC machine builder for which the company had developed its first motion control system went bankrupt. This obliged Motion-Control to lay off 20 people.
● In 1999, the main customer, a builder of printing machines, suddenly stopped placing orders. This was due to the unfortunate combination of three factors: an unexpected drop in demand for printing machines; excessive stocks of machine components; and change in logistics aimed at working with much lower stocks of components.

From 1998, Motion-Control decided to start building stronger sales capabilities which involved the creation of sales subsidiaries in England and Italy. At that time, the company was aiming at *reaching an 'optimal size' of SFr 20–25 million sales in the medium term*.[6] In 2001, the sales to the 10 largest customers still represented some 70% of total sales – with the largest customer representing 15% of total sales.

Figure N.1 (*continued*)

Notes
1. These machines had a 5–15 year life.
2. Motion-Mgt was manufacturing and selling both the separate module and the axis drives. Motion-Mgt drives were high accuracy drives that were also used for built-in control of specific axes (single axis vs. multi axis programming). Typical selling prices were SFr 2 to 3000 for axis drives and 5000 for separate control modules. Products prices were decreasing by some 5% a year but since the price of material was decreasing at the same rate, material had continued representing 32% of sales in recent years.
3. The total investment amounted to some SFr 1.5–2 million. This solution also involved the recruitment of some 5 to 10 more production people.
4. The builders of special machines were concentrated in a relatively limited number of countries: USA, Germany, Switzerland, Great Britain, Scandinavia, etc.
5. At that time machine builders used to place their orders months in advance. 'In the good old days machine builders were doing serious forecasts and were willing to wait for several months. Now they do not seem to make much forecasting and they want to get their components almost immediately!'
6. The market was not dominated by any one competitor. The three largest competitors had sales of SFr 120, 100 and 100 million. Motion-Control was the tenth largest company.

In June 2001 Motion-Control had been acquired by the industrial automation division of ABC, a large global industrial group. Since then, a new life had started for the management of Motion-Control: 'I did not believe that one could have so many meetings and travel so much!' However, Motion-Control's formal organization had not changed except for the fact that the company was now a 'product unit' of a global group. As a result the company now shared the responsibility for its foreign sales companies and sales offices within the integrated structure of the group. Maurice Dulac, the former president and one of the main former owners, had kept his position.

The situation at the end of 2001

As shown in Table N.1, 2001 was going to generate great results. Sales had developed better than expected in volume and prices had not decreased as much as they had done in the recent past when they were falling by 5% a year. This was very rewarding for Maurice Dulac and the whole Motion-Control team.

Following the acquisition, a team including people from ABC had been formed with a view to defining the strategy of the company for the coming years, and very ambitious goals had progressively emerged from the team's work.

The new Motion-Control was aiming to be one the five largest competitors in all the markets where it had decided to be. The work on strategy had enabled the company to

Table N.1 ● Motion-Control: past income statements (in SFr '000s)

	1996	1997	1998	1999	2000	2001
Net invoiced sales	13 087	11 501	12 860	8 781	11 124	16 617
Cost of goods sold	7 916	7 232	7 388	4 529	5 878	9 648
Gross profit	5 171	4 269	5 472	4 252	5 246	6 969
Administration	990	950	1 032	1 061	910	1 515
Marketing	1 450	1 150	1 393	906	1 565	1 708
R&D	1 800	1 500	1 775	1 493	1 704	1 786
Depreciation	275	513	480	489	647	560
Operating net income	656	156	792	303	420	1 400
Interest net	489	730	638	530	420	382
Net income before tax	167	−574	154	−227	0	1 018
Net income after tax	167	−574	154	−227	0	1 010
Growth in sales		−12.1%	11.8%	−31.7%	26.7%	49.4%
Growth in CGS		−8.6%	2.2%	−38.7%	29.8%	64.1%
Growth in administration costs		−4.0%	8.6%	2.8%	−14.2%	66.5%
Growth in marketing costs		−20.7%	21.1%	−35.0%	72.7%	9.1%
Growth in R&D		−16.7%	18.3%	−15.9%	14.1%	4.8%
CGS/sales	60.5%	62.9%	57.4%	51.6%	52.8%	58.1%
Functional costs/sales	32.4%	31.3%	32.7%	39.4%	37.6%	30.1%
Operating income/sales	5.0%	1.4%	6.2%	3.5%	3.8%	8.4%
Net income/sales	1.3%	−5.0%	1.2%	−2.6%	0.0%	6.1%

Table N.2 • Motion-Control: past cash flow statements

	1996	1997	1998	1999	2000	2001
Net income after tax	167	−574	154	−227	0	1010
Depreciation	275	513	480	489	647	560
Increase in receivables		−597	−868	−742	272	285
Increase in inventory		159	−492	228	−97	1777
Increase in non-interest-bearing liabilities		−67	−411	−807	484	819
Increase in activated R&D		332	−152	40	0	0
Capital expenditure		872	358	470	1610	1095
Free cash flow		−894	1377	−541	−654	−768
Dividend		0	0	0	0	0
New debt		901	−1403	544	−56	1196
New equity		0	0	750		0
Change in cash flow		7	−26	753	−710	428

Table N.3 • Motion-Control: past balance sheets

	1996	1997	1998	1999	2000	2001
Cash	22	29	3	756	46	474
Receivables	3 818	3 221	2 353	1 611	1 883	2 168
Inventory	3 026	3 185	2 693	2 921	2 824	4 601
Capitalized R&D	440	772	620	660	660	660
Net fixed assets	3 219	3 578	3 456	3 437	4 400	4 935
Total	10 525	10 785	9 125	9 385	9 813	12 838
Non-interest-bearing debt	2 234	2 167	1 756	949	1 433	2 252
Interest-bearing debt	7 260	8 161	6 758	7 302	7 246	8 442
Net worth	1 031	457	611	1 134	1 134	2 144
Total	10 525	10 785	9 125	9 385	9 813	12 838
Receivables in days	*105*	*101*	*66*	*66*	*61*	*47*
Inventory in days	*138*	*159*	*131*	*232*	*173*	*172*
Debt/equity	*7.0*	*17.9*	*11.1*	*6.4*	*6.4*	*3.9*

Note:
Following the acquisition, a number of provisions were made on inventory and receivables and capitalized R&D was charged to equity.

better define its products and product priorities, and to deepen its understanding of its markets.[2] During this process the company had also defined what could be considered to be its preferred customers, as well as its market and geographic priorities. The company had also defined its strengths[3] and weaknesses[4] as well as its basic beliefs and ways of working.

(a) Looking at trends with 2001 budgeted figures

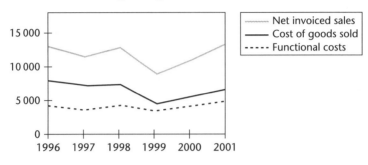

(b) with 2001 actual figures

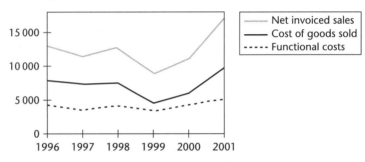

Figure N.2 Motion-Control: past trends
Note: 'functional' costs include administrative, selling and R&D costs.

Plans for growth

Maurice Dulac was expecting a 24% growth (+25% in volume and −1% on price) in 2002. 'As shown by experience, the market is now taking off and growth may actually even reach 30–40% as it did in 2001! We should be very careful and not miss that growth that we have been preparing for for so many years!' The initial assumptions made by Maurice Dulac when planning for growth as well as the corresponding financial statements are shown in Table N.2. Mr Dulac was aware that a lot of productivity gains could be achieved in production in 2002: *'The products that we are going to sell in 2002 belong to the "old" generation and our current production structure can absorb a substantial increase in volume.'* He was also aware that, in 2003, a new generation of products would be introduced and would use a different production technology. On the functional cost side, he believed that there was a need to strengthen the resources of Motion-Control and this was reflected in the initial assumptions which also showed the need for new investments.

Table N.4 ● Motion-Control: actual vs. budget figures for 2001

	2000	Budget 2001		Actual 2001	
Net invoiced sales	11 124	13 500	21%	16 617	49%
Cost of goods sold	5 878	6 710	14%	9 648	64%
Gross profit	5 246	6 790	29%	6 969	33%
Administration	910	1 100	21%	1 515	66%
Marketing	1 565	1 700	9%	1 708	9%
R&D	1 704	2 200	29%	1 786	5%
Depreciation	647	800	24%	560	−13%
Operating net income	420	990	136%	1 400	233%
Interest net	420	523	25%	382	−9%
Net income before tax	0	467		1 018	
Net income after tax	0	467		1 010	
Depreciation	647	800		560	
Increase in receivables	272	267		285	
Increase in inventory	−97	576		1 777	
Increase in non-interest-bearing	484	−83		819	
Increase in capitalized R&D	0	−110			
Capital expenditure	1 610	865		1 095	
Free cash flow	−654	−414		−768	

Human resources	2000	2001 B		2001 A	
Manufacturing staff	5	5	0%	6	20%
Manufacturing workers	16	20	25%	25	56%
Administration	8	8	0%	9	13%
Marketing	1	1	0%	1	0%
Sales	4	4	0%	3	−25%
Engineering support	3	4	33%	7	133%
Product development	15	16	7%	17	13%
	52	58	12%	68	31%

Table N.5 ● Assumptions for 2002

Expected sales volume growth	*25%*
Expected sales price change	*−1%*
Increase in volume development & design resources	*25%*
Increase in price development & design resources	*25%*
Increase in volume administration & marketing resources	*14%*
Increase in productivity administration & marketing resources	*10%*
Increase in price administration & marketing resources	*10%*
Increase in volume production resources	*0%*
Increase in productivity production resources	*25%*
Increase in price production resources	*0%*
Capital expenditure	*1550*
Depreciation	*614*
Increase in production volume	*25%*
Increase in purchase price	*−5%*
Increase in volume purchases	*12%*
Collection period (days)	*41*
Payment period (days)	*27*

Table N.6 ● Simulation for 2002

	2001	2002
Sales	**16 617**	**20 564**
Volume sales	*5 539*	*6 924*
Unit price sales	*3.0*	*3.0*
Development and design	**1 786**	**2 791**
Administration and marketing	**3 223**	**4 042**
Labour and other costs	**2 449**	**2 449**
Depreciation	**560**	**614**
Production level	5 871	7 339
Material costs		**8 983**
Inventory material end	3 143	2 068
Volume units	*2 483*	*1 720*
Price	*1.27*	*1.20*
Purchases		7 908
Volume purchases	*5 871*	*6 576*
Price purchases	*1.27*	*1.20*
Manufacturing cost		**12 046**
Unit manufacturing cost		*1.64*
Inventory finished goods	1 457	2 063
Volume	*842*	*1 257*
Price	*1.73*	*1.64*
CGS	**9 648**	**11 440**
Gross profit	**6 969**	**9 124**
Operating income	**1 400**	**2 291**
Interest	382	521
Income before tax	**1 018**	**1 770**
Net income after tax	**1 010**	**1 239**
Add back depreciation		614
Accounts receivable end	2 168	2 342
Inventory end	4 600	4 132
Non-interest-bearing liabilities	2 251	1 405
Capital expenditure		1 550
Free cash flow	**−768**	**−248**
Dividend		0
Change in debt		248
Change in cash		0
Cash	474	474
Receivables	2 168	2 342
Inventory	4 600	4 132
Net fixed assets	4 935	5 871
Total	12 177	12 819
Interest-bearing debt	8 442	8 690
Non-interest-bearing debt	2 251	1 405
Net worth	1 484	2 723
Total	12 177	12 819

Notes

1. The activity of Motion-Control is described in Figure N.1.
2. One of the challenges was to design an effective segmentation. One approach was to think in terms of type of machinery; business field of the final user of the machinery; general category of process; and finally type of working process of the machine (for example, for the general packaging category, there were specific processes like liquid filling, wrapping, etc.).
3. Among the strengths: high motion control expertise/technology, quality products, being part of a global industry group, strong presence in selected countries, good relationships with customers, references, openness with clients, application expertise, etc.
4. Among the weaknesses: package did not currently include motors and cables, products could be more user friendly, lack of sales personnel, distance from customers in some countries, lack of software and tools to support products in use, leading to too much support needed from the company, working system, lack of end-user recognition in some countries.

CASE

From 'strategic what-if' to 'real options' thinking

Growth sounds – and typically is – much more attractive than decline. However, in business both decline and growth are common dynamics and business leaders should be prepared to create value out of both. Experience actually proves that it is possible to create and destroy value out of both growth and decline. In growth and decline, the pace at which spending is accelerated or slowed down is critical and it often happens that:

- growing businesses that commit resources too fast end up destroying a lot of value;
- declining businesses that quickly commit to new business models that enable them to cut spending also succeed at creating value.

The challenges of growth and decline come from the fact that spending comes first. This is the case for the businesses, like Tyler Welding and Motion-Control, that operate according to a 'pay-then-collect' design. This is also partly the case for all those companies that operate according to a 'collect-then-pay' design. Even when operations are strictly collect-then-pay, it is generally impossible to avoid all sorts of commitment under uncertainty: R&D, core competencies building, business infrastructure development, and so on.

Because spending comes first, businesses have to select their trajectories of commitment before knowing what the growth or the decline will be. They have to embark on a spending trajectory without knowing when and by how much the pace of the receipts will accelerate or slow down.

Then, once they have committed to a specific trajectory of spending, they cannot easily flip flop from this trajectory to another. Before embarking on a trajectory of commitment, it is always a good idea to do sufficient **strategic what-if** and to check that this trajectory can fare well with any kind of 'bad surprise'!

Chapter 14 deals with two series of issues:

- How to use 'strategic what-if' for testing alternative trajectories of commitment. Strategic what-if is applied successively to Tyler Welding and to Motion-Control.
- **Risk as a key factor in the selection of effective trajectories of commitment**. When committing to a decision that cannot be easily reversed risk is negative. This is also

how most people perceive risk. However, when commitment can be deferred – when you think 'real options' rather than 'decisions' – then risk becomes a source of value and the management of commitment trajectories is a very powerful way to create value out of risk.

14.1 A model for Tyler Welding

A model for Tyler Welding is shown in Tables 14.1, 14.2 and 14.3. This model is very similar to the explicit price volume model of Delta Metal (Tables 10.2 and 10.3) except for

Table 14.1 ● Model for Tyler Welding: inputs and outputs

A	B	C	D	E	F	G	H	I
1	1999	2000	2001	2002	2003	2004		Cum.
2 Change in volume sold		–3%	–3%	–3%	–3%	–3%		
3 Change in selling price		–2%	–2%	–2%	–2%	–2%		
4 Change in volume produced		–40%	15%	20%	–3%	–10%		
5 Change in cost of material		–1%	–10%	–1%	–1%	–1%		
6 Change in variable unit cost		–1%	–1%	–1%	–1%	–1%		
7 Change in the number of people (production)	–44%	–5%	–5%	–5%	–5%			
8 Change in the cost per person		3%	3%	3%	3%	3%		
9 Change in other fixed production costs	–44%	–5%	–5%	–5%	–5%			
10 Change in the number of people (S&A)	–35%	–5%	–5%	–5%	–5%			
11 Change in cost per person		0%	0%	0%	0%	0%		
12 Change in other S&A costs		–35%	–5%	–5%	–5%	–5%		
13 Exceptional costs		41.5	0.0	0.0	0.0	0.0		41.5
14 Capital expenditure		6.0	1.0	1.0	1.0	1.0		10.0
15 Depreciation		7.0	7.0	7.0	7.0	7.0		35.0
16								
17 Sales	138	131	125	118	113	107		
18 Growth		–5%	–5%	–5%	–5%	–5%		
19 Gross margin/sales	25%	19%	22%	30%	30%	26%		
20 Operating income	0.7	–38.7	6.9	16.1	14.7	10.1		
21 Inventory WIP & FG volume	208	98	33	29	25	0		
22 Number of people	182	106	101	96	91	86		
23 **Value generated in 2000–4**								
24 Discount rate		12%						
25 Free cash flow (before interest)		–10	36	26	22	24		
26 Free cash flow 2000–4		–81	36	26	22	24	7	34
27 Receipts		108	126	119	114	108	19	593
28 **Value receipts**		425						
29 Payments		189	90	94	91	84	12	559
30 **Value payments**		418						
31 **Value generated in 2000–4**		6						

Table 14.2 ● Model for Tyler Welding: the model

33	1999	2000	2001	2002	2003	2004	Cum.
34 Volume sold (000 units)	345	334	324	314	305	296	
35 Unit selling price	400	392	384	376	369	362	
36 **Sales**	**137.8**	**131.0**	**124.5**	**118.4**	**112.5**	**107.0**	
37 Volume produced (000 units)	375	225	259	311	301	271	
38 Volume inventory material end	20	9	11	13	13	0	
39 Unit cost material	142	141	127	125	124	123	
40 Inventory end material	2.8	1.3	1.4	1.6	1.6	0.0	
41 Unit cost of material	142	141	127	125	124	123	
42 Volume material purchased	365	214	260	313	301	259	
43 Purchases of material	51.8	30.1	32.9	39.2	37.3	31.7	
44 Material consumed	53.3	31.7	32.9	38.9	37.4	33.3	
45 Other variable costs	8.0	4.8	5.4	6.4	6.2	5.5	
46 Number of people (production)	136	76	72	69	65	62	
47 Personnel costs	44.9	25.9	25.3	24.8	24.3	23.7	
48 Other fixed costs	7.0	3.9	3.7	3.5	3.4	3.2	
49 Depreciation	4.6	7.0	7.0	7.0	7.0	7.0	35
50 **Manufacturing cost**	**117.8**	**73.2**	**74.3**	**80.7**	**78.2**	**72.7**	
51 Inventory end volume	208	98	33	29	25	0	
52 Inventory end unit cost	314	325	287	260	260	268	
53 Inventory end	65.2	32.0	9.5	7.5	6.5	0.1	
54 **Cost of goods sold**	**103.6**	**106.4**	**96.9**	**82.6**	**79.2**	**79.2**	
55 **Gross result**	**34.2**	**24.6**	**27.6**	**35.8**	**33.4**	**27.8**	
56 Number of people in S&A	46	30	28	27	26	24	
57 Personnel cost S&A	20.5	13.3	13	12	11	11	
58 Other S&A costs	13.0	8.5	8.0	7.6	7.2	6.9	
59 **Selling & administrative costs**	**33.5**	**21.8**	**20.7**	**19.7**	**18.7**	**17.7**	
60 Exceptional costs	0.0	41.5	0.0	0.0	0.0	0.0	
61 **Operating income**	**0.7**	**−38.7**	**6.9**	**16.1**	**14.7**	**10.1**	
62 Interest	10.2	9.0	6.6	5.0	3.5	1.7	26
63 Income before tax	−9.5	−47.7	0.3	11.1	11.2	8.4	
64 **Net income**	**−9.5**	**−47.7**	**0.3**	**11.1**	**11.2**	**8.4**	−17
65 Collection period	2.1	2.1	2.1	2.1	2.1	2.1	
66 Accounts receivable	24.1	22.9	21.8	20.7	19.7	18.7	
67 Inventory end	68.0	33.3	10.8	9.2	8.1	0.1	
68 Payment period	1.7	1.7	1.7	1.7	1.7	1.7	
69 Payables end	21.8	13.3	12.6	13.4	12.9	12.0	
70 Capital expenditure	7.0	6.0	1.0	1.0	1.0	1.0	10
71 **Free cash flow**	**−24.7**	**−19.2**	**29.2**	**20.6**	**18.8**	**22.4**	
72 Dividend	0.0	0.0	0.0	0.0	0.0	0.0	
73 New equity	0.0	0.0	0.0	0.0	0.0	0.0	
74 New loans	23.7	19.2	−29.2	−20.6	−18.8	−22.4	
75 Change in cash	−1.0	0.0	0.0	0.0	0.0	0.0	
76							
77 Cash	1.5	1.5	1.5	1.5	1.5	1.5	
78 Receivables	24.1	22.9	21.8	20.7	19.7	18.7	
79 Inventory	68.0	33.3	10.8	9.2	8.1	0.1	
80 Net fixed assets	34.4	33.4	27.4	21.4	15.4	9.4	
81 Total assets	128.0	91.1	61.5	52.8	44.7	29.7	
82 Accounts payable	21.8	13.3	12.6	13.4	12.9	12.0	
83 Loans	93.0	112.2	83.0	62.4	43.6	21.2	
84 Equity	13.2	−34.5	−34.2	−23.0	−11.8	−3.5	
85 Total liabilities and equities	128.0	91.1	61.5	52.7	44.6	29.7	

Table 14.3 • Model for Tyler Welding: formulas

Rows 2 to 15: data[a]
Rows 65, 68, 72, 73 and 75: data

B17: +B36; Copy
C18: +C17/B17–1; Copy
C19: +C55/C17; Copy
C20: +C61; Copy
C21: +C51; Copy
C22: +C46+C56; Copy
C24: data
C25: +C71+C62
C26: +C25–B66–B67+B69; D26: +D25; Copy;
   H26: +G66+G67–G69
C27: +C36–C66; D27: +D36–D66+C66; Copy
C28: +NPV(C24,C27:H27)
C29: +C27–C26; Copy
C30: +NPV(C24,C29:H29)
C31: +C28–C30
B34: data (344.5); C34: +B34*(1+C2); Copy
B35: data (400); C35: +B35*(1+C3); Copy
B36: +B34*B35/1000; Copy
B37: data (375); C37: +B37*(1+C4); Copy;
   G38: 0
B38: data (20); C38: +C37/24[b]; Copy
B39: data (142); C39: +C41[c]; Copy
B40: +B38*B39/1000; Copy
B41: data (142); C41: +B41*(1+C5); Copy
B42: data (365), C42: +C37+C38–B38; Copy
B43: +B41*B42/1000; Copy
B44: +B43+4.3–B40; C44: +C43+B40–C40;
   Copy
B45: data (8); C45: +B45*(1+C6)*(1+C4);
   Copy
B46: data (136); C46: +B46*(1+C7); Copy
B47: 44.9; C47: +B47*(1+C7)*(1+C8); Copy

B48: 7; C48: +B48*(1+C9); Copy
B49: data (4.6); C49: +C15; Copy
B50: +B44+B45+B47+B48+B49; Copy
B51: +177+B37–B34; C51: +B51+C37–C34; Copy
B52: +B50/B37*1000; Copy
B53: +B51*B52/1000; Copy
B54: +B50+51–B53; C54: +C50+B53–C53; Copy
B55: +B36–B54; Copy
B56: 46; C56: +B56*(1+C10); Copy
B57: +B56*446/1000; C57:
   +B57*(1+C10)*(1+C11); Copy
B58: 13; C58: +B58*(1+C12); Copy
B59: +B57+B58; Copy
C60: +C13; Copy
B61: +B55–B59–B60; Copy
B62: data (10.2); C62: +C83*.08[d]
B63: +B61–B62; Copy
B64: +B63; Copy[e]
B66: +B36/12*B65; Copy
B67: +B40+B53; Copy
B69: +(B50–B49+B59+B70)/12*B68; Copy
B70: data; C70: +C14; Copy
B71: +B64+B49–B66–B67+B69+22+55.6–20–B70;
C71: +C64+C49–C66–C67+C69+B66+B67–
   B69–C70; Copy
B74: –B71+B72–B73+B75; Copy
B77: data (1.5); C77: +B77+C75
B78: +B66; Copy
B79: +B67; Copy
B80: +32+B70–B49; C80: +B80+C70–C49; Copy
B81: + B77+B78+B79+B80; Copy
B82: +B69;
B83: data (93); C83: +B83+C74; Copy
B84: data (13.2); C84: +B84+C64–C72; Copy
B85: +B82+B83+B84; Copy

Notes
[a] A large part of the exceptional costs is caused by the laying off of personnel: when laying off personnel, it is assumed that Tyler continues paying salaries for a full year.
[b] The target is to have 2 weeks of inventory of material.
[c] FIFO (First in, first out).
[d] This relation introduces a circular reference – see on page 146.
[e] It is assumed that Tyler Welding will not have to pay corporation tax.

the more detailed description of the manufacturing process. The manufacturing process is further described in Figure 14.1. The model assumes that:

- Tyler Welding experiences a continuous decrease in volume (–3% a year) and in selling prices (–2%). This is a very unfavourable sales scenario that, unfortunately, can materialize.
- The company commits to an immediate and aggressive transformation.

The three steps in the manufacturing process

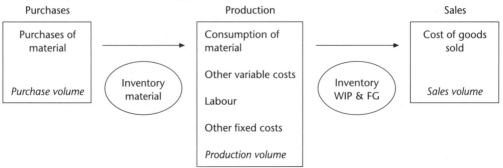

The three sets of relationships

Volume relationships
Volume purchases = volume consumption (production volume) – volume inventory material open + volume material end
Volume production = volume sales – volume inventory finished goods and work in progress open – volume inventory finished goods and work in process end

Unit cost relationships
Unit cost inventory material end = unit purchase price (FIFO)
Unit cost finished goods and work in progress inventory = unit production cost (FIFO)

Value relationships

Figure 14.1 Relationships in the manufacturing account

You can use the model to simulate what would happen if Tyler kept on the same spending trajectory as in 1999. To do so, set all the parameters in C4.G13 to zero and the capital expenditure to 6 in each year. The model confirms that a lot of value is destroyed in these conditions. It also shows in rows 27 and 29 that payments in this situation are higher than receipts:

● On a non-discounted basis, payments equal 665 million. This is 12% more than receipts (593).
● On a present value basis, payments equal 518 million. This is 22% more than receipts (425).

This very simple analysis gives a first idea of the magnitude of the reduction in spending that is needed at Tyler. You should also be aware that this analysis probably underestimates the reduction needed:

● When a company decides to get into downsizing, there is very often a lag between the decision to stop using a resource and the actual cessation of the payment for this resource.[1] In some cases, stopping using a resource also generates an additional one-off cost.
● Tyler Welding has an inventory of 68 million. The model assumes that the totality of the inventory can be turned into sales. The extreme adverse assumption would be that none of this inventory can be sold. In this case the spending needed to generate the 593 million of receipts becomes 665 + 68 = 733 million, which is 24% more than the receipts!

14.2 Strategic what-if analysis

The use of this case study in a variety of executive classroom situations has revealed that each executive is easily convinced that Tyler Welding faces a very serious situation that calls for radical transformation. With its unique access to the customers of Tyler Gas, the company seems to have the opportunity to harvest a valuable segment of a declining market. The problem though is that Tyler Welding cannot expect to capture this opportunity with the very poor operations it currently has. At the same time, many executives also like to focus their attention on the opportunity of a strategic alliance with Osvald. What is very attractive with this opportunity is that it would give more space and time to Tyler Welding for transforming itself. This opportunity could also enable Tyler to defer part of the restructuring and to make it contingent on the future evolution of the market.

Step 1: Using what-if to specify the possible futures and to design the strategies that fit these futures
The first step of any what-if analysis is to imagine and specify all the different future situations that one can expect to materialize. Let us assume that the management of Tyler considers that two situations and two only can materialize in the future[2]:

● Tyler continues to face a very hostile environment with sales continuously declining (–3% in volume and –2% in price). This is the situation depicted in Table 13.1.
● A strategic agreement is made with Osvald in 2000. This agreement brings the price war with Osvald to a halt and prices increase 12% in 2000. However, this is a short-term improvement only and prices start decreasing again: –2% each year from 2001 onwards. Volume decreases by 3% in 2000, but then the agreement with Osvald helps Tyler grow its gas welding equipment sales in all those markets where Osvald is strong with electric welding. The growth is modest however: +2% a year.

Once the possible futures have been specified, one needs to design for each of these futures the strategy that best fits the environment and enables the company to create the maximum possible value. Figure 14.2 contrasts the two possible future situations that Tyler

	The environment is hostile	A strategic alliance makes the environment easier
In 1999, Tyler goes for immediate total transformation . . . and sticks to this trajectory	Value created: 6	
In 1999, Tyler goes for alliance and progressive transformation . . . and sticks to this trajectory		Value created: 45

Figure 14.2 The outcomes of the two strategies

Table 14.4 ● Inputs for the progressive transformation strategy

	Aggressive transformation					Progressive transformation				
	2000	2001	2002	2003	2004	2000	2001	2002	2003	2004
Change in volume sold	–3%	–3%	–3%	–3%	–3%	–3%	2%	2%	2%	2%
Change in selling price	–2%	–2%	–2%	–2%	–2%	12%	–2%	–2%	–2%	–2%
Change in volume produced	–40%	15%	20%	–3%	–10%	–10%	–5%	–5%	–5%	–4%
Change in cost of material	–1%	–10%	–1%	–1%	–1%	–1%	–1%	–10%	–1%	–1%
Change in variable unit cost	–1%	–1%	–1%	–1%	–1%	–1%	–1%	–1%	–1%	–1%
Change in number of people (prodn)	–44%	–5%	–5%	–5%	–5%	–15%	–8%	–8%	–8%	–8%
Change in cost per person	3%	3%	3%	3%	3%	2%	2%	2%	2%	2%
Change in other fixed prodn costs	–44%	–5%	–5%	–5%	–5%	–15%	–8%	–8%	–8%	–8%
Change in number of people (S&A)	–35%	–5%	–5%	–5%	–5%	–17%	–8%	–8%	–8%	–8%
Change in cost per person	0%	0%	0%	0%	0%	0%	0%	0%	0%	0%
Change in other costs S&A	–35%	–5%	–5%	–5%	–5%	–17%	–8%	–8%	–8%	–8%
Exceptional costs	41.5	0.0	0.0	0.0	0.0	12.0	3.0	6.0	3.0	3.0
Capital expenditure	6.0	1.0	1.0	1.0	1.0	3.0	1.0	5.0	1.0	1.0
Depreciation	7.0	7.0	7.0	7.0	7.0	6.4	6.4	7.2	7.2	7.2

Welding expects to face as well as the strategies that fit each of these situations best. The inputs that correspond to these two strategies are in Table 14.4.

● The hostile environment calls for an aggressive transformation strategy that makes Tyler Welding immediately take advantage of all the 'opportunities to cut costs' described in the case. This transformation could enable Tyler to become the low-cost-high-quality player that would be in a position to harvest the niche corresponding to the business of the Tyler group.
● The situation of a strategic alliance with Osvald enables Tyler Welding to implement a more gradual transformation process. This strategy also aims at transforming Tyler into a low-cost-high-quality player: Tyler has poor operations and cannot continue to operate as it does in 1999.

The results in Figure 14.2 show that:

● As expected, the gradual transformation strategy within the more favourable environment seems to result in more value than the aggressive transformation strategy implemented within the hostile competitive environment.
● With an aggressive transformation strategy, it seems possible to create value out of a very hostile competitive environment. This is the unique advantage of strategies: they enable you to get organized for creating value out of the most challenging situations.

Step 2: Introducing strategy into the what-if analysis
The analysis presented in Figure 14.2 is very useful. It helps you prepare yourself to face different futures. It helps specify these futures as well as the strategies that fit each future best. However, it does not help you choose between these different strategies. What is best for Tyler Welding?

- To focus all its attention and energy towards a very fast and very deep re-engineering of its operations?
- To adopt a double focus? How to design and implement an effective strategic alliance with Osvald and, at the same time, how to organize a gradual transformation of the operations of the company?

In order to be able to choose between strategies, we have to recognize that strategies correspond to commitments that cannot be quickly and easily reversed:

- The first strategy is a commitment to an immediate and total transformation of the company – that is going to be made in one very large step. 'We want to reassess everything, now.' It means a commitment to action and speed. It requires the creation of a very strong sense of necessity and urgency: 'The industry is in crisis and this is the only way to survive.'
- The second strategy starts with a commitment to a different future for the industry. 'Growth and price increases are possible even in a declining industry.' It also means a commitment to a complete transformation of the company but through a step-by-step process that will enable valuable lessons to be learnt at each step, and so on.

Strategies are an explicit commitment to specific goals and to specific behaviours for reaching those goals. Strategies are expected to create value out of the **cumulative effect** of a series of consistent actions taken over a reasonably long period of time.

A first characteristic of strategies is focus. This is both positive and negative. When selecting a strategy a company commits itself to a specific vision of its business, of its customers, and so on. This is the **'lock-in'** effect of commitment. At the same time, as described by Mintzberg, Ahlstrand and Lampel,[3] 'Strategies are to organizations what blinders [blinkers] are to horses. They keep them going in a straight line but hardly encourage peripheral vision'. Strategies make companies ignore all the opportunities that are out of their intended focus. **'Lock-out'** is the mirror image of lock-in.

A second characteristic of strategies is **time lags** and inertia. Introducing a new strategy is a several-stage process[4] that takes time. Implementing a new strategy in an organization often requires a change in the patterns of interactions in this organization: this typically requires months or even years. And once a whole organization is set on a specific strategic trajectory, then there is a tendency for that organization to resist moving to a new trajectory: this is **'inertia'**.

Strategies have a paradoxical nature:

- They are designed in order to best fit a specific environment.
- And at the same time, since their essence is to persist over time, they need to be robust to a whole series of other possible environments. Even though they are not set for ever, strategies are set for a period of time and it is too costly to change them to accommodate temporary environmental 'turbulences'.

Deciding about strategies implies that we go beyond the results of Figure 14.2. If Tyler Welding knew what the future would be, then the company could decide based on the results of the figure. But since it has to decide without knowing what the future will be, Tyler has to pursue the what-if analysis and to fill up the two additional boxes that correspond to possible 'surprises' in Figure 14.3:

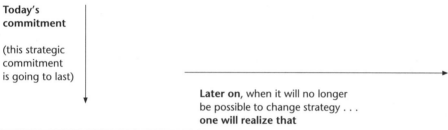

**Today's
commitment**

(this strategic
commitment
is going to last)

Later on, when it will no longer
be possible to change strategy . . .
one will realize that

	The environment is hostile	A strategic alliance makes the environment easier
In 1999, Tyler goes for immediate total transformation . . . and sticks to this trajectory	Value created: 6 *Strategy designed as the 'best' to fit this specific environment*	? Value created when the company is 'caught with the wrong strategy'
In 1999, Tyler goes for alliance and progressive transformation . . . and sticks to this trajectory	? Value created when the company is 'caught with the wrong strategy'	Value created: 45 *Strategy designed as the 'best' to fit this specific environment*

Figure 14.3 Assessing the robustness of strategies (1)

- What if Tyler were to commit to the aggressive transformation strategy and face the unexpected surprise of a strategic alliance with Osvald? Tyler expects a hostile environment, Tyler focuses all its attention on downsizing, and, surprise, the environment does not turn out to be hostile and Tyler has to face this new environment when it has committed to a completely different environment – and strategy.
- What if Tyler were to commit to the alliance with Osvald and to the progressive transformation strategy and, surprise, were then to see the perspective of this alliance collapse and the environment remaining hostile when the company has committed to a completely different environment – and strategy?

14.3 Tyler Welding: the case for immediate commitment

The full analysis of the two possible strategies is shown in Table 14.5 and Figure 14.4. Please note that the inputs in Table 14.5 are exactly the same as the inputs of Table 14.4 except for the environmental inputs (volume sold and selling price). The concept is to simulate a situation where the company is taken by surprise and does not want to – cannot – change its strategy to accommodate the new environment. The only variable that can be changed is production level.[5] Figure 14.4 shows for each strategy how it performs, first in the environment it has been designed for, and secondly in the other possible environment. How does the strategy cope with the 'surprises' that are necessarily going to materialize over its life cycle?

Table 14.5 ● Parameters for simulating the 'surprises'

	Aggressive transformation					Progressive transformation				
	2000	2001	2002	2003	2004	2000	2001	2002	2003	2004
Change in volume	−3%	2%	2%	2%	2%	−3%	−3%	−3%	−3%	−3%
Change in price	12%	−2%	−2%	−2%	−2%	−2%	−2%	−2%	−2%	−2%
Change in volume produced	−40%	20%	29%	2%	−6.4%	−15%	−10%	−6%	−6%	−6%
Change in cost of material	−1%	−10%	−1%	−1%	−1%	−1%	−1%	−10%	−1%	−1%
Change in unit variable cost	−1%	−1%	−1%	−1%	−1%	−1%	−1%	−1%	−1%	−1%
Change in number of people (p)	−44%	−5%	−5%	−5%	−5%	−15%	−8%	−8%	−8%	−8%
Change in cost per person	3%	3%	3%	3%	3%	0%	0%	0%	0%	0%
Change in other fixed costs	−44%	−5%	−5%	−5%	−5%	−15%	−8%	−8%	−8%	−8%
Change in number of people (S&A)	−35%	−5%	−5%	−5%	−5%	−17%	−8%	−8%	−8%	−8%
Change in cost per person	0%	0%	0%	0%	0%	0%	0%	0%	0%	0%
Change in other costs S&A	−35%	−5%	−5%	−5%	−5%	−17%	−8%	−8%	−8%	−8%
Exceptional costs	41.5	0.0	0.0	0.0	0.0	12.0	3.0	6.0	3.0	3.0
Capital expenditure	6.0	1.0	1.0	1.0	1.0	3.0	1.0	5.0	1.0	1.0
Depreciation	7.0	7.0	7.0	7.0	7.0	6.4	6.4	7.2	7.2	7.2

In order to simulate 'surprise', nothing is changed in the model except for:

● the environmental parameters – these are the 'surprise';
● the level of production: this is independent of the strategy and can be adjusted at once.

All the other parameters (grey zone) are kept the same in order to simulate the fact that the strategy is not reversed.

Today's commitment

(this strategic commitment is going to last)

Later on, when it will no longer be possible to change strategy . . . **one will realize that**

	The environment is hostile	A strategic alliance makes the environment easier
In 1999, Tyler goes for immediate total transformation . . . and sticks to this trajectory	Value created: 6	Value created: 97
In 1999, Tyler goes for alliance and progressive transformation . . . and sticks to this trajectory	Value created: −42	Value created: 45

Figure 14.4 Assessing the robustness of strategies (2)

Figure 14.4 shows that the aggressive transformation strategy dominates. The process for selecting strategies is to:

1. Select the dominant strategy when such a strategy exists.
2. Eliminate dominated strategies if such strategies exist. Once such strategies have been eliminated look again at the whole issue.
3. If there is no obvious dominating strategy, assign a weight to the different situations and calculate the expected value of each strategy and select the one with the highest value.

A final 'surprise'

The best strategy for the situation where an alliance with Osvald materializes is apparently not the strategy that we initially designed as the best fitted to this environment. The one that performs best in this environment is the aggressive restructuring. If Tyler manages to substantially reduce its cost base and also enjoys a more favourable environment, then its performance is really good! One problem with favourable environment scenarios is that they may not be sufficiently challenging. It often happens that organizations need a crisis to really go for radical change.[6]

Error of commission vs. error of omission

Another way to present the results of the strategic what-if analysis is to focus on the aggressive transformation strategy and to compare its outcomes with the outcomes of not implementing it. This is shown in Figure 14.5 with the identification of two possible errors:

● An **error of commission**: Tyler Welding commits to a strategy for a hostile environment while the environment ends up as non-hostile.
● An **error of omission**: Tyler Welding does not commit to the strategy that fits the hostile environment that actually prevails.

	The environment is hostile	The environment is not hostile
In 1999, Tyler goes for immediate total transformation . . . and sticks to this trajectory	Hit (Value: 6)	Error of commission (Value: 97)
In 1999, Tyler does not go for immediate total transformation . . . and sticks to this trajectory	Error of omission (Value: -42)	Hit (Value: 45)

Figure 14.5 Error of commission vs. error of omission

When selecting a strategy, one has to compare the relative costs of the two errors. For Tyler Welding, while the error of omission is costly, the error of commission is actually a blessing. There is very little risk for Tyler in committing to the aggressive transformation strategy.

14.4 A model for Motion-Control

Tables 14.6 and 14.7 display a model for Motion-Control. The format of this model is the same as the presentation of Table N.6 and is somewhat different from the ones we have built so far. Rather than mimicking the traditional accounting presentation, this model orders the different variables according to their position in the trajectory of commitment. Development and design is what you commit earliest: it comes on top of the model. Then come administrative and marketing resources, production resources and capital expenditure. Finally, the model envisages the levels of production and purchase that can be decided almost on time and that can be changed in case of 'surprises'. Production and purchase levels are actually the only two drivers that the model allows you to change in case of surprise.

Table 14.6 • Model for Motion-Control: drivers and selected outputs

A	B	C	D
1		**Strategy A**	
2		As expected	Surprise
3	2001	2002	2002
4 Sales volume growth (expected then actual)		25%	15%
5 Sales price change (expected then actual)		−1%	−5%
6 Increase in volume of development & design resources		25%	25%
7 Increase in price of development & design resources		25%	25%
8 Increase in volume of administrative & marketing resources		14%	14%
9 Increase in productivity of administrative & marketing resources		10%	10%
10 Increase in price of administrative & marketing resources		10%	10%
11 Increase in volume of production resources		0%	0%
12 Increase in productivity of production resources		25%	25%
13 Increase in price of production resources		0%	0%
14 Capital expenditure		1550	1550
15 Depreciation		614	614
16 Increase in production volume (expected then actual)		25%	10%
17 Increase in purchase price		−5%	−5%
18 Increase in volume purchased (expected then actual)		12%	0%
19 Collection period (days)		41	41
20 Payment period (days)		27	27
21			
22 Inventory material end (months of units produced)	5.1	2.8	3.5
23 Inventory finished goods end (months of units sold)	1.8	2.2	1.8
24 Net income	1010	1239	−113
25 Free cash flow	−768	−248	−1121

Table 14.7 ● Model for Motion-Control: the model

A	B	C	D
27		Strategy A	
28		Expected	Surprise
29	*2001*	*2002*	*2002*
30 **Sales**	**16 617**	**20 564**	**18 154**
31 *Volume sales*	*5 539*	*6 924*	*6 370*
32 *Unit price sales*	*3.0*	*3.0*	*2.9*
33			
34 **Development and design**	**1 786**	**2 791**	**2 791**
35 **Administration and marketing**	**3 223**	**4 042**	**4 042**
36			
37 **Labour and other costs**	**2 449**	**2 449**	**2 449**
38 **Depreciation**	**560**	**614**	**614**
39 Production level	5 871	7 339	6 458
40 **Material costs**		**8 983**	**7 924**
41 Inventory material end	3 143	2 068	2 280
42 *Volume units*	*2 483*	*1 720*	*1 896*
43 *Price*	*1.27*[a]	*1.20*	*1.20*
44 Purchases		7 908	7 061
45 *Volume purchases*	*5 871*	*6 576*	*5 871*
46 *Price purchases*	*1.27*	*1.20*	*1.20*
47 **Manufacturing cost**		**12 046**	**10 987**
48 *Unit cost*		*1.64*	*1.70*
49 Inventory finished goods	1 457	2 063	1 583
50 *Volume*	*842*	*1 257*	*930*
51 *Price*	*1.73*	*1.64*	*1.70*
52 **CGS**	**9 648**	**11 440**	**10 861**
53 **Gross profit**	**6 969**	**9 124**	**7 293**
54 **Operating income**	**1 400**	**2 291**	**460**
55 Interest	382	521	574
56 **Income before tax**	**1 018**	**1 770**	**−113**
57 **Net income after tax**	**1 010**	**1 239**	**−113**
58 Add back depreciation		614	614
59 Accounts receivable end	2 168	2 342	2 068
60 Inventory end	4 600	4 132	3 863
61 Non-interest-bearing liabilities	2 251	1 405	1 342
62 Capital expenditure		1 550	1 550
63 **Free cash flow**	**−768**	**−248**	**−1 121**
64 Dividend		0	0
65 Change in debt		248	1 121
66 Change in cash		0	0
67			
68 Cash	474	474	474
69 Receivables	2 168	2 342	2 068
70 Inventory	4 600	4 132	3 863
71 Net fixed assets	4 935	5 871	5 871
72 Total	12 177	12 819	12 275
73 Interest-bearing debt	8 442	8 690	9 563
74 Non-interest-bearing debt	2 251	1 405	1 342
75 Net worth	1 484	2 723	1 371
76 Total	12 177	12 819	12 275

[a] 1.266

Table 14.8 • Model for Motion-Control: formulas

The process for building the model is to:

1. Construct columns B and C.
2. Copy the whole column C into D (this is allowed by the use of absolute references).
3. Adjust D4.D20.

You can then copy the whole columns C and D into F and G, for example, in order to show simultaneously two different strategies.

C4.C8; C10,C11; C13.C20, C64, C66 data

C9: +(1+C4)/(1+C8)–1
C12: +(1+C4)/(1+C11)–1
C22: +C42/C39*12
C23: +C50/C31*12
C24: +C57
C25: +C63

B30, B32, B34.B39, B42.B46, B50.B68, B71, B73 and B75: data

B31: +B30/B32
B41: +B42*B43; Copy to C41
B43: +B46; Copy to C43
B49: +B50*B51; Copy to C49
B69: +B59, Copy to C69
B70: +B60; Copy to C70
B72: +B68+B69+B70+B71; Copy to C72
B74: +B61; Copy to C74
B76: +B73+B74+B75; Copy to C76

C30: +C31*C32
C31: +$B$31*(1+C4)
C32: +$B$32*(1+C5)
C34: +$B$34*(1+C7)*(1+C6)

C35: +$B$35*(1+C8)*(1+C10)
C37: +$B$37*(1+C13)*(1+C11)
C38: +C15
C39: +$B$39*(1+C16)
C40: +C44+$B$41–C41
C42: +$B$42+C45–C39
C44: +C45*C46
C45: +$B$45*(1+C18)
C46: +B$46*(1+C17)
C47: +C37+C38+C40
C48: +C47/C39
C50: +$B$50+C39–C31
C51: +C48
C52: +C47–C49–$B49
C53: +C30–C52
C54: +C53–C34–C35
C55: data first, then later: .06*C73[a]
C56: +C54–C55
C57: +IF(C56>0, +C56*.7,C56)
C58: +C38
C59: +C30/360*C19
C60: +C41+C49
C61: +(C34+C35+C37+C44+C62)/360*C20
C62: +C14
C63: +C57+C58–C62–C59+$B$59–
    C60+$B$60+C61–$B$61
C65: –C63+C64+C66
C68: +$B$68+C66
C71: +$B$71+C62–C58
C73: +$B$73+C65
C75: +$B$75+C57–C64

Once column C has been copied into column D:
D6: +C6; Copy into D7.D8,
C10.C11,C13.C15,C17 and C19.C20
All these cells have to be kept the same in case of surprise

Note

[a] This formula introduces a circular reference.
    In Excel, you need to activate the iteration option: Tools / Options / Calculations / Click on iterations that you can set at 5.

14.5 Motion-Control: the case for progressive commitment

Growth has been slow to come at Motion-Control. In the whole period 1996–2001, only 2001 has shown significant growth. The company's relations with its customers have been turbulent and as a result sales have declined twice in the period: –12% in 1997 and –31% in 1999. If Motion-Control has survived these two shocks, it is because the company has

Table 14.9 ● A more cautious commitment to growth: inputs and outputs

	2001	As expected 2002	Surprise 2002
Sales volume growth (expected then actual)		*15%*	*25%*
Sales price change (expected then actual)		*–5%*	*–1%*
Increase in volume development & design resources		*20%*	*20%*
Increase in price development & design resources		*20%*	*20%*
Increase in volume administrative & marketing resources		*10%*	*10%*
Increase in productivity administrative & marketing resources		5%	14%
Increase in price administrative & marketing resources		*10%*	*10%*
Increase in volume production resources		*–7.5%*	*–7.5%*
Increase in productivity production resources		24%	35%
Increase in price production resources		*0%*	*0%*
Capital expenditure		*1550*	*1550*
Depreciation		*614*	*614*
Increase in production volume (expected then actual)		*5%*	*20%*
Increase purchase price		*–5%*	*–5%*
Increase in volume purchases (expected then actual)		*–12%*	*–12%*
Collection period		*41*	*35*
Payment period		*27*	*27*
Inventory material end (months of units production)	5.1	2.9	1.0
Inventory finished goods end (months of units sold)	1.8	1.2	1.7
Net income	1010	249	1625
Free cash flow	–768	135	2144

effectively adjusted down the trajectory of its spending both in 1997 and 1999 (see Table N.1 and Figure N.2).[7] The exceptionally good results of 2001 (see Table N.4) result from a series of factors:

● The trajectory of sales has evolved much more favourably than expected (+47% rather than +21%).
● At the same time, the trajectory of marketing costs and of R&D has been kept according to plan for marketing and below plan for R&D (+5% actual vs. +29% planned).
● Unfortunately, the trajectory of production spending has got somewhat out of hand and as a result the gross margin has declined and the company has accumulated a large inventory of material and products at the end of 2001. The trajectory of administrative costs has also been unsatisfactory but Motion-Control probably had to implement more professional business systems following the change in ownership.

The simulation presented in Table N.6 shows a fairly conservative growth in sales (the change in volume at least is conservative) which corresponds to a substantially lower growth than in 2001. The resource commitment strategy is characterized by:

● a substantial growth in R&D (now called Development and Design) that is going to grow faster than the expected sales (56% vs. 24%);
● a 25% growth in administrative and selling expenses (slightly more than sales);

Today's commitment

(this strategic commitment is going to last)

Later on, in 2002, when it will no longer be possible to change strategy . . . **it will be realized that**

	Sales grow 24% (+25% in volume and –1% in price)	Sales grow 10% (+15% in volume and –5% in price)
In 2001, Motion-Control commits to growth . . . and sticks to this trajectory	Net earnings: 1239 Free cash flow: –248	Net earnings: –113 Free cash flow: –1121
In 2001, Motion-Control makes a more cautious commitment to growth . . . and sticks to this trajectory	Net earnings: 1625 Free cash flow: 2144	Net earnings: 249 Free cash flow: 135

Figure 14.6 Assessing the robustness of two commitment strategies

- no growth at all in production resources. This is probably caused by the large inventory and by the coming phasing out of the current products;
- an investment in capital expenditures 50% higher than in 2001.

Table 14.6 describes the commitment strategy in the case and the impact of a 'surprise'. What if the company implements an aggressive commitment strategy and has to face a lower growth? With a sales growth of 10% only (+15% in volume and –5% in prices) the company would experience a significantly lower income.[8] Table 14.9 shows a more progressive commitment strategy, as well as how it would resist surprise (higher growth). The two strategies are compared in Figure 14.6. The results are just the opposite of those that we have found for Tyler Welding: it seems that at Motion-Control deferred commitment creates more value than immediate commitment.

Risk is the factor that intuitively explains these different results:

- At Tyler Welding fast commitment is motivated by the fact that there is very little risk for the company in committing to a very deep transformation. There is not even much risk involved in deciding how deep the transformation should be: as deep as the company can take!
- The situation faced by Motion-Control is much more uncertain. There is uncertainty about the demand (sales have varied between –31% and +49% in the last three years).

There is uncertainty about the competition. There is uncertainty about the technology and about manufacturing, etc. And finally, the company is now part of an international group that probably has an opinion about the strategy that should be adopted. Immediate commitment is difficult when risk is very high.

The impact of risk is further analyzed below (see Section 14.6).

Growth, value and continuous improvement

You can also use the model to simulate a higher growth in sales – for example like that which was experienced in 2001 (54%). This will make you realize, if still needed, that:

- Even high growth may result in very little or no value.
- What is critical is to set the trajectory of spending on a lower growth trajectory, even if the company has to cope with the surprise of a lower sales growth. Trajectory models are the models that are needed for managing growth.

As growth may always be less than expected, some growing firms systematically base their plans on a fairly conservative growth forecast. This enables them to build plans that correspond to a relatively cautious commitment of resources. Doing so enables these firms to:

- Be better prepared to face lower sales growth surprises.
- Continuously stretch their organization. These companies expect that if, as is likely, the organization is confronted with a growth higher than in the plan, the whole organization will motivate itself to accommodate this 'success' and will innovate and find ways to deliver the additional activity with the resources it has. This will lead to excellent results!

This approach of always committing a little bit less resources than needed can be very effective for pushing an organization to continuously improve. The obvious danger of the approach is to create too much stress inside the organization and to lose business.

14.6 Creating value out of risk through an effective management of the trajectories of commitment

There is no single unique prescription when it comes to managing commitment effectively.

In some cases, fast commitment maximizes value. Tyler Welding should not wait; they should immediately exercise the option that it has to transform its old-fashioned operations. This will enable it to cease destroying value and will also create a platform for future growth that does not exist with its current operations. Using the language of decision trees, Tyler Welding is clearly positioned at a decision 'square' and it does not seem that it could create any value by trying to move this decision 'square' into the future, beyond some event 'circles'.

In other cases, it is a trajectory of progressive commitment that maximizes value. Rather than rush to commit a lot of new resources, Motion-Control should take a more cautious attitude and understand which commitments would be better deferred and made later when more information is available. In order to maximize value, Motion-Control should not exercise all the options it has. Using the language of decision trees, Motion-Control can create value by trying to move the decision 'square' into the future, beyond some event 'circles'.

Maygan

Maygan is operating in a declining industry. Current sales and costs are respectively €100 million and €80 million. Should the company commit now to a severe downsizing program or defer this decision until more is known about the evolution of the business?

● Next year, sales are expected to be either €101 million or €85 million (only two possible figures).

● Maygan can commit to downsizing now or defer this decision until it knows more about the evolution of the business (end of quarter 1 next year). If Maygan takes this latter route, then downsizing will be more expensive: 20% more.

● In any case, Maygan can accommodate small changes in the level of its activity. A higher level of activity can be accommodated by the same resources – provided this activity is not higher than 110% of the expected activity. If the activity is lower than expected, and even if it does not commit to downsize, Maygan can reduce its costs to 90% of what they were expected to be – a reduction in 'variable' costs.

Creative Products

Creative Products is operating in an emergent industry. Current sales and costs are respectively €100 million and €80 million. Should the company commit now to an aggressive resource building programme or defer this decision until more is known about the evolution of the business?

● Next year, sales are expected to be either €99 million or €115 million (only two possible figures).

● Creative Products can commit to building new resources now or defer this decision until it knows more about the evolution of the business (end of quarter 1 next year). If Creative Products takes this latter route, then resource building will be 20% more expensive.

● In any case, Creative Products can accommodate small changes in the level of its activity. A higher level of activity can be accommodated by the same resources – provided this activity is not higher than 110% of the expected activity. If the activity is lower than expected, and even if it does not commit to downsize, Creative Products can reduce its costs to 90% of what they were expected to be – a reduction in 'variable' costs.

Figure 14.7 Evaluating three different trajectories of commitment: the business issue

From the language of 'squares and circles' to the language of 'options'

The decision to select a trajectory of commitment should be based on a careful analysis of the unique characteristics of the specific business situation. This analysis should allow for:

● An identification of all the decision points – the 'squares'; the alternative courses of action at each of these decision points; and the risk factors for each of these alternatives – the event 'circles'.

● An exploration of the alternative ways to structure the sequence of decisions and events – or information. What are the possible trajectories of commitment? What are the alternatives to full commitment now? What are the commitments that can be deferred until more is known?

● An assessment of the value created by each possible trajectory of commitment.

This is the typical methodology of the decision tree that was introduced in Chapter 5.

Figure 14.7 describes two business situations where two companies, Maygan and Creative Products, consider two possible trajectories of commitment: commit now or defer commit-

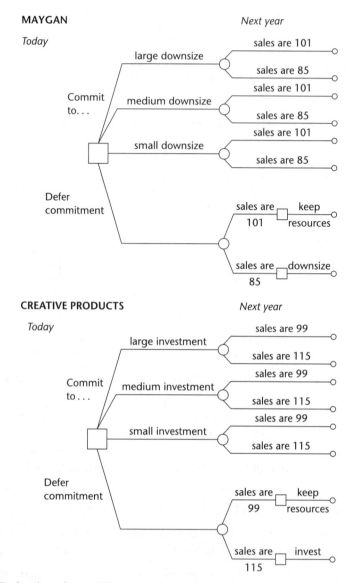

Figure 14.8 Evaluating three different trajectories of commitment: decision diagrams

ment until more is known. The decision diagrams corresponding to these trajectories of commitment are in Figure 14.8 and a spreadsheet model for assessing the end points of the decision diagram is in Tables 14.10 and 14.11.

The selection of a trajectory of commitment is an issue that can also be described in the language of options. The simplest financial options give the right, without the associated symmetric obligation, to buy (if a *call*) or to sell (if a *put*) a specified asset (e.g. a common stock, a stock index, a commodity) by paying a pre-specified price (the *exercise price* or *strike*

Table 14.10 • A spreadsheet model to assess the value of different trajectories of commitment (foreground)

A	B	C	D	E	F
1 *Current sales*	*100*				
2 *Current cost*	*80*				
3 *Expected additional sales (low)*	*1*				
4 *Expected additional sales (high)*	*−15*				
5 *% dealt with productivity increase*	*10%*				
6 *% dealt with cost reduction*	*10%*				
7 *Cost excess to increase capacity with information*	*20%*				
8 *Cost excess to decrease capacity with information*	*20%*				
9					
10		**Commit now**		**Defer commitment**	
11	*Low*	*Middle*	*High*		
12 Immediate commitment to additional resources	1	−6	−12		
13 Level of cost	81	74	68	80	
14					
15 **. . . and sales are actually**	**101**	**101**	**101**	**101**	
16 Resources that would have been needed	81	81	81	81	
17 . . . and that can be adjusted to	81	81	75	81	
18 . . . or rescaled at a cost of				0	
19 . . . which allows for sales of	101	101	94	101	
20 . . . and a profit of	20	20	19	20	
21					
22 **. . . and sales are actually**	**85**	**85**	**85**	**85**	
23 Resources that would have been needed	68	68	68	68	
24 . . . and that can be adjusted to	73	68	68	72	
25 . . . or rescaled at a cost of	0	0	0	−1	
26 . . . which allows for sales of	85	85	85	85	
27 . . . and a profit of	12	17	17	15	
28 Average profit	16	19	18	17	
29 . . . best average profit with commitment	19			−6%	

price) on or before a pre-specified date (the *expiration date*). Options and their pricing are discussed in the final appendix (see p. 482). Maygan and Creative Products have the option to change the level of their resources:

● Maygan has the option to downsize or sell part of its current resources. This is a put option.
● Creative Products has the option to invest and buy new resources. This is a call option.

The value of uncertainty

The model in Table 14.10 shows that it is better for both Maygan and Creative Products to exercise their options now:

Table 14.11 ● A spreadsheet model to assess the value of different trajectories of commitment (background)

B1.B8: data; B18.D18: data; F12: data

B12: =B3*(B2/B1); C12: =(B12+D12)/2; D12: =B4*(B2/B1)
B13: =$B$2+B12; copy to C13,D13,F13
B15: =$B$1+$B$3; copy to C15,D15,F15
B16: =B15*($B$2/$B$1); copy to C16,D16,F16
B17: =IF(B16<B$13,IF(B16>B$13*(1–$B$6), B16,B$13*(1–$B$6)), IF(B16>=B$13*(1+$B$5),
    B$13*(1+$B$5), B16)); copy to C17,D17,F17
F18: =IF(F16<$F$13*(1–$B$6), $B$8*($F$13–F16),IF(F16<$F$13*(1+$B$5), 0,$B$7*(F16–$F$13)))
B19: =IF(B16<B$13*(1+$B$5),B15($B$1/$B$2)*B17); copy to C19,D19,F19
B20: =B19–IF(B18=0,B17,B16)–B18; copy to C20,D20,F20
B22: =$B$1+$B$4. Copy to C22,D22,F22
Copy B16.F20 into B23.F27

B29: =(B30+B27)/2. Copy to C29.F29
B30: =MAX(B29.D29); F30: =F29/B30–1

● If Maygan downsizes it resources now by €5.6 million, then it will get a profit of either €17.0 million or €20.2 million: this is better than the €20.2 million or €14.6 million profit that it will get by deferring commitment.
● If Creative Products invests €5.6 million now, then it will get a profit of either €19.8 million or €23 million. This is better than the €19.8 million or €20.6 million profit that it will get by deferring commitment.

You can use the model for simulating another situation where both companies are confronted with a more uncertain environment:

● Maygan now expects a change in sales ranging from +€2 million to –€60 million.
● Creative Products now expects a change in sales ranging from –€2 million to +€60 million.

As shown in Table 14.12, both companies would be better to defer their commitment and keep their options alive. This is consistent with the theory of financial options that states that the value of options increases with uncertainty (see p. 512).

You can also use the model in Table 14.10 to test the impact of other drivers on the decision to manage the trajectory of commitment. You can assess in particular the impact of the level of margins and of the cost of waiting until information is available.

Managing the trajectory of commitment

It can be concluded that uncertainty is a key factor to consider in managing the trajectory of commitment:

● When uncertainty is low, then it is best to commit now and to adjust resources to a level that matches the expected future level of business. When the uncertainty is fairly

Table 14.12 • Uncertainty and management of trajectories of commitment

Low uncertainty		High uncertainty	
Decline situation (expected change in sales: +1 or −30)	Growth situation (expected change in sales: −1 or +30)	Decline situation (expected change in sales: +2 or −60)	Growth situation (expected change in sales: −2 or +60)
Better to commit now	Better to commit now	Better to defer	Better to defer

low, do not wait but downsize now and invest in new resources now. This is especially true when the margins of your business are on the low side.

• When uncertainty is high, then it is best not to commit now but to defer the decision until you have more information. When the uncertainty is very high, do not rush to downsize or to invest in new resources. This is especially true if the margins of your business are on the high side.

In the end, the management of the trajectory of commitment is more a function of uncertainty than of the situation you are in and it might be better to defer the decision to change the level of resources both in decline and growth situations. However, decline situations are most often characterized by a relatively low uncertainty – the range of sales decline is often narrower than the range of sales growth – and by low margins. As a result, immediate commitment is often the best solution in decline situations.

Notes

1. This is the case when laying off personnel, which is modelled in Tables 14.1 and 14.2 (see note 1).
2. This is just for the sake of simplicity: the process of the analysis would be the same with more alternatives.
3. In H. Mintzberg, B. Ahlstrand and J. Lampel (1998), *Strategy Safari*, The Free Press, p. 18.
4. See for example J. Kotter (1996) *Leading Change*, Harvard Business School Press.
5. A reduction in the production level will help decrease the inventory, but the existence of the fixed costs created by commitment will make the unit cost increase.
6. This is a standard recommendation of the literature of change in organizations: getting an organization to embark on a real change process requires that people perceive that there is a 'crisis'.
7. One should realize, however, that the spending has not been reduced as quickly as the costs – in the income statement. Inventories have increased in both 1997 and 1999 as well as 'activated' R&D.
8. As this evolution of sales is much more favourable than what actually happened in 1997 and 1999, one should realize that in the past the company has been very effective at curbing the trajectory of its spending very fast. It may also show that in 1997 and 1999, the company was not yet very much committed to growth. Maybe the risk created by a clear commitment to growth was just starting in 2001!

Decisions to commit to new products and new markets

Capital budgeting and strategy

There's no such thing as sustaining leadership;
it must be reinvented again and again.
Hamel and Prahalad[1]

Parts V and VI focus on models to help you manage the process of reinventing your business again and again. Part V deals with situations which are generally categorized as 'internal growth' or 'capital budgeting' situations. Part VI deals with 'external growth' situations: acquisitions, mergers, joint ventures and strategic alliances.

The two business cases analyzed in Part V focus on two very different stages of the development of a new product:

- *With the Eagle case (Case Q) we are at the early stage of the development of a new pharmaceutical product concept and the issue is to decide about the next phase of development: is it worth keeping committed to Eagle? How to capture the value of Eagle while keeping sufficient flexibility?*
- *At BA International (Case Q), they have now completed the development of P12, a new industrial compressor, and it is time to decide when and how to launch this new product.*

These two case studies are completed by a third case, CLS, in the appendices to Part V. The issue at CLS is to decide if it is valuable to commit to a large irreversible investment. How can ZBGas best capture the growth of the market: through an investment in a large multi-purpose plant or through a series of customer-specific facilities?

The models and the analyses in Part V build on the analyses of value and risk developed in Part II. The focus of this part is on:

- *the development and use of trajectory models that reflect strategic change situations. This is the central focus of BA International.*
- *the understanding, valuation and management of flexibility. This is the central focus of Eagle and of CLS. This discussion builds on the analysis of decision trees that we met in Chapter 5 and on the real options thinking presented in the appendices to Part II and in the General Appendix.*

Note

1. From G. Hamel and C.K. Prahalad (1994), *Competing for the Future Harvard Business School Press* (p. 17).

CHAPTER *15*

The challenge of evaluating new products and new markets

Financial analyses and models are very useful tools for assessing new products and markets but you should realize that commitments to new products and markets cannot solely be reduced to their financial dimension. Such commitments are typically the result of a series of complex strategic choices: commitment to an industry, to a competitive strategy, to a marketing strategy, and so on. New product/market decisions should be viewed as a general management issue that is part of the overall strategic planning process.

New product/market decisions are also the result of complex organizational processes. Commitments to new products and markets often change the power structure within an organization.

Finally, commitments to new products and markets are more often the result of a complex process than the outcome of an explicit decision that can be easily associated with a specific individual or a specific moment in time. This process makes it challenging to use financial tools and you should be aware that:

- You will get different financial results depending on when you make the calculation. What is the meaning of these different results?
- Risk will also generally look different at different stages of the process. At the beginning of the process of developing a totally new product, very little is known. Later on in the process, risk will still be present but it will generally be easier to portray it.

15.1 Challenges associated with the incremental approach

A very common and a very effective way is to use the additive property of value and to adopt an incremental approach for evaluating new product/market alternatives. It is just a matter of assessing the cash flows that they create and of discounting these cash flows at the relevant discount rate. Unfortunately, this is not always that easy in practice since the only cash flows to be considered are those which will be created by the decision to launch the new product or to enter the new market. As a result, all costs previously incurred should be ignored. In accounting/finance literature, these costs are called 'sunk' costs.

Before considering any cash flow, you should check that this cash flow is the direct result of your decision to go ahead with the new product or market you are studying. In particular, pay attention to:

● The nature of cost data you use. Much cost data in real life comes from accounting and is the result of allocation processes. This cost data is generally true on the average in the long run, but not necessarily on an incremental basis.
● The eventual impact of your decision on the existing business portfolio of your company. Many new activities create options to revisit the total organization of the business and cannot be considered as independent from the firm's existing business.
● The eventual impact of your decision on your company's future strategic opportunities. If the decision you contemplate is likely to create new options for the future development of your firm, you should recognize this additional value in your analysis.

Finally, a difficult problem with new product or market decisions is to select the adequate horizon for study. The theory gives you a clear answer. New products and markets should be studied over their entire expected life. But, again, doing it is not easy in practice, as we shall see when we analyze the BA International case.

15.2 The 'profitability of a new product' does not exist

The example in Figure 15.1 portrays a new product/market decision process. Financial studies are generally prepared at the various stages of such a process. In the example described in the figure, one could imagine that financial studies are prepared in at least four different stages:

● when the new product is made available to the selling subsidiaries (stage 4);
● when the decision to put the new product into production is about to be made (stage 3);
● when the new product idea is identified, or at least when it is identified with sufficient precision (stage 2);
● when the management periodically reflects about the position of the company on its markets and intends to increase its competitive edge, new products being one of the possible strategic moves (stage 1).

A large multinational company produces industrial products which are sold through a network of selling subsidiaries all over the world. For many years, this company has been selling products to a segment of customers and, in order to keep and improve its competitive edge, it has had to introduce new products every three to five years. This **product** introduction is a rather long process since it generally takes two to three years between the initial identification of the new product and the final decision to launch it. These two to three years are used for market research and product development. During this time, a number of ideas are abandoned. When the decision is finally made to start production, one to two more years are necessary to prepare the production facilities, organize the relationships with suppliers and develop the definitive marketing plan.

Figure 15.1 A new product decision process

Table 15.1 ● The company's cost structure

Sales	100
Cost of goods sold (CGS)	40
Research and development (R&D)	40
Administration at headquarters (HQ)	5
Administration at selling subsidiaries level	20
Profit	(5)

Further assumptions:
● All new product ideas lead to the same revenue and cost structure. (This structure is to be maintained in the future.)
● Revenues and costs can be assimilated to cash receipts and disbursements. There is no tax.
● In the short run, administrative costs at headquarters are fixed, administrative costs at selling subsidiaries level are divided into fixed (15) and variable (5).

Table 15.2 ● Four different stages of analysis

	Stage 1 Assessment of competitive position	Stage 2 A new idea is found	Stage 3 A new product is going to be launched in production	Stage 4 A new product is made available to selling subsidiaries
Cash inflows	100[a]	100[a]	100[a]	100[a]
Cash outflows	105[b]	85[c]	45[d]	90[e]
Net cash	−5	15	55	10

Notes
[a] Sales
[b] Since the company is operating on one market only all revenues and costs are to be taken into account over the long run.
[c] Disbursements envisaged are CGS (40), R&D (40), variable administrative costs at subsidiary level (5).
[d] Disbursements envisaged are CGS (40) variable administrative and selling costs in subsidiaries (5). All other costs are not taken into account since they are considered as sunk (R&D) or as fixed structure at both HQ and subsidiary levels.
[e] HQ charge to selling subsidiaries through the transfer price: CGS (40), R&D (40) and administration (5). Selling subsidiaries consider as outflows only the variable part of their selling costs (5).

The cash inflows and outflows depend on the assumptions made and other assumptions are possible.

Financial approaches aim to describe the *value of alternative decisions at a given moment in time*. Depending on the moment in time when the analysis is made, the results will differ quite significantly. Let us assume that the company described in Figure 15.1 has the cost structure shown in Table 15.1. The cash inflows and outflows that would be taken into account in the analysis at different stages are shown in Table 15.2. Financial analyses when made at different stages will therefore, as expected, lead to very different results:

- At stage 1, a financial analysis will conclude that the company destroys value with its present market/products.
- At stages 2, 3 and 4, the conclusion will be the opposite: the company creates value with its present market/products.

One has to realize, however, that the analysis itself is technically correct at each stage. For example, it is true that if one looks at stage 3, when the product has been developed, it makes sense to launch it since not launching it would make the situation even worse. What has to be understood is that the problem for this company is not really to decide whether or not products already developed should be launched but rather to examine why these products are not generating enough money to cover their costs of development and structure. If time has to be spent on financial analyses, it would be better in this case to spend time on decisions at stage 1, and to examine then whether the company should stay in this line of business.

15.3 Risk and commitment

As shown in Figure 15.2, risk and required commitment typically follow opposite trajectories over the process of developing most new products:

- **Risk typically decreases with the unfolding of the development process.** New products show different degrees of novelty, as they may range from simple line extensions to completely new-to-the-world concepts. However, whatever their degree of novelty, most new product have elements of discovery in their process of development and this makes them look more risky at the beginning. New products that correspond to disruptive technologies typically look extremely risky since many of their advantages are still hardly visible.[1] In the pharmaceutical industry, it is estimated that at the beginning of the process of drug discovery, a compound has something like one chance in 100 000 to reach the market. The product development process is a learning process that aims at generating knowledge[2] and reducing the risk of launching the product to an acceptable level.

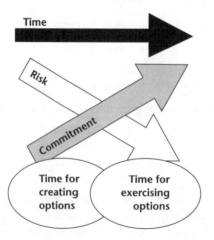

Figure 15.2 Risk and commitment trajectories

● **The need for irreversible commitment typically increases over time**. Fortunately enough, the development of most new product concepts does not require major financial commitment at the beginning. This is what renders possible the development of very innovative concepts. In many respects, the early stages of the development of new product ideas can often be viewed as a phase of creation and maintenance of options. The later stages of this development correspond more to the exercise of options: options to abandon the unsuccessful alternatives, options to switch to more promising alternatives, options to grow successful alternatives, and so on.

Even though of a considerable help, the natural opposite co-evolution of risk and of the need for irreversible commitment is generally not sufficient to guarantee a superior creation of value. Commitment has to be managed proactively in order to create and maintain flexibility.

The crucial need to manage commitment at the early stages of the process

When risk is very high one has to find ways to defer irreversible commitment and to create a whole series of options: options to abandon, options to switch, options to re-scale, and so on. The Eagle case study shows how flexibility can be created in the development of new pharmaceutical products. This case also shows that without the value attached to flexibility, it would not be valuable to commit to the development of this new product.

The need to create flexibility at all the stages of the process

Flexibility is often essential at the beginning of the development process of a new product. This does not mean that it is not also very important at the other stages of the process. Both the BA International and the CLS case studies show that valuable flexibility can always be created even at a very late stage.

Notes

1. For the difficulty that established businesses typically have to recognize the value of disruptive technologies, refer to C. Christensen (1997), *The Innovator's Dilemma*, Harvard Business School Press.
2. As noted by Nonaka and Takeuchi, 'The new product development process happens to be the core process for creating new organizational knowledge' (p. 231). In I. Nonaka and H. Takeuchi, *The Knowledge Creating Company* (1995), Oxford University Press. See also from the same authors, 'The new product development game', *Harvard Business Review*, Jan.–Feb. 1986.

BA International[1]

In December 2002, the time had come at BA International to submit the final report on P12, a new product to be introduced on the market in 2004, to the Board of Directors for their approval. Mr Keller, the Head of the Product Planning Department, was responsible for preparing this final report from the numerous memoranda about P12 as well as from the minutes of the New Product Committee.

The company

BA International was a large, German-based multinational corporation which specialized in the production and sales of industrial compressors. Its production facilities were located in Dusseldorf. The company sold through a network of wholly owned international sales subsidiaries in 40 countries, as well as through distributors.

In the past, BA International had been more successful in the more powerful end of the market (see Appendix O.1) selling to large industrial firms and/or those using large equipment (100–1000 kW range). It offered to these market segments products of high quality, in particular a very successful line of oil-free rotary screw compressors.

With P12, BA International was planning to offer the oil-free quality to a new market segment consisting of medium and small firms using medium size equipment (15–100 kW range).

Traditionally, BA International had a strong market position with a worldwide market share of about 15% in the 100–1000 kW range. In most of these markets, BA International had played the role of a price leader which resulted in high profitability. In recent years, however, growth had been sluggish and short-term prospects were not very favourable. As a consequence, BA International's profitability had declined recently, but to a lesser extent than its competitors. The worldwide stagnation of the compressor market, due to the economic recession, as well as the intense competition from dynamic compressors in the most powerful range, led management to believe that the basis for developing the group activities should lie in a downward extension rather than in a deeper penetration of the large or top power range markets.

P12

The introduction of P12 represented such a downward extension of its market position for BA International. It was not totally absent from the 15–100 kW segment. When the competition actively developed oil-lubricated rotary screw compressors for that segment, BA launched a line of comparable products with a view to preventing the competition in this segment from becoming too strong. In 2002, BA International was serving this segment through distributors rather than its own sales subsidiaries, except for the large firms served directly. But, although BA International had introduced a line of medium sized oil-lubricated rotary screw compressors, its long-term objective was to promote the oil-free solution in the entire 15–1000 kW range.

The concept for P12 was an old one at BA International. The first formal meeting about this product had taken place in the company as early as 1990. P12 was to be priced higher than the existing lubricated rotary screw compressors since it was providing a better service, oil-free air and lower maintenance costs. (BA International also provided maintenance services to its customers.)

BA International had been particularly concerned with the marketing of P12. Some questions had not been easy to answer

1. Were the prospective customers for P12 really sensitive to the oil-free argument? Apparently some were not, and that led BA International to conclude that P12 should be introduced only in those industries where specific characteristics required oil-free air (the electronics and food industries, for example). Another strategy, however, would be to promote P12 on a larger scale and invest in educating customers about the advantages of oil-free air. A spin-off effect of that effort would also help the sales of the more powerful equipment and reinforce BA International's image as a technological leader. However, the evaluation of such an effect was very difficult.

2. What premium over currently available products should P12 carry? The higher the premium, the more difficult P12 would be to sell in larger volume. In the end, a 15% premium over existing products was considered the most suitable.

3. Would P12 cannibalize the rotary screw compressors presently sold by BA International? As these were a profitable mature product this was a sensitive issue. The cannibalization issue depended very much on the strategy adopted for P12. If P12 were marketed only to those customers who were sensitive to the oil-free air argument, and if those customers were medium and small firms presently served by distributors, then it was felt that only limited cannibalization would take place. Obviously, if a higher price premium were charged, this would reinforce the argument for the absence of cannibalization. On the other hand, if BA International decided to aim at a larger market for P12, then it would be necessary to consider the impact of a cannibalization of the existing oil-lubricated compressors. Generally, when existing products are cannibalized, it is assumed that they are cannibalised in the proportion of their market share.

4. Would competition move in on this market? At present, no competitor seemed to have a product with a similar design. Even though it was finally considered at BA International that no competitor would offer a product similar to P12 in the near future, some engineers claimed that the major world competitor of BA International could well introduce such a product on the market at any time.

The new products development process

In a mature industry of the type in which BA International was operating, products have a long life cycle, some 10 to 15 years. During their life cycle, a number of the products require additional investment (engineering expenditures, change in the organization of production, even revamping of the product). In the case of P12, a 10-year life with no additional capital expenditures could reasonably be expected.

New product development and introduction was the responsibility of Headquarters which was frequently secretive about new product development since it was felt that, if sales subsidiaries knew about new products too early, they would put less effort into selling existing products and wait until the new product was available. As a result, sales subsidiaries were generally informed about new products only when these were available for sale (the end of 2003 for P12).

The Product Planning Department headed by Mr Keller was a staff department. Its mission was to co-ordinate the three functions involved in new product development, the technical, production and marketing functions. This co-ordination was formally made through a New Product Committee, the secretariat of which was provided by the Product Planning Department.

New product development was a long process, maybe too long, according to the new financial manager. It involved mainly Headquarters staff who were, in any case, the only ones concerned with technical and production problems. Marketing issues related to the introduction of new products were dealt with by the Marketing Department at Headquarters. When needed, this department tested new product ideas and characteristics (especially price) with the management of sales subsidiaries but had to remain discreet in order to avoid disclosing too much about the new products envisaged (the summary of the marketing studies for P12 is given in Appendix O.2).

During the process, numerous alternatives were explored until a consensus was reached on the most reasonable assumptions and strategy. These were the basis for the comprehensive profitability study submitted to the Board (see Appendix O.3). This profitability study was obviously not the first to be carried out in the product development process but was the only really comprehensive one.

Generally, this study presented one single set of assumptions and strategy, the one that had been progressively built up through successive consensus about the most realistic assumptions and the best strategic alternatives.

The final report on a project, including the profitability study, was not submitted to the Board so that they could decide whether or not the project should be launched. It was intended rather to:

● provide the senior management of BA International with the opportunity to summarize the various dimensions of the decision in a comprehensive and structured way;
● double-check the strength of the arguments in favour of the introduction of a new product on the market and the robustness of the consensual strategy that had progressively emerged.

In fact, substantial changes were often made to the consensual strategy during the process of preparing the final report.

Appendix O.1
The industrial compressor market

Air compressor technology, dating back to the industrial revolution of the nineteenth century, is based on a very simple idea. A given volume of air is confined in a cylinder, compressed by a piston usually driven by an electric motor) and the resulting energy, characterized by a volume of air at a given pressure, is used to drive a machine, move a piece of equipment or an air motor. Over the years, compressed air technology has evolved to the point where it is possible to distinguish three categories of product (in 2002 it appeared that technology had reached a stage of maturity).

1. Piston (reciprocating) compressors

Piston compressors are the oldest type but, even now, represent intrinsically the most energy-efficient solution (in terms of the number of kWs necessary to produce one cubic metre of air). Their main advantages (from the user's point of view) are their familiar technology and their lower purchasing cost. Their main disadvantages are:

● substantial installation costs (foundation mountings),
● vibration,
● noise level when in use,
● high maintenance costs. It can be estimated that a 100 kW piston industrial compressor has a life expectancy of 80 to 100 000 hours but must be checked on average every 8000 hours.

The piston compressor family covers a wide range, including oil-lubricated and oil-free (pure air), single- or double-acting, one- or two-stage compression, air- or water-cooled, etc.

2. Rotary screw compressors

Instead of being compressed in a cylinder, air is squeezed between two screws rotating in a housing. The main advantages of rotary screw compressors are their reduced installation cost (rotary screw compressors are packaged units which only need to be connected up to the electricity supply) and reduced maintenance costs (a major maintenance operation such as replacing a screw is necessary, on average, every 25 to 50 000 hours) as well as a reduced level of noise and vibration. The trade-off for this reduction in maintenance costs is that the initial capital cost is about 20% more than for a piston compressor.

Like piston compressors, rotary screw compressors include several types of machine, particularly oil-lubricated and oil-free machines. Oil-lubricated screw compressors have the advantage of being a packaged unit and are capable of delivering air at 7 to 10 bar pressure in a single stage of compression (such a performance would require a two-stage process for oil-free piston compressors), but the delivered air is not totally free from oil and must be purified through a series of filters, the effectiveness of which may vary considerably from one application to another. Since certain types of applications require very high quality air (the food and electronics industries) there also exist oil-free rotary screw compressors. Their main advantage is the purity of the compressed air delivered, but two compression stages are necessary as well as an intercooler in order to obtain a 7 to 10 bar final pressure. These compressors cost more than oil-lubricated ones (15% more than the sum of the costs of an oil-lubricated compressor and of the filters). The initial difference in capital cost between oil-lubricated and oil-free compressors is, however, compensated for by the savings obtained in energy consumption and maintenance. As the yearly maintenance costs are about 10% lower in the case of an oil-free screw compressor, the payback of selecting an oil-free solution lies somewhere between three and four years.

3. Dynamic compressors

The basic principle of dynamic compressors consists of an impeller accelerating air to a high velocity and converting the speed of the air into pressure in the diffuser. There are two main categories of dynamic compressor, centrifugal and axial. Given the high cost and level of sophistication, the dynamic compressor technology is only justified at a power range greater than 1000 kW. Dynamic compressors always deliver oil-free air. Their main advantage lies in their excellent input/output ratio and their compactness and limited number of components.

Industrial compressors may be driven by any type of motor, electrical or steam and gas turbine and are used in many applications in almost all industrial sectors. The different types of compressor correspond to different application areas.

(a) The market for **very small compressors** (smaller than 15 kW) is dominated by oil-lubricated piston technology. This market is highly competitive and a large number of manufacturers engage in price wars. Products which are technologically simple are sold in large quantities, most often through wholesalers at unit prices averaging a few thousand €. The bottom end of this line consists of small workshop compressors as well as do-it-yourself products. BA International was neither interested nor active in this market.

(b) The **middle range** (15–100 kW) compressor market worldwide was estimated at about 24 000 units in 2004. Given the standard nature of their product, manufacturers compete very actively with each other. Given the current economic situation, price and delivery criteria tend to be more important than company image and technical features. Traditionally dominated by piston technology, this market has changed fundamentally in the last ten years, under pressure from big international manufacturers who introduced oil-lubricated screw compressors to try to gain market share from the local producers. It was this development which prompted BA International to launch, slightly later than its competitors, its own line of oil-lubricated screw compressors. Most manufacturers sell directly through sales subsidiaries as well as through distributors.

(c) The market for **large compressors** (100–1000 kW) is more structured as far as demand and competition are concerned. Compressors in this range are often sold directly to customers by the manufacturer, to customer specifications. A potential customer interested in buying a compressor provides the specifications required for the particular application, a feasibility study is then made by each manufacturer interested in the contract and a proposal is made. If an agreement is reached, the contract is signed and the equipment is delivered and installed on site. The selection of a manufacturer is made on the basis of three criteria, technical (air quality, kW/m³ output), commercial (price, delivery) and reputation and image factors. This market segment is dominated by international companies.

(d) The market for **very large compressors** (greater than 1000 kW) is a market dominated by technical considerations and each sale is dealt with on an *ad hoc* basis. In 2002, BA International was not active in this segment.

Appendix O.2
Marketing studies

The determination of the potential market for P12 has been studied by the Marketing Department at Dusseldorf. This has been accomplished by desk and field research (interviews of managers in sales companies, industrial analysis). The conclusions of the studies on the market for P12 are summarized as follows:

● The total annual world market for compressors in the range of 40–100 kW is estimated at 5780 units in 2004. This market is estimated to grow at 3% per year (P12 was aimed at only part of the 15–1000 kW market).

● Within this total market, the users who need oil-free air represent 11%, corresponding to 635 units, the sales being equally shared between small and large firms. BA International currently sells to small firms through distributors (world market share 10%) and to large firms through subsidiaries (world market share 13%).

● There is potential for some other customers to be converted to the use of oil-free air since this solution could reduce their maintenance costs. This would, however, require BA International to undertake a major educational effort. If these customers were convinced, the potential market for P12 could progressively rise to 19% of the total market. If BA International were willing to spend about €17 m (equally spread over 2003 and 2004), P12's market segment could rise to 14% of total market in 2004, 16.5% of total market in 2005 and 19% of total market in 2006 and afterwards. Additional customers would be 50% small firms, 50% large firms although, given the technical characteristics of P12, BA International was planning to sell P12 directly and not through wholesalers.

● All other customers can be considered as non-sensitive to the oil-free argument, as long as oil-free compressors are more expensive than oil-lubricated ones.

● It is recommended that there is no education campaign. In which case, BA International could potentially change the size of P12's segment through its pricing policy.

Premium over present products	Estimated size of P12 segment
10% (sales price €32 140)	12%
15% (sales price €33 600)	11%
25% (sales price €36 520)	9%
35% (sales price €39 443)	7%

If the education campaign is carried out, the relationship between price premium and P12's additional segment size is estimated as follows:

Premium over present products	Estimated size of additional P12 segment (% of total market) 2006[2]
10%	12%
15%	8%
25%	5%
35%	2%

● It is recommended that a premium of 15% is charged which should ensure an 11% segment share for P12. Two factors influence the selection of the 15% premium:
  – The estimate of the cost of providing an alternative solution to P12 by using a rotary screw compressor plus filters plus higher maintenance costs.
  – BA International's experience with larger equipment which is selling at a similar premium.
● It is recommended that no account is taken of the possible introduction of a similar product to P12 by any competitor. The only possible competitor who could launch a similar product has a smaller market share than BA International (4 to 6 ratio).

Appendix O.3
Profitability studies

1. Sales assumptions
The volume of the market segment of P12 in 2004 is 635 units. This segment is assumed to grow at 3% a year after 2004. A 100% market share is assumed (no competitor present). A progressive market penetration is envisaged: 22.5% in 2004, 50% in 2005, 75% in 2006 and 100% in 2007 and afterwards.

2. Price assumptions
The average world price for P12 is estimated to be €33 600 (customers' price) in 2004. The entire profitability study is made at revenue and cost prices of 2004. Currency values considered are also 2004 values.

3. Costs
Production costs are determined on the basis of €17 013 per unit in 2004. No allowance has been made in future years for increases in prices. The calculation of costs is detailed in Appendix O.4. The cost of €17 013 represents the cost of P12 in 2004 for a volume of production of 100 units. This cost includes direct material, material overheads, direct labour, labour overheads, product costs (10% of the other costs) and packaging and transportation (9% of the total of the other costs). Since the volume of P12 is to remain small in comparison with other products, no attempt has been made to charge any cost relating to the structure of the production unit and Headquarters. The cost of goods sold is assumed to be equal to the cost of production.

Selling costs in the sales companies are estimated to be 20% of sales. No attempt has been made to charge any cost related to the general structure of the sales companies.

Other costs. No interest charges have been considered. Inflation and foreign exchange rate fluctuations have been considered as neutral, and their impact has been ignored.

Corporation tax is assumed to be paid at a rate of 40%, and no reduction of tax due to depreciation has been considered.[3]

4. Working capital needs

The collection period is assumed to be three months. Inventories are estimated at three months of production costs (excluding packaging and transport costs) at the factory and three months of production costs (including packaging and transport costs) in the sales companies. The profitability study does not consider any accounts payable, even though materials are paid for with a three month delay.

5. Capital expenditure

The only capital expenditure envisaged is related to the preparation of the production facilities, and amounts to €5.64 m, the disbursement of which takes place early 2004. The disbursements relating to the development of P12 were about €5 m, but by 2002 they are largely sunk costs. It has thus been decided to disregard them.

6. Profitability calculation

It was normal practice at BA International to calculate the internal rate of return over the first five years of the life of a new product. In 2002, even though there was no formal system of hurdle rate at BA International, it was felt that comparable projects to P12 should yield at least 14%. This yield could be considered as the risk adjusted cost of capital in 2002. Profitability is calculated for one set of assumptions and strategy. In case of doubt, the most cautious and conservative alternative is considered; this is why accounts payable are not considered. Cash flows beyond five years are also not considered.

Table O.1 shows the profitability model.

Appendix O.4
Production costs

When estimating unit costs of production, the engineering department envisaged these costs after the introduction phase was completed (after the production of 500 units). A new unit cost estimate was prepared at an earlier production stage (100 units). This led to a new unit cost estimate of €17 013. In order to take a cautious view, this unit cost estimate was then used in the profitability study.

Unit cost in € (2004 prices)	100 units	500 units
Direct material	12 151	11 168
Material overhead (2.7%)	328	302
Direct labour	786	786
Overhead labour	924	924
= Production cost	14 189	13 180
+ Product line cost (10% of production cost)	1 419	1 318
= Unit cost 1	15 608	14 498
+ Packaging, transport (9%)	1 405	1 305
= Unit cost 2	17 013	15 803

Table O.1 ● Profitability model

A	B	C	D	E	F	G	H
1	2004	2005	2006	2007	2008	2009	Cum.
2 Market growth		0.03	0.03	0.03	0.03		
3 Total market	5780	5953	6132	6316	6505		
4 P12 segment share	0.11	0.11	0.11	0.11	0.11		
5 Market penetration	0.225	0.5	0.75	1	1		
6 Sales volume	143	327	506	695	716		
7 Unit price	33.6	33.6	33.6	33.6	33.6		
8 SALES	4.8	11.0	17.0	23.3	24.0		
9 Unit cost	17.0	17.0	17.0	17.0	17.0		
10 CGS	2.4	5.6	8.6	11.8	12.2		
11 Selling costs/sales	0.2	0.2	0.2	0.2	0.2		
12 SELLING COSTS	1.0	2.2	3.4	4.7	4.8		
13 Tax rate	0.4	0.4	0.4	0.4	0.4		
14 **Profit after tax**	0.8	1.9	3.0	4.1	4.2		14.1
15 Collection period	3	3	3	3	3		
16 RECEIVABLES END	1.2	2.8	4.2	5.8	6.0		
17 Inventory period production	3	3	3	3	3		
18 Inventory period sales	3	3	3	3	3		
19 Inventory end	1.2	2.7	4.1	5.7	5.8		
20 **Cash flow**	−1.5	−1.1	0.0	1.0	3.9	11.8	14.1
21 **Capital expenditure**	5.6						
22 Discount rate	0.14						
23 NPV	0.2						
24 IRR	15%						

Background

C2: .03; D2: +C2; Copy across
B3: 5780; C3: +B3*(1+C2); Copy across
B4: .11; C4: +B4; Copy across
B5: .225; C5: .5; D5: .75; E5: 1; Copy across
B6: +B3*B4*B5; Copy across
B7: 33.6; C7: +B7; Copy across
B8: +B6*B7/1000; Copy across
B9: 17.013; C9: +B9; Copy across
B10: +B6*B9/1000; Copy across
B11: .20; C11: +B11; Copy across
B12: +B8*B11
B13: .4; C11: +B11; Copy across

B14: =(B8−B10−B12)*(1−B13); Copy across
B15: 3; C15; +B15; Copy across
B16: +B8/12*B15; Copy across
B17: 3; C17; +B17; Copy across
B18: 3; C18; +B18; Copy across
B19: =(B10/1.09/12*B17)+(B10/12*B18)[a]; Copy
B20: +B14−B16−B19
C20: +C14−C16−C19+B16+B19; Copy across
    D20.G20
B21: 5.64
B22: .14
B23: (NPV(B22;B20.G20)−B21)/(1+B22)[b]

[a] The 1.09 factor reflects that there is no transport and packaging cost for the production stock
[b] The NPV is calculated end of 2002. Capital expenditure is end of 2003.

Notes

1. This case was developed by the author and Bernard Dubois, Professor at Centre HEC-ISA (France). The pedagogy of this case has been developed by the author, Bernard Dubois, Sherwood Frey, Professor at Colgate Darden (USA) and Foster Rogers, Professor at IFL (Sweden).
2. For example if the educational campaign is undertaken, the total segment for P12 is equal to 24% (12 + 12) with a 10% price premium.
3. This is a cautious assumption, since the capital expenditure would be depreciated over five years. The actual average tax rate for the group was about 30%.

CASE

CHAPTER 16

Launching P12

Which model would help us best?

16.1 The environment of the problem

In December 2002, the time had come at BA International to make the final decision about the introduction of P12 and the strategy to adopt for this introduction. Over the years a consensual strategy had progressively emerged:

- P12 should be introduced.
- It should be targeted at those firms that need oil-free air. As a result there would be no need to undertake an educational campaign.
- It should be priced at a 15% premium above comparable oil-lubricated compressors.
- It should be sold direct through BA International's selling subsidiaries.

The key issues in 2002 can be described as follows:

- Is introducing P12 in 2004 the best alternative available? Is the consensual strategy the best strategy available? Even though a strong organizational commitment seems to exist, it would be useful to check that this is the best solution.
- How to include risk in the analysis?
- How to improve the initial model prepared at BA International and shown in Table O.1?

Before addressing these questions, let us briefly review what we know about P12, the industry and BA International.

P12

Table 16.1 describes the market segments at which BA International aims. P12 would be the first rotary oil-free compressor in the 40–100 kW segment. Potentially P12 can be targeted at either a part of this segment, the customers who need oil-free air (niche strategy), or to the whole segment. P12's selling point would in this case be its lower maintenance costs (volume strategy). The alternative strategies for the introduction of P12 are described in Figure 16.1. The figure calls for several comments.

- The diagram only shows decision nodes. This is because, if we believe the case, BA International does not seem to envisage any uncertainty, no competitive response, no manufacturing risk, etc.

Table 16.1 ● Market segments

Segment	Small <15 kW	Medium 15–100 kW	Large 100–1000 kW	Very large >1000 kW
Market size		24 000 units in 2003 5780 units in the 40–100 kW range		
Technology	Piston Oil-lubricated	Piston and rotary (new) Oil-lubricated	Rotary Oil-lubricated and oil-free	Dynamic Oil-free
Distribution	Independent distributors	Independent distributors and direct sales	Direct sales	Direct sales
BA International's position and competition	BA is not present	BA is strong but has been late introducing rotary. Worldwide competition, international and local firms	BA is very strong (15% market share worldwide). Competition: market dominated by international firms	BA is hardly present

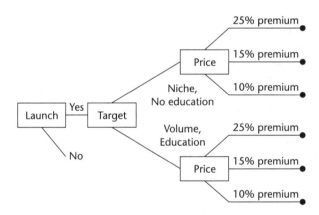

Figure 16.1 Alternative strategies

- The diagram does not show any decision related to distribution. The characteristics of P12 and the need to make use of the capacity of the selling subsidiaries (downward extension) eliminate the alternative of indirect selling.
- Some of the branches shown in Figure 16.1 seem to be meaningless. Why sell P12 at a low price when a niche strategy is adopted? Is it really reasonable to think that P12 can be sold at a 25% premium when a volume strategy is adopted?

The industry

The industry in which BA International operates seems to present many of the characteristics of a mature industry. A saturated mass market with limited growth. Standard products with limited innovation. Well segmented markets where service has become very important. Some production overcapacity with cyclicality. Falling profitability for manufacturers. Severe competition. What are the implications of this for the launch of a new product like P12?

In mature industries new products are not easy to find. Efforts are often more productive when concentrated on existing products. Competitors are not likely to surrender their market share. They may be ready to fight back and to engage in price wars. High quality, premium price strategies may be difficult to sustain. International competition increases and international companies try to eliminate local firms. Marketing changes and redistribution of power may occur between manufacturers and distributors. Profitability is at risk and manufacturers find it more and more difficult to create value. We may therefore consider that the introduction of P12 is not going to be easy for BA International. Consequently, we should not expect easily to find launch strategies corresponding to large NPVs. But we should not be too pessimistic, however.[1] It might well be that P12 is the chance for BA International to overcome the problems of maturity and to reinforce its competitive position. In particular, P12 might be the chance for BA International to achieve a dominant position on the 15–100 kW segment at the expense of local competition and of independent distributors as has already happened in the 100–1000 kW segment.

BA International

BA International is a successful firm in the industry. Its selling subsidiaries network is a definite strength when service becomes a key competitive weapon, and its price consciousness is also a strength in a mature industry. We might, however, have some worries when analyzing the data of the case. The company seems to perceive itself as the champion of oil-free air, but is that what the market really wants? The secrecy of the Headquarters when they introduce new products protects BA International against cannibalization but it may be unwise for the company not to take advantage of the knowledge subsidiaries have of their markets. The company also seems to perceive itself as a technology leader, but it was not the first to introduce the rotary technology in the 15–100 kW segment, and the decision to launch P12 has taken a long time in coming.

16.2 The need for a better model

The model prepared by BA International (Table O.1) raises a series of questions:

1. Why limit the period of study to five years?

At BA International they decided to limit the period of study to five years, based on the fact that cash flows beyond this are too uncertain to be considered. Even though future cash flows are uncertain, and probably more so as we go further into the future, what is the rationale behind so much discrimination between some cash flows (the first five) and the others? Why not analyze the decision to introduce P12 over the whole period during which this decision is expected to have an impact, the expected life of P12?

2. Why not build a trajectory rather than a per-cent-of-sales model?

The trajectory of **sales** that is portrayed in the initial model does not look like a typical product life cycle curve. This will be especially true if we extend the period of study to 10 years, the total expected life for P12. Why not start from the total expected sales over the life of P12 and use a product life cycle curve for creating a trajectory for the sales of P12? In the initial model, **selling costs** equal 20% of the sales in each of the years of P12's existence. When sales are low at the beginning of the life of P12 selling costs are also low. This will probably not be the case since BA International will need to make a special effort to promote P12 at the beginning of its life. Selling costs may be 20% of sales on average but we need to estimate their trajectory also and avoid estimating them as a percentage of current annual sales.

3. Is it right to assume that so many variables (unit selling price, unit production costs, collection period, inventory turnover, etc.) will remain constant over the whole period of study?

When evaluating the decision to launch P12 at BA International, they assumed that the **unit production cost** will remain constant and equal to €17 013. This is a cautious approach but is in contradiction to the data shown in Appendix O.4 which indicates that, at a production level of 500 units per year, the unit production cost should fall to €15 803. Since this level of production should be reached as early as 2006[2] keeping the unit cost at €17 013 creates a bias against the decision to launch P12. *It also creates a bias against any volume strategy, which is not acceptable as we want to choose between niche and volume strategies.* At the beginning of the life of P12, BA International probably needs large **inventories** (to cover the need to show the product to customers, uncertainty of demand, etc.). But later it should be possible to reduce inventories to a much lower level. Another problem related to inventories: it would be better to estimate them in relation to future sales rather than to current sales.

4. Is it right to ignore inflation and currency variations?

Can we reasonably expect that prices and exchange rates will remain constant over the period of study? How does this assumption relate to the assumption relative to the discount rate? Is the discount rate used at BA International consistent with the assumption that prices will not change over the period of study?

5. Is it correct to ignore cannibalization?

Almost all the sales of P12 will probably be made to customers who will buy P12 instead of buying another compressor. In other words, P12 will oust other compressors made by the industry, by both BA International's competitors and BA International itself. As a result of the introduction of P12, BA International will sell fewer of its existing compressors. Consequently, we should deduct from the cash flows of P12 the cash flows corresponding to existing compressors that will not be sold due to the introduction of P12.

6. Can risk be completely ignored?

There are several areas of uncertainty that should be investigated when analyzing the decision to launch P12: reaction from competition, manufacturing risk, etc. If BA International decides to introduce P12, its competitors may well not have an equivalent product in 2004. At BA International they consider that this is very likely and as a result do not even consider the risk that their competitors may have a similar product. This may be true in 2004 but one can seriously question the assumption that the competitors will *never* introduce a product similar to P12. In a mature industry where all firms have comparable technological capabilities, it seems far more reasonable to assume that the advantage BA International could achieve can only be temporary. If the competition does not have a similar product in 2004, it will probably develop and introduce one within a few years. The question asked should be *when* will it be introduced rather than *if*.

We should also consider manufacturing risk. P12 is a technological innovation, and whether the manufacturing of this new product will proceed smoothly or not is uncertain. This risk seems to be completely ignored by BA International. Introducing risk is necessary for understanding and assessing the real alternatives for P12.

7. Is it acceptable to ignore the impact of some variables with a view to remaining cautious?

BA International has ignored the tax impact of **depreciation** and envisaged a **pessimistic tax rate** of 40%. This creates biases against the decision to launch P12 and this is probably not acceptable. Ignoring the impact of **accounts payable** creates a further bias against the decision to introduce P12.

8. Is it correct to assimilate CGS and cost of production?

As P12 is a manufacturing project, the calculation of CGS cannot really be carried out in the same way as in the initial model. A more accurate way to calculate CGS would be to:

1. Evaluate first the total production cost. This could be done from an evaluation of the volume produced and of the unit production cost, volume produced being equal to the sum of volume sold and finished goods inventory build-up.
2. Then to calculate CGS as the difference between total production cost and increase in the value of inventory of finished goods.

9. Does the analysis focus on the relevant revenues and costs?

In the analysis of the decision to launch P12 we have followed BA International in envisaging only the incremental revenues and costs. As a result they have ignored:

● All allocated costs of structure. This was made on the basis that P12 should remain a small part of the overall activity of BA International. Is it realistic to consider that introducing P12 will not change these costs? Is it realistic in the particular case of a volume strategy?
● All costs incurred on P12 before the decision is made in 2002. The development costs of P12 are clearly sunk costs but does that mean that they should be completely ignored?
● Two further effects of the launching of P12 on the company's present businesses: first, that with P12, BA International will reinforce its image as the oil-free air champion. This might create valuable growth options for the company (opportunity to launch new products and services). At the same time, P12 might decrease the need for BA's maintenance services, a negative impact.[3]

10. Finally why not start with a simple global full life model?

Even though they are generally not sufficient, global evaluations are a very useful starting point. The expected profit over the entire life of P12 (10 years) can be estimated as follows:

Annual market volume	5 780
Number of years	8.5[1]
Total market	49 130
P12 segment share	0.11
Volume sold over entire life	5 404
Total sales (DM million)	182
Total CGS	92
Total selling costs	36
Total depreciation	5.6
Total profit before tax	48
Total profit after tax	**33**

1. In the first three years sales are less than 100% of the potential: 25% in the first year, 50% in the second and 75% in the third. As a result, 1.5 years are lost out of the 10 – or of the 5.

Table 16.2 ● Global evaluation over full life

	A	B	C	D	E	F	G	H	I	J
1			Niche					Volume		
2	Annual market	5 780								
3	Year factor	3.5								
4	Total market	20 230	20 230	20 230	20 230		20 230	20 230	20 230	20 230
5	Premium	0.35	0.25	0.15	0.10		0.35	0.25	0.15	0.10
6	P12 segment share	0.07	0.09	0.11	0.12		0.09	0.14	0.19	0.24
7	Total volume sold	1 416	1 821	2 225	2 428		1 821	2 832	3 844	4 855
8	Unit selling price	39.4	36.5	33.6	32.1		39.4	36.5	33.6	32.1
9	**Sales**	**55.9**	**66.5**	**74.8**	**78.0**		**71.8**	**103.4**	**129.1**	**156.0**
10	Unit cost	17.0	17.0	17.0	17.0		17.0	17.0	17.0	17.0
11	CGS	24.1	31.0	37.9	41.3		31.0	48.2	65.4	82.6
12	Selling costs	11.2	13.3	15.0	15.6		14.4	20.7	25.8	31.2
13	Education campaign	0	0	0	0		17	17	17	17
14	Depreciation	5.6	5.6	5.6	5.6		5.6	5.6	5.6	5.6
15	Profit before tax	15.0	16.6	16.3	15.5		3.8	11.9	15.3	19.6
16	**Profit after tax**	**10.5**	**11.6**	**11.4**	**10.8**		**2.7**	**8.3**	**10.7**	**13.7**

B4: +$B$2*B$3

B7: +B4*B6

B8: +33.6/1.15*(1+B5)

B9: +B7*B8/1000

B11: +B7*B10/1000

B12: +B9*.2

B15: +B9−B11−B12−B13−B14

B16: +B15*(1−.3)

As it ignores the cost of money, this approach tends to make P12 look a better opportunity than it probably is. The value of this approach is, however, to enable you to make a first and rough assessment of the various alternatives. In order to do so, you can build the simple spreadsheet model described in Table 16.2. With this model you can quickly generate results over the entire life of P12. Here are the results when you set the number of years at 8.5. The results are not the same as with 3.5 years.

	Niche strategy				Volume strategy			
Premium	0.35	0.25	0.15	0.10	0.35	0.25	0.15	0.10
Profit after tax	31.1	33.8	33.4	31.9	29.2	42.9	48.6	55.9

This suggests that:

● In order to give a volume strategy a fair chance, you have to study the alternatives over the entire life of P12. Volume strategies seem to be attractive, especially if we were accounting for a lower unit production cost. The problem though is that we need to know more about risk.
● The impact of pricing seems to differ with the envisaged target. Pricing does not seem to matter much with niche strategies but seems to become a key variable with volume strategy. When evaluating volume strategies, we should be prepared to investigate the impact of aggressive pricing strategies – even more aggressive than the ones introduced in the case.

16.3 What NPV figure should we aim at?

When we investigate the decision to launch P12, any positive NPV should satisfy us, and since we know that launching P12 is not going to be an easy task we should not expect to find very large NPVs. If we find large NPVs we have to be very cautious and check out possible errors in our calculations.

We do need to know whether we should be happy with a launching strategy which results in a slightly positive NPV. We should not forget that we make the study at a very late stage, which means that a lot of money has already been spent in relation to P12 (about €5 million). If when evaluated in 2002, the best strategy for launching P12 corresponds to a very small positive NPV, P12 should be launched as this will be better than forgetting about it, but it will not mean that the efforts devoted to P12 have been very successful. In order that these efforts should be successful in the end we need to find a strategy which generates an NPV significantly bigger than simply a positive one.

If BA International wants to recover its development costs, the NPV should be at least larger than €5 million, or more precisely larger than the present (2002) value of this 5 million.[4]

We may also want to take into consideration that in order to launch a new product a company like BA International will have explored many ideas and developed only a few. Then the NPV attached to the launching of P12 should be much more than €5 million if the company wants to justify its research and development activities. If one idea out of two results in the launching of a new product, P12 should generate at least a €10 m NPV; if it is one out of three, P12 should generate at least a 15 m NPV, and so on.

Notes

1. A major problem with maturity is its unexciting nature. Firms need a lot of managerial talent to break out into a dematurity stage. Refer to D. Quinn Mills, *The New Competition*, John Wiley (1985, Chapter 8, pp. 14–59).

2. Probably even earlier than 2006. In the initial model we assimilate cgs to cost of production and, as a result, we do not calculate the volume of production which is necessarily higher than the volume of sales, due to the need to build up inventories.
3. Which might, however, be compensated for by offering customers the option to pay for insurance against maintenance costs, a favourable deal for BA International, due to the very little maintenance expected.
4. If you consider that this €5 m has been spent over the past 10 years, then its present (2002) value is much higher than €5 m. If you assume that the 5 m has been equally spent over the past 10 years you find an NPV equal to €10 m.

CASE *P*

BA International (II)[1]
Additional data, experience and
theoretical background

Period of study

When reviewing the estimates of cash flows related to the decision to introduce P12, it was felt at BA International that limiting the period of study to five years was looking at the bad news only. Due to the working capital needs required by P12 at the beginning of its life, early cash flows were not very attractive. In order to make a better assessment of the decision it was necessary to analyze it over the whole expected life of P12. The memorandum sent by Mr Lefranc, the Financial Manager, is reproduced in Appendix P.1. The cash flows estimated over a period of 10 years are given in Table P.1.

Product life cycle

After checking the initial sales estimate of P12 against the concept of product life cycle and the experience of comparable products launched by BA International in the past, it had been felt that annual sales should be generated as follows:

1. Estimate of the total cumulated sales over the whole life of P12.
2. Estimate of the cumulated sales at the end of each year using a product life cycle model (see Appendix P.2).
3. Then estimate of the annual sales.

Cost/volume relationships[2]

When analyzing the manufacturing characteristics of P12, it had been concluded at BA International that an 85% experience curve would apply to both the material and assembly costs of P12.[3] Due to its very strong position with its suppliers, BA International would be able to reap most of their cost savings due to experience. P12 was, however, not a totally new product for the suppliers since a similar but larger product had already been manufactured. As a result, increasing the accumulated production of P12 from 100 to 500 units corresponded to a 43% increase in experience only (it could also be considered that 830 units had been produced before 2004).

Assembly costs were also to decrease in relation to an 85% learning curve but the previous experience was larger. It could be estimated that increasing the accumulated production of P12 from 100 to 500 units corresponded to a 17% increase in experience only (or that about 2200 units had been produced before 2004).

Selling costs

On average, it could be estimated that selling costs were equal to 20% of the sales of P12. Selling costs could not, however, be considered as equal to 20% of the sales of P12 each year. Only half of total selling costs could be considered as variable, mainly salespeople's commissions. The other half of the selling costs corresponded to launch costs and were to be incurred in the first three years of the life of P12 (in equal amounts). As they corresponded to a specific intensity of selling efforts, these launch costs were largely independent of the pricing policy. One could thus assume that they would not change if the price premium were modified. Consequently, it was decided to consider only two levels of fixed selling costs; one for the situation where the educational campaign was not undertaken and the other for the situation where it was undertaken.

Cannibalization[4]

In order to clarify this issue, Mr Keller had further meetings with managers responsible for marketing at Headquarters. Even though the situation was different on each national market it seemed possible to simplify it as follows when taking a worldwide view. The assumed segment for P12 was made up of 50% of small firms that BA International was presently serving through distributors and 50% of large firms that it served through its sales subsidiaries. As far as the first segment was concerned, BA International had a 10% market share only. In this market, the contribution after tax of each compressor sold could be estimated at about €4000. In the second segment, BA International had a 13% market share and a much higher contribution per unit, about €8000. If an educational campaign was undertaken, it would probably achieve results in both the first and second segments. Finally, no cannibalization was to be considered after 2008.

Competition

Even though it had been assumed in the initial study that no competitor was going to introduce a product similar to P12, discussions had shown that there was a chance that BA International's main world competitor could introduce a similar product. For some marketing people, that could happen as early as 2004. In this case, the market share of BA International would be equal to 0.6 throughout the period. To others, it seemed likely that this would happen within five years (in 2009). In a mature industry, major competitors had all mastered the technology, and five years was to be the maximum time needed by the major world competitor to find its answer to P12. In this case, BA International's market share would be equal to 0.8 in 2009 and to 0.6 afterwards.

If the major competitor was going to offer a product similar to P12, it could opt for two extreme types of pricing policy. It could decide to offer the competing product at the same price as P12, or, on the other hand, decide to price very aggressively. According to some marketing managers, this could mean a selling price never more than 175% of the cost per unit. It was also felt that the likelihood of a price war was much higher if BA International decided to make an aggressive bid for market share (educational campaign and low price premium).

Production risk

Production problems should never be ignored when putting a new product into manufacture. This was especially true in the case of P12 which introduced some innovative technological solutions which were not common in the industry. When this issue was discussed, one engineer reminded the committee about a previous manufacturing difficulty. SP4 had had a unit production cost 15% higher than expected and outputs significantly lower than expected. The company had expected to start with a 200/300 unit yearly output and rapidly reach 700/800 units per year, but had only achieved 25 units in the first year, 100 in the second, 200 in the third and 300 in the fourth year, and never managed to produce more than 400 units per year. However, the numerous meetings of the new product committee on P12 had convinced Mr Keller that it was likely that manufacturing would go smoothly, but he knew he must also remember the risk of the same difficulties as with SP4.

Discount rate

One could consider that the 14% discount rate used at BA International in 2002 embodied a 3% expected yearly inflation.

Inventories

After having carefully reviewed the logistics of P12, it had been felt that the inventory period estimates (in months) should be reconsidered as follows:

	2004	2005	2006 and subsequent years
Production	3	2	1
Sales companies	3	2	2

It was also felt that inventory estimates should be based on future rather than current sales.

Appendix P.1

Memorandum

FROM: M. Lefranc, Financial Manager
TO: M. Keller, Product Planning
SUBJECT: **P12 should be studied over a period of 10 years**

The length of the period of study has a significant impact on the net present value:

Period of study (years)	4	5	6	7	8	9	10	11	12
NPV (DM million)	−1.09	0.17	1.32	2.35	3.29	4.13	4.90	5.58	6.21

With a period of less than five years, the NPV criterion tells us that P12 should not be launched. With a period of five years or more, the same criterion indicates that P12 should be launched. As a consequence, we should not adopt any arbitrary time horizon but rather study P12 over its entire expected life of 10 years. When we do so, we obtain the cash flows shown in Table P.1. These cash flows correspond to an NPV at 14% of €4.9 m.

Appendix P.2

Memorandum

FROM: L. Lundquist, Marketing
TO: M. Keller, Product Planning
SUBJECT: **Re-examination of the initial sales estimates for P12 in the light of the product life cycle concept**

The concept

In industrial marketing, as for consumer goods, it is widely accepted that products experience a life cycle although the exact shape and duration of this cycle is not easy to predict.[5] The product life cycle (PLC) concept is an attempt to identify different stages in the sales history of a product to which correspond distinct opportunities and problems and therefore strategies and tactics. Although it is not possible to find in the marketing literature a universally accepted shape for the PLC, one may consider that a reasonably well accepted description is in terms of the bell-shaped (annual sales) and S-shaped (cumulative sales) curves shown in Figure P.1. The curves are then divided into several stages known as introduction, growth, maturity and decline. These stages are generally related to different steps of the innovation/diffusion process.

The experience of BA International

When considering the past experience of comparable products – see Figure P.2 – it appears that the PLC concept applies to our products. Testing the validity of the PLC concept on past data raises a major issue, however. *Past data shows the sales history that has resulted from the management of the PLC.* When the company feels that a product is going to reach decline, measures are taken in order to sustain the sales. A company like BA International

Table P.1 ● Assessment of value created over the whole expected life of P12

A	B	C	D	E	F	G	H	I	J	K	L	M
1	2004	2005	2006	2007	2008	2009	2010	2011	2012	2013		Cum
2 Market growth		0.03	0.03	0.03	0.03	0.03	0.03	0.03	0.03	0.03		
3 Total market	5780	5953	6132	6316	6505	6701	6902	7109	7322	7542		
4 P12 segment share	0.11	0.11	0.11	0.11	0.11	0.11	0.11	0.11	0.11	0.11		
5 Market penetration	0.225	0.5	0.75	1	1	1	1	1	1	1		
6 Sales volume	143	327	506	695	716	737	759	782	805	830		
7 Unit price	33.6	33.6	33.6	33.6	33.6	33.6	33.6	33.6	33.6	33.6		
8 SALES	4.8	11.0	17.0	23.3	24.0	24.8	25.5	26.3	27.1	27.9		211.7
9 Unit cost	17.0	17.0	17.0	17.0	17.0	17.0	17.0	17.0	17.0	17.0		
10 CGS	2.4	5.6	8.6	11.8	12.2	12.5	12.9	13.3	13.7	14.1		107.2
11 Selling costs/sales	0.2	0.2	0.2	0.2	0.2	0.2	0.2	0.2	0.2	0.2		
12 Selling costs	1.0	2.2	3.4	4.7	4.8	5.0	5.1	5.3	5.4	5.6		42.3
13 Tax rate	0.4	0.4	0.4	0.4	0.4	0.4	0.4	0.4	0.4	0.4		
14 **Profit after tax**	**0.8**	**1.9**	**3.0**	**4.1**	**4.2**	**4.4**	**4.5**	**4.6**	**4.8**	**4.9**		**37.3**
15 Collection period	3	3	3	3	3	3	3	3	3	3		
16 Receivables end	1.2	2.8	4.2	5.8	6.0	6.2	6.4	6.6	6.8	7.0		
17 Inventory period production	3	3	3	3	3	3	3	3	3	3		
18 Inventory period sales	3	3	3	3	3	3	3	3	3	3		
19 Inventory end	1.2	2.7	4.1	5.7	5.8	6.0	6.2	6.4	6.6	6.8		
20 **Cash flow**	**−1.5**	**−1.1**	**0.0**	**1.0**	**3.9**	**4.0**	**4.1**	**4.3**	**4.4**	**4.5**	**13.7**	**37.3**
21 **Capital expenditure**	5.6											
22 Discount rate	0.14											
23 NPV	4.90											

Note: The background of this model is the same as the model in Table O.1 on p. 292. In order to construct this model, start from the model in Table O.1, then insert five blank columns in between columns E and F. Finally copy column E into columns F to K.

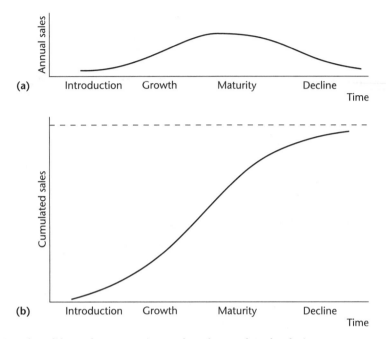

Figure P.1 Product life cycle curves (annual and cumulated sales)

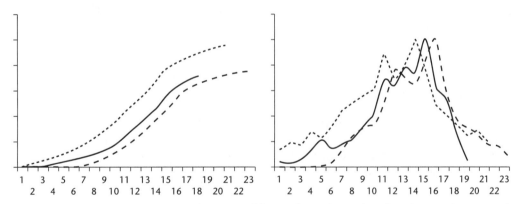

Figure P.2 Previous experience of comparable products (cumulated and annual volumes sold)

Note: Past products had long lives (20 years and more)

would never accept such a sharp decline in sales as that shown in Figure P.2. Production requirements lead to declining products being killed off quickly.

The approach used for estimating the penetration coefficients of P12 was that past data related to the introduction of the rotary oil-free compressors shows that cumulative sales have followed an S-shaped curve. The company decided to try to fit the curve generated by a popular substitution model, the Fisher and Pry model, to these data. As a good fit was found, it was decided to use this model to estimate the cumulated and annual sales of P12.

CASE

The Fisher and Pry model, a pure imitative diffusion model, aims to predict the rate at which the potential market is going to switch to a new substitute. It rests upon the assumption that the adoption process results from word-of-mouth activity initiated by the first adopters (the pioneers) and aimed at those who have not yet adopted (the followers).

In mathematical terms:

$$dF/dt = b \times F \times (1 - F)$$

where
F = the cumulative percentage of adopters of the new product at a given point in time

dF/dt = the percentage of those who are going to adopt the new product at that time

b = an industry related coefficient.

This mathematical formulation corresponds to the so-called bell-shaped curve, as can be seen from the following numerical values.

F	0%	10%	20%	30%	40%	50%	60%	70%	80%	90%	100%
$F \times (1 - F)$	0%	9%	16%	21%	24%	25%	24%	21%	16%	9%	0%

When F is small (when the pioneers are few), little word-of-mouth activity can take place and the number of new adopters is limited. When F grows, so does dF/dt, but beyond a certain threshold (50%) the number of new adopters decreases, not because word-of-mouth activity diminishes but because the market potential is now limited due to ceiling effects. In the end, only the laggards have yet to join the majority. To understand more about the industry-related coefficient b, let us consider again the numerical values below:

F		0%	10%	20%	30%	40%	50%	60%	70%	80%	90%	100%
$b = 1$	$b \times F \times (1 - F)$	0%	9%	16%	21%	24%	25%	24%	21%	16%	9%	0%
$b = 2$	$b \times F \times (1 - F)$	0%	18%	32%	42%	48%	50%	48%	42%	32%	18%	0%
$b = 1/2$	$b \times F \times (1 - F)$	0%	5%	8%	11%	12%	13%	12%	11%	8%	5%	0%

This is shown graphically in Figure P.3. Thus b plays the role of an amplifier or reducer of the impact of word-of-mouth activity. It is related to the tight, or loose, nature of contacts existing between companies in a given sector. In that respect it is an industry-related coefficient. Mathematically, the Fisher and Pry equation can be rewritten as:

$$F = \int \frac{dF}{dt} = \frac{1}{1 + e^{-b(t-t_0)}}$$

where t = time since introduction
t_0 = time when half of the market has switched to the new product.

The graphical representation of F results in the logistic curve (S-shaped) where t_0 corresponds to the inflection point (see Figure P.4).

Generating the annual coefficients

The best fit of the rotary oil-free compressors data with the curve generated by the above model was found when the b parameter was set to 1 and t_0 was set to 2008 (half of the

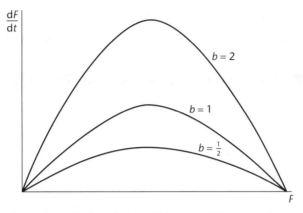

Figure P.3 Impact of the *b* coefficient in the Fisher and Pry model

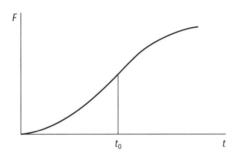

Figure P.4 Logistic curve

potential market having switched to oil-free four years after the introduction). As a result, the coefficients for generating cumulated sales at the end of each year are given by the formula:

Annual coefficient = $1 \ / \ (1 + \exp(-1 \times (\text{year} - 2008)))$

Appendix P.3

Memorandum

FROM: J. Muller, Production Engineer
TO: M. Keller, Product Planning
SUBJECT: **Re-examination of the cost/volume relationship for P12**

Cost/volume relationships constitute a very important issue in management and a voluminous amount of literature exists about them in at least two areas of management accounting and strategy.

The traditional accounting view: fixed and variable costs

In accounting, costs are traditionally analyzed into two basic categories: fixed and variable costs.

● Fixed costs are defined as those costs, the total of which does not depend on the volume of activity.
● Variable costs are defined as those costs, the total of which is a function of the level of activity.

The words fixed and variable are somewhat confusing and one should realize that they apply to total costs only. When looking at unit costs, fixed and variable costs are quite different.

● The unit cost of an item that accounting calls fixed is a function of the level of activity. Since the total cost is fixed, the unit cost is obviously low when the activity is high and high when the activity is low.
● The unit cost of an item that accounting calls variable is obviously fixed. It is because of this that the total cost is a function of the level of activity.

The concept of fixed and variable costs can be applied to P12. In the study of P12, we get the following information about the relationship between total production costs and volume:

Volume produced	Total production cost
100	1 701 300
400	6 321 200

(Data in the study actually refer to cumulative levels of production. Let us assume that these cumulative levels correspond to annual production levels of respectively 100 and 400 units.) These figures can be shown on a graph as in Figure P.5.
   When you assume that the relationship between total production cost and volume is linear, total production cost may be expressed as:

$$y = ax + b$$

where y = total production cost and x = volume.

You can calculate a and b:

$$a = (6\ 321\ 200 - 1\ 701\ 300) / (400 - 100) = 15\ 400$$
$$b = 6\ 321\ 200 - (15\ 400 \times 400) = 161\ 333$$

where a is the variable cost per unit and b the part of the total cost which is fixed and independent of volume.
   The relationship between total cost and volume enables us to derive the relationship between unit production cost and volume:

$$Y = 15\ 400 + 161\ 333 / x$$

where y = unit production cost and x = volume.

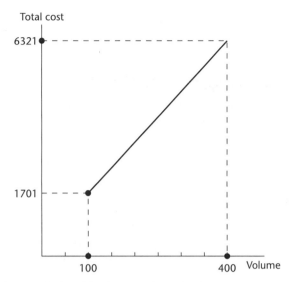

Figure P.5 Cost/volume relationship (accounting view)

The strategy approach: the concept of experience[6]

The distinction between fixed and variable costs fundamentally portrays the effect of economies of scale within a specific range of volumes. Within a specific range of volumes, among all the production costs some are fixed. When spread over more units, their impact is less and, as a result, the total unit cost decreases and ultimately tends towards the variable unit cost.

The effect of experience is a different concept that states that the unit production cost decreases, and tends towards no limit, when the cumulated volume of production increases. The relationship between unit production cost and cumulative production is known as the experience curve. The most popular way to describe the effect of experience is to say that: each time cumulated production doubles, unit production cost decreases by a constant percentage. If the learning rate is 80%, unit production cost decreases by 20% (100 – 80) each time cumulated production doubles.

The reasons why unit cost decreases with the accumulation of experience can be set out as follows:

● greater labour efficiency
● better work organization
● innovative processes
● better performance obtained from equipment
● better use of resources
● better product standardization
● product redesigns.

The concepts of experience and scale effects are not easy to distinguish since gains in experience occur at the same time as the size increases. The main difference between these two concepts is probably that the scale effect is more static and the experience effect more dynamic. The important things to realize about the experience effect are that:

- It is not automatic. Experience provides opportunities for decreasing the unit cost but these can be overlooked.
- The experience effect is difficult to measure.
  - As experience effects can generally only be observed over a long period, one should remove the impact of inflation, and also be careful with potential biases introduced by accounting measures.
  - Be careful with shared experience. A new product may benefit from the experience of products already manufactured and not correspond to a great deal of additional experience for the firm. As a result, its unit cost will not decline very quickly.
  - If it applies within an individual firm, the concept of shared experience may also apply within a whole industry.

The experience concept states that each time cumulated production doubles, the unit production cost decreases by a constant percentage. How can we express this relationship in mathematical terms? An example may help. A company has produced, as of today, 1000 units of the A product. The current unit production cost is €10. What will the unit production cost be when the company reaches production levels of 2000 and 4000 units, if the experience rate is 80%?

This question can be answered as follows:

	Current	Future	
Accumulated volumes	1000	2000	4000
Unit cost	10	$10 \times 0.8 = 8$	$8 \times 0.8 = 6.4$

You can define two variables:

X = future accumulated volume / current accumulated volume
Y = future unit cost / current unit cost

At present, X and Y are equal to 1. When cumulated volume doubles, X will be equal to 2 and Y to 0.8. When cumulated volume doubles again and becomes four times what it is today, X will be equal to 4 and Y equal to 0.64. When cumulated volume doubles again and becomes eight times what it is today X will $= 8$ and $Y = 5.12$. The values of X and Y can be plotted on a graph (Figure P.6).

The curve that fits the points corresponding to the points shown in Figure P.6 is a curve[7] corresponding to a function of the kind:

$Y = 1/X^n$ or $Y = X^{-n}$

The steepness of such a curve depends on the value of the exponent of X. Let us try with an exponent with an absolute value equal to 1:

X	1	2	4	8
$Y = X^{-1}$	1	0.5	0.25	0.125

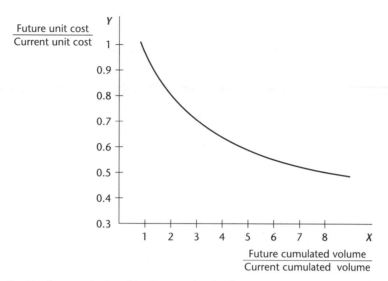

Figure P.6 Cost/volume relationship (strategic view)

This corresponds to a 50% learning curve, a curve much steeper than the 80% learning curve shown in Figure P.6. Let us now try with an exponent with an absolute value equal to 2:

X	1	2	4	8
$Y = X^{-2}$	1	0.25	0.0625	0.0156

In order to fit the points shown in Figure P.6, and, as a result, to portray an 80% experience curve, we should assign to the exponent of X an absolute value inferior to 1. Mathematics show that in order to get an experience curve of 80%, the exponent of X should have an absolute value of 0.322.[8] In this case, the relation between X and Y is: $Y = X^{-0.322}$.

Notes

1. This case was developed by the author and Bernard Dubois, Professor at Centre HEC-ISA (France). The pedagogy of this case has been developed by the author, Bernard Dubois, Sherwood Frey, Professor at Colgate Darden (USA) and Foster Rogers, Professor at IFL (Sweden).
2. Refer also to Appendix P.3.
3. Experience effects apply to existing products also. Given the large experience accumulated, the low growth and the severe competition, it was considered at BA International that the unit price of existing products would decrease by 1% per year in real terms in the coming years.
4. For more about cannibalization, refer to R. Kerin, M. Harvey and J. Rothe, 'Cannibalism and New Product Development', *Business Horizons* (Oct. 1978), pp. 25–31.
5. Models of innovation diffusion are described in Mahajan V. and Petreson R. (1985), *Models for Innovation Diffusion*, a Sage University Paper. Diffusion of innovation is discussed in E. Rogers (1995), *Diffusion of Innovations*, The Free Press. For more about the concept of substitution, refer to: M. Porter, (1985), *Competitive Advantage*, The Free Press, Ch. 8. For more about the modelling of

product life cycles, refer to V. Mahajan, E. Muller and F. Bass (1990), 'New Product Diffusion Models in Marketing: A review and directions for research', *Journal of Marketing*, January pp. 1–26; to R. Dolan and A. Jeuland (1981), 'Experience Curves and Dynamic Demand Models: Implications for optimal pricing strategies', *Journal of Marketing*, Winter, pp. 52–62; G. Lilien, P. Kotler and K. Sridhar Moorthy, *Marketing Models*, Prentice Hall (1992), and S. Mullick, G. Anderson, R. Leach and W. Smith, 'Life Cycle Forecasting', in *The Handbook of Forecasting*, S. Makridakis and S. Wheelwright (eds), John Wiley (1982).

6. For more about this concept, refer to: A. Hax and N. Majluf, 'Competitive Cost Dynamics: The experience curve', *Interfaces* (Oct. 1982), pp. 50–61; K. Clark and P. Adler (1991), 'Behind the Learning Curve: A sketch of the learning process', *Management Science*, March, pp. 267–81; W. Abernathy and K. Wayne, 'Limits of the Learning Curve' in *Survival Strategies for American Industries*, John Wiley (1983), pp. 114–31, and P.B. McNamee, *Tools and Techniques for Strategic Management*, Pergamon Press (1985), pp. 67–102.

7. The experience curve formula is usually presented as:

$$Cq = Cn \times (q/n)^{-b}$$

where Cq = cost of producing the qth unit
Cn = cost of producing the nth unit
b = experience parameter

8. The formula for calculating the exponent (n) is as follows: if ex is the experience rate (ex = 80 when learning rate is 80%)

$$n = (\ln(100) - \ln(ex))/\ln(2)$$

when the experience rate is 80: $n = (\ln(100) - \ln(80))/\ln(2) = (4.61 - 4.38)/0.69 = 0.322$

Some values of n:

Experience rate	90	85	80	75	70	65	60	50
Exponent (n)	0.152	0.234	0.322	0.415	0.515	0.621	0.737	1

CHAPTER 17

Designing a model of a new product decision

Reviewing the key design items

With the BA International II case, we now have all the data for building a trajectory model that will help us focus on the dynamics of this new product situation:

- How much spending in advance of sales is needed to get the innovation through? What is the trajectory of commitment required?
- How fast might the diffusion process develop? What might that mean in terms of volumes sold?
- How is it possible to set trajectories of prices (revenues and cost) in order to create, and maximize, value?

We also have all the data for introducing competition, both external and internal, with the issue of cannibalization. Finally, we also have data for dealing with issues such as inflation and foreign exchange, working capital, and so on.

Introducing improvements in a model is always very tempting. One should, however, always be cautious and check that such improvements make sense, that is have a significant impact on the outcome. So, let us consider each of these potential improvements one at a time and understand its unique impact on the value created.

17.1 Looking at one improvement at a time

Setting the selling costs trajectory

Launching P12 does not require BA International to commit to major new capital expenditure. However, the company will have to commit to commercial expenses: launch costs and a possible educational campaign. As discussed in Part IV, this spending that comes in advance of sales with a view to help sales materialize cannot be considered as 'driven by sales' as per-cent-of-sales models seem to assume.[1] In order to de-couple selling expenses from sales, we have to make two series of changes:

Starting from the model in Table P.1:

1. Introduce two blank rows above row 12.
2. Replace the heading in A11 by 'Variable selling cost/sales'. Enter 0.1 in B11.
3. Introduce a calculation of total cumulated selling cost in M11: =SUM(B8.K8)*0.20.
4. Use row 12 for calculating 'Variable selling costs': +B11×B8 in B12. Copy across.
5. Introduce 'Fixed selling costs' in row 13: +$M$11/6 in B13. Copy across to the range C13.D13. Erase the range E13.K13.
6. Correct the heading and formula in row 14: 'Total selling costs' in A14. Formula to be entered in B14 and to be copied: +B13+B12.
7. Put a formula in M14 and check that total selling cost is unchanged.

Figure 17.1 Introducing a more realistic timing of selling costs

Starting from the model in Table P.1:

1. Erase .11 in range C4.K4
2. Delete row 5 (market penetration)
3. Insert 3 rows above new row 5 (Sales volume)
4. Use new row 5 for 'Cumulated sales in segment'. In K5: +SUM(B3.K3)*B4
5. Use row 6 for 'Annual coefficient'. In B6: +1/(1 + EXP(−1*(B1−$F$1))); Copy across.
6. Use row 7 for 'Cumulated sales'. In B7: +B6*$K$5. Copy across.
7. Correct the formulas for sales volume. In B8: +B7; In C8: +C7−B7; Copy across.

Test: you should get the following figures:

	2004	2005	2006	2007	2008	2009	2010	2011	2012	2013
Cumulated sales in segment										7289
Annual coefficient	0.02	0.05	0.12	0.27	0.50	0.73	0.88	0.95	0.98	0.99
Cumulated sales	131	346	869	1960	3644	5328	6420	6943	7158	7240
Sales volume	131	215	523	1091	1684	1684	1091	523	215	82

Figure 17.2 Introducing a product life cycle driven sales volumes trajectory

1. We have to introduce the launch costs into the model. This is done in Figure 17.1. With the new timing of selling costs, the model returns an NPV of €1.38 m, 72% less than the base. You can check that this huge impact is a pure timing effect; cumulative profit and cash are still equal to €42.3 m.
2. We have to de-couple these launch costs from changes in selling prices. With the formula that we use for calculating fixed selling costs, these costs vary with both the volume and the price of sales. We will come back to this formula (see Chapter 19, Figure 19.4). Variable selling costs will probably also need to be somewhat de-coupled from changes in selling prices. This is done in Chapter 19.

Setting the trajectory of the volumes sold

Figure 17.2 shows how you can get sales generated according to a product life cycle concept. This makes the NPV go from €4.90 million to €7.43 million (a 52% increase)!

Starting from the model in Table P.1:

1. Insert 4 blank rows above row 9.
2. Introduce 'Cumulative volume sold' in row 9: +B6 in B9; +B9+C6 in C9; then copy across. Use a zero decimal format.
3. Use row 10 for cumulative sales at mid-year[1]: type +B9/2 in B10; +(B9+C9)/2 in C10, copy across.
4. Introduce unit material cost in row 11. Formula in B11 is: +12.151 * ((B10+830)/930)^–0.234. Copy across.

Test: you can check that you get the following unit material cost figures:

2004	2005	2006	2007	2008	2009	2010	2011	2012	2013
12.2	11.6	10.8	10.0	9.3	8.9	8.5	8.2	7.9	7.7

Format: one decimal

5. Introduce unit assembly packaging and transport costs in row 12. Formula to be entered in B12 is: +(17.013–12.151)*((B10+2200)/2300)^–0.234. Copy across.

Test: you can check that you obtain the following unit costs for assembly, packaging and transport:

2004	2005	2006	2007	2008	2009	2010	2011	2012	2013
4.9	4.8	4.6	4.4	4.2	4.1	3.9	3.8	3.7	3.6

Format: one decimal

6. Change the calculation of unit production cost in B13. This should become: +B11 +B12. Copy across.

Figure 17.3 How to set unit cost on a learning curve trajectory
1. Manufacturing cost is an average figure for the year, consequently you should not evaluate it from the end unit cost but from the unit cost at mid-year instead. Also note that cumulated volume drives both experience and product life cycle.

Setting the cost/prices trajectories: unit production costs and selling prices

In the base model, unit production cost is considered as a constant. This is hardly acceptable. The process for setting the unit production cost on a learning curve trajectory is described in Figure 17.3. When the impact of experience is introduced into the model, the NPV becomes €10.59 m, a very sharp increase compared to the base (a 116% increase).

When you have introduced formulas that describe the impact of experience, you can check that the results displayed behave as expected. You will see that unit material cost decreases quicker than unit assembly and other costs, because there is less accumulated experience for material, and that you have to wait until 2009 in order to double the experience related to assembly and other costs, and to gain 15% on unit costs. You can also draw a graph (see Figure 17.4) showing unit material cost, unit assembly and other costs and total unit production costs. One interesting thing to note in the graph is the small bump in the curves in 2005. *In order to obtain smooth curves you should plot unit cost against cumulative experience and not against time.*[2] The dramatic impact of experience calls for three questions:

1. How sure can we be about the fact that experience will be 85%?
   - If it were 80% (exponent = 0.322), NPV would be 12.32 m, 152% more than the base.
   - If it were 90% (exponent = 0.152), NPV would still be 8.79 m, 80% more than the base.

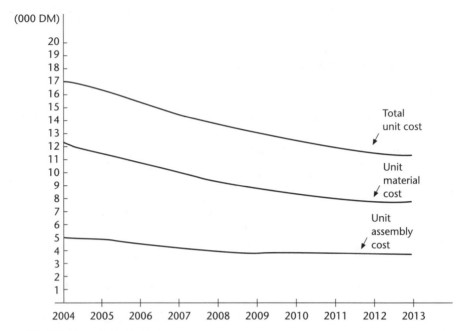

Figure 17.4 Unit costs trajectories

2. How sure can we be about the values assigned to previous experience?
   – If previous experience for material were 913 (10% more), NPV would be €10.41 m, 113% more than the base.
   – If previous experience for assembly were 2420 (10% more), NPV would be equal to €10.53 m, 115% more than the base.
3. How can we be sure that BA International is going to reap all the effects of experience from its suppliers? Since the company's operations consist mainly of assembly work, most of the experience effects are going to take place with the suppliers. In order to benefit from experience BA International will have to put a lot of pressure on its suppliers and get them to price their products along the experience curve. This is possible provided that BA International manages its relationships with suppliers effectively.

The need to take the experience on existing products into account: the concept of differential experience

The assumption in the model is that P12 is going to be sold at a premium of 15% above existing oil-lubricated products. This gives a price of €33 600 for P12 in 2004, but if experience applies to existing oil-lubricated products, their cost (and because of competition, their price) is going to decline with the increase in cumulative volume. Therefore, in order to keep a 15% premium above these products the P12 price should follow the same evolution as the existing oil-lubricated compressors (decreasing by 1% a year as indicated on page 313). The company is not going to benefit from its experience with P12 but rather from the differential between its experience with P12 and that of the existing products.

In order to introduce this into the model you have to change the calculation of unit selling price. To do so, starting from the model we adjusted for experience, in B7 enter +33.6*(1–0.01)^(B1–2004), and copy across. When you have done so, the model generates an NPV equal to €8.90 m: +82% more than the base (instead of +116%).

Using parity relations to eliminate the 'noise' caused by inflation and foreign exchange

As it is now, the initial model does not treat inflation[3] in a consistent way. Prices of revenue and cost items are considered as not affected by inflation: they are just constant in the model in P1 and they are changed in relation to 'real' (non-inflation-related) factors in the section above. Also, the discount rate embodies a 3% annual inflation.

In order to be consistent we should either:

• increase prices of revenue and cost items by 3% a year and keep the discount rate as it is;

or

• keep prices of revenue and cost items as they are and remove the 3% inflation from the discount rate.

Since the second alternative is much easier to implement, let us change the discount rate and make it equal to: $(1.14/1.03) – 1 = 0.107$. When you do so you get an NPV equal to €8.22 m, 68% more than the base. This 'real prices / real rate' approach is used a great deal in practice. Among its major advantages are its consistency and its simplicity.

Using the 'real prices / real rate' approach may introduce a bias in your models

Let us check, however, that the real price / real rate approach gives the same results as the current prices and discount rate equal to the current interest rate. In order to do so, you can modify the base model as follows:

1. Insert a row above row 2 and enter inflation rate in A2 and the value of the inflation rate 0.03 in B2.
2. Change, in row 8, the estimates of unit selling prices. In B8 enter: +33.6*(1+$B$2), in C8:+B8*(1+$B$2), copy across.
3. Change, in row 10, the estimates of unit production cost. In Bl0 enter: +17.013*(1+$B$2), in Cl0: +B10*(1+$B$2), copy across.
4. Introduce a formula to calculate the discount rate in B27: (1.14/1.03*(1+B2))–1.
5. Change the NPV calculation in order to get the NPV at the end of 2003: –B23+NPV(B24, B22.L22).

When you run the model, you find the following results:

NPV real prices / real rate (B2 = zero)   = 9.10 (the same as 8.22 at the end of 2002)
NPV current prices / current rate (B2 = 0.03) = 7.61

Contrary to what we were expecting, the two methods do not give the same results and the NPV estimated with current prices and current interest rate is 16% lower. Why is this? The two methods make the same assumption about inflation, and consider it as neutral, giving the same price evolution of revenue and cost items. But they differ in their treatment of the impact of inflation related to working capital needs. The constant prices method ignores this impact whereas the current prices method takes it into account. If this is not clear to you, you can make all the collection and inventory periods equal to zero, then you will get an NPV equal to 14.54 m with both methods. You can check further that you always get a 14.54 m NPV with both methods whatever the inflation rate is (provided that the discount rate remains equal to $(1.14/1.03) \times (1 + \text{inflation rate})$).

When there are no working capital needs, then the real/real method gives the correct result. When there are positive working capital needs, then the real/real method tends to overestimate the NPV and when there are negative working capital needs, it tends to underestimate the NPV.

What about the impact of depreciation?

Depreciation is ignored in the model as it is. You can check what would happen when it is introduced. Starting from the modified model with inflation set at 0 in B2 and collection and inventory periods also set to 0:

1. Insert a blank row above row 14 and use it for depreciation (1/5 of capital expenditures for the period 2004–8).
2. Correct the calculation of profit after tax: =(B9–B11–B13–B14)*(1–B15)
3. Correct the calculation of cash flow: +B16–B18–B21+B14 in B22 and +C16–B18–B21+ C18+C21+B14 in C22. Copy across.

When this is done you get an NPV equal to €16.22 m. With a 3% inflation rate the NPV decreases to 16.09 and with a 10% rate to 15.84.

Why does NPV decrease with inflation? This is due to the tax impact of depreciation[4] which gives a tax shield, the value of which is fixed (since it is based on the value of the acquisition cost of the assets). As a result the more inflation the less the value of the tax shield as compared to the overall cash flows.

What, then, can we conclude?

In spite of its consistency and simplicity the real / rate constant / price method somewhat overestimates the NPV (due to positive working capital needs and depreciation) or underestimates the NPV (due to negative working capital needs). This estimation error may be important especially when working capital needs are high. In the initial model the overestimation of the NPV may seem to be sufficiently high to make us prefer the current prices / current rate approach. We have to realize, however, that the initial model significantly overestimates working capital needs[5] (no impact of accounts payable, long inventory periods). When you compare the two methods with a more realistic description of working capital needs you realize that the difference between them is in the range of 10%. So let us keep the model simple and adopt the real / rate constant / price approach.

We must also consider **currency rate variations**. If BA International goes ahead with P12, it will sell this product in many different countries. The base model ignores this and assumes that all sales of P12 will be made in Europe, or, rather, that all sales made in any other country will be equivalent to sales made in Europe. This assumption is true provided that

● either sales to foreign countries will be made in euros, which is not realistic;
● or that sales to foreign countries will be made in foreign currencies at prices such that they will offset any future changes in the exchange rate between these foreign currencies and the euro.

This second assumption is consistent with a well-known principle in international economics and finance, the **purchasing power parity law**. This states that in the long run, on the average, changes in prices and in currency exchange rates offset each other.

Even though many deviations from purchasing power parity exist, this relationship is very important. First, it helps you to realize that currency exchange rate variations are not a problem in themselves. What really matters is the possible imbalance between changes in prices in the foreign currency and changes in exchange rates. Secondly, it helps you to simplify problems such as the one we are dealing with. Because BA International is strong in its markets, we can assume that, on average, and in the long run, it will be able, through price increases, to pass on the impact of exchange rate variations to its customers.

Although when modelling a problem like the decision to launch P12 it is generally acceptable to start by ignoring the impact of currency risk and to plan as if the product were to be sold in the local currency, it is necessary in practice to return to the model afterwards and to reflect on:

● the impact of short-term discrepancies between changes in prices and changes in exchange rates. The purchasing power parity law is fundamentally a law that is valid over the long term;

● the impact of medium-term discrepancies. Recent monetary history has shown that some currencies could be undervalued or overvalued over a relatively long period. Some companies have been able to build a competitive advantage from this whilst others have suffered losses. The problem remains, however, to know whether or not it is possible to predict such competitive advantages. Most of the theories available today tell us that this is not really possible.

Returning to BA International and P12, let us assume as a first step that it is reasonable to consider that the purchasing power parity law is going to hold. We can thus ignore currency rate variations, an assumption which simplifies the calculations. At a later stage, we will analyze the currency risk resulting from possible deviations from purchasing power parity (see the appendix to Chapter 19).

Cannibalization as a description of the interactions with current products

When you evaluate the impact of a new decision, you should evaluate the incremental cash flows caused by this new decision, and should account for the negative impact that this decision may have on the existing business. The process for introducing the impact of cannibalization is described in Figure 17.5. When cannibalization is introduced, the NPV is 3.95, that is 19% less than in the initial model. Is our description of cannibalization correct? In order to evaluate it, we need to make an assumption about who is going to buy P12. At present, we assume that P12 will be bought by a wide range of customers among whom the present customers of BA International will not represent a percentage higher than the present market share of the company. Consequently, the impact of cannibalization is relatively small.

Another assumption would be that P12 will be bought primarily by the existing customers of BA International. It might happen that any sale of P12 would replace the sale of an existing product, and then the impact of cannibalization would become much bigger, as shown in Figure 17.6. As we do not have detailed data about who the customers of P12 might be, let us consider that our description of cannibalization is correct.

1. In row 28 introduce 'Big firms as a % of total customers', 0.5 in B28; copy across (range C to F).
2. Use row 29 for 'Market share with big firms': 0.13 in B29; copy across (range C to F). (Format: two decimals.)
3. Put in row 30 'Market share with small firms': 0.10 in B30, copy across (range C to F).
4. Put in row 31 'Margin with big firms': 8 in B31. Copy across.
5. Put in row 32 'Margin with small firms': 4 in B32. Copy across.
6. Introduce in row 33 the calculation of 'Margin lost on existing products': type in B33: +((B6*B28*B29*B31)+(B6*(1−B28)*B30*B32))/1000. Copy across.
7. Calculate 'Cash flow after cannibalization' in row 34: +B23−B33 in B34 and copy across (range C to L).
8. Calculate 'NPV after cannibalization' in B35: +(NPV(B22,B34.L34)−B21)/(1+B22).

Figure 17.5 Introducing cannibalization

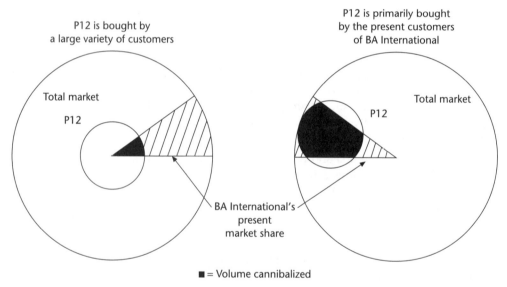

■ = Volume cannibalized

Figure 17.6 Two models of cannibalization

Introducing competitive interactions

The influence diagram in Figure 17.7 describes how BA International evaluates the sales of P12. This diagram calls for some comment. First, the size of the segment of P12 is not very dependent on the marketing strategy for P12. More precisely, it ignores the alternatives available to BA International in terms of the selection of specific national and/or industrial segments. The approach at BA International deliberately ignores one key concept in marketing, the concept of **market segmentation**. Even though one may question the existence of a homogeneous market for all countries and industries, one can accept such a homogeneity as an assumption necessary to keep the problem manageable. What should be kept in mind, however, is that because of this simplification, we will only be able to derive broad strategies for P12 at the worldwide level. These will not be very operational as they will not

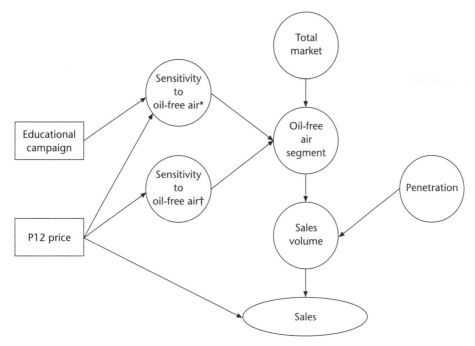

Figure 17.7 A model of the drivers of P12's sales
* Non-naturally oil-free sensitive customers (maintenance argument)
† Naturally oil-free sensitive customers

tell us which specific segments should be attacked. Detailed operational strategies will be elaborated at a later stage in the sales subsidiaries. When formulating these strategies, subsidiaries will have to identify the market segments for P12 and its positioning on these segments. This two-step approach obviously presents risks since the decision to launch P12 will be taken using simplified data which may not completely reflect the complex data of the different national and industrial market segments. The role of the Headquarters is to try to limit this risk, whilst keeping the worldwide model simple enough so as not to be submerged in details. So let us assume that the model used by BA International Headquarters is a fairly good compromise between simplicity and accuracy.

Secondly the penetration factor does not appear as a variable that can be influenced by BA International. Let us assume, as we have already done earlier, that this factor reflects a more general parameter related to the shape of the life cycle of P12.

A third point is that sales are driven by the market and not by production. This assumes that there will not be any major manufacturing problems, to which we shall return later.

Finally, competition is absent from the diagram. This seems an unrealistic assumption since competition may exist as early as 2004 and in any case will start to exist in 2009. The impact of competition can be entered in the model through an additional variable, market share. The process for doing so is described in Figure 17.8.

The new model returns a 3.24 m NPV, 34% less than the base. This description of competition corresponds to the minimum reaction of other manufacturers, and it might

1. Insert a blank row above row 6 and use it for market share: 1 in 2004; copy into range C6. F6; 0.8 in G6; 0.6 in H6. Copy across.
2. Change the formula for calculating sales volume in B7: +B3*B4*B5*B6. Copy across.

Figure 17.8 Introducing competition

1. Insert two rows above row 20; in row 20 introduce payment period (3 for 3 months).
2. In row 21 introduce accounts payable end. The formula to enter in B21 is:
   +(B10+B19)*12.151/17.013/12* B20.
   In C21: +(C10+C19−B19)*12.151/17.013/12*C20. Copy across.
3. Modify the formula for calculating Cash flow in B22: +B14−B16−B19+B21;
   In C22: +C14−C16+B16−C19+B19+C21−B21; copy across.

Test: you should get the following key figures:

	2004	2005	2006	2007	2008	2009	2010	2011	2012	2013	2014
Payables end	0.6	1.3	1.8	2.4	2.2	2.3	2.3	2.4	2.5	2.6	
Cash flow	−0.9	−0.5	0.6	1.6	3.7	4.1	4.2	4.3	4.5	4.6	11.2

Format: one decimal

Figure 17.9 Introducing accounts payable

well happen, as we have seen, that they offer a similar product as early as 2004. In this case the NPV falls to 0.96 m, 80% less than the base.

Correcting the inventories

There are two corrections to make at this level. First, you should introduce a formula that estimates inventories end in relation to next year's sales. In order to do so you have to modify the formulas in row 19: +((C10/1.09)/12*B18)+(C10/12*B19) in B19; then copy across. When this is done you can check that inventory end in 2013 is zero and that NPV becomes DM 4.67 m or 5% less than the base, a small difference. You should then correct the value of inventory periods. When this is done (with the new inventory calculations), you get an NPV of DM 5.85 m, 19% more than the base.

Introducing the impact of accounts payable

The procedure for introducing accounts payable in the base model is described in Figure 17.9. This modified model generates a DM 5.93 m NPV, 21% more than the base.

Correcting the impact of corporation tax

In order to introduce depreciation, you can proceed as described in Figure 17.10. When the tax rate is 0.4, NPV is equal to DM 6.25 m (28% more than the base). When the tax rate is 0.3, NPV is equal to DM 8.41 m (72 % more than base). When depreciation is introduced, profit before tax becomes negative and as the model is built, tax becomes negative also.

1. Insert a row above row 13 and introduce depreciation in B13: +$B$22/5; copy into C13.F13.
2. Correct the calculation of profit after tax in row 15: in B15: +(B8–B10–B12–B13)*(1–B14);
    then copy across.
3. Correct the calculation of Cash flow in row 21: In B21: +B15–B17–B20 + B13;
    in C21: +C15–C17–C20+B17+B20+B13.

Test. check that you get the following key figures (with a 30% tax rate):

	2004	2005	2006	2007	2008	2009	2010	2011	2012	2013	2014
Profit	0.2	1.5	2.7	4.0	4.2	5.1	5.2	5.4	5.6	5.7	
Cash	1.0	−0.5	0.9	2.0	4.9	4.7	4.9	5.0	5.2	5.3	13.7

Format: one decimal

Figure 17.10 Introducing depreciation

This is acceptable provided that the other activities of BA International are profitable; the loss due to P12 will provide the company with a tax credit which will decrease its overall corporation tax.

Is it worth introducing production and a better estimate of CGS?

BA International works according to a 'produce-then-sell' business model and production continuously leads on sales – by six months in the initial model.

In order to describe the operations of BA International more accurately, we could:

● estimate the trajectories of both sales and production, and
● calculate CGS as the difference between production cost and change in inventories (inventories of finished goods).

The process for modifying the initial model and introducing production and a better estimate of CGS is shown in Figure 17.11. When modified as described, the model returns an NPV equal to DM 4.67 m, which is exactly the NPV obtained when inventories are calculated on future sales. This equivalence was to be expected: prices do not change and as a result inventories do not cause the 'delaying' and 'catching-up' effects described in Chapter 10.

One should then check what happens when unit costs of production change. When you do so, you realize that the introduction of production and the better estimate of CGS do not really change the NPV. As a result, let us decide to keep our initial estimate of CGS.

Modelling the impact of an alternative design feature and realizing in the end that this feature is of no use is both useful and frustrating. For this reason I shall not describe in the main text the process for testing that the better calculation of CGS does not make a difference even when prices change. However, if you are interested in checking it by yourself, please go through the appendix to this chapter.

17.2 Reviewing all our design improvements

Many of the corrections we have made have a significant impact on the NPV, and at this stage it is very difficult to get any feeling about what the NPV attached to the launching of

1. Introduce 10 blank rows above row 9.
2. In row 9 introduce 'Inventory period production'.
3. In row 10 introduce 'Inventory period sales'.
4. In row 11 introduce 'Inventory end production'. The formula[1] in B12 is +C6/12*B9. (Format: zero decimal.) Copy the formula across.
5. In row 12 introduce 'Inventory end sales'. The formula in B12 is +C6/12*B10. Copy the formula across.
6. In row 13 introduce production volume. Type in B13: +B6+B11+B12.
   In C13: +C6+C11+C12–B11–B12. Copy across.
7. Use row 14 for 'Unit production cost 1'. Enter 15.608 in B14; +B14 in C14. Copy across.
8. Introduce 'Production cost 1' in row 15. The formula in B15 is +B13*B14/1000. Copy across.
9. Use row 16 for 'Packaging and transport'. The formula in B16 is: +B14*0.09*(B6+B12)/1000.
   In Cl6: +C14*0.09*(C6+C12–B12)/1000. Copy across.
10. Introduce 'Production cost 2' in row 17. The formula is: +B15+B16. You can copy across.

Test: you can check that you get the following key figures:

	2004	2005	2006	2007	2008	2009	2010	2011	2012	2013
Production volume	307	417	600	705	726	748	771	794	817	415
Production cost2	5.1	7.0	10.1	12.0	12.3	12.7	13.1	13.5	13.9	7.3

Format: zero decimal for production volume and one decimal for cost

11. Use row 18 for inventory end, the formula[2] in B18 is +((B11*B14)+(B12*B14*1.09))/1000. Copy across.
12. Correct CGS in row 20: +B17–B18 in B20; +C17–C18+B18 in C20. Copy across.
13. Delete row 19 (unit cost)

Test: you can check that you get the following figures for CGS:

	2004	2005	2006	2007	2008	2009	2010	2011	2012	2013
CGS	2.4	5.6	8.6	11.8	12.2	12.5	12.9	13.3	13.7	14.1

Format: one decimal

14. Change the formulas for inventory in row 28. In B30 type +B18 and copy across.
15. Delete rows 26 and 27 (inventory periods)

Figure 17.11 Introducing a better calculation of CGS
1. Inventory is related to expected sales.
2. The formula assumes that inventory end is evaluated at the average production cost during the year which is not adequate when unit production costs change significantly.

P12 could actually be once all the changes are incorporated in the model. The corrections made are reviewed in Table 17.1. Note that some changes impact the timing of the cash flows but not their cumulated value.

Appendix: Impact of alternative calculations of CGS when prices change

Towards the end of the chapter, we described the process for introducing production and a better calculation of CGS (Figure 17.11). Let us now introduce price changes in the model and compare the results with those of the initial model – with the same price changes. As shown in Figure 17.12, the NPV is not changed significantly.

Table 17.1 ● Reviewing all model improvements

	Total cumulated free cash flow	% difference with initial	NPV	% difference with initial
Initial model	31.7		4.90	
Trajectory of selling costs	31.7	no change	1.38	−72%
Trajectory of sales volumes	37.2	18%	7.43	+52%
Trajectory of:				
unit production costs (85% experience)	46.6	47%	10.59	+116%
differential experience	41.3	30%	8.90%	+82%
Cannibalization	29.9	−5%	3.95	−19%
Competition enters in 2009	23.3	−27%	3.24	−34%
Competition enters in 2004	16.7	−47%	0.96	−80%
Inventories (on future sales)	31.7	no change	4.67	−5%
Inventories (future + new periods)	31.7	no change	5.85	+19%
Accounts payable	31.7	no change	5.93	+21%
Depreciation (tax at 40%)	33.9	+7%	6.25	+28%
Depreciation (tax at 30%)	39.6	+25%	8.41	+72%
Alternative CGS calculation (and inventory on future sales)	31.7	no change	4.67	−5%

Introducing price changes in the model of Figure 17.11

1. Introduce three rows above row 14.
2. Use row 14 for cumulated production at year end: +B13 in B14; +B14+C13 in C14; Copy across.
3. Use row 15 for cumulated production at mid-year: +B14/2 in B15; +(B14+C14)/2 in C15; copy across.
4. In row 16, calculate unit production cost at year end 1. Let us not dissociate material and assembly and apply a single 80% experience rate: +15.608*((B14+830)/930)^−0.234 in B16. Copy across.
5. In row 17, Change the formula for unit production cost (mid-year): =15.608*((B15+830)/930)^−0.234 in B17. Copy across.
6. Calculate the inventories based on production cost at year end. In B21: ((B11*B16)+(B12*B16*1.09))/1000. Copy across.

Test: you should get an NPV of 11.155 with a three decimal format.

Introducing price changes in the initial model adjusted for future related inventory (p. 324)

1. Check that the inventory periods are all equal to 3.
2. Insert three rows above row 9. Calculate cumulated sales at year end in row 9 and cumulated sales at mid-year in row 10.
3. In row 11, introduce unit cost 1. Type in B11: =15.608*((B10+830)/930)^−0.234. Copy across.
4. In row 12, correct the formula for unit cost (unit cost 2): +B11*1.09: Copy across.

Test: you should get an NPV of 11.149 with a three decimal format, basically the same as with the other approach.

Figure 17.12 Alternative CGS estimates

Notes

1. One of the challenges that you often encounter when building models is the difficulty in identifying the real causes or *drivers* of the different revenues and costs. The accounting profession is now becoming aware of the need to understand the nature of the cost drivers. Among the rapidly growing literature on 'new' costing approaches and systems: R. Kaplan and R. Cooper (1998), *Cost and Effect*, Harvard Business School Press; C. Berliner and J. Brimson (eds), (1988), *Cost Management for Today's Advanced Manufacturing*, Harvard Business School Press; J. Borden, 'Review of Literature on Activity-Based Costing', *Cost Management* (Spring 1990) pp. 5–13; M. Bromwich and A. Hopwood (eds), (1986), *Research and Current Issues in Management Accounting*, Pitman; R. Cooper, 'You Need a New Cost System When . . .', *Harvard Business Review* (Jan.–Feb. 1989), pp. 77–82; T. Johnson and R. Kaplan (1987), *Relevance Lost,* Harvard Business School Press; R. Kaplan (ed.), (1990), *Measures for Manufacturing Excellence*, Harvard Business School Press; Y. Monden and K. Hamada, 'Target Costing and Kaizen Costing in Japanese Automobile Companies', *Journal of Management Accounting Research* (Fall 1991) pp. 16–34; M. Robinson (ed.), 'Contribution Margin Analysis: No Longer Relevant, Strategic Cost Management: The New Paradigm', *Journal of Management Accounting Research* (Fall 1990), 2: pp. 1–32.
2. You can obtain such a graph by using the X–Y type graph of your spreadsheet. In order to do so, define the X range as cumulative sales, and the Y ranges as the unit material cost, the unit assembly cost and the total unit cost.
3. By inflation we mean a global increase in prices which affects equally revenues and costs.
4. For more about this, you can refer to: C.R. Nelson, 'Inflation and Capital Budgeting', *Journal of Finance* (June 1976), 31: 923–31, and J.R. Ezzell and W.A. Kelly Jr, 'An APV Analysis of Capital Budgeting Under Inflation', *Financial Management* (Autumn 1984), pp. 49–54.
5. One danger of modelling. Looking at one improvement at a time is generally very effective. However, this process could have made us miss one of the impacts of inflation. Looking at one improvement at a time is fully acceptable only when the improvements are independent of one another.

CHAPTER *18*

Building an improved model

18.1 Building the model

It is now time to come back to the initial model and to incorporate in it all the new design improvements that we have analyzed so far. In order to do so, you have to go back to the base model and introduce successively into it each of the improvements described in Chapter 17 except for the alternative calculation of CGS. Before doing so, you should think about the best sequence for this. My proposal is to start, not with the base model but rather with the model adjusted for cannibalization (NPV = 3.95). You can then successively enter the following design improvements:

1. New sales volumes trajectory. NPV becomes 6.07 (the NPV before cannibalization is 7.43).
2. Competition enters in 2009. NPV becomes 4.58.
3. Differential experience. NPV becomes 9.60.
4. New trajectory of sales costs. NPV becomes 6.98.
5. Depreciation and 30% tax rate: NPV becomes 11.04.
6. Inventory. NPV becomes 11.91.
7. Accounts payable. NPV becomes 12.76.
8. Real discount rate. NPV is DM 17.85 m.

Obviously you may prefer to adopt another sequence. I shall not, therefore, give you the detailed steps to take, but you will find instead, in Tables 18.1 and 18.2, a description of the completed model.

329

Table 18.1 • Foreground of the improved model

A	B	C	D	E	F	G	H	I	J	K	L	M
1	2004	2005	2006	2007	2008	2009	2010	2011	2012	2013	2014	Cum.
2 Market growth		0.03	0.03	0.03	0.03	0.03	0.03	0.03	0.03	0.03		
3 Total market	5780	5953	6132	6316	6505	6701	6902	7109	7322	7542		
4 P12 segment share	0.11											
5 Cumulated sales in segment										7289		
6 Annual coefficient	0.02	0.05	0.12	0.27	0.50	0.73	0.88	0.95	0.98	0.99		
7 Cumulated sales at year end	131	346	869	1960	3644	5328	6420	6943	7158	7240		
8 Sales volume (no competition)	131	215	523	1091	1684	1684	1091	523	215	82		
9 Market share	1.0	1.0	1.0	1.0	1.0	0.8	0.6	0.6	0.6	0.6		
10 Sales volume	131	215	523	1091	1684	1347	655	314	129	49		
11 Unit price	33.6	33.3	32.9	32.6	32.3	32.0	31.6	31.3	31.0	30.7		
12 **SALES**	**4.4**	**7.1**	**17.2**	**35.6**	**54.4**	**43.1**	**20.7**	**9.8**	**4.0**	**1.5**		**198**
13 Cumulative volume sold	131	346	869	1960	3644	4992	5647	5960	6089	6139		
14 Cum. volume sold at mid-year	66	238	607	1415	2802	4318	5319	5803	6025	6114		
15 Unit material cost	12.3	11.8	11.0	9.9	8.8	8.1	7.8	7.7	7.6	7.6		
16 Unit assembly cost	4.9	4.8	4.6	4.4	4.1	3.8	3.7	3.6	3.6	3.6		
17 Unit cost	17.1	16.6	15.6	14.3	12.9	12.0	11.5	11.3	11.2	11.2		
18 CGS	2.2	3.6	8.2	15.6	21.7	16.1	7.5	3.5	1.4	0.6		80
19 Variable selling costs/sales	0.1	0.1	0.1	0.1	0.1	0.1	0.1	0.1	0.1	0.1		
20 Variable selling costs	0.4	0.7	1.7	3.6	5.4	4.3	2.1	1.0	0.4	0.2		40
21 Launch costs	6.6	6.6	6.6									

											Total
22 Selling costs	7.0	7.3	8.3	3.6	5.4	4.3	2.1	1.0	0.4	0.2	40
23 Depreciation	1.1	1.1	1.1	1.1	1.1						
24 Tax rate	0.3	0.3	0.3	0.3	0.3	0.3	0.3	0.3	0.3	0.3	
25 **Profit after tax**	**-4.2**	**-3.4**	**-0.3**	**10.7**	**18.3**	**15.8**	**7.8**	**3.7**	**1.5**	**0.6**	**51**
26 Collection period	3	3	3	3	3	3	3	3	3	3	
27 Receivables end	1.1	1.8	4.3	8.9	13.6	10.8	5.2	2.5	1.0	0.4	
28 Inventory period production	3	2	1	1	1	1	1	1	1	1	
29 Inventory period sales	3	2	2	2	2	2	2	2	2	2	
30 Inventory end	1.7	2.6	3.8	5.3	3.9	1.8	0.9	0.4	0.1	0.0	
31 Payment period	3	3	3	3	3	3	3	3	3	3	
32 Payables end	0.7	0.8	1.7	3.0	3.6	2.5	1.2	0.5	0.2	0.1	
33 Cash flow (before cannibalization)	-5.2	-3.8	-2.0	7.2	16.6	19.6	13.0	6.3	2.9	1.2	56
34 Capital expenditure	5.6										
35 **Free cash flow**	**-10.8**	**-3.8**	**-2.0**	**7.2**	**16.6**	**19.6**	**13.0**	**6.3**	**2.9**	**1.2**	**51**
36 Discount rate	10.7%										
37 NPV before cannibalization	19.4										
38 Big firms as % total	0.5	0.5	0.5	0.5	0.5						
39 Market share with big firms	0.13	0.13	0.13	0.13	0.13						
40 Market share with small firms	0.10	0.10	0.10	0.10	0.10						
41 Margin large firms	8	8	8	8	8						
42 Margin small firms	4	4	4	4	4						
43 Margin lost	0.1	0.2	0.4	0.8	1.2						
44 **Cash flow (after cannibalization)**	**-5.3**	**-3.9**	**-2.3**	**6.4**	**15.4**	**19.6**	**13.0**	**6.3**	**2.9**	**1.2**	**54**
45 **NPV**	**17.8**										

Table 18.2 ● Background of the improved model

C2; B3; B4; B9; B19; B24; B26; B28; B29; B31; B34; B38; B39; B40; B41; B42: Data

D2 =C2; Copy	B20: =B12*B19; Copy
C3: =B3*(1+C2); Copy	B21: =+$M$19/6; Copy to C21.D21; Copy
K5: =SUM(B3:K3)*B4	B22: =B20+B21
B6: =1/(1+EXP(−1*(B1−$F$1))); Copy	B23: =B34/5; C23: =B23; Copy
B7: =B6*$K$5; Copy	B25: =(B12−B18−B22−B23)*(1−B24); Copy
B8: =B7; C8: =C7−B7; Copy	B27: =B12/12*B26; Copy
B10: =B8*B9; Copy	B30: =(C18/1.09/12*B28)+(C18/12*B29); Copy
B11: =33.6*(1−0.01)^(B1−$B$1); Copy	B32: =(B18+B30)*12.151/17.013/12*B31
B12: =B10*B11/1000; Copy	B33: =B25+B23−B27−B30+B32
B13: =B10; C13: =B13+C10; Copy	B35: =B33−B34; Copy
B14: =B13/2; C14: =(B13+C13)/2; Copy	B36: =(1+0.14)/1.03−1
B15: =12.151*((B14+830)/930)^−0.234; Copy	B37: =(NPV(B36;B33:L33)−B34)/(1+B36)
B17: =B15+B16; Copy	B44: =B33−B43; Copy
B18: =B17*B10/1000	B45: =(NPV(B36;B44:L44)−B34)/(1+B36)
M19: =SUM(B12:K12)*0.2	

B16: =(17.013−12.151)*((B14+2200)/2300)^−0.234; Copy
C32: =(C18+C30−B30)*12.151/17.013/12*C31; Copy
C33: =C25+C23−C27−C30+C32+B27+B30−B32; Copy
B43: =((B10*B38*B39*B41)+(B10*(1−B38)*B40*B42))/1000; Copy

18.2 The results: how robust are they?

When you have incorporated all the improvements described in Chapter 17 (except for CGS) in the base model, you get an NPV equal to €17.8 m. Our previous analysis has shown how sensitive the NPV is. How confident can we be about this €17.8 m estimate? Let us perform some sensitivity analysis. The results are shown in Table 18.3.

What do the results indicate? NPV is most sensitive to unit price factors and especially to unit selling price. If we had the opportunity to check data and relationships further, we should give priority to these unit price data and relationships.

The €17.8 m result seems, however, fairly robust. P12 should be launched and this decision should allow BA International to do better than just recoup its development cost. One thing to note is that the same sensitivity analysis would have given different results if performed earlier. If performed, for example, on the initial model, a sensitivity analysis would have shown that NPV was extremely sensitive to unit price estimates and generally very sensitive to changes in any parameter. We actually had a chance of seeing this when working on improving the initial model.

Table 18.3 ● Sensitivity analysis

Driver	% change	NPV at 10.7%	% change with base
Base		**17.8**	
Market size (5780)	+10%	20.5	+15%
	−10%	15.2	−15%
Growth (3%)	+10%	18.2	+2%
	−10%	17.5	−2%
P12 segment size (11%)	+10%	20.5	+15%
	−10%	15.2	−15%
Diffusion	Faster (50% in 2007)[a]	23.6	+32%
	Slower (50% in 2009)	12.4	−30%
Life	1 year more[b]	21.3	+19%
	1 year less	15.0	−16%
Sales price[c]	+10%	23.3	+31%
	−10%	12.4	−31%
Unit production cost	+10%[d]	14.7	−18%
	−10%	21.0	+18%
	90% experience curve[e]	15.1	−15%
	80% experience curve	20.5	+15%
	10% more past experience[e]	18.1	+2%
	10% less past experience	17.7	−2%
Variable selling costs	+10%	17.1	−4%
	−10%	18.6	+4%
Fixed launch costs	+10%	16.8	−6%
	−10%	18.9	+6%
Margin cannibalized	+10%[f]	17.7	−1%
	−10%	18.0	+1%
Capital expenditure	+10%	17.5	−2%
	−10%	18.2	+2%
Collection period	+10%	17.6	−1%
	−10%	18.1	+1%
Discount rate	+10% (12%)	15.6	−13%
	−10% (9.3%)	20.4	+13%

[a] For faster, set coefficient at 0.9 and change $F$1 into $E$1. For slower, set coefficient at 1.1 and change $F$1 into $G$1.
[b] For 1 year more insert a column in between F and G and copy column F into G.H. Correct market share. For 1 year less, change the calculation of P12 segment: in J5: =sum(B3.J3)*B4. Change the formula for cumulated sales in row 6: +$J$5*B6. Then erase, not delete, K1.K32.
[c] The reference 33.6 is 10% more or less, and then the 1% decrease a year applies.
[d] The reference material and assembly costs in 2004 are 10% less or more.
[e] On both material and assembly.
[f] On both big and large firms.

Making the model work for us

Let us finally come back to the purpose of the model: to help us evaluate the end points of decision diagrams like the one in Figure 16.1 (page 295). In order to make such a task easier let us change the model again with a view to introducing a few selected drivers that correspond to the:

● **key decisions** that we want to consider (target, pricing, etc.);
● **critical risks** that we want to portray (entry and behaviour of competition, production risk, etc.). Currency risk is analyzed in the appendix to this chapter.

19.1 Improving the ability of the model to test targeting and pricing decisions

The impact of targeting and pricing decisions can be shown with the influence diagram in Figure 19.1.

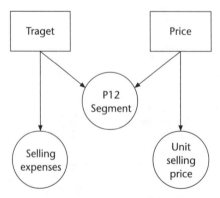

Figure 19.1 A model of the impact of the targeting and pricing decisions

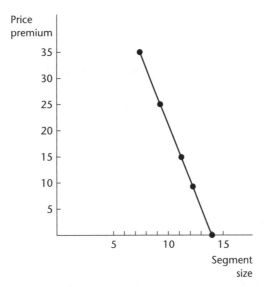

Figure 19.2 Segment size as a function of price premium (no education)

Price and segment size

Data in the BA International (i) case suggest the following relationship between the price premium and the size of the oil-free segment:

Price premium	10	15	25	35
Segment size	12	11	9	7

The data can be shown on a graph, as in Figure 19.2. This suggests that a linear relationship exists between price premium and segment size. This relationship corresponds to the following equation:

$$x = -0.2y + 14$$

where x is segment size and y is price premium.

Introducing such a relationship into the model will make it easier to test different pricing strategies. It will also allow us to test the impact of more than four price premiums and to explore the impact of extreme pricing strategies.

Price, segment size and education

When the educational campaign is undertaken, the data suggest the following relationship between the price premium and the size of the additional segment:

Price premium	10	15	25	35
Additional segment size	12	8	5	2

These data can also be shown on a graph as in Figure 19.3. This suggests the existence of a turning point. One can assume that the turning point either corresponds to a 15% price premium (Figure 19.3a), or is somewhere between a 15% and a 10% premium (Figure 19.3b).

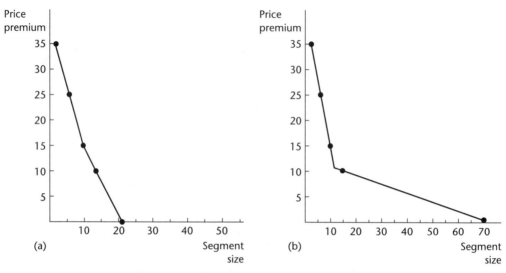

Figure 19.3 Segment size as a function of price premium (with education)

If you assume that the turning point corresponds to a 15% premium, then the relationship between the premium and the additional segment is:

for $y > 15$: $x = -0.3y + 12.5$
for $y < 15$: $x = -0.8y + 20$

This means that even with the educational campaign and a 0% premium, BA International cannot expect to capture more than 34% of the market with P12: 14% for the oil-sensitive customers and 20% for all the other customers. This somewhat contradicts the intuitive idea one may have about P12. As P12 is a better product than the existing ones (lower maintenance costs), almost all customers should theoretically buy it if it is sold at no premium.

Alternatively, you can consider that the turning point is somewhere between a 10% and a 15% premium. You get a new relationship between the premium and the additional segment. This relationship is a function of the maximum market share that can be captured by P12:

for $y > 15$: $x = -0.3y + 12.5$
for $y < 15$: $x = (26 - \text{maximum})/10y + \text{maximum} - 14$

If P12 can capture 100% of the market, then the second equation is $x = -7.4y + 86$. If it can capture 70% of the market, then it is $x = -4.4y + 56$.

For the moment, let us assume that the turning point corresponds to the 15% premium.

Modifying the model

To make it easy to test the impact of alternative targeting and pricing decisions, you can add two new drivers to the model:

---

1. Insert three blank rows above row 1.
2. Type in Al: 'Educational campaign, no=1, yes=2'. Type in El: 2.
3. Type in A2: 'Premium'. Type in E2: 15.
4. Type in A3: 'NPV'; type in B3: +B48; in D3: 'NPV before cannibalization'; in H3: +B40; in J3: 'Total cash'; in L3: +M47–B37.
5. Introduce a calculation of P12 segment share. In B7, type: +(–0.2*E2+14+IF(E1=2, IF(E2<15, –0.8*E2+20, –0.3*E2+12.5),0))/100.

Test: check that P12 segment share is equal to: 19.
Also check that with no educational campaign (F1=1) and a price premium equal to 0, P12 segment share is equal to: 14.

6. Change the price calculation in row 14: in B14 type: =(33.6*(1–0.01)^(B4–2004))/1.15*(1+$E$2/100). Copy across.
7. Calculate the amount of fixed selling cost with the educational campaign and a price premium of 15: when you set El to 2 and E2 to 15 you get an annual fixed selling cost of €11.389 m. It is 6.594 with no educational campaign and a 15 premium. Change the calculation of fixed selling costs in row 24; type in B24: +IF(E1=1, 6.594, 11.389+8.500). The 8.5 comes from the fact that half of the educational campaign budget is spent in 2004. Then type in C24: +IF(E1=1, 6.594, 11.389). Finally in D24: +C24.
8. De-couple variable selling costs/sales from price changes. In B22: +0.1/(1+$E$2/100)*1.15; Copy across.
9. Change the calculation of the NPVs to introduce the educational campaign in 2003: you should have after that in B40: =(NPV(B39,B36..L36)–B37–IF(E1=2, 8.5*(1–B27), 0))/(1+B39). Check the computer returns €30.5 m (with E1=2 and E2=15).

   In B48: (NPV(B39,B47..L47)–B37–IF(E1=2, 8.5*(1–B27), 0))/(1+B39). Check the computer returns €27.8 m (with E1=2 and E2=15).
11. Change the calculation of total cash in L3: +M47–B37–IF(E1=1,0,8.5*(1–B27)). Check that the computer returns a total net cash of €81.8 m (with E1=2 and E2=15).

Figure 19.4 Introducing the drivers corresponding to two decisions (target market and pricing)

- Educational campaign. This driver will have two values only: for example, 2 when the campaign is undertaken and 1 when it is not.
- Price premium. This driver will take any value and will drive both the segment size and the selling prices.

In order conveniently to see the value of these two drivers and their impact on the NPV, you can also build at the top of your model a small control panel displaying both the key drivers and the key outcomes of the model. This is described in Figure 19.4.

Selling costs

The educational campaign driver should trigger additional costs:

- Half of the educational campaign (€8.5 m) is going to take place in 2004 and can be included in the fixed selling costs.

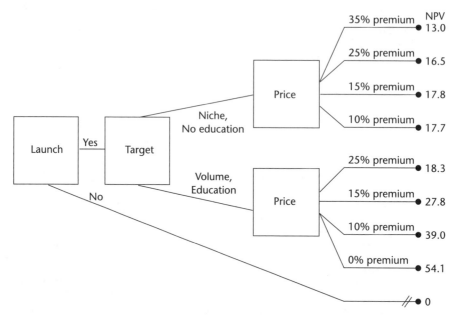

Figure 19.5 First evaluation of the alternative strategies

● The remaining half of the campaign is going to take place in 2003 and its after tax value can be taken into account in the NPV formula without creating a new column.

We still have to de-couple the selling costs from the pricing decisions. As suggested in the case, let us assume that the fixed selling costs or launch costs depend on the target selected (niche or volume) but not on the price. Their annual amount will be €6.594 m for the niche target and €11.389 m for the volume target.

Let us also assume the 10% variable selling costs to sales relationship is true when the premium is 15% and that selling costs will not be reduced by lower prices or increased by higher prices. This leads to the adjustment of the variable selling costs to sales that is described in Figure 19.4.

The results of the new model

The results of the new model are shown in Figure 19.5.

● When there is no educational campaign the final outcome is not very sensitive to the price premium but a price premium equal to 15% (or a bit less) seems to be best.[1]
● When the educational campaign is undertaken, there is a strong argument in favour of a very low price premium.
● The strategy corresponding to the educational campaign and a very low price premium seems to dominate the others.[2]

It is interesting to compare these results with the ones we got a long time ago with our very first simple global model (Chapter 16, section 2.10): this is done in Figure 19.6. The good news is that all the analysis we have done has confirmed our initial intuition. The bad

			Global full life model (profit after tax)	First NPV model (NPV)
Do not launch			0	0
Launch	Niche	35% premium	31	13
		25% premium	34	17
		15% premium	33	18
		10% premium	32	18
	Volume	35% premium	29	
		25% premium	43	18
		15% premium	49	28
		10% premium	56	39
		0% premium		54

Figure 19.6 Comparing the results of two models

news is that we might have the feeeling that we have not made much progress. In a way this is true except for one very important thing: the sophisticated model that we have built is going to help us do something that simple models are totally unfit for: an analysis of the uncertainties.

19.2 Improving the ability of the model to help us understand risk

Competitive risk

Competitive risk is easier to test if we introduce two additional drivers:

● Date of entry of competition. We can assign two values to this driver: 1 for a late entry (2009) of competition and 2 for early entry (2004).
● Competition's pricing policy. Two values also: 1 when competition adopts a conservative pricing policy and 2 when competition is aggressive. In this latter case BA International will be obliged to follow the competition, and selling price will never be more than 1.75 times the unit cost. Let us assume that such a situation can only occur if BA International itself pursues an aggressive strategy (i.e. undertakes the educational campaign), and when the competition enters early (in 2004). The process for introducing these two new variables is described in Figure 19.7 and the results are shown in Figure 19.8.

Returning to cannibalization

Should we always consider the NPV after cannibalization? This is acceptable when competition enters late, but may not be when competition enters as early as 2004. If competition enters in 2004 our existing products will probably be attacked by competition and

1. Start from the model in Figure 19.4 and introduce two blank rows above row 3.
2. In A3 type: 'Entry of competition 1=2009, 2=2004'; in E3 type 2.
3. In A4 type: 'Competition pricing 1=conservative, 2=aggressive'; in E4 type 2.
4. Change the calculation of market share in row 14: in B14 type: +IF($E$3=2, 0.6, 1) copy into range C1.F1 1 in G1 type: IF(E3=2, 0.6, 0.8).

Test: check that when there is no educational campaign and a 15% price premium NPV is equal to DM 6.8 m when competition enters in 2004.

5. Introduce a row above row 17. In Al 6 type: 'Competitive price'. In B17 type: =IF($E$1=1, B16;IF($E$3=1, B16, IF($E$4=1, B16, IF(B16<1.75*B23, B16, 1.75*B23)))); Copy across.

Test: check that where the educational campaign is undertaken, a premium of 15% is selected, competition enters in 2004 and follows an aggressive pricing policy, competitive prices are:

2004	2005	2006	2007	2008	2009	2010	2011	2012	2013
30.0	28.9	27.2	24.8	22.4	20.6	19.6	19.1	18.9	18.8

6. Change the calculation of sales in row 18: in B18 type: +B15×B17/100 and copy across.

Test: check that when the educational campaign is undertaken, a premium of 15% is selected, competition enters in 2004 and follows an aggressive pricing policy, NPV is equal to DM −15.5 m.

Figure 19.7 Improving the ability of the model to portray competitive risk

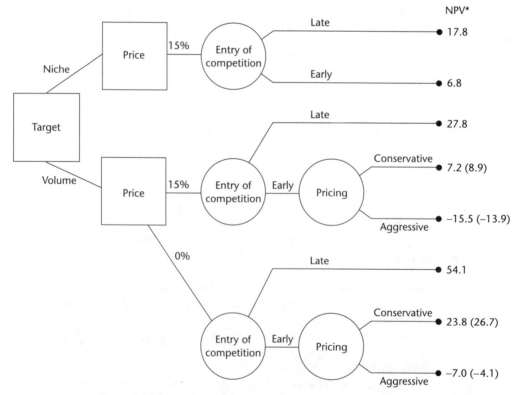

Figure 19.8 Evaluation of the alternative strategies when competition is introduced
* NPVs before cannibalization are shown in parentheses.

launching P12 would cause no further reduction of their sales, so why not consider NPV before cannibalization for all situations which correspond to early entry of competition?

Production risk

In our model, sales are always driven by the market which is acceptable provided that there are no production problems. If there are, sales would no longer be driven by the market, but by production capacity instead. We do not have any estimate of what the maximum production volumes could be in the case of production difficulties. The only thing we can do is extrapolate from the experience of 5P4 as described in the BA International (II) case. Let us therefore assume that in case of production problems, the maximum volumes produced would be as follows:

2004	2005	2006	2007	2008	2009	2010	2011	2012	2013
25	100	200	300	400	400	400	400	400	400

Another problem is to account for the increase in unit cost. Again we have little data for doing so. In our model, however, we calculate unit production cost as a function of cumulative production. Let us assume that this relationship would adequately reflect the increase in unit production cost when manufacturing problems occur.

The final problem with production difficulties is to know whether such difficulties can occur at BA International only, or at BA International and its competitor as well. In the latter case there is no risk of the competitor engaging in a price war while BA International is struggling with its production problems. In the former case the competitor may well take advantage of its ability to produce large volumes with no manufacturing difficulties to engage in a price war that would affect BA International when it is unable to produce P12 at a competitive price. The process for changing the model to evaluate situations with manufacturing problems is described in Figure 19.9.

---

1. Start from the model in Figure 19.7 and introduce a blank row above row 5. In A5 type 'Production problems, 2=Yes , 1=No '; in E5 type 2.
2. Insert two blank rows above row 16. In A16 type: 'Theoretical sales volume'. In B16 type: +B14*B15 and copy across.
3. In Al7 type: 'Volume if production problems'. Enter the following values: 25 in B17, 100 in C17, 200 in D17, 300 in E17, 400 in F17.K17.
4. Change the calculation of sales volume in B18: IF($E$5=2, B17, B16). Copy across.
5. Insert a row above row 20. Type in A20: 'Aggressive price with production problems'. Enter the following values in row 20:

B20	C20	D20	E20	F20	G20	H20	I20	J20	K20
30.0	28.9	27.2	24.8	22.4	20.6	19.6	19.1	18.9	18.8

6. Change the calculation of competitive price in row 21. Change the formula in B21: =IF(AND($E$5=2;$E$3=2;$E$4=2);B20;IF($E$1=1 . . . the rest unchanged except for an additional closing parenthesis at the end. Copy across.

Test: check that the model returns a –10.6 NPV (with no educational campaign, 15% price premium, 2004 entry of competition, aggressive pricing and production problems).

Figure 19.9 Adapting the model to test production risk

		2004	2005	2006	2007	2008	2009	2010	2011	2012	2013	2014 Cum.

1 Decision and risk variables
2 Educational Campaign, no=1, yes=2   1
3 Premium   15
4 Entry of competition, 1=2009; 2=2004   2
5 Comp. pricing, 1=conservative; 2=aggressive   1
6 Production problems, 2=yes; 1=no   1
7
8 Outcomes
9 NPV 17.8   NPV before cannibalization 19.4   Total cash 47.9
10

	2004	2005	2006	2007	2008	2009	2010	2011	2012	2013	2014 Cum.
11											
12 Market growth		0.03	0.03	0.03	0.03	0.03	0.03	0.03	0.03	0.03	
13 Total market	5780	5953	6132	6316	6505	6701	6902	7109	7322	7542	
14 P12 segment share	0.11										

Figure 19.10 Control panel with decision and risk drivers and outcomes

19.3 Finalizing the presentation of the model

We now have a model which adequately describes the impact of the decision to launch P12 and enables us easily to test the various options related to this decision. We can at this stage carry out a last modification which will improve the presentation of the model. To do so:

1. Insert one blank row above row 1.
2. Insert two blank rows above row 7.
3. Insert one blank row above row 10.
4. Type in titles:
   – Decision and risk variables
   – Outcomes

Finally, you can have, as shown in Figure 19.10, a summary on top of your model and you can concentrate on this summary when testing alternative strategies. A further step would be to protect the model except for the decision and environment variables.

Appendix: Portraying currency risk

As discussed in Chapter 17, it is a good idea to use purchasing power parity in order to simplify your models and remove the 'noise' caused by currency variations. You cannot, however, ignore that deviations from purchasing power parity do materialize and are actually common for economies as a whole and even more common for specific markets and products. When dealing with a decision like the launch of P12, you have to portray the currency risk involved, i.e. the risk that purchasing parity does not hold. The process for doing so is described in Figure 19.11.

Purchasing power parity deviations and competition: the strategic dimension of currency risk

Analyzing the full impact of deviations from purchasing power parity is actually very difficult as the impact of these deviations depends very much on the competitive context:

Start from the model in Tables 18.1 and 18.2.

1. Insert two rows above row 11 (unit price).
2. In row 11, introduce a set of deviations from purchasing power parity: 0 in B11, −.2 in C11, −.6 in D11, −.6 in E11, −2 in F11, +2 in G11, +.6 in H11, +.6 in I11, +.2 in J11 and 0 in K11. If you sum all these deviations you get 0. The idea is that deviations from PPP tend to offset each other over the long run.
3. In B12, indicate the percentage of business that BA International does in USD: let us assume it is 40%.
4. Change the calculation of the selling price in B13:
(33.6*(1−0.01)^(B1−$B$1))*(1− $B$12)+(33.6*(1−0.01)^(B1−$B$1))*$B$12*(1+B11).
Copy across.

You should get an NPV of €14.7 m which is 18% less than the original value (17.8). If you change the set of deviations to: 0, +20%, +60%, +60%, +20%, −20%, −60%, −60%, −20% and 0, you get an NPV of 21.0 which is 20% more than the initial value.

Figure 19.11 Portraying currency risk

- A firm with a very strong competitive position will definitely be better placed to adjust its prices with a view to offsetting changes in exchange rates. In the present situation, the fact that P12 has some unique features might help decrease the currency exposure.
- Deviations from purchasing parity may have complex consequences on the respective positions of competitors in an industry. If the main international competitor of BA International is a US firm that sources its products from the USA, then a temporary overvaluation of the US dollar can jeopardize its short-term position and also encourage it to improve which could reinforce its long-term position.
- The deviations from purchasing power parity that really matter are not easy to identify and may even affect those purely domestic competitors who operate in one currency only. If the US dollar becomes temporarily overvalued, then BA International will suddenly enjoy a stronger competitive position vis-à-vis its local competitors in the USA. Even though they do not deal in foreign currency, the local competitors of BA International have a significant currency exposure.

Notes

1. If you try different price premiums, you get the highest NPV for a 13% premium. Let us not try to make the model say too much and let us accept the idea that a 15% price premium is adequate if we go for a niche strategy.
2. This is even more true when you assume a more optimistic relationship between price premium and market share.

CHAPTER *20*

Deciding about the new product

20.1 Making a decision

You may feel that the time has come for us to make a decision about the launching of P12. This feeling is justified since it seems that we now know enough to make a well-argued decision. When you run the model we built, you get the results shown in Figure 20.1.

What shall we decide?

It seems that we have two basic options:

- niche strategy with a standard price premium, the consensus strategy which emerged at BA International;
- volume strategy with no price premium.

The first strategy appears to be less risky than the second one, but is it really superior? In order to explore this issue, we have to try to weigh the different situations. Since we have very little idea about the probabilities, we can build a model which helps us understand the impact of different probabilities. Such a model is described in Table 20.1.

This model considers that, since the industry is mature, all competitors are faced with similar problems. As a result if there are production problems, they will be shared by BA International and its major competitor, and consequently there will be no price war in such a situation. *We should not overestimate the manufacturing risk. If at BA International they thought that production problems were likely to occur, they would not even have considered launching P12.* Let us assign a 0.9 probability to the absence of production difficulties.

As shown in Table 20.2, the volume strategy is always superior unless you think that it is extremely likely that the competition will offer a similar product to P12 in 2004 and it is likely that the competition is going to adopt an aggressive pricing strategy. This contradicts the consensus strategy which emerged at BA International. Did they refuse the volume strategy because they were afraid of the possibility of adverse outcomes? Let us examine the risk profiles attached to the niche and volume strategies which are shown in Figure 20.2.

344

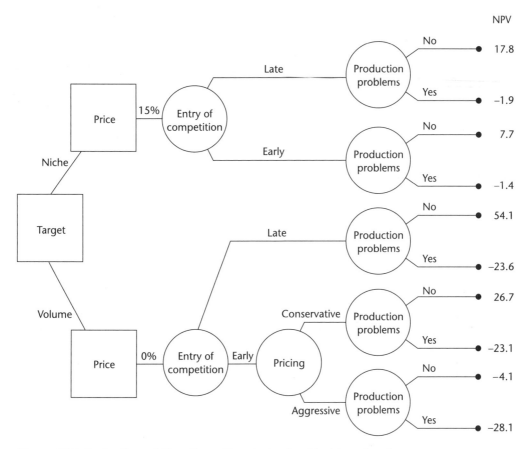

NPV

Figure 20.1 Evaluation of the alternative strategies (decision stage)

Once more, the analysis does not generate any definite answer. You have to make up your own mind. It is clear that the volume strategy may generate very adverse outcomes, but the probability of such outcomes is low and if successful the volume strategy would generate a great value.

20.2 Have we missed something?

When you review the analysis you may have three worries, at least:

- How sure can we be that capital expenditures are not going to change, whatever the strategy?
- Have we made a fair assessment of the volume strategies?
- Have we given a fair assessment to the niche strategies?

The capital expenditure issue

In our analysis, we have assumed that capital expenditure is not going to change when volume strategies are chosen. The problem is, however, that volume strategies imply a

Table 20.1 ● Model for calculating expected values

	A	B	C	D	E	F	G	H	I
1	Probability late competition entry	0.20							
2	Probability conservative pricing (large target)	0.80							
3	Probability no production problems	0.90							
4		Entry	Pricing	Pr. Pb	Weight	NPV			Expected NPV
5	**Niche**								
6	Probability late competition entry	0.20							
7	Probability no production problems			0.90	0.18	17.80	3.20		
8	Probability production problems			0.10	0.02	-1.90	-0.04		
9	Probability early entry	0.80							
10	Probability no production problems			0.90	0.72	7.70	5.54		
11	Probability production problems			0.10	0.08	-1.40	0.11	8.60	
					1				
12	**Large target**								
13	Probability late entry	0.20							
14	Probability no production problems			0.90	0.18	54.10	9.74		
15	Probability production problems			0.10	0.02	-23.60	-0.47		
16	Probability early entry	0.80							
17	Probability conservative pricing		0.80						
18	Probability no production problems			0.90	0.58	26.70	15.38		
19	Probability production problems			0.10	0.06	-23.10	-1.48		
20	Probability aggressive pricing		0.20						
21	Probability no production problems			0.90	0.14	-4.10	-0.59		
22	Probability production problems			0.10	0.02	-28.10	-0.45	**22.13**	2.6

B1,B2,B3 and F7,F8,F10,F11,F14,F15,F18,F19,F21 and F22: data

B6: =B1
D7: =B3
E7: =B6*D7
G7: =E7*F7.Copy into G8, G10, G11, G14, G15, G18, G19, G21, G22
D8: =1-D7
E8: =B6*D8
B9: =1-B6

D10: =B3
E10: =B9*D10
D11: =1-D10
E11: =B9*D11
B13: =B1
D14: =B3
E14: =B13*D14
D15: =1-D14

E15: =B13*D15
B16: =1-B13
C17: =B2
D18: =B3
E18: =B16*C17*D18
D19: =1-D18
E19: =B16*C17*D19
C20: =1-C17

D21: =B3
E21: =B16*C20*D21
D22: =1-D21
E22: =B16*C20*D22
H11: =SUM(G7.G11)
H22: =SUM(G14.G22)
I22: =H22/H11

Table 20.2 ● Expected values

Probabilities			Results (expected values)	
Late competitive entry	Conservative pricing	No production problems	Niche	Volume
		0.9	14	40
	0.8	0.8	12	33
		0.7	10	26
		0.9	14	39
0.8	0.5	0.8	12	32
		0.7	11	25
		0.9	14	37
	0.2	0.8	12	30
		0.7	11	23
		0.9	11	31
	0.8	0.8	10	25
		0.7	8	19
		0.9	11	27
0.5	0.5	0.8	10	21
		0.7	8	16
		0.9	11	23
	0.2	0.8	10	17
		0.7	8	12
		0.9	9	22
	0.8	0.8	8	17
		0.7	6	12
		0.9	9	15
0.2	0.5	0.8	8	11
		0.7	6	6
		0.9	9	9
	0.2	0.8	8	5
		0.7	6	1

much higher capacity, as shown in Table 20.3. If you believe the results in the table and consider that some additional capacity may be required by volume strategies, then those strategies look less attractive.

Have we made a fair assessment of the volume strategies?

One could argue that we might have underestimated the value of volume strategies. When assessing volume strategies, we have not considered the possibility of a negative price

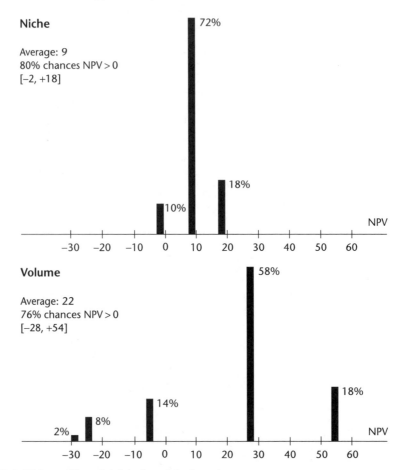

Figure 20.2 Risk profiles of 'niche' and 'volume'

Table 20.3 ● Cumulative volumes over ten years

	Cumulated volumes over life	Index	Required capital expenditure according to index
Niche strategy:			
15% premium, late competition entry	6 139	100	5.64
15% premium, early competition entry	4 334	71	
Volume strategy:			
0% premium, late competition entry	18 974	309	17.43
0% premium, early competition entry	13 427	219	12.34

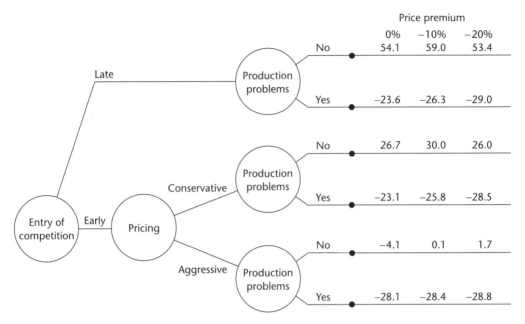

			Price premium		
			0%	−10%	−20%
Late	Production problems	No	54.1	59.0	53.4
		Yes	−23.6	−26.3	−29.0
Conservative	Production problems	No	26.7	30.0	26.0
		Yes	−23.1	−25.8	−28.5
Aggressive	Production problems	No	−4.1	0.1	1.7
		Yes	−28.1	−28.4	−28.8

Figure 20.3 Impact of negative price premiums (volume strategy)

premium. When you do so (see Figure 20.3) you realize that selling P12 at a price 10% lower than substitute products would lead to a better result. If you are attracted by volume strategies and think that P12 might be the chance for BA International successfully to attack local competition then you might consider that we have not given a fair chance to extremely low price strategies. If we retained the idea expressed in Chapter 19 (see page 336) and consider that the P12 segment could reach, for example, a maximum share of 70% (with five times the capital expenditures initially planned), then, as shown in Figure 20.4, the results would look quite different. But this would correspond to a grand strategic move for BA International and would probably require much more costs of structure. As no mention of the possibility of such a grand strategic move is made in the case, let us be cautious and not dream too much about it.

20.3 The need to recognize the option value of the niche strategy

In our analysis we have considered that an early entry of the competition would only result in the sharing of an unchanged total market. But what if this also changed the size of the segment of P12 as shown in the influence diagram of Figure 20.5?

When you analyze the level of fixed selling costs, you realize that they are very significant when compared with the amount of the educational campaign. If BA International's competitor introduces a product similar to P12 in 2004 it will probably also incur fixed selling costs. The combined impact of its effort and that of BA International may well be as effective as the impact of an educational campaign undertaken by BA International alone, and fought by competition. If you accept this idea, you have to carry out further modifications to the model in order to give a fairer assessment to the niche strategies. The process

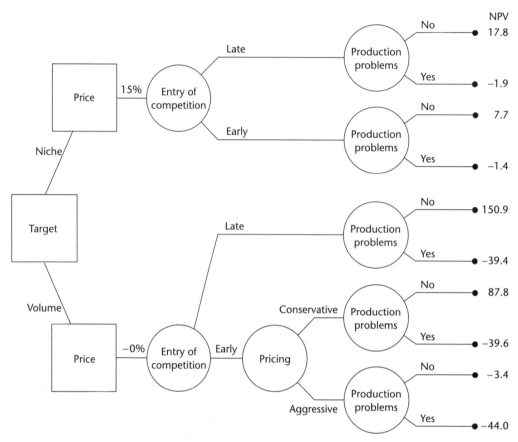

Figure 20.4 Impact of an extremely low price premium strategy

Note: In order to get these results you need to make two modifications to the model in Figure 9.10. (1) In B14: =(−0.2*E2+14+IF(E1=2, IF(E2<15,−4.4*E2+56,−0.3*E2+12.5),0))/100. Check that you get a 70% segment share with the educational campaign and a 0% premium. (2) In B48: +5.64*5.

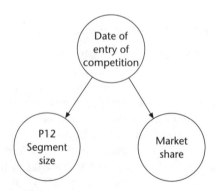

Figure 20.5 Impact of competition

The three things you need to do (starting from the model in Figure 19.10) are to change the calculation of P12 segment share in row 14 and the calculation of fixed selling costs in row 35.

1. In order to change the calculation of P12 segment share, type in B14:
   =(−0.2*E3+14+IF(OR(E2=2,AND(E2=1,E4=2));IF(E3<15 . . . the rest unchanged
2. In order to change the calculation of fixed selling costs, type in B35:
   =IF(E2=1,IF(E4=1, 6.594, 11.389), 11.389+8.5)
   type in C42:
   =IF(OR(E2=2, AND(E2=1, E4=2)), 11.389, 6.594)
3. Change the calculation of competitive price in order to introduce the possibility of a price war in the situation corresponding to: production difficulties, no educational campaign and early entry of competition. In order to do so, change the calculation of competitive price in row 25:
   =IF(OR(AND($E$6=2, $E$4=2, $E$5=2), AND($E$2=1, $E$4=2, $E$5=2)),B24 . . . the rest unchanged. Copy across.

Test: After these modifications, your model should return a DM 19.1 m NPV (before cannibalization). (No educational campaign, 15% premium, early entry of competition, conservative pricing, no production difficulties.)

Figure 20.6 Introducing the idea of sharing a bigger market

for this is described in Figure 20.6. The results are given in Figure 20.7. If you believe in the idea that an early entry of competition would result in the opportunity to share a bigger market then, as shown in Figure 20.7, the niche strategy looks much better than we thought – but still inferior to the volume strategy. When analyzing the results in the figure, you find something interesting. In the case where there are no production problems, the outcome of the niche strategy looks better when competition enters the market early. If competition offers a product similar to P12 in 2009 the NPV is 17.8 m but if it offers the same product as early as 2004, the NPV is €19.1 m. Within our new framework the situation:

● niche strategy is decided in 2002
● and competition enters in 2004

does not result in P12 being sold to a niche market! This situation actually results in P12 being sold to a large market! This is clear when you look at the value of the segment of P12. It is equivalent to what could be achieved by BA International if it undertakes the educational campaign. This has several implications.

1. Figure 20.7 should be modified in order to acknowledge that the market becomes a volume market in this situation.
2. Figure 20.7 has to be further modified in order to show **the option which becomes available to BA International if competition enters in 2004**. Why keep the premium at 15%? As the nature of the market has changed under the pressure of competition, why not cut the price premium to enlarge the P12 segment size further? In the decision diagram language, we should introduce a new square (decision) on the right side of the circle that portrays the entry on competition (once we know if competition actually enters in 2004). The decision to target a volume market and to decide at what price we want to do it is no longer to be taken now (in 2002). We only need to take this decision in 2004 when we will really know about competition! One further problem though: if,

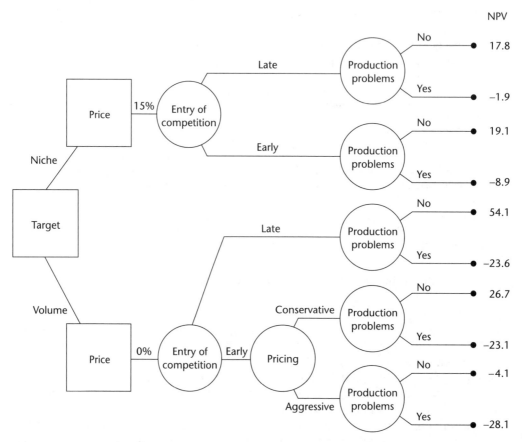

Figure 20.7 Impact of sharing a bigger market
Note: Volume strategy is as shown in Figure 20.1.

in 2004, BA International decides to go for volume through an aggressive pricing, then the competition may react and cut its prices further and a price war might start. We probably need to introduce a new circle – competitive pricing – very much the same as we have in the diagram for the volume strategy.

3. Not only the diagram has to be changed but also the model, since we should introduce this possibility ŏf a price war in the situation where there is no production problem, no educational campaign and early entry of competition (this was already in Figure 20.6).

What do the results in Figure 20.8 suggest?

In 2002, BA International can choose between two courses of action:

● either to commit irreversibly to a volume strategy,
● or to commit to a niche strategy keeping the option to switch to a volume strategy in 2004.

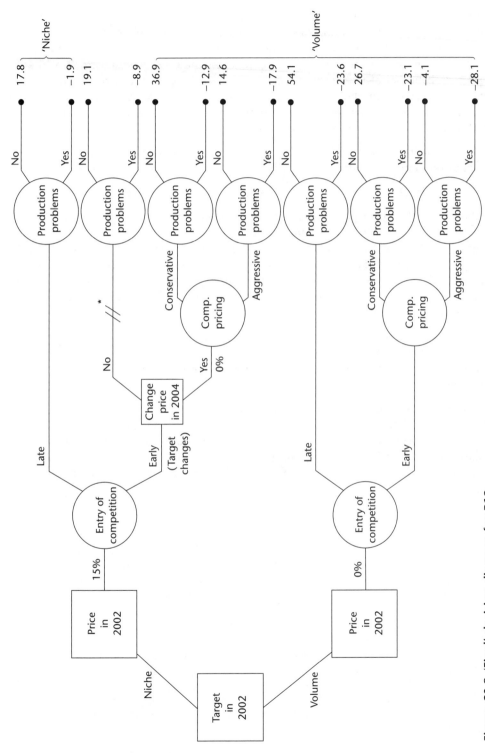

Figure 20.8 'Final' decision diagram for P12

* This branch is less valuable than 'change price – yes'.

You can use the model in Table 20.1 to calculate the expected NPV of the alternative 'go for niche while keeping the option to switch to volume'. You can either modify the model and introduce the competitive pricing branches in the evaluation of the niche strategy, or just use the lower part of the model (volume) to assess the new niche strategy. If you keep the same probabilities of late entry of competition (20%), conservative pricing (80%) and absence of production problems (90), then you can see that the expected value of the niche strategy now is €25.41 m. You can decompose this value into the value of the 'naked' niche strategy (Table 20.1) and the value of the option to switch:

Value of going for niche while = Value of the naked + Value of the option
keeping the option to switch   niche strategy   to switch

25.41   =   8.60   +   16.81

This shows that the major part of the value of the decision to go for niche in 2002 is the value of the option to switch to volume in 2004.

Figure 20.8 shows a decision diagram comparing the two possible courses of action in 2002: 'go for niche while keeping the option to switch to volume' and 'commit irreversibly to volume'. This confirms the value of the niche strategy. Maybe, this was what they had in mind at BA International with their consensual strategy. It is interesting to compare the two most likely outcomes of the two strategies:

1. They correspond to the situation: early entry of competition (80%), conservative pricing (80%) and absence of production problems (90%).
2. The outcome of 'commit irreversibly to volume in 2002' is some €10 m less – the after tax value of the educational campaign!

You may now think that we have dissected the problem sufficiently, so let me end the analysis with one final remark. The comments that we have made on the hidden value of the volume strategy (Section 20.2) are valid for both strategies (commit irreversibly to volume and go for niche while keeping the option to switch to volume). Consequently, they do not change the situation in favour of committing irreversibly to volume in 2004.

Eagle

On 14 August 2002 John Reich, the CEO of Norge Pharma, a medium-sized niche pharmaceutical company, was trying to evaluate Eagle, a new neuroprotective therapy to prevent neuronal death in acute conditions, such as stroke. Eagle has successfully gone through pre-clinical development and now it was time to review the situation:

- What were the value creation prospects of Eagle?
- What were the main drivers and destroyers of value?
- How to 'play with' these drivers and maximize value?

A business with a high potential value

Table Q.1 shows the potential value that could be created by Eagle:

- The present value of its development costs was estimated to be $23.50 million.
- The present value of the profit generated by the sales of Eagle over its life was estimated to be $108.60 million.

Eagle's sales were expected to start in 2007, to reach half their full potential in 2011 and to continue growing until the end of the period of patent protection (2018). Based on expert advice, it had been decided to estimate Eagle's annual sales with the following diffusion model:

$$\text{Annual sales} = 1/(1 + \exp(-0.9 \times (\text{year} - 2011)))$$

It was impossible at this stage to come up with one single estimate of the product's possible sales. A panel of experts had come up with two extreme estimates that actually corresponded to two different product profiles:

- The first estimate allied Eagle's maximum global volume to 75% of 900 000 procedures. Within this scenario, the average unit price was estimated at $312.
- The second estimate linked Eagle's maximum volume to 20% of these same 900 000 procedures and the unit average price to $30 only.

Cost of goods sold (excluding depreciation) and other operating expenses were expected to amount to $56 and $6 per unit respectively. In order to launch Eagle, the company would also have to invest in new production facilities ($18 million in 2006) and in significant initial marketing and sales costs. A pre-launch campaign and building of a sales force of

Table Q.1 ● Eagle's potential value

	Cum.	2002	2003	2004	2005	2006	2007	2008	2009	2010	2011	2012	2013	2014	2015	2016	2017
Discount rate	0.12																
Spending committed before commercial launch																	
Phase 1 trials	1.20	1.20															
After tax	−0.84																
NPV (end 2001) (1)	−0.75																
Phase 2 trials	3.40		3.40														
After tax		0.00	−2.38														
NPV (2)	−1.90																
Phase 3 trials	17.70			8.50	9.20												
After tax			0.00	−5.95	−6.44												
NPV (3)	−8.33																
Pre-launch costs	8.00				8.00												
After tax			0.00	0.00	−5.60												
NPV (4)	−3.56																
Production facility	18.00				18.00												
Depreciation						3.60	3.60	3.60	3.60	3.60							
After tax		0.00	0.00	0.00	−18.00	1.08	1.08	1.08	1.08	1.08							
NPV (5)	−8.97																
Total NPV (1+2+3+4+5)	−23.50																

Spending and receipts after commercial launch

Launch costs	**44**	0	0	22	22	0	0	0.0	0.0	0.0	0.0	0.0	0.0	0.0	0.0
After tax	**–31**	0.0	0.0	–15.4	–15.4	0.0	0.0	0.0	0.0	0.0	0.0	0.0	0.0	0.0	0.0
NPV (6)	**–16.54**														
Profile 1															
Annual sales volume		0.00	0.02	0.04	0.10	0.20	0.34	0.48	0.58	0.63	0.66	0.67	0.67	0.67	0.67
Selling price		312	312	312	312	312	312	312	312	312	312	312	312	312	312
Annual sales	**1576**	0.0	0.0	5.6	13.3	29.9	60.9	105.3	149.7	180.7	197.3	205.0	208.3	209.7	210.2
Unit cost		56	56	56	56	56	56	56	56	56	56	56	56	56	56
CGS & Operating	**283**	0.0	0.0	1.0	2.4	5.4	10.9	18.9	26.9	32.4	35.4	36.8	37.4	37.6	37.7
Profit before tax	**1293**	0.0	0.0	4.6	10.9	24.5	49.9	86.4	122.9	148.3	161.9	168.2	170.9	172.0	172.5
Profit after tax/cash flow	**905**	0.0	0.0	3.2	7.6	17.2	35.0	60.5	86.0	103.8	113.3	117.7	119.6	120.4	120.7
NPV (7)	**229.16**														
Profile 2															
Annual sales volume	**1**	0.00	0.00	0.00	0.01	0.03	0.05	0.09	0.13	0.15	0.17	0.18	0.18	0.18	0.18
Selling price	**420**	30	30	30	30	30	30	30	30	30	30	30	30	30	30
Annual sales	**40**	0.0	0.0	0.1	0.3	0.8	1.6	2.7	3.8	4.6	5.1	5.3	5.3	5.4	5.4
Unit cost		6.0	6.0	6.0	6.0	6.0	6.0	6.0	6.0	6.0	6.0	6.0	6.0	6.0	6.0
CGS & Operating	**8**	0.00	0.00	0.03	0.07	0.15	0.31	0.54	0.77	0.93	1.01	1.05	1.07	1.08	1.08
Profit before tax	**32**	0.0	0.0	0.1	0.3	0.6	1.2	2.2	3.1	3.7	4.0	4.2	4.3	4.3	4.3
Profit after tax/cash flow	**23**	0.0	0.0	0.1	0.2	0.4	0.9	1.5	2.1	2.6	2.8	2.9	3.0	3.0	3.0
NPV (8)	**5.73**														
Expected NPV	*108.60*														
$(6+7)/2 + (8 \times 0.8/2)$															

8 million was planned for 2006. A launch campaign was also planned after the product was launched: $22 million in 2007 and 2008. The plant was going to be depreciated over five years. The tax rate was 30%.

Research and development costs for Eagle were estimated at $22.30 million:

- $1.20 million in 2003 for phase 1 clinical trials;[1]
- $3.40 million in 2004 for phase 2 clinical trials; and
- $17.70 million in 2005 and 2006 (8.50 and 9.20 respectively) for phase 3 clinical trials.

A very risky business

As was typical in the pharmaceutical industry, the chances of ever commercializing Eagle were low: something like 13% only. This was the combined probability of Eagle successfully going through phase 1 (70%) and phase 2 (50%) and phase 3 (50%) and of being approved by the FDA (75%). Had one looked at these probabilities one year earlier – before the company knew the results of the pre-clinical trials – then the chances of Eagle reaching the market would have looked even more remote (something less than 5%). The additional problem was that Eagle could end up in different product profiles and that one of these profiles – profile 2 – was not creating any value.

John Reich could anticipate the reactions of some of the members of the Board to the prospect of investing in the further development of Eagle: 'How can you expect to create value from a business that requires an investment of 23.5 million[2] and gives you 13 chances out of 100 to earn 108.6 million. Investing 23.5 to get 14 does not look attractive to me!'

Reviewing the issue

John Reich decided to look again at the opportunity to go ahead and start phase 1 clinical trials. In so doing, he wanted carefully to look at the full sequence of decisions, uncertainties, decisions, uncertainties, and so on that would correspond to the long process of bringing Eagle to the market.

The only irreversible commitment that the company had to make in 2003 was to invest $0.75 million in phase 1 studies. All the other irreversible commitments would come at later dates and would be made in the light of much better information than was available today. The development of new knowledge that was missing today was the central purpose of the development of Eagle!

A case in point was the decision to commit to $16.50 million launch expenses:

- As seen from today's perspective, this decision was very risky: there was only a 13% chance that the product would be launched and only a 50% chance that the launch expenses would fit the product profile.
- In 2007, however, the situation would be totally different. Then, the company would have full information about the possibilities of launching Eagle and its product profile. If Eagle could not be launched, then the company would obviously not commit to the launch expenses. If Eagle profile 1 could be launched, then the company would commit to the launch expenses. Finally, if only Eagle 2 could be launched, then the company would not commit to the launch expenses but would rather license the product to one of its partners. This would enable the company to capture 80% of the value estimated for Eagle profile 2 ($5.73 million).

Notes

1. Phase 1 clinical trials aim at assessing the toxicity of the drug in humans at different doses. At this stage the drug is tested on a small group of people, usually 20 to 80 healthy volunteers. Phase 2 clinical trials are done on a bigger scale (100 to 300) of patients. They aim at verifying the side-effects, obtaining dosing information and getting an indication of efficacy in patients. Phase 3 trials are even larger (1000 to 3000 patients). Their main goal is to demonstrate statistical significance of the drug. Phase 3 studies are designed to conclusively document the efficacy of the drug.
2. One can argue that the total investment for Eagle is even higher. With the launch expenses ($16.54 million) the total investment is $40.04 million. Then the argument becomes: 'Why invest 40.04 million in order to have a 13% chance to earn 117.44 million (229.16/2 + 5.73/2)?'

CHAPTER 21

The value of flexibility

With Eagle we are at an early stage of the development of an innovation. Is it valuable for the company to commit to the development of a concept that, a few years from now, may result in the launch of a new product? The decision to invest in Eagle has two features that are common to most early commitment decisions:

- On the one hand, risks are substantial. In 2002, very little is known about Eagle.
- On the other hand, one has to recognize that there are many opportunities to manage these risks through acting in a flexible way. At this early stage, the decision to go for Eagle requires very little immediate and irreversible spending. If it commits to developing Eagle, the company has to invest $0.75 million only in 2003. This is less than 2% of the $40.04 million apparently needed to develop and launch Eagle. The remaining investments will be decided later, when the company has developed much more knowledge and understanding of the project. The possibility to defer 98% of the commitment that might ultimately be needed creates plenty of opportunities for acting flexibly, for example for deciding to commit resources only when one knows for sure that these resources will create value.

When there is a lot of flexibility, risk is not that much of a problem and, as we shall see below, risk may even become a source of value. However, turning risk into a source of value is not automatic. It requires a very specific management of time and 'speeding up' the process often stops being an attractive alternative. Let us analyze the Eagle case with the help of two powerful tools: the 'old' decision diagram analysis and the new real options framework.

21.1 Assessing the value of investing in development

On 2 August 2002 John Reich wants to assess the value of committing to Eagle's further development. Investing in the development of Eagle is a matter of: committing to a total investment of $40.04 million (23.50 for development and 16.54 for launch) with a series of options to abandon and restructure the project and to avoid investing up to 39.29 m if the company learns that the project is not valuable at the end of phase 1. On 2 August 2002 the only irreversible commitment is to invest $0.75 m in the phase 1 clinical trials. Figure 21.1

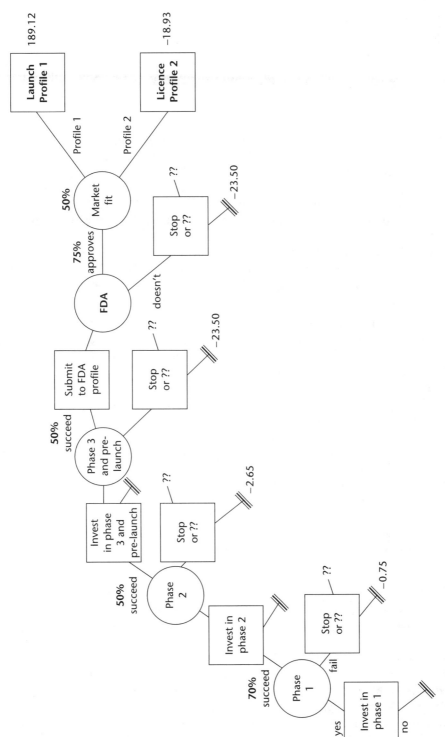

Figure 21.1 The 'decision–events–options' sequence that may lead to operating Eagle

portrays the process of events and options that will take place during the development and launch of Eagle:

1. Once phase 1 trials are completed at the end of 2003, the company will know the results of testing Eagle in a small group of healthy volunteers. These results will enable the company to decide what is most valuable: to continue and invest in phase 2 trials or to exercise a first option to abandon the project.
2. Should it commit to a further irreversible investment of $1.90 m in 2004, the company will then be able to run phase 2 trials, to learn more about Eagle's effectiveness, its side-effects and its dosing. At the end of 2004, the company will be able to exercise a second option to abandon the project.
3. In order to pursue the development of Eagle, the company will have to commit to a first large irreversible investment of $20.86 m (8.33 for phase 3 trials, 3.56 for pre-launch and 8.97 for the production facility). At the end of 2006, the company will be able to exercise its last option to abandon the project.
4. If Eagle is launched in 2007, the company will then have sufficient information to decide which is most valuable: to launch it according to 'Profile 1' or to exercise the option to license Eagle out to a partner. In order to launch Eagle Profile 1, the company will commit to a final irreversible investment of $16.54 m in launch costs.

The decision diagram in Figure 21.1 shows a remarkable sequence of 'squares' (decisions) and of 'circles' (events/information). There is only one square that is not preceded by a circle. This is the square that pictures the only irreversible commitment: the 0.75 m investment in phase 1 trials. All the other squares are preceded by one or more circles. This portrays a very flexible process. Except for phase 1, all investments remain discretionary. They will be decided later on, when the company knows more about Eagle. The events (results of phase 1, results of phase 2, FDA approval, etc.) that are pictured by the various circles will reveal a lot of information about Eagle and will help the company understand whether it is worth continuing to invest in the project. If it is not worth continuing, then the company will have the option to stop investing and to abandon the project. The circle 'market fit' that immediately precedes the decision to launch shows that there will not be any uncertainty left about the profile of Eagle when the company will plan for the launch.

The decision diagram can be used to estimate the range of values and the expected value associated with investing in Eagle's development.

Expected value

The first step is to calculate the values of the end points of the diagram. These values are shown in Table Q.1 and Figure 21.1. A model to calculate these end points is provided in Table 21.1.

The second step is to weight the values of the end points by their respective probabilities and to fold the diagram back. Two alternative models are proposed for estimating the expected value: Table 21.2 is organized according to the structure of the decision diagram, while Table 21.3 takes advantage of the decision diagram's very simple structure where decisions are always limited to a binary choice: 'continue towards the launch of Eagle' or 'recognize failure and abandon'.

Table 21.1 ● A model to estimate the values of the end points

	A	B	C	D	E	F	G	H	I	J	K	R
		Cum.	2003	2004	2005	2006	2007	2008	2009	2010	2011	2018
1												
2	Discount rate	0.12										
3	**Spending committed before commercial launch**											
4	*Phase 1 trials*	1.20	1.20									
5	After tax		−0.84									
6	NPV (end 2002)	−0.75										
7	*Phase 2 trials*	3.40		3.40								
8	After tax		0.00	−2.38								
9	NPV (end 2002)	−1.90										
10	*Phase 3 trials*	17.70			8.50	9.20						
11	After tax			0.00	−5.95	−6.44						
12	NPV (end 2002)	−8.33										
13	*Pre-launch costs*	8.00				8.00						
14	After tax			0.00	0.00	−5.60						
15	NPV (end 2002)	−3.56										
16	*Production facility*	18.00				18.0						
17	Depreciation						3.60	3.60	3.60	3.60	3.60	
18	After tax		0.00	0.00	0.00	−18.0	1.08	1.08	1.08	1.08	1.08	
19	NPV (end 2002)	−8.97										
20	Total NPV spending before	−23.50										
21	**Spending and receipts once Eagle is launched**		Year of first sales					**2007**				
22	*Launch Profile 1*											
23	Launch costs	44			0	0	22	22	0	0	0	
24	After tax	−31	0.0	0.0	0.0	0.0	−15.4	−15.4	0.0	0.0	0.0	0.0
25	NPV	16.54										

Table 21.1 continued

A	B	C	D	E	F	G	H	I	J	K	R
	Cum.	2003	2004	2005	2006	2007	2008	2009	2010	2011	2018
25											
26 *Profile 1*											
27 Annual sales volume			0.00	0.00	0.02	0.04	0.10	0.20	0.34	0.67	
28 Selling price				312	312	312	312	312	312	312	312
29 Annual sales	1576			0.0	0.0	5.6	13.3	29.9	60.9	105	210
30 Unit cost				56	56	56	56	56	56	56	56
31 CGS & Operating	283			0.0	0.0	1.0	2.4	5.4	10.9	18.9	37.7
32 Profit before tax	1293			0.0	0.0	4.6	10.9	24.5	49.9	86.4	172
33 **Profit after tax/cash flow**	905	0.0	0.0	0.0	0.0	3.2	7.6	17.2	35.0	60.5	121
34 NPV	229.16										
35 NPV	212.62										
36 *License Profile 2*											
37 Annual sales volume	1			0.00	0.00	0.00	0.01	0.03	0.05	0.09	0.18
38 Selling price	420			30	30	30	30	30	30	30	30
39 Annual sales	40			0.0	0.0	0.1	0.3	0.8	1.6	2.7	5.4
40 Unit cost				6.0	6.0	6.0	6.0	6.0	6.0	6.0	6.0
41 CGS & Operating	8			0.00	0.00	0.03	0.07	0.15	0.31	0.54	1.08
42 Profit before tax	32			0.0	0.0	0.1	0.3	0.6	1.2	2.2	4.3
43 **Profit after tax/cash flow**	23	0	0	0.0	0.0	0.1	0.2	0.4	0.9	1.5	3.0
44 NPV	5.73										
45 80% of NPV	4.58										
46 Expected value launch	108.60										

47	*Profile 1*							
48	Sales volumes 2005 launch	0.02	0.04	0.10	0.20	0.34	0.48	0.58	0.67
49	Sales volumes 2006 launch	0.00	0.02	0.04	0.10	0.20	0.34	0.48	0.67
50	Sales volumes 2007 launch	0.00	0.00	0.02	0.04	0.10	0.20	0.34	0.67
51	Sales volumes 2008 launch	0.00	0.00	0.00	0.02	0.04	0.10	0.20	0.67
52	Sales volumes 2009 launch	0.00	0.00	0.00	0.00	0.02	0.04	0.10	0.67
53	*Profile 2*							
54	Sales volumes 2005 launch	0.00	0.01	0.03	0.05	0.09	0.13	0.15	0.18
55	Sales volumes 2006 launch	0.00	0.00	0.01	0.03	0.05	0.09	0.13	0.18
56	Sales volumes 2007 launch	0.00	0.00	0.00	0.01	0.03	0.05	0.09	0.18
57	Sales volumes 2008 launch	0.00	0.00	0.00	0.00	0.01	0.03	0.05	0.18
58	Sales volumes 2009 launch	0.00	0.00	0.00	0.00	0.00	0.01	0.03	0.18

Background

B4: =SUM(C4:R4); Copy in B7, B10, B13, B16 and B23

C5: =–C4*.70. You have to introduce similar formulas in rows 8, 11, 14 and 24. For the production facility in row 18: +F16 in F18 and +$F$16/5 in G17,G18+G17*.30; Copy across

B6: =NPV($B$2, C6:R6); Copy into B9, B12, B15, B19, B25, B34, and B44. Be sure to have zeros in the years where the cash flows are nil

B20: =B6+B9+B12+B15+B19

E27: =IF($I$21=2005,E48,IF($I$21=2006,E49,IF($I$21=2007,E50,IF($I$21=2008,E51,E52)))). Copy

E29: +E27*E28; Copy across and in row 39; E31: +E30*E27. Copy across and in row 41; E32: +E29–E31; Copy across and in row 42.
E33: +E32*.7; Copy across and in row 43. B35: =B25+B34

⋮

E37: =IF($I$21=2005,E54,IF($I$21=2006,E55,IF($I$21=2007,E56,IF($I$21=2008,E57,E58)))). Copy

B45: =.8*B44; B46: =B35/2+B45/2

E48: =(0.9*0.75)/(1+EXP(–0.9*(E1–2009))). Copy
G50: =(0.9*0.75)/(1+EXP(–0.9*(G1–2011))). Copy
I52: =(0.9*0.75)/(1+EXP(–0.9*(I1–2013))). Copy
E54: =(0.9*0.2)/(1+EXP(–0.9*(E1–2009))). Copy
G54: =(0.9*0.2)/(1+EXP(–0.9*(G1–2011))). Copy
I54: =(0.9*0.2)/(1+EXP(–0.9*(I1–2013))). Copy

F49: =(0.9*0.75)/(1+EXP(–0.9*(F1–2010))). Copy
H51: =(0.9*0.75)/(1+EXP(–0.9*(H1–2012))). Copy

F55: =(0.9*0.2)/(1+EXP(–0.9*(F1–2010))). Copy
H54: =(0.9*0.2)/(1+EXP(–0.9*(H1–2012))). Copy

Table 21.2 ● A first model to estimate the expected value

A	B Value	C Value if stopping at this step	D Prob.	E Prob. of stopping at this step	F Weighted value
1					
2 Phase 1	−0.75	−0.75	70%	30.0%	−0.23
3 Phase 2	−1.90	−2.65	50%	35.0%	−0.93
4 Phase 3 and pre-launch	−20.86	−23.51	50%	17.5%	−4.11
5		−23.51	75%	4.4%	−1.03
6 Launch Profile 1	212.62	189.11	50%	6.6%	12.41
7 Launch Profile 2	4.58	−18.93	50%	6.6%	−1.24
8 **Expected value**				100%	**4.87**

Background
Column B and D: data
Column B: data from Table 21.1
B2: −.75; B3: −1.90; B4: −8.33−3.56−8.97
B6: +229.17−16.54; B7: 4.58
Column D: data from Figure 21.1 in D2.D6
D7: =1−D6

C2: =B2; C3: =C2+B3; Copy to C4.
C5: =C4; C6: =C4+B6; C7: =C4+B7

E2: =1−D2; E3: =D2*(1−D3)
E4: =D2*D3*(1−D4); E5: =D2*D3*D4*(1−D5)
E6: =D2*D3*D4*D5*D6
E7: =D2*D3*D4*D5*D7

F2: =C2*E2; Copy to E3.E7
E8: =SUM(E2.E7); Copy to F8

Risk profile

The decision diagram with the values and probabilities of its end points also enables us to generate the risk profile reproduced in Figure 21.2.

What do the results tell us?

Commercializing Eagle Profile 1 could generate a very large value ($189 million). At the same time, investing in the phase 1 clinical trials is, as expected, a very risky proposition:

● There is less than a 7% chance of turning the current Eagle concept into a commercial product and capturing its value.
● There are a few ugly possible outcomes (−19 million, −24 million) and, together, they account for almost 30% of the chances. They correspond to the late discovery that Eagle cannot be turned into a success.
● There is a majority of small negative outcomes (65% chance). They correspond to the early discovery that Eagle is an uninteresting idea.

In spite of the fact that there is a lot of value attached to a successful Eagle, the expected value of investing in its development in 2003 is relatively small (5.63 million for an investment of 0.75 million which corresponds to a net value of $4.88 million). It is interesting

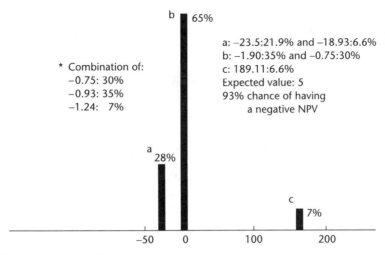

Figure 21.2 Eagle's risk profile

to realize that this positive value is largely due to the flexibility created by the embedded options to abandon and to license the project.

A first assessment of the value of flexibility

We can use the model in Table 21.3 to estimate the value created by the option to license Eagle. We can say that if this option did not exist the company would have to commit to the launch expenses whatever the profile of Eagle may actually be. As shown in Table 21.4, this would make the value of investing in the development of Eagle decrease by 1.01 m. You could also say that the option to license creates a value of 1.01 million.

21.2 Assessing the value of flexibility created by all the options combined

In order to assess the value of the flexibility created by all the options associated with Eagle's development, you need to compare:

● the value of developing Eagle according to the current flexible process, with
● the value of doing it with a totally inflexible process. What if the company were to decide to commit irreversibly to the totality of the $40.04 m investments in 2003?

The result is shown in Table 21.5. The data in the table come from the model in Table 21.6 which is directly derived from the model in Table 21.3. These data show:

● The value of flexibility is very high (29.50 million). This value is such that it is does better than compensate the negative value of developing Eagle in an inflexible way. Without the value created by flexibility, it is not possible to invest in Eagle's development.
● The value of flexibility comes from the fact that it allows investment only when the investment makes sense. For example, if the results of phase 1 are not satisfactory, one has the option to abandon the project. As a result, one will invest in phase 3 only if the results of phase 2 tell one that it is valuable to do so.

Table 21.3 ● An alternative model to estimate the expected value

A	B	C	D	E	F
1	2003	2004	2005	2006	2007
2 **Phase 1**	100%				
3 Value	−0.75				
4 Weighted value	−0.75				
5 **Phase 2**		70%			
6 Cumulated probability		70%			
7 Value		1.90			
8 Weighted value		−1.33			
9 **Phase 3**			50%		
10 Cumulated probability			35%		
11 Value			−8.33		
12 Weighted value			−2.91		
13 **Pre-launch**					
14 Value			−3.56		
15 Weighted value			−1.25		
16 **Factory**					
17 Value			−8.97		
18 Weighted value			−3.14		
19 **Launch Profile 1**					19%
20 Cumulated probability					7%
21 Value					212.62
22 Weighted value					13.95
23 **Licence Profile 2**					
24 Value					4.58
25 Weighted value					0.30
26					
27 **Expected value**	4.87	5.62	6.95		14.25

Background

B4: =B2*B3; Copy in C8, D12; and F22.
In D15: =D14*D10; in D18: =D17*D10; in F25: = F24*F20
C6: =B2*C5
D10: =D9*C6
F19: =.5*.75*.5
F20: =F19*D10

Backwards, from F to B:
F27: =F22 + F25
D27 =F27 + D12 + D15 + D18
C27: =D27 + C8
B27: =C27 + B4

- The value of flexibility is created by the fact that 98% of the irreversible commitment can be deferred. Table 21.4 shows a very interesting result: while an investment that is committed irreversibly today has a 100% weight, any investment that is deferred into the future has a weight equal to the probability of that future only. Investing in phase 1 has a weight of 100% but investing in phase 3, a decision that will be made only if phases 1 and 2 are successful, has a weight of 35% only (35% is the combined probabilities of success of phases 1 and 2).
- Without flexibility it is difficult to create value in high-risk contexts. While revenues are not very likely and therefore have a small weight (less than 7% here), all irreversible

Table 21.4 ● Estimating the value of the option to license Eagle

Base case

	2003	2004	2005	2006	2007
Phase 1	100%				
Value	-0.75				
Weighted value	-0.75				
Phase 2		70%			
Cumulated probability		70%			
Value		-1.90			
Weighted value		-1.33			
Phase 3			50%		
Cumulated probability			35%		
Value			-8.33		
Weighted value			-2.91		
Pre-launch			50%		
Value			-3.56		
Weighted value			-1.25		
Factory			50%		
Value			-8.97		
Weighted value			-3.14		
Launch Profile 1					19%
Cumulated probability					7%
Value					212.62
Weighted value					13.95
Licence Profile 2					19%
Value					4.58
Weighted value					0.30
Expected value	4.87	5.62	6.95		14.25

Case with no option to license

	2003	2004	2005	2006	2007
Phase 1	100%				
Value	-0.75				
Weighted value	-0.75				
Phase 2		70%			
Cumulated probability		70%			
Value		-1.90			
Weighted value		-1.33			
Phase 3			50%		
Cumulated probability			35%		
Value			-8.33		
Weighted value			-2.91		
Pre-launch			50%		
Value			-3.56		
Weighted value			-1.25		
Factory			50%		
Value			-8.97		
Weighted value			-3.14		
Launch					38%
Cumulated probability					13%
Value					-16.54
Weighted value					-2.17
Profile 1					50%
Cumulated probability					7%
Value					229.16
Weighted value					15.04
Profile 2					
Value					5.73
Weighted value					0.38
Expected value	3.86	4.61	5.94		13.24

Table 21.5 ● Assessing the value of flexibility

	Flexible development process	Inflexible development process	Value created by flexibility
Commitment to phase 1	−0.75	−0.75	
Other commitments			
Phase 2	−1.33	−1.90	0.57
Phase 3	−2.91	−8.33	5.41
Pre-launch	−1.25	−3.56	2.31
Factory	−3.14	−8.97	5.83
Campaign	−1.09	−16.54	15.46
Expected revenues			
Expected revenues Profile 1	15.04	15.04	0.00
Expected revenues Profile 2	0.30	0.38	−0.08
Value	5.63	−23.88	**29.50**
Net value	4.87	−24.64	

investments have a 100% weight. Flexibility is of a considerable help in such situations. Through deferring commitment, flexibility decreases the weights of the investments and brings these weights close to the weight of the receipts. A case in point is the launch expenses in Table 21.5. The commitment to this large spending is deferred until one is really sure that Eagle Profile 1 is launched. As a result launch expenses have the same weight as the net revenues of Eagle Profile 1.

21.3 Checking that risk increases the value of flexibility

It is an important result of the theory of finance that the value of financial options increases with risk. This result is also valid for real options and we can check that the value of the flexibility of Eagle increases with risk.

Commercial risk creates value

The case states that the present value of the commercial outcomes from Eagle can be 5.73 or 229.16 million. The middle of this range is 117.45. Let us assume two alternative situations with the same middle point but with less or more dispersion around the middle point:

● *Situation A*: the present value of the commercial outcome of Eagle can take one value only: 117.45 m.
● *Situation B*: the present value of the commercial outcomes can be either −94.27 m or 329.16 m. If the extremely low outcome materializes the company has the option to abandon the project: Eagle is not launched and the actual value is zero.

We can use the model of Table 21.3 to estimate the new values of investing in Eagle's development. The results are shown in Table 21.7 and compared with the results without flexibility. As the middle point is the same (117.45), the value of the situation without flexibility also remains the same (−24.63). The important result of Table 21.7 is that the

Table 21.6 ● A model to assess the value of flexibility

#	A	B	C	D	E	F	G	H	I	J	K	L	M
		2003	2004	2005	2006	2007			2003	2004	2005	2006	2007
1	Base							No flexibility					
2													
3	Phase 1	100%						Phase 1	100%				
4	Value	-0.75						Value	-0.75				
5	Weighted	-0.75						Weighted	-0.75				
6	Phase 2		70%					Phase 2		100%			
7	Cum. prob.		70%					Cumulated		100%			
8	Value		-1.90					Value		-1.90			
9	Weighted		-1.33					Weighted		-1.90			
10	Phase 3			50%				Phase 3			100%		
11	Cum. prob.			35%				Cumulated			100%		
12	Value			-8.33				Value			-8.33		
13	Weighted			-2.91				Weighted			-8.33		
14	Pre-launch			50%				Pre-launch			100%		
15	Value			-3.56				Value			-3.56		
16	Weighted			-1.25				Weighted			-3.56		
17	Factory			50%				Factory			100%		
18	Value			-8.97				Value			-8.97		
19	Weighted			-3.14				Weighted			-8.97		
20	Launch Profile 1					19%		Launch			100%		
21	Cum. prob.					7%		Cumulated			100%		
22	Value					212.62		Value			-16.54		
23	Weighted					13.95		Weighted					
24	Licence Profile 2					19%		Profile 1					7%
25	Value					4.58		Cumulated					
26	Weighted					0.30		Value					229.16
27								Weighted					15.04
28								Profile 2					
29								Value					5.73
30								Weighted					0.38
31		4.87	5.62	6.95		14.25			-24.64	-23.89	-21.99		15.41

Note: If you introduce a formula in M25: +F21, you can use the model to test estimate the value of flexibility when the probabilities of success change.

Table 21.7 ● The value of flexibility with less and more commercial risk

	Less commercial risk			More commercial risk		
	Flexibility	No flexibility	Value created by flexibility	Flexibility	No flexibility	Value created by flexibility
Commitment to phase 1	−0.75	−0.75		−0.75	−0.75	
Other commitments						
Phase 2	−1.33	−1.90	0.57	−1.33	−1.90	0.57
Phase 3	−2.91	−8.33	5.41	−2.91	−8.33	5.41
Pre-launch	−1.25	−3.56	2.31	−1.25	−3.56	2.31
Factory	−3.14	−8.97	5.83	−3.14	−8.97	5.83
Campaign	−2.17	−16.54	14.37	−1.09	−16.54	15.46
Expected revenues						
Expected revenues Profile 1	7.71	7.71	0.00	21.60	21.60	0.00
Expected revenues Profile 2	7.71	7.71	0.00	0.00	−6.19	6.19
Value	4.62	−23.88	**28.49**	11.89	−23.88	**35.76**
Net value	3.87	−24.63		11.14	−24.63	

value of flexibility and *the value of investing in the development of Eagle increases with commercial risk*. This is a very important result. When considering committing to a development project, and provided that the investments needed by the project do not require major immediate and irreversible commitments, then the risk of the commercial outcome should not be seen as a destroyer but as a creator of value. As soon as the existence of options enables you to capture the upside of risk while avoiding its downside, you obviously prefer risky situations. When there is flexibility, risk becomes an opportunity!

Secondly, the impact of risk depends very much on the nature of the commitment required. When a situation calls for immediate and irreversible commitment, then risk destroys value. This is the typical feeling most people have of risk. However, when the situation allows for deferring commitment, then risk may become a source of value. This is a less intuitive result that both decision diagrams and option valuation models help us to understand.

Eagle (II)

Why not make a step-wise investment in the production facility?

In order to avoid investing too early in a full production facility, the company investigated the possibility of a staged approach. A solution was to start with an investment of $10 million in 2006 in a test factory that could be approved by the FDA. This would be followed by a further investment of $13 million in additional capacity in 2009. The present end of 2002 values of these investments had been estimated at 4.98 and 4.61 million respectively.[1]

Should one try to combine phases 1 and 2 and accelerate Eagle's introduction?

When analyzing Table Q.1 and considering the very large cash flows generated by Eagle at the end of its life, John Reich could not prevent himself from thinking that it would be very valuable to benefit from one more of these cash flows at least! The end of the life of Eagle was caused by the end of the patent protection in 2018. As a result, there was only one way to gain one more year: to introduce the product earlier. A possibility of doing that could be to run simultaneously clinical trials phases 2 and 3. This had a cost however: in order to do that, the company would have to commit to the large investments of phase 3 without knowing the results of phase 2.

Further growth options

John Reich was not sure that it was correct to assume that at the end of each step of Eagle's development there were two alternatives only. Either:

- 'we produce knowledge that enables us to push Eagle to its next stage of development', or
- 'we do not produce any useful knowledge' and we stop.

John Reich wanted to find out if some of the knowledge that was not useful in pushing Eagle to its next stage of development could trigger the launch of other products.

Note

1. You can generate these values with the model in Table 21.1. It is just a matter of introducing a few blank rows and creating two areas for the investments in production facilities: first step in 2006 and second step in 2009.

21.4 Time and risk/flexibility value of cash flows

The contribution of any cash flow to the total value of a decision is the result of three factors:

- its **absolute value**,
- its **date of occurrence**,
- its **risk/flexibility**. A cash flow that will occur for sure, or that is committed irreversibly, has a one-to-one contribution to value. A cash flow that is uncertain or not irreversibly committed contributes in proportion to its probability (a factor less than one).

When you draw decision diagrams and portray the usual decisions–events–options–events sequences, then you realize that, as shown in Figure 21.3, the risk/flexibility of cash flows increases with time.

Accelerate receipts and delay payments!

At the level of any single cash flow risk/flexibility and time value of money typically reinforce each other. This makes it really valuable to:

- bring the receipts forward;
- push the payments as far as possible into the future! When considering pushing payments away into the future, what really matters is to try to time commitments in such a way that they always follow the revelation of information. Making payments 'contingent' on information or 'flexible' is a powerful source of value creation.

Be careful with the cost of losing flexibility!

When accelerating receipts, you have to assess the impact of this acceleration on the timing of payments:

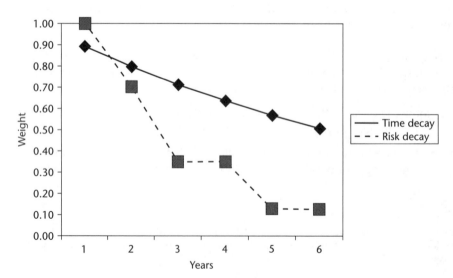

Figure 21.3 Time and risk decay of Eagle's cash flows

● Accelerating payments cause a loss due to time value of money. As payments are typically smaller than receipts, this loss is generally smaller than the gain caused by the acceleration of payments.

● Accelerating payments may also cause a loss due to the change in the risk/flexibility of a payment. Instead of being contingent on information, a payment can suddenly become irreversible. The cost of losing flexibility can be larger than the gain derived from an acceleration of the payments.

21.5 Value of speed vs. value of flexibility

Eagle (II) offers two opportunities for assessing the relative values of speed and flexibility.

Should one make a staged investment in production?

From the point of view of the absolute amount of the investment, the staged approach is not a good idea: you have to spend $23 million instead of 20 m. When time value of money is taken into account, the staged approach is still not a good idea: in present value terms, you have to spend $9.59 million (4.61 + 4.98) instead of 8.97 m.

But, as shown in Table 21.8, when you introduce the value of flexibility, then the stepwise approach looks like a good idea. Increased flexibility decreases the weighted value of the investment in the factory from $3.14 million to 2.04 m, a 1.10 million increase in the value of committing to the development of Eagle.

Should one try to accelerate Eagle's launch?

Creating value out of speeding up the launch of a new product sounds almost like common sense.[1] The problem, however, is that speeding up the launch of Eagle has both advantages and disadvantages. The clear advantage is that the receipts of Eagle are going to be accelerated. The disadvantage is that the payments are also going to be accelerated. Speeding up payments will actually not be a problem in all cases:

● Accelerating the payments that are contingent on the launch (launch expenses, cost of goods sold, etc.) will not be much of a problem. Speeding these payments will increase their value in proportion to time value of money but their flexibility weight will not change. The weight of these payments will remain the same as the weight of the receipts and since these payments are smaller than the receipts, the acceleration will have a net positive effect on value.

● The problem will come with the acceleration of the other payments and in particular of the payments for phase 3 clinical trials. With the present flexible development process these payments are contingent on the success of phase 2 trials. If one now wants to start phase 3 before the information that is needed (success of phase 2) is available, then the payments of phase 3 are no longer contingent and their flexibility weight changes considerably (from 35% to 70%).

You can use the model in Table 21.1 to estimate the values of launching Eagle one year early. It is 257.85 m for profile 1 and 5.83 million for profile 2. You can then modify the model in Table 21.3 and make it describe the situation of an early launch. If you do so you get the results shown in Table 21.9. They show that the loss of value due to the loss of flexibility is greater than the gain of value due to the speeding up of the project. This is

Table 21.8 ● Assessing the value of a staged investment in production

	2003	2004	2005	2006	2007
Phase 1	100%				
Value	−0.75				
Weighted value	−0.75				
Phase 2		70%			
Cumulated probability		70%			
Value		−1.90			
Weighted value		−1.33			
Phase 3			50%		
Cumulated probability			35%		
Value			−8.33		
Weighted value			−2.91		
Pre-launch					
Value			−3.56		
Weighted value			−1.25		
Factory					
Value			−4.98		−4.61
Weighted value			−1.74		−0.30
Launch Profile 1					19%
Cumulated probability					7%
Value					212.62
Weighted value					13.95
Launch Profile 2					
Value					4.58
Weighted value					0.30
Expected value	5.97	6.72	8.05		13.95

obviously not a general result. Value is often created by speeding up projects. However, you have to keep in mind that:

- speed and flexibility affect both receipts and disbursements;
- speeding up receipts and the disbursements that are contingent on these receipts is valuable;
- speeding up disbursements that are not contingent on receipts may make them less flexible – or even irreversible – and this can create a large loss of value.

Risk, flexibility and speed

In very risky situations speeding up is often a very poor idea. If that seems counter-intuitive to you, consider again the process of developing Eagle. Most of the value of investing in Eagle's development is created by the flexibility of this process. Eagle is valuable only because spending is phased in a very smart way:

- The fact that development is organized in a series of successive phases definitely delays the launch of the product as compared to an alternative solution where all the development would be done in parallel. Phasing definitely destroys value.

Table 21.9 • Assessing the value of trying to speed up Eagle

	2003	2004	2005	2006
Phase 1	100%			
Value	−0.75			
Weighted value	−0.75			
Phase 2		70%		
Cumulated probability		70%		
Value		−1.90		
Weighted value		−1.33		
Phase 3				
Cumulated probability		70%		
Value		−9.33		
Weighted value		−6.53		
Pre-launch				
Value		−3.99		
Weighted value		−2.79		
Factory				
Value		−10.04		
Weighted value		−7.03		
Launch Profile 1				
Cumulated probability				7%
Value				257.85
Weighted value				16.92
Licence Profile 2				
Value				5.53
Weighted value				0.36
Expected value	−1.14	−0.39		17.28

- But the succession of steps also creates flexibility and enables the company to render its investments contingent on its progressive discovery of Eagle. This creates more value than the value that is destroyed by the implied delay in the launch of the product.

Even though it creates a lot of value at the beginning of the process of developing Eagle, flexibility will not be as important once most of the uncertainty is resolved. As soon as the company knows that Eagle can be launched, then speed will become the main driver of value. The interplay between risk, flexibility and speed is depicted in Figure 21.4. Flexibility and speed are two powerful ways to create value. They are somewhat opposite forces and should be used in different circumstances:

- When risk is high, flexibility often creates more value than speed. It is often a good idea to go for progressive commitment and to accept the loss of the positive effect of speed.
- When risk is low, speed becomes the main driver of value. It is then a good idea to go for full commitment, to accept the risk and forget about flexibility which is a non-issue in such a situation.
- When risk is high, one should be careful with speed: is it really good to increase an already high risk with full commitment?

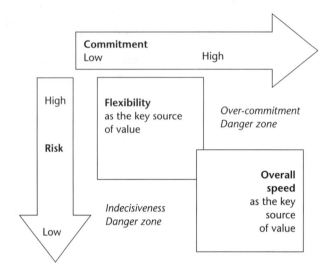

Figure 21.4 Risk, speed, flexibility and commitment

● When risk is low, one should be careful with looking for flexibility: this can easily become indecisiveness.

The paradox with flexibility

Contrary to what some people think, going for flexibility does not mean being slow. Going for flexibility actually means starting immediately with experimentation and learning. When you go for flexibility you have to break the whole issue into a series of small parts that can be immediately implemented and tested. This is the paradox with flexibility:

● Organizations that act flexibly do not spend much time analyzing each of their moves. They just go, experiment, correct and progressively develop the whole thing by trial and error. Such organizations generally give an impression of very high activity – and speed.
● Organizations that go for big moves necessarily need more time for analyzing each of their moves. During the periods when they analyze their moves these organizations often look slow.

21.6 Have we accounted for all the flexibility?

This is a critical question and the Eagle (III) case suggests an additional source of value: what of the possibility to generate knowledge that could be used for launching new products? One can imagine that at some stage, the clinical studies may reveal that the knowledge developed could enable the company to develop another product instead of Eagle or in addition to Eagle. If you believe that such a possibility exists, then you have to redraw the decision diagram, estimate the new end points, assess the probabilities and re-estimate the expected value.

When analyzing a situation like Eagle, you can never be sure that all flexibility has been accounted for. The only way you can be confident that no major option has been ignored is to make sure you go through a sufficient number of brainstorming exercises with colleagues and experts using decision diagrams as a tool for structuring your thinking.

21.7 Why not simply discount at a higher rate?

Figure 21.3 shows that time and risk have the same type of effect: they both decrease the value of cash flows and for both of them this negative impact on cash flows increases with time. This is the rationale that has often been used for combining the effects of time and risk into a higher discount rate: when discounting risky cash flows, one adds a 'risk premium' to the discount rate. Which premium should we use for Eagle?

Table 21.10 shows the value of investing in Eagle as obtained with different discount rates. As one might expect, it is possible to find the value of investing in phase 1 clinical trials (4.87) by applying a risk adjusted discount rate to the non-discounted after tax cash flows of the project. However, this is of relatively little practical value and the questions remain:

● How to find out the relevant risk premium?
● How to account for the fact that the risk decay is generally not as smooth as assumed by the risk premium?
● Should you use one single or several risk-adapted rates?

Even if the risk premium idea looks attractive to you, let me strongly recommend that you use decision diagrams rather than risk adjusted discount rates. Decision diagrams are most

Table 21.10 ● Using a risk adjusted discount rate

	2002	2003	2004	2005	2006	2007
Time decay	89%	80%	71%	64%	57%	51%
Risk decay	100%	70%	35%	35%	13%	7%
Combined	89%	56%	25%	22%	7%	3%
Rate with same effect	12%	34%	59%	46%	68%	76%

	2002	2003	2004	2005	2006	2007
Cash flows	−0.84	−2.38	−5.95	−30.04	203.56[a]	−15.40

[a] This is the average value of cash flows at their 2006 value: (407.89 − 15.4 + 14.63)/2. The 407.89 and 14.63 are calculated using a 12% rate.

You get the following NPVs for these cash flows:

Discount rate	NPV
76%	6.07
68%	8.16
59%	11.43
71%	7.31

effective at helping you find the 'right' number, and most important, they have the unique advantage of making you think about alternative sequences of decisions–events–options and so on.

Thinking about alternative sequences and progressively discovering better ones is the most rewarding exercise that you can do when confronted with an issue like Eagle. Finding how much value is created is important but the process of discovery is even more so.

Note

1. There is a wide literature focusing on 'speeding up' new products and the process of new product development. Refer for example to: P. Smith and D. Reinertsen (1998), *Developing Products in Half the Time*, John Wiley.

Appendices to Part V
Using a new technology to capture growth while keeping flexibility

APPENDIX

CLS produces and sells oxygen, nitrogen and other air gases. In 2003, CLS is contemplating an investment in a new plant in Peru. This investment, which is aimed at capturing the expected growth in the Peruvian market, is a large and risky investment.

Case S and the model attached enables you to assess the magnitude of the risk involved. While the analysis of the value created is done, as one should, incrementally, the analysis of the risk envisages the impact of a price war on the totality of the business.

Case T introduces an alternative way to serve the market. A recent technology would enable CLS to serve its large customers with small dedicated plants. As the growth is expected to come mainly from such large customers, why not drop the large plant and be prepared to build small plants when needed?

CASE *S*

The CLS project

On 11 May 2003 Rick De Jong was preparing the board meeting of the daughter company of ZB Gas in Peru that was scheduled for two weeks later, on 25 May.

Rick De Jong was a senior vice-president of ZB Gas, a global company producing and selling oxygen, nitrogen and other air gases. He headed the Process Industry division of ZB Gas and was also the chairman of the board of several local companies and of the local Peruvian company in particular. A key item on the agenda was the decision to invest in the CLS project, a new air separation unit. As usual the financial numbers were telling that ZB Gas should go ahead and invest some US$22 million, an amount 30% higher than the sales made by ZB Gas Peru in 2002!

Rick De Jong had a long experience of the gas business and he was fully aware that this was one of the most capital intensive businesses. The problem though was that it was not easy to create value out of these large investments. Over the last few months Rick De Jong had heard about many new air separation unit projects – inside and outside ZB Gas – and he was feeling somewhat nervous:

- What if the investment in CLS were to fail to deliver the results shown in the financial study? He wanted to play with the spreadsheet of the CLS project and generate a good sensitivity analysis.
- Was the decision limited to an 'invest now or never in a new plant' option? Would it be possible to defer this investment until the company was in a better position to load it with firm customer contracts? Why was the choice apparently limited to a large all purpose air separation unit solution? Why not try also to benefit from the recent membrane technology that was allowing for smaller customer dedicated units?

Producing and selling air gases

The industrial gas industry (oxygen, nitrogen, argon and other air gases) was often referred to as an industry with more robust earnings than those of other industrial companies. This was due to some unique characteristics of the industry and in particular to its competitive structure and the nature of the contracts that the gas companies had with their customers.

Industrial gas was a global industry but while companies were global in spread, national markets were often dominated by just two or three players. In addition, unlike most chemical markets, the end products could not be transported over large distances. The cost was just too high.

Gas companies were supplying their products to customers through three main delivery methods:

- **On-site.** The very large customers – steel works, chemical plants, etc. – were supplied via pipeline from a large (typically dedicated) air separation unit.[1] Contracts with customers often ran for 10 to 15 years with a 'take-or-pay' clause. In recent years, a new form of on-site business had been developed with medium sized customers. In this case the gas was not produced by the traditional cryogenic process but by a new separation process – for example through membranes – developed in the 1980s.[2]
- **Merchant.** Most medium sized customers received their supplies in tankers: the gas was delivered in liquid form to a storage tank on the customer's premises. The merchant market was the most volatile form of income for gas companies.
- **Cylinders.** This was the solution for small customers who generally also paid a rental charge for the use of the cylinder. For the gas companies that were involved in this business, it was a capital intensive, logistics intensive activity.

ZB Gas in Peru

In 2002 the merchant and cylinder market[3] for industrial gases in Peru had amounted to $27 million. The market was dominated by two companies of equal size: ZB Gas and IMC, a subsidiary of a large local diversified industrial group. In 2002, one of the large global companies had established a representative office in Lima.

ZB Gas had two plants with a total capacity of 10.9 million m^3 for oxygen – a capacity that was going to be increased to 14 million in 2004. The ZB Gas plants were not modern, which meant a higher electricity consumption.

IMC had invested in a new plant in 2001. This was the largest plant in Peru for the merchant market. In 2003, IMC had twice as much capacity as ZB Gas.

The management of ZB Gas was concerned about the company's low pace of investment. This was especially worrying since they expected the market in Peru to grow fast in the coming decade. Table S.1 shows the financial statements of ZB Gas Peru, and their forecasts for the development of the Peruvian market are shown in Table S.2.

Table S.1 ● Financial performance of ZB Peru

	1998	1999	2000	2001	2002	2003 (budget)
Sales ($ million)	10.5	12.0	13.7	14.7	16.9	20.8
Operating income	2.8	2.9	4.0	4.2	3.9	4.3

Table S.2 ● Expected development of the demand for oxygen

	2003	2005	2008	2011
Demand for oxygen that can be captured by ZB Gas (million m^3)	7.1	14.0	23.4	31.7

CASE

384 • Business Finance: Applications, Models and Cases

The CLS project

CLS was a $21.7 million investment in a new merchant air separation unit in Lima. CLS was going to replace the two existing gas plants of ZB Gas. It was planned to start the operations of this plant in 2005. The financial study made in support of the investment decision is shown in Figure S.3.

Notes

1. The cryogenic technology used for air gas production is based on the air being compressed and cooled to −190°C where it becomes liquefied. The air gases boil at different temperatures and can therefore be separated from the liquid gas. This process consumed a little less than 1 kWh of electricity per cubic metre of liquid gas.
2. This was a much more energy efficient process than the traditional cryogenic one. However, it could not be used for applications requiring 100% pure gases.
3. One distinctive feature of the Peruvian market was the large number of plants which supplied industries in isolated areas – mines in particular – with oxygen. These plants were owned by the oxygen-consuming industries and generally had no impact on the merchant gas market. ZB Gas expected to grow its business through taking charge of more and more of these private plants in the future.

Appendix V.1
Risk analysis of a major capital expenditure

The model in Figure S.3 is designed for performing sensitivity and risk analyses. Please note the feature that allows you to simulate two types of uncertainties on variables such as volume of demand (rows 3 to 7), power costs (row 34) etc. The first type of uncertainty relates to the absolute level of the variable: you can adjust the initial level of the variable by changing the first parameter (change of initial level in column B for the volume of demand). The second type of uncertainty refers to the trajectory of evolution of this variable. As an example the base version of the model assumes that the demand of oxygen will grow very fast in the initial years of study and then grow much slower: what if this were to be just the opposite: slow growth in the initial years followed by faster growth in the later years?

Also note the feature that allows you to simulate the impact of a price war on the totality of the business and not only on the incremental business that is described in the financial analysis. This a problem with incremental analyses: they properly describe the additional value created by a decision (value is additive). They do not necessarily properly describe risk (risk is not an additive).

When people in the gas industry discuss this case and are asked to identify the three major uncertainties, they typically come up with:

● The risk of a price war. With CLS, ZB Gas is going to create a lot of capacity in the market. This could trigger a price war that could well bring the prices down to 80%–60% of their current levels. Prices will probably not stay at these low levels for ever but it might take many years before they come back to a more reasonable level. Contrary to what is assumed in the model, prices of gas on the merchant market tend to decrease over time. When asked about the chances of a price war occurring, most people state that it is very likely.

Table S.3 ● Financial study to support CLS

	A	B	C	D	E	F	G	H	I	J	K	L	M	N	O	P	Q
1		2003	2004	2005	2006	2007	2008	2009	2010	2011	2012	2013	2014	2015	2016		
2	Forecast demand (volume)																
3		I Lev Annual change														Average	
4	Cylinder oxygen	0%	3%	3%	3%	3%	3%	3%	3%	3%	3%	3%	3%	3%	3%	3.0%	
5	Liquid oxygen	0%	49%	32%	29%	16%	12%	11%	11%	10%	6%	5%	4%	4%	4%	14.2%	
6	Liquid nitrogen	0%	41%	150%	38%	10%	9%	5%	10%	3%	5%	3%	3%	3%	3%	17.6%	
7	Liquid argon	0%	10%	10%	10%	16%	24%	14%	6%	6%	6%	5%	5%	4%	4%	9.1%	
8	Cylinder oxygen	3.1	3.2	3.3	3.4	3.5	3.6	3.7	3.8	3.9	4.0	4.2	4.3	4.4	4.6		
9	Liquid oxygen	7.1	10.6	14.0	18.0	20.9	23.4	26.0	28.8	31.7	33.6	35.3	36.7	38.2	39.7		
10	Liquid nitrogen	2.9	4.1	10.2	14.1	15.5	16.9	17.8	19.5	20.1	21.1	21.8	22.4	23.1	23.8		
11	Liquid argon	0.2	0.2	0.2	0.3	0.3	0.4	0.4	0.4	0.5	0.5	0.5	0.5	0.6	0.6		
12	Production needed (volume)																
13	Oxygen (6% losses)	10.9	14.7	18.4	22.8	25.9	28.7	31.6	34.7	37.9	40.1	42.0	43.6	45.3	47.1		
14	Nitrogen (9% losses)	3.2	4.5	11.2	15.5	17.1	18.6	19.5	21.5	22.1	23.2	23.9	24.6	25.4	26.1		
15	Argon	0.2	0.2	0.2	0.3	0.3	0.4	0.4	0.4	0.5	0.5	0.5	0.5	0.6	0.6		
16																	
17	Capacity of the current plants																
18	Oxygen	10.9	14.0	14.0	14.0	14.0	14.0	14.0	14.0	14.0	14.0	14.0	14.0	14.0	14.0	168.0	
19	Nitrogen	3.2	1.7	2.0	3.9	3.9	3.9	3.9	3.9	3.9	3.9	3.9	3.9	3.9	3.9	44.9	
20	Argon	0.2	0.2	0.2	0.2	0.2	0.2	0.2	0.2	0.2	0.2	0.2	0.2	0.2	0.2	2.4	
21	Capacity of the new plant																
22	Oxygen			37.5	37.5	37.5	37.5	37.5	37.5	37.5	37.5	37.5	37.5	37.5	37.5	450.0	
23	Nitrogen			26.0	26.0	26.0	26.0	26.0	26.0	26.0	26.0	26.0	26.0	26.0	26.0	312.0	
24	Argon			0.4	0.4	0.4	0.4	0.4	0.4	0.4	0.4	0.4	0.4	0.4	0.4	4.8	
25	Volume gained with the new plant																
26	Oxygen			4.4	8.8	11.9	14.7	17.6	20.7	23.5	23.5	23.5	23.5	23.5	23.5	219.1	
27	Nitrogen			9.2	11.6	13.2	14.7	15.6	17.6	18.2	19.3	20.0	20.7	21.5	22.1	203.7	
28	Argon			0.0	0.1	0.1	0.2	0.2	0.2	0.2	0.2	0.2	0.2	0.2	0.2	1.9	
29	New plant oxygen prod.			18.4	22.8	25.9	28.7	31.6	34.7	37.5	37.5	37.5	37.5	37.5	37.5		
30	Capacity used (%)			49	61	69	77	84	93	100	100	100	100	100	100		
31																	

CASE

Table S.3 continued

A	B	C	D	E	F	G	H	I	J	K	L	M	N	O	P	Q
	2003	2004	2005	2006	2007	2008	2009	2010	2011	2012	2013	2014	2015	2016		
32 Costs																
33 **Current plants**			I.Lev	Annual	change											
34 Change in power costs			0%	0%	0%	0%	0%	0%	0%	0%	0%	0%	0%	0%		
35 Power			1.76	1.76	1.76	1.76	1.76	1.76	1.76	1.76	1.76	1.76	1.76	1.76		
36 Change in fixed costs			0%	4%	5%	5%	5%	5%	6%	6%	6%	6%	7%	7%		
37 Fixed costs			0.83	0.86	0.91	0.95	1.00	1.05	1.11	1.18	1.25	1.32	1.41	1.51		
38 Transport costs			0.02	0.02	0.02	0.02	0.02	0.02	0.02	0.02	0.03	0.03	0.03	0.03		
39 **New plant**			I.Lev	Annual	change											
40 Change in power costs			0%	0%	0%	0%	0%	0%	0%	0%	0%	0%	0%	0%		
41 Unit power cost			0.10	0.09	0.09	0.08	0.07	0.07	0.07	0.07	0.07	0.07	0.07	0.07		
42 Power			1.84	1.94	2.21	2.30	2.34	2.43	2.63	2.63	2.63	2.63	2.63	2.63		
43 Change in fixed costs			0%	0%	0%	0%	0%	0%	0%	0%	0%	0%	0%	0%		
44 Fixed costs			0.44	0.44	0.44	0.44	0.44	0.44	0.44	0.44	0.44	0.44	0.44	0.44		
45 Change in transport costs			0%	0%	0%	0%	0%	0%	0%	0%	0%	0%	0%	0%		
46 Transport costs			0.59	0.73	0.83	0.92	1.01	1.11	1.20	1.20	1.20	1.20	1.20	1.20		
47 Change in selling expenses	0%		50%	33%	25%	10%	10%	10%	10%	10%	10%	10%	10%	10%	Average	
48 Selling expenses	0.1		0.15	0.20	0.25	0.27	0.30	0.33	0.37	0.40	0.44	0.49	0.53	0.59	16%	

Background

B4:B7: coefficient for adjusting the initial level (data)
C4:O7: annual changes (data)
P4: =(O8/B8)^(1/13)−1. Copy to P5:P7
B8: =3.1*(1+B4); C8: +B8*(1+C4); Copy
B9: =7.1*(1+B5); C9: +B9*(1+C5); Copy
B10: =2.9*(1+B6); C10: +B10*(1+C6); Copy
B11: =.19*(1+B7); C11: +B11*(1+C7); Copy
B13: =(B8+B9)/(1−.06); Copy
B14: +B10/(1−.09); Copy
B15: +B11; Copy

B18: O20 and D22:O24: data.
D26: =IF(D13<D22,+D13−D18,D22−D18); Copy
D27: =IF(D14<D23,+D14−D19,D23−D19); Copy
D28: =IF(D15<D24,+D15−D20,D24−D20); Copy
D29: =D26+D18; Copy
D30: =D29/D22; Copy
D35: =1.759*(1+D34); E35: =D35*(1+E34); Copy
D37: =.829*(1+D36); E37: =D37*(1+E36); Copy
D38: =.017; E38: =D38*(1+E36); Copy

D41: =IF(D30<0.5,0.1,IF(D30<0.6,0.09,IF(D30<0.7,0.085,IF(D30<0.8,0.08,IF(D30<0.9,0.074,0.07))))); Copy
D42: =D41*D29*(1+$D$40); E42: =E41*E29*(1+$D$40); F42: =F41*F29*(1+$D$40)*(1+$E$40)*(1+$F$40); etc.
D44: =.444*(1+D43); E44: =D44*(1+E43); Copy
D46: =0.032*(1+$D$45)*D29; E46: =0.032*(1+$D$45)*(1+$E$45)*E29; F46: =0.032*(1+$D$45)*(1+$E$45)*(1+$F$45)*F29; etc.
C48: =.1*(1+C47); D48: =C48*(1+D47); Copy; P48: =(O48/C48)^(1/12)−1

		2003	2004	2005	2006	2007	2008	2009	2010	2011	2012	2013	2014	2015	2016	Total
49																
50	**Prices**			I.Lev	Annual	change										
51																
52	Change in liquid oxygen price			0%	0%	0%	0%	0%	0%	0%	0%	0%	0%	0%	0%	
53	Change in liquid nitrogen price			0%	0%	0%	0%	0%	0%	0%	0%	0%	0%	0%	0%	
54	Change in liquid argon price			0%	0%	0%	0%	0%	0%	0%	0%	0%	0%	0%	0%	
55	Liquid oxygen price			0.20	0.20	0.20	0.20	0.20	0.20	0.20	0.20	0.20	0.20	0.20	0.20	
56	Liquid nitrogen price			0.15	0.15	0.15	0.15	0.15	0.15	0.15	0.15	0.15	0.15	0.15	0.15	
57	Liquid argon price			2.00	2.00	2.00	2.00	2.00	2.00	2.00	2.00	2.00	2.00	2.00	2.00	
58	**Capital expenditure**	0%														Total
59	Change in equipment															
60	Equipment	5.6	13.8	0.2												19.6 21.9
61	Building	0.2	1.5													1.8
62	Land	0.6														0.6
63	**Value analysis – everything incremental:**															
64	Incremental sales			2.3	3.6	4.5	5.5	6.3	7.2	7.8	8.0	8.1	8.2	8.3	8.4	78.3
65	Losses on price			0.0	0.0	0.0	0.0	0.0	0.0	0.0	0.0	0.0	0.0	0.0	0.0	0.0
66	Incremental power costs			0.1	0.2	0.4	0.5	0.6	0.7	0.9	0.9	0.9	0.9	0.9	0.9	7.7
67	Incremental fixed costs			-0.4	-0.4	-0.5	-0.5	-0.6	-0.6	-0.7	-0.7	-0.8	-0.9	-1.0	-1.1	-8.0
68	Incremental transport costs			0.6	0.7	0.8	0.9	1.0	1.1	1.2	1.2	1.2	1.2	1.2	1.2	12.1
69	Incremental selling costs		0.1	0.2	0.2	0.2	0.3	0.3	0.3	0.4	0.4	0.4	0.5	0.5	0.6	4.4
70	Incremental op. income before depn			1.9	2.9	3.5	4.3	4.9	5.7	6.1	6.3	6.4	6.6	6.7	6.9	**62.2**
71	Incremental depreciation			3.4	3.4	3.4	3.4	3.4	3.4	0.1	0.1	0.1	0.1	0.1	0.1	20.7
72	Incremental operating income	-0.1		-1.5	-0.4	0.1	0.9	1.6	2.3	6.0	6.2	6.3	6.5	6.6	6.8	**41.4**
73	Incremental tax savings	15%		-0.2	-0.1	0.0	0.1	0.2	0.4	0.9	0.9	1.0	1.0	1.0	1.0	6.2
74	**Incremental cash flow**	-6.4	-15.4	1.9	3.0	3.5	4.1	4.7	5.3	5.2	5.4	5.5	5.6	5.7	5.8	**5.8**
75	Discount rate	12%														
76	NPV	4.8		IRR	16%											
77	**Base NPV**	**4.8**														
78	Difference with base		0.00													
79	Losses on price															
80	Liquid oxygen prices	0.28	0.28	0.28	0.28	0.28	0.28	0.28	0.28	0.28	0.28	0.28	0.28	0.28	0.28	
81	Liquid nitrogen prices	0.18	0.18	0.18	0.18	0.18	0.18	0.18	0.18	0.18	0.18	0.18	0.18	0.18	0.18	
82	Argon prices	2.00	2.00	2.00	2.00	2.00	2.00	2.00	2.00	2.00	2.00	2.00	2.00	2.00	2.00	
83	In case of price war, do you believe that the low price will apply to all sales, no=1, yes=2														1	

CASE

Table S.3 continued

Background
D52: O54: Data.
D55: =.2*(1+D52); E55: =D55*(1+E52); Copy
D56: =.15*(1+D53); E56: =D56*(1+E53); Copy
D57: =2*(1+D54); E57: =D57*(1+E54); Copy
B60: =5.61*(1+C59); C60: =13.757*(1+C59); D60: =.232*(1+C59)
B61, C61, B62: data
C69: +C48
B74: -B60-B61-B62
D71: =($B$60+$C$60+$D$60)/6+($B$61+$C$61)/20;
Copy into E71:I71; J71: =($B$61+$C$61)/20; Copy into K71.O71

D64: =D26*D55+D27*D56+D28*D57
D65: =(IF(D55<D80,(D80-D55)*D18,0)+IF(D56<D81,(D81-D56)*D19,0)+IF(D57<D82,(D82-D57)*D20,0))*IF($N$83=2,1,0)
D66: =D42-D35
D67: =D44-D37
D68: =D46-D38
D69: =D48
D70: =D64-D66-D67-D68-D69
Copy D64: =D70 into E64: O64

C72: =C64-C65-C66-C67-C68-C71-C69; Copy
D73: =D72*$B$73; Copy
C74: -C60-C61-C62+C64-C65-C66-C67-C68-C69-C73;
Copy into D74:O74. P74: =O74; Copy into Q74
B76: =NPV(B75,B74,Q74)
Copy B76 into B77; Copy / paste special / value
E76: =IRR(B74.Q74,0.15)
C78: =B76/B77-1
B80: N82: data

- The risk of a slower build up of demand. Even though most industry people who have discussed the case tend to agree with the average growth rates of the demand, they tend to identify the risk that demand may just continuously grow at this average rate – and not build up very fast in the initial years.
- Finally, most people mention that erecting such a plant is always a major project for a local company. As a result, cost overruns are not uncommon (+15%). It can also happen that cost savings materialize (–5%). But this is much less frequent.

If you build a decision tree with these three key uncertainties, you will most likely find a negative expected value for CLS!

CASE *T*

The CLS project (II)

Building a large merchant plant was not the only solution for capturing the expected growth of the Peruvian market. Another solution was to rely on on-site oxygen generators: these generators were using new non-cryogenic technologies:

● There existed a large variety of sizes for these generators. It was easy to find the capacity that would provide most medium sized customers with maximum cost effectiveness.
● These generators were delivering oxygen with purities in the range 90–95%, which was perfectly adequate for most customers.
● Finally, these generators were more adapted to serve fairly constant demands for gas: most process industries have fairly constant consumption patterns.

ZB Gas was used to install these on-site oxygen generators and Rick De Jong was now reviewing two contracts that had just been signed with customers in another South American country. The spreadsheets of these contracts are shown in Tables T.1 and T.2. The pessimistic and optimistic assumptions that had been envisaged when signing these contracts are in Table T.3. When testing these pessimistic and optimistic assumptions Rick De Jong was surprised to see how robust the value creation ability of these contracts was. But when comparing the contracts with the CLS alternative he realized that they did not have any of the major risks of CLS. With the on-site oxygen generators, there was:

● no risk of triggering a price war;
● no risk of building up idle capacity;
● no risk of facing the cost overruns of a large project.

Value-wise, the small on-site generators were quite satisfactory especially when considering that a similar on-site solution could be used for satisfying the needs of the nitrogen customers.[1] Obviously the problem of replacing the two current plants with a new more energy effective plant remained to be solved but this could be done later with a smaller plant.

Finally, Rick De Jong used the models in Tables T.1 and T.2 to calculate the minimum price at which ZB Gas could contract the small on-site generators and still break even. The answer he came up with was $0.12 per cubic metre of oxygen, which was substantially less than the $0.20 assumed in the CLS study which was not sufficient to break even due to the high level of risk. The superior flexibility of the on-site solution was making it a real win-win solution: lower price for the customer and superior value for ZB Gas.[2]

Table T.1 ● Model of a small on-site oxygen generator

A	B	C	D	E	F	G	H	I	J	K	L	M	N	O	P	Q
1 Volume sold	4.38															
2 Price	0.2															
3 Investment	1.68															
4 *Year*		*1*	*2*	*3*	*4*	*5*	*6*	*7*	*8*	*9*	*10*	*11*	*12*	*13*	*14*	*15*
5 Sales		0.88	0.88	0.88	0.88	0.88	0.88	0.88	0.88	0.88	0.88	0.88	0.88	0.88	0.88	0.88
6 Energy costs		0.2	0.2	0.2	0.2	0.2	0.2	0.2	0.2	0.2	0.2	0.2	0.2	0.2	0.2	0.2
7 Other costs		0.04	0.04	0.04	0.04	0.04	0.04	0.04	0.04	0.04	0.04	0.04	0.04	0.04	0.04	0.04
8 Depreciation		0.24	0.24	0.24	0.24	0.24	0.24	0.24								
9 Profit before tax		0.40	0.40	0.40	0.40	0.40	0.40	0.40	0.64	0.64	0.64	0.64	0.64	0.64	0.64	0.64
10 Profit after tax		0.28	0.28	0.28	0.28	0.28	0.28	0.28	0.45	0.45	0.45	0.45	0.45	0.45	0.45	0.45
11 Cash flows	−1.68	0.52	0.52	0.52	0.52	0.52	0.52	0.52	0.45	0.45	0.45	0.45	0.45	0.45	0.45	0.45
12 Rate	0.12															
13 NPV	1.68															

Background

C5: =$B$2*$B$1; Copy
C6: =data; D6: =C6; Copy
C7: =data; D7: =C7; Copy
C8: =$B$3/7; Copy

C9: =C5−C6−C7−C8; Copy
C10: =C9*.7; Copy
B11: −B3; C11: =C10+C8; Copy
B13: =B11+NPV(B12, C11.Q11)

CASE

Table T.2 ● Model of a large on-site oxygen generator

A	B	C	D	E	F	G	H	I	J	K	L	M	N	O	P	Q
Volume sold	8.64															
Price	0.2															
Investment	3.36															
Year		1	2	3	4	5	6	7	8	9	10	11	12	13	14	15
Sales		1.73	1.73	1.73	1.73	1.73	1.73	1.73	1.73	1.73	1.73	1.73	1.73	1.73	1.73	1.73
Energy costs		0.36	0.36	0.36	0.36	0.36	0.36	0.36	0.36	0.36	0.36	0.36	0.36	0.36	0.36	0.36
Other costs		0.07	0.07	0.07	0.07	0.07	0.07	0.07	0.07	0.07	0.07	0.07	0.07	0.07	0.07	0.07
Depreciation		0.48	0.48	0.48	0.48	0.48	0.48	0.48								
Profit before tax		0.82	0.82	0.82	0.82	0.82	0.82	0.82	1.30	1.30	1.30	1.30	1.30	1.30	1.30	1.30
Profit after tax		0.57	0.57	0.57	0.57	0.57	0.57	0.57	0.91	0.91	0.91	0.91	0.91	0.91	0.91	0.91
Cash flows	–	1.05	1.05	1.05	1.05	1.05	1.05	1.05	0.91	0.91	0.91	0.91	0.91	0.91	0.91	0.91
	3.36															
Rate	0.12															
NPV	3.49															

Note: the background is the same as in the model of Table T.1.

Table T.3 ● Optimistic and pessimistic scenarios for the on-site oxygen generators

	Pessimistic scenario	Optimistic scenario
Small on-site generator	Energy cost increases by 30% overnight, we cannot pass any of this increase on to the customer Maintenance costs (other costs) are 20% higher than expected	Energy saving (10% lower energy cost) The customer needs 10% more gas. A very small/cheap modification enables us to increase the annual fee by 10%
Large on-site generator	Energy cost increases by 30% overnight, we cannot pass any of this increase on to the customer The performance of the plant is lower than expected. Energy costs are 15% higher Installation costs are 15% higher	Energy savings are possible (10% lower energy cost) Superior preventive maintenance enables us to reduce the other costs by 15% Installation costs are 10% lower

Note: As the price is guaranteed by a contract there is no price risk. There is no volume risk either for ZB Gas.

Notes

1. There was no such solution, yet, for argon however.
2. This is similar to the Gatefield project: a more flexible solution avoids destroying value which benefits both customer and supplier. The superior flexibility of the on-site technology makes it a very tough competitor for the current technology that might end up becoming a 'niche' technology: high purity applications.

CASE

Deciding to commit to external growth opportunities

Models for acquisitions, divestments, mergers, joint ventures and strategic alliances

External growth is one of the critical weapons of corporate strategy and is a popular approach for trying to reinvent companies. Experience seems to show, however, that external growth is a risky activity[1] that does not easily result in value creation. Part VI is about designing transactions that can help manage the many risks involved in external growth:

- *How to use models in order to understand the situation from both your point of view and also – and emphatically – from the point of view of the other party?*
- *How to avoid deals that create unnecessary irreversible commitments?*
- *How to use contingent deals in order to reduce risk?*

Part VI is organized around 'I in the United Kingdom', a case study developed from negotiations that took place between two major automotive groups.[2] F, the leader of the truck industry in the United Kingdom has offered I to acquire its operations. For I, the second largest European manufacturer of trucks, this is a unique opportunity to build a very strong position in a key market and to close the overall market share gap it has with the industry leader in Europe. Even though they both have a lot to gain from an agreement, I and F have to solve a series of difficult problems:

how to structure an agreement that minimizes the risk of the acquisition, how to fix a price that satisfies both parties, etc. Our task is to help I capture this strategic opportunity. Part VI starts with a framework for evaluating companies. Then the case introduces the situation as it is viewed by I.

I suggest that you read the case very carefully and prepare the negotiation with F as if you were going to run it. If you follow this advice, Part VI will provide you with a unique advantage over most real-life situations.

Case V, 'F Trucks', will enable you to discover what was the actual position of F.

And finally, Case W, 'The negotlation between I and F', will tell you how the actual negotiations developed and reached a critical stage. This will enable you to reassess the conditions of a successful deal between the two companies.

Appendix VI expands on the idea that businesses that change owner do not all have the same risks and that this probably calls for different approaches. The RFa case presents two potential divestment deals. While one looks very much like the I and F deal, the other one probably calls for a more traditional kind of deal where irreversible commitment and speed are essential. How can RFA maximize the value that it can get from these divestments?

Competition in a co-operative system

It is a specific feature of external growth situations to require one or several acquirers and one or several sellers to reach an agreement for creating and sharing value or for 'co-operating and competing'. We have introduced this important process of co-operation and competition or 'co-opetition'[3] in Appendix I.1 in Part I. Let us explore it further now.

As shown by Axelrod,[4] this process of competing and co-operating is a very pragmatic and effective rule for action. It does not require altruism, friendship or the existence of a central authority. It only requires that 'egoists', or self-interested and opportunistic people, driven by their own interests, recognize that:

● *They are not alone, there are many other 'egoists' around.*
● *Life is not a zero-sum game, i.e. there are other ways to create value than to grab it from somebody else.*
● *Their interactions with other egoists will be durable, or as expressed by Axelrod, the 'shadow of the future' is large. When interaction with others is sufficiently durable, co-operation is the most effective strategy to advance one's own interests.*

Competing and co-operating is a process that does not necessarily require the existence of negotiated agreements[5] between the parties, it may simply grow out of the interactive behaviour of the parties.[6] In the business world of today this process has become a very important strategic and operational issue:

● *When adopting innovative manufacturing technologies, numerous companies have discovered that a critical success factor is the creation and effective management of more co-operative, long-term – or repeat – relationships with their suppliers.[7]*
● *Companies operating in complex, rapidly changing industries have realized that effective competition should not necessarily aim at simply destroying other companies, it sometimes requires the establishment and successful implementation of strategic alliances with some key competitors.[8]*
● *In complex, decentralized and global organizations, accountability is increasingly concentrated, while authority and resources are more and more shared or diffused. In such organizations, managers can only succeed through co-operation and influence.*

Successful competition and *co-operation requires a series of attitudes that can be greatly enhanced by effective modelling and simulation. Successful competition* and *co-operation requires careful preparation, the main elements of which are: know yourself, know the other parties, give thought to the negotiating conventions, consider the logistics of the situation, use simulated role playing, iterate and set your aspiration levels.*[9]

Spreadsheet modelling is the powerful and flexible tool you need to perform the many simulations that can help you imagine how to design and implement valuable competition and co-operation. It is also the tool that can help you enhance your negotiating skills and in particular your ability to simulate the point of view of the other parties and your capacity to reformulate business situations into win-win solutions.[10]

Notes

1. In his classic 'From Competitive Advantage to Corporate Strategy', *Harvard Business Review*, May–June 1987, pp. 43–59, M. Porter states that 'the track record of corporate strategy has been dismal' and that his records of 33 large, prestigious US companies over the 1950–86 period show that most of them have divested many more acquisitions than they have kept. Several studies of the post-merger performance of acquiring firms are not encouraging either. In 'The market for Corporate Control: The scientific evidence', *Journal of Financial Economics*, 11, 1983, pp. 5–50, M. Jensen and R. Ruback report an average abnormal return of –5.5% during the 12 months after takeover. However, in 'The Post Merger Share Price Performance of Acquiring Firms, *Journal of Financial Economics*, 29, 1991, pp. 83–96, J. Franks, R. Harris and S. Titman argue that poor performance after takeover is probably due to benchmark errors. In 'Why Mergers Fail?', *The McKinsey Quarterly*, 2001 no. 4, pp. 6–9, M. Bekier, A. Bogardus and T. Oldham argue that even though it may look impressive, the sales growth of merged companies seems to be well short of what might have happened had the acquirer and the target remained separate.
2. This material has been developed from the negotiations that took pace between Iveco, the truck company of the Fiat group, and Ford in the mid-1980s. The situation and the data have been modified in order to preserve business confidentiality.
3. See *Co-opetition* by A. Brandenburger and B. Nalebuff, Currency Doubleday, 1996. The term co-opetition was actually coined by Ray Noorda. The essence of 'negotiation' situations is to entwine two dimensions: creation of value and sharing of value. The problem with the word 'negotiation' is that for many people it is associated with sharing of value, conflict of wills, compromise, etc. Consequently I prefer using the expression 'co-operation *and* competition'.
4. *The Evolution of Cooperation*, R. Axelrod, Basic Books, New York, 1984.
5. Actually, as stated by P. Rubin in *Managing Business Transactions*, The Free Press, New York, 1990, 'it is impossible to write complete contracts which take account of any and all possible events and which eliminate all forms of opportunism or cheating'. Processes other than negotiated agreements are needed to control opportunism. Among those processes, Rubin mentions the 'creation of a reputation', a concept which is very close to the 'shadow of the future'.
6. In *The Selfish Gene*, Oxford University Press, Oxford, 1989, R. Dawkins shows that co-operative strategies apply in the world of nature also: consciousness is irrelevant to the development of co-operative strategies.
7. Refer for example to 'ABB and Ford: Creating value through cooperation', S. Frey and M. Schlosser, *Sloan Management Review*, Fall 1993, pp. 65–72; 'Mixed Motive Marriages: What's next for buyer-supplier relations?', J. Henke, R. Krachenberg and T. Lyons, *Sloan Management Review*, Spring 1990, pp. 29–36; 'Managing Suppliers: Incentive systems in Japanese and US industry', J. McMillian, *California Management Review*, Summer 1990, pp. 38–55; 'How Much Has Really Changed Between U.S. Automakers and their Suppliers', S. Helper, *Sloan Management Review*, Summer 1991, pp. 15–28.
8. Refer for example to *Power and Influence – Beyond Formal Authority*, J. Kotter, The Free Press, New York, 1985; *The Manager as a Negotiator – Bargaining for Cooperation and Competitive Gain*, D.A. Lax,

and J.K. Sebenius, The Free Press, New York, 1986; *Influence Without Authority*, A. Cohen and D. Bradford, John Wiley & Sons, New York, 1990.

9. See H. Raiffa, *The Art and Science of Negotiation*, The Belknap Press of Harvard University Press, 1982, Chapter 9.

10. Research shows that most negotiators tend to make similar mistakes, or have similar biases:

   ● assumption of a 'fixed pie';
   ● framing of the situation in term of potential losses rather than in terms of potential gains;
   ● belief that too much has been invested to quit;
   ● belief that their positions will prevail in the end, provided they do not give in;
   ● underestimation of the importance of accurate information;
   ● assumption that the other party is fairly inactive.

These biases are analyzed in *Judgement in Managerial Decisions*, M.H. Bazerman, John Wiley, New York, 1986.

CHAPTER 22

A framework for evaluating companies[1]

22.1 Evaluating companies: modelling opportunities and challenges

The value of a company that you are considering acquiring is equal to the difference between two present values:

- the present value of the additional free cash flows that *you* expect to generate as a result of this acquisition;
- the price that you need to pay for acquiring this company.

Assessing a company creates unique modelling opportunities and challenges.

When considering acquiring a company, you need to build models that help you understand how this company works and what its risks are. If, as is often the case, you envisage changing the strategy of the acquired company, you need to assess the possible outcomes of the new strategy as well as the results of the transition to the desired new situation.

Structuring and implementing acquisition or merger agreements mean that several parties decide to co-operate. Establishing effective co-operation requires that each party understands its own interests as well as the interests of all the other parties involved. Models can help you role-play the situation of the other parties and further your understanding of their specific points of view.

Acquisitions and mergers present specific modelling challenges: unique situations, need for innovative solutions, high uncertainty, incomplete or unreliable information, and so on. A further problem is that companies generally have very long lives – infinite, or at least long and indefinite lives. When assessing the value of an acquisition opportunity, you need to build and use genuine long-term, strategic models.

When, as is usually the case, the seller is paid in cash at the date of acquisition,[2] the immediate payment creates an asymmetry in the risk exposures of the two parties. When you are in the position of the buyer and are asked for an immediate cash payment, you need to assess your risk in a systematic fashion.

Finally, a warning; acquiring companies sounds like a very exciting activity, but it is a difficult business. Even though it does not give any definite answers, the literature suggests that it is not easy to create value through mergers and acquisitions and that buyers tend to pay a premium over market prices.[3] As a consequence, be very careful with your acquisition models.

- Do not use models so as to become overconfident about the value that you can achieve. Positive net present values only result from superior competitive strategies. Believing that you can derive a positive value from an acquisition should mean that you are confident that this acquisition will lead to a superior performance: either superior future performance and/or exceptionally low acquisition price.
- Specify very clearly the key assumptions that drive your value estimates and make explicit decisions regarding the complexity of your models. When evaluating a very uncertain situation it is generally not a good idea to use very detailed models. Detailed models require a lot of data and when these data are not reliable the final result might be misleading.
- Do not rely on one single valuation method. When you are confronted with a new and unique situation the methods you are comfortable with might be challenged. A useful precaution is to use a variety of methods and check that they lead to similar results.
- Finally, make sure that your models envisage all the tax implications.[4]

22.2 Breaking the value of an acquisition into three components

The future free cash flows[5] that you expect to derive from an acquisition belong to two main categories.

- The cash flows that will be generated by the future activity. It is common practice to break these cash flows into two successive periods:
  - an initial, or explicit, planning period corresponding, for example, to the first five years after the acquisition, and
  - a second period corresponding to all subsequent years beyond the initial planning period. The value of these cash flows is often called the continuing or terminal value.
- The future cash flows that will result from the pre-acquisition activity. When acquiring a company, you generally inherit from debts raised in the past, from accounts receivable, from accounts payable, etc.

When estimating the value of an acquisition prospect, it is a good idea to:

- Evaluate successively each of the three value components: (1) *present value of the cash flows during the initial planning period*, (2) *continuing value* and (3) *value of the inheritance from the pre-acquisition activity*.
- Estimate the value as the sum of these three components and frame your estimate through a comparison with similar transactions or any other relevant benchmark. This enables you to put your valuation in perspective and to check that it is not excessive – or that there are good reasons for it being very high.

22.3 Assessing the present value of the cash flows during the initial or explicit planning period

Three common reasons for using an initial or explicit planning period

A first, and not necessarily valid, reason for singling out an initial planning period, relates to the belief that the initial cash flows are the ones that matter most. One thing to

Table 22.1 ● Proportion of the total value captured by the planning period

Model

A		B
1 Length of the planning period		5
2 Constant annual growth		3%
3 Discount rate		10%
4 Total value of the future cash flows		14
5 Value captured by the planning period		4
6 Percentage of value captured by the planning period		28%

Formulas
B4: +1/(B3–B2). For the formula see page 90.
B5: +(1–((1+B2)/(1+B3))^B1)/(B3–B2). For the formula see page 90.
B6: +B5/B4

Results
Percentage of value captured by the planning period:
1 When future cash flows grow 3% each year

Discount rate	Length of the planning period (in years)		
	5	10	15
10%	28%	48%	63%
15%	42%	67%	81%
20%	53%	78%	90%

2 When future cash flows are constant

Discount rate	Length of the planning period (in years)		
	5	10	15
10%	38%	61%	76%
15%	50%	75%	88%
20%	60%	84%	94%

3 When future cash flows decline 5% each year

Discount rate	Length of the planning period (in years)		
	5	10	15
10%	62%	77%	89%
15%	62%	85%	94%
20%	69%	90%	97%

remember is that even though each of the early cash flows has a much greater weight than any more distant one, it is not necessarily true that discounting makes the sum of all the distant cash flows negligible. Table 22.1 shows the proportion of the total value of a potential acquisition that is captured by the initial planning period depending on the profile of the future cash flows, the length of the initial planning period, and the discount rate.[6]

Table 22.1 shows that there are many situations where the value of the cash flows beyond the planning period matters and should get all your attention.

● When you evaluate an acquisition with high growth prospects, the long-term cash flows are the ones that matter most. When acquiring a business in an emerging industry, the value of the cash flows during the first years might even be negative.
● Even when the future cash flows decline by 5% a year, the value of the cash flows beyond five years represents as much as 38% of the total value when you use a 15% discount rate!

A second, and very good reason for singling out an initial planing period relates to the fact that you, as the new owner, plan to change the strategy or the operations of the acquired company or to integrate this company into another company. This will cause the years immediately following the acquisition to be transition years that should be modelled in great detail. When the rationale for the initial planning period is the modelling of a transition:

● the length of the initial planning period should correspond to the time needed for the transition;
● the cash flows should probably be modelled according to the traditional accounting approach (like the one we used for the analysis of Delta Metal) which is well adapted to a detailed, short-term assessment of a business. Long-term strategic modelling approaches based on concepts like product life cycle profiles and learning cost dynamics (like the approach that we used for the analysis of BA International) are probably more adapted to the longer term when a more stable situation has been reached.

A third very good reason for using an initial planning period relates to the belief that superior strategies cannot be sustained for ever. It is not easy for a company to maintain a superior competitive position that enables it to generate above market returns, and economic theory tells us that, in the long run, companies' returns tend towards their cost-of-capital or industry-required return. As a consequence you may decide to break the future cash flows into two successive periods:

● the period during which you believe that the acquired company will sustain a superior competitive performance;
● the subsequent years in which performance will just equal the cost of capital.

In this case you should probably use a relatively long planning period – as long as the superior competitive position will last – and you should probably adopt a long-term modelling approach similar to the one we used in the BA International case.

A three-step approach for assessing the value of the free cash flows in the initial planning period

The first step is to ask yourself why you want to use an initial planning period and how long you want this initial planning period to be. You can then simulate the strategy of the acquired company during the planning period. Which are the underlying competitive ideas? How can these ideas be implemented and sustained? What are the expected revenues and costs – including the potential synergies? What are the capital expenditures needed? What are the resulting free cash flows? You should also choose a modelling approach suited to the problem: traditional accounting approach, long-term strategic approach or a mixture of both.

Finally, if you plan to change the strategy of the acquired company, you should carefully simulate the transition from the old to the new strategy: how much of the existing inventories can be used? (Any inventory used will decrease the expected future disbursements.) Are the existing fixed assets suited to the new strategy? Do some of these assets need to be modified? Are some fixed assets not needed any longer? How much cash can be derived from their disposal? More generally, what are the costs involved in adapting the existing structure and resources to the new strategy; people-related costs (training, recruitment, dismissals), administrative systems costs, and so on. The simulation of the transition process and of its financial implications is generally very difficult and requires a lot of what-if analyses.

The inflation issue

As in any financial model you have the choice between the constant prices / real rate and the current prices / current rate approaches (see p. 319). When the initial planning period is short and when the cash flows are modelled according to an accounting approach, it is common practice to use the current prices / current rate approach. When you use a long initial planning period and a long-term strategic modelling approach, it is probably better to use the constant prices / real rate approach and eventually adjust the value in order to remove the bias introduced by this approach.

22.4 A series of approaches for assessing the continuing or terminal value

A variety of approaches are used in practice to assess the value of the cash flows beyond the initial planning period. The price-to-earnings (PE)[7] ratio and the cash flow or profit perpetuity formula approaches are probably the most widely used but various approaches based on an explicit assessment of the free cash flows or profits beyond the initial planning period are gaining acceptance. Other methods are also used.

The explicit cash flow or profit forecast approaches

These approaches are the ones that we recommend you to use whenever possible; they can be more or less detailed. A detailed approach would be similar to the one we have used to assess the value of P12 at BA International. A non-detailed approach is the one shown in Table 22.2. Rather than building a full cash flow model, you make a direct estimate of the annual free cash flows after the initial planning period.

1. You start with the estimate of three interrelated parameters: return, cash flow before new investments (or profit), and capital needed to generate such a cash flow – or capital or assets in place – at the end of the initial planning period.
2. Then, you estimate the annual free cash flows as the difference between the cash flow before investments generated by the capital in place at the beginning of the year and the additional investments required by growth.
3. Finally, you estimate the continuing value as the net present value of the free cash flows. The difference between this value and the value of the capital in place at the end of the planning period corresponds to the additional value created by growth.

It is worth noting that the annual free cash flow increases as long as the return is higher than the cost of capital. But as soon as the return becomes equal to the cost of capital, the annual free cash flow does not increase any longer.[8] This is due to the fact that the additional investments become exactly equal to the increase in cash flow.

Table 22.2 ● A model for assessing the continuing value

A	B	C	D	E	F	G	H	I	...	CU	CV	CW
1 Return of acquired company during planning period					0.2							
2 Length of the period of above market return (years)					5							
3 Annual growth					0.04							
4 Cost of capital					0.12							
5 Base profit in year 1 after planning period					10							
6												
7 **Free cash flow approach**												
8 Year (after planning period)	1	2	3	4	5	6	7	8		98	99	100
9 Return	0.2	0.2	0.2	0.2	0.2	0.12	0.12	0.12		0.12	0.12	0.12
10 Capital invested open	50	52	54	56	58	61	63	66		2245	2335	2428
11 Additional capital needed	2	2	2	2	2	2	3	3		90	93	97
12 Cash flow before investments	10	10	11	11	12	12	13	13		449	467	486
13 Cash flow above market return	8	8	9	9	9	10	10	11		359	374	388
14 Actual free cash flow	8	8	9	9	9	7	7	7		7	7	7
15 NPV (last year planning period)	65											
16 NPV capital in place	50											
17 NPV growth	15		Growth as a %			24%						
18												
19												
20												
21												
22 **Profit approach**												
23 Year (after planning period)	1	2	3	4	5	6	7	8		98	99	100
24 Return	0.2	0.2	0.2	0.2	0.2	0.12	0.12	0.12		0.12	0.12	0.12
25 Profit	10	10	11	11	12	7	8	8		269	280	291
26 Capital invested open	50	52	54	56	58	61	63	66		2245	2335	2428
27 Additional capital needed	2	2	2	2	2	2	3	3		90	93	97
28 Cost of capital	6	6	6	7	7	7	8	8		269	280	291
29 Above market profit	4	4	4	4	5	0	0	0		0	0	0
30 NPV (above market profit)	15											
31 NPV capital in place	50											
32 NPV (last year planning period)	65											

Formulas

B9: =IF(B8<=$F$2,$F$1,$F$4); Copy to C9..CW9
B10: +F5/F1; C10:+B10+B11; Copy to D10..CW10
B11: +B10*$F$3; Copy to C11..CW11
B12: +F5; C12: +C10*$F$1; Copy to D12..CW12
B13: +B10*$F$1–B11; Copy to D13..CW13
B14: =F(B8<=$F$2,B13, ($B$10*(1+$F$3)^(F2))*$F$4)
B15: =NPV(F4,B14.CW14)
B16: +B10
B17: +B15–B16 in G17:+B17/B15

B24: =IF(B23<=$F$2,$F$1,$F$4); Copy to C24..CW24.
B25: +F5 C25: +C24*(B26+B27); Copy
B26: +B25/B24; C26: +B26+B27; Copy
B27: +B26*$F$3; Copy
B28: +B26*F4. C28: +$F$4*(B26+B27); Copy
B29: +B25–B28; Copy
B30: =NPV(F4,B29..CW29)
B31: +B26
B32: +B30+B31

An alternative model based on annual profits is also shown in Table 22.2. The value is estimated as the sum of the value of the capital in place at the end of the planning period and the value of growth. The value of growth is equal to the present value of the additional annual profits caused by growth. As long as the return is higher than the cost of capital, the additional investments required by growth generate an additional profit equal to the difference between the above-market return and the cost of capital. As soon as the return becomes equal to the cost of capital, the additional investments break even and additional profit is no longer created. Since working capital needs are ignored, the cash flow and profit approaches give similar results.

The model in Table 22.2 assumes:

- a very long modelling period. This enables you to assess the impact of the length of the period of above-market returns and growth;
- constant above-market returns and growth. If you want to test the impact of variable returns and growth, we advise you to use the profit model and (1) insert a blank row above row 27 and use it to introduce annual growth, (2) correct the formula for additional capital, and (3) introduce the annual return and growth rates.

Growth is not always a source of value

The model in Table 22.2 can help you check once more that growth has a positive impact on value only when the company generates a return higher than the industry-required return of cost of capital. If the company has no superior competitive advantage and just generates the industry-required return, its value is not increased by growth. If the company generates a return lower than its cost of capital, then growth reduces its value.

The cash flow and profit perpetuity formula approaches

These approaches also estimate continuing value as the present value of a stream of annual free cash flows or profits. But they further assume that cash flows or profits behave steadily after the end of the planning period: i.e. constant or growing at a constant rate up to infinity which enables you to use simple perpetuity formulas[9] (see page 90). Even though they look very simple, these approaches pose a series of problems.

Which variable should you discount: profit or cash?

Cash is obviously the variable to be discounted but since the only difference between cash and profit is time, you may assume that beyond the planning period cash will lag behind (or lead) profit by a constant period of time. Consequently, you can discount either annual profits or annual free cash flows, keeping in mind that the profit-based NPV will differ from the cash-based NPV by a factor corresponding to the cash–profit timing difference. When assessing long-term outcomes, you might find it easier to focus on profit and assess the continuing value as the present value of the stream of future annual profits. You may eventually decide to adjust this present value through discounting: for example, if you believe that cash will lag by one year behind profit, you may discount the profit-based present value by one additional year in order to get the cash-based NPV.

The inflation issue

Here again you have to decide which approach you want to use: constant prices / real rate or current prices / current rate. When doing so, be careful to check the internal consistency of your assumptions beyond the planning period (profit or cash flow level, superior return, growth, cost of capital) as well as their consistency with the assumptions made for the initial planning period.

The case when performance is equal to the industry-required return

When you assume that the company will not have a superior competitive position beyond the planning period and as a result will generate a return just equal to the industry-required return or cost of capital, you actually mean that future growth will not matter. If sales grow after the planning period, the company will have to invest in order to sustain this growth and:

● the additional investments will return exactly as much as they cost (i.e. their net present value will be nil) and the annual profit will remain constant for ever;
● the additional investments will be exactly equal to the additional cash flows and as a result the annual cash flow will remain constant for ever.

When profit is constant for ever, the calculation of the continuing value is very simple:

$$\text{Continuing value} = \frac{\text{PAT1}}{rr}$$

where PAT1 = profit after tax in the first year after the planning period
rr = industry required return (cost of capital).

Even though it looks simplistic, this assessment of the continuing value is, and should be, of a wide use. It corresponds to the reasonable assumption that, in the long run, the return of a company is equal to the industry-required return or cost of capital. It is the formula you should always use when you believe that the superior performance of the acquired company will not extend beyond the initial planning period.

A problem, however, is that the perpetuity formula assumes that the company will generate the industry required return up to infinity. If the company generates the industry-required return for a limited period of time only, then the perpetuity formula overestimates the true value:

Actual period of industry-required returns	Overestimation of the true value (with a 10% discount rate)
40 years	2%
30	6%
25	10%
29	17%
15	31%

Since there are few companies and industries which have been around for a very long period of time, these results should encourage you to be careful when using a perpetuity formula.

The case where you believe that the company can sustain a superior performance for ever

As the company generates a return higher than its cost of capital, then growth is valuable and should be taken into account. The perpetuity formula to be used is the following:

$$\text{Continuing value} = \frac{\text{PAT1}}{r} + \frac{\text{PAT1} \times (r - rr)}{r} \times \frac{1}{(rr - g)}$$

where PAT1 = profit after tax in the first year after the explicit planning period
g = growth rate
r = above market return
rr = required return (cost of capital).

To derive this formula, you should consider that the continuing value is equal to the sum of the values of:

● the capital in place at the end of the planning period, i.e.

PAT1/r, and

● the additional profits that will result from valuable growth. In the first year, the additional profit is equal to the value of the capital in place multiplied by the difference between the above market return of the additional investments required to sustain the growth and the cost of capital

PAT1/r × (r − rr)

As annual additional profits grow at a constant rate g, and provided that g is small[10] and lower than rr (the cost of capital) their present value can be approximated by

PAT1/r × (r − rr) × 1/(rr − g)

The perpetuity formula can be rewritten as:

$$\text{Continuing value} = \text{PAT1} \times \frac{(1 - g/r)}{(rr - g)}$$

Introducing the perpetuity formula into the model

To introduce the perpetuity formula in the model shown in Table 22.2, the inputs are the following:

In A18: NPV perpetuity formula
In B18: +B12 × (1 − F3/F1)/(F4 − F3)
In C18: Difference with exact formula
In G18: +B18/B15 − 1

The finite period of superior performance approach

As you might find it difficult to believe that superior performance can be maintained for ever, you might feel more comfortable using a formula[11] that assumes that the superior performance is limited to a period of P years.

$$\text{Continuing value} = \text{PAT1} \times (1/r + \frac{(r - rr)}{r \times (rr - g)} \times (1 - ((1 + g)/(1 + rr))^{\wedge}P)$$

where P = length of the period of superior performance.

This formula assumes that return and growth rates are constant but, contrary to the perpetuity formula, is not an approximation.

Introducing the finite period formula into the model

To introduce the finite period formula in the model shown in Table 22.2, the inputs are:

In A19: NPV finite period formula
In B19: +F5 × (1/F1 + (F1 − F4)/(F1 × (F4 − F3)) × (1 − ((1 + F3)/(1 + F4))^F2))

The price-to-earnings (PE) ratio approach

This approach assumes that the value of the company at the end of the initial period is equal to its profit after tax multiplied by the relevant PE ratio. Profit after tax might correspond to a single estimate (profit after tax in the first year after the explicit planning period), or to an average of several – usually three to five – estimates. The PE ratio might be the PE ratio observed in the industry, the PE ratio of 'comparable' companies, or a purely judgemental PE ratio. Multiplying the profit after tax in the first year following the planning period by a PE ratio is the same as using a perpetuity or finite period formula.

● When you believe that the company has no superior competitive position after the planning period, then the PE ratio is equal to: $1/rr$ (rr = cost of capital). Some PE ratios and their corresponding implied cost of capital are:

PE ratio	Implied cost of capital
12.5	8%
10	10%
8.3	12%
6.7	15%
5	20%

Even though it looks simplistic, this approach is of wide use and is the one you should use when you assume that the superior competitive position of the company will not be maintained beyond the initial planning period.

● When you believe that the company will be able to sustain a superior competitive position and benefit from growth for a very long period of time, then the PE ratio is equal to: $(rr - g)/(1 - g/r)$.

● When you believe that the company will be able to sustain a superior return during a finite period of time P only, then the PE ratio is equal to:

$$1/(1/r + (r - rr)/r \times (rr - g) \times (1 - ((1 + g)/(1 + rr))\textasciicircum P)$$

Introducing PE calculations into the model

To introduce PE calculations in the model shown in Table 22.2, the inputs are the following:

In A20: PE ratio (based on exact formula)
In B20: +B15/F5
In D20: PE ratio (based on perpetuity formula)
In I20: +B18/F5

You can also calculate the PE to be applied to the normalized profit, that is the profit that would be generated by the capital in place if the return were equal to the cost of capital:

In C20: +B15/(F5 × F4/F1)

The problem with the PE approach is that it fails to specify its assumptions, which might be misleading. In Table 22.3 you will find the correspondence between some PE ratios and the values of their key drivers: above market returns, length of the period of superior performance, growth and cost of capital.

Table 22.3 ● Growth, above-market returns, cost of capital and PE ratios

Period		5 years				10 years				15 years				Ever		
Cost of capital	Growth Return	10%	15%	20%	25%	10%	15%	20%	25%	5%	10%	15%	20%	2.5%	5%	10%
12%	15%									8.4 / 10.5	9.0 / 11.3	9.9 / 12.4	11.2 / 14.0			
	20%	6.7 / 11.2	6.9 / 11.5	7.1 / 11.8	7.3 / 12.1	8.3 / 13.8	9.0 / 15.1	10.0 / 16.6	11.1 / 18.6	8.5 / 14.2	9.7 / 16.2	11.5 / 19.1	14.1 / 23.5	8.8 / 11.0	9.5 / 11.9	13.9 / 17.4
	25%	6.2 / 13.0	6.4 / 13.4	6.7 / 13.9	6.9 / 14.4	8.3 / 17.3	9.2 / 19.3	10.5 / 21.8	12.0 / 25.0	8.6 / 17.9	10.2 / 21.2	12.4 / 25.9	15.8 / 32.9	9.2 / 15.3	10.7 / 17.8	20.9 / 34.8
	30%	5.9 / 14.8	6.2 / 15.4	6.4 / 16.1	6.7 / 16.8	8.3 / 20.7	9.4 / 23.5	10.8 / 27.0	12.6 / 31.4	8.6 / 21.6	10.4 / 26.1	13.1 / 32.7	16.9 / 42.4	9.5 / 19.7	11.4 / 23.8	25.1 / 52.2
	40%	5.5 / 18.4	5.8 / 19.3	6.1 / 20.3	6.4 / 21.5	8.3 / 27.6	9.6 / 31.9	11.2 / 37.3	13.3 / 44.2	8.7 / 29.0	10.8 / 36.0	13.9 / 46.2	18.4 / 61.3	9.6 / 24.1	11.9 / 29.7	27.8 / 69.6
	Growth Return	10%	15%	20%	25%	10%	15%	20%	25%	5%	10%	15%	20%	2.5%	5%	10%
15%	20%	6.0 / 8.0	6.1 / 8.1	6.2 / 8.2	6.3 / 8.4	6.8 / 9.1	7.2 / 9.6	7.7 / 10.2	8.3 / 11.0	6.9 / 9.1	7.4 / 9.9	8.3 / 11.0	9.5 / 12.6	7.0 / 9.3	7.5 / 10.0	9.9 / 13.2
	25%	5.6 / 9.3	5.7 / 9.6	5.9 / 9.8	6.1 / 10.1	6.9 / 11.5	7.5 / 12.5	8.2 / 13.7	9.2 / 15.3	7.0 / 11.6	7.9 / 13.2	9.2 / 15.4	11.1 / 18.6	7.2 / 12.0	8.0 / 13.3	11.9 / 19.8
	30%	5.3 / 10.7	5.5 / 11.0	5.7 / 11.4	5.9 / 11.8	6.9 / 13.8	7.7 / 15.4	8.6 / 17.3	9.8 / 19.7	7.1 / 14.1	8.2 / 16.4	9.9 / 19.7	12.3 / 24.5	7.3 / 14.7	8.3 / 16.7	13.2 / 26.4
	40%	5.0 / 13.3	5.2 / 13.9	5.5 / 14.6	5.7 / 15.3	7.0 / 18.6	7.9 / 21.2	9.1 / 24.4	10.6 / 28.4	7.2 / 19.1	8.6 / 22.9	10.7 / 28.4	13.7 / 36.4	7.5 / 20.0	8.7 / 23.3	14.8 / 39.5

Note
The first PE is the PE to apply to the actual profit, the second PE is the PE to apply to the normalized profit.

The results in the table show that you should be careful and not use unrealistically high PE ratios.

- A high (let us say higher than 10) PE ratio is justified only if you are very confident that the superior performance of an acquisition target is sustainable.
- A high PE ratio is not justified for a company with a short-lived superior performance. Expecting that the company will soon return to a normal performance means that its profits will soon fall from their exceptionally high current level. When you set the above-market return to 30%, the length of period of superior return to 5, the growth to 15%, and the cost of capital to 12%, you get a PE of 6.2. This is less than the PE of 8.3 that you would use if the same profit were the profit of a company generating a 12% return for a very long period of time. Using a PE higher than 8.3 would be valid only if this PE were applied to a normalized profit.

A paradox to finish with PEs: even though the results in Table 22.3 show that high PE ratios are not easy to justify, some companies listed on the stock market do enjoy very high PEs.[12] This might be due to the fact that

- the market really expects stellar performance from these companies;
- the current profit of these companies is abnormally low due to the occurrence of some exceptional events. When recalculated on a more 'normal' level of profit, the PE of these companies is much lower.

Some other approaches[13]

The *value-to-book-value* approach estimates the value as the result of the multiplication of the book value at the end of the planning period by an adequate multiple. This approach poses several problems. A first difficulty is that the book value primarily reflects what has been achieved so far and not the future prospects which drive the continuing value. A second problem is how to find an adequate multiple. There is however one – but not unusual – situation where the book value might be relevant: this is the case when you assume that the acquired company will generate a return equal to its cost of capital after the initial planning period. In this case, the continuing value is equal to the capital in place which should be close to the book value. The multiple you should use in this situation is 1.

The *value-to-sales* approach assesses the continuing value as the result of the multiplication of the estimated sales by an adequate multiple. This approach requires the estimate of sales only, which might be an advantage when the cost structure is very uncertain. The problem though is to find an adequate sales multiple.

The *liquidation-value* approach assumes that the continuing value is equal to the proceeds that could be obtained from the liquidation of the assets. This approach poses a series of problems. A first problem is that the liquidation value remains a mere estimate for as long as the company is actually not liquidated. Another difficulty is that the liquidation value is nothing more than an estimate of the lower limit of the continuing value; if the operations are considered as worth being pursued, it is because the continuing value is higher than the liquidation value.

Formula-based approaches. All over the world, investment bankers, tax authorities and courts often use formulas which derive value as a weighted average of the capitalized value of earnings, dividends, book value, and so on. A formula used by the US courts to value privately held stock is the one reported by K. Hickman and G. Perry:[14]

$$\text{Value} = (A \times \text{EPS} \times \text{PE} + B \times \frac{\text{Div}}{\text{Divy}} + C \times \text{BV} \times \text{BVM}) \times \text{Disc}$$

where A, B and C are weighting coefficients $(A + B + C = 1)$. Typically, A has the highest share value (often 0.5)

    EPS = earnings per share or average of the most recent earnings per share (last 5 years for example)
    PE   = industry related price earnings ratio
    Div = dividend per share
    Divy = dividend yield
    BV   = book value per share
    BVM = industry-related book value multiple
    Disc = discount factor reflecting the lack of liquidity.

Formula-based approaches are sometimes also called 'rules of thumb': their main value is to reflect expert knowledge.

22.5 Assessing the value of the inheritance from the pre-acquisition activity

When you buy a company, you generally inherit the consequences of some of its pre-acquisition operations. The inheritance that matters is the one which will result in future cash flows.

Starting with an analysis of the opening balance sheet

In order to assess the future cash flows that will result from past activities, you should probably start from the balancce sheet at the date of acquisition. Some balance sheet items are easy to deal with:

- Cash and marketable securities. Except for the cash balance that might be required by the operations, this is a potential cash inflow (book value of cash and market value of marketable securities), the present value of which increases the value of the acquired company.
- Accounts and notes receivable. Their collection will result in cash inflows, the present value of which also increases the value of the company.
- Accounts payable and other debts. Their payment will cause cash outflows, the present value of which decreases the value of the company.

Some balance sheet items are more difficult to deal with:

- Inventories. The inventories that are going to be used in the new operations enable you to save on future operating costs (as this might already have been taken into account when assessing future operations, be careful to avoid double counting). The inventories that are not going to be used should be liquidated, their liquidation value increases the value of the acquisition.

- Fixed assets. As with inventories, you should make a distinction between those assets that are going to be used for future operations and those that are going to be liquidated. As the value of the assets to be kept has already been implicitly taken into account in the assessment of the future operations, the only additional thing to take into consideration is the present value of the tax savings caused by their depreciation. The value of the assets that are not going to be kept is equal to their liquidation value.

The need to go beyond the analysis of the opening balance sheet

All future cash flows resulting from pre-acquisition activities are not necessarily reflected in the balance sheet. In its past relationships with its customers, banks, competitors, local authorities, personnel, and so on, the acquisition candidate might have concluded contracts, created a reputation or conflictual situations that can result in future cash flows – or that might affect future cash flows.

22.6 A final precaution: framing the value estimate

Because the value of an acquisition prospect depends on your unique perspective and ideas, it is very difficult to check that your assessment is correct. Even when you plan to acquire a company listed on the stock market, you might come up with a value that differs from the market value and be very confident – and rightly so – in your estimate. A reason for that might be that you are the only one in the position to merge this company with other operations and capture significant synergies.

When trying to frame an estimate of the value, you should probably:

- actively look for other estimates, keeping in mind they are probably going to be different from yours;
- check that you are able to explain why your own estimate differs from these other estimates. If you are not able to explain the differences, check your estimate and revise it if needed.

Among the benchmarks you should use are: value of other transactions, market value, value-to-current earnings, value-to-sales of comparable companies, or even value-to-real parameters.

When the uncertainty is very high, it can be very useful to estimate a few value-to-real parameters relationships, such as 'pops'. In the absence of other reliable figures, 'pops', or the number of inhabitants in a geographical area, have been used by the mobile telecoms industry to frame the value of smaller operators or even of licences. Industry-wide models have been developed by experts[15] to assess the value of such 'pops'.

Notes

1. For an analysis of acquisitions from a strategic perspective, refer to: P. Haspeslagh and D. Jemison (1991). *Managing Acquisitions: Creating Value Through Corporate Renewal*. The Free Press and to M. Forsgren (1989). *Managing the Internationalization Process: The Swedish Case*. Routledge (Chapters 4 and 5).
2. Cash is a very popular way of paying for mergers. According to *Mergers & Acquisitions*, almost 60% of the acquisition deals in the USA were all cash financed in 1989. May/June 1990, p. 63.
3. The idea that overconfidence may lead managers to overpay acquisitions is documented in several studies. See for example: 'The Hubris Hypothesis of Corporate Takeovers', R. Roll, *Journal of Business*, 59, 1986, pp. 197–216 and 'Do Managerial Objectives Drive Bad Acquisitions?', R. Morck, A. Shleifer and R. Vishny, *The Journal of Finance*, March 1990, pp. 31–48. In 'Do Bidder Managers Knowingly Pay Too Much for Target Firms?', *Journal of Business* Vol. 63, 1990, H. Nejat Seyun argues that it does not seem that bidder managers pay too much knowingly.

   In 'Merger Bids, Uncertainty, and Stockholder Returns', *Journal of Financial Economics*, 11, pp. 51–83, P. Asquith shows that while selling firms receive substantial premiums, stockholders of buying firms roughly break even. The literature suggests that the value which corresponds to the target gains is created either by synergies or by the shifting of the control of the business to more effective managers (see for example: 'Synergy, Agency, and the Determinants of Premia Paid in Mergers', A. Slusky and R. Caves, *The Journal of Industrial Economics*, XXXIX, March 1991, pp. 277–95).
4. In spite of its critical importance, this issue cannot be dealt with in a general text like this one. When dealing with an acquisition, make sure that you understand all the tax implications of the transaction.
5. The need to value acquisitions from their future cash flows is now well accepted. See for example: *Valuation: Measuring and Managing the Value of Companies*, McKinsey, T. Copeland, T. Koller and J. Murrin, 2000, John Wiley, and *The Dark Side of Valuation*, A. Damodaran, 2001, Prentice Hall.
6. It is worth noting that the approach shown in Table 22.1 is not easy to use and can result in over-optimistic estimates. The difficulty stems from growth: when assessing the growth of the future free cash flows, you need to recognize the impact of the additional investments required by growth. Due to these investments, the annual free cash flow increases only when the additional investments generate a return higher than the cost of capital. This is shown in the model in Table 29.2.
7. See page 90.
8. 'Capital' or 'Assets in Place' are the same as Capital Employed and 'Return' is the same as Return on Capital Employed. Estimating return and capital in place is not easy and estimates derived from income statements and balance sheets can be misleading.
9. This means that the NPV of the free cash flows could be calculated as the sum of:

   - the NPV of the free cash flows during the period of above market returns;
   - the NPV of the capital in place at the end of that period. The value of the capital in place is the present value of a perpetuity; the stream of constant cash flows after the period of above market returns.

   You can modify the model in Table 22.2 and check that you get the same results.
10. Lower than 5–6%, which is not a major problem since it is difficult to imagine high growth rates lasting for ever and always corresponding to above market return situations.
11. The formula is derived as follows:

$$\text{Value} = \text{Value of capital in place} + \text{Value of growth}$$
$$= \text{PAT1}/r + \text{VG}$$

$$\text{VG} = \frac{\text{PAT1} - \text{C1}}{(1 + rr)} + \frac{\text{PAT2} - \text{C2}}{(1 + rr)^2} + \ldots + \frac{\text{PAT}p - \text{C}p}{(1 + rr)^p}$$

with C1, C2, Cp = cost of financing the capital in place.

$$\text{PAT1} - \text{C1} = \text{PAT1} \times (1 - rr/r)$$
$$\text{PAT2} - \text{C2} = \text{PAT1} \times (1 - rr/r) \times (1 + g)$$
$$\text{PAT}p - \text{C}p = \text{PAT1} \times (1 - rr/r) \times (1 + g)^{p-1}$$

$$VG = PAT1 \times (1 - rr/r) \times \left(\frac{1}{(1 + rr)} + \frac{(1 + g)}{(1 + rr)^2} + \ldots + \frac{(1 + g)^{p-1}}{(1 + rr)^p} \right)$$

$$VG = PAT1 \times \frac{(1 - rr/r)}{(1 + g)} \times \left(\frac{(1 + g)}{(1 + rr)} + \frac{(1 + g)^2}{(1 + rr)^2} + \ldots + \frac{(1 + g)^p}{(1 + rr)^p} \right)$$

$$VG = PAT1 \times \frac{(1 - rr/r)}{(1 + g)} \times \left(\frac{1 - (1 + g)/(1 + rr)^p}{1 - (1 + g)/(1 + rr)} \right)$$

$$VG = PAT1 \times \frac{(r - rr)}{r \times (rr - g)} \times (1 - (1 + g)/(1 + rr)^p)$$

12. Consult for example 'The Global 1000' published each year by *Business Week*. On line at www.businessweek.com.
13. Approaches to business valuation are extremely numerous. For an overview of the very many approaches used in practice, refer to: T. West and J. Jones (1999), *Handbook of Business Valuation*, Wiley & Sons, and to R. Reilly and R. Schweihs (1999), *The Handbook of Advanced Business Valuation*, Irwin.
14. K. Hickman and G. Perry (1990), 'A Comparison of Stock Price Predictions Using Court Accepted Formulas, Dividend Discount, and P/E Models', *Financial Management* (Summer), pp. 76–87.
15. One of the expert models was developed by Donaldson, Lufkin & Jenrette Securities Corporation, 140 Broadway, New York, NY 10005.

I, in the United Kingdom[1]

On 16 June 1985, Mr Corsi, the Managing Director of I, the second largest truck manufacturer in Europe, was replacing the phone after a conversation with Mr Jones, the president of F. He Had just agreed to a meeting in Torino on 29 June 1985, to discuss the conditions of an eventual takeover of F by I. The two companies had been discussing this question since the end of 1984, when F approached I. From the very beginning, I had shown interest, but the value of an acquisition of F's truck operations was not easy to assess, and now Mr Corsi was a bit puzzled by F's pressure to strike a deal. Mr Corsi asked his secretary to organize quickly a meeting with the two senior managers who had represented I at the last meeting at F's UK headquarters in May, 1985.

I's strategy in Europe

In 1985, I was one of the leading manufacturers of trucks in Europe with a 16% share of the market:

Market shares of the main manufacturers of trucks in Europe (according to the numbers of units sold. 3.5 tons and above)

Daimler Benz	23.5%	Scania	4.6%
I	16.2%	Daf	4.0%
Renault	10.7%	Leyland	3.7%
Man-VW	7.1%	GM-Bedford	1.8%
Volvo	6.5%	Japanese	4.7%
F	4.6%	Others[1]	12.6%

1. Including car manufacturers for light vehicles.

I's policy was to offer a full range of trucks to all national markets in Europe as well as to a number of markets outside Europe. In 1985, I was present on all European markets and, except for the UK, had achieved strong positions in the main markets: 16% in France, 12% in Germany, 69% in Italy, 6% – but rapidly growing – in Spain. Increase in market share was seen at I as one of the key conditions for improving profitability and recouping the high cost of new product development.

I had been formed in 1975 from the integration of Italian, French and German truck companies. Since its creation, I's strategy had been to increase its size and to rationalize its

Table U.1 ● Key financial data of I

	1979	1980	1981	1982	1983	1984	1985
Sales (£ million)[a]	2203	2459	3097	2725	2362	2373	2543
Annual growth		12%	26%	−12%	−13%	0%	7%
Profit before tax	−121	−98	16	5	−67	−113	43
As a % of sales	−5%	−4%	1%	0%	−3%	−5%	2%
Number of vehicles sold (000)[b]	110	110	113	102	96	90	99
Annual growth		0%	3%	−10%	−6%	−6%	10%
Personnel (000)	50	47	46	42	39	36	35

[a] I was selling products other than trucks: buses, military vehicles, engines, spare parts, fire-fighting equipment, fork lifts, etc. In 1985, I had sold about 56 000 trucks on the European market and had exported some 20 000 more units outside Europe. As an estimate, one could consider the average unit selling price of I trucks to be equal to about £17 000 in 1985.
[b] Trucks, buses, military vehicles, etc.

operations, which involved closures of plants in France and Germany. Rationalization had enabled I to cut the number of product lines from 21 to 6, the number of engine groups from 12 to 6 and the variety of cabs from 21 to 4. In 1985, I had manufacturing and R&D facilities in Italy, France and Germany, which was both a disadvantage (complexity of operations) and an advantage (image of a national manufacturer able, for example, to sell to armed forces in three key European markets). I's policy was to manufacture, or at least to control the manufacturing of the main components, engines and drivelines.

I was spending 3% of its sales on R&D – and was planning an increase to 4% to keep ahead of the technology and to introduce new products. The cost of new product introduction was very high; I estimated that they would need to spend about £900 million to introduce the new generation of trucks they were planning to launch in the early 1990s.

The very high cost of new product introduction was making the long-term survival of smaller truck manufacturers very unlikely, with the exception of those which had been able to focus on the most profitable segments and to achieve a wide geographic coverage. The early 1980s had been very difficult for most European truck manufacturers. Even for a market leader like I, profitability had been unsatisfactory (see Table U.1). Fortunately, the late 1980s were expected to be more favourable.

● For the first time since 1979, demand in Europe was increasing again in 1985. A further increase of about 5% was expected in 1986, but I remained very cautious about the future. Though confident in the long-term prospects of the commercial vehicle industry, I's management believed that it was a low-growth industry: the long-term growth trend of the overall European market was slightly below 1% a year.
● The industry was likely to go through a difficult restructuring phase during the next few years, as a number of competitors unable to renew their product lines would have to leave the industry. It was expected at I that this restructuring would improve the overall profitability of the industry.

A brief description of the industry is in Appendix U.1.

I, on the UK market

The UK market was one of the largest in Europe and the share and status of the different Competitors was as follows:

Company	Share	Status
F	20%	Foreign-owned, local production
Leyland	16%	UK, state-owned, local production
Daimler Benz	13%	Foreign, importer
GM-Bedford	8%	Foreign-owned, local production
Renault-Dodge	8%	Foreign, local production
Volvo	6%	Foreign, importer
Daf	4%	Foreign, importer
I	3%	Foreign, importer
Scania	3%	Foreign, importer
Seddon Atkinson	2%	UK, local production
Man	2%	Foreign, importer
Erf	2%	UK, local production
Foden-Paccar	1%	Foreign-owned, importer

The UK market was characterized by its large number of competitors, the largest in Europe, and the growing importance of large fleet operators. The UK market was not very profitable (more so than France but significantly less than Finland or Italy). During the early 1980s continental European manufacturers increased their pressure on the UK market: Daimler Benz managed to get ahead of GM-Bedford, while Renault acquired Dodge, and became aggressive on prices. In 1985, F, Leyland and GM-Bedford were making losses.

There were several reasons why I was weak on the UK market:

● Late entry and relatively low priority given to this market so far. However, in the early 1980s, I had merger talks with Leyland and tried to acquire Seddon Atkinson.
● Strength of competitors such as F, Bedford or Leyland. Leyland had been the largest truck company in the world immediately after World War II.
● The relative weakness of I's dealer network in the UK. In 1985, I had 40 dealers in the UK who were not always located in prime sites and were often lacking in financial strength.

I was not satisfied with its position in the UK and was planning to become more aggressive in this market over the next five years. Its objective was to capture share and to be in a stronger position when the new generation of products was introduced. I was aware of the obstacles it would have to face.

● In spite of their good reputation, I's products were not well known in the UK.
● As the margins in the UK market were not very high, there was not much room for implementing an aggressive strategy.
● The UK market presented some specific characteristics which differed from the ones I was used to in continental Europe.

However, as it expected several competitors to leave the market, the management of I believed that it was the right time to focus its attention on the UK market and do better than the initial plan shown in Table U.2.

CASE

Table U.2 ● I's plans for the UK market

The initial and conservative plan
To compare this plan with other alternatives and in particular with the acquisition of F, the management of I had estimated the value that would result from this strategy. The value as of the end of 1985 had been estimated as the net sum of:

● the value of the working capital needs as of 31 December 1985;
● the present value of the cash flows that the company was expecting to generate in the period 1986–90;
● the present value of the cash flows to be achieved beyond 1990. This value had been estimated on the basis of £10 milion per point of market share.

In £ million, except for unit prices in £000:

	1986	1987	1988	1989	1990	1991	Cum.
Growth	5.0%	5.0%	5.0%	3.0%	3.0%		
Total market	84 000	88 200	92 610	95 388	98 250		
Market share	3.00%	3.25%	3.50%	3.75%	4.00%		
Unit selling price	18 000	18 000	18 000	18 000	18 000		
Sales	45	52	58	64	71		
Unit cost	12 780	12 780	12 780	12 780	12 780		
CGS	32	37	41	46	50		
CGS/sales	71%	71%	71%	71%	71%		
Operating expenses	14	14	14	15	16		
Operating expenses/sales	31%	27%	24%	23%	23%		
Profit before tax	−1	1	3	4	5		
Profit after tax	−1	1	2	2	3		7
Working capital open	0	5	5	6	6	7	
Working capital/sales	10%	10%	10%	10%	10%		
Working capital end	5	5	6	6	7		
CFO 1986–90	−5	0	1	2	2	7	7
Discount rate	0.10						
NPV 1986–90 cash flows	3						
Working capital open	4						
Market share in 1990	0.04						
Value cash flows beyond 1990	40						
Total value (£ million)	47						

An alternative and aggressive plan
The management of I had prepared an aggressive plan for bringing its share of the UK market from 3 to 8% in 1990. Though difficult to achieve, this goal did not seem unrealistic: I had a share higher than 8% in most European markets and had been able to progress quickly in those markets where local competitors were losing ground. As an example, I had been able to increase its share of the Spanish market from less than 2% in 1982 to more than 6% in 1985 even though it operated as an importer. The plan envisaged:

● an increase in marketing and selling expenses: 15 million in 1986 and 1987, 16 million in 1988, 17 million in 1989 and 18 million in 1990;
● a reduction in prices. Average selling price would be reduced from £18 000 in 1985 to £14 000 in 1986 (a 20% reduction), kept at this level for three years, then brought back to £15 000 in 1989 and £18 000 in 1990.

Table U.3 ● Evolution of the UK market and of the position of F Trucks

UK market
(number of units)

	1979	1980	1981	1982	1983	1984	1985
Heavy (≥16 tonnes)	37 300	27 200	19 300	20 800	24 200	26 900	27 900
Annual growth		−27%	−29%	8%	16%	11%	4%
In % of total UK market	40%	36%	34%	34%	35%	36%	35%
Medium (5–15.9 tonnes)	37 700	29 800	22 900	21 800	23 200	23 600	24 600
Annual growth		−21%	−23%	−5%	6%	2%	4%
In % of total UK market	40%	40%	40%	35%	34%	32%	31%
Light (3.5–4.9 tonnes)	18 100	18 400	14 800	19 400	21 300	24 200	27 500
Annual growth		2%	−20%	31%	10%	14%	14%
In % of total UK market	19%	24%	26%	31%	31%	32%	34%
Total	93 100	75 400	57 000	62 000	68 700	74 700	80 000
Annual growth		−19%	−24%	9%	11%	9%	7%
F Trucks							
F Sales							
(number of units sold)	24 000	19 000	14 000	15 000	16 400	15 400	16 000
Annual growth		−21%	−26%	7%	9%	−6%	4%
Market share	26%	25%	25%	24%	24%	21%	20%

CASE

One alternative was to implement an aggressive pricing strategy (see Table U.2) but this was risky and was falling short of reaching the long-term goal of the company, to capture at least 20% of the market. Under current conditions such a goal could only be reached by external acquisitions. However, acquiring market share was not easy, and past experience had shown that it was generally impossible to maintain the market share of the acquired company: losing 25% to 50% of this share was not unusual.

The negotiations with F

At the end of 1984, F offered I to acquire its truck operations. The management of I responded that such an acquisition might fit their strategy but that there was debate within the senior management of the company as to the real value of such a deal for I.

F Trucks was part of the international automotive group F. Within the F group, the commercial vehicle business had traditionally been centred on the UK market, where it enjoyed a very strong position. However, its market share had declined under the pressure of competition (see in Table U.3 the evolution of the UK market and of F sales). In the UK, F was operating as an integrated manufacturer focusing on the medium range since the discontinuation of the heavy trucks in 1983.

The financial data of F Trucks, as they were given to I, at the May meeting are in Table U.4. As F Trucks was integrated into the other activities of F, these data had to be considered with some caution and during the meeting, the representatives of I had the feeling that the management of F did not have full knowledge of their costs and were over-optimistic about their ability to reach a break-even situation.

Table U.4 ● Key financial data of F

(£ million)		
Income statements	1984	1985
Sales	187	192
Cost of goods sold	167	169
Other expenses	30	27
Profit before tax	−11	−4
Balance sheets		End 1985
Inventory and receivables		44
Accounts payable		24

It was not F's intention to sell their plant to I. In the case of an acquisition, the plant would be leased, and the annual lease payments had been included in the financial forecasts.

As far as F's products were concerned, they were very good and very well accepted by the market. F's problem was that:

● The products were produced in insufficient quantities to allow adequate economies of scale. When it had introduced these products, F had planned for much higher volumes, but it had to face disappointing export markets as well as some erosion of its domestic position.
● Introduced four years earlier, these products could not be expected to be sold beyond an horizon of five to six years without major capital investments which F was not ready to make.

The main strength of F was actually its dealer network which was among the best in the UK: F had 120 dealers, most of whom were car and truck dealers.

I was considering the following strategy in the case of an acquisition:

● Continue to produce the current F products for as long as they sold. The continuation of these products which were well accepted by the market would obviously help maintain the relationships with the dealers. I believed that the profitability of F's operations could not be improved during the next five years.
● When these products reached the end of their lives, I would invest in F's manufacturing facilities which would then assemble the new generation of products developed by I.

I's position *vis-à-vis* F

As the value of acquiring F's truck operations was obviously very dependent on the price to be paid, I wanted to avoid falling into the trap of paying too much.

Acquiring F was a unique opportunity for I to build a strong position in the UK market without having to exert pressure on prices and threatening the profitability of the market. Among all the UK companies, F was probably the best company to acquire. But acquiring the operations of F was a very risky move.

- Experience in other countries had taught I's management that up to half of the market share might be lost. Even though F's products were enjoying a good market response, it was not easy to predict how they would sell when manufactured by a not very well known foreign company. How would fleet operators and large customers like the Post Office react? Would they trust the new company to maintain the level of service presently provided by F?
- How would the dealers react to the prospect of working with I instead of F, a company with a strong and long-established reputation? Would the wealthy individuals owning F dealerships be willing to invest in the risky business of developing a new brand on the UK market? Would it be possible to integrate the F and the I networks?
- How would the management and personnel of F react to a takeover by I? F had a reputation as a very good company to work for, and some people could find the change in ownership difficult to accept. People might actually believe that I was only interested in the dealer network and was going to close the manufacturing facilities as soon as the first recession occurred.
- Finally, what growth could be expected in the UK market? Growth had been better than in other European countries recently, but this could mean bad news for the future as the UK market could not grow forever.

On the other hand, there were also arguments that the risks of this specific acquisition were limited.

- Because of its car business, F did not want its dealers to be frustrated and leave for competition. I could probably expect F to arrange for a smooth transition process, but it was clear also that F could do nothing as far as its customers were concerned.
- F's narrow product range made it difficult for the F dealers to compete; the full range of I would put them in a much better competitive position against Daimler Benz.
- As the truck business had never been a core activity for F, that company's employees in this sector might actually welcome the idea of being part of a company totally committed to the commercial vehicle industry.

The management of I had estimated the value of an eventual acquisition. This estimate, which is reproduced in Table U.5, shows that given the risks involved, I could not reasonably agree to pay very much for this acquisition. However, this was not necessarily a problem, since F was generating losses: an estimate of the value of F's operations if not acquired by I is in Table U.6.

Obviously, the situation would have been completely different had the acquisition of the truck operations of F really meant acquiring 20% of the UK market. In such a case, I would obviously have been prepared to pay much more!

Finally, Mr Corsi was wondering why Mr Jones and the management of F in general were so optimistic about the future and apparently so confident that I would succeed with the acquisition. The attitude of F's management could well be just negotiation tactics, but since the beginning of his discussions with F, Mr Corsi had had two somewhat conflicting feelings. One was telling him he had to find ways to help F adopt more realistic views, the other one was that he should not waste his time trying to change their views. After all, they were perfectly entitled to their own opinions about the future. Perhaps Mr Corsi should fully accept the optimism of the other party and find ways to take advantage of it for the benefit of both parties. This was obviously possible only if F's optimism was genuine.

Table U.5 ● The value of the combined operations of I and F

The value of the combined operations of I and F, as of the end of 1985, had been estimated as the net sum of:

- the value of the working capital as of 31 December 1985;
- the present value of the cash flows that the operations were expected to generate in the period 1986–90;
- the present value of the cost of reorganization (£30 million), to be incurred in 1990;
- the present value of the cash flows to be achieved beyond 1990. This value had been estimated on the basis of £10 million per point of market share.

The most likely scenario
In £ million, except for unit prices in £000:

	1986	1987	1988	1989	1990	1991	Cum.
Growth	5.0%	5.0%	5.0%	3.0%	3.0%		
Total market	84 000	88 200	92 610	95 388	98 250		
Share I	3.5%	4.0%	4.5%	5.0%	5.5%		
Share F	18.0%	16.0%	14.0%	12.0%	10.0%		
Unit price I	18 000	18 000	18 000	18 000	18 000		
Unit price F	12 000	12 000	12 000	12 000	12 000		
SALES	234	233	231	223	215		
Unit cost I	12 780	12 780	12 780	12 780	12 780		
Unit cost F	10 407	10 643	10 956	11 468	12 189		
CGS	195	195	195	192	189		
CGS/sales	83%	84%	85%	86%	88%		
Operating expenses	54	46	46	44	40		
Operating expenses/sales	23%	20%	20%	20%	19%		
Profit before tax	−15	−8	−11	−13	−14		
Profit after tax	−15	−8	−11	−13	−14		−60
Working capital open	0	23	23	23	22	22	
Working capital/sales	10%	10%	10%	10%	10%		
Working capital end	23	23	23	22	22		
CFO 1986–90	−38	−8	−10	−12	−13	22	−60
Discount rate	0.10						
NPV 1986–90 cash flows	**−53**						
Working capital open	**24**						
Reorganization cost					30		
NPV reorganization	**19**						
Tax shield	11						
NPV tax shield					21		
Market share in 1990	0.155						
Value cash flows beyond 1990	**155**						
TOTAL VALUE (£ million)	**118**						

Note
The unit cost of F's products had been estimated with the following formula: 7100 + 50 000 000/volume.

Other scenarios
A pessimistic scenario with the following assumptions had also been prepared:

	1986	1987	1988	1989	1990
Share I	0.03	0.03	0.03	0.03	0.03
Share F	0.16	0.12	0.10	0.08	0.07
Operating expenses	54	46	46	44	40
Market share beyond 1990	0.10				
Cost of reorganization	40 (in 1990)				

Table U.5 • continued

This scenario – which was not the most pessimistic – would lead to catastrophic results. Finally, the management of I had prepared an optimistic scenario:

	1986	1987	1988	1989	1990
Share I	0.04	0.05	0.06	0.07	0.12
Share F	0.19	0.18	0.17	0.16	0.11
Operating expenses	54	46	46	46	46
Market share beyond 1990	0.23				
Cost of reorganization	30 (in 1990)				

Table U.6 • Value of the operations of F if not acquired by I

The value of the operations of F had been estimated as the net sum of:

● the value of the working capital as of 31 December 1985;
● the present value of the cash flows that the company was expecting to generate in the period 1986–90. It has been assumed that the present products could not be sold beyond 1990;
● the present value of the cost of closure: 30 million, to be incurred in 1990.

In £ million, except for unit prices in £000:

	1986	1987	1988	1989	1990	1991	Cum.
Growth	5.0%	5.0%	5.0%	3.0%	3.0%		
Total market	84 000	88 200	92 610	95 388	98 250		
Market share	18.0%	16.0%	14.0%	12.0%	10.0%		
Unit selling price	12 000	12 000	12 000	12 000	10 000		
Sales	181	169	156	137	98		
Unit cost	10 407	10 643	10 956	11 468	12 189		
CGS	157	150	142	131	120		
CGS/sales	87%	89%	91%	96%	122%		
Operating expenses	30	25	23	20	15		
Operating expenses/sales	17%	15%	15%	15%	15%		
Profit before tax	−6	−6	−9	−14	−37		
Profit after tax	−4	−4	−6	−9	−24		−47
Working capital open	0	18	17	16	14	10	
Working capital/sales	10%	10%	10%	10%	10%		
Working capital end	18	17	16	14	10		
CFO 1986–90	**−22**	−3	−5	−7	−20	10	−47
Discount rate	0.10						
NPV 1986–90	**−37**						
Working capital open	**20**						
Cost of closure					30		
NPV closure	**19**						
TOTAL VALUE (£ million)	**−36**						

Notes
The unit cost of F's products had been estimated with the following formula: 7100 + 50 000 000/volume.
As F's other operations in the UK were profitable, any loss on the truck operations would generate a tax credit.

Appendix U.1
The European truck industry

Since the 1950s when they were as many as 55, competitors in the European truck industry had not found it easy to create value, as the overall industry had been characterized by its low margins, large and increasing capital expenditures and low growth and volatile demand.

In this difficult market, competitors had traditionally adopted a variety of strategies ranging between two extremes:

● Strategies for overall market dominance. In the mid-1980s two companies were emerging as overall market leaders with respective shares of 20 and 16% of the number of new vehicles delivered.

● Focused strategies. Focus on specific segments and/or specific national markets. Among the competitors, one had been very successful at pursuing a strategy focusing on the heavy-vehicle segment.

In the mid-1980s several competitors were facing an even more difficult challenge as they had to invest in the renewal of their product lines at a time when profitability had been depressed by the price wars of the early 1980s. This was expected to force several competitors out of the industry.

Salient features of the commercial vehicle industry

A low growth and cyclical market
The annual number of new commercial vehicles registered in western Europe had evolved as shown in Figure U.1 during the period 1970–85. For the European manufacturers, the situation had been made worse by the collapse of the export markets, which fell from 175 000 units in 1981 to less than 75 000 units in 1985. It was expected that these exports would further decrease in 1986.

In spite of the rapid development of road transportation and the growing importance of this form of transport in the infrastructure of modern economies, the commercial vehicle industry was a very low-growth industry: slightly less than 1% a year on average over a

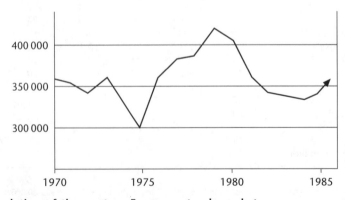

Figure U.1 Evolution of the western European truck market

Table U.7 ● Segments of the European truck market

New registrations	1979	1980	1981	1982	1983	1984	1985
Total market							
Number of units (000)	425	405	362	340	339	333	343
Annual growth		−5%	−11%	−6%	0%	−2%	3%
Heavy (≥16 tonnes)							
As a % of total	31%	31%	30%	30%	32%	34%	34%
Annual growth		−7%	−13%	−5%	7%	3%	1%
Medium (5–15.9 tonnes)							
As a % of total	38%	38%	35%	33%	33%	32%	31%
Annual growth		−6%	−16%	−12%	0%	−6%	1%
Light (3.5–4.9 tonnes)							
As a % of total	30%	32%	35%	37%	34%	34%	36%
Annual growth		0%	−3%	0%	−6%	−2%	7%

20-year period. As a basis for comparison, the GNP of OECD countries grew by 3.8% a year in the period of 1950–73 and 1.9% in the period 1973–87. The different segments of the market were not behaving in the same way and, as shown in Table U.7, the trend seemed to be towards a polarization of the market: heavy trucks for long-distance haulage and light trucks for city transportation.

In 1984, the size of the respective national markets (in 000 units) was:

UK	75	Italy	40
France	75	Spain	19
Germany	56	Others	68

Because of the registration procedures, volume date were easily available in the industry. While more difficult to obtain and probably much less reliable, value data were very interesting, since they showed a different picture:

Average unit selling price for the manufacturer (£000):

Heavy (≥16 tonnes)	34
Medium (5–15.9 tonnes)	17
Light (3.5–4.9 tonnes)	10

Relative size of segments (sales as a % of total sales):

Heavy (≥16 tonnes)	57%
Medium (5–15.9 tonnes)	26%
Light (3.5–4.9 tonnes)	18%
Total	100%

Numerous laws and regulations

The truck industry was affected by numerous national laws related to:

● Standards for commercial vehicles in each country: maximum weight (from 28 tonnes in Switzerland to 52 tonnes in Sweden), maximum width and length, number of axles,

Table U.8 • Typical breakdown of ownership cost over full life	
Driver	30
Fuel	21
Tax	12
Maintenance	10
Tyres	7
Insurance	7
Depreciation	7
Interest	6
Total	100

speed, noise levels, exhaust emissions, etc. Pollution-control factors had become very important; according to industry sources, more than one-third of the cost of designing new truck engines was spent on pollution control.

• The organization of the road transport industry. In several European countries, like Germany, regulations were keeping numerous inefficient companies in existence, while in countries like the Netherlands and the UK, the transport industry had been largely deregulated.

The impact of the creation of a unified market in Europe was difficult to assess:

• On the one hand, there were forecasts suggesting that cross-border transportation could grow by more than one-third in Europe before the end of the century and that the share of freight moved by trucks could increase to 55% from its current 40% level.

• On the other hand, improvement in logistics and the removal of regulations would keep trucks from operating empty. Disappearance of borders would also mean that the speed of operations would increase dramatically. Therefore, some industry experts believed that the volume of road transport in 2000 could be handled by the same number of vehicles as at the present time. Another unfortunate consequence for European manufacturers would be that a unified European market might become more attractive to Japanese manufacturers.

Demanding customers
Commercial vehicles were industrial products sold to:

• Well-informed customers. Large fleet operators and leasing companies had built up extensive statistics of the ownership costs of the different makes and models. A typical breakdown of the ownership costs of a truck over its full life is in Table U.8.

• Customers requiring ever-increasing productivity. The industry of road transportation, or large sectors of it, had become very efficient.

There were numerous specification requirements and very few trucks were identical.

Higher technology products requiring very high investments
The 1985 Frankfurt Motor Show witnessed attempts by European truck manufacturers to outdo each other in their claims to superiority in advanced engineering.

After the car industry, the truck industry was now being penetrated by electronics, and the hot issues in Frankfurt were vehicle management systems – aimed at improving performance and fuel efficiency – and computer-aided gearchange systems. Electronics were also present in the anti-skid systems. Diesel engines had progressed also; they were becoming cleaner, quieter and more efficient. Use of exhaust-gas-driven turbochargers allowed engines to burn fuel more completely and efficiently. Intercoolers, which reduce the temperature of the air delivered by the turbocharger before it goes into the engine, had also improved efficiency.

European manufacturers had invested a lot in manufacturing technology, in order to deal with erratic demand and to benefit from vertical integration. Competitors like Scania and Volvo were producing all their driveline components (engines, gearboxes and rear axles) and had dramatically reduced the number of basic components, thus achieving scale effects comparable to those of higher volume manufacturers often plagued by manufacturing diversity. Advances in product and manufacturing technology had made the development of new products very expensive: Scania and Volvo had announced that they each had invested £900 million for the development and introduction of their new generation of trucks launched in 1984–5.

A variety of competitive strategies . . . and very few successes so far
According to many industry observers, the economics of the market (limited growth, volatility of demand, low margins and large investment requirements) were going to lead to a further reduction of the number of competitors. Competitors could be classified according to their positioning on the market:

- Full product and geographic coverage (I)
- Full product range but limited geographic coverage (II)
- Focused product range and full geographic coverage (III)
- Focused product range and limited geographic coverage (IV)

According to most observers in the industry, only those companies which had positioned themselves in I or III had strong chances of survival in the long run. These two groups of competitors had very different strategies:

- Stralegies aimed at succeeding through maximizing volume and achieving economies of scale, on the one hand.
- Focused strategies aimed at creating high customer value (superior product design, high quality, service, etc.), premium pricing and innovative manufacturing, on the other.

Table U.9 shows the positioning of the European manufacturers in 1985.

Another characteristic of the industry was the strong presence of state-owned and state-supported companies:

France:	Renault
Spain:	Enasa, Pegaso
UK:	Leyland
Austria:	Steyr
Finland:	Sizu
Netherlands:	Daf

Table U.9 ● Positioning of the European truck manufacturers in 1985

Product coverage	Market coverage	
	All countries	**Selected countries**
Full range	Mercedes Benz	RVI
	Iveco	British Leyland
Selected segment	Scania	Man
	Volvo	Ebro
		Pegaso/Seddon
		Sizu
		ERF
		Foden
		Ford
		Astra
		Daf
		Steyr
		Bedford

Fights for market shares, attempts at maintaining workloads in volatile markets, priority given to volume over profitability, and so on had triggered numerous price wars which had eroded the margins of all competitors. In 1985, very few competitors were profitable.

- Scania and Volvo were showing operating profits equal, respectively, to 13% and 7% of their sales.
- Daimler Benz was not publishing profitability data on its truck operations. I was expecting to report a small profit.
- Renault was expecting to sustain losses of £270 million in 1985. The company had lost 640 million in the period 1983–5.
- Man had to sell assets to Daimler Benz in order to resist an acquisition by GM.
- Daf was expecting to make a marginal profit after heavy losses in 1984.

Key financial data of the main competitors are shown in Table U.10.

Europe and the world market

In the mid-1980s, the world truck industry was fragmented into regional markets, each having its specific regulations and demand characteristics but, as shown in Table U.11, all equally volatile.

The US market

The US was quite a different market from Europe.

- The products were very different (for example, the traditional cab behind the engine was still popular in the USA).
- US competitors were much less integrated than their European counterparts. Paccar, the most profitable competitor, was one of the less vertically integrated companies.

Table U.10 ● Key financial data of the main European truck manufacturers

	Strategy	Output	Estimate average selling price (authors' estimates)	Operating profit/sales
Daimler Benz	Strategy for world market dominance. Numerous production sites. Wide range of products.	110–150 000	£19 000	Not published, did not seem very high
I	Strategy for European market dominance plus exports outside of Europe.	76 000 in 1985 56 000 in Europe	£17 000	5% in 1985
F	Activity limited to the UK market (plus some exports) and to medium trucks. Suffered from over-capacity.	16 000 in 1985	£12 000	Loss
Volvo	Leadership in heavy/medium segment. Strong vertical integration.	28 700 European trucks and 13 200 American trucks, e.g. 41 900 in 1985 42 200 in 1984	£32 000 (European trucks)	6% in 1985 7% in 1984
Scania	Leadership in the heavy segment in Europe and Latin America. High-quality products, high level of service, premium prices. Strong vertical integration with the lowest number of components in the industry. Distribution through independent dealers.	22 970 in 1985 21 800 in 1984 17 500 in 1983	£35 000	13% in 1985 13% in 1984

- The US market was more heavily dominated than Europe by large fleet operators (Ryder, for example, had a fleet of more than 100 000 trucks).

In the late 1970s, most US competitors were suffering from the collapse of the market, and this allowed several European competitors – Volvo, Renault, Daimler Benz – to strengthen their position through acquisitions. However, the substantial differences between the US and European markets prevented these companies from achieving much industrial integration of their European and US operations.

The Japanese market
This was another market with its own specific features. There were four competitors, three with a share slightly higher than 25%: Hino (part of the capital of Hino was held

Table U.11 ● World truck markets. Annual number of new registrations (3.5 tonnes and above)

	1979	1980	1981	1982	1983	1984	1985
Total world market (000 vehicles)	1315	1205	1162	1000	995	1083	1138
Annual growth		–8%	–4%	–14%	–1%	9%	5%
Western Europe							
As a % of world market	32%	34%	31%	34%	34%	31%	30%
Annual growth		–5%	–11%	–6%	0%	–2%	3%
USA							
As a % of world market	42%	30%	26%	28%	31%	38%	39%
Annual growth		–35%	–17%	–7%	11%	32%	7%
Rest of the world							
As a % of world market	26%	37%	43%	38%	35%	31%	31%
Annual growth		29%	14%	–24%	–9%	–1%	4%

Slightly less than half of the 'rest of the world' was accounted for by Japan, the second largest market in the world.

by Toyota), Isuzu and Mitsubishi; the fourth with a share somewhat lower than 20%: Nissan.

Japanese truck competitors were less aggressive than the Japanese car competitors on the world market. However, they were very active in south eastern Asia, and they had started actively looking for niches in the European and US markets. Hino entered the US market in 1984. Other Japanese companies had established joint ventures with US companies. Nissan had signed an agreement to supply a new generation of medium-weight trucks to International Harvester, and GM, which had a 40% interest in Isuzu, was distributing Isuzu's light- and medium-weight trucks.

The European market in the mid-1980s

At the end of the 1970s, the truck market had been very buoyant all over the world, and manufacturers installed new capacity in expectation of a continually expanding market. According to some industry sources, the total capacity of the industry had risen to as much as 600 000 vehicles per year. Starting in 1980, the market collapsed as, one after another, key export markets in Africa and the Middle East ran out of foreign currency to pay for imports. To make things worse, demand also fell on most European markets. This led the European truck manufacturers to:

● cut part of their production capacity; about one-fourth was eliminated between 1980 and 1985;
● compete more intensely among themselves;
● rely more on the European market.

The first year to show some improvement was 1985, with demand expected to grow by 3% above its level in 1984. Another improvement in 1985 was related to the fact that capacity reductions were beginning to have an impact, and it was expected that several manufacturers who had been incurring heavy losses would break even. However, the feeling was that the restructuring of the industry would continue and even accelerate with a recovery, which could encourage potential buyers to invest. Another reason for further industry restructuring to occur was the fact that several competitors were no longer able to renew their product range and would therefore be in a critical position in the late 1980s or early 1990s. The industry was expecting further recovery in 1986, but in spite of the feeling that demand should come back to a 'normal' level, many people in the industry were taking a very cautious view of the future.

In the mid-1980s, one US truck manufacturer, GM, was attempting to implement the same acquisition strategy that had allowed some European competitors to establish themselves on the US market five years earlier. GM was aiming at building a worldwide truck business and had been engaged in acquisition and collaboration talks with several companies in Europe, particularly those finding it more difficult to compete: Enasa, Leyland and Man.

Note

1. This case has been prepared by Damir Borsic, Professor of Business Administration at Isvor Fiat: at (Italy) and the author from a real business situation which has been modified in order to serve as a basis for class discussion. The pedagogy of this case has been developed by the author, Damir Borsic and Sherwood Frey, Professor at Darden (USA). This document is not intended to reflect the real business situation of the truck industry at the time of the case.

CASE

CHAPTER *23*

A step-by-step analysis of the dynamics of an opportunity for co-operation

23.1 Recognizing the motivations to co-operate

Case U suggests that a deal would be beneficial to both companies.

- I is the second largest competitor, it holds a 16% share of the European market but is weak in the UK, one of the biggest European markets. To be consistent with its strategy, I has to reinforce its position in the UK. When considering an acquisition, F is probably the best candidate: leading market share, superior dealer network, strong local reputation, quality products, private ownership, and so on. A more debatable advantage is the local manufacturing capacities brought by F: producing in the UK would increase the complexity of the operations of I for a benefit that Daimler Benz does not seem to need to succeed in the UK.

  By acquiring F and retaining its market share, not only would I build up a strong local position but it would also close its overall European market share gap with Daimler Benz. If it misses the acquisition of F, I will probably not have such an opportunity in the near future, i.e. before the introduction of the new product generation.
- F has decided to withdraw but still commands a leading share of the UK market. This is a short-lived but precious asset provided that an adequate buyer is found. I is obviously the ideal buyer and it is no surprise that it is I that F decided to approach.

The case also suggests that the two companies have further motives to co-operate.

- For both companies the issue at stake is of strategic importance. Because it will continue working with most of its current truck dealers through its car business, F cannot only be interested in getting a high price from I. F most probably also wants the acquisition to succeed.

● The positions of the two companies are equally strong and their respective strengths depend on the other party. The value of the market share of F is created by the interest of I and the acquisition of F is a unique opportunity for I. Neither I nor F can use the threat of time. If an agreement is not reached, F's customers may quickly lose interest in a brand that is going to disappear. But if F's market share collapses, a great opportunity will be lost for I as the customers leaving F will turn more to the market leaders – and to Mercedes Benz in particular – than to marginal competitors like I. Both F and I are working under the pressure of time.

● Both companies are key players in the world automotive industry, both have a long-term view about the industry, both have a reputation to keep and both probably consider the present deal as part of a long-term competitive and co-operative relationship. At the same time I and F compete with each other and each want to gain as much as possible from the potential agreement.

23.2 Mapping the alternatives available to each party

Figure 23.1 shows a tentative mapping of the alternatives available to I and F.

● I does not seem to be in a position to buy any other company than F. If it does not acquire F, I will have to rely on internal growth. When considering internal growth, I might decide to pursue its current conservative strategy or adopt a more aggressive approach. When analyzing alternatives, and in particular the acquisition of F, I has to realize that these alternatives may result in a variety of outcomes.

● F does not seem to be able to sell its operations to any other company than I. If F fails to reach an agreement with I, its only option will be to decide when to close its operations.

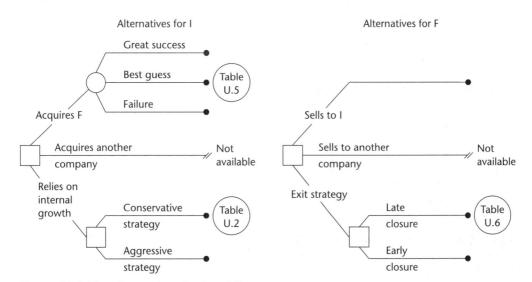

Figure 23.1 The alternatives for I and F

23.3 Understanding the integrative and distributive dynamics of the situation

In order to understand a co-operative situation you should analyze its two critical dimensions:

● What is the value, or 'the pie', to be shared? What are the critical factors that drive the value to be shared? How can this value be increased? This is the **integrative dimension** of co-operative and negotiation situations.
● How can this value be shared? This is the **distributive** or **claiming dimension**.

Even though it is too often reduced to its claiming dimension, negotiation is primarily a powerful approach for creating value. Value can be created by various means:[1]

● Identification of *common interests*. I and F have several common interests: reaching an agreement quickly, retaining the current customers of F, satisfying the current dealers of F, and so on. I and F should not find it difficult to discover that they want the same resolution of several issues and are in a position to work at creating common value. One interesting property of common – or 'public' – value is that it can be shared by all parties simultaneously; no one can be excluded unless all are.
● Recognition of *valuable differences*. A classic image is the one suggested by M.P. Follett:[2] two sisters quarrel over an orange until they realize that one wants only the fruit to eat and the other only the peel for baking.
● *Redefining* the situation. The negotiating parties might reformulate their apparent conflict and invent new options that can fulfil their underlying interests.

Means to create value – or to enlarge the pie – are like alternatives to decisions. They do not appear spontaneously but are created out of the analysis and imagination of managers. Experience and research actually show that most negotiators find it difficult to see all the opportunities for creating value and the literature prescribes a series of rules of hygiene.

1. Start with the analysis of the integrative dimension.
2. Define the goal as 'designing an outcome that fits the needs of the parties involved'.[3]
3. Invent first, decide later, focus on interests, not on positions, separate the problem from the people.[4]
4. Listen and question.[5]

The integrative dynamics: value, BATNAs and zone of agreement

The mapping of the alternatives of I and F shown in Figure 23.1 enables us to understand the integrative dimension of the situation. The value of an agreement between I and F is equal to the difference between:

● the value of the combined operations of I and F and
● the sum of the maximum values that I and F could achieve by themselves in the absence of an agreement or using the term coined by Fisher and Ury,[4] the sum of their BATNAs – Best Alternatives to a Negotiated Agreement.

For I, the value of an agreement with F is equal to the difference between the value of the combined operations of I and F, the value of the best internal growth strategy I can choose (I's BATNA), and the price paid to F. The maximum price that I can pay is equal to the difference between the value of the combined operations and the value of its best internal

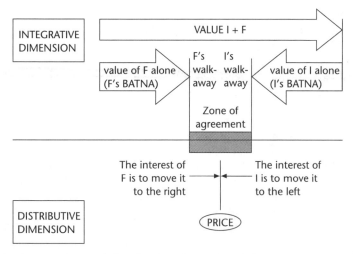

Figure 23.2 The integrative and distributive dynamics of the situation

growth strategy. Any price above this maximum, or **walk-away**, or **reservation** price should be rejected by I as it would render an agreement with F less valuable than the best internal growth option.

For F, the value of an agreement with I is equal to the difference between the price paid by I and the best exit strategy F can adopt. The minimum price that F can accept is equal to the value of the best exit strategy it can select. This is the walk-away price of F.

The integrative dimension of the situation is driven by three critical values:

● the value of the combined operations of I and F;
● the value of the BATNA of I (best internal growth strategy);
● the value of the BATNA of F (best exit strategy).

As shown in Figure 23.2, the first two critical values drive the walk-away price of I, the third value drives the walk-away price of F and the two walk-away prices drive the existence and size of a **zone of agreement**.

What does this tell us about the dynamics of the situation?

A zone of agreement should exist in order that a deal be possible. This zone is bounded by three critical values combined operations, BATNA of I and BATNA of F. The zone of agreement shows the value of the deal, or the size of the potential pie to be shared. It is increased by any increase in the value of the integrated operations and by any decrease in the value of each stand-alone company.

The concept of zone of agreement is actually more complicated than shown in Figure 23.2 as you should realize that:

● Both I and F probably have their own *perceived* zones of agreement. These perceived zones depend on the opinions that I and F have on the three critical values. As a result, the two parties may see quite different zones of agreement which may overlap or not. A further complication is that neither I not F knows what is the perceived zone of agreement of the other party. Trying to unveil the expected zone of agreement of the other party is one of the very important parts of the negotiation process.[6]

● The perceived zones of agreement of each party are not necessarily stable as their perception of each of the three critical values may change over time and in particular may change with new information unveiled during the negotiation process.

The distributive dimension and the 'fair' price issue

Figure 23.2 also shows the distributive dimension of the situation. An interesting question is what I and F would consider as a fair sharing. Even though it may appeal to intuition a 50–50% sharing is not easy to justify and some buyers systematically aim at a 100–0% sharing: 'We never pay for synergies'.

Another issue with sharing is that the true value of the pie is not known for sure today. This value will only be known a few years from now when the major uncertainties will be resolved. Sharing the expected value can be done in two ways:

● either you agree today on a rule for sharing and wait until the uncertainties are resolved in order to determine the actual amount to be shared and to proceed with the actual payments;

● or you make the actual payments today. When doing so, you create an asymmetry between the two parties since the buyer acquires a share of an expected value in exchange for an certain payment. This is a further reason for the buyer not to be satisfied with a 50–50% sharing.

23.4 A model for evaluating the three critical alternatives

We can use the model described in Tables 23.1 and 23.2 to assess the value of the three critical alternatives: the BATNA of I, the BATNA of F and the combined operations of I and F. The model breaks the value of each alternative into three components.

● The value of the inheritance from the pre-acquisition activity. Here the value of the inheritance is limited to the working capital needs at the date of acquisition. Neither of the companies carries debt obligations, owns fixed assets, holds significant cash balances, or faces potential costs of litigation.

● The value of the cash flows during the transition period up to the introduction of the new product generation. If it does not acquire F, I will try to take advantage of the expected restructuring of the UK market in order to increase its share. If I acquires F there will be additional costs related to the integration of the two dealer networks and to the reinforcement of the brand image of I in the UK. Costs of reorganizing the production facilities of F will have to be faced also. If it does not reach an agreement with I, F will have to design and implement an exit strategy.

● The continuing value. This value is based on the expected gains from the new generation of products. There is obviously no continuing value for F in case it does not reach an agreement with I.

Table 23.1 • The foreground of a model to evaluate the alternatives of I and F

	1986	1987	1988	1989	1990	1991	Cum.
Growth	5.0%	5.0%	5.0%	3.0%	3.0%		
Total market	84 000	88 200	92 610	95 388	98 250		
Share I	3.5%	4.0%	4.5%	5.0%	5.5%		
Share F	18.0%	16.0%	14.0%	12.0%	10.0%		
Competitive price change	0						
Unit price I	18 000	18 000	18 000	18 000	18 000		
Unit price F	12 000	12 000	12 000	12 000	12 000		
Sales	234	233	231	223	215		
Unit cost I	12 780	12 780	12 780	12 780	12 780		
Unit cost F	10 407	10 643	10 956	11 468	12 189		
CGS	195	195	195	192	189		
CGS/sales	83%	84%	85%	86%	88%		
Operating expenses	54	46	46	44	40		
Operating expenses/sales	23%	20%	20%	20%	19%		
Profit before tax	−15	−8	−11	−13	−14		
Profit after tax	−15	−8	−11	−13	−14		−60
Working capital open	0	23	23	23	22	22	
Working capital/sales	10%	10%	10%	10%	10%		
Wording capital end	23	23	23	22	22		
CFO 1986–90	−38	−8	−10	−12	−13	22	−60
Discount rate	0.10						
NPV 1986–90	**−53**						
Working capital open	**24**						
Reorganization cost					30		
NPV reorganization	**19**						
Tax shield					21		
NPV tax shield	**11**						
Market share in 1990	0.155						
Market share in 1991	0.155						
Adjustment continuing value	0.0%						
Value cash flows beyond 1990	**155**						
Total value (£ million)	**118**						

The model uses a constant prices / real rate approach for assessing both the initial planning period and the continuing value. It also includes parameters aimed at simulating different industry scenarios and in particular the impact of a possible price war.

23.5 Understanding the continuing value

The importance of the continuing value in the total value of both I and I and F suggests that we spend some time trying to understand why the management of I believes that a point of market share is worth £10 million. Table 23.3 shows a model to frame this estimate of the continuing value.

Table 23.2 ● The background of a model to evaluate the alternatives of I and F

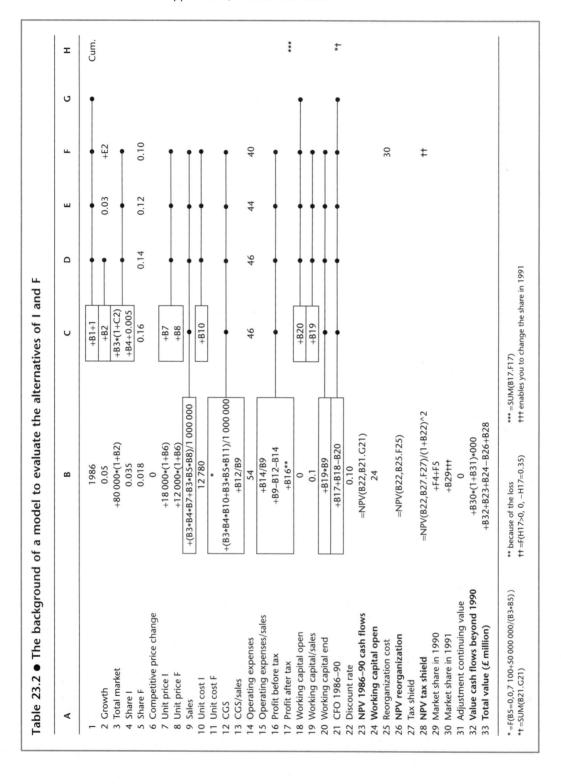

	A	B	C	D	E	F	G	H
1		1986						Cum.
2	Growth	0.05	+B1+1		0.03	+E2	•	
3	Total market	+80 000*(1+B2)	+B2	•	•	•	•	
4	Share I	0.035	+B3*(1+C2)	0.14	0.12	0.10	•	
5	Share F	0.018	+B4+0.005	•	•	•	•	
6	Competitive price change	0	0.16	•	•	•	•	
7	Unit price I	+18 000*(1+B6)	+B7					
8	Unit price F	+12 000*(1+B6)	+B8					
9	Sales	+(B3*B4*B7+B3*B5*B8)/1 000 000		•	•	•	•	
10	Unit cost I	12 780	+B10	•	•	•	•	
11	Unit cost F	*		•	•	•	•	
12	CGS	+(B3*B4*B10+B3*B5*B11)/1 000 000	•	•	•	•	•	
13	CGS/sales	54	46	46	44	40	•	
14	Operating expenses	+B14/B9	•	•	•	•	•	
15	Operating expenses/sales	+B9–B12–B14						
16	Profit before tax	+B16**	•	•	•	•	•	
17	Profit after tax	0		•	•	•	•	
18	Working capital open	0.1	+B20	•	•	•	•	***
19	Working capital/sales	+B19*B9	+B19	•	•	•	•	
20	Working capital end	+B17+B18–B20	•	•	•	•	•	*†
21	CFO 1986–90	0.10						
22	Discount rate	=NPV(B22,B21.G21)						
23	**NPV 1986–90 cash flows**	24						
24	**Working capital open**							
25	Reorganization cost	=NPV(B22,B25.F25)				30		
26	**NPV reorganization**							
27	Tax shield	=NPV(B22,B27.F27)/(1+B22)^2						
28	**NPV tax shield**	+F4+F5				††		
29	Market share in 1990	+B29†††						
30	Market share in 1991	0						
31	Adjustment continuing value	+B30*(1+B31)*000						
32	**Value cash flows beyond 1990**	+B32+B23+B24–B26+B28						
33	**Total value (£ million)**							

* =F(B5=0,0,7 100+50 000 000/(B3*B5))
** =SUM(B21.G21)

** because of the loss
†† =F(H17>0, 0, –H17=0.35)

*** =SUM(B17.F17)
††† enables you to change the share in 1991

Table 23.3 ● Understanding the continuing value

A	B	C	D	E	F	G	H	I	J	K	L	M
1 Year	1	2	3	4	5	6	7	8	9	10	11	12
2 Growth	0.01											
3 Market volume	100	101	102	103	104	105	106	107	108	109	110	112
4 Market share	20%											
5 Unit price	20											
6 Sales	400	404	408	412	416	420	425	429	433	437	442	446
7 Operating income/sales	11%											
8 Net income	29	29	29	29	30	30	30	31	31	31	32	32
9 NPV 1990	204											
10 **NPV 1985**	**126**											
11 Value beyond (1990)	112											319
12 **Value beyond (1985)**	**69**											
13 **Continuing value**	**196**											

C3: =B3*(1+$B$2); Copy across   B9: =NPV(.1, B8.M8)

B6: =B3*$B$4*$B$5; Copy across   B10: =B9/(1.1)^5; Copy in B12

B8: =B6*$B$7*.65   M11 =M8/.1; B11: =M11/(1.1)^11; B13: =B10+B12

Notes

1. In *The Manager as Negotiator*, Lax and Sebenius claim that all joint gains derive from transactions involving various combinations of four basic factors:

   ● values and attitudes toward risk and time;
   ● beliefs and forecasts;
   ● original endowments of the parties; and
   ● the capabilities of the parties to produce.

2. 'Constructive Conflict', M.P. Follett, in *Dynamic Administration: the Collected Papers of Mary Parker Follett*, H.C. Metcalf and L. Urwick (eds), New York, Harper, 1940.

3. Refer to *Conflicts, A Better Way to Resolve Them*, Edward De Bono, Penguin Books, London, 1985.

4. *Getting to Yes, Negotiating Agreement without Giving In*, R. Fisher and W. Ury, Houghton Mifflin Company, Boston, 1981.

5. The art of questioning is critical to the unveiling of creative solutions; for the use of questioning in negotiation, refer to Chapter 8, *Fundamentals of Negotiating*, G. Nierenberg, Hawthorn Books, Inc., New York, 1968.

6. For a treatment of this issue, refer to Chapter 4, *The Art and Science of Negotiation*, H. Raiffa, The Bellknap Press of Harvard University Press, Cambridge, 1982.

CHAPTER *24*

Designing a co-operative strategy and preparing for its implementation

When preparing for the negotiation, I should understand both its interests and the interests of F. The problem is that understanding the interests of another party is extremely difficult. First, taking the other party's perspective is not easy. Secondly, what you need to understand is not what the interests of the other parties should be, but *what the other parties think their interests are.*

In order to try to understand how F views its interests, I should like to propose a three-step approach.

1. Let us start with an 'objective' analysis of the situation and let us design a deal that should satisfy their interests and ours.
2. Then, let us put ourselves in their shoes and imagine how they might react to our 'objective' deal. This should help us go one step further in the process of understanding their perceived interests and perhaps make us revise or strategy.
3. Finally, let us make sure that we devise a negotiation strategy that will enable us to ask them, directly or indirectly, what they think their interests are. Even though it is essential, a careful preparation should never make you believe that you can guess what is in other people's minds:

24.1 Starting with an 'objective' analysis of the interests of the two parties

Specifying the industry risk

The data suggested in the case for making 'best guess' assessments are reproduced in Table 24.1.

Both the history of the market and its current situation (a competitor seems to be willing to start a price war) encourage us to explore more than one industry scenario. Even though

Table 24.1 ● Sets of data for 'best guess' assessments

I Grows internally and pursues a conservative strategy

	1986	1987	1988	1989	1990
Growth	5.0%	5.0%	5.0%	3.0%	3.0%
Share I	3.00%	3.25%	3.50%	3.75%	4.00%
Share F					
Unit price I	18 000	18 000	18 000	18 000	18 000
Unit price F					
Unit cost I	12 780	12 780	12 780	12 780	12 780
Operating expenses	14	14	14	15	16
Working capital/sales	10%	10%	10%	10%	10%
Working capital open	4				
Cost of reorganization					

TAX: loss in 1986, carry forward in 1987, normal tax in 1988–90

I Grows internally and adopts an aggressive strategy

	1986	1987	1988	1989	1990
Growth	5.0%	5.0%	5.0%	3.0%	3.0%
Share I	4.0%	5.0%	6.0%	7.0%	8.0%
Share F					
Unit price I	14 400	14 400	14 400	15 000	18 000
Unit price F					
Unit cost I	12 780	12 780	12 780	12 780	12 780
Operating expenses	15	15	16	17	18
Working capital/sales	10%	10%	10%	10%	10%
Working capital open	4				
Cost of reorganization					

TAX: no tax losses during the whole period 1986–9

F closes its operations as late as possible

	1986	1987	1988	1989	1990
Growth	5.0%	5.0%	5.0%	3.0%	3.0%
Share I					
Share F	18.0%	16.0%	14.0%	12.0%	10.0%
Unit price I					
Unit price F	12 000	12 000	12 000	12 000	10 000
Unit cost I					
Operating expenses	30	25	23	20	15
Working capital/sales	10%	10%	10%	10%	10%
Working capital open	20				30
Cost of reorganization					

TAX: losses create tax credits for the other operations of the group

F closes its operations as early as possible

	1986	1987	1988	1989	1990
Growth	5.0%	5.0%			
Share I					
Share F	16.0%	10.0%			
Unit price I					
Unit price F	12 000	10 000			
Unit cost I					
Operating expenses	30	28			
Working capital/sales	10%	10%			
Working capital open	20				
Cost of reorganization		30			

TAX: losses create tax credits for the other operations of the group

Table 24.1 continued

I acquires F: the best guess case

	1986	1987	1988	1989	1990
Growth	5.0%	5.0%	5.0%	3.0%	3.0%
Share I	3.5%	4.0%	4.5%	5.0%	5.5%
Share F	18.0%	16.0%	14.0%	12.0%	10.0%
Unit price I	18 000	18 000	18 000	18 000	18 000
Unit price F	12 000	12 000	12 000	12 000	12 000
Unit cost I	12 780	12 780	12 780	12 780	12 780
Operating expenses	54	46	46	44	40
Working capital/sales	10%	10%	10%	10%	10%
Working capital open	24				30
Cost of reorganization					
Market share in 1991	15.5%				

TAX: no tax, losses during the whole period

I acquires F and the acquisition is a great success

	1986	1987	1988	1989	1990
Growth	5.0%	5.0%	5.0%	3.0%	3.0%
Share I	4.0%	5.0%	6.0%	7.0%	12.0%
Share F	19.0%	18.0%	17.0%	16.0%	11.0%
Unit price I	18 000	18 000	18 000	18 000	18 000
Unit price F	12 000	12 000	12 000	12 000	12 000
Unit cost I	12 780	12 780	12 780	12 780	12 780
Operating expenses	54	46	46	46	46
Working capital/sales	10%	10%	10%	10%	10%
Working capital open	24				30
Cost of reorganization					

TAX: loss in 1986, carry forwards in 1987–8, normal tax afterwards

I acquires F and the acquisition is a failure

	1986	1987	1988	1989	1990
Growth	5.0%	5.0%	5.0%	3.0%	3.0%
Share I	3.0%	3.0%	3.0%	3.0%	3.0%
Share F	16.0%	12.0%	10.0%	8.0%	7.0%
Unit price I	18 000	18 000	18 000	18 000	18 000
Unit price F	12 000	12 000	12 000	12 000	12 000
Unit cost I	12 780	12 780	12 780	12 780	12 780
Operating expenses	54	46	46	44	40
Working capital/sales	10%	10%	10%	10%	10%
Working capital open	24				40
Cost of reorganization					

TAX: no tax, losses during the whole period

it is very difficult to anticipate the evolution of such a volatile market, let us specify a very optimistic and a very pessimistic scenario.

● 'Profitable boom'. A temporary market upswing will result in the following growth rates: 15% in 1986 and 1987, 10% in 1988, –5% in 1989, and –10% in 1990. This temporary

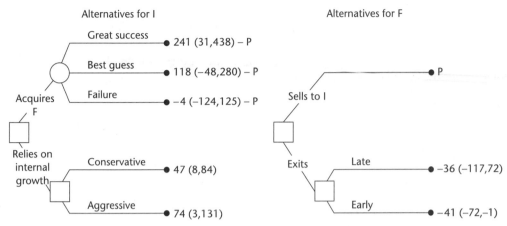

Notes
1. The first number corresponds to the 'best guess' scenario, the second to the 'cutthroat recession', the third to the 'profitable boom'.
2. To generate the results of the very difficult integration:
For 'cutthroat recession', assume a 14 400 unit selling price for I and a 9600 unit selling price for F (whole period).
For 'profitable boom', take the 1990 loss into account for the tax shield.
3. To generate the results of aggressive internal growth with 'cutthroat recession', assume that in spite of a unit selling price of 14 400, I keeps the same market share as with the conservative strategy.
4. To generate the results of late closure, make the tax shields and the value beyond 1990 equal to zero. For 'cutthroat recession', make all unit prices 20% less than with the best guess scenario, for 'profitable boom', make them 20% higher.
5. To generate the results of early closure, erase the range C1.F16.

Figure 24.1 Outcomes of the alternatives available to I and F

boom will not lift the total market in 1991 which will remain equal to 100 000 units. Taking advantage of the boom, the industry will be able to increase its average selling price by 20% in 1986.
● 'Cutthroat recession'. There will be no market growth at all in the period 1986–90. A price war will cause a 20% price reduction in the period 1986–90 and the overall market value in 1991 will be 15% less than expected.

Figure 24.1 shows the results of the simulations of the situations of I, F, and of the combined operations of I and F within the three industry scenarios.

Assessing the BATNA of I
A 3–4% share of the UK market does not fit the ambition of I. It is why some managers are in favour of a more aggressive strategy. Is such a strategy a valuable alternative for I? Figure 24.1 suggests that the outcomes of the aggressive strategy are attractive but you should consider risk also and recognize that the aggressive strategy may start an industry-wide price war. In order to compare the conservative and the aggressive strategies, you should assign a much higher probability to the pessimistic industry scenario[1] in case I adopts the aggressive strategy. As risk easily destroys the advantage of the aggressive strategy, let us assume that the BATNA of I corresponds to the conservative internal growth strategy with a £47 million best guess value and an £8 to 84 million range.

Assessing the 'objective' BATNA of F

Figure 24.1 compares two exit strategies: closing as late as possible and closing as early as possible, i.e. within the next two years. The late closing strategy exposes F to a risk of very large losses, which might even be higher than shown by the model as the market may drastically lose confidence in products which are about to be discontinued. If, as seems reasonable, F adopts an early closing strategy, then its BATNA corresponds to a negative value: £–36 million for the best guess industry scenario.

The interesting thing, though, is that only a late closing strategy would give F a chance to leave the market without a loss (in the case of a market boom). As a result, it is difficult to guess what F perceives as its BATNA.

- Our analysis suggests that F had better close as early as possible. As this BATNA corresponds to a negative value, F should be willing to pay a price for getting rid of its operations.
- However, one may also imagine that if it believes that there is a good chance of a market upswing, F might be tempted to continue for as long as it can. If that were the case, F might consider that its BATNA is a positive number (if F assigns a 60% probability to the 72 million outcome, a 35% probability to the –36 million outcome and a 5% probability to the –117 million outcome, then its BATNA is as high as £25 million).

Assessing the 'objective' value of the combined operations of I and F

Figure 24.1 shows nine possible outcomes for the combined operations: three acquisition scenarios (best guess, very successful integration and very difficult integration) and three values for each acquisition scenario (one for each industry scenario). These nine values are also shown in Figure 24.2 together with the three estimated outcomes of the BATNA of I.

Figure 24.2 confirms that, even though it might create a significant value, the acquisition is a risky option for I. If the industry becomes difficult, only a very successful integration process can avoid a disaster. Even though they are difficult to assess, the probabilities attached to the different integration and industry scenarios are critical. As shown in Table 24.2, when you assign the same probability to each of the nine scenarios, you get an expected value of some 116 million which is about the same as the 118 million of the best guess scenario (best guess industry and best guess integration scenario). However, when you take a more pessimistic view, the expected value of the combined operations becomes equal to 57 million only. At the opposite, when you take a more optimistic view, the expected value of the combined operations almost doubles.

A model for assessing the zone of agreement: initial assessments of the situation

The model in Table 24.3 can help us assess the value of an agreement, the walk-aways of I and F and a 'fair' price (corresponding to an equal sharing of the value created) depending on:

- the values and probabilities of the outcomes of the three critical alternatives: integrated operations, BATNA of I and BATNA of F;
- the values and probabilities of the three industry scenarios. (The industry and integration outcomes are assumed to be independent.)

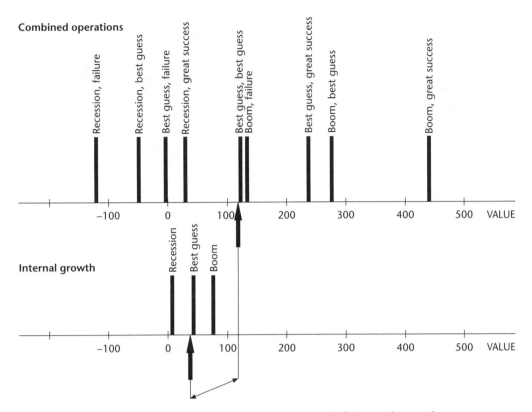

Figure 24.2 Outcomes of the integrated operations and of internal growth

Table 24.2 ● Value of the combined operations of I and F

	Equal weights	Pessimistic view	Optimistic view
Industry scenario			
Cutthroat recession	33%	40%	20%
Best guess	33%	40%	30%
Profitable boom	33%	20%	50%
Integration scenario			
Failure	33%	40%	20%
Best guess	33%	40%	30%
Great success	33%	20%	50%
Value (in £ million)	117	57	225

Table 24.3 ● A model to assess the integrative dynamics

A	B	C	D	E	F	G	H
1	Recession			Best guess			Boom
2 INTEGRATED OPERATIONS							
3 VERY DIFFICULT	−124			−4			129
4 Probability	0.33						
5 BEST GUESS	−48			118			280
6 Probability	0.33						
7 GREAT SUCCESS	31			241			438
8 Probability	0.33						
9 Expected value	−47			118			282
10							
11 BEST INTERNAL GROWTH (I'S BATNA)	8			47			84
12							
13 BEST EXIT STRATEGY (F'S BATNA)	−72			−41			−1
14							
15 Value created	17			112			199
16 Probability industry scenarios	0.33			0.33			0.33
17							
18 **Value created (expected)**	**110**			Walk-aways	F	−38	I 72
19 **Fair price (equal sharing of value)**	**17**			Value for	F	17	I 101
20				Additional value for	F	55	I 55

Formulas
B9: +B3*$B$4+B5*$B$6+B7*$B$8; copy into E9 and H9
B15: +B9−B11−B13; copy into E15 and H15
B18: +B15*B16+E15*E16+H15*H16
F18: +B13*B16+E13*E16+H13*H16
B19: +B18/2+F18
F19: +B19
H18: +(B9−B11)+B16+(E9−E11)*E16+(H9−H11)*H16
H19: +B9*B16+B9*E16+H9*H16−B19
F20: +F19−F18
H20: +(B9−B11−B19)*B16+(E9−E11−B19)*E16+(H9−H11−B19)*H16

When the probabilities of each integration and industry scenarios are set to 1/3, the model suggests that:

● A deal between I and F would create a substantial expected value: £110 million. The value is especially high when the market becomes better. A large portion of the value is created by the suppression of the losses of F.

● F should accept any price above −£38 million (i.e. F should be prepared to pay up to 38 million to I in order to get rid of its truck operations) and I should be willing to pay as much as 72 million: this creates a large zone of agreement and suggests a fair price of £17 million.

The model in Table 24.3 enables you to test the robustness of this initial assessment. Let us assume that a pessimistic view of the industry or of the integration would make I assign

Table 24.4 • Sensitivity analysis

	£ million		
	Value created	Zone of agreement	Fair price
I is pessimistic about the integration and			
pessimistic about the industry	32	−53 to −21	−37
optimistic about the industry	93	−24 to 68	22
I is optimistic about the integration and			
pessimistic about the industry	115	−53 to 62	5
optimistic about the industry	200	−24 to 176	76

a 50% probability to the worst outcome, a 40% probability to the middle outcome and a 10% probability to the best outcome. Let us further assume that an optimistic view of the same scenarios would make I assign a 10% probability to the worst outcome, a 40% probability to the middle outcome and a 50% probability to the best outcome. When you run the model with these assumptions you get the results shown in Table 24.4. The sensitivity of the value created by a deal has a series of implications:

- I has to assess the risks involved very carefully. What are these risks? How can they be reduced? Is it possible to design a deal that can accommodate the remaining risks?
- If they happen to have different views about the risks of the integration or of the industry, I and F will find it very difficult to make a deal.

Let us assume, for the time being, that I assigns a 1/3 probability to the different integration and industry scenarios and therefore aims at a 'fair' price of £17 million (see Table 24.3).

24.2 Trying to introduce the subjectivity of the other party

Reversing roles

If you were F, would you easily agree that £17 million is a fair price for your business?

When you realize that your working capital has a value of 20 million and that each point of market share is worth £10 million, i.e. that a 20% share is worth 200 million, you might consider that 17 million is a very low price! It seems obvious that F will find it difficult to understand that I believes that the costs and risks of transferring their operations are so high that they wipe out almost all the intrinsic value of these operations.

If you were F, how would you evaluate the combination of your operations with those of I?

F's assessment should present many similarities to I's. The valuation model of F should have the same general structure, similar key relationships and numbers (value of initial working capital, value of each percentage point of market share, size of the market in 1986, market shares of F and I in 1986, selling prices of F and I trucks in 1986, unit costs of F and

I trucks in 1986, operating costs of F and I in 1985 and possibly in 1986, etc.). When you consider it, it is not unreasonable to assume not only that I and F have similar valuation models but also that the numbers shown in the first year of their models are very close.

However, it is likely that F's models present some fundamental differences also as there is no reason for F to share I's views regarding the future of the UK market and the potential for integrating the operations.

- F has built a leading position in the UK; I has always been marginal in this market.
- F has access to the best network of dealers in the UK; I's dealers are of a relatively low quality.
- F has a very strong brand in the UK; I's brand is hardly known on this market.
- F has strong management capabilities in the UK; I has never devoted much management attention to this market.
- F has no experience of integrating the operations of another truck company; I has been built through a series of acquisitions and some of these acquisitions have not been easy to integrate.
- If it sells its operations to I, and gets paid in cash, F will be able to forget about the truck business; I will have to implement the merger.

What if F were more optimistic than we are?

Let us formulate an extreme, but not necessarily unrealistic, scenario. Let us assume that F, who never had a difficult integration experience and who has an intimate knowledge of the market, believes that:

- The integrated operations of I and F could result in a market share bigger than the sum of the individual shares of I and F. In order to simulate the impact of this synergy, you can run again the very successful integration scenario and set the market share of I in 1990 at 14% (using the model in Table 23.2).
- This new very successful scenario is the most likely: 60% chances against 35% for the middle scenario and 5% for the difficult scenario.
- The most likely industry scenario is the 'profitable boom': 60% chances against 35% for the middle scenario and 5% for the pessimistic one.
- Running their operations until 1990 is their best alternative to an agreement with I.

The model in Table 24.3 can help you simulate the consequences of this optimistic view of F. As shown in Table 24.5, F now requests a price higher than 25 million and aims at a 'fair' price of £129 million. If I sticks to the view corresponding to our initial assessment (see Table 24.3) and if F adopts the optimistic view, an agreement becomes much more difficult.

- F wants to get a price between 25 and 233 million, while I is willing to pay a price between −38 and 72 million.
- As a result there is a narrow zone of agreement: between 25 and 72 million. However, it might be difficult to find a price within that zone that would satisfy both I and F as any price in the zone might look a bit low for F and a bit high for I.

Table 24.5 ● What if F were to be more optimistic?

	Recession	Best guess	Boom
INTEGRATED OPERATIONS			
Very difficult	−124	−4	129
Probability	0.05		
Best guess	−48	118	280
Probability	0.35		
Great success	49	265	465
Probability	0.60		
Expected value	6	200	383
BEST INTERNAL GROWTH (I'S BATNA)	8	47	84
BEST EXIT STRATEGY (F'S BATNA)	−117	−36	72
Value created	115	189	227
Probability industry scenarios	0.05	0.35	0.6
Value created (expected)	208	Walk-aways F 25 I 233	
Fair price (equal sharing of value)	129	Value for F 129 I 171	
		Additional value for F 104 I 104	

	I's view	F's view
Integrated operations	118	300
Best internal growth	46	67
Best exit strategy	−38	25
Value created	110	208
I's walk-away	72	233
F's walk-away	−38	25
Fair price	17	129
Zone of agreement		
F's walk-away	25	
I's walk-away		72

The danger of negotiating over positions

A typical negotiation process is to have each party state its position, argue for it and engage in a 'dance' of concessions aimed at reaching a compromise somewhere in the middle of the initial positions.

Where could such a process lead I and F? Let us now assume that while F considers that the results of Table 24.5 give a fair assessment of the situation, I wants to be cautious and ends up espousing the most pessimistic view described in Table 24.4 (pessimistic view about the integration and the market). Let us further assume that I and F are so confident in their analyses that they decide to state their respective positions regarding a 'fair' price at the very beginning of the negotiation:

F: 'We estimate that you should pay 129 million to us'
I: 'We estimate that you should pay 37 million to us'

This could obviously upset both parties and jeopardize the whole negotiation even though both I and F are perfectly able to understand the rationale behind such distant positions.

In the present situation, *it is better for I and F to decide to defer the statement of any position regarding a 'fair' price*. The priority for I and F is to design a process that will enable them to work together at establishing the integrative dimension of the situation they are dealing with.

24.3 Designing a co-operative strategy for negotiation

The analysis suggests the following negotiating agenda:

● I should acquire a better understanding of F's perspective: how does F see the future of the market, its own future and the potential of a merger?
● I should try to close part of the potential gaps between its point of view and the point of view of F. If, as is likely, I is more concerned with risk than F, the two companies should define joint actions that they could undertake for helping reduce the risks for I.
● The two companies should design a solution to create value out of their remaining differences.
● Finally, I and F should find a solution for claiming a fair share of the value created by the negotiation.

As the priority is to create the value of a potential deal and not to share this value, I should adopt a co-operative approach. This requires the implementation of a specific strategy and of specific behavioural characteristics.

● Axelrod[1] has established that the negotiating strategy that works best in most cases is a very simple co-operative one: adopt a co-operative attitude from the very beginning and continue co-operating for as long as the other party reciprocates. In case the other party stops co-operating and 'attacks', retaliate immediately but be forgiving and turn again to co-operation straightaway after retaliation.
● Co-operation also requires specific behavioural attitudes aimed at building mutual trust: clear distinction between facts that can be agreed on and beliefs that can be accepted as being different, honesty in the presentation of facts and beliefs, openness to new information and differences in beliefs, joint problem solving, establishment of jointly accepted criteria and . . . patience. One thing I has to decide is how much information it is prepared to share with F; for example, is I willing to show its business plans (BATNA and integrated operations) to F?

When trying to simulate the discussions with F, I should realize that not all critical issues are to be dealt with in the same way.

● If they show mutual respect, the two parties should probably recognize that the other party knows best about its own situation. F should probably easily accept the value stated by I regarding its best internal growth scenario and I should probably do the same for the value of the best exit strategy stated by F. I should also probably realize that the discussion of the eventual liquidation of the operations of F is difficult as such a discussion can easily turn into an investigation of the weaknesses of F and destroy the co-operative climate.

- On the other hand, the evaluation of the combined operations is the real opportunity for I and F to recognize their shared interests, to go for a two-way exchange of information and to engage in joint problem-solving activities. One very important thing that the two companies should quickly realize is that they have a common interest: the success of the merger of the operations of I and F. This means that F should be willing to help I reduce the risks of the merger. Consequently, I should identify how F could help reduce the risk and think about what it could reasonably request from F in the negotiation: authorization to use the F brand name for a period of time, guarantee that the key managers will not leave, assistance in the negotiation with the dealers, and so on.

Finally, I should think about how to deal with the differences that will probably remain in the end. Because the uncertainties are very big, I should probably remain flexible and wait until more is known to decide about the best structure for a deal. The problem, however, for I is to be aware that the great uncertainty will probably make it look for either:

- a straight buy-out solution with a relatively low payment made to F at the date of signature (less than 50% of the value created paid to F and/or conservative assessment of the value created);
- or a merger of the operations of F and I that would keep F involved for a period of time and would defer the payment to F to a future date when the major uncertainties are resolved. F might actually be interested in such a solution. If it is very confident about the success of the merger, F could see such a deal as an opportunity to get a higher payment. F could also realize that such a solution could help it contribute to the success of the merger and make sure that no damaging conflicts surface with its dealers.

These two extreme solutions are consistent with different negotiation climates (distributive vs. co-operative). If as seems reasonable, I decides that the second type of solution is preferable, then the need for establishing a co-operative climate is even greater.

A final problem that I should consider is the chance that F is not willing to adopt a co-operative approach. Analysis says that F should adopt an integrative approach, but there is at least one indication in the case which suggests that F might have decided to adopt a calming approach: F is putting pressure on for a quick deal. This might mean that F believes that the value is easy to assess and that the only thing to do is to agree on how to share it, a pure distributive issue. If it has this view, F will probably show impatience with the efforts of I to establish a co-operative climate and will push for a price. F might even come very quickly with a price proposal. Such a proposal would help I understand F's perspective but could also create difficulties associated with position bargaining. Dealing with a difficult other party[2] might make I's task much more complicated but should not make I abandon its co-operative strategy.

Notes

1. R. Axelrod, *The Evolution of Co-operation*, Basic Books. New York, 1984.
2. For how to negotiate with difficult people, refer to *Getting Past No, Negotiating with difficult people*, W. Ury, Business Books, London, 1991.

F Trucks[1]
(Abridged version)

On 28 June 1985, Reginald Jones, the president of F in the United Kingdom was busy reviewing his files before leaving for Torino where he was going to meet the senior management of I on the following day. Reginald Jones was optimistic about the issue of the meeting which he had pressed I's management to organize before the summer break. Since a deal was very clearly beneficial to both parties, Reginald Jones was confident that it should be easy to agree quickly about a fair price.

F Trucks was part of the international automotive group F. Within the F group, the truck business had traditionally been centred on the UK market where it enjoyed a strong position. However, the market share of F Trucks had progressively declined under the pressure of competition. Since it discontinued its heavy truck product line in 1984, F was selling medium trucks only. One of the major strengths of F was its network of dealers which was probably the strongest car and truck dealers network in the UK. In 1985, F had 120 truck dealers, most of whom were car dealers also. Like most companies in the automotive sector, F had to face difficult labour relations in the 1970s, but these improved a lot in the early 1980s and the company launched a major change programme aimed at reaching world-class quality. The programme was successful and in 1985, F Trucks had been able to suppress quality inspectors, to reduce the number of its suppliers from 15 000 to 400 and to operate with three unions instead of nine in the early 1980s. F had also taken measures for reducing its capacity and lowering its break-even point. In particular, F had decided to abandon the manufacturing of its own axles.

The divestment plan

In November 1984, the Board of F made the decision not to develop a new generation of trucks as the investment required would not be profitable due to the insufficient size of F's operations. Following this decision, F started preparing a divestment plan. The obvious option for F was to try to sell their operations to one of their competitors. Among those, I appeared to be the one which would benefit most from the acquisition of F Trucks. F approached I at the end of 1984 and as expected by F, I expressed interest in exploring the issue further. During the first meeting that took place between the representatives of the two companies in January 1985, I tried to show that:

Table V.1 ● Evaluation of an exit strategy at F

	1986	1987	1988	1989	1990	1991	Cum.
Growth	5.0%	5.0%	5.0%	3.0%	3.0%		
Total market	84 000	88 200	92 610	95 388	98 250		
Share F	19.0%	19.0%	18.0%	17.0%	15.0%		
Unit price F	12 000	12 000	12 000	12 000	10 000		
SALES	192	201	200	195	147		
Unit cost F	10 233	10 084	10 099	10 183	10 493		
CGS	163	169	168	165	155		
CGS/sales	85%	84%	84%	85%	105%		
Operating expenses	25	20	15	15	10		
Operating expenses/sales	13%	10%	7%	8%	7%		
Profit before tax	3	12	17	14	−17		
Profit after tax	2	8	11	9	−11		19
Working capital open	0	19	20	20	19	15	
Working capital/sales	10%	10%	10%	10%	10%		
Working capital end	19	20	20	19	15		
CFO 1986–90	−17	7	11	10	−6	15	19
Discount rate	0.10						
NPV 1986–90 cash flow	**9**						
Working capital open	**20**						
Reorganization cost					20		
NPV reorganization	**12**						
Total value (£ million)	**17**						

Notes
This scenario corresponds to the best guess industry scenario.
With the 'profitable boom' scenario, the value is £151 million.
With the 'cutthroat recession' scenario, the value is −£84 million.
The expected value is (−84+17+151)/3=28 million.

- F was in a weak position;
- the benefits that I world derive from the acquisition were not that great.

It was not the first time that Reginald Jones had been involved in such negotiations and he was convinced that the young I team who took part in the first meeting had been playing tough to prepare for a quick agreement in their favour. As far as F's position was concerned, Reginald Jones did not believe it was that weak. Even though I was the only possible buyer, F could very well implement a plan for closure, and as shown in Table V.1, achieve reasonable results. As it did not include some opportunities to export to South Africa and Turkey (about 1500 vehicles), this plan could be considered as conservative.

The potential benefits for I

Reginald Jones was convinced that the acquisition of F was a great opportunity for I: the estimate of the value of the combined operations of F and I that had been prepared by F is in Table V.2.

Table V.2 ● Estimate of the value of a merger between F and I

	1986	1987	1988	1989	1990	1991	Cum.
Growth	5.0%	5.0%	5.0%	3.0%	3.0%		
Total market	84 000	88 200	92 610	95 388	98 250		
Share I	4.0%	4.0%	5.0%	6.0%	12.0%		
Share F	19.0%	19.0%	19.0%	18.0%	11.0%		
Unit price I	18 000	18 000	18 000	18 000	18 000		
Unit price F	12 000	12 000	12 000	12 000	12 000		
Sales	252	265	294	309	342		
Unit cost I	12 780	12 780	12 780	12 780	12 780		
Unit cost F	10 233	10 084	9 942	10 012	11 726		
CGS	206	214	234	245	277		
CGS/sales	82%	81%	79%	79%	81%		
Operating expenses	45	43	43	43	43		
Operating expenses/sales	18%	16%	15%	14%	13%		
Profit before tax	1	8	17	21	22		
Profit after tax	0	5	11	14	14		44
Working capital open	0	25	26	29	31	34	
Working capital/sales	10%	10%	10%	10%	10%		
Working capital end	25	26	29	31	34		
CFO 1986–90	–25	4	8	12	11	34	44
Discount rate	0.10						
NPV 1986–90 cash flow	21						
Working capital open	24						
Reorganization cost					30		
NPV reorganization	19						
Market share in 1991	0.23						
Adjustment continuing value	0.0%						
Value cash flows beyond 1990	230						
Total value (£ million)	256						

Through acquiring F, I would be able to get access to a 20% market share without having to put any pressure on the prices. Obviously, a critical success factor was that I would be able to retain F's dealers and customers, but according to Reginald Jones, this should not present any major difficulty.

The continuation of F's current products until 1990–1 should allow for a smooth transition and Reginald Jones was convinced that the dealers would welcome the business of I which, contrary to F, was offering a full range of products. As they were generally selling both trucks and cars, dealers were very important to F and Reginald Jones was prepared to make all the efforts needed to ensure a smooth transition and to avoid any of the dealers going to the competition. There was obviously a risk related to the integration of the two operations but since I, contrary to F, was strongly committed to the truck business, management and employees should welcome their new owner. Finally, the manufacturing facilities of F were among the most modern in Europe and could easily be converted to assemble the new products of I in the 1990s. In any case, acquiring F trucks was a much

Table V.3 ● Estimate of the value that can be achieved through internal growth by I

	1986	1987	1988	1989	1990	1991	Cum.
Growth	5.0%	5.0%	5.0%	3.0%	3.0%		
Total market	84 000	88 200	92 610	95 388	98 250		
Market share	3.0%	5.0%	7.0%	9.0%	10.0%		
Unit selling price	14 400	13 680	13 680	13 680	14 000		
Sales	36	60	89	117	138		
Unit cost	12 780	12 780	12 780	12 780	12 780		
CGS	32	56	83	110	126		
CGS/sales	89%	93%	93%	93%	91%		
Operating expenses	10	15	20	22	22		
Operating expenses/sales	28%	25%	23%	19%	16%		
Profit before tax	−6	−11	−14	−14	−10		
Profit after tax	−6	−11	−14	−14	−10		−55
Working capital open	0	4	6	9	12	14	
Working capital/sales	10%	10%	10%	10%	10%		
Working capital end	4	6	9	12	14		
CFO 1986–90	−10	−13	−17	−17	−12	14	−55
Discount rate	0.10						
NPV 1986–90 cash flow	**−44**						
Working capital open	**4**						
Market share in 1991	0.1						
Value cash flows beyond 1990	**100**						
Total value (£ million)	**60**						

better solution for I than relying on internal growth (an assessment of what I could achieve without acquiring F is in Table V.3).

Reginald Jones's intuition was that in such a situation, where a deal was clearly beneficial to both parties, the best approach was to try to strike the deal quickly. This is why he pressed for a meeting to take place before the summer break.

Note

1. This case is an abridged version of the F Trucks case which was developed by the author and Damir Borisic, Professor at ISVOR-FIAT (Italy). The F Trucks case can be obtained from the author on www.michel-schlosser.com.

CASE *W*

The negotiation between
I and F[1]

On 15 October 1985, Mr Corsi was very happy. I and F had agreed to form a 50–50 joint venture to run the merged operations of F Trucks and of I in the UK and were going to meet at the end of the month to finalize the agreement. It had been already agreed that the joint venture would be managed by I.

The joint venture proposal was made by Mr Corsi when opening the meeting held on 29 June. The discussions that took place during the meeting and several subsequent meetings during the autumn, allowed the two parties to:

- agree to form a 50–50 joint venture;
- exchange a lot of information. I and F exchanged their strategic plans agreed about their respective positions in case they failed to reach and agreement.
  - The value of the best internal growth strategy for I was estimated at £47 million according to I's strategic plan.
  - The value of the best exit strategy for F was estimated at £28 million according to F's strategic plan.
- recognize their common interest in reducing the risk of the future merged operations. F agreed that the joint venture would be allowed to use the F brand name for a period of three to five years; F agreed to play an active role in the negotiation of the new contracts with the dealers and confirmed that the key managers of its truck operations were enthusiastic about the opportunity to work for I.
- agree on the sharing of the results of the joint venture: at the end of each year, any profit would be distributed to the two partners, any loss would be covered by a new equity issue subscribed equally by the two partners.

However, the two parties had not been able to agree on the value of the expected outcome of the operations of the joint venture. The solutions found with F to limit the risks of the merger had made Mr Corsi disregard the failure scenario that he had envisaged initially but as shown in Tables W.1 and W.2, I was still more pessimistic than F about the future of the joint venture. As the two parties were not willing to change their views, it was decided to keep two scenarios for planning the future of the joint venture. Rather than 'I' and 'F', these two scenarios were called 'pessimistic' and 'optimistic'.

Table W.1 • The 'optimistic' scenario for the joint venture

	1986	1987	1988	1989	1990	1991	Cum.
Growth	5.0%	5.0%	5.0%	3.0%	3.0%		
Total market	84 000	88 200	92 610	95 388	98 250		
Share I	4.0%	4.0%	5.0%	6.0%	12.0%		
Share F	19.0%	19.0%	19.0%	18.0%	11.0%		
Competitive price change	0						
Unit price I	18 000	18 000	18 000	18 000	18 000		
Unit price F	12 000	12 000	12 000	12 000	12 000		
Sales	252	265	294	309	342		
Unit cost I	12 780	12 780	12 780	12 780	12 780		
Unit cost F	10 233	10 084	9 942	10 012	11 726		
CGS	206	214	234	245	277		
CGS/sales	82%	81%	79%	79%	81%		
Operating expenses	45	43	43	43	43		
Operating expenses/sales	18%	16%	15%	14%	13%		
Profit before tax	1	8	17	21	22		
Profit after tax	0	5	11	14	14		44
Working capital open	0	25	26	29	31	34	
Working capital/sales	10%	10%	10%	10%	10%		
Working capital end	25	26	29	31	34		
CFO 1986–90	−25	4	8	12	11	34	44
Discount rate	0.10						
NPV 1986–90 cash flows	21						
Working capital open	24						
Reorganization cost					30		
NPV reorganization	19						
Tax shield					0		
NPV tax shield	0						
Market share in 1990	0.23						
Market share in 1991	0.23						
Adjustment continuing value	0.0%						
Value cash flows beyond 1990	230						
Total value (£ million)	256						

The above assessment of the optimistic integration scenario corresponded to the 'best guess' market scenario. When run within different market scenarios, the optimistic integration scenario was giving the following values:

- 'profitable boom' £454 million
- 'cutthroat recession' £47 million

The average value of this optimistic integration scenario was equal to (47+256+454)/3 i.e. £252 million. This scenario is the same as the integration scenario prepared by F (see Table W.2).

CASE

Table W.2 ● The 'pessimistic' scenario (same as I's best-guess integration)

	1986	1987	1988	1989	1990	1991	Cum.
Growth	5.0%	5.0%	5.0%	3.0%	3.0%		
Total market	84 000	88 200	92 610	95 388	98 250		
Share I	3.5%	4.0%	4.5%	5.0%	5.5%		
Share F	18.0%	16.0%	14.0%	12.0%	10.0%		
Competitive price change	0						
Unit price I	18 000	18 000	18 000	18 000	18 000		
Unit price F	12 000	12 000	12 000	12 000	12 000		
Sales	234	233	231	223	215		
Unit cost I	12 780	12 780	12 780	12 780	12 780		
Unit cost F	10 407	10 643	10 956	11 468	12 189		
CGS	195	195	195	192	189		
CGS/sales	83%	84%	85%	86%	88%		
Operating expenses	54	46	46	44	40		
Operating expenses/sales	23%	20%	20%	20%	19%		
Profit before tax	−15	−8	−11	−13	−14		
Profit after tax	−15	−8	−11	−13	−14		−60
Working capital open	0	23	23	23	22	22	
Working capital/sales	10%	10%	10%	10%	10%		
Working capital end	23	23	23	22	22		
CFO 1986–90	−38	−8	−10	−12	−13	22	−60
Discount rate	0.10						
NPV 1986–90 cash flows	**−53**						
Working capital open	**24**						
Reorganization cost					30		
NPV reorganization	**19**						
Tax shield					21		
NPV tax shield	**11**						
Market share in 1990	0.155						
Market share in 1991	0.155						
Adjustment continuing value	0.0%						
Value cash flows beyond 1990	**155**						
Total value (£ million)	**118**						

The above assessment of the pessimistic integration scenario corresponded to the 'best guess' market scenario. When run within different market scenarios, the pessimistic integration scenario was giving the following values:

● 'profitable boom' £280 million
● 'cutthroat recession' −£48 million

The average value of this pessimistic integration scenario was equal to (−48+118+280)/3, i.e. £117 million.

Note

1. This case has been prepared from a real business situation by Damir Borsic, ISVOR FIAT (Italy) and the author.

CHAPTER 25

Creating value out of shared interests and differences: the rationale for a joint venture[1]

The essence of a joint venture is to entwine agreement and disagreement. A joint venture has the same fabric as the negotiation that led to its establishment. With the joint venture, the co-operative relationship between I and F will continue and develop within a new frame.

25.1 The positions on 29 June 1985

With the I and F cases, we are in the unusual situation of knowing what the two parties to a negotiation were thinking when they started to discuss. Table 25.1 shows the initial positions of I and F as they can be assessed with the help of the model in Table 24.3. I and F had a narrow zone of agreement and the design of a distributive agreement was very difficult.

25.2 The joint venture enables I and F to implement a series of agreements for creating common value

Even though they had reached different positions regarding a 'fair' price, I and F were agreeing on many critical factors when they met on 29 June 1985. The negotiation process enabled them to discover that:

- They had the same basic understanding of the situation. This shows in the scenarios developed by the two companies. I and F were sharing similar views about the market, they were considering the same alternatives, and they were making almost the same assumptions for future revenues and costs.

Table 25.1 ● Positions before the June negotiation

	I's View	F's View
Integrated operations	118	252
Best internal growth	46	59
Best exit strategy	−38	28
Value created	110	166
I's walk-away	72	194
F's walk-away	−38	28
Fair price	17	111
Zone of agreement		
F's walk-away	28	
I's walk-away		72

Note
It is assumed that F considers the same three industry scenarios as I (equal probabilities). For F, there is only one integration scenario.

● Both companies were recognizing the risks involved in an acquisition as well as the common interest they had in limiting these risks. This led them to organize a process for an effective transfer of know-how from F to I. As they have decided to stay, the key managers of F will make I benefit from their unique knowledge of the market, the use of the F brand name will help I build its position in the UK, F will make I benefit from its successful experience in managing a network of dealers in the UK.

The joint venture institutionalizes the agreement reached by I and F for limiting the risks of the merger, it provides them with the time they need to implement a successful transfer of know-how. Finally it creates for both of them, and for F in particular, a strong incentive to succeed.

25.3 The joint venture also enables I and F to disagree and to create value out of this disagreement

In spite of the agreements that they managed to establish during the negotiation, I and F were still in disagreement regarding the risks involved.

Table 25.2 shows the impact of the joint actions decided by I and F to reduce the risks of a merger: as a result of these actions I values the integrated operations at £172 million (i.e. 44% more than its initial estimate). These joint actions have reduced the gap between the points of views of I and F. The paradox, however, is that the value of an agreement, as seen by I, has decreased; this is due to the fact that I has revised its assessment of the BATNA of F which contributes now much less to the value of an agreement.

At this stage of the negotiation, I and F were in a much better position to agree on a fair price. A first approach for reaching an agreement would have been to continue discussing the risks involved with the hope that the two companies would manage to resolve their remaining differences, that is that at least one of the parties would change its mind. A

Table 25.2 ● Positions after the June negotiation

	I's View	F's View
Integrated operations	171	238
Best internal growth	46	46
Best exit strategy	28	28
Value created	97	164
I's walk-away	125	192
F's walk-away	28	28
Fair price	76	110
Zone of agreement		
F's walk-away	28	
I's walk-away		125

possible solution could have been that F finally agrees with I that a merger is always a risky venture and accepts a price of £76 million, a price significantly higher than its walk-away.

A second and more creative approach was to design the deal in such a way that neither F nor I had to change its mind. As nobody can claim to know what the future will be, *why not agree to disagree about the future* and find a way to create a deal that can leave each party free to believe what it wants regarding the future? The key to the creation of such a deal was to take advantage of time. A few years after I and F decide to merge their operations, that is in 1990–1, there will no longer be any uncertainty about the success of the deal. Both I and F will know perfectly the situation of the integrated company: market share, dealers network, internal climate, selling prices, costs, profits, and so on. Consequently, there will no longer be any major difficulty for I and F to agree on a fair price.

- If the acquisition has enabled I to capture 23% of the UK market and to derive a large profit from this position, I will have no objection to paying a high price to F.
- If at the other extreme, the UK market has collapsed, a severe price war has occurred and if these adverse events have made the combined operations of F and I, and the rest of the industry, generate losses, F will easily agree that its operations have a very low value.

I and F decided to take advantage of time and of their disagreement regarding risk. They agreed to form a joint venture and to get through its future dividends whatever these future dividends might be. This is a very effective approach for creating value and belongs again to the option framework.

25.4 The value of the joint venture agreement[2]

A model to assess the value of the joint venture

You can compare the value of the joint venture with the value of the following two alternative situations: no deal, and a 76 million fixed price deal (the case in which F would

Table 25.3 ● A model to evaluate the joint venture

	A	B	C	D	E	F	G	H	I	J
1	Industry scenarios	R	BG	B						
2	Probabilities	0.33	0.33	0.33						
3	**Point of view of I**						Point of view of F			
4	Integrated operations									
5	Success	47	256	454			47	256	454	
6	Probability of success	0.4					0.9			
7	Difficulties	−48	118	280			−48	118	280	
8		−10	173	350	171		38	242	437	239
9	BATNA I	8	47	84	46		8	47	84	46
10	BATNA F	−84	17	151	28		−84	17	151	28
11	Value created	66	109	115			114	178	202	
12	Expected value	97					164			
13	Fair price	76					110			
14	**No deal** Value for I	46			Value for F		28	Total		74
15	Fixed price deal	Price	76.3							
16	Value, success	−29	180	378			76	76	76	
17	Value, difficulties	−86	97	273			76	76	76	
18										
19	Additional value, success	−37	133	294			160	59	−75	
20	Additional value, difficulties	−132	−5	120			160	59	−75	
21	**Fixed price** Value for I	48			Value for F		48	Total		97
22	% of I in the joint venture	0.5								
23	Value, success	24	128	227			24	128	227	
24	Value, difficulties	−24	59	140			−24	59	140	
25	Expected net dividends	Paid by I			85		Received by F			119
26	Additional value, success	16	81	143			108	111	76	
27	Additional value, difficulties	−32	12	56			60	42	−11	
28	**Joint venture** Value for I	39			Value for F		91	Total		122

B8: +B5*$B$6+B7*(1–$B$6). Copy to C8.D8

G8: +G5*$G$6+G7*(1–$G$6). Copy to H8.I8

E8: +B8*$B$2+C8*$C$2+D8*$D$2. Copy to E9,E10,J8,J9 and J10

B11: +B8–B9–B10. Copy to C11,D11,G11, H11 and I11

B12: +B11*$B$2+C11*$C$2+D11*$D$2. Copy to G12

B13: +E10+B12/2. Copy to G13

B14: +E9

G14: +E10

J14: +G14+B14

B16: +B5–$C$15. Copy to C16.D16

G16: +$C$15. Copy to H16,I16 and G17.I17

B17: +B8–$C$15. Copy to C17.D17

B19: +B5–B9–$C$15. Copy to C19.G19

G19: +$C$15–G10. Copy to H19.I19

B20: +B7–B9–$C$15. Copy to C20.D20

G20: +G19. Copy to H20.I20

B21: +B6*(B19*$B$2+C19*$C$2+D19*$D$2)
    +(1–B6)*(B20*$B$2+C20*$C$2
    +D20*$D$2). Copy to G21

J21: +B21+G21

B23: +B5–B5*(1–$B$22). Copy

G23: +G5*(1–$B$22). Copy

B24: +B7–(1–$B$22)*B7. Copy

G24: +G7*(1–$B$22). Copy

E25: +B6*(B5–B23)*$B$2+(C5–C23)*$C$2
    +(D5–D23)*$D$2)+(1–B6)*((B7–
    B24)*$B$2+(C7–C24)*$C$2+(D7–
    D24)*$D$2)–H22

J25: +G6*(G23*$B$2+H23*$C$2
    +I23*$D$2)+(1–G6)*(G24*$B$2
    +H24*$C$2+I24*$D$2)–H22

B26: +B5–B9–(1–$B$22)*B5. Copy

G26: +G23–G10. Copy

B27: +B7–B9–(1–$B$22)*B7. Copy

G27: +G24–G10. Copy

B28: +B6*(B26*$B$2+C26*$C$2
    +D26*$D$2)+(1–B6)*(B27*$B$2
    +C27*$C$2+D27*$D$2)+H22

G28: +G6*(G26*$B$2+H26*$C$2
    +I26*$D$2)+(1–G6)*(G27*$B$2
    +H27*$C$2+I27*$D$2)–H22

J28: +B28+G28

finally accept I's view regarding the risk of the merger). A model for establishing this comparison is shown in Table 25.3.

● In the no agreement situation, the values for I and F are equal to their BATNAs and the total value for I and F is equal to the sum of their BATNAs.
● In the fixed price deal situation, I gets the difference between the outcome of the integrated operations and the price paid to F. To estimate the additional value created by the deal for I you have to further deduct the outcome of the best internal growth strategy of I.

F gets the fixed price whatever the final outcome of the merger is. The additional value of the deal for F is equal to the difference between the price and what F would have obtained with its best exit strategy.
● In the joint venture situation, I gets the difference between the outcome of the integrated operations and the dividend paid to F (or the new equity contributed by F). To estimate the additional value created by the deal for I, you have to further deduct the outcome of its best internal growth strategy. In this situation, F receives a dividend or contributes new equity depending on the outcome of the integrated operations. The additional value created by the deal for F is obtained by further deducting the outcome of the best exit strategy.

The joint venture reduces risk

With a £76 million price paid in 1985, the merger creates an additional expected value of 48 million for I, but this is a very risky solution as the additional value may range between a loss of 132 million and a profit of £294 million.

Table 25.3 shows that the expected value of the joint venture agreement is equal to 39 million. This value is 17% lower than the value of the fixed price deal but is less risky as it only varies between −32 and 143 million. If the joint venture agreement creates value through a reduction of the risk for I, it is worth noting that this reduction of risk is not achieved at the expense of a reduction of the expected value. The 17% difference with the fixed price solution is only due to the fact that the dividend paid to F is based on the value of the joint venture and not, as it should be, on this value adjusted for the difference between the two BATNAs of I and F. To avoid the bias introduced by the basis for calculating the dividend, I and F could either agree on slightly different shares in the joint venture (you can check that 55–45 would do), or on a compensating payment made by F to I at the date of signature. In order to introduce such a payment in the model, you can:

1. Enter in H22 the amount of this payment: set it to half of the differences between the two BATNAs (9 million).
2. Correct the joint venture values: +H22 for I and −H22 for F (already done in Table 25.3).

When you do so, you will check that the value for I of a 50–50 joint venture is equal to £48 million: the 50–50 joint venture creates the same value as the fixed price deal but is much less risky. With the compensating payment, the additional value for F is equal to £82 million.

As with most conditional agreements, the joint venture is valued differently by I and F

Another interesting result of Table 25.3 is that:

● I believes that it will pay a net amount of £76 million to F (85 million dividend minus the 9 million initial payment) and values the agreement at 48 million. I has obtained exactly what it wanted and has obtained it at a lower risk than it was willing to take.

● F believes that it will get a net amount of £110 million from the joint venture with I (119 million dividend minus the 9 million initial payment). F has obtained exactly what it wanted, i.e. £82 million more than its 28 million BATNA.

This is a great advantage of the joint venture solution. It enables I and F to keep believing that they will get the amounts they wanted to reach. As the amounts they will ultimately obtain will not be known until a much later date, why quarrel about them? I and F know that they are going to get half of the future results but they have been wise enough not to try to force an agreement on what each of them mean by 'half of the future results'. They have agreed on a process for sharing the results and since nobody can predict the future, they fully accept that the other party may genuinely have its own opinion about the future – a very personal matter which should not prevent serious people from doing business together. This recognition of and respect for individual differences is materialized by the decision to have two business plans for the joint venture: an optimistic plan (F's preferred scenario) and a pessimistic one (I's preferred scenario).

A potential problem with contingent agreements is their sustainability: how will I and F react when the final outcomes are known? The real issue is to make sure that both I and F have exchanged all the information which was available to them and will continue doing so. If this is the case neither I or F should have any problem accepting that the future might be full of surprises!

The joint venture is a genuine 'win-win' agreement

A final result of Table 25.3 is the sum of the values for I and F or total value of the different situations:

● The no-deal situation corresponds to a total value of £74 million.

● The 76 million fixed price deal corresponds to a 97 million total value, 31% more than the no-deal situation.

● The joint venture solution corresponds to a 131 million total value, 35% more than the fixed price deal and 77% more than the no-deal situation. With the joint venture solution, both I and F get a better deal than with the fixed price solution.

25.5 The superiority of joint venture over profit sharing and other types of conditional agreements

As an alternative to their joint venture agreement, I and F could have crafted a profit sharing agreement: F could have brought its operations to I which would have then paid a share of the profit of the merged operations to F. Even though it is very close to a joint venture agreement, such a profit sharing agreement is not as effective for I if the losses are not shared also. This is shown in the model in Table 25.4 which is an extension of that in Table 25.3.

Table 25.4 • A model to evaluate alternative deals

	A	B	C	D	E	F	G	H	I	J
1	Industry scenarios	R	BG	B						
2	Probabilities	0.33	0.33	0.33						
3	**Point of view of I**						Point of view of F			
4	Integrated operations									
5	Success	47	256	454			47	256	454	
6	Probability of success	0.4					0.9			
7	Difficulties	−48	118	280			−48	118	280	
8		−10	173	350	171		38	242	437	239
9	BATNA I	8	47	84	46		8	47	84	46
10	BATNA F	−84	17	151	28		−84	17	151	28
11	Value created	66	109	115			114	178	202	
12	Expected value	97					164			
13	Fair price	76					110			
14	**No deal** Value for I	46			Value for F		28	Total		74
15	Fixed price deal	Price	76.3							
16	Value, success	−29	180	378			76	76	76	
17	Value, difficulties	−86	97	273			76	76	76	
18										
19	Additional value, success	−37	133	294			160	59	−75	
20	Additional value, difficulties	−132	−5	120			160	59	−75	
21	**Fixed price** Value for I	48			Value for F		48	Total		97
22	% of I in the joint venture	0.5			Initial payment		9			
23	Value, success	24	128	227			24	128	227	
24	Value, difficulties	−24	59	140			−24	59	140	
25	Expected net dividends	Paid by I		85			Received by F			119
26	Additional value, success	16	81	143			108	111	76	
27	Additional value, difficulties	−32	12	56			60	42	−11	
28	**Joint venture** Value for I	48			Value for F		82	Total		122
29	% Profit for I	0.5								
30	Value, success	24	128	227			24	128	227	
31	Value, difficulties	−48	59	140			0	59	140	
32										
33	Additional value, success	16	81	143			108	111	76	
34	Additional value, difficulties	−56	12	56			84	42	−11	
35	**Profit sharing value for I**	34			Value for F		92	Total		127

B30: +B5–IF(B5>0,(1–$B$29)*B5,0). Copy
G30: =IF(G5>0,(1–$B$29)*G5,0). Copy
B31: +B7–IF(B7>0,(1–$B$29)*B7,0). Copy
G31: =IF(G7>0,(1–$B$29)*G7,0). Copy
B33: +B30–B9. Copy
G33: +G30–G10. Copy
B34: +B31–B9. Copy
G34: +G31–G10. Copy
B35: +$B$6*(B33*$B$2+C33*$C$2+D33*$D$2)+(1–$B$6)*(B34*$B$2+C34*$C$2
     +D34*$D$2)+H29
G35: +$G$6*(G33*$B$2+H33*$C$2+I33*$D$2)+(1–$G$6)*(G34*$B$2+H34*$C$2
     +I34*$D$2)–H29
J35: +G35+B35

Other types of conditional agreements could also have been designed by I and F:

- in 1985, F brings its operations to I;
- at a later date, 1990 for example, I pays to F a price linked to some critical performance indicator (for example, the market share of the combined operations in 1990).

How does such a conditional sale agreement compare with a joint venture solution? If it aims at the same risk sharing goal as a joint venture, a conditional sale agreement has a number of drawbacks.

- A first difficulty is to specify the critical performance indicator(s). In addition to being 'objective' and easily measurable, critical performance indicator(s) should be relevant also. In the I–F negotiation, the 1990 market share is definitely critical to the overall performance of the integrated operations but other parameters can greatly influence the overall performance, for example, levels of selling price and cost of goods sold, operating expenses, and other factors that we are not even able to imagine now! On the other hand the joint venture solution naturally organizes the sharing of the overall results without requiring that the two parties specify how these results will be generated.
- A further difficulty is to find and agree on a performance indicator that enables the two parties to share both profits and losses. A major advantage of joint venture solutions is that their very nature implies the sharing of both profits and losses.
- A final difficulty with conditional sales is that the seller is generally no longer part of the operations which are under the sole control of the buyer. This asymmetry is not consistent with the idea of risk sharing and in case things turn sour, here is a great danger that the seller believes that the bad results were caused by the poor management of the buyer (even though the latter has no real motivation to mismanage the operations). Again this danger is probably less in the case of a joint venture.

25.6 Some implementation problems

The need to enable F to withdraw from the joint venture

Even though it looks like a very good solution, the joint venture does not enable F to achieve one of its key objectives, that is to divest its truck operations. A solution for this is to decide, in 1985, when and how F could withdraw from the joint venture.

The very rationale of the joint venture implies that F stays for a sufficiently long period of time, that is, until the major risks are resolved. In both scenarios the major risks should be resolved fairly early, in 1987 or 1988, even though one might argue that a very important risk will only be resolved when the market adopts or not I's new generation of products. This will not be known until 1992 or 1993. However, F might not be willing to share this latter risk as the success of the new products of I is very much out of the control of F.

If F leaves the joint venture, there will be a need to value its equity in the joint venture. An approach for assessing the equity price is to estimate the present value of the future dividends that F would have received had it stayed in the joint venture. The problem is that F and I might disagree on the forecast of these future dividends which might bring them back to the problem they managed to avoid with the joint venture solution. As this could be a difficult problem, you cannot believe that F will enter a joint venture if the rules

Table 25.5 ● Optimistic vs. pessimistic scenarios

F – or optimistic – scenario (Table W.1)

		1986	1987	1988	1989	1990
Value claimed by F	128					
Profit after tax		0	5	11	14	14
Dividends/new equity		0	3	6	7	7
Value achieved during 1986–90	15					
Value still to be claimed	113					
in 1990 value	181					
Price to 1990 earnings ratio	26					
Price to 1990 sales ratio	1.06					

I – or pessimistic – scenario (Table W.2)

		1986	1987	1988	1989	1990
Value claimed by F	59					
Profit after tax		–15	–8	–11	–13	–14
Dividends/new equity		–8	–4	–6	–7	–7
Value achieved during 1986–90	–23					
Value still to be claimed	82					
in 1990 value	132					
Price to 1990 earnings ratio	Negative					
Price to 1990 sales ratio	1.23					

for evaluating its equity are not fixed in the joint venture agreement. Table 25.5 shows the nature of the problem.

● If the optimistic scenario materializes, F will get 15 million (1985 value) of dividends during the period 1986–90 and will therefore still have 111 million to claim if it leaves in 1990.

● If the pessimistic scenario materializes, then F will have invested 23 million (1985 value) and will therefore still have 82 million to claim if it leaves in 1990.

It is worth noting that the values to be claimed in 1990 have a lower dispersion (82–113) than the values claimed in 1985 (59–128). As the dispersion reflects the difference between the points of view of I and F, this means that I and F differ more on the short than on the long term. Both consider that in the long run the joint venture will succeed; they differ on the assessment of the costs and risks of the transition.

Among the possible solutions that can be specified in the joint venture agreement to value the equity of F are:

● A price based on the results achieved. Even though this seems to be the most adequate solution, this is not easy to implement: a multiple of profit will not work if the pessimistic scenario materializes. A multiple of sales could eventually be used but the relationship between value and sales is not a very good one.

● A fixed price; even though I and F have different opinions about the future, Table 25.5 shows that I and F differ more on the short than on the long term. Consequently, an agreement on a fixed price might not be impossible to reach, especially if F is not allowed to leave the joint venture too soon. (Extending the model in Table 25.5 to a few more years would probably reduce the dispersion of the values to be claimed by F.)

The joint venture agreement also has to specify the conditions in which F will be able to get out of the joint venture. Many solutions are possible. The agreement may specify that F will leave at a given date, it may give F an option to leave at that date (or starting from that date), it may give F an option to leave and I an option to force F to leave, and so on.

The need to protect the interests of I and F

Even though I and F will have an equal share in the joint venture, their interests are fundamentally different. I has a long-term commitment to the truck market while F has decided to leave this market. This asymmetry in interests explains why the management of the joint venture has been entrusted to I. Even though it might give F the option to reconsider its decision to leave the market, the joint venture solution also exposes F to the consequences of decisions made by I in its own interest. In 1989–91, I will focus on the launch of its new generation of products and might be willing to engage in heavy investments. As these investments will pay only in the long run F might find that 1989–91 is not a good time for leaving the joint venture. F might therefore either:

● impose a right to veto the decisions made by I, and in particular the investment decisions of I. Such a veto would not necessarily be a useful protection for F as it could just cause conflict; or
● choose an earlier or later date for leaving the venture (mandatory or optional exit).

25.7 How to assess the quality of the deal

Even though it has enabled I and F to reach a deal, the joint venture solution is not exempt from problems as conflicts between the two partners may easily surface in the future. Assessing the value of the deal from I's point of view is a difficult matter: is I getting a good deal? Is I getting a better deal than F? Is I getting the best deal it could get? and so on. In *The Evolution of Co-operation*, R. Axelrod suggests that the relevant standard for evaluating a deal is to ask yourself 'how you are doing relative to how well someone else could be doing in your shoes'.[2] As there were plenty of opportunities for I and F to fail to agree and as I and F have managed to create a significant value out of their agreement, you should probably conclude that both I and F have done very well.

Notes

1. There exists a considerable literature on the creation and management of strategic alliances and joint ventures and especially in the area of international management. Among many useful references: K. Harrigan (1986), *Managing for Joint Venture Success*, Lexington Books; J. Carter, R. Cushman and C.S. Hartz (eds) (1988), *The Handbook of Joint Venturing*, Dow Jones Irwin; J. Lewis (1990), *Partnerships for Profit*, The Free Press (this book contains useful information on the Iveco–Ford deal); and F. Contractor and P. Lorange (1988), *Cooperative Strategies in International Business*, Lexington Books.
2. On the choice between a full takeover and the creation of a joint venture: J.-F. Hennart (1991), 'The Transaction Costs Theory of Joint Ventures: An empirical study of Japanese subsidiaries in the United States', *Management Science* (April), pp. 483–97. On joint ventures and strategic alliances as a learning process, refer to: J. Badaracco Jr (1991), *The Knowledge Link: How Firms Compete through Strategic Alliances*, Harvard Business School Press.

Appendix to Part VI

Dealing differently with different types
of divestment situations

RFa[1]

On 15 June 1993, Georges Paris, the president of RFa was sitting on flight AF 289 to Munich. He was going to meet with Johan Ericsson, the president of Atlas Robotics, in order to finalise the sale of RFa's robotics and body-in-white businesses to Atlas Robotics. RFa and Atlas Robotics are described in Figures X.1 and X.2. While the plane was landing, Georges Paris was remembering the long process that finally made both companies realize that they 'had to' make a deal together.

The first round of negotiation

In 1992, Georges Paris approached several companies with a view to exploring their interest in acquiring RFa. Atlas Robotics was the fastest to make an offer: 'We are willing to take over Mars, the robots activity of RFa. We plan to keep a minimum of 50 persons in the new Atlas-Mars company, and we expect RFa to take care of all the other persons. Atlas is willing to pay €8.8 million to RFa: €4.8 million for the goodwill and €4 million for the inventory. Half of the payment for the goodwill is conditional on the sale of 600 robots to

---

RFa was the factory automation business of R, the second largest French automotive group selling passenger cars (81% of the total sales in 1991), trucks (16%) and other industrial products (3%). With an annual production of more than 1.5 million cars, R was the sixth largest car manufacturer in Europe* with a 10% share of the market.

Following heavy losses experienced in the mid-1980s, a newly-appointed president embarked on a programme of change. The diversification strategy implemented in the 1970s was drastically curtailed and all non-core activities were critically reassessed. Most non-core activities were divested, some put into partnership (the bearings business became a joint venture with a Japanese company) and, finally, some were retained.

When he was appointed as the president of RFa in 1986, Georges Paris received the brief to rationalise the company, to bring it back to profitability and to prepare it for a possible future change in ownership. Then, in January 1992, Georges Paris was given two years to divest RFa.

In 1992, RFa was made up of a cluster of four loosely-related units: robots, body-in-white, machining, and engine and transmission shops.

Figure X.1 RFa
* and the tenth largest in the world.

In 1992, Atlas Robotics was the largest non-Japanese company among the world's leading producers of industrial robots and robot systems. In 1991 Atlas sold 2160 robots, which made it the largest competitor in Europe (1500 robots sold and a 25% share of the market) and the second largest competitor in the USA (with a 23% share).

The robots industry was a young industry. Originally created in the 1960s, this industry developed slowly until the early 1980s, when it started to grow explosively. In 1986–87, the market sharply declined, but then began to grow again slowly. In 1991, the total sales of the world robots industry equalled $1800 million (four-fifths of these sales being made up of 'naked' robots). In 1989–91, an average of 24 000 robots had been sold each year in the world, with more than 60% of them being sold in one single country: Japan. With the very great size of the Japanese market, it was no surprise that several Japanese companies had managed to build a very strong position: Yaskawa was producing some 4000 robots per year, and Fanuc and Kawazaki some 3000 robots each. The larger Japanese robot manufacturers were also present in Europe and the USA.* The robot industry was very competitive and even a large competitor like Atlas was not in a comfortable position: Atlas lost money in 1985 and 1986. In 1992, there were more than 200 manufacturers of robots in the world, but this number was expected to fall sharply.

In the early 1990s, Atlas designed a new strategy aimed at building a global leadership. This strategy had a few critical goals:

- bridging the size gap with the largest Japanese competitors through both internal and external growth;
- entering the business of applications and systems in a more aggressive way;
- continuing the aggressive programmes of unit cost reduction. In 1986, Atlas decided to regroup all its manufacturing in one single plant.

In 1992, the automotive industry (car and truck manufacturers and their sub-suppliers) was still the main customer group for the robot suppliers and for Atlas in particular. Atlas was present in France but had only been able to capture 10% of the market and was weak in relation to the French car manufacturers. In 1991, Atlas sold 246 robots in France (as against 206 in 1990). At the end of 1991, it employed 104 people (as against 93 at the end of 1990).

Figure X.2 Atlas Robotics and the robots industry
* Prices of robots were much lower in Japan: if the price of a robot was 100 in Europe, it was only 70 in Japan.

R during the period 1993–95. The payment for the stock is based on 50% of its book value. Atlas and RFa still have to agree on the implementation of the phasing out of the current Mars products. The preference of Atlas is for a very fast phasing out. The reserve for the orders under warranty of 2.4 million is transferred to Atlas. The R group commits to buy 80% of its total robot needs from Atlas-Mars in the next five years. The R group will also help Atlas-Mars to sell their robots to the other French automotive group. Finally, Atlas is interested in continuing to analyse the opportunity of acquiring the body-in-white building business.'

The robots and body-in-white businesses of RFa are described in Figures X.3 and X.4.

The senior management of R decided to reject this offer: 'Atlas is definitely not interested in acquiring the whole RFa business. They are not even interested in acquiring the whole of Mars but only in buying the access to its customers – and in buying this access at a fairly low price.'[2] The only thing that Georges Paris did not fully understand was the reason why Atlas intended to keep as many as 50 people: 'As they want to stop the production of robots in France, why keep so many people?'

With its Mars robots, RFa was the market leader for industrial robots in France, where it commanded a 30% share of the market. RFa was especially strong in the automotive segment, where it had an 80% share of the business of the car and truck manufacturers.[1] In spite of its very strong position in France, RFa's robot business was very small: in 1991 RFa supplied only 269 robots! In 1991, the robots business generated sales of FF238 million and an operating loss of FF32 million.

R had been one of the companies that pioneered the development of robots in the early 1970s. With the help of government funding, R pursued an aggressive programme of new product development.

However, in the mid-1980s, the robot activity of R came under scrutiny. Seriously. In spite of all the noise – and the press coverage – surrounding robots, the business was not developing as fast as expected.[2] At the same time, prices were falling, and more and more money was needed to develop new products. In spite of its high selling prices (typically 30% more than the competition) the robot activity of RFa never managed to generate a profit in its whole history! In 1985, RFa realized that it had to prepare itself for 'gracefully exiting' the robot business and, in 1986, Paul Ledoux, the newly-appointed manager of the robots division, was given the explicit mission: 'to make the business as attractive as it could possibly look to its future owner'. Paul Ledoux immediately initiated two parallel strategies:

● A co-operative strategy aimed at trying to develop a 'common understanding' with other robot companies that could turn into future owners. A case in point was the co-operation that took place between the development teams of RFa and C in the early 1990s. This co-operation was a non-binding agreement aimed at the co-development of a new robot for spot welding applications: each of the two partners was free to use the outcome of the joint development.
● A very tough 'slimming down' strategy. Paul Ledoux decided to focus all the activity of the company on its main product and to cut everything that was not critical to its maintenance in the short term. The plan was also to bring down the number of people in the robot division from 200 to 60–80. Paul Ledoux was well aware that this strategy was risky and he believed that the 'slimmed down' company could probably not survive for very long in the future as an independent entity: 'With such a strategy, we had better find a new owner some time between 1993 and 1995!'

Figure X.3 RFa's robots business
Notes:
1. RFa had a much smaller share (10%) of automotive sub-suppliers. Sub-suppliers represented about the same volume of robots as the automotive manufacturers. Together sub-suppliers and manufacturers represented about half the total volume of robots.
2. Several departments at R were actually resisting this innovation and, in 1991, robots had not managed to find as many applications as in most other automotive groups. While there were about 25 robots per person employed in Japan, there were only 5 robots per person employed in France.

From Spring 1992 to Spring 1993, discussions took place with a number of other potential partners and in April 1993 an agreement for the sale of the whole of RFa was about to be signed. However, at the last minute the potential buyer suddenly withdrew from the negotiation.

The second round of negotiation

The failure of the first round of discussions made Georges Paris realize that it would be much easier to break up the company and sell it in sections. RFa was split into two new companies:

With sales of FF350 million in 1991, body-in-white was RFa's largest business, located in Beauchamp, 50 km north of Paris. In 1991, this activity had enjoyed a very special position in the face of the divestment climate at RFa. The body-in-white activity was started in 1986 as a result of the coming together of a series of unique factors:

- A request from the engineering and methods division at R. In the mid-1980s, R realized that the improvement in the quality of its vehicles was very dependent on the improvement in the geometry of the car body and R was looking for a new body-in-white partner.
- The need to 'save' the industrial site at Beauchamp. In 1986, Henri Maurice, the new manager who was appointed to run the site of Beauchamp, quickly realized that without a major new activity the site would have to be closed. In spite of his lack of experience in this business, he managed to convince R that Beauchamp was the body-in-white partner that they needed.
- And the drive of an entrepreneur: from the beginning, Henri Maurice had been eager to find other customers than R and he managed to do so in Europe and in the USA.

Henri Maurice was convinced that there was a great need for strong and competent independent body-in-white specialists. Automotive companies had decided to build new, high-quality, cost-effective factories at a time when they had also decided to reduce their in-house engineering resources. The development of the body-in-white business was presenting a number of challenges also:

- Body-in-white was a large-project[1] business involving a large number of components[2] bought from many sub-suppliers.[3] In the future, and with the apparent desire of auto manufacturers to go for 'one single step', 'turnkey' equipment supplies, the size of the orders could increase very significantly.
- The business was expected to become global: some auto manufacturers were talking about the 'world car' and wanted their plants all over the world to adopt similar processes. In 1992, none of the European body-in-white builders was able to supply globally. There were hundreds of independent[4] line builders in Europe and the largest in Europe was 10 times smaller than the largest one in the USA.

In the business plan that they prepared in 1991 for the period 1992–96, the management of Beauchamp was expecting the European line building industry to go through a consolidation process and they wanted to take advantage of it and to grow through gaining new customers outside France. The overall European market for the construction of automotive plants was not expected to grow: in the first three years of the plan (1992–94) the market was expected to be stable (growth in the East compensating the decline in the West), then in the subsequent three years, the market was expected to decrease by 15% to 20% (increased Japanese car manufacturers' penetration, more effective operation of the plants, redeployment of equipment from one plant to another, etc.). A further challenge was that prices were expected to fall.

Figure X.4 The body-in-white business

Notes:
1. A typical order was in the range of €10 million to €40 million.
2. External purchases represented 70% of the project costs. Robots typically represented some 10% to 15% of the total cost of the project.
3. Beauchamp had 700 such sub-suppliers.
4. Some were linked to car manufacturers.

Table X.1 ● Financial data

Income statements

	1990	1991	1992	1993
Body-in-white				
Sales	52.0	63.2	113.0	70.0
Profit after tax	1.0	1.0	0.8	−0.2
Profit after tax/sales	1.9%	1.6%	0.7%	−0.3%
Robots				
Sales (FF million)	58.4	47.6	38.8	28.8
Profit after tax	−1.6	−7.6	1.0	5.0
Profit after tax/sales	−2.7%	−16.0%	2.6%	20.8%
Consolidated				
Sales	110.4	110.8	151.8	98.8
Profit after tax	−0.6	−6.6	1.8	5.8
Robots				
Volume of robots sold	308	269	230	179
Number of people	195	137	95	83

Balance sheets

	31 December 1992			31 December 1993 (estimate)		
	Consolidated	Body-in-white	Robots	Consolidated	Body-in-white	Robots
Net fixed assets	15.0	5.0	10.0	14.0	4.4	9.6
Inventories	16.0	10.0	6.0	16.0	9.0	7.0
Receivables	63.4	44.0	19.4	50.4	36.0	14.4
Total	94.4	59.0	35.4	80.4	49.4	31.0
Equity	11.0	10.0	1.0	16.8	9.8	7.0
Provision	6.0	3.0	3.0	5.4	3.0	2.4
Loans	25.4	8.0	17.4	13.6	8.0	5.6
Payables	52.0	38.0	14.0	44.6	28.6	16.0
Total	94.4	59.0	35.4	80.4	49.4	31.0

● *Robots and body-in-white* This was the company that was now on sale. The financial statements of the new company are in Table X.1.
● *Other activities* This part of the business would probably have to be kept by R for a while.

In May 1993 Johan Ericsson, the president of Atlas Robotics, called and enquired about the situation at RFa. Georges Paris was happy to explain why the offer from Atlas had not been put on top of the list: 'In their offer, Atlas appears to be interested only in robots while the other potential buyers are interested in robots and body-in-white. Atlas seems to be interested only in buying a market while the other companies seem to be willing to be more equal partners. Finally some people at R have the fear that Atlas is planning to take drastic restructuring action that will result in turmoil.'

In subsequent conversations, Atlas was advised to reconsider its initial offer and: 'Make an offer for both body shop line building and robots. Make an offer at a "fair" price with "normal" conditions.'

Atlas Robotics as the best potential buyer

During the progress of the negotiations, it appeared that Atlas was the best potential partner for both the body-in-white and the robot activities. For the management of body-in-white, Atlas had a lot of advantages:

- Contrary to the other potential buyers, Atlas had no body-in-white activity. They were the ones who had the strongest interest in acquiring the expertise of the RFa Beauchamp site.
- Atlas was the strongest and most global company among the possible buyers: the Beauchamp site needed a strong global partner to develop its business. The fact that Atlas was not linked with any automotive company would also make it easier for the Beauchamp site to work with all companies.
- Atlas was bringing the best possible robot offer to the party. It was actually fair to say that none of the other potential buyers was coming up with a good solution for robots.

As far as the robot business was concerned, only Atlas was offering a solution for the long term. Georges Paris was convinced that a deal with any of the other companies would not result in the creation of any viable robot manufacturer in the long run. 'In the final analysis, it may be better to implement a good long-term solution for 50 people rather than implement a bad solution for everybody. In any case, the robot activity is now close to having the 50 people that Atlas wants to have!' (See Figure X.3.)

And finally, from the point of view of R, the owner, Atlas could be a very good partner in the future. Atlas could well be one of those strong and competent equipment suppliers that R wanted to work with. The problem though was that the discussion had not started on the best footing. Now the issue was to change the whole climate and to start exploring how to implement a more 'equal partner' approach.

Issues to be resolved

A number of issues had still to be resolved:

- *The integration of the RFa businesses into Atlas Robotics and the future of the body-in-white and robot teams.* How would body-in-white be run within Atlas? What would the role of the current Mars robot team? It seemed clear that the Beauchamp site would be maintained, but there was a problem with the location of the robot team, as agreements with the unions stipulated 'that the people employed by Mars could only be moved within the same town'. As regards the robots, there was also a need to decide about the phasing out of the current products.
- *Guarantees to be given by R.* Atlas wanted a commitment from the R group to buy robots from them in the future. If it was difficult for R to commit to a fixed number of robots, it was no problem for R to guarantee that a large proportion of their robot needs would be sourced from Atlas.[3] Georges Paris was also willing to accept that part of the price paid by Atlas would be conditional on the success of the new business: this can often be the best way for the seller to get a fair price!
- *The price to be paid by Atlas Robotics.* Georges Paris expected the price to be a delicate issue, so he decided to read once more the analysis prepared by the controller of RFa (see in Exhibit X.1).

Exhibit X.1 ● Price to be obtained from Atlas

Memorandum
To Mr Georges Paris, President
From André Louis, Controller

Summary
Assessing the price that we can get from the sale of the company is a matter of deciding the minimum price that we can accept and of trying to guess the maximum price that Atlas is prepared to pay. As shown below, we believe that:

● Atlas is willing to pay as much as €180.8 million for the body-in-white and robot businesses.
● We cannot accept any deal below €43.6 million.

This leaves substantial room for negotiation and we would recommend aiming at a price of €72.6 million.

Assessment of value
All values have been assessed based on future cash flows. Values have been estimated as equal to the present value (using a 15% discount rate) of the future cash flows.[4] According to standard practice, we have split the future cash flows into two components:

● Future cash flows inherited from the past: the value of those flows has been estimated as equal to the net worth reported in the opening balance sheet of the acquired business (31 December 1993). In this opening balance sheet, inventories and land and buildings have not been adjusted.
● Future cash flows resulting from future sales. The net present value of these cash flows is shown as 'goodwill'. In most calculations, we have split these flows into two subsequent sets of flows:
  – Flows generated by the sales to be made in the next five years ('the planning period'): those flows have been estimated for each of the years of the planning period and their present value has been calculated.
  – Flows generated by the sales to be made beyond the planning period. These flows have not been explicitly estimated but have been summarized as a lump sum ('terminal value') estimated as ten or twelve times the profit in the last year of the planning period. This lump sum has then been discounted for assessing the present value of the flows beyond the planning period.

Assessing the price for the body-in-white business

Value of the future cash flows generated by future sales
As shown in Table X.2, the 1994–98 business plan which has been communicated to Atlas results in a value of €26.8 million.

In our minds, this is the value that R would get from this business should it continue to own it. It is therefore equal to the minimum price that we should get from Atlas or our 'walk-away' price. Should Atlas come up with a lower offer than

---

Table X.2 ● Value of body-in-white (according to business plan)

	1994	1995	1996	1997	1998	
Sales (€ million)	80.0	60.0	100.0	120.0	160.0	
Profit after tax	2.0	0.6	2.2	3.4	4.4	
Profit after tax/sales	2.5%	2.0%	2.2%	2.8%	2.8%	
Multiple					10	
Terminal value						44.0
Profit after tax + terminal value	2.0	0.6	2.2	3.4	4.4	44.0
Discount rate	0.2					
NPV	26.8					

Note: 1994 and 1995 sales correspond to orders already booked.

CASE

this, we would be better to refuse the deal, keep the business and create that value by ourselves.[5] However, we believe that we should not limit ourselves to obtaining this minimum price but also try to capture part of the additional value (synergy) that is going to be created by this business under the new ownership and leadership of Atlas. We have identified two main sources of synergy:

● The ownership by Atlas will enable the business to grow faster (global support, strong robot offer, etc.) and also to generate better margins (larger projects, project management experience, etc.)
● For the Atlas Group, the business will also create an additional value owing to the contribution from each additional robot sold.

This is shown in the spreadsheet in Table X.3. As a result of its new ownership, the future activity of the business will generate a value of €56 million, which is €29.2 million more that the value of the business as run by R. This value of €56 million is the maximum price that Atlas can expect to pay for the future cash flows, i.e. its 'walk-away' price.

Price to be obtained for the body-in-white business
Table X.4 shows the estimates of the walk-away prices: €36.6 million for R and €65.8 million for Atlas. We propose to aim at a price of €44 million (walk-away price plus one-quarter of the synergy).

Assessing the price of the robotics business (Mars)

Our walk away
We have prepared a business plan for this business in case we do not sell it (see Table X.5). The results suggest that we should not walk away provided that Atlas offers at least €1 for the goodwill! These figures have not been communicated to Atlas and we should try to conclude the deal on another basis and to capture a share of the benefits that Atlas will generate should they acquire our business.

Table X.3 ● A model to assess the value of body-in-white

A	B	C	D	E	F	G
1	1994	1995	1996	1997	1998	
2 Sales (€ million)	80.0	100.0	120.0	160.0	200.0	
3 Profit after tax/sales	2.6%	2.0%	2.2%	2.8%	2.8%	
4 Profit after tax	2.1	2.0	2.6	4.4	5.5	
5 Multiple					12	
6 Terminal value						66.0
7 Profit after tax + terminal value	2.1	2.0	2.6	4.4	5.5	66.0
8 Additional robots	60	75	90	120	150	
9 Contribution per robot (€000)	15.8	15.8	15.8	15.8	15.8	
10 Additional profit after tax	0.9	1.2	1.4	1.9	2.4	
11 Multiple					12	
12 Terminal value						28.4
13 Profit after tax + terminal value	0.9	1.2	1.4	1.9	2.4	28.4
14 Total profit after tax + terminal value	3.0	3.2	4.1	6.3	7.9	94.4
15 Discount rate	0.2					
16 NPV	56.1					

Background

B2.F3: data
B4: =B2*B3; Copy
F5: data
G6: =F5*F4
B7: =B4+B6; Copy

B8.F9: data
B10: =B9*B8/1000; Copy
B13: =B10+B12; Copy
B14: =B7+B13; Copy
B16: +NPV(B15,B14:G14)

Table X.4 ● Walk-away prices for the body-in-white business

	R walk-away price	Atlas walk-away price
Goodwill*	26.8	56.0
Net worth	9.8	9.8
Total	36.6	65.8

* From the balance sheets (Figure 5).

Table X.5 ● Value of the robots business

	1994	1995	1996
Sales	40.0	30.0	7.0
Profit after tax	4.0	1.0	−6.4
Discount rate	0.15		
NPV	0		

Table X.6 • Data communicated to Atlas Robotics

	1994	1995	1996	1997	1998
Number of robots	300	400	450	500	600
Average revenues per unit (000)	150.0	160.0	160.0	160.0	160.0
Sales	45.0	64.0	72.0	80.0	96.0

Atlas's estimated walk away

In July, we established together with Atlas a forecast of the sales that a new Mars-Atlas company could expect to make in the next five years. This is shown in Table X.6. When a reasonable contribution after tax for each robot is applied (both at the French subsidiary and the factory levels) then, as shown in Table X.7, a value of €107.9 million is obtained. There are a few problems with these calculations, however:

● The contributions have been assessed by our own people: there is no guarantee that these estimates are correct.
● The number of robots taken into account in this calculation will be questioned by Atlas. Atlas is likely to claim that the only figure to be taken into account is that which the new company will generate over and above what Atlas could generate by itself. There is actually one argument in favour of this and one argument against:
  – The argument in favour is that Atlas is very weak in relation to French car manufacturers. Should we stop doing business, our share will probably not go to Atlas, but is most likely to go to those of our competitors who are in a stronger position in regard to the car manufacturers and especially to C, who now has a product that these French car manufacturers like very much (our own new robot).
  – The argument against is that the French car manufacturers cannot do anything else but turn to Atlas, the world leader in robots, in the future. The only thing that Atlas gains by acquiring us is time. In the long run Atlas will serve the French car manufacturers anyway. With us, they are going to serve them earlier and therefore the only numbers to be taken into account are the additional robots expected to be sold in the next three to five years.

Price to be obtained for the robots business

Table X.8 shows the estimates of the walk-away prices: €7.0 million for R and €115 million for Atlas. We propose to aim for a price of €28.6 million (walk-away price plus one-fifth of the synergy).

Price for the whole business

We propose to establish our target price for the whole business at €72.6 million (€44 million for body-in-white and €28.6 million for robots). This is significantly above our walk-away price (€43.6 million) and well below Atlas's estimated walk away (€180.8 million).

Table X.7 ● A model to assess the value of the robots business

A	B	C	D	E	F	G
1	1994	1995	1996	1997	1998	
2 Number of robots	300	400	450	500	600	
3 Unit selling price	150.0	160.0	160.0	160.0	160.0	
4 Sales	45.0	64.0	72.0	80.0	96.0	
5 Unit cost	127.4	134.4	132.8	132.8	132.8	
6 Costs	38.2	53.8	59.8	66.4	79.7	
7 Profit before tax	6.8	10.2	12.2	13.6	16.3	
8 Profit after tax	3.7	5.6	6.7	7.5	9.0	
9 Multiple					10.0	
10 Terminal value						89.8
11 Profit after tax and terminal value	3.7	5.6	6.7	7.5	9.0	89.8
12 Discount rate	0.2					
13 NPV	59.5					
14 Contribution in the factory						
15 Contribution per unit (after tax)	12.0	12.0	12.0	12.0	12.0	
16 Contribution	3.6	4.8	5.4	6.0	7.2	
17 Multiple					10.0	
18 Terminal value						72.0
19 Profit after tax and terminal value	3.6	4.8	5.4	6.0	7.2	72.0
20 Discount rate	0.2					
21 NPV	48.4					
22 Total value	107.9					

Background
B2.F3: data
B4: =B2*B3/1000
B5.F5: data
B6: =B2*B5/1000
B7: =B4–B6
B8: =B7*.55
G10: =F9*F8

B11: =B8+B10; Copy
B13: =NPV(B12,B11.G11)
B15.F15: data
B16: =B15*B2/1000
B18: =F16*F17
B19: =B15+B18
B21: =NPV(B20,B19.G19)
B22: =B13+B21

Table X.8 ● Walk-away prices for the robots business

	R walk-away price	Atlas walk-away price
Goodwill	0	108.0
Net worth	7.0	7.0
Total	7.0	115.0

Notes

1. This case has been developed by the author. The Atlas case can be obtained from Michel Schlosser on www.Michel-schlosser.com.
2. Georges Paris had calculated that the price proposed of €8.8 million was less than the value of a 10% rebate given to R on its purchases of robots over the next three years.
3. The R group had estimated the following purchases of robots in the next three years: 1994: 200; 1995: 300; 1996: 350. Georges Paris had also estimated the future purchases of the other French automotive group: 1994: 100; 1995: 100; 1996: 100.
4. Actually I have discounted future profits instead of future cash flows. The rationale for this is that the impact of working capital needs and capital expenditure is not significant in this specific case. In such a case, working with profits has the great advantage of simplifying the calculations.
5. Some people would argue however that this is a bit theoretical: it is very difficult to develop a new business in the current divestment climate.

CASE

General Appendix
Evaluating business opportunities
Summary and background material on cost of capital, financial and real options

1 Recommendations for evaluating business opportunities: a summary

1.1 A well-disciplined creative process

Evaluating business opportunities is a matter of evaluating all the possible sets of possible future cash flows. The approach for that is to:

(a) Draw an initial decision tree mapping the sequence of decisions and uncertainties. Failing to start with a decision tree is taking the risk of missing most of the issues.
(b) Assess the end points and the probabilities.
(c) Draw a risk profile – and estimate the expected value.
(d) Reflect on how to improve the sequence of decisions and events.
(e) Draw a new decision tree – assess the end points, etc. until you feel that you can decide what is the best trajectory of commitment. This may result in the decision not to pursue the opportunity.

This is the approach that we have followed in the book and in particular in Chapter 21. As you will realize when working with the book, this is very much a process and what counts most is to progressively understand an opportunity and to construct a valuable business out of it.

Even though the ultimate goal is to create the maximum possible value – as expressed by a hard number – one should definitely not rush to calculate this number. When starting the analysis, value can only be estimated within a range and, in general, the bigger the range, the better the opportunity! The central purpose of the analysis is to find ways to increase the width of the range and to capture its upper part without being exposed to its lower part. When the range has been transformed in your favour, and only then, is it time to summarize it with one single expected value. Many textbooks focus on estimating *the* value of assets: this is definitely an important issue but certainly not as important as the creative process of finding the best ways to create this value.

1.2 Assessing the end points: the cash flows issue

This is an issue that is extensively dealt with in the book. For a summary, you may want to refer to Chapter 15 and the analysis of the case BA International in Chapter 16. A list of critical recommendations would be as follows:

● Select a period of study that corresponds to the life of the decision.
● Adopt an incremental approach (what is changed by the decision to go and capture the opportunity).
● Use 'trajectory' rather than 'per cent of sales' models to generate the numbers.
● Ignore inflation and foreign exchange rates – work with 'real' prices and costs – i.e. prices and costs that are not adjusted for inflation.
● Consider the real trajectories of the different unit prices and costs: very few things keep constant over time!
● Check that the cash–income parity relation is respected.

1.3 Assessing the end points: the discount rate issue

The rationale for deferring the issue

Throughout the book, we use a discount rate but we never really discuss where this rate comes from. We introduce the idea in Chapter 2 that discounting is a way to account for the cost of money/capital. We suggest in Chapter 4 that equity should cost more than debt. Finally, in Chapter 17, we recommend the use of a 'real' rate, i.e. a rate that does not include inflation.

The rationale for dealing with the discussion of the discount rate in a final appendix is that:

● Non-financial managers typically have a limited influence on the discount rate. Managers can – and are very much expected to – create a lot of value through effectively structuring the business and its cash flows. They generally have no comparable impact on the discount rate, that is typically a 'given'.[1]
● Providing reliable estimates of the discount rate and minimizing this cost are specific responsibilities of the finance department.[2] This is an issue that is heavily impacted by institutional, tax and legal matters which contributes to making it an issue for specialists.
● Finally, it is also fair to say that the theory of finance is not totally clear about the discount rate issue. For a few years, there has been a widely accepted paradigm known as 'modern finance'. Within this paradigm, the 'capital asset pricing model', CAPM, was

offering an elegant solution to the discount rate issue. Nowadays, the modern finance paradigm is attacked and some authors claim they have now started the 'new finance'.[3] Today the CAPM looks a bit old fashioned but, unfortunately, no new model has really replaced it! To make the situation even more complicated, there is now a widespread interest in 'real option' approaches, which also question the CAPM approach of the discount rate – and have also failed, so far, to come up with a widely accepted alternative model!

The material that follows will help you to navigate through this challenging issue, to ask valuable questions of the specialists, and prepare yourself to understand the future developments in the field.

Selecting the relevant discount rate: six practical rules of action and a word of caution

1 Use the cost of equity as the discount rate. We have already met this idea in Chapter 2. Capital is no different from all the other resources needed for running a business: it has a cost that is equal to the price asked for by its suppliers. Chapter 1 starts with the idea that maximization of value is a responsibility and a discipline for every manager. In order to maximize value, you should: (a) assess the cost of equity – what is required by the shareholders; and (b) capture all the opportunities that have a positive present value at this cost.

2 Use the cost of equity that corresponds to the market risk of your opportunity. Use the expected return/risk relationship of the capital asset pricing model (CAPM) to estimate your equity cost (refer also to Section 2.5 below):

$$E(i) = R_f + \beta_i (R_m - R_f)$$

Where, $E(i)$ = Return required by those institutions who invest in business activities carrying the same risk as the opportunity you are analyzing. As each industry generally has its specific risk characteristics, a typical simplification is to use the return required by institutions who invest in the industry to which your opportunity belongs.

R_f = Risk-free rate for the same time period as the project. Ideally the rate of a zero-coupon government bond.[4]

R_m = The return on the market portfolio. This is typically the return from a stock market index in which each stock's performance is weighted by its capitalization, or market value. In the USA, the S&P 500 is such a 'value weighted' index.[5]

$R_m - R_f$ = The equity premium – average premium for all the shares. Historically this premium has been around 6% in the USA. Many experts consider that this was exceptional and recommend the use of a lower premium (3%–4%). $R_m - R_f$ is also known as the 'price of market risk'.

β_i = A coefficient[6] that expresses the quantity of market risk brought to shareholders by the opportunity that you analyze. Market risk is only a part of the total risk of the opportunity but, since it can be diversified, the specific idiosyncratic/diversifiable risk should not be considered:[7] in a competitive market there is no reward for holding inefficient portfolios.

Please note that the discount rate for evaluating an **opportunity depends only on the market risk of this opportunity**. In order to estimate the rate at which you are going to discount the cash flows of a business opportunity you have to identify a company that is listed on the market and that has the same market risk: this is the so-called 'twin security'. The discount rate is the return that shareholders require from the twin security. If the twin security has a high market risk, then the discount rate will be high. If the twin security has no market risk, then the discount rate will be the risk free rate. As we discuss below, options are typically valued from the construction of a riskless portfolio that is then evaluated at the risk free rate. What about using the cost of equity of your company? You should actually use the return that shareholders require from your company only when two conditions are met: (a) your company is specialized in one single industry, and (b) you consider investing in that same industry.[8]

When they look at your projects, shareholders are concerned with their 'market' or 'systematic' risk only. They do not care about the 'diversifiable' or 'idiosyncratic' risk of your projects. As a manager you typically have a different point of view: you are concerned with the total risk for your projects that is made up of both the market and the diversifiable parts.[9]

● The risk of losing market share is very important for the management of a company that is attacked by the competition. This risk, however, is of no importance to the investor: they can invest in several competing companies in the industry and diversify this risk away. This kind of risk is not rewarded by any premium. Symmetrically this kind of risk does not affect the cost of equity.[10]
● The risk created by inflation is a concern for both management and shareholders. Diversification cannot totally eliminate the effect of inflation which impacts the value of any portfolio. Inflation, however, affects different companies in different ways: some are very much hurt and, when part of a portfolio, they contribute more than the average to the inflation risk of the portfolio. Some other companies even benefit from inflation: when part of a portfolio, they contribute to reducing its exposure to inflation risk. Inflation risk is called a 'market risk'. Market risks are compensated by the market. Symmetrically market risks increase or decrease the cost of equity.

Risk should be taken into account once only. In order to avoid double counting risk, it is a good idea to.

● Systematically analyze all the idiosyncratic risks when building your decision trees: you want to understand these risks that matter to you – even if they do not matter to the shareholders and are not taken into account by the market in the cost of equity.
● Ignore the market risks when building the decision tree: these risks are already included in the discount rate.

3 Do not make any difference between internally and externally generated capital. Externally and internally raised capital basically have the same cost.[11] Each time you envisage committing new capital you should ask yourself if the investment is better than what the shareholders can achieve by themselves. If your answer is negative do not commit capital even if you 'have the money'. If there are internal funds available and no competitive opportunity to invest them in, then these funds should be distributed to the shareholders through dividend payments.[12] Capital markets have both a manifest and a latent function. Companies use capital markets both as a source of capital – not that often – and as a source of information every day. Even in the absence of capital transactions, capital markets help to co-ordinate decentralized decision-making in the economy.

4 Do not adjust the rate of equity for 'unprofitable' investments. When a company invests in all the opportunities that have positive net present values, it creates the maximum possible additional value.

What about the existence of unprofitable investments? Let us assume that a company operating in a single line of business has a 15% cost of capital. Now its competitive position has become very shaky, so the company decides to keep a large amount of cash uninvested that represents 25% of its capital expenditure budget. For the sake of simplicity let us assume that this cash has a zero return.

In such a situation some people are tempted to think that since the 'profitable' projects – the 75% – have to contribute to the financing of the idle cash – the 25% – why not increase the return required from the profitable projects and use a higher hurdle rate: 20% (0.15/0.75)?

This would actually be wrong since doing so would make the company reject projects that have positive net present values at rates ranging between 15% and 20% that could contribute to creating the additional value that is needed for financing the non-value creating investment.

5 Do not adjust the cost of equity for the impact of financing. Most businesses are not financed by equity alone but also use debt that typically induces tax allowances. A common approach is to adjust the cost of equity and estimate a weighted average cost of capital (WACC). As you can see below in section 2.8, this approach is a crude approximation only and it can result in significant errors.[13] A much better approach is to leave the cost of equity intact and to adjust the NPV instead: this is the 'adjusted present value' (APV) approach.

6 In the end, always ask yourself why the NPV is positive. Theory tells us that when an industry settles into long-term competitive equilibrium, all assets are expected to earn their opportunity cost of capital and, as a result, to generate zero net present values. Finding a strategy that generates a positive net present value is a matter of discovering how to outperform the market and to create what economists call a rent, and that is not easy. This has some practical implications:

● Never take it for granted that the NPV attached to a decision is positive: always make sure that this does not result from over-optimistic forecasts. Make sure that you can always explain a positive NPV by a unique and sustainable competitive advantage.
● Specialists are not the ones who should make NPV calculations. Value calculations should be performed by the managers who design the strategy: who is in a better position to claim that the NPV corresponds to a genuine competitive advantage?

Finally, a word of caution – please remember that even though it is probably the most widely-used model for estimating the discount rate, the CAPM is no longer popular with investors on the stock market, who now prefer various types of factor models. It is therefore crucial to check that your decisions are not critically dependent on the choice of the discount rate.[14]

Be especially cautious when your decision tree pictures a lot of flexibility – or options. As explained below in section 3, the CAPM-based discount rate is not adapted to the valuation of options that generally have a high and very unstable beta.

1.4 Reviewing the decision tree: fully leveraging the option framework

Decision trees are a very powerful tool for analyzing the flexibility of decisions and you should always use them to try to 'push the squares ahead of the circles'! The recent popularity of the 'real option' approaches makes decision trees more useful than ever as they are the only practical and easy-to-use tool available for portraying flexibility and options. The unique advantage of the real option framework is to renew the language of strategic and operational flexibility and to invite you systematically to look for, and to create, a variety of options.

- When you consider committing to any course of action, to capture any opportunity, etc., there is at least one option that you should always take into account: is it the best time to commit or should you keep the option open and defer your commitment. In *Investment under Uncertainty*,[15] Dixit and Pindyck recommend replacing the old rule: 'invest when the net present value is positive' with 'invest when the net present value is higher than the value of keeping the option alive'.
- There are typically many more potential options than the option to defer commitment. This is the list of the most common real options as identified by Trigeorgis:[16] options to defer, time-to-build or staged investment, option to expand, option to contract, option to shut down and restart, option to abandon, option to switch inputs and outputs, growth options and multiple interacting options.

APPENDIX

2 Background material on the discount rate or cost of capital issue

2.1 Is the stock market efficient?

The debate about the predictability of the stock market is not new. Almost exactly a century ago:

- In 1900, L. Bachelier stated in his dissertation that the fluctuations of the stock market are unpredictable and that stock prices move in a random fashion. This is the famous *random walk hypothesis*.
- In 1900–02, C. Dow published a series of articles that were going to form the basis of what was later called the 'Dow theory' and is the ancestor of *modern technical analysis* or *charting*. According to this approach, it is possible to partly predict the future prices by analyzing the previous price history.[17]

Both approaches have enjoyed a happy life up to now, even though it is fair to say that the random walk hypothesis completely dominated the financial academic literature for some time. The dominance of the random walk hypothesis was reinforced by a series of related concepts. In the second part of the twentieth century, the *efficient market hypothesis* (EMH) was formulated: assets are always priced correctly and they incorporate the expectations and information of all participants. If prices always fully reflect all available information, changes in prices can only come from totally new information and, as a consequence, price changes are necessarily random and unpredictable.[18] The more efficient the market, the more random the changes in prices! Another important idea is that in an efficient market there should be no *arbitrage* opportunities – no opportunities to gain without taking risk or committing money, because professional investors move their money around to close any pricing gaps. Arbitrage is the process that enforces the 'law of one price': two identical assets necessarily have the same price.

However, starting in the mid-1980s, the EMH–random walk paradigm came under serious attack:

● Stock prices do not really change in a random fashion. This was established in particular by A. Lo and C. MacKinlay in their 1988 article: 'Stock market prices do not follow random walks: Evidence from a simple specification test'.[19]
● The financial markets show a number of anomalies that are not consistent with the EMH paradigm. Volumes of trading are higher and stock prices are more volatile than advocates of the EMH theory would predict.[20] There exist limits to arbitrage.[21] It seems that prices change not only in relation to interest rates and risk premiums but according to other patterns also: 'day-of-the-week' effect,[22] 'January' effect,[23] etc. Most trading rules fail but 'value investing'[24] seems to work very well. Finally, it seems that in some cases professional investors do outperform the market – but this is not easy to replicate![25] The markets do not always respond instantly and accurately to the receipt of new information.[26] When it takes time for markets to respond, then studying their dynamics[27] becomes more important than studying their equilibrium. And studying past dynamics is one of the ways to approach the issue. Technical analysis is not dead!

As stated by Lo and MacKinlay:[28] *'Financial markets are predictable to some degree, but far from being a symptom of inefficiency or irrationality, predictability is the oil that lubricates the gears of capitalism.'*

What should you do when it comes to estimating cost of capital? In spite of the fact that market efficiency is an idealized model of the existing financial markets, competition in these markets is such that it is a good idea to start from the assumption that markets are efficient. This has some very practical implications. Trust the market prices. Try to learn as much as you can from the prices and the reactions of the market. Do not believe that the market will pay for things that you do and that markets can also do by themselves. Do not believe in financial and accounting illusions.

2.2 It is not because it has no explicit cost that equity is free!

There are many sources of capital: debt, equity, convertible debt, leasing,[29] etc. While the cost of some sources is stated explicitly, the cost of many other sources – and the cost of equity in particular – cannot be observed directly and can only be estimated by analysis.

When you borrow, the lender specifies the cost of the loan and you can observe this cost directly: it is the IRR of the cash flows of the loan. This is shown in Table 1. When a company raises equity, nothing is specified regarding future cash flows:

Table 1 ● Calculation of the explicit return required by a lender

Cash flows of a loan (from the lender's point of view)					
	2003	2004	2005	2006	2007
Cash outflows	−1020				
Cash inflows (interest and repayment of capital)		329	329	329	329
Net cash flows	−1020	329	329	329	329
IRR	11%				

● There is a promise of future dividends but the numbers are not specified and it is made clear that they are contingent on the performance of the company.
● Shareholders keep the option to discontinue their investment at any time through selling their shares but the selling price is not guaranteed.[30]

The lack of specification of the payoffs of equity investments sometimes leads inexperienced people to believe that equity comes for free! This is obviously wrong. To assess the cost of equity, you have to put yourself in the position of an institution that is analyzing the opportunity to invest in shares. This institution can either use an 'absolute' or 'relative' approach.

The absolute approach

When using an absolute approach to valuation, investors estimate the future cash flows that they will receive as a result of holding the share. These cash flows correspond to future dividends and selling price or, more simply, to all the future dividends up to eternity. Since any future selling price will necessarily be based on subsequent future dividends, you can simplify the problem and consider the flow of future dividends only. A number of models have been proposed that link the stock price, the expected return and the future dividends. The most famous among these models is the so-called 'Gordon model':

$S = D/(k - g)$ or $R = D/S + g$

Where: R = return required by the investor D = expected dividend next year
       S = current share price g = expected growth rate
       k = rate of return on shares

If you are:

● a shareholder, you estimate the dividends, you discount them with your required return and you decide if the price is right for you.
● a company, you look at the share price, try to guess what dividends are expected[31] by investors and infer the return they require. This is the cost of your equity.

The problem with this approach is that future dividends are very uncertain. It is why it is always a good idea to benchmark these absolute estimates with relative approaches.

The relative approach

The relative approach to valuation consists in comparing the opportunity to invest in equity with a well-specified opportunity: debt. Should equity return the same as debt, or less or more? How much more? This approach is described in the section below.

2.3 Equity necessarily costs more than debt

Investors are 'risk adverse'.[32] They want risky deals to promise more than a fair bet and they want their compensation to increase with the risk they take.

When they provide a firm with capital through a debt contract, investors exchange money today against the commitment of the firm to pay future amounts of interest and capital reimbursements. The amounts and the dates of these future payments are explicitly defined in the debt contract. As a result, investors know from the very first day what return they will get from their investment and this return will materialize whatever the perform-ance of the company – provided, however, that it does not encounter severe financial problems. Debt contracts put all the burden of risk on the borrower.

When they provide a firm with equity capital, investors can only estimate the return they will obtain. When investing in equity, investors exchange money today for the right to future dividends – and the rights attached to being the partial owners of the firm. Future dividends are basically uncertain and depend on the future performance of the firm. Equity enables companies and investors to share the burden of risk. In order to get out of the investment, investors need to sell their share at a price that is also unknown at the moment of the investment. Risk adverse investors are willing to provide equity capital only if equity is promising a higher expected return than debt.

There is a perfect symmetry between the position of the investors and the position of the companies that raise capital:

● Investors can either invest in debt, a lower risk–lower return investment, or in equity – a higher risk, higher return investment.
● Companies can either raise debt, a higher risk–lower cost financing, or equity – lower risk, higher cost financing.

The arguments above apply to expected returns. Studies of the past behaviour of capital markets[33] all show that there has been a substantial historical **equity premium**. We repro-duce in Table 2 data from *Stocks for the Long Run*, by J. Siegel.[34] They show that, in the USA:

● Equities have returned an average real return of 7% in the period 1802–1997.
● The average real return of long-term government bonds has been 3.5% over the same period but falling from 5% in the period 1802–70 to 2% in the period 1926–97.

This corresponds to an equity premium (equities minus government bonds) of 3.5% over the very long period (1802–1997) and of 6.4% since the Second World War. Comparable data can be found in Damodaran, who reports a 6.05% equity premium over the period 1928–99.[35]

With many authors, one cannot extrapolate these historical premiums into the future: historical premiums are affected by the survival bias[36] and this is especially true of the US markets which have not been exposed to all the shocks that many other countries

Table 2 ● Returns on equities, government bonds and government bills

Year	Equities		Long-term government bonds		Short-term government bills[3]		Inflation
	Return[1]	Risk[2]	Return	Risk	Return	Risk	
1802–1997	7.0	18.1	3.5	8.8	2.9	6.1	1.3
1802–1870	7.0	16.9	4.8	8.3	5.1	7.7	0.1
1871–1925	6.6	16.8	3.7	6.4	3.2	4.8	0.6
1926–1997	7.2	20.4	2.0	10.6	0.6	4.2	3.1
1946–1997	7.5	17.3	1.1	11.3	0.5	3.4	4.3
1966–1997	6.0	17.1	2.5	13.2	1.4	2.5	5.2
1966–1981	−0.4	18.7	−4.2	8.1	−0.2	2.1	7.0
1982–1997	12.8	13.2	9.6	13.6	2.9	1.9	3.4

1. Compounded return (compounded).
2. Standard deviation.
3. Short-term government bonds.
Source: Jeremy Siegel, Stocks for the Long Run.

have experienced. When it comes to 'forward-looking' estimates of the equity risk premium, it seems to be a general opinion that 6% is on the high side,[37] but then opinions differ![38]

Measuring the risk of stocks and portfolios – volatility
The standard procedure for measuring the risk of stocks and portfolios is to calculate their variances (VAR or σ^2) and standard deviations (σ). The volatility of a stock price is usually defined as the standard deviation of the return provided by the stock in one year when the return is expressed as continuous compounding. A spreadsheet model for estimating the volatility of a stock from historical data is in Table 3.[39]

A paradox: over the very long run, equity seems to be less risky than debt
One interesting thing to note is that the analysis of past performance shows that one cannot say that investments in equity are always more risky than investments in debt. For long holding periods – beyond 10 years – investments in equity have been less risky than investments in bonds. For example, J. Siegel[40] estimates that, between 1802 and 1997, the real holding period return of equities held for 10 years ranged between −4% and +17% vs. a −5% to 12% range for bonds. For 30-year holding periods the range was +3% to +11% for equities and −2% to +7% for bonds. When the holding period gets longer, the risk of stocks declines faster than predicted by the assumption that their returns would follow a random walk. This is a manifestation of the mean reversion of the equity returns, which also explains their remarkable stability over the long term. As opposed to this, the risk of bonds does not fall as fast as predicted by the random walk theory. This is a manifestation of the mean aversion of bonds returns.

Table 3 ● A spreadsheet model for assessing volatility

	A	B	C	D	E
1	Day	Price	Daily return		(Daily return – average)^2
2	0	157			
3	1	158	0.00635		0.0000000
4	2	163	0.03116		0.0006189
5	3	160	−0.01858		0.0006177
6	4	162	0.01242		0.0000378
7	5	170	0.04820		0.0017577
8	6	168	−0.01183		0.0003280
9	7	170	0.01183		0.0000309
10	8	167	−0.01780		0.0005799
11	9	164	−0.01813		0.0005956
12	10	164	0.00000		0.0000394
13	11	160	−0.02469		0.0009591
14	12	165	0.03077		0.0006000
15	13	168	0.01802		0.0001379
16	14	172	0.02353		0.0002977
17	15	175	0.01729		0.0001213
18	16	176	0.00570		0.0000003
19	17	176	0.00000		0.0000394
20	18	176	0.00000		0.0000394
21	19	177	0.00567		0.0000004
22	20	178	0.00563		0.0000004
23					
24	Average return			0.006277	
25	Sum of (daily return-average)^2			0.006802	
26	Variance			0.000358	
27	Standard deviation (daily volatility)			0.018921	
28	Assuming there are 252 trading days per year, annual volatility				30%

Formulas

B2 to B22: data; C3 =LN(B3/B2); Copy; D24: =AVERAGE(C3:C22); E3: =(C3−$D$24)^2; Copy. D25: =SUM(E3.E22); D26: =D25/19 (number of returns minus 1); D27: =D26^.5; E28: =D27*252^.5

2.4 Diversification enables shareholders to get rid of a large part of the risk

As discussed in Chapter 5 (section 5.1), risk is not additive and risk cannot be analyzed in isolation. For shareholders, what counts is not the individual risk of each individual share but the contributions of each share to the total risk of their total portfolio. This was one of the ideas developed in 1952 by H. Markovitz in 'Portfolio selection',[41] the paper that was to be the foundation of the relationship between risk and return in modern finance.

As investors hold portfolios, they are able to suppress a large part of the risk of each individual share that they hold. As we have seen above, this part of the risk is called

In February 2003 Maurice Dulac, a French investor, wants to invest €10 000 on the Paris stock market. He considers the following three course of action:

1. Invest 10 000 in the shares of Alma
2. Invest 10 000 in the shares of Opera
3. Diversify and invest 5000 in Alma and 5000 in Opera

The analysis of Alma and Opera shows that even though they are totally different and completely independent from each other, the two companies have an identical risk profile.

Expected returns:

Alma	Oil price decreases	Oil price increases
New product A succeeds	30%	5%
New product A fails	10%	−15%

Opera	Oil price decreases	Oil price increases
New product X succeeds	30%	5%
New product X fails	10%	−15%

The probability of an oil price decrease is 50% – Alma and Opera are equally exposed to a change in oil price. At Alma, the chance that product A succeeds is 60%. At Opera, the chance that product X succeeds is 60%. The success or failure of products A and X is independent.

Figure 1 Diversification: the issue

'specific risk' or 'idiosyncratic risk'. It is obviously not compensated for in a competitive market. The example in Figures 1, 2 and 3 and Table 4 helps to illustrate the impact of diversification:

● investing in either Alma or Opera generates an expected return of 9.5%, with a standard deviation of 16% (see Table 4);
● sharing the investment between Alma and Opera generates the same 9.5% return but reduces the standard deviation to 14%.

The risk of the combined portfolio of Alma (A) and Opera (O) can be estimated by its variance:

$$VAR(aA + bO) = a^2\ VAR(A) + b^2\ VAR(O) + 2\ ab\ COV\ (A, O)$$

$$VAR(\tfrac{1}{2}A + \tfrac{1}{2}O) = 0.25\ VAR(A) + 0.25\ VAR(O) + 0.5\ COV\ (A, O)$$

$$= 0.25 \times 0.0252 + 0.25 \times 0.0252 + 0.5 \times 0.0156 = 0.0204$$

Alma and Opera are partly correlated: they similarly respond to changes in oil prices. What is the impact of this correlation?

Table 4 • Diversification: the spreadsheet model

	A	B	C	D	E	F	G	H	I	J	K
1	Oil price	INC	INC	INC	INC	DEC	DEC	DEC	DEC		
2	*Probabilities*	0.5	0.5	0.5	0.5	0.5	0.5	0.5	0.5		
3	Alma	npS	npS	npF	npF	npS	npS	npF	npF		
4	Return Alma	5%	5%	-15%	-15%	30%	30%	10%	10%		
5	*Probabilities*	0.6	0.6	0.4	0.4	0.6	0.6	0.4	0.4		
6	Opera	npS	npF	npS	npF	npS	npF	npS	npF		
7	Return Opera	5%	-15%	5%	-15%	30%	10%	30%	10%		
8	*Probabilities*	0.6	0.4	0.6	0.4	0.6	0.4	0.6	0.4		
9	Return Alma + Opera	5%	-5%	-5%	-15%	30%	20%	20%	10%		
10	*Probabilities*	0.18	0.12	0.12	0.08	0.18	0.12	0.12	0.08		
11	**ALMA**										
12	Return×probability	0.02		-0.03		0.09		0.02		Expected return	9.50%
13	(Return- e.v.)^2×probability	0.00		0.01		0.01		0.00		Variance	0.0252
14										Standard deviation	15.88%
15	**OPERA**										
16	Return×probability	0.02	-0.03			0.09	0.02			Expected return	9.50%
17	(Return- e.v.)^2×probability	0.00	0.01			0.01	0.00			Variance	0.0252
18										Standard deviation	15.88%
19	**ALMA + OPERA**										
20	Return×probability	0.01	-0.01	-0.01	-0.01	0.05	0.02	0.02	0.01	Expected return	9.50%
21	(Return- e.v.)^2×probability	0.00	0.00	0.00	0.00	0.01	0.00	0.00	0.00	Variance	0.0204
22										Standard deviation	14.29%
23	Deviations from expected value										
24	Alma	-5%	-5%	-25%	-25%	21%	21%	1%	1%	Covariance	0.0156
25	Opera	-5%	-25%	-5%	-25%	21%	1%	21%	1%	Correlation coeff.	0.62
26	Dev Alma×Dev Opera×prob	0.00	0.00	0.00	0.00	0.00	0.00	0.00	0.00		

Background

```
B2,B4,D4,H4,B5,B7,C7,F7,G7,B8:data
C2: =B2; Copy to D2.E2;
F2: =1-B2; Copy to G2.I2
C4: =B4; E4: =D4; G4: =F4; I4: =H4
C5: =B5; D5: =1-B5; E5: =1-C5;
F5: =B5; Copy to G5.I5
D7: =B7; E7: =C7; H7: =F7; I7: =G7
C8: =1-B8; D8: =B8; E8: =C8; F8: =B8;
G8: =C8; Copy to H.I
B9: =(B4+B7)/2. Copy
B10: =B2*B5*B8; Copy
B12: =B4*B5*B2; Copy in D,F,H

B13: =(B4-$k$12)^2*B5*B2; Copy in D,F,H
B16: =B7*B8*B2; Copy in C,F,G
B17: =(B7-$k$16)^2*B8*B2 Copy in C,F,G
B20: =B9*B10; Copy
B21: =(B9-$k$20)^2*b10; Copy
B24: =(B4-$k$12);
B25: =(B7-$k$16)
B26: =B24*B25*B10
K12: =SUM(B12.I12); Copy to 13,16,17,20,21
K14: =K13^(1/2); Copy to 18 and 22
K24: =SUM(B26.I26)
K25: =K24/(K14*k18)
```

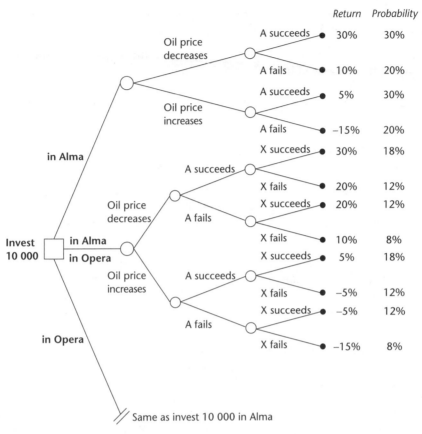

Figure 2 Diversification: the decision tree

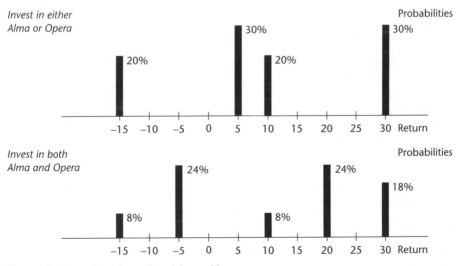

Figure 3 Diversification: the risk profiles

- Without this correlation, the variance of the portfolio would have been cut by 50%.
- With this correlation it is cut by 19% only.

By buying a large number of equities, shareholders can diversify the risk specific to each equity (such as the risk linked here to the launching of new products by Alma and Opera). However, they cannot diversify the part of the risk that corresponds to the correlation factor. This market or system risk is the only part of the risk that is compensated for by a higher return.

Does it matter whether companies manage risk and hedge?
According to the logic of diversification, risk is either specific or systematic:

- Specific risk does not matter for shareholders: there is no need for the management of companies to attempt to manage or hedge that risk.
- Systematic risk matters for shareholders but they can manage this risk by themselves: there is no need either for companies to manage or hedge this risk.

The rationale for managing risk comes from its indirect effects. Risk in itself is not a problem for diversified investors: uninsured losses are actually spread across the capital market and across taxpayers as well! However risk has indirect effects that lower the value of the firm. In *Integrated Risk Management*,[42] N. Doherty lists the following main indirect effects:

- Tax burden: as higher levels of corporate earnings typically face higher tax rates, a volatile pattern of earnings results in higher taxes.
- Cost of bankruptcy and of financial distress.
- Crowding out of new investment by unhedged loss. After it suffers a loss of its assets, a firm needs funds both for replacing assets and investing in new assets. This may result in the company missing some valuable investment opportunities.
- Inefficiencies arising from managerial risk aversion: managers do not enjoy the benefits of diversification.

2.5 Expected return is a linear function of risk: expected return-beta models

There exist many models which try to describe how investors are rewarded for their patience (the risk-free rate) and their willingness to take risks (the risk premium). Most of these models share the same idea: investors who hold equity are rewarded by a risk premium that depends on the quantity of non-diversifiable risk – or beta – of the security they hold. The most famous of these models is the 'old' CAPM developed in the early 1960s by W. Sharpe, J. Lintner and J. Mossin.

The CAPM
We have shown in section 1.2 above the expected return – the non-diversifiable risk relationship stated by the CAPM:

$$E(i) = R_f + \beta_i (R_m - R_f).$$

Please refer to section 1.2 for the meaning of the variables. The relationship is also depicted in the graph in Figure 4. According to the CAPM:

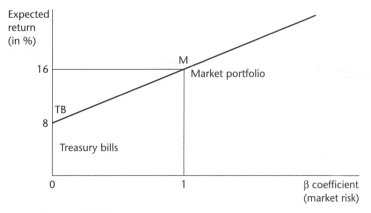

Figure 4 The security market line

- All individual securities are plotted on the RF-M security market line. The security market line describes the cost of capital for all companies, projects and business opportunities in a given economy at a specific date.
- As a result, estimating the cost of capital for evaluating a business opportunity is a matter of: (1) estimating the security market line, a general economic relationship that is valid for all companies and that can be obtained from a specialized financial services firm; and (2) estimating the beta coefficient of the business opportunity.

It has now been many years since the CAPM was declared dead[43] but it is still widely used to estimate cost of capital – probably because no good substitute has yet imposed itself. A number of authors have criticized the assumptions behind its construction[44] and, more importantly, a series of studies has revealed facts that contradict the predictions of the CAPM. One of the most disturbing facts is that while the CAPM predicts that beta is the only reason why expected returns differ, several studies have shown that other reasons also seem to matter. For example, E. Fama and K. French have shown that small companies' stocks perform substantially better than large companies' stocks, and that stocks with low ratios of market value to book value – value stocks – also perform much better than stocks with high market value to book value-growth stocks.

Consumption-based models
Consumption-based models are probably the most general of these models. They start from the idea that investors care for the volatility of their overall consumption. They are not concerned with the volatility of each of their individual assets, provided that they retain a steady rate of consumption. Assets whose payoffs co-vary positively with consumption are not very desirable: they pay off when they are already wealthy and they do badly when they are feeling poor. Only a high expected return might induce investors to buy such assets. On the contrary, assets whose payoff co-varies negatively with consumption are much more desirable and are bought even if they carry a low rate of return: insurance is an extreme case of such an asset. One of the models proposed by J. Cochrane in *Asset Pricing*[45] is:

$$E(R_i) = R_f + \beta_{i,m} \, \lambda_m$$

Where, $E(R_i)$ = expected return of security i

  R_f = risk-free rate

  $\beta_{i,m}$ = beta factor, the correlation coefficient of security i with m, the discount factor.
      This beta factor represents the quantity of risk in security i;

  λ_m = often called the price of risk, is a factor common to all securities that is determined by risk aversion and the volatility of consumption.

Even though not very much used yet in practice, consumption-based models have triggered the '**equity premium puzzle**' controversy. As shown by R. Mehra and E.C. Preston, the equity premiums observed in the past appear to be too high in relation to the volatility of consumption, given the typically assumed attitudes to risk.[46]

Arbitrage pricing theory (APT)

Formulated by Ross in 1976,[47] the APT model assumes that each security's return depends partly on events that are unique to that security and partly on pervasive macroeconomic factors. The fact that they respond in similar ways to macroeconomic factors result in the stocks being correlated and one can define a series of macroeconomic factors' betas. The formula is:

$$E(R) = R_f + {'}\beta_1 (R_{\text{factor 1}} - R_f) + \beta_2 (R_{\text{factor 2}} - R_f) + \ldots \text{etc.}$$

Where

  β_1, β_2, etc. = various beta coefficients
  $(R_{\text{factor 1}} - R_f)$, $(R_{\text{factor 2}} - R_f)$, etc. = expected risk premiums for the different factors

The APT does not say what the underlying macroeconomic factors are. Its only prediction is that, because of arbitrage, the relationship between expected returns and the various factor premiums should be linear (betas). An example of an APT model and its factors is given by Elton, Gruber and Mei.[48] Their six factors are:

● yield spread (return on long government bonds minus return on 30-day Treasury bills);
● interest rate (change in Treasury bill return);
● exchange rate (change in value of USD relative to a basket of currencies);
● real GNP (change in forecasts of real GNP);
● inflation (change in forecasts of inflation); and
● stock market return.

Factor models

The CAPM introduced the idea that risk can be segmented into index-related risk and residual risk. However, very few people would now use a single explanatory variable to model the risk of an asset. They would use instead more than one variable or factor. These models are sometimes classified into the following categories:[49]

● *Fundamental factor models*: these models use as factors the company or asset characteristics that, according to experts, explain the differences in asset returns: book-to-price value, market capitalization, recent performance, volatility, etc.

- *Macroeconomic factor models* that use macroeconomic variables as factors: industrial production, interest rates, investor confidence, etc.
- *Statistical factor models* which rely upon pure statistical analysis to identify the factors.

These models look very much like the APT model above. You can refer to Haugen[50] for an example of a factor model with five families of factors: risk factors, measures of cheapness, liquidity factors, measures of profitability and technical factors. Factor models are very much used for portfolio management but not really for estimating cost of capital.

2.6 Debt models look cheap but this may be an illusion

From a pure cost point of view, debt is cheaper: one could be tempted to use it in preference to other forms of financing. An analysis of the impact of using debt shows, however, that this would not be a very good idea.

The case with no corporation tax
As early as 1958, Modigliani and Miller demonstrated that, in the absence of corporate taxes, a company cannot achieve any advantage by using cheap debt. Shareholders who want to take a high level of risk – in order to achieve a higher return – can either buy the shares of highly indebted companies or buy the shares of all-equity financed companies and then finance this investment with borrowing. As a result, shareholders are indifferent to whether firms borrow or not. They merely require more return from levered firms – exactly the return they would achieve by borrowing themselves.

The leverage effect
Figure 5 shows the example of two identical companies with the same business activity, the same size and the same operating profitability. The two companies differ in one respect only: while Al Shirawi uses no debt, Al Kantara finances its assets with debt. Table 5 shows a model for estimating the return achieved by the two companies and their shareholders.
  Figure 5 displays the popular 'leverage' or 'gearing' effect:

- When the book return of assets is higher than the cost of debt, using debt increases the book return on equity, and the more the debt, the higher the return on equity.
- When the book return on assets is lower than the cost of debt, the effect is just the opposite: using debt decreases the book return on equity.

Table 5 also shows the position from the point of view of the shareholders, who can achieve the same results by themselves:

- They can invest in the all-equity company, leverage their investment and achieve the same return as an investment in the leveraged company.
- They can invest in the leveraged company, undo its leverage and achieve the same return as with an investment in the all-equity company.

Shareholders do not need companies to achieve the effects of leverage.

APPENDIX

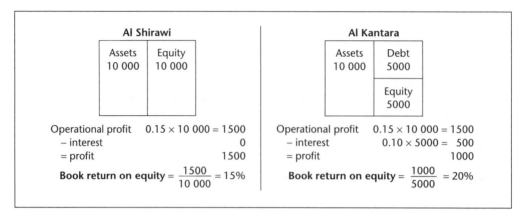

A suggestion: Construct a small spreadsheet model for comparing the return on equity of Al Shirawi and Al Kantara in various situations. Design your model in such a way that return on assets, interest rate and debt to equity ratio can easily be changed. Use your model to test:

1. What happens to the return of equity of Al Kantara when the return on assets is lower than the interest cost.
2. The impact of higher debt ratios when:
   (a) Return on assets is higher than interest.
   (b) Return on assets is lower than interest.

You can then compare your model with the one in Table 5 (rows 1 to 9).

Figure 5 The leverage effect

With the model in Table 5, you can check that using debt increases the risk or volatility of the return on equity:

● When the return on assets is 25%, then the return on equity of the all-equity company is also 25%, while the return on equity of the leveraged company jumps to 40%. When the return on assets is 6%, then the returns on equity are respectively 6% and 2%.
● You can also check this from the point of view of the shareholders: they experience the same volatility if they buy the shares of a leveraged company or buy the shares of an all-equity company and do their own home leverage.

Whatever companies do in terms of leverage, shareholders can easily achieve their own objectives. What are the consequences of this?

● Companies should not be able to create any additional value from the use of debt.
● Shareholders should not be sensitive to the increase in book return created by leverage. As they can easily achieve the same levered return at the price of additional risk, shareholders should adjust the return they require from leveraged companies in relation to the amount of debt these companies use. Shareholders should actually require from leveraged companies exactly the same return as they would get by borrowing themselves.

The effect of borrowing on the cost of equity and on the combined cost of any mix of equity and debts is shown in Figure 6. The combined cost of any mix of equity and debt remains consistent and equal to the cost of equity when the business is all-equity financed.

Table 5 ● Company, shareholders and leverage

A	B	C	D	E
1 Return on assets	0.15			
2 **COMPANY AL SHIRAWI**			**COMPANY AL KANTARA**	
3 Total assets	10 000		Total assets	10 000
4 Debt/equity ratio	0.0		Debt/equity ratio	1.0
5 Operational profit	1 500		Operational profit	1 500
6 Interest cost	0		Interest cost	500
7 Profit after interest	1 500		Profit after interest	1 000
8 Equity	10 000		Equity	5 000
9 **Return on equity**	0.15		**Return on equity**	0.20
10				
11 **SHAREHOLDER BAHRAIN HLDs**			**SHAREHOLDER MANAMA HLDs**	
12 Own equity investment	10 000		Own equity investment	5 000
13 Debt/own investment	1.0		Debt/own investment	0.0
14 Total equity investment	20 000		Total equity investment	5 000
15 Own debt investment	0		Own debt investment	5 000
16 Income from equity	3 000		Income from equity	1 000
17 Interest paid	1 000		Interest paid	0
18 Income from debt	0		Income from debt	500
19 Total income	2 000		Total income	1 500
20 **Return on own investment**	0.20		**Return on own investment**	0.15

Formulas
B1: 0.15
B3: 10 000
B4: 0
B5: +B3*B1
B6: +B4/(B4+1)*0.1*B3
B7: +B5−B6
B8: 1/(1+B4)*B3
B9: +B7/B8
B12: +B8
B13: 1
B14: (1+B13)*B12
B15: 0.0
B16: +B14*B9
B17: +B12*B13*0.1
B18: +B15*0.1
B19: +B16−B17+B18
B20: +B19/(B12+B15)

E3: +B3
E4: 1
E5: +E3*B1
E6: +E4/(E4+1)*0.1*E3
E7: +E5−E6
E8: +1/(1+E4)*E3
E9: +E7/E8
E12: +E8
E13: 0.0
E14: +(1+E13)*E12
E15: 5000
E16: +E14*E9
E17: +E12*E13*0.1
E18: +E15*0.1
E19: +E16−E17+E18
E20: +E19/(E12+E15)

The proportion of debt and equity in the total capital of a company is known as the **capital structure**. Using financial language, we can say that Table 5 shows that, in the absence of corporate taxes, the capital structure of a company does not seem to matter.

The consequence of borrowing on the cost of capital can also be shown within the framework of the CAPM. As shown in Figure 7, companies which use debt will increase

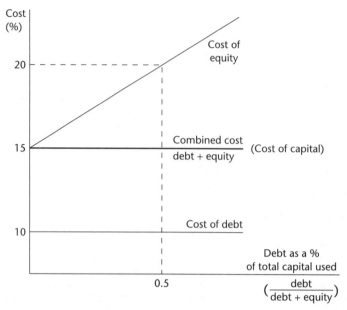

Figure 6 Impact of borrowing on the cost of capital

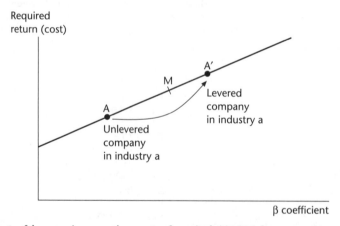

Figure 7 Impact of borrowing on the cost of capital (CAPM framework)

their beta, and the relationship between the beta of a levered company and the beta of the same company if all-equity financed is as follows:

$$\beta'_A = \beta_A + D/E \times (\beta_A - \beta_D)$$

Where

   β'_A = beta coefficient of the levered company
   β_A = beta of the unlevered company
   D = amount of debt used
   E = amount of equity used
   β_D = beta of debt

Table 6 • Impact of debt (without and with tax)

	No debt		Debt = 50% of total capital used	
No corporation tax	Cost of debt:	0.10	Cost of debt:	0.10
	Cost of equity:	0.15	Cost of equity:	0.20
	Aggregate cost:		Aggregate cost:	
	(equity cost)	0.15	$(0.5 \times 0.1) + (0.5 \times 0.2) =$	0.15
Corporation tax (50% rate)	Cost of debt:	0.10	Cost of debt:	0.10
	Cost of equity:	0.15	Cost of equity:	0.20
	Tax savings:	0.00	Tax savings: $0.5 \times (0.1 \times 0.5) =$	0.025
	Aggregate cost:	0.15	Aggregate cost: $0.15 - 0.025 =$	0.125*

* This is equal to either:

Cost of unlevered equity – tax savings: $0.15 - 0.025 = 0.125$

or to:

Weighted sum, of cost of equity and debt after tax: $0.5 \times 0.20 + 0.5 \times 0.05 = 0.125$

As most companies use some debt, observed betas are the result of both the risk of their business and the risk of their financing. As a result, you need to adjust observed betas before you can use them to estimate the cost of equity for a business opportunity.

The case with corporate taxes and other factors

Corporation tax exists in most countries and generally does not have a neutral effect on financing, since it treats the various sources of capital differently. In most countries, interest related to debt financing is tax deductible, whereas dividends related to equity financing are not.

When interest is tax deductible, debt financing suddenly becomes attractive to companies. Using debt enables companies to create an additional value equal to the present value of the tax savings created by the tax deductibility of interest charges. This is shown in Table 6.

An alternative way to describe the advantage of debt financing is to say that debt-induced tax shields reduce the combined cost of debt and equity – or cost of capital. This is shown in Table 6. The problem with this alternative method is that it is not correct because it wrongly assumes that returns are additive.

So, when corporation tax is considered, companies should theoretically borrow as much as they can. The issue is more complicated than this, however, because using debt also increases the chances of the company running into financial difficulties. As it commits the company to compulsory cash outflows in the future, borrowing reduces the company's operational flexibility. This may result in the loss of valuable opportunities, or, even worse, in payment difficulties. Ultimately, an excessive use of debt can result in bankruptcy. Consequently, the value of a firm that uses debt should be expressed as follows:

$$
\begin{array}{ccccc}
\text{Present value} & \text{Present value} & & \text{Present value} & \text{Present value of} \\
\text{of the levered} = & \text{if all-equity} & + & \text{of debt induced} & + \text{ cost of financial} \\
\text{firm (APV)} & \text{financed} & & \text{tax shields} & \text{inadequacy}
\end{array}
$$

Table 7 ● Assessing the impact of debt

Gamma is contemplating an investment in its usual and unique line of business. The expected after tax cash flows attached to this opportunity are (in €000):

2003	2004	2005	2006
−900	400	950	520

The unlevered cost of equity of Gamma is 15%. The corporate tax rate is 50%. Gamma believes that, if implemented, this opportunity will enable the company to borrow €569 000 at a rate of 10%. This borrowing will result in an annual interest payment of €56 900 which will itself cause an annual tax shield of 28 450 or 56 900 × 0.50.

As both the value of tax shields and of financial inadequacy increase with the quantity of debt used, this formula suggests the existence of an optimal capital structure – an intuitively appealing idea which is unfortunately not consistent with actual practices.

2.7 How should the APV be estimated in practice?

A typical situation involving financing is described in Table 7.

The most effective way to model the impact of the effects of financing is to estimate the adjusted present value (APV) of this opportunity:

- You start by assessing the net present value of the operational cash flows, using the unlevered cost of equity as the discount rate:

$$NPV = -900 + 400/1.15 + 950/1.15^2 + 520/1.15^3 = 508$$

- You then assess the present value of the tax shield, using the debt rate as the discount rate:

$$PV_{tax\ shields} = 56.9 \times 0.5(1/1.10 + 1/1.10^2 + 1/1.10^3) = 71$$

- You finally estimate the APV as the sum of the NPV of the project and the PV of the tax shields:

$$APV = NPV + PV_{tax\ shields} = 508 + 71 = 579$$

Note that there are a number of challenges involved in the estimation of the APV:

1. The first series of difficulties relates to the validity of attaching a debt to a project. For example, in Table 7, what makes Gamma believe that a debt of €569 000 is attached to the project?

   - Is there a specific debt opportunity tied to this project? This is the easiest case but, unfortunately, not the most common.
   - Is it an attempt to reflect the idea that this project is going to increase the debt capacity of the company? If this is the case, then some further questions arise. Does the amount of €569 000 actually reflect an intended capital structure? If so, how has this number been calculated: in relation to the amount initially invested (569/900)?

Or in relation to the value of the project (569/1408)? This becomes a very delicate issue that, in the first place, assumes the existence of a target capital structure – something that is not an obvious concept.

2. The second series of challenges relates to the rate that should be used. In the example above we have used the debt rate on the basis that the tax shields are certain. How sure can we be about this?

3. Finally, what about the present value of the costs of financial inadequacy? In general these costs are small and can be ignored.[51] It is what we do here.

2.8 Avoid using the WACC

A very popular alternative to calculating the APV is the weighted average cost of capital (WACC). The idea with the WACC is to say that the use of debt reduces the cost of capital (equity + debt). When using the WACC approach, you first estimate the cost of capital; then you discount the cash flows at this rate. Let us apply this approach to the situation described in Figure 7.

A formula for calculating the WACC:

$$\text{WACC} = \text{Cost of equity} \times E/(E+D) + \text{After-tax cost of debt} \times D/(E+D)$$

Where:

Cost of equity = cost of levered equity
E = equity
D = debt.

The cost of levered equity can be estimated as follows:

$$\frac{\text{cost of}}{\text{levered equity}} = \frac{\text{cost of}}{\text{unlevered equity}} + D/E \times \left(\frac{\text{cost of}}{\text{unlevered equity}} - \frac{\text{cost of}}{\text{debt}} \right)$$

One issue is the choice of values for equity and debt: should we use book values (the initial amounts) or the market values instead? It is generally recommended to use the market values. In the example in Table 7, the total market value of the project is 1408 and the debt 569. The debt to total capital ratio ($D/(D+E)$) is therefore 40%.

$$\text{Cost of levered equity} = 15\% + 0.4/(1-0.4) \times (15\% - 10\%) = 18.3\%$$

$$\text{WACC} = 18.3\% \times 60\% + 10\% \times 0.5 \times 40\% = 13\%$$

$$\text{NPV} = 558$$

This NPV is not equal to the APV (579), the main reason being that the WACC approach assumes that the debt ratio is kept constant over the life of the project, which is not true with the loan considered by Gamma. A reconciliation of the WACC and APV approaches is shown in Exhibit 2 on p. 532.

3 Background material on option valuation: from financial to real options

3.1 Financial options: what is an option?

An option is a contract between two parties in which:

- one party (the *holder* or *buyer*) is given the *right* – and not the obligation – to buy or sell an asset. This right has a price: the option price or *premium*.
- and the other party (the *writer* or *seller*) assumes the obligation to buy or sell that same underlying asset or underlying security at a certain price by a certain date. The price in the contract is known as the *exercise price* or *strike price*. The date in the contract is known as the *expiration date* or *maturity date*.

The two simplest forms of options (or *vanilla options*) are *calls* and *puts*:

- A call option gives the holder the right to buy (or to call away) the underlying security from the writer at a fixed price on or before a certain future date.
- A put option gives the holder the right to sell to (or to put to) the writer the underlying security at a fixed price on or before a certain date.

Puts and calls can be European, American or Bermudan: *European* options can be exercised at expiry only; *American* options can be exercised any time before expiry; and *Bermudan* options can be exercised at specific dates or in specific periods during their lives. The complete transaction between the writer and the holder of a European call and of a European put are described in Table 8.

Table 8 ● Transactions between the writer and the holder of an option

	European call	European put
The contract	Created on 1 June 2003 Underlying stock: 1 RTB share Price of the option: €1 Exercise date: 30 September 2003 Strike price: €10	Created on 1 June 2003 Underlying stock: 1 RTB share Price of the option: €0.9 Exercise date: 30 September 2003 Strike price: €10
On 1 June	The holder pays €1 to the writer in order to receive the call option contract	The holder pays €0.9 to the writer in order to receive the put option contract
On 30 September	The holder either: ● Does nothing, or ● Exercises the option. In this case the holder pays €10 (the strike price) to get 1 RTB share against the call option contract	The holder either: ● Does nothing, or ● Exercises the option. In this case the holder gets €10 (the strike price) for 1 RTB share against the put option contract

Options on financial instruments have been around for years but until 1973 it was not really possible to trade them. Since the creation of exchange-traded options by the Chicago Board of Exchange in 1973, options have experienced a dramatic growth. They are traded on many exchanges around the world and huge volumes are also traded over the counter by banks and financial institutions.

Options of very many different kinds are now available on a wide variety of financial instruments. Some options are also available on more than one asset: these are known as *rainbow* or *basket* options.

3.2 Value of options: payoffs at expiry

Calculating the value of an option is either very easy or very difficult, depending on when you want to do it: at expiry, it is very easy:

- The value of a call is either zero, if the stock price is lower than the exercise price, or equal to the difference between the stock price and the exercise price.
- Similarly, the value of a put is either zero if the stock price is higher than the exercise price, or equal to the difference between the exercise price and the stock price.

Figure 8 shows the values at expiry for six investment strategies:

- Buy and write a call.
- Buy and write a put.
- Buy and sell the underlying security (stock).

It is interesting to compare the payoff diagrams for the options and the stock. Contrary to the payoff diagrams for the share, the payoff diagrams for the options have a kink that reflects the fact that they are contingent on a future decision: the decision whether or not to exercise the option. Options create unique opportunities for managing risk:

- Options create asymetric exposures to risk. When buying a call, you put yourself in the position either to make an unlimited gain if the stock price exceeds the strike price or to lose – almost[52] – nothing. When buying a put, you put yourself in the position either to gain if the stock price falls below the strike price or, again, to lose almost nothing. On the other hand, when writing a call you put yourself in the position to gain little while taking a huge risk: writing calls with a high exercise price may give you the feeling that you can 'easily' win the premium, but beware!
- Combining the underlying asset with various proportions of various options, enables you to build portfolios that have your desired level of risk. This includes the possibility of building portfolios that have no risk ('risk-free' portfolios). Figure 9 shows the payoffs of some portfolios combining options and the underlying asset.

3.3 Value of options during their lives: a one-step binomial model

In-the-money, out-of-the-money and at-the-money

An in-the-money option is an option that would lead to a positive cash flow to the holder if it were exercised immediately. Similarly, an at-the-money option would lead to a zero cash flow and an out-of-the-money option would lead to a negative cash flow. A call is in

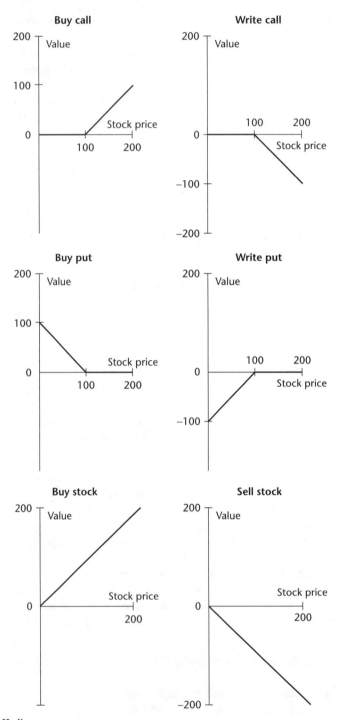

Figure 8 Payoff diagrams

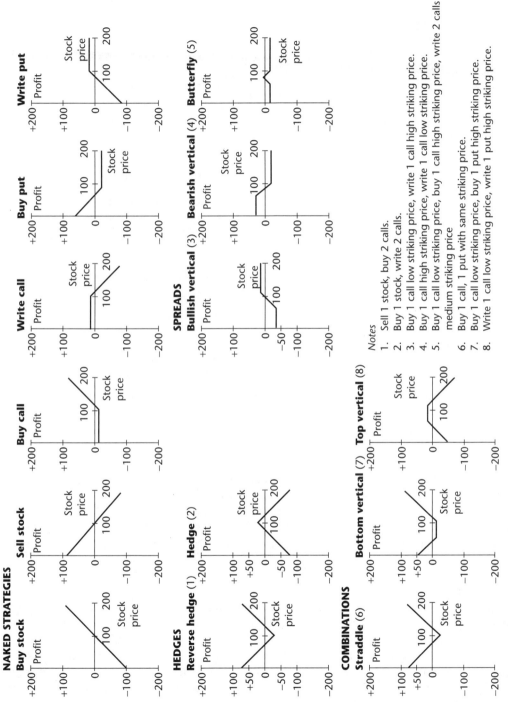

Figure 9 Payoffs of various portfolios of options and the underlying asset

Notes
1. Sell 1 stock, buy 2 calls.
2. Buy 1 stock, write 2 calls.
3. Buy 1 call low striking price, write 1 call high striking price.
4. Buy 1 call high striking price, write 1 call low striking price.
5. Buy 1 call low striking price, buy 1 call high striking price, write 2 calls medium striking price
6. Buy 1 call, 1 put with same striking price.
7. Buy 1 call low striking price, buy 1 put high striking price.
8. Write 1 call low striking price, write 1 put high striking price.

APPENDIX

What is the value of:

- a one-year European call written on a non-paying dividend stock that has a €10 exercise price?
- a one-year European put written on the same stock and also with a €10 exercise price?

The current value of the stock is €10. We are in a binomial world in which the stock can only tick up and take a value of 14 or tick down and take a value of 6. The risk-free rate is 4%.

Figure 10 A one-step binomial example

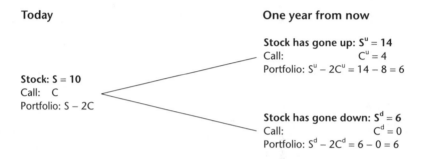

Today

One year from now

Stock: S = 10
Call: C
Portfolio: S − 2C

Stock has gone up: $S^u = 14$
Call: $C^u = 4$
Portfolio: $S^u − 2C^u = 14 − 8 = 6$

Stock has gone down: $S^d = 6$
Call: $C^d = 0$
Portfolio: $S^d − 2C^d = 6 − 0 = 6$

Notes:
According to the binomial assumption, the stock can only take two values: $S^u = 14$ or $S^d = 6$
Consequently the call can also take two values: $C^u = 4$ or $C^d = 0$
The number of calls, n, to be bought in order to build the riskless hedge can be calculated with the formula:

$n = (S^u − S^d)/(C^u − C^d) = (14 − 6)/(2 − 0) = 2$

This formula is obtained by expressing that the portfolio has the same value whatever the value of the stock:

$S^u − nC^u = S^d − nC^d$

Figure 11 A riskless portfolio for valuing a call

the money when the stock price is higher than the exercise price. A put is in the money when the stock price is lower than the exercise price.

The **intrinsic value** of an option is the maximum of zero and the value it would have if exercised now. An in-the-money American option that is not exercised has a value higher than its intrinsic value: its value is equal to the sum of its intrinsic value and of its **time value**.

Valuing a call

A simple one-step binomial example is in Figure 10. The general approach for pricing options is to use the fact that they enable us to build a portfolio with the level of risk we want and in particular portfolios with no risk – or *riskless hedges*. In the example above, 'buying one stock and writing two calls' is a riskless investment. As shown in Figure 11, the payoff is €6, whatever the value of the stock (only two values, 6 or 14, are possible for the stock). The next step is to realize that since it is risk free this investment can only return the risk-free rate (4%). This enables you to calculate the value of the call:

If C = value of the call: $10 − 2C = 6/1.04 = 5.77$ and $C = 2.12$

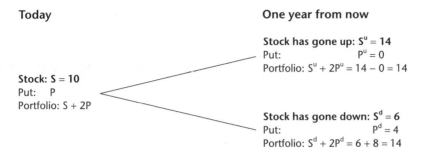

Today

Stock: S = 10
Put: P
Portfolio: S + 2P

One year from now

Stock has gone up: $S^u = 14$
Put: $P^u = 0$
Portfolio: $S^u + 2P^u = 14 - 0 = 14$

Stock has gone down: $S^d = 6$
Put: $P^d = 4$
Portfolio: $S^d + 2P^d = 6 + 8 = 14$

Notes:
According to the binomial assumption, the stock can only take two values: $S^u = 14$ or $S^d = 6$
Consequently the call can also only take two values: $P^u = 4$ or $P^d = 0$
The formula for n:

$n = (S^u - S^d)/(P^d - P^u)$

Figure 12 A riskless portfolio for valuing a put option

Valuing a put
We can use the same thinking for valuing a put. Figure 12 shows that 'buy one stock and buy two puts' is a risk-free investment that returns 14, whatever the value of the stock (6 or 14). Once again this investment should return the risk-free rate which enables us to value the put:

If P = value of the put: $10 + 2P = 14/1.04 = 13.46$ and P = 1.73

Put–call parity
If we buy one stock, buy one put and write one call, we again get an investment that always returns the exercise price 10.

● When the price of the stock is 14, the put is worth 0, write one call is worth −4 and the portfolio is worth 10.
● When the price of the stock is 6, the put is worth 4, write one call 0 and the portfolio 10.

This investment should again return the risk-free rate:

$S + P - C = K/(1 + R_f)$

Where,

S = stock price   K = exercise price
P = price of the put R_f = risk-free rate
C = price of the call

This formula can be generalized to more than one period:

$S + P - C = K/(1 + R_f)^T$

Where,

T = number of periods

The difference between the price of the call and the price of the put is:

$$C - P = S - K/(1 + R_f)^T \text{ or in continuous time: } C - P = S - Ke - R_fT$$

This assumes the options are European, and that the put and the call are on the same stock and have the same exercise price and date of expiry.

3.4 Value of options: using the one-step binomial model to understand what drives the value of an option

We can use the simple example in Figure 10 to simulate the impact of three key drivers on the value of an option.

1 *The risk of the stock increases the value of the option.* What if the value of the stock at expiration were either 2 or 18 instead of 6 or 14? After having checked that the portfolios 'buy one stock and writes two calls' and 'buy one stock and buy two puts' are still riskless,[53] let us use the same formulas for assessing the value of the call and the put. The new values are given by:

$$10 - 2C = 2/1.04 \quad \text{which leads to C} = 4.04 \text{ vs. } 2.12$$
$$10 + 2P = 18/1.04 \quad \text{which leads to P} = 3.65 \text{ vs. } 1.73$$

The value of a call and of a put increases with risk: when you can manage risk and avoid its downside, then risk becomes an opportunity and the higher it is the more value you can create out of it.

In spite of its simplicity, our example also shows one very important result when it comes to the risk of the underlying asset: **what counts is the range – or volatility, not the probabilities and the expected return**. We have not used these probabilities and expected returns, and generally they do not impact on the price of the option. This is shown in Figure 13.

2 *Interest rate.* What if the interest rate were 10% instead of 4%? The new values of the call and the put are given by:

$$10 - 2C = 6/1.1 \quad \text{which leads to C} = 2.27 \text{ vs. } 2.12$$
$$10 + 2P = 14/1.1 \quad \text{which leads to P} = 1.36 \text{ vs. } 1.73$$

An increase in interest rate increases the value of the call and decreases the value of the put.

3 *Exercise price.* What if the exercise price were 12 instead of 10? This requires new compositions for the portfolios: we now need to buy one share and write four calls and to buy three shares and four puts to achieve the riskless portfolios.[54] The new values of the call and the put are given by:

$$10 - 4C = 6/1.04 \quad \text{which leads to C} = 1.16 \text{ vs. } 2.12$$
$$30 + 4P = 42/1.04 \quad \text{which leads to P} = 2.60 \text{ vs. } 1.73$$

When the exercise price increases in relation to the stock price, then the value of the call decreases and the value of the put increases.

In Figures 11 and 12, we have valued options by referring to the volatility – or range of variation – of the stock (between €6 and €14) but not to the probabilities of the stock taking these two values. Why is it that these probabilities do not matter?

Let us assume two possible situations:

Situation 1: the probability of the stock reaching a value of €14 is 70%
Situation 2: the probability of the stock reaching a value of €14 is 80%

Let us value the same call option with a €10 exercise price in these two situations, using the same approach as used throughout the book, i.e. using genuine probabilities.

Situation 1	Situation 2
• The expected return from the stock is equal to: $40\% \times 70\% - 40\% \times 30\% = 16\%$	• The expected return from the stock is equal to: $40\% \times 80\% - 40\% \times 20\% = 24\%$
• The expected return from the option is equal to: $(4 - C)/C \times 70\% + (0 - C)/C \times 30\% = ((4 \times 70\%) - C)/C$	• The expected return from the option is equal to: $(4 - C)/C \times 80\% + (0 - C)/C \times 20\% = ((4 \times 80\%) - C)/C$
• Let us now estimate the beta of the option[1] in relation to the stock. $\beta_0 = ((4 - C)/C - (-1))/(40\% - (-40\%)) = 5/C$	• Let us now estimate the beta of the option in relation to the stock: $\beta_0 = ((4 - C)/C - (-1))/(40\% - (-40\%)) = 5/C$
• This enables us to estimate the return required from the option: $R = 5/C \times (16\% - 4\%) + 4\% = 32\%$	• This enables us to estimate the return required from the option: $R = 5/C \times (24\% - 4\%) + 4\% = 51\%$
• This also enables us to calculate the value of the option: $C = 4 \times 70\%/(1 + 32\%) = 2.12$	• This also enables us to calculate the value of the option: $C = 4 \times 80\%/(1 + 51\%) = 2.12$

Whatever the probability of the high (14) and low (6) values of the stock, we get the same value for the option – the same value as the one we calculated earlier with the 'risk neutral probabilities'. When the high value of the stock is more likely, then the expected return of the stock is higher. It follows that the risk of the investment in stock is higher and that the risk of the option is also higher. As a consequence, the outcome of the option has to be discounted at a higher rate that exactly offsets the benefit of the higher probability.

What counts for the valuation of an option is the volatility – or range of variation of the underlying asset. The probabilities of the underlying asset reaching these values, and as a consequence the expected return on the underlying asset, do not matter.

Note
1. The beta of the option is equal to the difference in the option's excess returns, given the stock's excess returns divided by the difference in the stock's excess returns. Refer to M. Kritzman (2000), *Puzzles in Finance: Six practical problems and their remarkable solutions.* John Wiley.

Figure 13 The expected return on the underlying asset does not impact on the value of the option

3.5 Value of options: binomial tree and risk-neutral evaluation

This generalizes the construction of a riskless portfolio and introduces risk-neutral probabilities.

Figure 14 describes the payoffs for a stock and a call option on this stock. As in section 3.4, the stock and the option can take two values only.

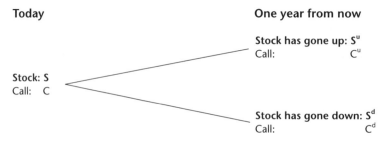

Figure 14 The payoffs for a stock and a call option on this stock

The first step is to determine the composition of the riskless investment. Let us assume that this consists of investing in n stocks and writing one call. In order to be riskless the portfolio should have the same payoff in the two possible situations:

$$S^u - nC^u = S^d - nS^d$$

Where,

n = number of calls written
S = value of the stock today; S^u its value if it goes up; S^d its value if it goes down
C = value of the call today; C^u its value if it goes up; C^d its value if it goes down

This is equivalent to:

(a) $n = (S^u - S^d)/(C^u - C^d)$

If $S^u = Su$ and $S^d = Sd$, with u = coefficient up and d = coefficient down, then (a) becomes:

$$n = S(u - d)/(C^u - C^d)$$

The second step is to show that the portfolio earns the risk-free rate. Let us assume that the portfolio earns the risk-free rate:

$$S - nC = (S^u - nC^u)/(1 + R_f)$$

When you replace n with its value in equation (a) and simplify, you find:

(b) $C = (C^u p + C^d(1 - p))/(1 + R_f)$ where $p = (1 + r - d)/(u - d)$

An equivalent alternative to these two steps is to find out the composition of a '**tracking portfolio**' consisting of buying N shares and of borrowing against them an amount of B dollars at the risk-free rate so that this portfolio would exactly replicate the future payoffs of the option. This is the idea of constructing a synthetic or 'home-made' equivalent to the option, composed of assets of which we know the value. This alternative leads to the same results (N = 1/n) and N is known as the option's **delta hedge ratio**.

The final step is to introduce 'risk-neutral' probabilities. Equation (b) looks familiar to people who are used to estimating an expected value based on probabilities . . . This is why people used the term 'probabilities'. This term is misleading, however, since p and $1 - p$ do not reflect the actual probabilities; p and $p - 1$ are just coefficients that help you to express the fact that, since you have built a riskless investment, the return is equal to the risk-free rate. This is where 'risk neutral' comes from. For the purpose of calculations, these coefficients work the same way as probabilities.

Let us check that we get the same results as in section 3.3:

$C^u = 4$; $u = 1.4$; $d = 0.6$; $R_f = 0.04$
$p = (1 + 0.4 - 0.6)/(1.4 - 0.6) = 0.55$
$C = 4 \times 0.55/1.04 = 2.12$

u, d, volatility and risk-neutral probabilities

When constructing a binomial tree, it is important to select values of u and d that correspond to the volatility of the stocks. These values are:

$u = e^{\sigma \sqrt{t}}$
$d = e^{-\sigma \sqrt{t}}$ and
$u = 1/d$

where t = length of time corresponding to one binomial step and σ = volatility.

An example: The volatility of a stock is 30% per annum and we want to construct a binomial tree with one-month steps. In this case, t = 1/12 and the formula for Excel is as follows:

u: =exp $(0.4 * (1/12)^{0.5}) = 1.09$

The value of the risk-neutral probability is obtained with the formula:

$p = (e^{rt} - d)/(u - d)$

In the example above, assuming that the interest-free rate is 4%, then the risk neutral probability is equal to: $(1.0033 - 0.9170)/(1.0905 - 0.9170) = 0.498$

3.6 Option price: several steps binomial trees

When using binomial trees in practice, typically the life of the option would be divided into 30 or more time steps. In each time step one assumes a binomial stock price movement (up or down). In order to give you a taste of the process, we display a four-step binomial tree in Table 9. The 'mechanics' are very much the same as in the decision tree:

1. You evaluate the stock prices at each node.
2. You evaluate the option price at each node.
3. You indicate the risk-neutral probabilities.
4. You fold back.

The meaning of N – Delta and of the Greeks

Greek letters are used to measure the different dimensions of the risk involved in option positions: managing these risks – or 'managing the Greeks' – is essential for traders in options.

The *delta* of a stock option – or a portfolio of options – is the ratio of the change in price of the option to the change of price of the underlying stock. It is the number of units of the stock we should hold for each unit of the option written: this is N.[55] The construction of a riskless hedge is called delta hedging.

Table 9 ● A four-step binomial process

This is a spreadsheet for evaluating an American put on a non-dividend-paying stock. The option has a 4-month maturity and is analyzed according to a 4 × one-month steps binomial process. Other data: stock price today: €10, exercise price 10. Annual volatility of the stock: 30%. Risk-free rate: 4%.

	A	B	C	D	E	F	G
1	Stock price today	10					
2	Strike price	10					
3	Risk free rate	4%					
4	Δt (I month)	0.083333					
5	Volatility	30%					
6	**Step 1**: evaluation of the stock price at each node:						
7	u =	1.090463		d =	0.917042		
8	**Step 2**: evaluation of the option prices at the final nodes (month 4)						
9	**Step 3**: evaluation of the probabilities and folding back (month 3, then month 2, then month 1, then now)						
10	The option prices at a node are equal to the present value of the prices at the subsequent node – weighted by the neutral probabilities						
11	p =	0.497616		1 − p =	0.502384		
12	*Time*	*0*	*1*	*2*	*3*	*4*	
13						14.14	
14						*0.00*	
15					12.97		
16					*0.00*		
17				11.89		11.89	
18				*0.00*		*0.00*	
19			10.90		10.90		
20			*0.20*		*0.00*		
21		10.00		10.00		10.00	
22		*0.58*		*0.40*		*0.00*	
23			9.17		9.17		
24			*0.96*		*0.80*		
25				8.41		8.41	
26				*1.52*		*1.59*	
27					7.71		
28					*2.25*		
29						7.07	
30						*2.93*	

Formulas

B4(Δt): =1/12
B7(u): = EXP(B5*B4^0.5)
E7(d): = 1/B7
B11(p): = (EXP(B3*B4)–E7)/(B7–E7)
E11: = 1–b11
B21: =B1

C19: +B21*$B$7. Copy
C23: +B21*$E$7. Copy
F14: = IF(F13>$B$2,0,$B$2–F13). Copy
E16: =(F14*$B$11+F18*$E$11)*EXP(–$B$3*$B$4). Copy
    in columns E,D,C, and B

The other Greek letters measure the change of the option, or portfolio, value with respect to one specific risk – the change in value with respect to:

- The passage of time: *theta*
- The price of the underlying asset: *gamma*
- The volatility of the underlying asset: *vega*
- The interest rate: *rho*

3.7 Value of options – the Black and Scholes model

Published in 1973, this was the first exact model for evaluating options. The model is also based on the construction and evaluation of a riskless hedge.[56] One of the key results of the model is that the value of an option depends on six parameters only:

- Current stock price (S)
- Exercise price (K)
- Total risk – or volatility – of the stock (σ)
- Time to expiration (T)
- Risk-free interest rate (R_f)
- Dividend

The impact of the first five parameters (the stock is assumed to pay no dividend) on the value of a call and a put is shown in Figure 15. Black and Scholes' formula is as follows:

$$C = SN(d1) - Ke^{-rf\,T}\,N(d2)$$

Where:

$$d1 = (\ln(S/K) + R_f\,T)/\sigma T^{1/2} + \tfrac{1}{2}T^{1/2}$$
$$d2 = d1 - \sigma T^{1/2}$$

C = current value of the call
S = current value of the stock
$N(d)$ = probability that a normally distributed variable z will be less than or equal to d[57]
K = exercise price
T = time to expiration
R_f = risk-free rate (continuously compounded)
σ = volatility of the stock

Table 10 shows a spreadsheet of the Black and Scholes model.

3.8 What is a real option? Calculating the value of a real option

Many business situations can be described in option terms: option to defer commitment, option to expand, option to shut down temporarily, option to abandon, etc. In all these situations, options create flexibility and add value. Also, as we have seen with Eagle, there are situations where flexibility becomes the deciding factor: without the value of flexibility, Eagle would not be viable. The 'real option' approach aims to bring the language and methodologies of financial options into the operational and strategic decision-making process of business firms.

APPENDIX

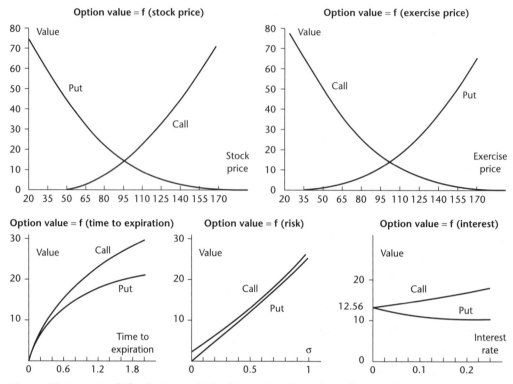

Figure 15 Impact of the factors which determine the value of an option

A definition
A real option can be defined[58] as the right, but not the obligation, to take an action (e.g. deferring, expanding, contracting, abandoning) at a predetermined cost called the exercise price, for a predetermined period of time – the life of the option. Figure 16 contrasts the characteristics of real and financial options.

Real options bear much resemblance to financial options: this explains the strong interest in trying to use knowledge of financial options in business decisions.

At the same time, real options have characteristics that make it difficult to directly use the financial options valuation approach. This is due in particular to the fact that business opportunities:

● are often unique, which makes it difficult to build riskless hedges;
● have a risk that depends on a large number of factors which cannot be easily described by a geometric Brownian process assumed by the binomial tree;
● generally correspond to very complex options.

These are the reasons why we still prefer the 'classical decision tree' method that is used throughout this book.

How to use the real option approach
Figure 17 describes two real option problems: an option to expand and an option to scale down. The solution to these problems is in Figure 18.

Table 10 • A spreadsheet model for using the Black and Scholes formula

	A	B	C	D	E	F	G
1							
2			Option Valuation Model				
3			(According to the Black-Scholes formula)				
4							
5							
6	PARAMETERS:						
7							
8							
9	CURRENT STOCK PRICE			100			
10	TIME TO EXPIRATION			0.4 (expressed in year)			
11	STRIKING PRICE			100			
12	VOLATILITY (standard deviation)			0.5			
13	RISK FREE RATE			0.05 (per year)			
14							
15							
16	RESULTS:						
17							
18	CURRENT VALUE OF CALL			13.45			
19	CURRENT VALUE OF PUT			11.52			
20							
21	CALCULATION OF D1 AND D2:						
22							
23	CALCULATION OF D1:						
24	D1 = D11/D12 + D13						
25	D11 = LN(STOCK PRICE/STRIKING PRICE) RISK FREE RATE * TIME TO EXPIRATION						
26	D11 =						0.02
27	D12 = VOLATILITY (standard deviation) * (TIME TO EXPIRATION)^0.5						
28	D12 =						0.316227
29	D13 = 1/2 * VOLATILITY (standard deviation) * (TIME TO EXPIRATION)^0.5						
30	D13 =						0.158113
31	D1 = D11/D12 + D13						0.221359
32							
33	CALCULATION OF D2:						
34	D2 = D1 − VOLATILITY (standard deviation) * (TIME TO EXPIRATION)^0.5						
35	D2 =						−0.09486
36							
37	POLYNOMIAL APPROXIMATION OF THE STANDARD NORMAL DISTRIBUTION FUNCTION:						
38							
39	CONSTANTS:						
40	B1	0.31938153	B4		−1.821255978		
41	B2	−0.356563782	B5		1.330274429		
42	B3	1.781477937	A		0.2316419		
43							
44			D1	D2			
45	z(D1 or D2)		0.221359	−0.09486			
46	Absolute value of z		0.221359	0.094868			
47	K = 1/(1 + A * z)		0.951224	0.978497			
48	N(absolute value of z)		0.587593	0.537790			

Table 10 continued

	A	B	C	D	E	F	G
49	N(z)		0.587593	0.462209			
50							
51	Value of call		13.45363				
52	Value of put		11.52095				

Width of columns: global, 9; B and E, 13.

Formulas
D9: 100
D10: 0.4
D11: 100
D12: 0.5
D13: 0.05
C18: +C51
C19: +C52
G26: =LN(D9/D11)+D13*D10
G28: +D12*(D10^0.5)
G30: 0.5*G28
G31: (G26/G28)+G30
G35: +G31−G28
B40: 0.31938153
E40: −1.821255978
B41: −0.356563782
E41: 1.330274429
B42: 1.781477937
E42: 0.2316419
C45: +G31
D45: +G35
C46: =ABS(C45)
D46: =ABS(D45)
C47: 1/(1+C46*$E$42)
D47: 1/(1+D46*$E$42)
C48: 1−(1/((2*pi)^0.5)*EXP(−(C46^2)/2)*($B$40*C47+($B$41*C47^2)+($B$42*C47^3)
+($E$40*C47^4)+($E$41*C47^5)))
D48: 1−(1/((2*pi())^0.5)*EXP(−(D46^2)/2)*($B$40*D47+($B$41*D47^2)+($B$42*D47^3)
+($E$40*D47^4)+($E$41*D47^5)))
C49: =IF(C45>0,C48,1−C48)
D49: =IF(D45>0,D48,1−D48)
C51: +D9*C49−EXP(− D13*D10)*D11*D49
C52: +C51−D9+(D11/(1+D13)^D10)

	Financial options	Real options
Similarities – focusing on the derivative on an underlying asset		
Underlying asset(s)	One or several financial assets: stock, currency, index, future contract, another option, etc.	One or several real assets: a project – Gatefield on page 100; a business – F on page 415; a new product – Eagle on page 355; etc.
The right to use time to make a better decision	Right to wait and right to buy an asset (call option); right to wait and right to sell (put); etc.	Right to wait and fix the price (Gatefield and F); right to wait and decide about the best ways to proceed with the different steps in Eagle; right to wait and invest; right to wait and adjust size or operating mode; etc.
Exercise price	The amount to be paid/to receive for the financial asset if the option is exercised.	The 'initial cash flow(s)': the value of the real asset is the value of all the cash flows except for the initial cash flow(s).
Differences and modelling challenges		
Asset specification	Financial assets exist before – and independently of – the derivative that is created. Financial assets are well specified and easily observable – they often have a history. They are, typically, widely traded.	Real assets are often created by the creator of the derivative at the same time he/she creates the derivative. Real assets are often unique and difficult to specify. They have no history. They are not easy to observe. They are typically not traded.
Modelling the risk of the asset	For the sake of option pricing, financial assets are typically assumed to behave according to a geometric Brownian motion process in which the uncertainty gets resolved continuously, and smoothly, over time.	For most real assets, uncertainty is resolved through critical events occurring at critical moments in time (results of a study, competitor's move, regulatory approval, etc.) when the value of the asset experiences sudden and dramatic changes[1].
Tracking portfolio	Relatively easy to build and to adjust (transaction costs may become a problem, however).	Difficult to build and to adjust in spite of the growing variety of financial instruments. Additional complications are created by cash payments – similar to the dividend for a financial asset, the need for cash infusions, convenience yield[2], the cost of holding, etc.
Modelling risk	The risk of model errors is not negligible[3].	The risk of model errors seems to be very great.

Notes

1. However, a number of authors make the assumption that the behaviour of financial assets can be modelled as the risk of financial assets. For the view that the changes in the present value of a project follow a random walk – regardless of the pattern of its cash flows, refer to: P. Samuelson (1965) 'Proof that properly anticipated prices fluctuate randomly', *Industrial Management Review*, Spring, pp. 41–9.
2. Convenience value arises from the ability to store a commodity and to sell it at will in the spot market.
3. In 'A calculus of risk', *Scientific American*, May 1998, pp. 70–5, G. Stix estimates the cumulative dollar figures for losses attributable to incorrect valuation of derivatives (modelling risk) to be 20% of all publicly disclosed losses on derivatives in the period 1987–97.

APPENDIX

Figure 16 Real vs. financial options

The management of RTM intends to assess the value of various options attached to a new project. This project, which requires an immediate investment of €72 million, may result in a value of either €94.50 million (with a 60% probability) or €51.80 million, one year from now. RTM has identified a 'twin security' for this project, i.e. a non-dividend paying stock that is perfectly correlated to the project. This stock has a value of €10 today. A year from now it is expected to have gone up to a value of €13.50 (u = 1.35) or to have gone down to a value of €7.40 (d = 0.74). The risk-free rate is 6%.

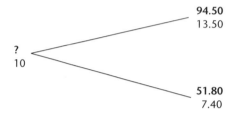

Estimation of the cost of capital (risk-adjusted rate)

The twin security enables us to estimate the required return
Required return = (13.5 × 60% + 7.40 × 40%)/10 − 1 = 10.6%

Value of the project without options (the 'decision tree approach')

Value = −72 + (94.50 + 60% + 51.80 × 40%)/(1 + 10.6%) = −72 + 70 = −2

Value of the project without options (the 'option/risk-neutral probabilities approach')
Risk-neutral probabilities:

p = (1 + 0.06 + 1.35)/(1.35 − 0.74) = 52.46%; 1 − p = 47.54%

Value = −72 + (94.50 × 52.46% + 51.80 × 47.54%)/(1 + 6%) = −72 + 70 = −2

When flexibility is not considered, the traditional 'decision tree approach' and the 'option/risk-neutral approaches' give exactly the same result.

What is the value of:
1. **The option to expand the project? In year 1, management has the option to double the size of the project and receive 94.5.**
2. **The option to scale down? The investment of 72 can be made in two steps: 42 million today and 31.80 million (30 × 1.06) one year from now. In the event of an unfavourable development, the second step of the investment can be abandoned at no cost.**

Figure 17 A real option problem

Comparing the decision tree approach and the real option approach
Figure 19 describes an option to defer a commitment of capital. The background data are the same as in Figure 17. Figure 20 contrasts the 'decision tree' approach with the 'real option' approach. An initial comment before looking at Figure 20: as shown in Figure 17, both approaches gives the same result when flexibility is ignored. In the absence of flexibility, both approaches tell us that the investment should not be undertaken. Now, when you look at Figure 20 you will realize that:

● both approaches use the same tree with very similar end points: the only difference in the value of end points is due to the different discount rates;

The value of an option to expand (growth option)

Drawing the tree and calculating the end points

-72.00

$94.50 - 70 + 94.50 = \mathbf{119.00}$

$\mathbf{51.80}$

Estimating the value of the option
If we use the risk-neutral probabilities estimated in Figure 17:

New value $= -72 + (119 \times 52.46\% + 51.80 \times 47.54\%)/(1 + 6\%) = 13.12$
Value without flexibility $= -2$
Value of option to expand $= 12.12 - (-2) = \mathbf{14.12}$

The value of an option to downsize

Drawing the tree and calculating the end points

-42.00

$94.50 - 31.80 = \mathbf{62.70}$

$\mathbf{51.80}$

Estimating the value of the option
Using the neutral probabilities estimated in Figure 17:

New value $= -42 + (62.70 \times 52.46\% + 51.80 \times 47.54\%)/(1 + 6\%) = 12.26$
Value without flexibility $= -2$
Value of option to expand $= 12.26 - (-2) = \mathbf{14.26}$

Figure 18 Evaluating an option to expand and an option to downsize

- a first major difference is in the probabilities: while the approach in the book uses the actual probabilities, the real option approach uses risk neutral probabilities;
- a second major difference is in the selection of the discount rate: while the approach in the book uses a risk-adjusted discount rate, the real option approach uses the risk-free rate.

You should, however, realize that both approaches give the same signal: flexibility is very valuable. They also tell us that we should take the same course of action: defer investing until we know more about the outcome of the project. The only difference in the two approaches is a 6%–7% disagreement on the value of flexibility.

APPENDIX

The situation is the same as in Figure 17

The management of RTM intends to assess the value of various options attached to a new project.

This project, which requires an immediate investment of €72 million, may result in a value of either €94.50 million (with a 60% probability) or €51.80 million, one year from now.

RTM has identified a 'twin security' for this project, i.e. a non-dividend paying stock that is perfectly correlated to the project. This stock has a value of €10 today. A year from now it is expected to have gone up to a value of €13.50 (u = 1.35) or to have gone down to a value of €7.40 (d = 0.74). The risk-free rate is 6%.

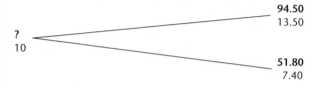

The cost of capital is 10.6% and the risk-neutral probabilities are 52.46% (up) and 47.54% (down). See Figure 17.

What is value of the option to defer investing by one year until we know which of the two possibilities (up or down) will materialise?

Figure 19 A real option problem: the value to defer commitment

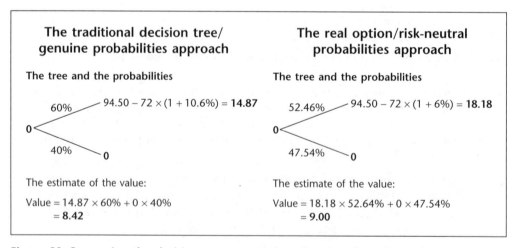

The traditional decision tree/ genuine probabilities approach	The real option/risk-neutral probabilities approach
The tree and the probabilities	The tree and the probabilities
60% ⟋ 94.50 − 72 × (1 + 10.6%) = **14.87** 0 ⟨ 40% ⟍ 0	52.46% ⟋ 94.50 − 72 × (1 + 6%) = **18.18** 0 ⟨ 47.54% ⟍ 0
The estimate of the value:	The estimate of the value:
Value = 14.87 × 60% + 0 × 40% = **8.42**	Value = 18.18 × 52.64% + 0 × 47.54% = **9.00**

Figure 20 Comparing the decision tree approach and real option approach

Notes

1. This is obviously not totally true. Shareholders and banks definitely trust some management teams more than others.
2. What are the unique responsibilities of the finance function?

   • To maintain an adequate system of information on the cash flows, the value creation process and the risks within the whole organization. Which units and projects generate cash excesses? Which ones generate cash needs? How do cash excesses compare with cash needs? Which are the expected future cash flows? What are the risks attached to these cash flows? And so on.
   • To manage the relationships with all the providers of capital, the providers of risk management instruments and all the agents in the capital markets in general. What are the solutions available? What are their benefits and costs? How can they be best used to create value?

   Please also refer to 'The role of the Chief Financial Officer in 2010' available on the website of the International Federation of Accountants, *www.ifac.org*
3. See for example: R. Haugen (1999) *The New Finance*, Prentice Hall.
4. A riskless asset is an asset with (a) no default risk – assets issued by government are normally, but not always, risk free; (b) no reinvestment rate risk: a zero coupon bond has no cash flows prior to maturity and consequently no reinvestment risk.
5. This is not the case with the Dow-Jones Index, which is price weighted (the index is established as the sum of the prices divided by the number of stocks in the index).
6. The beta of an asset i relative to a portfolio M is the ratio of the covariance between the return on the security and the portfolio to the variance of the portfolio: $Bi = cov(Ri,RM)/Var(RM)$.
7. One of the problems is that published betas are not readily usable as their value depends on the level of indebtedness of the company.
8. See E.F. Fama (1977) 'Risk-adjusted discount rates and capital budgeting under uncertainty', *Journal of Financial Economics*, August, pp. 3–24.
9. This obviously raises a number of interesting issues regarding the compensation of managers, e.g. shares vs. options. Refer to N. Doherty (2000) *Integrated Risk Management*, McGraw-Hill, pp. 214–21.
10. This probably means that managers should not overreact to diversifiable risk. This has implications for hedging.
11. Except for the transaction cost associated with raising external capital.
12. See M. Jensen (1989) 'The eclipse of the public corporation', *Harvard Business Review*, 67 (September–October), pp. 61–74.
13. This approach also violates the maximization rule. Lowering the cost of capital tends to result in acceptance of non-value creating projects.
14. The good news is that they are generally not. See S.C. Myers (1984) 'Finance theory and financial strategy', *Interfaces*, 14 (January–February), pp. 126–37.
15. *Investment Under Uncertainty* by A. Dixit and R. Pindyck. Princeton University Press, 1994.
16. *Real Options* by Lenos Trigeorgis. MIT Press, 1997.
17. A quick introduction is in Paul Wilmott (2000) *Paul Wilmott on Quantitative Finance*. John Wiley, Chapter 13, Vol 1. Refer also to J. Murphy (1999) *Technical Analysis of the Financial Markets*, New York Institute of Finance.
18. See P. Samuelson (1965) 'Proof that properly anticipated prices fluctuate randomly', *Industrial Management Review*, Spring, pp. 41–9.
19. Reproduced in *A Non-Random Walk Down Wall Street*, Princeton University Press, 1999, Chapter 2.
20. See J. Shiller (1989) *Market Volatility*, MIT Press, and R. Thaler, *The End of Behavioral Finance*, Association for Investment Management and Research, 1999.
21. See N. Barberis and R. Thaler, *A Survey of Behavioral Finance*, August 2001, on R. Thaler's website at the University of Chicago Graduate School of Business.
22. See K. French, 'Stock returns and the week-end effect', *Journal of Financial Economics* (March 1980).
23. See W. DeBondt and R. Thaler, 'Does the stock market overreact?', *Journal of Finance* (July 1985).
24. Investing in stocks with a low market value to book value ratio. See, for example: J. Lakonishok, A. Schleifer and R. Vishny, 'Contrarian investment extrapolation and risk', *Journal of Finance* (December 1994).

APPENDIX

25. See M. Cahart, 'On persistence in mutual funds performance', *Journal of Finance* (March 1997).
26. See for example how investors react to earnings announcements in R. La Porta, J. Lakonishok, A. Schliefer and R. Vishny, 'Good news for value stocks: further evidence of market efficiency', *Journal of Finance* (June 1997).
27. See for example: K. Ilinski (2001) *Physics of Finance*, John Wiley.
28. In *A Non-Random Walk Down Wall Street* (note 19).
29. See 'how to assess a financial lease' in Exhibit 1 to this Appendix.
30. The option to discontinue the investment is more problematic when you invest in a company that is not listed on the stock market.
31. Stock market analysts often make public what they expect from companies. This is what is called the 'consensus forecast'.
32. For more about risk aversion, see M. Rabin and R. Thaler, 'Risk Aversion', *Journal of Economic Perspectives*, 15, pp. 219–32 (Winter 2001).
33. The most widely-used database is from Ibbotson Associates (www.ibbotson.com). It has data going back to 1926. In *Stocks for the Long Run*, J. Siegel analyses data starting in 1802.
34. J. Siegel (1998) *Stocks for the Long Run*, McGraw-Hill.
35. A. Damodaran (2001) *The Dark Side of Valuation*, Prentice-Hall, p. 62. Damodaran reports equity risk premiums of 6.05% for the period 1928–99, of 5.36% for the period 1962–99 and 13.16% for the period 1990–99.
36. Think about comparing two random samples of people aged 65, one group of smokers, one of non-smokers. To assess the impact of smoking, you can track the health of each group going forward. In particular you can determine which group lives longer on average. Surprisingly enough, one study found it was the smokers! This is the impact of the survival bias. For the impact of the survival bias on the equity premium, refer to: S. Brown, W. Goetzmann and S. Ross 'Survival', *The Journal of Finance* (1995) 50(3), pp. 353–73.
37. In spite of the very high equity premiums experienced during the equity bubble of the late 1990s.
38. For a review of this issue, refer to B. Cornell (1999) *The Equity Risk Premium*, John Wiley.
39. For more about volatility, refer to: J. Hull (2000) *Options, Futures and Other Derivatives* (4th edn), Prentice-Hall, and to C. Alexander (1996) 'Volatility and correlation: measurement models and applications', in *Risk Management and Analysis*, C. Alexander (ed.) John Wiley.
40. See J. Siegel (1998) *Stocks for the Long Run*, McGraw-Hill, p. 17.
41. H. Markovitz (1952) 'Portfolio selection', *Journal of Finance*, 7 (March), pp. 77–91.
42. N. Doherty (2000) *Integrated Risk Management*, McGraw-Hill.
43. See for example A. Wallace, 'Is Beta Dead?', in *Institutional Investor* (July 1980) 14, pp. 22–30.
44. See for example R. Haugen (1999) *The Inefficient Stock Market*, Prentice Hall, pp. 15–20.
45. J. Cochrane (2001) *Asset pricing*; Princeton University Press.
46. R. Mehra and E.C. Preston (1985) 'The equity risk premium: a puzzle', *Journal of Monetary Economics*, 15, pp. 145–61.
47. S. Ross, 'The arbitrage theory of capital asset pricing', *Journal of Economic Theory* (December 1976) 13, pp. 341–60.
48. E. Elton, M. Gruber and J. Mei, 'Cost of capital using arbitrage pricing theory: A case study of nine New York utilities', *Financial Markets, Institutions and Instruments* (August 1994) 3, pp. 46–73.
49. S. Bekers (1998) 'A Survey of Risk Measurement Theory and Practice', pp. 39–60 in *Risk Management and Analysis*, Carol Alexander (ed.), John Wiley.
50. In *The Inefficient Stock Market*. See note 44.
51. For an estimation of bankruptcy costs, refer to J. Warner, 'Bankruptcy costs: some evidence', *Journal of Finance* (May 1977) 32, pp. 337–48.
52. The only loss is the premium – typically a small amount.
53. This is generally not the case: you have to recheck this and use the formula in Figure 19 for a call and in Figure 20 for a put.
54. For the call n = (14 − 6)/(2 − 0) = 4; for the put n = (14 − 6)/(6 − 0) = 4/3.
55. The delta of a call is positive and the delta of a put is negative.
56. At its limit, when the number of steps is large, the binomial model approaches Black and Scholes' model.

57. The meaning of N(d) can be illustrated with the density function of a normal distribution.

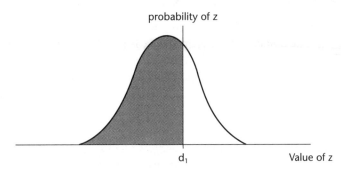

probability of z

d_1 Value of z

N(d_1) or the probability that z be equal to d_1 or less than d_1 is equal to the shaded surface below the curve. N(d) can be either estimated from tables or from the following polynomial approximation:

$$N(d) \approx 1 - (1/\sqrt{2\pi})e^{-d^2/2}(b_1k + b_2k^2 + b_3k^3 + b_4k^4 + b_5k^5)$$

where $b_1 = 0.31938153$ $b_4 = -1.821255978$ $k = 1/(1 + ad)$
$b_2 = -0.356563782$ $b_5 = 1.330274429$
$b_3 = 1.781477937$ $a = 0.2316419$

This calculation is valid for $d_1 > 0$. For $d_1 < 0$, the result is equal to 1 – the result of the above calculation for the absolute value of d_1.

58. This definition is borrowed from T. Copeland and V. Antikarov (2001) *Real Options*, Texere Publishing Limited.

APPENDIX

Exhibit 1 ● Assessing a financial lease

The literature of accounting and finance has devoted considerable attention to the issue of leasing. The objective of this appendix is limited to the definition of leasing, and the presentation of a spreadsheet model for assessing a financial lease. For more about leasing, refer to the references given at the end of this Further Model.

What is leasing?

A lease is a contract between the owner of an asset called the lessor and another party called the lessee who is given the right to use the asset against the promise to make a series of payments (the first payment being generally made as soon as the lease is initiated). Provisions of leasing contacts depend very much on the country in which you operate. In the USA, where leasing is well established since the mid-1960s, it is common to make a distinction between financial leases and operating leases.[1]

Financial leases

Even though there exist many varieties of financial leases, we can consider that, in general, financial leases have most of the following characteristics:

- Long-term contract between the lessee and the lessor. Generally, financial leases are concluded for most of, or all, the useful life of the asset. Consequently, total lease payments are close to the value of the asset.
- Non-cancellable contract.
- The lessee is responsible for maintenance, insurance and the payment of property taxes, if any (net lease as opposed to full-service lease).
- The lessee may acquire the full ownership of the asset at the end of the lease (strict transfer of property or bargain purchase option).

Contracting a financial lease is therefore very close to buying an asset and borrowing money from a bank. In most cases, leased assets are new ones. But it sometimes happens that firms sell an asset which they already own to another party and then lease it back from the buyer. This arrangement is called sale and lease back, as opposed to direct leasing. In some cases, the lessor borrows part of the price of the leased asset, using the lease contract as security for the loan. Such arrangements are called leveraged leases.

Operating leases

Operating leases are short term leases (the contract term is only a small fraction of the useful life of the asset). In general, they provide for both financing and other services (maintenance, insurance, property tax, etc.), and are cancellable during the contract at the option of the lessee. Vehicles, computers, copiers are among the assets commonly acquired through operating leases.

Accounting and tax issues

One dubious advantage of leasing is that it represents off balance sheet financing. Rentals are included in the income statement but neither the leased asset nor the lease obligation are shown in the balance sheet (though a footnote to the accounts indicates the existence of the lease). In many countries, and in particular in the USA (since 1976), this way to account for leases is only allowed for operating leases. For finance (or capital leases) the firm should explicitly show the lease in its assets and liabilities. In any case, it is somewhat naive to consider that external investors can be fooled by off balance sheet financing.

As far as tax is concerned, and even though this again very much depends on the country you operate in, it can be said in general that the lessor retains the tax benefit of ownership (depreciation, tax investment credit, etc.) whereas the lessee is entitled to deduct the lease rentals from its taxable income.

Leasing is not a miracle form of financing and as stated by Miller and Upton[2] 'The decision to lease or buy is neither a matter of indifference for the typical firm nor one for which any general presumption can be established a priori. Each case must be examined on its merit.'

An example of a financial lease

The Constructor Company has decided to execute a project which requires the use of a piece of equipment worth $125 000. Constructor has the option of entering the following financial lease scheme, rental fee is $22 500 to be paid from 2003 to 2008, maturity six years with no cancellation clause. The leasing company does not provide Constructor with any maintenance, insurance or tax property service (a net lease). Should Constructor buy the equipment, it would have to pay the asset cost in 2003, and would benefit from a tax credit equal to 10% of the value of the asset. If it owned the equipment, Constructor would be able to depreciate it over five years for 15%, 22%, 21%, 21%, and 21% of its depreciable value each year (the depreciable value being equal to the asset cost minus half of the investment tax credit taken). The tax rate is 46%. How can we approach this problem?[3]

1. The actual choice for Constructor is between leasing, or buying and borrowing. Prior to the financing decision Constructor has assessed that the project was worth being undertaken and the operational cash flows of the project did not depend on the financing solution. These operational cash flows can therefore be ignored in the lease vs. borrow analysis.
2. What are the differential cash flows of the solution lease vs. the solution buy and borrow?
   - Lease payment.
   - Equipment acquisition cost.
   - Loss of investment credit.
   - Loss of depreciation tax shield.

   These differential cash flows and the net differential cash flows are shown in the spreadsheet model presented in Table 11.
3. If we believe that financial leasing is a form of debt, then we can consider that the net differential cash flows are equivalent to the interest and repayment cash flows caused by a loan. Since the after tax interest rate to Constructor is 0.054, we can calculate the present value of a loan which would cause the same cash outflows as the net differential cash flows. Such a loan would be equivalent to the leasing proposal. As shown in Table 11, this present value is equal to $92 850.
4. The advantage of leasing over the equivalent loan can be calculated as the difference between the present value of the leasing ($92 160) and the present value of

Table 11 ● Evaluation of a financial lease: a spreadsheet model

A	B	C	D	E	F	G
1 PARAMETERS						
2 Capital outlay	125					
3 Tax credit rate	0.1					
4 Depreciation rates	0.15	0.22	0.21	0.21	0.21	
5 Tax rate	0.46					
6 Debt rate	0.1					
7 Annual lease fee	22.5					
8						
9 CALCULATIONS						
10 Years	2003	2004	2005	2006	2007	2008
11 Capital outlay	125.00					
12 Lease payment	22.50	22.50	22.50	22.50	22.50	22.50
13 Tax shield lease	10.35	10.35	10.35	10.35	10.35	10.35
14 Loss investment credit	12.50					
15 Loss tax shield depreciation	8.19	12.02	11.47	11.47	11.47	
16 DIFFERENTIAL CASH FLOWS	92.16	−24.17	−23.62	−23.62	−23.62	−12.15
17						
18 After tax interest rate	0.05					
19 PRESENT VALUE EQUIVALENT LOAN	92.85					
20 PRESENT VALUE LEASE	−0.69					

Background
  Width of columns: A30, global 7
  Format: fixed two decimals
  Range B2.G10: data
  Formulas:
    B11: +B2; B12: +$B$7 (to be copied across)
    B13: +B12*$B$5, (to be copied across)
    B14: +B2*B3
    B15: +($B$2−0.5*$B$2*$B$3)*B4*$B$5 (to be copied in the range C15.F15)
    B16: +B11−B12+B13−B14−B15 (to be copied across)
    B18: +B6*(1−B5)
    B19: −NPV(B18,C16.G16)
    B20: +B16−B19

the equivalent loan ($92 850). In the present case, leasing is not an attractive proposal.

What can make leasing a worthwhile solution? It is difficult to generalize but we may, however, say that: the potential advantage of leasing is not due to a miraculous financial or tax trick, but to the fact that in some cases companies are not in a position to take advantage of all tax subsidies available. In this case they may use the services of leasing companies which specialize in the maximum utilization of these subsidies, a maximum utilization which is in turn reflected in the rental rates. You can, for example, check that if Constructor plans not to pay tax (set the tax rate and the investment credit to zero), then the lease becomes a valuable proposal.

A final note

Until the recent development of option valuation theory, most of the literature concentrated on the analysis of valuation of financial, non-cancellable, leases. More recently, attention has shifted towards the analysis of operating leases and of their cancellable features.[4]

Notes

1. In the USA, the distinction between capital and operating leases has been defined by the Financial Accounting Standards Board (SFAS no. 13, Nov 1976). For more about accounting for leases in the USA, refer to J. Williams (2000) *2000 Miller GAAP Guide*, Harcourt Professional Publishing. For a discussion of some problems encountered with the distinction between capital and operating leases in the USA, refer to: Richard Dieter, 'Is lessee accounting working?' *The CPA Journal* (Aug 1979), pp. 13–15, 17–19.
2. M.N. Miller and C.W. Upton, 'Leasing, buying and the cost of capital services', *Journal of Finance* (June 1976), **31**: 761–86.
3. This lease valuation method is derived from: S.C. Myers, D.A. Dill and A.J. Bautista, 'Valuation of financial lease contracts, *Journal of Finance* (June 1976), **31**: 799–819, and from: J.R. Franks and S.D. Hodges, 'Valuation of financial lease contracts: a note', *Journal of Finance* (May 1978), **33**: 657–69. There are many proposed approaches for evaluating a financial lease contract. For a review, refer to: R Bower, 'Issues in lease financing', *Financial Management* (Winter 1973), pp. 25–33.
4. For an example of such an analysis, refer to J.J. McConnell and J.S. Schallheim, 'Valuation of asset leasing contracts', *Journal of Financial Economics* (1983), **12**: 237–61.

Exhibit 2 ● WACC and APV[1]

In order to help you understand the difficulties of using the WACC and the APV, we would like to invite you to build a spreadsheet model for calculating the NPV attached to a new project opportunity available to Gamma. The cash flows attached to this project are:

In €000	2004	2005	2006
Operational profit	500	1600	740
Depreciation	300	300	300
Operational profit before tax	200	1300	440
Profit after tax (50% rate)	100	650	220
CFE/CFO (no working capital needs)	400	950	520

Capital expenditures amount to 900 (to be made in 2003). There is no residual value. The risk adjusted cost of unlevered equity for such a project is 15%. Let us assume further that Gamma aims at a debt to total capital ratio of 39% (or debt to equity ratio of 64%), and thinks that the new project opportunity will sustain the same level of debt as the overall company. Consequently, it considers that the project will generate an additional debt constantly equal to 39% of its value. A spreadsheet model for comparing the WACC and APV approaches when a constant debt to equity ratio (market values) is assumed is shown in Tables 12 and 13.

Notes on the model
The upper part of the model shows the parameters:

● Discount rate for unlevered equity (0.15)
● Tax rate (0.5)
● Interest rate (0.10)
● Leverage rate (0.39).

The second part shows the cash flows and their present values. The loan is calculated each year as 39% of the present value of the project, this present value including the present value of the debt-related tax shields (hence the circular reference in the model).[2]

The third part shows the results of the APV and WACC approaches. The WACC is calculated according to the formula proposed by Miles and Ezzel (a close alternative to the popular formula shown on page 504).

$$\text{WACC} = \frac{\text{unlevered}}{\text{equity rate}} - \frac{\text{debt to}}{\text{total funds}} \times \frac{\text{interest}}{\text{rate}} \times \frac{\text{tax}}{\text{rate}} \times \frac{1 + \text{unlevered equity rate}}{1 + \text{interest rate}}$$

As far as APV is concerned, you should note that the tax shields are discounted at the unlevered equity rate except for the first year they materialize.[3]

A fourth part shows the annual cash flow statements, income statements and balance sheets of the project.

Table 12 ● WACC and APV: foreground of the model

	A	B	C	D	E	F	G	H
1	Discount rate (unlevered)			0.15	interest rate			0.10
2	Corporation tax rate			0.50	debt/total funds			0.39
3					implied D/E ratio			0.64
4								
5	OPERATING PROFIT BEFORE DEPRECIATION				500	1600	740	
6	DEPRECIATION				300	300	300	
7	PROFIT AFTER TAX				100	650	220	
8	CASH FLOWS			−900	400	950	520	
9	PRESENT VALUE AT UNLEVERED RATE			1408	1219	452		
10	PRESENT VALUE INTEREST TAX SHIELDS			51	29	8		
11	ADJUSTED PRESENT VALUE (APV)			1459	1249	460		
12	DEBT			569	487	180		
13	INTEREST AFTER TAX				28	24	9	
14	INTEREST TAX SHIELDS				28	24	9	
15								
16	APV					WACC		
17								
18	NPV			508				
19	INTEREST TAX SHIELDS			51		RATE		0.130
20	APV			559		NPV		559
21	NET CASH			−900	372	926	511	
22	DEBT			569	487	180	0	
23	EQUITY			331				
24	LOAN REPAYMENT			0	569	487	180	
25	DIVIDEND			0	0	0	0	
26	CHANGE IN CASH (BALANCE SHEET)			0	289	618	331	
27								
28	PROFIT BEFORE TAX				500	1600	740	
29	INTEREST				57	49	18	
30	DEPRECIATION				300	300	300	
31	PROFIT AFTER TAX				72	626	211	
32								
33	CASH			0	289	908	1239	
34	NET FIXED ASSETS			900	600	300	0	
35	TOTAL ASSETS			900	889	1208	1239	
36								
37	DEBT			569	487	180	0	
38	NET WORTH			331	402	1028	1239	
39	TOTAL EQUITIES			900	889	1208	1239	
40								
41	Book debt/equity ratio			1.7	1.2	0.2	0.0	
42	Book debt/total funds ratio			0.6	0.5	0.1	0.0	

Width of columns: Global: 7; A:23.
Format: 0 decimal, except for rates and ratios.

APPENDIX

Table 13 • Constructing the WACC/APV spreadsheet model

1 D1, D2, H1, H2: data; H3: +H2/(1–H2).
Operating profit before depreciation: data.

2 Depreciation: in E6: –D8/3; in F6: +E6; in G6: +F6.

3 Profit after tax: in E7: (E5–E6)*(1–$D$2) (to be copied).

4 Cash flows: in D8: –900; in E8: +E6+E7; etc.

5 Unlevered present value is the present value of the future cash flows (not including the cash flow of the current year) in F9: +G8/(1+D1); in E9: (F9+F8)/(1+$D$1) (you can copy into D9).

6 Present value interest tax shields: it is assumed that the company keeps an amount of borrowing equal to the target debt equity ratio times its present levered value (the latter being equal to the present unlevered value plus the value of the interest tax shields). In order to model this assumption you have to build a circular reference.* The formulas for interest tax shields are starting from F10:
   in F10: +F11*$H$2*$H$1*$D$2/(1+$H$1)
   in F10: +E11*$H$2*$H$1*$D$2/(1+$H$1)+F10/(1+$D$1)
   in D10: copy the formula from E10.

7 Present levered value: +D9+D10 in D11 (to be copied).

8 Borrowing: +D11*$H$2 in D12; to be copied.

9 Interest after tax: +D12*$H$1*(1–$D$2) in E13 (to be copied).

10 Interest tax shields: +D12*$H$1*$D$2 in E14 (to be copied).

11 NPV: +D9+D8 in D18; interest tax shield in D19:
   +G14/((1+H1)*(1+D1)^2+F14/((1+H1)*(1+D1))+E14/(1+H1)
   Apv: +D18+D19 in D20.

12 Rate for WACC: +D1–D2*H1*H2*(1+D1)/(1+H1) in H19;
   NPV: =NPV(H19,E8.G8)+D8 in H20.

13 Cash flow statements:
   Net cash: +D8–D13 in D21 (to be copied).
   Borrowing: +D12 in D22 (to be copied).
   Equity: –D21–D22 in D23.
   Loan repayment: 0 in D24; then +D22 (to be copied).
   Dividend: a data.
   Change in casb: +D21+D22+D23–D24–D25 in D26 (to be copied).

14 Income statements:
   Profit before tax: +E5 in E28 (to be copied).
   Interest: +E13+E14 in E29 (to be copied).
   Depreciation: +E6 in E30 (to be copied).
   Profit after tax: (E28–E29–E30)*(1–$D$2) in E31 (to be copied).

15 Balance sheets:
   Cash: +D26 in D33; then +D33+E26 in E33 (to be copied).
   Net fixed assets: –D8 in D34; +D34–E30 in E34 (to be copied).
   Total assets: +D33+D34 in D35 (to be copied).
   Debt: +D12 in D37 (to be copied).
   Net worth: +D23–D25 in D38; +D38+E31–E25 in E38 (to be copied).
   Total equities: +D37+D38 in D39 (to be copied).

16 Debt equity ratio: +D37/D38 in D41 (to be copied).

17 Debt total funds ratio: +D37/D39 in D42 (to be copied).

---

* Because of the circular reference you may obtain slightly different values for the APV and the NPV. In order to get the same value depress the F9 key as many times as necessary.

Comments

So it is possible, with hard work, to get the same results through the WACC and APV approaches, provided that you assume in both cases that the debt to equity ratio (with market values) is kept constant over the life of the project.

You can use the model to check that this result is true whatever the timing of the cash flows (you only have to change the operational profit before depreciation in the range EG.G4).

Two points are worth noting:

1. Borrowing 39%[4] of the market value of the project leads to borrowing much more than 39% of the 900 initially needed. Actually, the model shows that borrowing 39% of the market value of the project leads to financing the initial 900 by more debt than equity.[5] This phenomenon is fairly general, since, as soon as a project has a positive net present value, the present value of its expected cash flows is necessarily higher than the initial investment.
2. Borrowing 39% of the market value does not imply that the book debt to equity ratio will be 64%. In the present case, this ratio is 170%, then 120%, then 20% then 0%.

Notes

1. This model uses the approach presented by J. Miles and R. Ezzell in 'The weighted average cost of capital perfect capital markets and project life: a clarification', *Journal of Financial and Quantitative Analysis* (Sept 1980), **15**: 719–30.
2. Because of this circular reference, you may get slightly different values for the APV and the NPV implied by the WACC. If this happens, press F9 and the two values will converge.
3. The rationale for this is that, since the rule is to borrow in relation to the present value of the project, the level of borrowing becomes uncertain.
4. The reason why a 569 000 FFR loan corresponds to a 39% debt ratio rather than a 40% ratio, is due to the fact that, in the model, the value of the project incorporates the present value of the tax shields.
5. The model also shows that, beyond a 0.60 debt to total funds ratio, you no longer need to invest any equity.

APPENDIX

Bibliography
and References

Abernathy, W. and Wayne, K. (1983) 'Limits of the Learning Curve', in Abernathy, W. (ed.) *Survival Strategies for American Industries*, New York: John Wiley.

Ackoff, R. (1978) *The Art of Problem Solving – Accompanied by Ackoff's Fables*, New York: John Wiley.

Alexander, C. (1996) 'Volatility and Correlation: Measurement Models and Applications' in Alexander, C. (ed.) *Risk Management and Analysis*, New York: John Wiley.

Amram, M. and Kulatilaka, N. (1999) *Real Options: Managing Strategic Investment in an Uncertain World*, Boston, MA: Harvard Business School Press.

Anderson, J. and Narus, J. (1999) *Business Market Management: Understanding, creating and delivering value*, Upper Saddle River, NJ: Prentice-Hall.

Anthony, R. (1982) 'Equity interest – its time has come', *Journal of Accountancy*, December.

Asquith, P. (1983) 'Merger bids, uncertainty, and stockholders' returns', *Journal of Financial Economics*, 11, pp. 51–83.

Axelrod, R. (1984) *The Evolution of Co-operation*, Harmondsworth: Penguin Books/New York: Basic Books.

Axelrod, R. and Cohen, M.D. (1999) *Harnessing Complexity*, New York: The Free Press.

Badaracco, J. (1991) *The Knowledge Link: How Firms Compete Through Strategic Alliances*, Boston, MA: Harvard Business School Press.

Bazerman, M.H. (1986) *Judgement in Managerial Decisions*, New York: John Wiley.

Bekers, S. (1998) 'A survey of risk measurement theory and practice' in Alexander, C. (ed.) *Risk Management and Analysis*, New York: John Wiley.

Bekier, M., Bogardus, A. and Oldham, T. (2001) 'Why mergers fail', *The McKinsey Quarterly*, 4, pp. 6–9.

Bell D., Raiffa, H. and Tversky, A. (eds) (1988), *Decision Making: Descriptive, normative and prescriptive interactions*, Cambridge: Cambridge University Press.

Bell, D. (1988) 'Disappointment in decision making under uncertainty' in Bell, D., Raiffa, H. and Tversky, A. (eds) *ibid* (see p. 358).

Beniger, J.R. (1986) *The Control Revolution*, Boston, MA: Harvard Business School Press.

Benninga, S. (2000) *Financial Modelling*, Cambridge, MA: MIT Press.

Berliner, C. and Brimson, J. (eds) (1988) *Cost Management for Today's Advanced Manufacturing*, Boston, MA: Harvard Business School Press.

Best, P. (1998) *Implementing Value at Risk*, Chichester/New York: John Wiley.

Bodie, Z. and Merton, C. (2000) *Finance*, Upper Saddle River, NJ: Prentice-Hall.

Bodily, S.E., Carraway, R.L. and Frey, S.C. (1998) *Quantitative Business Analysis: Text and Cases*, Boston, MA: Irwin/McGraw-Hill.

Bohm, D. (1992) *Thought as a System*, London/New York: Routledge.

Borden, J. (1990) 'Review of literature on activity-based costing', *Cost Management*, Spring, pp. 5–13.

Brandenburger, A.M. and Nalebuff, B.J. (1996) *Co-opetition*, New York: Doubleday.

Brealey, R., Myers, S. and Marcus, J. (2001) *Fundamentals of Corporate Finance*, Irwin Series in Finance, Boston, MA: Irwin/McGraw-Hill.

Brennan, M. and Trigeorgis, L. (2000) *Project Flexibility, Agency and Competition*, Oxford: Oxford University Press.

Bromwich, M. and Hopwood, A. (eds) (1986) *Research and Current Issues in Management Accounting*, London: Pitman Publishing.

Brown, S., Goetzmann, W. and Ross, R. (1995) 'Survival', *The Journal of Finance*, 50(3), pp. 353–73.

Brown, S.L. and Eishenhardt, K.M. (1998) *Competing on The Edge*, Boston, MA: Harvard Business School Press.

Cahart, M. (1997) 'On persistence in mutual funds performance', *Journal of Finance*, March.

Carter, J., Cushman, R. and Hartz, C.S. (eds) (1988) *The Handbook of Joint Venturing*, Homewood, IL: Dow Jones-Irwin.

Chew, D. (1993) *The New Corporate Finance: Where Theory Meets Practice*, New York: McGraw-Hill.

Christensen, C. (1997) *The Innovator's Dilemma*, Boston, MA: Harvard Business School Press.

Clark, K. and Adler, P. (1991) 'Behind the learning curve: A sketch of the learning process', *Management Science*, March, pp. 267–81.

Cochrane, J. (2001) *Asset Pricing*, Princeton, NJ: Princeton University Press.

Cohen, A. and Bradford, D. (1990) *Influence Without Authority*, New York: John Wiley.

Collis, D.J. and Montgomery, C.A. (1998) *Corporate Strategy*, Boston, MA: Irwin/McGraw-Hill.

Contractor, F. and Lorange, P. (1988) *Co-operative Strategies in International Business*, Lexington, MA: Lexington Books.

Cooper, R. (1989) 'You need a new cost system when . . .', *Harvard Business Review*, January–February, pp. 77–82.

Copeland, T.E. and Joshi, Y. (1996) 'Why derivatives don't reduce FX risk', *The McKinsey Quarterly*, 1, pp. 66–79.

Copeland, T., Koller, T. and Murrin, J. (2000) *Valuation: Measuring and managing the value of companies*, New York: John Wiley.

Cornell, B. (1999) *The Equity Risk Premium*, New York: John Wiley.

Culp, C. (2001) *The Risk Management Process*, New York: John Wiley.

Damodaran, A. (2001) *Corporate Finance: Theory and Practice*, Wiley Series in Finance, New York: John Wiley.

Damodaran, A. (2001) *The Dark Side of Evaluation*, Upper Saddle River, NJ: Prentice-Hall.

Dawkins, R. (1989) *The Selfish Gene*, Oxford: Oxford University Press.

DeBondt, W. and Thaler, R. (1985) 'Does the Stock Market Overeract?', *Journal of Finance*, July.

Deming, W.E. (2000) *The New Economics: for industry, government, education*, Cambridge, MA: MIT Press.

DeRosa, D. (1992) *Options on Foreign Exchange*, Chicago, IL: Irwin; (2000), New York: Wiley.

Dixit, A. and Pindyck, R. (1994) *Investment under Uncertainty*, Princeton, NJ: Princeton University Press.

Dixit, A. and Pindyck, R. (1995) 'The options approach to capital investments', *Harvard Business Review*, May–June.

Doherty, N.A. (2000) *Integrated Risk Management: Techniques and strategies for managing corporate risk*, New York: McGraw-Hill.

Dolan, A. and Jeuland, A. (1981) 'Experience curves and dynamic demand models: Implications for optimal pricing strategies', *Journal of Marketing*, Winter, pp. 52–2.

Dolan, R.J. and Simon, H. (1996) *Power Pricing – How Managing Price Transforms the Bottom Line*, New York: The Free Press.

Donaldson, G. (1961) *Corporate Debt Capacity*, Boston, MA: Harvard University Press.

Downes, L. and Mui, C. (1998) *Unleashing the Killer App*, Boston, MA: Harvard Business School Press.

Drucker, P. (1959) 'Long Range Planning', *Management Science*, April.

Duffie, D. (1996) *Dynamic Asset Pricing Theory*, Princeton, NJ: Princeton University Press.

Eccles, R., Hertz, R., Keegan, M. and Philips, D. (2001) *The Value Reporting Revolution*, New York: John Wiley.

Ehrbarr, A.L. (1998) *Stern Stewart's EVA: The Real Key to Creating Wealth*, New York: John Wiley.

Eisenhardt, K. and Sull, D. (2001) 'Strategy as simple rules', *Harvard Business Review*, January, pp. 107–16.

Elliott, B. and Elliott, J. (2000) *Financial Accounting and Reporting*, Upper Saddle River, NJ: Prentice-Hall.

Elton, E., Gruber, M. and Mei, J. (1994) 'Cost of capital using arbitrage pricing theory: A case study of nine New York utilities', *Financial Markets, Institutions and Instruments*, 3, August, pp. 46–73.

Epstein, B.J. and Mirza, A.A. (2002) *Wiley IAS 2002*, New York: John Wiley.

Evans, P. and Wurster, T.S. (2000) *Blown to Bits*, Boston, MA: Harvard Business School Press.

Ezzell, J.R. and Kelly, W.A. Jr (1984) 'An APV analysis of capital budgeting under inflation', *Financial Management*, Autumn, pp. 49–54.

Fama, E. (1977) 'Risk adjusted discount rates and capital budgeting under uncertainty', *Journal of Financial Economics*, August, pp. 3–24.

Figlewski, S., Silber, W. and Subrahmanyam, M. (1990) *Financial Options: From Theory to Practice*, Chicago, IL: Irwin.

Forrester, J.W. (1961) *Industrial Dynamics*, Portland, Oregon: Productivity Press.

Forsgren, M. (1989) *Managing the Internationalisation Process: The Swedish Case*, London/New York: Routledge.

Franks, J., Harris, R. and Titman, S. (1991) 'The post merger share price performance of acquiring firms', *Journal of Financial Economics*, 29, pp. 83–96.

Freeman, R.E. (1984) *Strategic Management: a Stakeholder Approach*, London: Pitman.

French, K. (1980) 'Stock returns and the week-end effect', *Journal of Financial Economics*, March.

Frey, S. and Schlosser, M. (1993) 'ABB and Ford: Creating value through cooperation', *Sloan Management Review*, Fall, pp. 65–72.

Ghemawat, P. (1991) *Commitment: The Dynamic of Strategy*, New York: The Free Press.

Goldratt, E. (1992) *The Goal* (2nd edn), Great Barrington, MA: North River Press.

Haeckel, S.H. (1999) *Adaptive Enterprise: Creating and Leading Sense-and-Respond Organizations*, Boston, MA: Harvard Business School Press.

Hall, R. (1987) *Attaining Manufacturing Excellence*, Homewood, IL: Dow Jones-Irwin.

Hamel, G. and Prahalad, C.K. (1994) *Competing for the Future*, Boston, MA: Harvard Business School Press.

Hammer, M. (1996) *Beyond Reengineering*, New York: Harper Business.

Harmon, R. and Peterson, L. (1990) *Reinventing the Factory*, New York: The Free Press.

Harrigan, K.R. (1986) *Managing for Joint Venture Success*, Lexington, MA: Lexington Books.

Harris, M. and Raviv, A. (1991) 'The theory of capital structure', *Journal of Finance*, March, pp. 297–355.

Haspeslagh, P. and Jemison, D. (1991) *Managing Acquisitions: Creating Value Through Corporate Renewal*, New York: The Free Press.

Haugen, R. (1999) *The Inefficient Stock Market*, Upper Saddle River, NJ: Prentice-Hall.

Haugen, R. (1999) *The New Finance*, Upper Saddle River, NJ: Prentice-Hall.

Haugen, R. (2001) *Modern Investment Theory*, Upper Saddle River, NJ: Prentice-Hall.

Hax, A. and Majluf, N. (1982) 'Competitive cost dynamics: the experience curve', *Interfaces*, October, pp. 50–60.

Hayes, R., Wheelwright, S. and Clark, K. (1988) *Dynamic Manufacturing*, New York: The Free Press.

Helper, S. (1991) 'How much has really changed between US automakers and their suppliers?', *Sloan Management Review*, Summer, pp. 15–28.

Henke, J., Krachenberg, R. and Lyons, T. (1990) 'Mixed motive marriages: What's next for buyer-supplier relations?', *Sloan Management Review*, pp. 29–36.

Hennart, J.F. (1991) 'The transaction cost theory of joint ventures: An empirical study of Japanese subsidiaries in the United States', *Management Science*, April, pp. 483–97.

Hickmann, K. and Perry, G. (1990) 'A comparison of stock price predictions using court accepted formulas, dividend discount, and P/E models', *Financial Management*, Summer, pp. 76–87.

Holland, J.H. (1995) *Hidden Order*, Reading, MA: Addison-Wesley.

Horngren, C.T., Sundem, G.L. and Elliott, J.A. (1999) *Introduction to Financial Accounting*, Upper Saddle River, NJ: Prentice-Hall.

Hull, J. (2000) *Options, Futures, and Other Derivative Securities*, Upper Saddle River, NJ: Prentice-Hall.

Hunter, V. and Tietyen, D. (1997) *Business-to-business Marketing: Creating a Community of Customers*, Lincolnwood, IL: NTC Business Books.

Ilinski, K. (2001) *Physics of Finance*, Chichester: Wiley.

Jensen, M. (1986) 'Agency costs of free cash flow: corporate finance and take-overs', *American Economic Review*, May.

Jensen, M. (1989) 'The eclipse of the public corporation', *Harvard Business Review*, 67, September–October, pp. 61–74.

Jensen, M. (2000) *Value Maximization and the Corporate Objective Function*, Harvard Business School Working Papers 00–058, Boston, MA: Harvard Business School Press.

Jensen, M. and Meckling, W. (1976) 'Theory of the firm: managerial behaviour, agency costs and capital structure', *Journal of Financial Economics*, 3, pp. 305–60.

Jensen, M. and Ruback, R. (1983) 'The market for corporate control: the scientific evidence', *Journal of Financial Economics*, 11, pp. 5–50.

Johnson, T. and Kaplan, R. (1987) *Relevance Lost*, Boston, MA: Harvard Business School Press.

Kaplan, R. (ed.) (1990) *Measures for Manufacturing Excellence*, Boston, MA: Harvard Business School Press.

Kaplan, R.S. and Cooper, R. (1999) *Cost and Effect*, Boston, MA: Harvard Business School Press.

Kaplan, R.S. and Norton, D.P. (1996) *The Balanced Score Card*, Boston, MA: Harvard Business School Press.

Katzenbach, J. (1995) *Real Change Leaders*, London: Nicholas Brealey.

Keen, P. (1997) *The Process Edge*, Boston, MA: Harvard Business School Press.

Keeney, P.L. and Raiffa, H. (1976) *Decisions with Multiple Objectives: preferences and tradeoffs*, New York: John Wiley.

Knight, J.A. (1997) *Value Based Management*, New York: McGraw-Hill.

Kotter, J. (1985) *Power and Influence – Beyond Formal Authority*, New York: The Free Press.

Kotter, J. (1996) *Leading Change*, Boston, MA: Harvard Business School Press.

Kritzman, P. (2000) *Puzzles of Finance*, New York: John Wiley.

Labovitz, G. and Rosanssky, V. (1997) *The Power of Alignment*, New York: John Wiley.

Lakonishok, J., Schleifer, A. and Vishny, R. (1994) 'Contrarian investment extrapolation and risk', *Journal of Finance*, December.

Langer, E. (1989) *Mindfulness*, Reading, MA: Addison Wesley.

La Porta, R., Lakonishok, J., Schliefer, A. and Vishny, R. (1997) 'Good news for value stocks: Further evidence of market efficiency', *Journal of Finance*, June.

Larsen, J. (1999) *Modern Advanced Accounting*, New York: McGraw-Hill.

Lax, D.A. and Sebenius, J.K. (1986) *The Manager as a Negotiator – Bargaining for Cooperation and Competitive Gain*, New York: The Free Press.

Levy, H. and Robinson, M. (1998) *Stochastic Dominance: Investment Decision Making Under Uncertainty*, Boston, MA: Kluwer Academic Press.

Lewis, J. (1990) *Partnerships for Profit*, New York: The Free Press.

Lilien, G., Kotler, P. and Sridhar Moorthy, K. (1992) *Marketing Models*, Englewood Cliffs, NJ: Prentice-Hall.

Lo, A. and MacKinlay, G. (1999) *A Non-Random Walk Down Wall Street*, Princeton, NJ: Princeton University Press.

Lubben, R. (1988) *Just-in-time Manufacturing*, New York: McGraw-Hill.

Luca, C. (2000) *Trading in the Global Currency Markets*, Upper Saddle River, NJ: Prentice-Hall.

Luehrman, T. (1998) 'Investment opportunities as real options: Getting started on the numbers', *Harvard Business Review*, July–August, pp. 51–67.

Luehrman, T. (1998) 'Strategy as a portfolio of real options', *Harvard Business Review*, September–October, pp. 89–99.

MacCrimmon, K.R. and Wehrung, W.A. (1988) *Taking Risks: The Management of Uncertainty*, New York: The Free Press.

McMillian, J. (1990) 'Managing suppliers: incentive systems in Japanese and US Industry', *California Management Review*, Summer, pp. 38–55.

McNamee, P.B. (1985) *Tools and Techniques for Strategic Management*, Oxford/New York: Pergamon Press.

Mahajan, V., Muller, E. and Bass, F. (1990) 'New product diffusion models in marketing: A review and directions for research', *Journal of Marketing*, January, pp. 1–26.

Mahajan, V. and Peterson, R. (1985) *Models for innovation diffusion*, Beverly Hills: Sage.

Malkiel, B. (2000) *A Random Walk Down Wall Street*, New York: WW Norton.

Markovitz, H. (1952) 'Portfolio selection', *Journal of Finance*, 7, March, pp. 77–91.

Mason, S., Merton, M., Perold, A. and Tufano, P. (1995) *Cases in Financial Engineering*, Englewood Cliffs, NJ: Prentice Hall.

Mehra, R. and Preston, E.C. (1985) 'The equity risk premium: a puzzle', *Journal of Monetary Economics*, 15, pp. 145–61.

Miles, J. and Ezzell, J.R. (1980) 'The Weighted Average Cost of Capital – perfect capital markets and project life: a clarification', *Journal of Financial and Quantitative Analysis*, 15, September, pp. 719–30.

Mintzberg, H., Ahlstrand, B. and Lampel, J. (1998) *Strategy Safari: A guided tour through the wilds of strategic management*, New York: The Free Press.

Monden, Y. and Hamada, K. (1991) 'Target costing and Kaizen costing in Japanese automobile companies', *Journal of Management Accounting Research*, Fall, pp. 16–34.

Moore, P.G. (1977) 'The manager struggles with uncertainty', *Journal of the Royal Statistics Society*, Series A (General), 140, pp. 129–48.

Morck, R., Schleifer, A. and Vishny, R. (1990) 'Do managerial objectives drive bad acquisitions?', *Journal of Finance*, March, pp. 31–48.

Moss Kanter, R. (1989) *When Giants Learn to Dance*, New York: Simon and Schuster.

Mulford, C. and Comiskey, E. (2002) *The Financial Numbers Game: Detecting Creative Accounting Practices*, New York: John Wiley.

Mullick, S., Anderson, G., Leach, R. and Smith, W. (1982) 'Life cycle forecasting', in Makridakis, S. and Wheelwright, S. (eds) *The Handbook of Forecasting*, New York: John Wiley.

Murphy, J. (1999) *Technical Analysis of the Financial Markets*, New York: New York Institute of Finance.

Myers, S.C. (1984) 'Finance theory and financial strategy', *Interfaces*, 14, January–February, pp. 126–37.

Myers, S.C. (1984) 'The capital structure puzzle', *Journal of Finance*, 39, July, pp. 575–92.

Nagle, T.T. and Holden, R.K. (1995) *The Strategy and Tactics of Pricing* (4th edn, 2002), Upper Saddle River, NJ: Prentice Hall.

Neftci, S. (2000) *An Introduction to the Mathematics of Financial Derivatives*, San Diego: Academic Press.

Negroponte, N. (1995) *Being Digital*, New York: Knopf.

Nejat Sejun, H. (1990) 'Do bidder managers knowingly pay too much for target firms?', *Journal of Business*, 63.

Nelson, C.R. (1976) 'Inflation and capital budgeting', *Journal of Finance*, 31, June, pp. 923–31.

Nicolis, G. and Prigogine, I. (1989) *Exploring Complexity: An Introduction*, New York: WH Freeman.

Nolan, R. and Croson, D. (1995) *Creative Destruction: a Six-stage Process for Transforming the Organization*, Boston, MA: Harvard Business School Press.

Nonaka, I. and Takeuchi, H. (1995) *The Knowledge Creating Company*, Oxford: Oxford University Press.

Pascale, R.T. (1990) *Managing on the Edge: How the smartest companies use conflict to stay ahead*, Englewood Cliffs, NJ: Prentice-Hall.

Pinchot, G. and Pinchot, E. (1993) *The Intelligent Organisation*, Berrett-Koehler Publishers.

Porter, M.E. (1980) *Competitive Strategy*, New York: The Free Press.

Porter, M.E. (1985) *Competitive Advantage*, New York: The Free Press

Porter, M.E. (1987) 'From competitive advantage to corporate strategy', *Harvard Business Review*, May–June, pp. 43–59.

Prigogine, I. and Stengers, I. (1990) *Order Out of Chaos*, London: Flamingo.

Quinn Mills, D. (1985) *The New Competition*, New York: John Wiley.

Rabin, M. and Thaler, R. (2001) 'Risk aversion', *Journal of Economic Perspectives*, 15, Winter, pp. 219–32.

Raiffa, H. (1970) *Decision Analysis: Introductory Lectures on Choices Under Uncertainty*, Reading, MA: Addison Wesley.

Raiffa, H. (1982) *The Art and Science of Negotiation*, Boston, MA: Belknap Press of Harvard University Press.

Rajan, R.G. and Zingales, L. (1995) 'What do we know about capital structure? Some evidence from international data', *Journal of Finance*.

Rappaport, A. (1986) *Creating Shareholder Value*, New York: The Free Press.

Reichheld, F. (1996) *The Loyalty Effect*, Boston, MA: Harvard Business School Press.

Reilly, R. and Schweihs, R. (1999) *The Handbook of Advanced Business Valuation*, Chicago, IL: Irwin.

Resher, N. (1999) *Predicting the Future: An Introduction to the Theory of Forecasting*, New York: State University of New York Press.

Rivett, P. (1980) *Model Building for Decision Analysis*, New York: John Wiley.

Robinson, M. (ed.) (1990) 'Contribution margin analysis: no longer relevant. Strategic cost management: the new paradigm', *Journal of Management Accounting Research*, 2, Fall, pp. 1–32.

Rogers, E. (1995) *Diffusion of Innovations*, New York: The Free Press.

Roll, R. (1986) 'The hubris hypothesis of corporate takeovers', *Journal of Business*, 59, pp. 197–216.

Rosenberg, M. (1996) *Currency Forecasting*, Chicago, IL: Irwin.

Ross, S. (1976) 'The arbitrage theory of capital asset pricing', *Journal of Economic Theory*, 13, December, pp. 341–60.

Ross, S., Westerfield, R. and Jordan, B. (2002) *Fundamentals of Corporate Finance*, New York: McGraw-Hill.

Rothenberg, A. (1979) *The Emerging Goddess: The creative process in art, science and other fields*, Chicago, IL: University of Chicago Press.

Rubin, P. (1990) *Managing Business Transactions*, New York: The Free Press.

Russo, E. and Schoemaker, P. (1989) *Decision Traps*, New York: Doubleday; (1990) New York: Simon and Schuster.

Samuelson, P. (1965) 'Proof that properly anticipated prices fluctuate randomly', *Industrial Management Review*, Spring, pp. 41–9.

Sanders, T.I. (1998) *Strategic Thinking and the New Science*. New York: The Free Press.

Schlaifer, R. (1969) *Analysis of Decisions under Uncertainty*, New York: McGraw-Hill.

Schoemaker, P.H.J. (1982) 'The Expected Utility Model: its variants, purposes, evidence and limitations', *Journal of Economic Literature*, XX, June.

Schrage, M. (2000) *Serious Play – How the World's Best Companies Simulate to Innovate*, Boston, MA: Harvard Business School Press.

Schroeder, R. and Clark, M. (1997) *Accounting Theory*, New York: John Wiley.

Schwartz, G.P. (1995) *Shareholder Rebellion*, Burr Ridge, IL: Irwin.

Senge, P. (1990) *The Fifth Discipline*, London: Century Business (see p. 10).

Shapira, Z. (1995) *Risk Taking: A Managerial Perspective*, New York: Russell Sage Foundation.

Shapiro, A. (1998) *Foundations of Multinational Financial Management*, Upper Saddle River: Prentice Hall; (4th edn (2002), New York: John Wiley).

Sharpe, W.F., Alexander, G.J. and Bailey, J.V. (1998) *Investments*, Upper Saddle River, NJ: Prentice-Hall.

Shiller, J. (1989) *Market Volatility*, Cambridge, MA: MIT Press.

Shingo, S. (1988) *Non Stock Production: the Shingo system for continuous improvement*, Portland, Oregon: Productivity Press.

Siegel, J. (1998) *Stocks for the Long Run*, New York: McGraw-Hill.

Simmel, G. (1908) *Conflict and the Web of Group Affiliations*, New York: The Free Press (1955).

Slusky, A. and Caves, R. (1991) 'Synergy, agency and the determinants of premia paid in mergers', *Journal of Industrial Economics*, XXXIX, March, pp. 277–95.

Slywostzky, Ä.J. and Morrison, D.J. (1999) *Profit Patterns*, New York: Times Business, Random House.

Smith, P. and Reinertsen, D. (1998) *Developing Products in Half the Time*, New York: John Wiley.

Smith, T. (1992) *Accounting for Growth: Stripping the camouflage from company accounts*. London: Century Business.

Stalk, G. and Hout, T. (1990) *Competing against Time*, New York: The Free Press.

Stewart, III, G.B. (1991) *The Quest for Value: The EVA™ Management Guide*, New York: Harper Business.

Stewart, T.A. (2000) 'Making decisions in real time', *Fortune*, 26 June.

Suzaki, K. (1987) *The New Manufacturing Challenge*, New York: The Free Press.

Thaler, R. (1999) 'The end of behavioral finance', *Financial Analysts Journal* (November–December).

Tigeorgis, L. (1996) *Real Options, Managerial Flexibility and Strategy in Resource Allocation*, Cambridge, MA: MIT Press.

Treacy, M. and Wiersema, F. (1995) *The Discipline of Market Leaders*, Reading, MA: Addison-Wesley.

Tversky, A: (1972) 'Elimination by aspect: a theory of choice', *Psychological Review*, 79, pp. 281–99.

Ury, W. (1991) *Getting Past No: Negotiating with Difficult People*, New York: Bantam Books.

Vives, X. (ed.) (2000) *Corporate Governance, Theoretical and Empirical Perspectives*, Cambridge/New York: Cambridge University Press.

Wallace, A. (1980) 'Is beta dead?', *Institutional Investor*, 14, July, pp. 22–30.

Walmsley, J. (2000) *The Foreign Exchange and Money Markets Guide*, New York: John Wiley.

Warner, J. (1977) 'Bankruptcy costs: some evidence', *Journal of Finance*, 32, May, pp. 337–48.

Wayland, R. and Cole, P. (1997) *Customer Connections*, Boston, MA: Harvard Business School Press.

Weber, M. (1905) *The Protestant Ethic and the Spirit of Capitalism*, New York: Charles Scribner (1958–1976).

West, T. and Jones, J. (1999) *Handbook of Business Valuation*, New York: John Wiley.

Williams, J.R. (2002) *2002 Miller Gaap Guide*, New York: Harcourt Professional Publishing.

Wilmott, P. (2000) *Quantitative Finance*, Chichester: Wiley.

Zeff, S. and Keller, T. (1985) *Financial Accounting Theory*, New York: McGraw-Hill.

Index